The
ECONOMICS
of
WELFARE

Classics in Economic Series

The ECONOMICS *of* WELFARE

Arthur Cecil Pigou

With a new introduction by
Nahid Aslanbeigui

 Routledge
Taylor & Francis Group

LONDON AND NEW YORK

Originally published in 1952 by Macmillian and Co. Limited

First published 2002 by Transaction Publishers

Published 2019 by Routledge
2 Park Square, Milton Park, Abingdon, Oxon OX14 4RN
52 Vanderbilt Avenue, New York, NY 10017

Routledge is an imprint of the Taylor & Francis Group, an informa business

New material this edition copyright © 2002 Taylor & Francis

Library of Congress Catalog Number: 00-049102

Library of Congress Cataloging-in-Publication Data

Pigou, A. C. (Arthur Cecil), 1877-1959.
    The economics of welfare / Arthur Cecil Pigou; with a new introduction by Nahid Aslanbeigui.—Transaction ed.
        p. cm.
    Includes bibliographical references and index.
    ISBN 0-7658-0739-4 (alk. paper)
    1. Welfare economics. I. Title.
HB99.3 .P58   2000
330.15'5—dc21   00-049102

ISBN 13: 978-0-7658-0739-7 (pbk)

ANALYTICAL TABLE OF CONTENTS

PART I

WELFARE AND THE NATIONAL DIVIDEND

CHAPTER I

PAGE

WELFARE AND ECONOMIC WELFARE 3

§ 1. The main motive of economic study is to help social improvement. §§ 2-3. Economic science will, therefore, be "realistic" rather than "pure"; but not merely "descriptive." § 4. It is very difficult to make its analysis quantitative. § 5. Economic welfare may be defined roughly as that part of welfare that can be brought into relation with the measuring rod of money. §§ 6-9. Instances can be multiplied in which economic causes, that affect economic welfare in one way, affect total welfare in a different way. § 10. Nevertheless there is a presumption that qualitative conclusions about effects upon economic welfare will hold good also of effects upon total welfare. § 11. And reasonably adequate conclusions about effects upon economic welfare can often be obtained by economic science, in spite of the partial and limited character of that science.

CHAPTER II

DESIRES AND SATISFACTIONS 23

§ 1. The relation between satisfaction and the money measure is not direct, but is mediated through desires, the intensity of which need not always bear the same proportion to the satisfactions that their fulfilment yields. § 2. For the most part this circumstance is not important. § 3. But for the choice between using resources for the present and for the distant future it is very important. § 4-5. Coupled with the fact of individual mortality, it suggests that people are likely to save less and to use up nature's exhaustible stores more quickly than consists with the general interest. § 6. There is a presumption, therefore, against taxes that differentiate against saving. § 7. And in favour of State action to conserve natural resources.

V

CHAPTER VIII

§§ 1-2. Changes in the distribution of the national dividend in
favour of the poor may be brought about in several ways, the most
important of which is by a transference of purchasing power to
them from richer persons. §§ 3-4. Except in very special circumstances such a transference must increase economic welfare. §§ 5-6.
Particularly in a country where income is distributed as unevenly as
it is in England. § 7. This, however, is not quite the same thing
as saying that a diminution in the inequality of distribution must
increase economic welfare.

CHAPTER IX

§ 1. It may be objected that the consequences of an increase in
the dividend accruing to any group, particularly to a poor group,
discussed in Chapters VII. and VIII. are nullified by reactions on the
numbers of the population. § 2. Even apart from changes induced
by greater wealth in wants and tastes, this thesis is not tenable.
§ 3. And, when account is taken of them, the case for it is further
weakened. § 4. But the fact of migration between countries complicates the issue. § 5. And transferences of income present difficulties.

CHAPTER X

§ 1. The conclusions reached in Chapters VII. and VIII. must now
be reviewed in the light of modern biological knowledge. § 2. That
knowledge warrants the belief that general welfare and economic
welfare alike could be increased by measures restricting propagation
among the obviously degenerate. This belief, however, is additional
to, and does not disturb, our results. § 3. It is sometimes held that
modern biology, by demonstrating the dominant part played by
heredity as compared with environment, has proved economic
inquiries, which are, in the main, concerned with environment, to
be unimportant. Reasons are offered for rejecting this view. §§ 4-6.
It is sometimes held, further, that the advantage to economic welfare
claimed in Chapters VII. and VIII. to result from (1) an increase in
the magnitude and (2) an improvement in the distribution of the
national dividend are cancelled by indirect biological effects.
Reasons are offered for rejecting these views.

CHAPTER XI

PART II

THE SIZE OF THE NATIONAL DIVIDEND AND THE DISTRIBUTION OF RESOURCES AMONG DIFFERENT USES

CHAPTER I

§§ 1-2. The general problem of this Part is to ascertain how far the free play of self-interest, acting under the existing legal system, tends to distribute the country's resources in the way most favourable to the production of a large national dividend, and how far it is feasible for State action to improve upon "natural" tendencies.

CHAPTER II

§§ 1-4. The meaning of the term *marginal net product* is explained. § 5. Marginal social and marginal private net products are distinguished. § 6. As also their respective values.

CHAPTER III

§ 1. In the absence of costs of movement, it can be shown that, provided there is only one arrangement of resources which makes the values of the marginal social net products equal in all uses, that arrangement will maximise the national dividend. § 2. There is difficulty in extending this analysis to differences in degrees of inequality. § 3. In so far as there are costs of movement, the *optimum* arrangement, which is, of course, not so good as the *optimum* arrangement in the absence of costs, is different, and, within limits, indeterminate. § 4. In real life there are likely to be a number of different arrangements of resources, each one of which will make the values of the marginal social net products equal in all uses. Hence, equality of values of marginal social net products does not imply that the national dividend is maximised. § 5. There is here a possible opening for the beneficial use of bounties.

CHAPTER IV

§ 1. Values of marginal private net products are, in general, equal to rates of return. § 2. In the absence of costs of movement, self-interest tends to make rates of return everywhere equal ; where there are costs of movement to make them as nearly equal as those costs allow. § 3. This implies that, except in so far as marginal private and marginal social net products diverge, anything that obstructs the free play of self-interest is likely to damage the dividend.

CHAPTER V

§§ 1-5. In a general way the elimination of obstacles, in the form of costs of movement or lack of knowledge, to the free working of self interest is likely to promote equality of returns. But this statement is subject to qualifications. § 6. It is important to distinguish between the effects on economic welfare of a real reduction in costs and those of a mere transference of costs from the persons who control the movement of resources to the State.

CHAPTER VI

§§ 1-5. The tendency towards equality of returns in different occupations is obstructed by imperfect knowledge, resulting partly from the character of business accounts, and partly from the general organisation of business finance. § 6. The intervention of banks, which naturally look to permanent and not merely to immediate profit, in the work of promotion may, if other conditions allow, do something to improve matters. § 7. The control exercised in minor fields of investment by People's Banks of the Raiffeisen type is a safeguard against the wasteful employment of borrowed resources.

CHAPTER VII

§ 1. When the units in which transactions are made are large, or when they are compounded of two factors in a fixed proportion, the tendency of self-interest to make the rate of returns equal in all uses is obstructed. § 2. In modern times the size of the unit in which transactions in respect of capital take place has been diminished in a twofold manner, partly with the help of the Stock Exchange. § 3. The compound character which formerly belonged to this unit has also, in great part, been eliminated by arrangements which the great growth of securities adapted to serve as collateral has facilitated. §§ 4-5. The device of dividing shares into several grades and the holding of them in their riskiest early age by financiers, who afterwards pass them on, work in the same direction. § 6. In general, in present conditions, imperfect divisibility in the units of transactions has but little effect.

CHAPTER XV

§ 1. Under monopolistic competition, self-interest does not tend to make the value of the marginal social net product of resources in the industry affected equal to the value of the marginal social net product of resources in general. §§ 2-3. Rather, it leaves the value of the marginal social net product indeterminate over a range, the extent of which depends upon certain influences that are briefly discussed.

CHAPTER XVI

§§ 1-5. Under simple monopoly *plus* restriction of entry to the industry affected it is probable that the value of the marginal social net product of resources in that industry will diverge from the value of the marginal social net product of resources in general more widely than it would do under simple competition. § 6. If the entry to the monopolised industry is not restricted, the national dividend will also suffer in another way.

CHAPTER XVII

§ 1. Under certain conditions monopolists are able to charge discriminating prices. §§ 2-4. The nature of these conditions, which depend essentially upon the non-transferability of the commodities affected, is discussed. §§ 5-7. Of three distinguishable forms of discriminating monopoly, the only one of practical importance is discriminating monopoly of the third degree, under which different prices are charged between markets, the composition of which is determined otherwise than by the monopolist's own choice. §§ 8-11. But a brief analysis of the other two forms is given. §§ 12-16. Under discriminating monopoly of the third degree, *plus* restriction of entry to the industry affected, the output may, not improbably in certain circumstances, approach more nearly to the ideal output, which makes the value of the marginal social net product of resources in that industry equal to the value of the marginal social net product of resources in general, than it would do under simple monopoly ; but it is unlikely to approach more nearly to this output than it would do under simple competition. § 17. Under discriminating monopoly, without restriction of entry to the industry affected, the situation is still less favourable.

CHAPTER XVIII

§ 1. The discussion of the preceding chapter throws light on the controversy between advocates of "the cost of service principle" and of "the value of service principle" in respect of railway rates. § 2. The meaning in concrete form of "the cost of service principle" is explained, and this principle is shown to imply uniform charges to different purchasers of ton-miles of transportation, so far as the ton-miles sold to different purchasers are not "jointly supplied." §§ 3-4. The common view that railway services are in large part jointly supplied—that the carriage of copper and the carriage of coal, or the carriage of coal destined for A and the carriage of coal destined for B, over a given piece of line are joint products—is incorrect. § 5. However, some measure of jointness, as, for instance, between out and home journeys, does in fact prevail. § 6. The meaning in concrete form of "the value of service principle" is explained. §§ 7-8. "The cost of service principle" corresponds to simple competition, and "the value of service principle" to discriminating monopoly of the third degree. In general, the former is the more advantageous to the national dividend; but, as stated in the preceding chapter, circumstances may arise in which the latter is the more advantageous. §§ 9-10. These circumstances, however, are less common than writers on railway economics usually suppose. § 11. Moreover, such benefit as the "value of service principle" is competent to bring about can often be attained more satisfactorily by means of a bounty. § 12. The policy of permitting discriminating charges, subject to the condition that profits are prevented from rising above the normal, is discussed. § 13. Lastly, something is said of zone systems of railway tariffs.

CHAPTER XIX

§ 1. The preceding chapters have shown that, in many industries, neither simple competition, nor monopolistic competition, nor simple monopoly, nor discriminating monopoly will make the value of the marginal social net product of resources invested in them equal to the value of the marginal social net product of resources in general. We have next to inquire whether this result can be secured by resort to the device of Purchasers' Associations. § 2. The answer is clearly in the affirmative; but no inference follows as to the effect on the national dividend, until the comparative advantages in respect of productive efficiency of Purchasers' Associations and ordinary commercial businesses have been ascertained. § 3. Not much light can be thrown on that matter by historical examples. §§ 4-5. Purchasers' Associations have advantages in respect of production, so far as they save costs in advertisement, are exceptionally well fitted to spread knowledge of the best methods of production among their members, and have exceptionally small need of bargaining and safeguards against fraud. These advantages have led to their successful establishment over a considerable field. § 6. But for various reasons this field is limited, and a study of further remedies for the imperfections of ordinary business forms is, therefore, still required.

CHAPTER XX

§ 1. This chapter is concerned with the general merits of public intervention in industry, including both control and operation, as a remedy for the failures of private enterprise. § 2. For various reasons the experience of the war can afford much less guidance on this

CHAPTER XXI

CHAPTER XXII

joint-stock operation of industry cannot be successfully compared by reference to statistics. §§ 6-9. The public operation of industries may assume a number of different forms, and, from the point of view of technical efficiency, it need not be inferior to private operation—particularly controlled private operation. § 10. But, first, under public operation there is a danger that the operating authority may be tempted to maintain its enterprise by the use of unfair extra-commercial methods at the expense of rival enterprises capable of satisfying the same wants more cheaply. § 11. Secondly, under public operation efficiency is likely to suffer through unwillingness to take risks and make experiments. §§ 12-13. Thirdly, efficiency is likely to suffer through the establishment of units of management of an uneconomical size ; though, in industries where the normal state of things is monopolistic competition, public operation is, in this respect, superior to joint-stock operation. § 14. On the whole, apart from a few special exceptions, the proposal for public operation is a live one only where there is monopoly ; and here the case for it, as against that for public control, works out differently in different industries. § 15. When public operation is determined upon for a concern hitherto in private hands, the determination of a proper purchase price presents difficulties. § 16. But, even when a heavy ransom has to be paid to vested interests, it may still be for the general good that a public authority should buy up a private monopoly, in order to stop artificial restriction of output.

PART III

THE NATIONAL DIVIDEND AND LABOUR

CHAPTER I

Industrial peace being obviously relevant to the magnitude of the national dividend, the machinery designed for maintaining it must be examined.

CHAPTER II

§§ 1-5. Various possible lines of classification are compared and discussed.

CHAPTER III

§ 1. The United Kingdom is the classical home of voluntary arrangements for dealing with differences about broad general questions. § 2. A permanent organ of negotiation is more effective than *ad hoc* meetings called specially to deal with differences as they arise. §§ 3-4. The constitution of this organ and methods of procedure are discussed. § 5. Agreements for conciliation alone are compared with agreements which also provide for arbitration in the last resort. § 6. The qualities required in arbitrators, their number, and the best method of appointing them, are discussed. §§ 7-8. Also the question of a referendum, and the question of monetary guarantees.

CHAPTER IV

§§ 1-5. In the event of a failure on the part of employers and workpeople in an industry to reach agreement, mediation may be usefully undertaken by eminent outsiders, non-governmental Boards or governmental agencies. But care should be taken not to allow the existence of this machinery to check the development of direct voluntary arrangements between the parties.

CHAPTER V

§ 1. Coercive intervention may provide for disputants to enter a court of compulsory arbitration if both of them wish to do so. § 2. Or for "extending" agreements made between associations of employers and employed so as to make them binding on outside employers and workpeople. § 3. Or it may follow the model of the Canadian Industrial Disputes Investigation Act. § 4. Or it may take the form of compulsory arbitration as understood in Australasia.

CHAPTER VI

§ 1. Disputes between associations of employers and employed are in some respects analogous to disputes between nations. § 2. Within limits the wage rate subject to a bargain between two organisations is indeterminate. §§ 3-11. The influences by which the *range of indeterminateness* and the *range of practicable bargains* are determined are examined. § 12. The bearing of this study upon the prospects of industrial peace in various circumstances is explained. § 13. And also its bearing upon a common view of an arbitrator's functions.

CHAPTER VII

§ 1. In each several industry for each class of workers there is some length of working day, varying with the circumstances of different occupations, the overstepping of which is disadvantageous to the national dividend. § 2. There is evidence that in fact this limit tends to be passed. § 3. The way in which this can and does happen is explained. § 4. The length of day best for the national dividend may be too long for economic welfare. § 5. There is a *prima facie* case for State intervention to prevent unduly long hours. § 6. In this connection the problem of overtime is discussed.

CHAPTER VIII

§ 1. Broadly speaking, the worker's output will be larger, and the national dividend more advantaged, the more nearly his remuneration is adjusted to services rendered. § 2. Adjustment is complicated by the fact that a man's services to his firm include more than his immediate physical output. § 3. By the fact that output is liable to vary in quality as well as in quantity. § 4. And by the fact that even quantity of output cannot, in some occupations, be measured. § 5. Under time-wages some degree of adjustment is feasible. §§ 6-7. Under piece-wages adjustment could be made closer if it were not for the difficulty created by the "cutting" or "nibbling" of rates. §§ 8-9. Premium bonus plans and piece-rate plans are compared. § 10. The difficulty of "cutting" and "nibbling" may be dealt with by means of collective bargaining. §§ 11-12. The task-wage system is discussed. § 13. The conclusion reached is that the interests of the national dividend will be best promoted under a system of piece - wage scales controlled by collective bargaining.

CHAPTER IX

§ 1. In general the national dividend is injured by causes that prevent labour being so distributed that the demand prices for and the wages of labour of any given grade are equal in different places and occupations. §§ 2-3. This is subject to an important qualification. § 4. The chief of the above causes are ignorance, costs of movement and restrictions imposed upon movement. §§ 5-6. The most fundamental way in which ignorance operates is by impairing the initial distribution of new generations of workpeople as they flow into industry. § 7. Ignorance also interferes with the correction of errors in the initial distribution of labour by subsequent movement. § 8. The extent to which it does this depends upon the form in which wage-contracts are made. §§ 9-10. The effects of "costs of movement" as an obstacle to adjustment are studied. § 11. Including the peculiar element of cost involved in the geographical unity of the family. § 12. The most important instance of restrictions imposed from without is afforded by the traditional and customary exclusion of women workers from certain occupations. § 13. The foregoing obstacles to what may be called the ideal distribution of labour may (1) crumble from within, (2) be pulled down at public cost, or (3) be leapt over. § 14. When they crumble from within, the national dividend is practically certain to be increased. § 15. When they are pulled down at public cost, there is a presumption that it will be diminished, but this presumption may be rebutted. § 16. When they are leapt over, the effect on the dividend is bound to be beneficial if the obstacle is ignorance, but there is a presumption that it will be injurious if the obstacle is costs.

CHAPTER X

§ 1. Workpeople are liable, not merely to be distributed badly between different employments, but, sometimes, to be unemployed altogether. § 2. Their liability to this, and the loss of dividend associated with it, can be lessened by the development of Employment Exchanges. § 3. And by the utilisation of them as centres of engagement. §§ 4-5. Some principal influences upon which the efficiency of these Exchanges depends are considered.

CHAPTER XI

§ 1. The analysis of the two preceding chapters is relevant to a comparison of the three principal ways open to employers of meeting periods of depression : namely, (1) working full time and dismissing some of the staff; (2) working full time and rotating employment among the whole staff; (3) working short time with the whole staff. § 2. The causes determining the choice between the short-time plan and both the other two plans are considered. §§ 3-4. Those determining the choice between the dismissal plan and both the others. § 5. And those determining the choice between the rotation plan and both the others. § 6. The short-time plan and the dismissal plan are the most usual. § 7. *Prima facie* the dismissal plan seems certain to be the more injurious to the national dividend, because, through the unemployment it creates, it reacts adversely on the quality of the workpeople. § 8. But against the other method is to be set its tendency to prevent workpeople from moving to other jobs or places when the interests of the dividend require that they should do so. § 9. The suggestion that manual workers should be placed in the same position as the permanent salaried staff is discussed.

CHAPTER XII

§ 1. The "natural course of wages" is understood to mean the system of wage rates that would prevail in the absence of interference on the part of some person or body of persons external to the workmen and employers involved in the discussion of them. § 2. Interference may be attempted by consumers' associations or by governmental authorities. § 3. In some conditions interference can be baffled by undetected evasion ; but this cannot generally be done when workpeople are organised. § 4. There are special opportunities for evasion when the regulating authority is only able to determine minimum day-rates for "ordinary" workers. § 5. Where undetected evasion is not practicable, there are various sanctions by which interference can be made effective.

CHAPTER XV

§ 1. Inside any industry fair wages as between different men engaged on the same class of job mean wages proportionate to efficiency. § 2. Under time-wages more can be accomplished in this sense than is sometimes supposed. § 3. Under piece-wages the difficulties are less, and several allowances must be made. § 4. First, an allowance for differences in the assistance which different men receive in their work from machinery and nature. This allowance can be calculated closely. §§ 5-6. Secondly, an allowance for differences in the exact character of the operation which different men perform. This also, with the help of "elementary rate-fixing," can be calculated closely. § 7. Thirdly, an allowance for differences in the assistance they receive from the co-operation of managing power. The calculation of this is much more difficult; but something can be done by the establishment, alongside of the piece-rate scale, of a minimum day wage.

CHAPTER XVI

§ 1. What is fair as between dissimilar persons of given characteristics depends not only on what those characteristics are, but also on the surrounding circumstances. §§ 2-3. This is worked out as regards persons possessing different degrees of the same kind of ability. § 4. And as between persons possessing different kinds of ability. § 5. The practical significance of this analysis is illustrated.

CHAPTER XVII

§§ 1-2. Interference to raise wages that are already fair may benefit the national dividend if, as a result of it, employers are stimulated to improve their organisation and technique. §§ 3-4. General movements may occur of a kind that would make a change in all wage rates advantageous for the national dividend; and that, therefore, the existence of fairness in a wage rate cannot be regarded as a conclusive reason against change. § 5. This consideration is especially important when general prices have been suddenly and largely altered by currency changes; but there are several distinctions to be borne in mind. § 6. It is sometimes claimed that, even when the wages in an industry are fair, they should, nevertheless, always be forced up if they are less than "living wages." §§ 7-10. This claim is examined in detail; and the general conclusion is reached that to act on it effectively would injure the national dividend. § 11. The system of "family wages" is discussed.

is smaller the more elastic is the supply of labour in the occupation. The practical implications of this proposition are drawn out. § 12. Automatic machinery for making adjustments to fluctuations in the demand for labour is provided by sliding scales. §§ 13-18. A detailed study is made of the various forms which these may assume and of the problems connected with them. § 19. When relations between the parties are sufficiently good, better results may be obtained by arrangements under which joint-committees adjust wages at two- or three-monthly intervals, not merely in accordance with a mechanical index, but also with a view to other factors of which this may fail to take account.

PART IV

THE DISTRIBUTION OF THE NATIONAL DIVIDEND

CHAPTER I

The purpose of this Part is to inquire whether any important causes can be distinguished which affect in different senses the size of the national dividend as a whole and the size of that part of it which accrues to the poor; and to study the practical problems which the existence of such causes suggests.

CHAPTER II

§ 1. Certain statistical investigations conducted by Pareto seem, at first sight, to show that the magnitude and distribution of the dividend are rigidly bound together, in such wise that it is impossible for the dividend as a whole and the real income of the poor to move otherwise than in the same direction. § 2. But the statistics set out are not adequate to support this conclusion. §§ 3-5. Nor are its logical foundations sound. § 6. The possible openings for disharmony must, therefore, be studied in detail.

CHAPTER III

§ 1. The distribution of income among people is analytically quite distinct from the distribution among factors of production discussed in economic text-books. Nevertheless no great error is introduced if we identify the income of the poorer classes with the receipts from wages of the factor labour. §§ 2-6. In an elaborate discussion it is shown that a cause operating to increase the national dividend by increasing the supply of capital cannot, in present conditions, at the same time diminish the real income of labour. § 7. A cause facilitating the investment of capital abroad *may* act discordantly from the standpoint of a short period, though hardly from that of a long period. § 8. On the basis of a proof that the demand for labour in general in any one country is likely to be highly elastic, it is shown that a cause operating to increase the national dividend by increasing the supply of labour cannot at the same time diminish the real income of labour. § 9. A complicating side-issue is examined. § 10. And some practical implications of the results attained are noticed.

CHAPTER IV

§ 1. The problem of this chapter is to determine in what, if any, conditions, an invention or improvement, which increases the aggregate dividend, will diminish the absolute share of labour. § 2. This problem is not settled by determining whether an invention increases or decreases employment in the industry in which it is made. § 3. Its solution turns on the *comparative proportions* in which the quantities of labour and capital respectively available in occupations outside the one to which the invention applies are affected. §§ 4-6. An analysis on this basis is carried out in detail. § 7. The conclusion is reached that an invention that benefits the national dividend may at the same time lessen the real income of the poor ; but that this is a very improbable contingency.

CHAPTER V

§ 1. It is next required to determine in what, if any, conditions the forcing-up of the wage rate of a group of workpeople will at the same time injure the national dividend and increase the real income of labour as a whole. § 2. The particular workpeople directly concerned, if they are not themselves purchasers of the commodity they produce, will be benefited if the demand for their labour has an elasticity less than unity. § 3. The influences which determine this elasticity in different circumstances are examined. § 4. The whole body of workpeople, if they are not purchasers of the commodity, will be benefited if the demand for the labour of the particular workpeople has an elasticity less than unity. § 5. Since, in fact, workpeople are themselves purchasers of most of the things that workpeople make, the prospect of a net gain is not, *prima facie,* very bright. § 6. Moreover, when account is taken of the cumulative reactions set up on the side of capital, this prospect, and with it the likelihood of disharmony between the effect on the dividend and the effect on the absolute share of the poor, is lessened. § 7. This conclusion must, however, be qualified, in so far as the State undertakes to help with public funds persons thrown into distress through unemployment.

CHAPTER VI

CHAPTER VII

CHAPTER VIII

CHAPTER IX

CHAPTER X

CHAPTER XI

CHAPTER XII

§§ 4-6. But transferences in the form of training or of care in sickness to normal adult workers may yield a large return. § 7. And well-managed transferences in the form of education and nurture to children a very large return. § 8. Transferences in the form of general purchasing power are less likely to be employed effectively. § 9. Some friendly supervision over the use made of them seems to be desirable.

CHAPTER XIII

§ 1. The establishment of a national minimum standard of real income may affect the aggregate dividend disadvantageously at the same time that it benefits the poor. § 2. The nature of the national minimum that is contemplated is described. § 3. The theoretical considerations relevant to the level at which it should be placed are analysed. § 4. Practically we may conclude that it can safely be set higher the larger is the real income per head of the community. §§ 5-6. This conclusion is developed with special reference to the United Kingdom. §§ 7-8. Its relation to international labour legislation is discussed. § 9. And its relation to the problem of immigration.

APPENDICES

INTRODUCTION TO THE TRANSACTION EDITION (2001)

PIGOU, *THE ECONOMICS OF WELFARE*, AND THE GENESIS OF WELFARE ECONOMICS*

Arthur Cecil Pigou: A Life Sketch

THE author of the book you hold in your hands lived a long life (1877-1959), occupying the Chair of Political Economy at Cambridge for thirty-five years (1908-1943), and publishing more than thirty books and 100 pamphlets and articles. In his lifetime, he witnessed the rise and demise of Marshallian economics, which he embraced wholeheartedly, systematized, and extended to areas unexplored by Marshall himself.

Arthur Cecil Pigou was born November 18, 1877 on the Isle of Wight to Nora Frances Sophia Lees and Clarence George Scott Pigou. His mother descended from a family in Irish administration, his father from a French Huguenot family engaged in trade with India and China. Educated at Harrow (1891-1896), Pigou earned many distinctions as a scholar and athlete, and was a contemporary of Winston Churchill, G.M. Trevelyan, and Leo Amery. He entered King's College, Cambridge on a Minor Scholarship in History and Foreign Languages (1896). At Cambridge, he studied poetry, moral philosophy, and political economy with Oscar Browning, Lowes Dickinson, and Alfred Marshall. His achievements were stunning: A First Class degree in the History Tripos (1899), a First Class degree in Part II of the Moral Sciences Tripos with special distinction in Political Economy (1900), the Burney Prize for his essay on "Robert Browning as a Religious Teacher" (1901), the Cobden Prize for "The Causes and Effects of

xxix

Changes in the Relative Values of Agricultural Produce in the United Kingdom during the last Fifty Years" (1901), a King's Fellowship in 1902, and the Adam Smith Prize for "The Principles and Methods of Industrial Peace" (1903).

In his youth, Pigou was a fun-loving athlete who spent his leisure hours playing cricket, tennis, and golf, and touring Brittany on his bicycle. As an undergraduate, he was often "engaged in composing lengthy English poems" during lectures (Pigou, 1953, p. 3) and later recited them in debates on national issues in the Union, of which he was secretary and president (1899-1900). By the 1940s, Pigou had become a recluse, reading mystery novels, playing chess, and writing stories for his friends' children. This dramatic change had many causes: his experience as an ambulance driver at the front during the Great War; a fibrillating heart that made him seriously ill in 1928 and 1937 and severely restricted his mountaineering—Pigou was an enthusiastic and experienced climber; and the bitter hostility among the Keynesians and the "classics" at Cambridge following the publication of the *General Theory* (1936).

Alfred Marshall, who discovered Pigou's "exceptional genius" in 1900, hired him to teach the general course in economics at Cambridge from 1901 until 1904, when he became the first Girdlers lecturer. In 1908, Pigou succeeded Marshall in the Chair of Political Economy at the youthful age of thirty, thanks in part to his master's sophisticated manipulation of the election process.[1] *Wealth and Welfare* (1912), his first major book as the Professor of Political Economy, laid the groundwork for Pigou's later work: *Unemployment* (1913), *The Economics of Welfare* (1920, 1924, 1929c, 1932), *Industrial Fluctuations* (1927a, 1929b), *A Study in Public Finance* (1928b, 1929a, 1947), the *Theory of Unemployment* (1933), and *Employment and Equilibrium* (1941, 1949).[2]

According to Pigou, economics is a realistic science designed to lead, directly or indirectly, to "practical results in social improvement" (Pigou, 1932, p. 4): "When we elect to watch the play of human motives that are ordinary—that are sometimes mean and dismal and ignoble—our impulse is not the philosopher's impulse, knowledge for the sake of knowledge, but rather the physiologist's, knowledge for the healing that knowledge may help to bring." However, economics is not an art, nor does it "directly enunciate percepts of government." Economists discover new truths and advance economic knowledge (ibid., p. 5) independent of political considerations, and without committing the "intellectual crime" of changing their theory to conform to political exigencies (1935a, pp. 9-10).

According to Pigou, it is philosopher-kings who "build up policies directed to the common good" based on economic and other data (Pigou, 1939, p. 220). However, he increasingly lost hope that "an advance in economic knowledge will appreciably affect actual happenings" (ibid.). Although he served on several government committees early in his career—the Board of Trade (1916-1917), the Cunliff Committee on the Foreign Exchange (1918-1919), the Royal Commission on the Income Tax (1919-1920), the Chamberlain Committee on the Currency and Bank of England Note Issues (1924-1925), and a committee of the Economic Advisory Council (1930)—events of the 1930s (such as the return to protectionism in 1931) increased his aversion to advising the government. Politicians did not behave like philosopher-kings: "To how small an extent the conduct of affairs is the result of thought!" (ibid.). From the early 1930s, Pigou's only connection to public policy was through letters to the editor of *The Times* and occasional appearances before a commission when he was called upon.

Unlike his contemporary, John Maynard Keynes, Pigou was a reluctant participant in public debates over economic issues. In his view, they diminished the influence of economists by creating the impression that they "are hopelessly divided" (1935a, p. 24).[3] Nor did he favor private debates among economists that involve disciplinary novitiates: "before he has learnt to swim, he is tossed to a turbulent sea." Debate on theoretical issues proves valuable only among mature economists "breaking down dogmatic slumber" and leading to "a progressive, if irregular, advance towards clearer understanding" (1939, p. 220). However, theoretical debate has its etiquette. Economists should try to improve "on what has been done ... build on it ... strengthen and test its foundations," but not "cavil and depreciate" it (1935a,

p. 23). It is only in light of these views that the moral and emotional tone of Pigou's review of Keynes's *General Theory* can be understood.[4]

Pigou followed these guidelines for much of his career. Occasionally he responded to his critics, either to correct flaws in his theoretical arguments (Young, 1913) or in response to a seminal article (Sraffa, 1926). In other cases, he incorporated new theories, at least partially, into his own work (the IS-LM model). However, he did not respond to some controversies for many years (interpersonal comparisons of utility and modern welfare economics). For the most part, Pigou avoided "the give-and-take of discussions with others" in favor of "undisturbed concentration on solution of intellectual problems" (Saltmarsh and Wilkinson, 1960, p. 12).

Pigou saw himself as a theoretical economist whose main task was to develop "a set of fairly general ideas, a machinery or method of thinking" that could be used to analyze "particular issues ... more clearly" (Pigou, 1952a, p. 65). As a general rule, he entered analytical territory only if it had not already been explored by Marshall: "What was the use, for example, of anyone working at Money, when we knew that in his head, if not in his drawer, there was an analysis enormously superior to anything that we could hope to accomplish?" (Pigou, 1939, p. 220). Marshall, perhaps consciously, had been reluctant to pursue a theory of economic policy. Following Sidgwick, Pigou investigated Adam Smith's "system of natural liberty" and its limits. For most of his life, Pigou constructed and reconstructed the many theoretical components of this research program, which became welfare economics. Neither economic fashions nor the historical upheavals of his times altered Pigou's research agenda. During the Great Depression of the 1930s, for example, he published *The Economics of the Stationary States* (1935b), a theoretical book dealing with the workings of a fully employed economy under stationary state conditions. During World War II, he did not follow the lead of his British and American contemporaries by concentrating on the questions posed by a war economy. Instead he wrote *Employment and Equilibrium* (1941), which contrasted the Keynesian and the classical models.

The Economics of Welfare: **History**

The Economics of Welfare established welfare economics as a field of study. Its beginnings lie in Pigou's *Wealth and Welfare* (1912). If originality "set its unmistakable mark" on *Wealth and Welfare*, as Edgworth claimed (1913, p. 62), this was not due to its novel philosophy or methodological tools. The book was heavily influenced by Henry Sidgwick's utilitarian philosophy and Alfred Marshall's marginalist analysis. Sidgwick, who had argued that self-motivated economic pursuits do not necessarily lead to the most efficient or just results (Sidgwick, 1901), identified areas in which the government can increase total welfare. Pigou's contribution was to build a framework for analyzing Sidgwick's list of divergences between private and social interests by employing Marshall's "engine for the discovery of concrete truths" (Pigou, 1925, p. 86).[5]

It is difficult to establish the origins of Pigou's systematic thought about welfare economics. In the preface to *Wealth and Welfare*, he stated that shortly after beginning the book as an investigation into the causes of unemployment, he realized that "these causes are so closely interwoven with the general body of economic activity that an isolated treatment of them is scarcely practicable" (1912, p. vii). Pigou's interest in labor issues may be traced to "The Principles and Methods of Industrial Peace," which was started in spring 1902 and formed the basis of his 1903-1904 Jevons Memorial Lectures at the University College, London (Pigou, 1905). In 1906, *Protective and Preferential Import Duties*[6] introduced the major themes of *Wealth and Welfare*, including the impact of tariffs on national welfare through possible repercussions on the size, distribution, and variability of the national dividend.

The first edition of *The Economics of Welfare* appeared in 1920. However, Pigou had worked out most of its analysis during 1913-1914, rewriting *Wealth and Welfare* "partly with the objective of making it less difficult to understand and partly with that of including a number of topics not originally discussed in it" (Pigou, 1915). At a formidable length of nearly one thousand pages, *The Economics of Welfare* was twice as long as its predecessor. Pigou included the sections of the earlier book on the relationship between total welfare, the national dividend, and the allocation of resources (Parts I and II), the distribution of national dividend (Part V) and its variability (Part VI), and added sections on the relationship between the organization of labor and public finance (Parts III and IV) and the size of the national dividend.

Edwin Cannan's review of *The Economics of Welfare* criticized Pigou severely for its length: "The sage who observed that of the making of books there is no end, was a child in these matters. In Professor Pigou's paradise each author will scrap his *magnum opus* by superseding it with another twice its size every eight years. Most of us will sigh for a little of Malthus' 'prudential restraint.' It would surely have been better to let *Wealth and Welfare* remain in its old form and to have supplemented it with entirely new books of more moderate dimensions" (Cannan, 1921, pp. 206-207).

In the second edition (1924), Pigou made the book more manageable by eliminating two major components.[7] His analysis of the variability of the national dividend was incorporated into *Industrial Fluctuations,* a book on which he had been working since 1922; and his discussion of public finance, which was reproduced in *The Political Economy of War* (1921), became the subject of the now classic *A Study in Public Finance.* Pigou also attempted to improve the exposition of the second edition. The technical analysis that "was found confusing by some students" was eliminated and the terminology simplified (Pigou, 1924, p. v). The "threefold distinction between social, trade, and individual net product," for example, was replaced by "a single distinction between social and private net product" (ibid., p. vi). Pigou also "substantially" revised his theoretical treatment of the laws of returns (ibid.). The third and fourth editions (1929c, 1932) retained the structure of the second, with minor modifications in the number of chapters.

The composition and successive revisions of *The Economics of Welfare* began in the first decade of the twentieth century and ended in the fourth edition of 1932. Thus the book remained substantially unaffected by the revolution in economic theory that began in the 1930s. Why did Pigou produce no fifth edition? There are several explanations: the advent of the Great Depression, the effect of the Keynesian revolution on economists at Cambridge, Pigou's ill health, World War II, and his mandatory retirement in 1943. By his retirement, Pigou was sixty-five and "incapable" of the "amount of concentrated effort" necessary for a thorough revision. Rather than producing a "botched patchwork," he left the text of the book intact (1952b, p. viii). Some recent theoretical developments, such as the theory of imperfect competition or the new welfare economics, were addressed in new appendices (the 1952 reprint included eight). He considered employment and income issues raised by Keynes's *General Theory* that lay outside the scope of the 1932 edition in his *Employment and Equilibrium,* and also in a series of popular books: *Lapses from Full Employment* (1945), *Income* (1946), and *Income Revisited* (1955).

The Economics of Welfare: Content

The Economics of Welfare has four Parts: Part I analyzes the relationship between the national dividend and economic and total welfare. Parts II and III link the size of the dividend to the allocation of resources in the economy and the institutional structure governing labor-market operations. Part IV explores the relationship between the national dividend and its distribution. A summary of each Part follows.

Part I—Welfare and the National Dividend

Part I provides a definition of the general concpet of welfare and a distinction between economic and total welfare. Pigou examines the imprecisions associated with these definitions and frames criteria for establishing differences in degrees of welfare.

For Pigou, welfare and good are cognates (Pigou, 1912, p. 3). Like G. E. Moore's concept of the good, Pigou's concept of welfare is indefinable: "welfare" refers to unanalyzable "states of consciousness." Unlike Moore's concept of the good, Pigou's welfare "can be brought under the category of greater and less" (Pigou, 1932, p. 10). Since an inchoate concept such as welfare cannot form an object of investigation, Pigou limits his analysis to economic welfare: that part of total welfare consisting of a group of "satisfactions and dissatisfactions which can be brought into relation with a money measure" (ibid., p. 23). According to Pigou, money measures the intensity of desires, not the satisfaction derived from the consumption of products. These two variables coincide except in cases involving "attitudes toward the future." In general, people suffer from defective "telescopic faculty," preferring a present sum of satisfactions to an equal and certain future sum (ibid., pp. 24-5). Hence, inter-temporal allocation of resources is based on an irrationality that has significant implications: the level of savings is inadequate, there is insufficient investment in forests or tunnels, natural resources are used wastefully, and animal species can be extinguished.[8]

Economic welfare has an "objective counterpart:" the national dividend (ibid., p. 31). Pigou maintains that in most cases it is reasonable to assume that economic welfare increases with an increase in the size of the dividend. However, it does not follow that economic welfare is an index of total welfare. Economic causes that enhance economic welfare, such as an increase in the length of the average work-day, could have deleterious effects on workers' quality of life and non-economic welfare, which is the portion of total welfare that cannot be "brought into relation with a money measure.""Efforts devoted to the production of people who are good instruments may involve a failure to produce people who are good men" (ibid., p. 14). This proviso notwithstanding, Pigou concludes it is safe to assume that "the effect of any cause on economic welfare ... is ... *probably* equivalent in direction, though not in magnitude, to the effect on total welfare" (ibid., p. 20; emphasis in the original).

Although the analytical primacy Pigou ascribes to the national dividend has the advantage of avoiding the difficult issue of utility measurement, this concept is not without problems of its own. Under what conditions could it be established that the dividend of period II is higher than that of period I? Pigou offers the following criterion:

> ... we say that the dividend in period II. is greater than in period I. if the items that are added to it in period II. are items *to conserve which*

they would be willing to give more money than they would be willing
to give to conserve the items that are taken away from it in period II.
(ibid., p. 52; emphasis in the original)

Such a criterion produces an unambiguous ranking of the national
dividend if tastes and the distribution of income remain unchanged.   If they change, a paradox may result from the
proposition that the dividend of period I is both higher and
lower than the dividend of period II (ibid., pp. 52-3).   In
response to this problem, Pigou assumes constant tastes and
distributions of income; when this assumption is violated, he finds
it reasonable to believe that the dividend would usually change
in the same direction from the point of view of both periods (ibid.,
pp. 53-54).

    A criterion of change in the size of the dividend should not
be confused with a measure of this change.   As measures, Pigou
uses the Paasche (P)—$(\Sigma p_2 q_2 / \Sigma p_2 q_1)$—and the Laspeyre (L)—
$(\Sigma p_1 q_2 / \Sigma p_1 q_1)$—index number ratios.   If both ratios are higher than
one, Pigou argues, then the national dividend of period II is
higher than that of period I.   If they are both less than 1, the
dividend of period I is higher.[9]

    After dealing with definitional problems, Pigou proposes two
welfare criteria.   Economic welfare can improve under either of
two conditions: the national dividend increases without changing
the absolute share of the dividend allocated to the poor; or the
allocation of the national dividend to the poor increases without
reducing its size (ibid., pp. 82, 89).   Before discussing these two
criteria in Parts II-IV, Pigou anticipates two objections to his
analysis.   The first is the Malthusian argument that any improvement in the average income of the poor leads to higher marriage
rates, lower mortality rates, population increases, and a lower
average income.   However, empirical evidence shows Pigou that
poverty and high birth rates go hand in hand (ibid., pp. 99-102).
In the long-run, higher incomes for the poor may "bring about the
development of a higher spiritual and cultural level, in which
more forethought is exercised about the children and more
satisfactions rival to that of having children come to the front"
(ibid., p. 101).

Second, Pigou rejects claims made by biologists of his time that "alterations in the size, composition, or distribution of the national dividend, affect environment only; and environment is of no importance, because improvements in it cannot react on the quality of the children born to those who enjoy the improvements" (ibid., p. 110). In Pigou's assessment, environments, much like people, "have children."

> Though education, and so forth, cannot influence new births in the physical world, they can influence them in the world of ideas; and ideas, once produced or once accepted by a particular generation, whether or not they can be materialised into mechanical inventions, may not only remodel from its very base the environment which succeeding generations enjoy, but may also pave the way for further advance. For, whereas each new man must begin where his last ancestor began, each new invention begins where its last ancestor left off. In this way a permanent or, rather, a progressive change of environment is brought about, and since environment is admittedly able to exert an important influence on persons actually subjected to it, such a change may produce enduring consequences (ibid., pp. 113-4).

Part II—The National Dividend and the Allocation of Resources

In part II, Pigou investigates "how far the free play of self-interest ... tends to distribute the country's resources in the way most favourable to the production of a large national dividend, and how far it is feasible for State action to improve upon" it (ibid., p. xii). Pigou analyzes the efficiency of resource allocation by using his innovative concepts of marginal social net product (MSNP)—output resulting from the investment of an increment of a resource regardless of its beneficiaries—and marginal private net product (MPNP)—output created by a resource increment accrued to the person undertaking the investment. The national dividend can be maximized only if the MSNP of resources is brought to equality in all their uses. However, the pursuit of self-interest in a market economy—assuming perfect knowledge and zero costs of movement (see below)—equalizes the MPNP, not the MSNP, across productive activities: "industrialists are interested, not in the social, but only in the private, net product of their operations" (ibid., p. 172). When there are divergences between MPNP and

MSNP, therefore, the national dividend is not at its maximum, and "certain acts of interference with normal economic processes may be expected, not to diminish, but to increase the dividend" (ibid.).[10]

Pigou qualifies this conclusion in three important respects. First, any act of reallocation entails costs of movement; for example, costs involved in retraining and relocating workers, psychological costs of moving a home, and job losses for other members of the family. Second, actions directed at reducing costs of movement and increasing mobility, if combined with imperfect knowledge (ignorance), may prove counterproductive by allocating capital and labor to lower productivity sectors. Third, since government subsidy of such efforts imposes costs on taxpayers, it is justifiable only when the private sector fails to take the initiative to improve mobility or knowledge (ibid., pp. 148, 510-11).

Marginal private and social net products diverge because a portion of the marginal product of a resource accrues, positively or negatively, to people who have not employed that resource. But divergences differ depending on the market structure.

Misallocation of Resources Under Simple Competition. Under competitive conditions, involuntarily affected parties "may fall into any one of three principal groups: (1) owners of durable instruments of production, of which the investor is a tenant; (2) persons who are not producers of the commodity in which the investor is investing; (3) persons who are producers of this commodity" (ibid., p. 174).

The first class of divergences occurs when the investor is not the same person as the owner of the durable means of production. In such cases, the MSNP is higher than the MPNP because the tenant's investment benefits the owner upon the termination of the lease. Since tenants do not capture the total benefit of their investment, they fail to make the socially desirable levels of expenditure to improve the durable means of production. According to Pigou, such divergences can be "mitigated by a modification of the contractual relation between any two contracting parties," including compensation schemes that would internalize the external benefits of the tenant's investment (ibid., p. 192). Pigou's real-world examples show the defects that plague such modifications: owners, for example, may increase rents to recapture the compensation made to the tenant. These imperfections notwithstanding, Pigou suggests only one solution to the problems posed by this class of divergences: modifying contractual specifications by the tenant and the owner.[11]

The second class of divergences occurs because it is either impossible (public goods) or technically difficult (externalities) to exact payment from the parties who have captured incidental benefits or to extract compensation for those who have been burdened by incidental costs (ibid., pp. 183, 185).[12] The MPNP of public goods—lighthouses, parks, roads, forests, street lamps, prevention of pollution, and scientific research—is less than their MSNP. In the case of externalities—rabbits overrunning a neighbor's land, factories located in crowded residential areas, motor cars wearing out the surface of roads, crimes induced by the sale of alcoholic drinks, wars designed to protect a country's foreign investments, and pregnant women's factory work—the MPNP is higher than the MSNP. It is obvious to Pigou that this class of divergences "cannot, like divergences due to tenancy laws, be mitigated by a modification of the contractual relation between any two contracting parties" (ibid., p. 192). The reasons vary from technical difficulty in exacting payment "from the benefited parties" or compensating "the injured parties" (ibid., pp. 183-4) to the highly complex "inter-relations of the various private persons affected" (ibid., p. 194).

Given the impossibility of reducing or eliminating this group of divergences by contractual arrangements, Pigou suggests alternatives such as government action. It is possible, although not always advisable, for the government to close such a gap by "extraordinary encouragements"—most obviously subsidies—and "extraordinary restraints"—most obviously taxes (ibid., p. 192). However, other means can achieve the same goals: urban planning and zoning laws, cleaning of slums, providing information and training, paid maternity leaves, patents, or holding companies responsible for health-care costs if the high disease rates can be linked to their operations (ibid., pp. 184-96).

The third group of divergences occurs when the return to employing an incremental unit of resource benefits or harms other producers within a certain industry. In the decreasing-cost industries, the change in the output of one firm may create external economies for other firms, including technical or managerial breakthroughs, that would lower the cost of production of the equilibrium firm.[13] Given competitive conditions, the size of the firm is small, and its activity cannot decrease factor prices. As a result, the reduced cost of production (the gain to the firms) is not offset by the loss of income for owners of factors of production. It follows that the external economies created by decreasing-cost industries are a real gain to society as a whole (ibid., pp. 222-3). The MSNP of production in such industries is higher than its MPNP.

Increasing-cost industries are on a different plane. A firm's production could create external diseconomies for other firms by increasing the price of factors of production in fixed supply, mainly land. However, the increased cost of production does not necessarily represent a divergence between private and social costs. As long as the owners of the fixed factor are citizens of the home country, the increased rents represent transfers of purchasing power from producers to owners of these factors. Divergence is possible only if rents accrue to foreign nationals (ibid., pp. 220-221).

The ideal output occurs when the MSNP and MPNP are equal. An increasing-cost industry produces more than the socially ideal level of output if it transfers purchasing power to other countries. A tax on such industries could promote economic welfare by cutting the level of output. A decreasing-cost industry produces less than the socially ideal level. Subsidies could increase output, assuming they are funded by taxes that leave the size of the national dividend unchanged (ibid., p. 224). However, Pigou warns that industries should not be considered in isolation. If, for example, social and private benefits diverge at the same rate in all industries, taxes or subsidies would not increase the size of the dividend (ibid., p. 225).

Misallocation of Resources under Monopolistic Conditions. In industries where one or more sellers produce a large share of the total output, Pigou argues, actual output is generally less than its ideal level (ibid., pp. 266-8). The welfare implications of monopolies that practice price discrimination—of the first, second, or third degree—are ambiguous and require a case-by-case analysis: output levels can be less than, equal to, or greater than the ideal level (ibid., pp. 275-89). In the case of public utilities or railway transportation, where monopolies may become necessary, Pigou offers a lengthy discussion of whether they should be publicly controlled or operated. Here as well, the welfare implications are nebulous. Judgment should be suspended until detailed analyses of the industry and the government body that would assume public control or operation are conducted (ibid., pp. 405-406).

A monopolistically competitive market structure (in Pigou's terminology duopoly and oligopoly) may cause social and private interests to diverge for reasons unrelated to the level of output. Firms may engage in wasteful advertising, exploit their workers, or deceive their customers instead of attempting to achieve managerial efficiency. The formation of trusts may drive out small- and medium-size enterprises, preventing capable working class entrepreneurs from moving up a learning ladder (ibid., pp. 196-207). Standardization of production, which has the direct effect of increasing productivity, may indirectly inhibit "inventions and improvements," thereby diminishing the productivity of future generations (ibid., pp. 209-210). Finally, scientific management may reduce workers' productivity by ignoring the diversity of their "psychological and physical qualities." The elimination of "opportunities for the exercise of initiative," if carried too far, may destroy workers' "capacity for initiative" (ibid., pp. 211-212).

Both voluntary or involuntary arrangements—agreement among firms, taxes, or prohibition—can reduce or eliminate competitive advertisement. Exploitation and deception may be reduced (taxes) or eliminated (prohibition) by the government (ibid., pp. 199-201). Aside from vague references to the role of government or philanthropic institutions in encouraging the formation of small businesses or reducing the negative impacts of scientific management, Pigou offers no solutions to the problems posed by trusts and Taylorism (ibid., pp. 206-207, 212).

Part III-the National Dividend and Labor

In Part III of *The Economics of Welfare*, Pigou links the size of the national dividend to the institutional structure that governs labor-market operations. This structure includes the "machinery of industrial peace," hours of work, distribution of unemployment and labor across occupations, the method for compensating labor, and labor unions.

The Machinery of Industrial Peace. According to Pigou, strikes or lock-outs diminish output in the industries directly affected. There are spillover effects as well: the supply of raw material or equipment to other industries is reduced or cut off, the unemployed decrease their demand for goods produced by other industries, and workers' children may suffer lasting injury induced by malnutrition (ibid., pp. 411-413). To "build up and fortify the machinery of industrial peace" (ibid., p. 414), therefore, would increase the national dividend and economic welfare.

As a means of enhancing industrial peace, Pigou recommends permanent labor boards, composed of workers' and employers' representatives, that meet regularly to consider "conditions of work, methods of remuneration, technical education, industrial research, improvement of processes" as well as the settlement of disputes between labor and capital (ibid., p. 421). To ease decision making and conflict resolution, Pigou suggests that lawyers be excluded from membership on the boards since they would increase time and cost and create an appearance of opposition between the two sides. He also advocates private meetings and decisions based on more than a simple majority (ibid., pp. 422-4). Arbitration should be available as a last resort. Arbitrators should be impartial, competent, and preferably make their decisions alone (ibid., pp. 424-30).

In the absence of conciliation or arbitration, or when these voluntary arrangements prove ineffectual, Pigou suggests friendly mediation prior to strikes or lock-outs. An "eminent outsider" or a governmental or non-governmental board could mediate. Although each of these methods has its own weaknesses, each may be appropriate in certain circumstances (ibid., pp. 434-7). Finally, in the event that all efforts at reconciling labor and capital fail, the government may intervene coercively. Pigou identifies four options: sanctions imposed on labor and capital; generalization of an agreement that has been made between a subset of employers and workers; legislation requiring that before work stoppages, all disputes be submitted to a tribunal that collects facts, mandates negotiations, and submits reports; and prohibition of strikes and imposition of binding judgments through compulsory arbitration (ibid., pp. 439-47).

Arbitration or mediation over wage disputes should begin by discovering what Pigou calls "the range of practicable bargains." The upper limit of this range—the employers' sticking point— is determined by the maximum wage they are willing to pay in order to avoid the cost of a strike; the lower limit— the employees' sticking point—is determined by the minimum wage workers are willing to accept in order to avoid a strike. Without a range of practicable bargains, no agreement is possible without conflict. However, even on the basis of such a range, a peaceful outcome is not guaranteed (ibid., pp. 451-61).

Hours of Labor. Excessive hours of labor, the deleterious effects of which are much more severe for women and children, affect physical vigor and efficiency and contribute to absenteeism, tardiness, and alcoholism. Pigou argues on many grounds that private self-interest fails to establish socially desirable hours of labor. Workers and employers alike discount future damages resulting from excessively long work-days. Poor workers are often willing to work for longer hours (ibid., pp. 463-7). Where labor is unskilled and casually employed, "the lack of durable connection between individual employers and their workpeople makes it to the employers' interest to work longer hours than are in the long run to the interest of production as a whole" (ibid., p. 466). Finally, employers are often reluctant to reduce the length of the work-day because any such concession would have to be extended to all workers (ibid., p. 467).

In light of these considerations, Pigou sees a *prima facie* case for government action to reduce the length of the work-day. Legislation is less likely to lead to the firing of workers than measures to increase wages. A business would be forced to employ workers until it develops more capital-intensive technology. However, workers might not be fired if capacity to produce improved significantly during the interval necessary for the development of technology. The case for government intervention, Pigou stresses, remains a *prima facie* one. "It is still necessary to consider how far governmental authorities are competent to frame the delicately adjusted regulations which analysis shows to be desirable" (ibid., pp. 468-9).

Methods of Compensation. Pigou regards piece-rates as the best method of compensating labor since they provide the most accurate link between wages and productivity. However, the measurement of workers' marginal product poses several problems: it is difficult to separate the productivity of labor from that of capital; workers' productivity can vary in quality; and the marginal product is intangible in service-oriented or supervisory occupations (ibid., pp. 475-7). Even when piece-rates are practical, their introduction may have negative consequences. Workers who are paid the value of their marginal product have the incentive to increase productivity and expect higher wages. Employers who think that workers are being paid "too much" may attempt to lower wages. In turn, workers may anticipate the probable reduction in wages and deliberately curb their output. Although piece-rates may be the ideal method of compensation, it may prove useless in increasing the national dividend (ibid., pp. 479-80).

Distribution of Labor and Unemployment. According to Pigou, the elimination of inefficiencies in the distribution of labor can increase the national dividend. These inefficiencies have several causes. Imperfect knowledge makes workers ignorant of vacancies or better job opportunities elsewhere and leads parents to miscalculate the future needs of labor markets and their children's capacities (ibid., pp. 492-97; 512). Costs of movement—"equivalent to an annual (or daily) sum spread over the period during which the workman who has moved may expect to find profit in staying in his new place or occupation" (ibid., p. 500)—may prevent a more satisfactory allocation of labor. Unions may create artificial restrictions on the movement of labor by reserving specific jobs for union members. Finally, "traditions and customs" may restrict certain occupations to workers of a specific race, color, or gender (ibid., pp. 507-508).

Ignorance, costs of movement, and artificial or traditional restrictions can be remedied by government action. General progress improves information availability, diminishes the costs of transportation, and breaks down traditional attitudes. Governments can actively promote mobility and the availability of information, employment exchanges, and compulsory reallocation of labor at taxpayer expense. Pigou argues that the latter measures are advisable only if their benefits outweigh the cost to taxpayers (ibid., pp. 509-518).

The distribution of unemployment, similar to the distribution of labor, influences the size of the national dividend. During depressions, which Pigou dos not distinguish from recessions, demand for output is diminished. Employers can obtain the requisite reduction in output either by employing part of their workforce full time and dismissing the remainder or by maintaining the entire workforce for shorter work periods.[14] The choice between the two methods is dictated by technical factors such as the cost of suspending production for part of the day; the sophistication of worker skills such as their ability to handle expensive equipment, their possession of firm-specific human capital, and their knowledge of the firm's manufacturing secrets; and the accuracy with which wages are tied to workers' efficiency—if the time-rate method is used, layoffs of less productive workers are more likely (ibid., pp. 519-21).

Pigou argues that a *prima facie* case can be made for the method of shorter work period. A long spell of unemployment concentrated on a certain group is much more injurious to the national dividend than unemployment of short duration that is shared by everyone. A prolonged deprivation of basic needs may produce long-lasting physical effects for workers and their families; and vagrancy, dependence on charity, or government subsidies may lead to a "permanent weakening of the moral fibre" (ibid., pp. 524-7). However, Pigou warns against adopting the short-term method "out of hand." If workers are mobile and the costs of movement low, layoffs may reduce the national dividend less than the introduction of shorter work periods (ibid., pp. 527-8).

Raising "Unfair" wages. The natural wage rate is mutually determined by workers and employers without the external interference of the government or consumers (ibid., p. 531). However, the natural rate is not necessarily fair. Pigou identifies two types of unfair wage. In the first case, the wage is equal to the value of the workers' marginal product in their current occupation, but less than they would have received had they been engaged in other industries. In the second case, the natural rate is unfair because it is less than the value of workers' marginal product in their present occupation. Pigou regards the second case as exploitative (ibid., pp. 551). Government intervention to increase wages has different implications for the national dividend depending on the type of unfairness.

The first type of unfairness may be due to high costs of labor mobility. Family obligations or retraining costs, for example, may prevent relocation to high-wage areas. Since wage increases in these areas would do nothing to reduce costs of movement or to increase mobility, they would also reduce the national dividend (ibid., p. 554). Workers may also be uninformed about alternative higher paying jobs. In this case, the impact of a wage increase on the national dividend depends on the method of labor engagement. If employers hire workers based on a preference list—workers are irreplaceable—a wage increase will not attract other workers to this occupation, since the mathematical expectations of earnings (aggregate worker earnings/number of workers) is equal to zero. In addition, workers who are laid off as a result of such a wage increase would be compelled to move elsewhere because they know that their release is permanent. Hence, the wage increase would create the incentive for movement to better jobs, the distribution of labor would improve, and the national dividend would increase. But if workers are hired on a casual basis—they are perfectly substitutable—and the elasticity of the demand for labor is less than one, an increase in wages would reduce the size of the dividend. A wage increase raises the mathematical expectations of earnings for laid-off workers as well as workers engaged in other industries. Unemployment would increase and the national dividend would diminish in size. With an elasticity higher than one, the result is indeterminate (ibid., pp. 553-5).

The second type of unfairness, exploitation, may occur when workers are uninformed, immobile, unorganized, poor, or geographically scattered. Under these circumstances, employers have monopoly power, and "considerably greater strategic strength than [their] opponents." They are rich, better trained in bargaining, and can tolerate adverse conditions better than workers can (ibid., p. 559). Eliminating exploitation would improve the size of the national dividend. Increasing the wage to its efficiency level would increase the supply of labor and force business to increase profits by introducing technological improvements. Monopolistic firms unable to survive the wage increase would be replaced by more efficient firms (ibid. pp. 561-3).[15]

Although wage increases may in some cases increase unemployment for the short-term, Pigou argues that they may produce long-term benefits by increasing efficiency through improvements in physical, mental, and psychological capacities. Common sense shows that such improvements are more likely in the case of exploited and very poor workers, especially women and children, who are trapped in a vicious circle of exploitation, low capacity, and inferior bargaining power. A long-term net gain in the dividend, effected by improved worker capacity, is also possible for workers who are not exploited in Pigou's sense. However, Pigou is reluctant to make such generalizations in the absence of consistent empirical data. The effect of higher wages on the short- and long-term demand for labor should be determined after careful examination of each case (ibid., pp. 607-611).

Pigou objects to increasing wages by means of a national minimum-wage law. Because every worker faces different circumstances and needs, a mandatory minimum wage would not provide most workers with a "living income." Moreover, a minimum wage may increase unemployment rates for the elderly, the unskilled, and women. Instead of adopting such an imperfect measure, the government can secure "for all families of its citizens, with the help, if necessary, of State funds, an adequate minimum standard in every department of life" (ibid., p. 618). The combination of a minimum standard of living and flexible wages would provide a better outcome for the economy: less poverty and more efficient labor markets.[16]

Part IV-The Distribution of the National Dividend

In part four, Pigou studies the relationship between changes in the national dividend and the absolute share of the dividend distributed to the poor. In order to increase the national dividend by changing the distribution of income, both the rich and the poor—a distinction that Pigou uses interchangeably with that of capital and labor—would have to benefit. When the interests of the two groups conflict, the change in the national dividend is indeterminate.

In general, Pigou believes that changes resulting from general progress increase the share of one group—capital or labor—without diminishing either the share of the other group or the national dividend. Technological change may temporarily displace some workers, but it also reduces prices and increases the demand for products and labor: "Disharmony, as a result of inventions, is a possible, but a decidedly improbable, contingency. Nobody would seriously propose to interfere with, or to obstruct, inventions in order to provide a safeguard against it" (ibid., p. 680). Government initiatives (e.g., forcing up non-exploitative wages) produce similar results in the sense that capital and labor are both negatively affected in the long run. A higher share of the dividend distributed to workers leaves a smaller share for capital and less capital to assist labor in the long run (ibid., pp. 683-93).

Unlike Pareto, Pigou does not believe that there is always harmony between the changes in the size of the national dividend and the changes in the absolute share distributed to the poor (ibid., p. 648). Pigou finds the most important area of inconsistency between the interests of capital and labor in the transfer of income from the rich (mostly in the form of income or inheritance taxes) to the poor (in the form of direct cash transfers, maternity leaves, social security, or public goods such as parks). Such a transfer has the potential to increase aggregate welfare because "it enables more intense wants to be satisfied at the expense of less intense wants," if it does not reduce the size of the national dividend (ibid., p. 89). However, both the expectation and the fact of such transfers may influence the size of the national dividend.

If the intersts of capital and labor conflict, it is impossible to generalize about the net impact of redistributive measures on economic welfare (ibid., pp. 719, 730).

The expectation of income transfers is likely to "modify the dividend of any year by reacting both on the contribution of work provided during that year and on the quantity of capital equipment made ready in former years against the needs of that year" (ibid., p. 742). The rich may work less, capital may leave the country, savings may be reduced, and the poor may become "idle and thriftless" (ibid., pp. 715-20). In Pigou's judgment, these effects can be exaggerated. The danger of capital flight is not very serious since money sent abroad will be taxed twice: by the foreign and the national governments (ibid., p. 715). The rich care about relative as well as absolute levels of income. If "the incomes of all rich people are diminished together" through income taxes, then the loss of satisfaction to them will be much smaller than the gain to the poor (ibid., p. 90). Inheritance taxes do not discourage saving as much as commonly believed. Most people target a level of savings that can provide a good future for their family. Once that target is reached, the rich "engage in business enterprises because of a love of action and a love of power. Accumulated capital becomes then one of the instruments of the game. So long as the player is left in possession of this instrument while he is one of the players, he is not likely to be discouraged from accumulation merely by the fact that the State, rather than his heirs, gets it after he is through with it" (ibid., pp. 718-9).

The argument that the poor become idle and thriftless if they expect a redistribution of income is "based on defective analysis" (Ibid., p. 720). What the poor will do depends on the incentive structure of the relief scheme. Transfers that differentiate against idleness and thriftlessness can tie productivity to relief: the more productive workers are, the more relief they receive (ibid., p. 721). Neutral transfers involve "the attainment of some condition not capable of being varied by voluntary actions in the economic sphere, on the part of possible beneficiaries" (ibid., p. 722). If they are made in cash, or in forms that can be sold or pawned, they promote idleness. However, it is also possible to structure these transfers with no negative impact on the national dividend. Examples include public parks, "general sanitary measures," public education, medical care for children, and vacations for boys in the countryside (ibid., pp. 722-8). Transfers that differentiate in favor of idleness include compensating people more the further they fall below a poverty line. If the government creates such a social safety net, it would have to include measures that make it disadvantageous for workers to quit their jobs (no voluntary leave pay). The government may also expect transfer recipients to work for the help they receive. Refusal to do so may occasion extreme measures such as detention (ibid., pp. 732-6).

The fact of the transfer produces its own effects by reducing the share of the national dividend used to accumulate capital for future production (ibid., p. 742). The impact on the national dividend would be positive if "the return yielded by investment in the poor ... is not less than the return yielded by investment in material capital—that is to say, roughly, than the normal rate of interest" (ibid., p. 745). The return can be very high if the transfer is made to train select groups of low-wage workers who demonstrate uncommon abilities, to provide medical care and food for workers in danger of becoming permanently ill, or to offer "training and nurture to the normal children of the poor" (ibid., pp. 747-51). Pigou recommends oversight by the government to ensure that the poor do in fact invest in the required areas (ibid., pp. 755-7).

The Economics of Welfare: **The Critical Response**

The Economics of Welfare (1932) provided a framework for analyzing two sets of factors that can improve welfare: those that increase the size of the national dividend and those that alter its distribution. The first set became the subject of a theoretical debate involving many economists, including Pigou himself despite his aversion to controversy. This debate began in 1913 and continued in the 1920s as well as in 1960. The second set of factors was criticized by Lionel Robbins in 1932; Pigou did not reply until 1951. The following provides a summary of these criticisms and their impact on *The Economics of Welfare*.[17]

The Controversy over the Laws of Returns

In his *Wealth and Welfare*, Pigou argued that private and social net products coincide for constant-cost (returns) industries. Increasing- and decreasing- cost (returns) industries produce inefficient resource allocations; government policies such as taxes or subsidies may be necessary to bring output to its socially ideal levels.

Pigou used two curves to demonstrate his arguments. The marginal supply price curve—which represents the "difference between the aggregate expenses of the annual production of x units and (x + Δ x) units respectively"—and the supply price curve—which represents "the price which tends to call out the production of" any quantity of output (1912, pp. 176, 174). Under increasing-cost conditions, the curve of supply price is below the marginal supply price. It follows that a small increase in the output of one firm would create external diseconomies for the industry as a whole by increasing the price of land (or other factors in fixed supply). In the case of decreasing costs, the supply price curve is above the marginal supply price curve: an increase in the output of the firm would create external economies for the industry as a whole (ibid., p. 176). In both cases, the fact that the two curves do not overlap signifies a divergence between marginal social and private net products.

Critics of *Wealth and Welfare* and its successor, *The Economics of Welfare*, pointed out that increasing and decreasing returns are essentially different phenomena (Robertson, 1924; Schumpeter, 1928; Young, 1928). External economies, such as increased division of labor and technological change, are irreversible and represent a real social gain. External diseconomies, such as an increased price of a fixed factor of production, "do not represent an increased *using up* of resources in the work of production. They merely represent *transferences* of purchasing power" from the producers to the owners of land.[18] Pigou accepted this position in the second edition of *The Economics of Welfare*, arguing that in increasing-cost industries the private and social net products are the same as long as the increased rents do not accrue to foreigners (1924, pp. 194-6).

In 1926, Sraffa showed that this revised version of Pigou's analysis was flawed.   Increasing and decreasing returns are incompatible with the Marshallian (and Pigouvian) simple competition, partial-equilibrium analysis.   This framework implies that the demand for and the supply of a product must be mutually independent and also independent of the demand for and supply of other commodities.   When increasing costs (decreasing returns) rule, increased output in industry A implies that the price of a fixed factor of production increases not only for industry A but for any industry B that uses this factor.   If A and B produce products that can be substituted, the change in relative prices will also influence the demand for industry A's output (Sraffa, 1926, p. 539). Decreasing-cost (increasing-returns) industries have problems of their own, Sraffa argued.   Internal economies must be ruled out because they lead to monopoly, and external economies due to general economic progress are not compatible with partial-equilibrium analysis.   The only acceptable category is economies internal to the industry but external to the firm.   This is "the class which is most seldom to be met with" (ibid., p. 540).

Within six months of the publication of Sraffa's article, Pigou accepted some of Sraffa's arguments: "it is *impossible* for production anywhere to take place under conditions of increasing costs.   In this matter my conclusion agrees with that reached by Professor Sraffa" (Pigou, 1927, p. 193; emphasis in the original). The output of a competitive firm is negligible by assumption and "no practicable changes in the scale of ... output could sensibly affect the relative values of ... factors" (ibid., p. 192).   Pigou disagreed with Sraffa on the incompatibility of external economies and simple competition.   Theoretically, increased industry output may result in "inventions, improved technique, increased specialisation among the makers of the machines used in the industry and so on" (ibid., p. 195).   The extent to which this analysis is realistic should be determined by a combination of theoretical and statistical analysis (ibid., p. 196).

In 1928, Pigou produced the standard textbook analysis of a competitive firm's stable equilibrium conditions, a discussion he later added to *The Economics of Welfare* (1929, 1932) as part of appendix III.   The analysis was conducted through a mathematical cost function for the equilibrium firm that is defined to be in equilibrium when the industry is in equilibrium (1928, p. 239). The equilibrium firm's costs are a function of its own output as well as the output of the industry. Although the industry may experience increasing, decreasing, or constant costs, the equilibrium firm is always at equilibrium when the industry price is equal to its marginal and (the minimum of) average costs. Pigou combined this mathematical analysis with diagrams of the equilibrium firm's U-shaped average and marginal cost curves, perhaps the first time such an apparatus was published in English. Decreasing costs and external economies shift the equilibrium firm's cost curves.[19]

The Problem of Social Cost

The year after Pigou's death (1960), Ronald Coase criticized the analysis of externalities by Pigou and his followers. Pigou's conception of the problem, according to Coase, is to declare that there is a divergence between social and private costs, and that the producer creating the externality should be discouraged by government policies such as taxes, subsidies, or regulation. With the employment of these measures, the efficiency of resource allocation will improve and output will move toward the socially optimal level.

Coase finds this analysis defective for many reasons. First, Pigou's framework compares a laissez-faire state, where externalities are not internalized, to an ideal state, where externalities are corrected by a government policy. "A better approach would seem to be to start our analysis with a situation approximating that which actually exits, to examine the effects of a proposed policy change and to attempt to decide whether the new situation would be, in total, better or worse than the original one" (1960, p. 43). Second, externalities are reciprocal, not uni-directional as Pigou argues. The question is not: what should be done to prevent A from inflicting the externality on B? The question is, rather: since helping B will have harmful effects on A as well, "should A be allowed to harm B or should B be allowed to harm A?" (ibid., p. 2). Third, remedies that are directed at internalizing the externality can also be harmful. Government action is not cost-free; in some cases, the cost of the policy designed to internalize the externality may be more than the benefit acquired by reducing or eliminating the externality (ibid., p. 18).

With these criticisms, Coase offers an alternative approach to analyzing and solving the problem of externalities. In a zero transaction-costs world, the right to produce the externality becomes a factor of production much like labor and land (ibid., p. 44). Once that right is assigned to either producer—from the point of view of efficiency it does not matter who has the right—the two parties negotiate, the externality is internalized, and the total value of the output is maximized. In a world of positive transaction costs, the cost of reaching an agreement may be so high that even a well defined right to the production of externality may fail to improve on market outcomes (ibid., pp. 2-16). Under these circumstances, three solutions are possible. First, one firm can take over the other, and externalities are resolved within the newly formed organization; however, the administrative costs of such a solution may be unacceptably high (ibid., pp. 16-17). Second, the government may act to remedy the externality; however, there is no guarantee that government action would produce an optimal solution. Government regulations are costly, politicians are responsive to political pressure, and regulations may be misapplied. It is very likely, therefore, that "direct governmental regulation will not necessarily give better results than leaving the problem to be solved by the market or the firm" (ibid., p. 18). These considerations notwithstanding, Coase does not rule out the possibility that the government may improve over market outcomes (ibid.). The third alternative is to do nothing about the externality. The gain from government regulation may be far less than the cost imposed by the externality (ibid.).

Although Pigou died before the publication of Coase's article, it is not too difficult to construct a Pigouvian reply to some of his criticisms. First, for Pigou, a condition of laissez-faire does not entail a complete absence of government. A market economy has an "organised system of civilised government and contract law" that direct self-interest into beneficial channels "in considerable detail." A more efficient allocation of resources implies only a different degree of government action, reducing the remaining "imperfections" and "failures," and increasing the size of the national dividend (ibid., pp. 128-9). Moreover, to expect factual details from Pigou is to misunderstand the purpose of *The Economics of Welfare*. Pigou's book developed a framework for analysis, identifying areas of divergence between private and social benefits, and pointing out some possible remedies. Even if Pigou had intended to do real-world case studies, the state of the discipline at the time would not have allowed it. Professional economics was in its infancy, and without adequate or consistent data. This is one reason he spoke with an "uncertain voice" on practical issues (Pigou, 1932, pp. 9-10).

Second, Pigou's analysis of social costs is much closer to Coase's position than the latter admits. This essay has shown that Pigou begins with a class of divergences in which the number of parties is small (a tenant and a landlord), in Coase's terminology, a situation of low transaction costs. The externality in this case is treated by modifying the terms of the contract between the two parties, a voluntary arrangement. Pigou then moves to the second group of divergences, which "cannot, like divergences due to tenancy laws, be mitigated by a modification of the contractual relation between any two contracting parties" (ibid., p. 192). Externalities are due to difficulties in exacting payment "from the benefited parties," compensating "the injured parties," or the highly complex "inter-relations of the various private persons affected" (ibid., pp. 183-4, 194), resembling Coase's high transaction-costs scenario. In such cases, the government may act through taxes, subsidies, zoning laws, urban planning, or comparable measures. Pigou is always engaged in a cost-benefit analysis of government action as well as a cost-benefit analysis of reallocating resources.

Third, Coase is correct in arguing that Pigou does not see externalities as reciprocal. However, even if Pigou accepts reciprocity, his arguments may not alter significantly. Suppose, accepting Coase's position, that the government either assigns the externality right to the injuring party or refuses to address the externality. A polluted environment increases infant mortality and morbidity rates and produces long-lasting physical and moral consequences for the majority of the population. Total welfare, in Pigou's world, has both economic and non-economic components; the quality and character of the people are no less important than economic efficiency. A short-term focus on maximizing the dividend may reduce non-economic, and therefore total, welfare.[20]

Inter-personal Comparisons of Utility

Pigou, like other economists, used the law of diminishing marginal utility as a basis for policy proposals that redistribute income and progressively tax the rich. His argument assumes that the first units of income are spent on satisfying urgent and intensive needs. As income increases, the utility gained by the expenditure of the last units rises, but less than proportionately. The transfer of income from the rich to the poor damages the former; nevertheless, such a transfer—if it does not decrease the size of the national dividend—increases aggregate satisfaction, "since it enables more intense wants to be satisfied at the expense of less intense wants" (Pigou, 1932, p. 89).

Heavily influenced by positivism, Robbins's *Essay on the Nature and Significance of Economic Science* challenged the scientific status of these proposals. It is one thing to use diminishing marginal utility to determine the order of preferences of one individual. It is quite another to "compare the arrangements of one such individual scale with another" (Robbins, 1935, p. 138). The latter strategy makes an assumption that "can never be verified by observation or introspection. The proposition we are examining begs the great metaphysical question of the scientific comparability of different individual experiences" (ibid., p. 137). Inter-personal comparisons, Robbins argued, are commonplace, but they are based on the conventional, unscientific idea that people have the same capacity for satisfaction. How could a dispute be settled between a Brahmin, who believes himself to be ten times more capable of satisfaction than an untouchable, and a Benthamite, who believes everyone to be equally capable of pleasure? (Robbins, 1938, p. 636) Given the impossibility of intuitive or empirical tests, inter-personal comparisons of utility, and propositions based on them are excluded from the domain of

economics as a science. Even if redistributive measures qualify as
science, it does not follow that they should be carried out.
Propositions "involving 'ought' are on an entirely different plane
from propositions involving 'is'" (ibid., p. 140).

Pigou largely ignored Robbins's criticisms and the development of the new (Paretian) welfare economics sparked, at least
partly, by the publication of Robbins's *Essay*. It was obvious to
Pigou that any policy prescription takes the economist beyond
"the narrow boundaries of his science. He must necessarily base
himself in part upon judgments about what is good and what is
bad, what is better and what is worse, thus trespassing on the
domain of ethics" (Pigou, 1935a, p. 107). And once "you have
decided what things ... are ultimately good, it becomes your duty
to try and bring about these things" (in Pigou, 1925, p. 82).
Pigou, who had entered economics from the moral sciences tripos,
was not scandalized by his violation of positivist strictures:
"Professor Robbins ... seems to allow that such comparisons can
be made; merely wishing to call them value judgements—a
difference of name which does not seem to me to matter."[21]

In addition, in *The Economics of Welfare* Pigou had considered but rejected the argument that the rich are "inherently
capable of securing a greater amount of economic satisfaction
from any given income than the poor" (1932, p. 91). For him,
ephemeral differences between the rich and the poor do not matter.
In the long run, especially if "long enough to allow a new
generation to grow up," a transfer of income to the poor will
"make possible the development in them, through education and
otherwise, of capacities and faculties adapted for the enjoyment of
the enlarged income. Thus in the long run differences of temperament and taste between rich and poor are overcome by the very fact
of a shifting of income between them" (1932, pp. 91-2).

At the request of the editor of *The American Economic
Review*, Pigou published "Some aspects of Welfare Economics"
(1951), a portion of which was added to the 1952 reprint of *The
Economics of Welfare* as Appendix XI. In this article, he argued
that a rejection of the assumption of equal capacities for satisfaction— "In all practical affairs we act on that supposition" (1951,
p. 292)—has significant and perhaps disastrous implications. Not

only welfare economics but "the whole apparatus of practical thought" would collapse (ibid., p. 292).

Pigou maintained that satisfaction or utility is an unmeasurable intensive magnitude. With Bertrand Russell as an authority, he argued that this position does not preclude economists from ranking an individual's utilities, or differences in his or her utilities, either in principle or in fact (ibid., pp. 290-1). Inter-personal comparisons of utility, on the other hand, are not possible in fact, only in principle. But "analogy, observation, and intercourse" showed him that inter-personal comparisons "can ... properly be made" (ibid., p. 292). Furthermore, "unless we have a special reason to believe the contrary, a given amount of stuff may be presumed to yield a similar amount of satisfaction, not indeed as between *any* one man and any other, but as between representative members of groups of individuals." If, as Pigou claimed, there are objective tests showing that representative members of randomly selected groups are similar "in many features," there is no reason to believe that they are different in other respects, including their capacities for satisfaction. The burden of proof, according to Pigou, rests on those who claim dissimilarity (ibid.).

The Economics of Welfare: Place in the History of Economics

The Economics of Welfare occupies a privileged position in economics for various reasons. First, it contributed to the professionalization of economics, a goal aggressively and effectively pursued by Pigou's predecessor and teacher Alfred Marshall. Marshall's synthesis of classicism and marginalism, although "supreme" from Pigou's point of view, lacked a theory of economic policy. His account of market departures from the maximum social advantage was limited, inconclusive, and qualified by "a list of methodological objections" (Maloney, 1985, p. 169). *The Economics of Welfare* founded welfare economics by systematically analyzing such departures and their potential remedies. It also represented a significant departure from Marshall's attempts to make economics accessible to "ordinary people, business men, politicians, and so on" (Pigou, 1953, p. 6). It is well known that

Marshall confined his technical discussions to footnotes and appendices. Pigou's analysis was much more abstract and ahistorical; it was more mathematical and grounded in the new disciplinary jargon of economics. Pigou believed that Marshall's approach invited laypeople to eavesdrop on conversations between economists that they were not competent to understand: "might it not be better not to understand and know that they do not, rather than to roll about, self-satisfied and complaisant, in a sea of mental cotton-wool?" (ibid., p. 7).

Second, in writing *The Economics of Welfare*, Pigou built a bridge between the old and the new economics at Cambridge and in Britain. The British brand of the theory of imperfect competition grew out of the debate over the laws of returns, which were more elaborately and carefully analyzed in Pigou's book than in Marshall's *Principles* (1920). In fact, Joan Robinson saw her *Economics of Imperfect Competition* (1933) as "a complete restatement of the Pigovian system" (Robinson, 1978, p. x). The same debate generated the perfect-competition model. Its assumptions, stability conditions, and diagrammatic and mathematical analysis were clarified and developed in the 1920s, in part on the basis of contributions made by Pigou. The main problems of modern welfare theory—ranking of national income over time, inter-personal comparisons of utility, and welfare criteria—were all posed by Pigou.

Finally, much of *The Economics of Welfare* remains relevant for contemporary economics. The list of Pigouvian analyses that continue to play an important role in economics is impressive. To name a few of the more important: public goods and externalities, welfare criteria, index number problems, price discrimination, the theory of the firm, the structure of relief programs for the poor, and public finance. Pigou's discussion of the institutional structure governing labor-market operations in his *Wealth and Welfare* prompted Schumpeter to call it "the greatest venture in labor economics ever undertaken by a man who was primarily a theorist" (Schumpeter, 1954, p. 948).

The book you hold in your hands is long, laborious, and perhaps daunting. But it is a classic that will repay careful study.

NAHID ASLANBEIGUI

Endnotes

*   The author is grateful to Guy Oakes for valuable comments on the various drafts of this paper. The usual disclaimer applies.

1.   Pigou was elected Professor over the much older Herbert Foxwell. For Marshall's electoral maneuvers on behalf of Pigou and the rationales on which they were based, see Coats (1968, 1972), Coase (1972), and Jones (1978). For Foxwell's attempts to replace Pigou during World War I, see Aslanbeigui (1992a).

2.   For biographical information on Pigou, see Saltmarsh and Wilkinson (1960) and Collard (1981).

3.   The unfavorable public reaction to his own stance on a number of controversial issues—advocacy of free trade in 1903, and support for an honorable peace with Germany in 1915—doubtless contributed to this opinion.

4.   In his review of the *General Theory*, Pigou wrote: "Einstein actually did for Physics what Mr. Keynes believes himself to have done for Economics. He developed a far-reaching generalisation, under which Newton's results can be subsumed as a special case. But he did not, in announcing his discovery, insinuate, through carefully barbed sentences, that Newton and those who had hitherto followed his lead were a gang of incompetent bunglers. The example is illustrious: but Mr. Keynes has not followed it. The general tone *de baut en bas* and the patronage extended to his old master Marshall are particularly to be regretted. It is not by this manner of writing that his desire to convince his fellow economists ... is best promoted" (Pigou, 1936, p. 115).

5.   On parallels between Sidgwick's and Pigou's work, see O'Donnell (1979).

6.   This book was written in reaction to Joseph Chamberlain's 1903 tariff reform proposal, which called for preferential tariffs for the British colonies.

7.   Some of the significant changes introduced in the second edition were criticized: "Such constant rearrangement of a treatise is disconcerting to the constant reader. The continual change in the order of topics breaks the links of memory, tangles the chains of reasoning, and is fatal to artistic form" (Edgeworth, 1925, p. 30).

8.   In Pigou's view, government regulation of exhaustible natural resources for the benefit of future generations may restrict the choices of the present generation. This consequence may reduce economic welfare (Pigou, 1932, pp. 25-30). On Pigou and the future generations, see Collard (1996).

9.   Subsequently, Paul Samuelson showed that $P>1$ is a sufficient measure for a higher dividend in period II. Along the same lines, $L<1$ is sufficient to show that the dividend of period I is higher.

P<1 and L>1 do not prove either proposition (Samuelson, 1950, pp. 21-29).

10. Equalization of the MSNP across activities does not necessarily entail that the national dividend will be at the highest possible level. Resources could be allocated in several ways, each of which could lead to a local (relative) maximum. Only one of these allocations could generate the global maximum. It might be better to try and reallocate resources to increase the size of the national dividend (getting closer to the global maximum) instead of attempting to achieve equality of marginal net social products for a local maximum (Pigou, 1932, pp. 139-40).

11. For Pigou's treatment of land tenancy, see Victor Goldberg (1981).

12. Although Pigou did not distinguish between public goods and externalities, the subgroups included in his analysis did in effect make such a distinction.

13. Pigou's typical firm was the equilibrium firm, a theoretical construct defined as a unit that would be in equilibrium whenever the industry is in equilibrium (Pigou, 1928a, pp. 239-40).

14. Pigou dismisses a third method, "rotating employment so that only a proportion ... is actually at work at any one time" (1932, p. 519) on the ground that it "involves a good deal of organisation and collaboration with the workpeople" (ibid., p. 522).

15. For a discussion of Pigou's views on male-female wage differentials, see Aslanbeigui (1997).

16. Pigou realizes that there are "insuperable practical obstacles" (collection of statistics is time-consuming, and book-keeping is costly) to an ideally flexible wage system. Practical considerations dictate that wages be adjusted not on a daily basis, but generally after two or three months (1932, p. 625).

17. *Wealth and Welfare* (1912) and the first edition of *The Economics of Welfare* included a third set of factors that reduce fluctuations of national income and employment, a position attacked by Keynes in his *General Theory*. This set is not addressed here because Pigou eliminated it from the later editions. On Pigou's *Theory of Unemployment* (1933) and Keynes's criticisms, see Aslanbeigui (1992b) and Cottrell (1994). On Pigou's later response to Keynes, which includes both concessions and criticisms, see Pigou (1950) and Aslanbeigui (1998).

18. Young (1913, p. 683). For Marshall's criticism of Pigou's treatment, see Bharadwaj (1972).

19. For a more elaborate discussion of the laws of returns and their implications, see Ellis and Fellner (1952) and Aslanbeigui (1996). Richard Kahn (1935) has explored the welfare implications of these laws under imperfect competition. Aslanbeigui and Naples (1997) have examined the implications of this controversy for costs and supply curves.

20.   For a comparison of Pigou's and Coase's treatments of social costs, see Aslanbeigui and Medema (1998).

21.   Pigou (1953, p. 45, n3); see also Pigou (1935a, p. 22). Pigou's intolerance of methodological debates is nicely demonstrated in an exchange with J.H. Clapham. See Clapham (1922) and Pigou (1922).

References

Aslanbeigui, N.   (1992a) "Foxwell's Aims and Pigou's Military Service: A Malicious Episode?" *Journal of the History of Economic Thought*, 14 (Spring), 96-109.

Aslanbeigui, N.   (1992b) "Pigou's Inconsistencies or Keynes's Misconceptions?" *History of Political Economy*, 24 (2), 413-433.

Aslanbeigui, N.   (1996) "The Cost Controversy: Pigouvian Economics in Disequilibrium," *The European Journal of the History of Economic Thought*, 3 (2), 275-95.

Aslanbeigui, N.   (1997) "Rethinking Pigou's Misogyny," *Eastern Economic Journal*, 23 (3), 301-316.

Aslanbeigui, N.   (1998) "Unemployment through the Eyes of a Classic," in Ahiakpor, J.C.W.   (ed.) *Keynes and the Classics Reconsidered*, Boston: Kluwer Academic Publishers, 85-99.

Aslanbeigui, N.   and Medema, S.G.   (1998) "Beyond the Dark Clouds: Pigou and Coase on Social Cost," *History of Political Economy*, 30 (4), 601-25.

Aslanbeigui, N.   and Naples, M.I.   (1997) "Scissors or Horizon: Neoclassical Debates about Returns to Scale, Costs, and Long-Run Supply, 1926-1942," *Southern Economic Journal*, 64 (2), 517-530.

Bharadwaj, K.   (1972) "Marshall on Pigou's *Wealth and Welfare*," *Economica*, 39 (154), 32-46.

Cannan, E.   (1921) "Review of *The Economics of Welfare*," *The Economic Journal*, 31 (122), 206-214.

Clapham, J.H.   (1922) "Of Empty Economic Boxes," *The Economic Journal*, 32 (127), 560-63.

Coase, R.H.   (1960) "The Problem of Social Cost," *Journal of Law and Economics*, 3 (October), 1-44.

Coase, R.H.   (1972) "The Appointment of Pigou as Marshall's Successor," *Journal of Law and Economics*, 15, 473-85.

Coats, A.W.   (1968) "Political Economy and the Tariff Reform Campaign of 1903," *Journal of law and Economics*, 11, 181-229.

Coats, A.W.   (1972) "The Appointment of Pigou as Marshall's Successor," *Journal of Law and Economics*, 15, 487-95.

Collard, D.   (1981) "A.C. Pigou, 1877-1959," in O'Brien, D.P. and J.R. Presley (eds) *Pioneers of Modern Economics in Britain*, Totowa, NJ: Barnes and Noble Books.

Collard, D. (1996) 'Pigou and Future Generations: A Cambridge Tradition', *Cambridge Journal of Economics*, 20, 585-97.

Cottrell, A. (1994) "Keynes's Appendix to Chapter 19: A Reader's Guide," *History of Political Economy*, 26 (4), 681-95.

Edgeworth, F.Y. (1913) "Review of *Wealth and Welfare*," *The Economic Journal*, 23 (89), 62-70.

Edgeworth, F.Y. (1925) "The Revised Doctrine of Marginal Social Product," *The Economic Journal*, 35 (137).

Ellis, H.S. and Fellner, W. (1952) "External Economies and Diseconomies," in Stigler, G.J. and Boulding, K.E. (eds) *Readings in Price Theory*, Chicago: Richard D. Irwin, Inc., 242-63.

Goldberg, V.P. (1981) "Pigou on Complex Contracts and Welfare Economics," *Research in Law and Economics*, 3, 39-51.

Jones, T.W. (1978) "The Appointment of Pigou as Marshall's Successor: The Other Side of the Coin," *Journal of Law and Economics*, 21, 235-43.

Kahn, R.F. (1935) "Some Notes on Ideal Output," *The Economic Journal*, XLV (177), 1-35.

Keynes, J.M. (1936) *The General Theory of Employment, Interest, and Money*, New York: Harcourt, Brace, and World.

Maloney, J. (1985) *Marshall, Orthodoxy and the Professionalisation of Economics*, Cambridge: Cambridge University Press.

O'Donnell, M.G. (1979) "Pigou: An Extension of Sidgwickian Thought," *History of Political Economy*, 11 (4), 588-605.

Pigou, A.C. (1905) *Principles and Methods of Industrial Peace*, London: Macmillan.

Pigou, A.C. (1906) *Protective & Preferential Import Duties*, London: Macmillan.

Pigou, A.C. (1912) *Wealth and Welfare*, London: Macmillan.

Pigou, A.C. (1913) *Unemployment*, London: William and Norgate.

Pigou, A.C., (1915) Letter from Pigou to Macmillan, in the Macmillan Archive, ADD55199, vol. CDXIV, The British Library.

Pigou, A.C. (1920) *The Economics of Welfare*, London: Macmillan.

Pigou, A.C. (1921) *The Political Economy of War*, London: Macmillan.

Pigou, A.C. (1922) "Empty Economic Boxes: A Reply," *The Economic Journal*, 32 (128), 458-65.

Pigou, A.C. (1924) *The Economics of Welfare*, 2nd ed., London: Macmillan.

Pigou, A.C. (ed.) (1925) *Memorials of Alfred Marshall*, London: Macmillan.

Pigou, A.C. (1927a) *Industrial Fluctuations*, London: Macmillan.

Pigou, A.C. (1927b) "The Laws of Diminishing and Increasing Costs", *The Economic Journal*, 38 (146), 188-97.

Pigou, A.C. (1928a) "An Analysis of Supply," *The Economic Journal*, 38 (150), 238-57.

Pigou, A.C. (1928b) *A Study in Public Finance*, London: Macmillan.

Pigou, A.C. (1929a) *A Study in Public Finance*, 2nd ed., London: Macmillan.

Pigou, A.C. (1929b) *Industrial Fluctuations*, 2nd ed., London: Macmillan.

Pigou, A.C. (1929c) *The Economics of Welfare*, 3rd ed., London: Macmillan.

Pigou, A.C. (1932) *The Economics of Welfare*, 4th ed., London: Macmillan.

Pigou, A.C. (1933) *The Theory of Unemployment*, London: Macmillan.

Pigou, A.C. (1935a) *Economics in Practice: Six Lectures on Current Issues*, London: Macmillan.

Pigou, A.C. (1935b) *The Economics of Stationary States*, London: Macmillan.

Pigou, A.C. (1936) "'Mr. J. M. Keynes' General Theory of Employment, Interest and Money', *Economica*, (May), 115-132.

Pigou, A.C. (1939) "Presidential Address," *The Economic Journal*, 49 (194), 215-221.

Pigou, A.C. (1941) *Employment and Equilibrium*, London: Macmillan.

Pigou, A.C. (1945) *Lapses from Full Employment*, London: Macmillan.

Pigou, A.C. (1946) *Income: An Introduction to Economics*, London: Macmillan.

Pigou, A.C. (1947) *A Study in Public Finance*, 3rd ed., London: Macmillan.

Pigou, A.C. (1949) *Employment and Equilibrium*, 2nd ed., London: Macmillan.

Pigou, A.C. (1950) *Keynes's "General Theory:" A Retrospective View*. London: Macmillan.

Pigou, A.C. (1951) 'Some Aspects of Welfare Economics', *The American Economic Review*, 41(3), 287-302.

Pigou, A.C. (1952a) *Essays in Economics*, London: Macmillan.

Pigou, A.C. (1952b, reprint) *The Economics of Welfare*, 4th ed., London: Macmillan.

Pigou, A.C. (1953) *Alfred Marshall and Current Thought*, London: Macmillan.

Pigou, A.C. (1955) *Income Revisited*, London: Macmillan.

Robbins, L. (1935) *An Essay on the Nature and Significance of Economic Science*, 2nd ed., London: Macmillan.

Robbins, L. (1938) "Interpersonal Comparisons of Utility: A Comment," *The Economic Journal*, 48 (192), 635-41.

Robertson, D.H. (1924) "Those Empty Economic Boxes: A Rejoinder," *The Economic Journal*, 34 (133), 16-30.

Robinson, J.V. (1933) *The Economics of Imperfect Competition*, London: Macmillan.

Robinson, J.V. (1978) *Contributions to Modern Economics*, Oxford: Basil Blackwell.

Saltmarsh, J. and Wilkinson, P. (1960) *Arthur Cecil Pigou, 1877-1959*, Cambridge: Cambridge University Press.

Samuelson, P.A. (1950) "A Note on Pigou's Treatment of Income," *Oxford Economic Papers*, (January), 21-29.

Schumpeter, J.A. (1928) "The Stability of Capitalism," *The Economic Journal*, 38 (151), 361-86.

Schumpeter, J.A. (1954) *History of Economic Analysis*, New York: Oxford University Press.

Sidgwick, H. (1901) *The Principles of Political Economy*, 3rd ed., London: Macmillan.

Sraffa, P. (1926) "The Laws of Returns Under Competitive Conditions," *The Economic Journal*, 36 (144), 535-50.

Young, A. (1913) "Pigou's Wealth and Welfare," *Quarterly Journal Of Economics*, 27, 672-86.

Young, A. (1928) "Increasing Returns and Economic Progress," *The Economic Journal*, 38 (152), 527-42.

PREFACE TO THE THIRD EDITION (1928)

IN preparing this revised third edition, I have removed a number of minor errors and have made, I hope, some improvements in analysis and exposition. I have also tried, so far as possible, to bring my references to facts and laws up to date. The main changes in the structure of the book are as follows. A portion of what used to be Chapter VIII. of Part IV. and the Appendix entitled "Taxes on Windfalls" are omitted, as the matters there discussed are now dealt with in *A Study of Public Finance*. The following Chapters are new: Part I., Chapter IV.; Part II., Chapter VIII.; Part III., Chapter XVI.; Part IV., Chapter VII. Chapter XI. of Part II. replaces, under a new title, what used to be Chapter X. and has been entirely rewritten. The first five divisions of Appendix III., which are concerned with the subject-matter of that Chapter, are also new. In these divisions I have made free use of an article entitled "An Analysis of Supply," which appeared in the *Economic Journal* in June 1928 ; and in the new Chapter VII. of Part IV. I have used part of an article on "Wage Policy and Unemployment," which appeared in the same journal in September 1927.

The scheme of the book, which is displayed in more detail in the Analytical Table of Contents, is as follows. In Part I. it is argued, subject, of course, to a large number of qualifications, that the economic welfare of a community of given size is likely to be greater (1) the larger is the volume of the national dividend, and (2) the larger is the absolute share of

that dividend that accrues to the poor.   Part II. is devoted
to a study of certain principal influences of a general kind by
which the volume of the dividend is affected, and Part III. to
a study of influences specifically connected with labour.   In
Part IV. the question is raised in what circumstances it is
possible for the absolute share of the dividend accruing to
the poor to be increased by causes which at the same time
diminish the volume of the dividend as a whole; and the
relation of disharmonies of this character, when they occur,
to economic welfare is discussed.   The two Parts contained
in the first edition, which discussed respectively the Variability of the National Dividend and Public Finance, are
omitted from this, as they were from the second edition.
Their subject-matter is now treated more fully in my *Industrial
Fluctuations* and *A Study in Public Finance.*

I have done my best, by restricting as far as possible the
use of technical terms, by relegating specially abstract discussions to Appendices, and by summarising the main drift of
the argument in an Analytical Table of Contents, to render
what I have to say as little difficult as may be.   But it would
be idle to pretend that the book is other than a severe one.
In part, no doubt, the severity is due to defects of exposition.
But in part also it is due to the nature of the problems
studied.   It is sometimes imagined that economic questions
can be adjudicated upon without special preparation.   The
"plain man," who in physics and chemistry knows that he
does not know, has still to attain in economics to that first
antechamber of knowledge.   In reality the subject is an
exceedingly difficult one, and cannot, without being falsified,
be made to appear easy.

In publishing so comprehensive a book, I have had to face
one somewhat special difficulty.   Legislative and other changes
both here and abroad are so numerous and rapid that some of
the legal enactments and general conditions to which I have
referred in the present tense are certain, by the time the book

is in the reader's hands, to have been superseded. I do not think, however, that the impossibility of being completely up to date in a world of continuous change matters very greatly. For the illustrations I have used are not brought forward for their own sake. The service I ask of them is to throw light on principles, and that purpose can be performed as well by an arrangement or a fact that lapsed a year or two ago as by one that is still intact.

I would add one word for any student beginning economic study who may be discouraged by the severity of the effort which the study, as he will find it exemplified here, seems to require of him. The complicated analyses which economists endeavour to carry through are not mere gymnastic. They are instruments for the bettering of human life. The misery and squalor that surround us, the injurious luxury of some wealthy families, the terrible uncertainty overshadowing many families of the poor—these are evils too plain to be ignored. By the knowledge that our science seeks it is possible that they may be restrained. Out of the darkness light! To search for it is the task, to find it perhaps the prize, which the "dismal science of Political Economy" offers to those who face its discipline.

A. C. P.

King's College,
Cambridge, *November* 1928.

NOTE TO THE FOURTH EDITION (1932)

The principal changes made in this edition affect Chapter IV. and Chapter VI. §§ 12-13 in Part I.; Chapter XI. § 2 and Chapter XV. in Part II.; and Chapter IX. §§ 2-3 and Chapter XIV. § 1 in Part III.

NOTE TO REPRINT (1952)

THE last revised edition of this book was published in 1932, since when there have been a number of reprints. As the book is still in demand, I should naturally have liked to undertake a thorough revision of it, taking account both of recent writings and of changes that have taken place in the facts and in the laws to which I have referred. But, apart from the fact that the printing has been stereotyped, that would have involved an amount of concentrated effort of which I am not now capable. Rather than a botched patchwork, it seems better to leave the body of the book as it is. There are, however, several matters on which I should like to emend or amplify what I have written and several more recent approaches to which I should like to refer. I have therefore added new Appendices (numbers IV to XI), mostly reproducing or based on articles written by me and relevant to the subject-matter of the book. Except in Appendices VIII and IX, I have not drawn on *The Economics of Stationary States*. Nor have I added anything about monetary analysis or the ideas associated with Keynes's *General Theory*. In the main these relate to a terrain—covered to some extent in my *Employment and Equilibrium*—outside the scope of this book. Recent difficult discussions about utility and " the new welfare economics " are, of course, relevant ; but I have not felt competent to discuss them in their technical aspects, only in the " plain man " manner of Appendix XI.

A. C. P.

Sept. 1951

PART I

WELFARE AND THE NATIONAL DIVIDEND

CHAPTER I

WELFARE AND ECONOMIC WELFARE

§ 1. When a man sets out upon any course of inquiry, the object of his search may be either light or fruit—either knowledge for its own sake or knowledge for the sake of good things to which it leads. In various fields of study these two ideals play parts of varying importance. In the appeal made to our interest by nearly all the great modern sciences *some* stress is laid both upon the light-bearing and upon the fruit-bearing quality, but the proportions of the blend are different in different sciences. At one end of the scale stands the most general science of all, metaphysics, the science of reality. Of the student of that science it is, indeed, true that "he yet may bring some worthy thing for waiting souls to see"; but it must be light alone, it can hardly be fruit that he brings. Most nearly akin to the metaphysician is the student of the ultimate problems of physics. The corpuscular theory of matter is, hitherto, a bearer of light alone. Here, however, the other aspect is present in promise; for speculations about the structure of the atom may lead one day to the discovery of practical means for dissociating matter and for rendering available to human use the overwhelming resources of intra-atomic energy. In the science of biology the fruit-bearing aspect is more prominent. Recent studies upon heredity have, indeed, the highest theoretical interest; but no one can reflect upon that without at the same time reflecting upon the striking practical results to which they have already led in the culture of wheat, and upon the far-reaching, if hesitating, promise that they are beginning

3

to offer for the better culture of mankind. In the sciences whose subject-matter is man as an individual there is the same variation of blending as in the natural sciences proper. In psychology the theoretic interest is dominant—particularly on that side of it which gives data to metaphysics ; but psychology is also valued in some measure as a basis for the practical art of education. In human physiology, on the other hand, the theoretic interest, though present, is subordinate, and the science has long been valued mainly as a basis for the art of medicine. Last of all we come to those sciences that deal, not with individual men, but with groups of men ; that body of infant sciences which some writers call sociology. Light on the laws that lie behind development in history, even light upon particular facts, has, in the opinion of many, high value for its own sake. But there will, I think, be general agreement that in the sciences of human society, be their appeal as bearers of light never so high, it is the promise of fruit and not of light that chiefly merits our regard. There is a celebrated, if somewhat too strenuous, passage in Macaulay's Essay on History : " No past event has any intrinsic importance. The knowledge of it is valuable, only as it leads us to form just calculations with regard to the future. A history which does not serve this purpose, though it may be filled with battles, treaties and commotions, is as useless as the series of turnpike tickets collected by Sir Matthew Mite." That paradox is partly true. If it were not for the hope that a scientific study of men's social actions may lead, not necessarily directly or immediately, but at some time and in some way, to practical results in social improvement, not a few students of these actions would regard the time devoted to their study as time misspent. That is true of all social sciences, but especially true of economics. For economics " is a study of mankind in the ordinary business of life " ; and it is not in the ordinary business of life that mankind is most interesting or inspiring. One who desired knowledge of man apart from the fruits of knowledge would seek it in the history of religious enthusiasm, of martyrdom, or of love ; he would not seek it in the market-place. When we elect to watch the play of human motives that are ordinary—that are sometimes mean and dismal and ignoble —our impulse is not the philosopher's impulse, knowledge for the sake of knowledge, but rather the physiologist's, knowledge for the healing that knowledge may help to bring. Wonder, Carlyle declared, is the beginning of philosophy. It is not wonder, but rather the social enthusiasm which revolts from the sordidness of mean streets and the joylessness of withered lives, that is the beginning of economic science. Here, if in no other field, Comte's great phrase holds good: "It is for the heart to suggest our problems; it is for the intellect to solve them. . . . The only position for which the intellect is primarily adapted is to be the servant of the social sympathies."

§ 2. If this conception of the motive behind economic study is accepted, it follows that the type of science that the economist will endeavour to develop must be one adapted to form the basis of an art. It will not, indeed, itself be an art, or directly enunciate precepts of government. It is a positive science of what is and tends to be, not a normative science of what ought to be. Nor will it limit itself to those fields of positive scientific inquiry which have an obvious relevance to immediate practical problems. This course would hamper thorough investigation and shut out inquiries that might ultimately bear fruit. For, as has been well said, "in our most theoretical moods we may be nearest to our most practical applications."[1] But, though wholly independent in its tactics and its strategy, it will be guided in general direction by practical interest. This decides its choice of essential form. For there are two main types of positive science. On the one side are the sciences of formal logic and pure mathematics, whose function it is to discover *implications*. On the other side are the realistic sciences, such as physics, chemistry and biology, which are concerned with actualities. The distinction is drawn out in Mr. Russell's *Principles of Mathematics*. "Since the growth of non-Euclidean Geometry, it has appeared that pure mathematics has no concern with the question whether the

---

[1] Whitehead, *Introduction to Mathematics*, p. 100.

axioms and propositions of Euclid hold of actual space or not: this is a question for realistic mathematics, to be decided, so far as any decision is possible, by experiment and observation. What pure mathematics asserts is merely that the Euclidean propositions follow from the Euclidean axioms, *i.e.* it asserts an implication: any space which has such and such properties has also such and such other properties. Thus, as dealt with in pure mathematics, the Euclidean and non-Euclidean Geometries are equally true: in each nothing is affirmed except implications. All propositions as to what actually exists, like the space we live in, belong to experimental or empirical science, not to mathematics." [1] This distinction is applicable to the field of economic investigation. It is open to us to construct an economic science either of the pure type represented by pure mathematics or of the realistic type represented by experimental physics. Pure economics in this sense—an unaccustomed sense, no doubt—would study equilibria and disturbances of equilibria among groups of persons actuated by any set of motives *x*. Under it, among innumerable other subdivisions, would be included at once an Adam-Smithian political economy, in which *x* is given the value of the motives assigned to the economic man—or to the normal man—and a non-Adam-Smithian political economy, corresponding to the geometry of Lobatschewsky, under which *x* consists of love of work and hatred of earnings. For pure economics both these political economies would be equally true; it would not be relevant to inquire what the value of *x* is among the actual men who are living in the world now. Contrasted with this pure science stands realistic economics, the interest of which is concentrated upon the world known in experience, and in nowise extends to the commercial doings of a community of angels. Now, if our end is practice, it is obvious that a political economy that did so extend would be for us merely an amusing toy. Hence it must be the realistic, and not the pure, type of science that constitutes the object of our search. We shall endeavour to elucidate, not any

[1] *Principles of Mathematics*, p. 5. I have substituted *realistic* for Mr. Russell's word *applied* in this passage.

generalised system of possible worlds, but the actual world of men and women as they are found in experience to be.

§ 3. But, if it is plain that a science of the pure type will not serve our purpose, it is equally plain that realism, in the sense of a mere descriptive catalogue of observed facts, will not serve it either. Infinite narration by itself can never enable forecasts to be made, and it is, of course, capacity to make forecasts that practice requires. Before this capacity can be obtained facts must be passed upon by reason. Besides the brute facts, there must be what Browning calls, " something of mine, which, mixed up with the mass, made it bear hammer and be firm to file." It is just the presence of this *something* which is essential to a realistic science as distinguished from mere description. In realistic science facts are not simply brought together ; they are compelled by thought to *speak*. As M. Poincaré well writes : " Science is built up of facts as a house is built of stones ; but an accumulation of facts is no more a science than a heap of stones is a house." [1] Astronomical physics is not merely a catalogue of the positions which certain stars have been observed to occupy on various occasions. Biology is not merely a list of the results of a number of experiments in breeding. Rather, every science, through examination and cross-examination of the particular facts which it is able to ascertain, seeks to discover the general laws of whose operation these particular facts are instances. The motions of the heavenly bodies are exhibited in the light of the laws of Newton ; the breeding of the blue Andalusian fowl in the light of that of Mendel. These laws, furthermore, are not merely summaries of the observed facts re-stated in a shorthand form. They are *generalisations*, and, as such, extend our knowledge to facts that have not been observed, maybe, that have not as yet even occurred. On what philosophical basis generalisations of this sort rest we are not here concerned to inquire. It is enough that in every realistic science they are *made*. As Mr. Whetham, speaking of physics, puts it, any such science " seeks to establish general rules which describe the sequence of phenomena in *all* cases." [2] It is only by

[1] *Science and Hypothesis*, p. 141.
[2] *Recent Developments in Physical Science*, p. 30. The italics are mine.

reference to these general rules that the forecasts, which practice needs, are rendered possible. It is in their fundamental aspect as an organon of laws, and not in their superficial aspect as a description of facts, that the realistic sciences have bearing upon the conduct of affairs. The establishment of such an organon adapted and ready for application to particular problems is the ideal at which they aim.

§ 4. To say this without saying something more would, however, be very misleading. It is not pretended that, at the present stage of its development, economic science is able to provide an organon even remotely approaching to what it imagines for itself as its ideal. Full guidance for practice requires, to borrow Marshall's phrase, capacity to carry out *quantitative*, not merely *qualitative*, analysis. " Qualitative analysis tells the ironmaster that there is *some* sulphur in his ore, but it does not enable him to decide whether it is worth while to smelt the ore at all, and, if it is, then by what process. For that purpose he needs quantitative analysis, which will tell him *how much* sulphur there is in the ore." [1] Capacity to provide information of this kind economic science at present almost entirely lacks. Before the application of general laws to particular problems can yield quantitative results, these laws themselves must be susceptible of quantitative statement. The law is the major premiss and the particular facts of any problem the minor. When the statement of the law lacks precision, the conclusion must generally suffer from the same defect ; and, unfortunately, the task of setting out economic laws in precise form has scarcely been begun. For this there are three reasons. First, the relations which have to be determined are extremely numerous. In physics the fundamental thing, the gravitation constant, expressing the relation between distance and attractive force, is the same for all sorts of matter. But the fundamental things in the economic world—the schedules expressing the desires or aversions of groups of people for different sorts of commodities and services — are not thus simple and uniform. We are in the position in which the physicist would be if tin attracted iron in the inverse ratio of the cube of its distance, lead in that of the square of its

---

[1] Marshall, *The Old Generation of Economists and the New*, p. 11.

distance, and copper in some other ratio. We cannot say, as he can of his attractions, that the amount offered or required of every several commodity is one and the same specified function of the price. All that we can say in this general way is that it is *some one* of a specified large family of functions of the price. Hence, in economics there is not, as in dynamics, one fundamental law of general application, but a great number of laws, all expressible, as it were, in equations of similar form but with different constants. On account of this multiplicity, the determination of those constants, or to put the matter broadly, the measurement of the elasticities of demand and supply of the various commodities in which economics is interested, is a very large task. Secondly, this task is one in attacking which the principal weapon employed by other sciences in their inquiries cannot be fully used. "Theory," said Leonardo da Vinci, "is the general; experiments are the soldiers." Economic science has already well-trained generals, but, because of the nature of the material in which it works, the soldiers are hard to obtain. "The surgeon dissects a dead body before he operates on a living one, and operates upon an animal before he operates upon a human being; the mechanic makes a working model and tests it before he builds the full-sized machine. Every step is, whenever possible, tested by experiment in these matters before risks are run. In this way the unknown is robbed of most of its terrors." [1] In economics, for the simple reason that its subject-matter is living and free men, direct experiment under conditions adequately controlled is hardly ever feasible. But there is a third and even more serious difficulty. Even if the constants which economists wish to determine were less numerous, and the method of experiment more accessible, we should still be faced with the fact that the constants themselves are different at different times. The gravitation constant is the same always. But the economic constants—these elasticities of demand and supply—depending, as they do, upon human consciousness, are liable to vary. The constitution of the atom, as it were, and not merely its position, changes under the influence of environment. Thus the real injury done to Ireland by

[1] Lord Hugh Cecil, *Conservatism*, p. 18.

the earlier English administration of that country was not the
destruction of specific industries or even the sweeping of its
commerce from the seas.   " The real grievance lies in the fact
that something had been taken from our industrial character
which could not be remedied by the mere removal of the
restrictions.   Not only had the tree been stripped, but the
roots had been destroyed." [1]   This malleability in the actual
substance with which economic study deals means that the
goal sought is itself perpetually shifting, so that, even if it
were possible by experiment exactly to determine the values of
the economic constants to-day, we could not say with confidence
that this determination would hold good also of to-morrow.
Hence the inevitable shortcomings of our science.   We can,
indeed, by a careful study of all relevant facts, learn *something*
about the elasticities of demand and supply for a good number
of things, but we cannot ascertain their magnitude with any
degree of exactness.   In other words, our fundamental laws,
and, therefore, inferences from these laws in particular conditions,
cannot at present be thrown into any quantitatively precise
form.   The result is that, when, as often happens, a practical
issue turns upon the balancing of opposing considerations, even
though these considerations are wholly economic, economic
science must almost always speak with an uncertain voice.

§ 5. The preceding paragraph has been somewhat of a
digression.   It has now to be added that, just as the
motive and purpose of our inquiry govern its form, so
also they control its scope.   The goal sought is to make
more easy practical measures to promote welfare—practical
measures which statesmen may build upon the work of the
economist, just as Marconi, the inventor, built upon the
discoveries of Hertz.   Welfare, however, is a thing of very
wide range.   There is no need here to enter upon a general
discussion of its content.   It will be sufficient to lay down
more or less dogmatically two propositions; first, that the
elements of welfare are states of consciousness and, perhaps,
their relations; secondly, that welfare can be brought under
the category of greater and less.   A general investigation of all
the groups of causes by which welfare thus conceived may be

---

[1] Plunkett, *Ireland in the New Century*, p. 19.

affected would constitute a task so enormous and complicated as to be quite impracticable. It is, therefore, necessary to limit our subject-matter. In doing this we are naturally attracted towards that portion of the field in which the methods of science seem likely to work at best advantage. This they can clearly do when there is present something measurable, on which analytical machinery can get a firm grip. The one obvious instrument of measurement available in social life is money. Hence, the range of our inquiry becomes restricted to that part of social welfare that can be brought directly or indirectly into relation with the measuring-rod of money. This part of welfare may be called economic welfare. It is not, indeed, possible to separate it in any rigid way from other parts, for the part which *can* be brought into relation with a money measure will be different according as we mean by *can*, "can easily" or "can with mild straining" or "can with violent straining." The outline of our territory is, therefore, necessarily vague. Professor Cannan has well observed : "We must face, and face boldly, the fact that there is no precise line between economic and non-economic satisfactions, and, therefore, the province of economics cannot be marked out by a row of posts or a fence, like a political territory or a landed property. We can proceed from the undoubtedly economic at one end of the scale to the undoubtedly non-economic at the other end without finding anywhere a fence to climb or a ditch to cross." [1] Nevertheless, though no precise boundary between economic and non-economic welfare exists, yet the test of accessibility to a money measure serves well enough to set up a rough distinction. Economic welfare, as loosely defined by this test, is the subject-matter of economic science. The purpose of this volume is to study certain important groups of causes that affect economic welfare in actual modern societies.

§ 6. At first glance this programme, if somewhat ambitious, appears, at all events, a legitimate one. But reflection soon shows that the proposal to treat in isolation the causes affecting one part of welfare only is open to a serious objection. Our ultimate interest is, of course, in the effects

[1] *Wealth*, pp. 17-18.

which the various causes investigated are likely to have upon welfare as a whole. But there is no guarantee that the effects produced on the part of welfare that can be brought into relation with the measuring-rod of money may not be cancelled by effects of a contrary kind brought about in other parts, or aspects, of welfare; and, if this happens, the practical usefulness of our conclusions is wholly destroyed. The difficulty, it must be carefully observed, is *not* that, since economic welfare is only a part of welfare as a whole, welfare will often change while economic welfare remains the same, so that a given change in economic welfare will seldom synchronise with an equal change in welfare as a whole. All that this means is that economic welfare will not serve for a *barometer* or *index* of total welfare. But that, for our purpose, is of no importance. What we wish to learn is, not how large welfare is, or has been, but how its magnitude would be affected by the introduction of causes which it is in the power of statesmen or private persons to call into being. The failure of economic welfare to serve as an *index* of total welfare is no evidence that the study of it will fail to afford this latter information: for, though a whole may consist of many varying parts, so that a change in one part never *measures* the change in the whole, yet the change in the part may always *affect* the change in the whole by its full amount. If this condition is satisfied, the practical importance of economic study is fully established. It will not, indeed, tell us how total welfare, after the introduction of an economic cause, will differ from what it was before; but it will tell us how total welfare will differ from what it would have been if that cause had not been introduced: and this, and not the other, is the information of which we are in search. The real objection then is, not that economic welfare is a bad *index* of total welfare, but that an economic cause may affect non-economic welfare in ways that cancel its effect on economic welfare. This objection requires careful consideration.

§ 7. One very important aspect of it is as follows. Human beings are both "ends in themselves" and instruments of production. On the one hand, a man who is attuned to the beautiful in nature or in art, whose character is simple and sincere, whose passions are controlled and sympathies developed, is in himself an important element in the ethical value of the world; the way in which he feels and thinks actually constitutes a part of welfare. On the other hand a man who can perform complicated industrial operations, sift difficult evidence, or advance some branch of practical activity, is an instrument well fitted to produce things whose use yields welfare. The welfare to which the former of these men contributes directly is non-economic; that to which the latter contributes indirectly is economic. The fact we have to face is that, in some measure, it is open to the community to choose between these two sorts of men, and that, by concentrating its effort upon the economic welfare embodied in the second, it may unconsciously sacrifice the non-economic welfare embodied in the first. The point is easy of illustration. The weak and disjointed Germany of a century ago was the home of Goethe and Schiller, Kant and Fichte. "We know what the old Germany gave the world," says Mr. Dawson in a book published several years before the war, "and for that gift the world will ever be grateful; we do not know what modern Germany, the Germany of the overflowing barns and the full argosies, has to offer, beyond its materialistic science and its merchandise. . . . The German systems of education, which are incomparable so far as their purpose is the production of scholars and teachers, or of officials and functionaries, to move the cranks, turn the screws, gear the pulleys, and oil the wheels of the complicated national machine, are far from being equally successful in the making of character or individuality."[1] In short, the attention of the German people was so concentrated on the idea of learning to *do* that they did not care, as in former times, for learning to *be*. Nor does Germany stand alone before this charge; as witness the following description of modern England written by an Englishman from the standpoint of an Oriental spectator. "By your works you may be known. Your triumphs in the mechanical arts are the obverse of your failure in all that calls for spiritual

[1] *The Evolution of Modern Germany*, pp. 15-16.

insight. Machines of every kind you can make and use to perfection; but you cannot build a house, or write a poem, or paint a picture; still less can you worship or aspire. . . . Your outer man as well as your inner is dead; you are blind and deaf. Ratiocination has taken the place of perception; and your whole life is an infinite syllogism from premises you have not examined to conclusions you have not anticipated or willed. Everywhere means, nowhere an end. Society a huge engine and that engine itself out of gear. Such is the picture your civilisation presents to my imagination." [1] There is, of course, exaggeration in this indictment; but there is also truth. At all events it brings out vividly the point which is here at issue; that efforts devoted to the production of people who are good instruments may involve a failure to produce people who are good men.

§ 8. The possibility of conflict between the effects of economic causes upon economic welfare and upon welfare in general, which these considerations emphasise, is easily explained. The only aspects of conscious life which can, as a rule, be brought into relation with a money measure, and which, therefore, fall within economic welfare, are a certain limited group of *satisfactions* and *dissatisfactions*. But conscious life is a complex of many elements, and includes, not only these satisfactions and dissatisfactions, but also other satisfactions and dissatisfactions, and, along with them, cognitions, emotions and desires. Environmental causes operating to change economic satisfactions may, therefore, either in the same act or as a consequence of it, alter some of these other elements. The ways in which they do this may be distinguished, for purposes of illustration, into two principal groups.

First, non-economic welfare is liable to be modified by the manner in which income is earned. For the surroundings of work react upon the quality of life. Ethical quality is affected by the occupations—menial service, agricultural labour, artistic creation, independent as against subordinate economic positions,[2]

---

[1] Dickinson, *Letters of John Chinaman*, pp. 25-6.

[2] Thus it is important to notice that machinery, as it comes to be more elaborate and expensive, makes it, *pro tanto*, more difficult for small men, alike in industry and agriculture, to start independent businesses of their own. Cf. Quaintance, *Farm Machinery*, p. 58.

monotonous repetition of the same operation,[1] and so on—into
which the desires of consumers impel the people who work to
satisfy them.   It is affected, too, by the influence which these
people exert on others with whom they may be brought into
personal contact.   The social aspect of Chinese labour in the
Transvaal and of the attempt by Australian pastoralists to
maintain the convict system, as a source of labour supply,[2]
had relevance to welfare.   So, too, have the unity of interest
and occupation which characterise the farm family as distinguished from the town-dwelling family.[3]   In the Indian
village "the collaboration of the family members not only
economises expenses, but sweetens labour.   Culture and
refinement come easily to the artisan through his work amidst
his kith and kin."[4]   Thus the industrial revolution, when it
led the cottager from his home into the factory, had an effect
on other things besides production.   In like manner, increased
efficiency in output was not the only result which the
agricultural revolution, with its enclosures and large-scale
farming, brought about.   There was also a social change in
the destruction of the old yeoman class.   The human relations
that arise out of industrial relations are also relevant.   In the
great co-operative movement, for example, there is a non-
economic side at least as important as the economic.   Whereas
in the organisation of ordinary competitive industry opposition of interest, both as between competing sellers and as
between sellers and buyers, necessarily stands in the fore-
front, and results at times in trickery and a sense of mutual
suspicion, in a co-operative organisation unity of interest

[1] Munsterberg writes "that the feeling of monotony depends much less upon
the particular kind of work than upon the special disposition of the individual"
(*Psychology and Industrial Efficiency*, p. 198).   But, of course, the *ethical effect*
of monotony must be distinguished from the unpleasantness of it.   Marshall
maintains that monotony of life is the important thing, and argues that variety
of life is compatible with monotony of occupation, in so far as machines take
over straining forms of work, with the result that "nervous force is not very
much exhausted by the ordinary work of a factory" (*Principles of Economics*,
p. 263).   Obviously much turns here on the length of the working day.
Smart held that "the work of the majority is not only toilsome, monotonous,
undeveloping, but takes up the better part of the day, and leaves little energy
for other pursuits" (*Second Thoughts of an Economist*, p. 107).

[2] Cf. V. S. Clark, *The Labour Movement in Australia*, p. 32.

[3] Cf. *Proceedings of the American Economic Association*, vol. x. pp. 234-5.

[4] Cf. Mukerjee, *The Foundations of Indian Economics*, p. 386.

is paramount. This circumstance has its influence on the
general tone of life. " As a member of a society with interests
in common with others, the individual consciously and unconsciously develops the social virtues. Honesty becomes
imperative, and is enforced by the whole group on the individual, loyalty to the whole group is made an essential for
the better development of individual powers. To cheat the
society is to injure a neighbour." [1] In the relations between
employers and workpeople in ordinary industry the non-economic
element is fully as significant. The *esprit de corps* and interest
in the fortunes of the firm, which animate the workpeople in
establishments where the personal intercourse of employers and
employed is cordial, besides leading to increased production of
wealth, *is* in itself an addition to welfare. As large-scale
industry extended during the eighteenth and nineteenth
centuries, employers and employed became more distant in
station, and their opportunities of meeting one another
diminished. In the wake of this inevitable physical separation there followed a moral separation—" the personal aliena-
tion of the employer from his fellow-men whom he engages to
work for him in large numbers." [2] This spirit of hostility
was an obvious negative element in non-economic welfare due to
an economic cause; and the partial suppression of it through
Boards of Conciliation, Whitley Councils and Copartnership
arrangements is an equally obvious positive element. Nor is
this all. It is more and more coming to be recognised that, if
one root of " labour unrest " has been dissatisfaction with rates of
wages, a second root, also of great importance, has been dissatisfaction with the general *status* of wage-labour—the feeling that
the industrial system, as it is to-day, deprives the workpeople of
the liberties and responsibilities proper to free men, and renders

---

[1] Smith-Gordon and Staples, *Rural Reconstruction in Ireland*, p. 240. Cf.
the enthusiastic picture which Wolff draws of the general social benefits of
rural co-operation on the Raiffeisen plan : " How it creates a desire and readiness
to receive and assimilate instruction, technical and general, how it helps to raise
the character of the people united by it, making for sobriety, strict honesty,
good family life, and good living generally." It has been seen, he says, to
produce these effects " among the comparatively educated peasantry of Germany,
the illiterate country folk of Italy, the primitive cultivators of Serbia, and it is
beginning to have something the same effect among the ryots of India" (*The
Future of Agriculture*, p. 481).

[2] Gilman, *A Dividend to Labour*, p. 15.

them mere tools to be used or dispensed with at the convenience
of others : the sense, in short, as Mazzini put it long ago, that
capital is the *despot* of labour.[1] Changes in industrial organisation that tend to give greater control over their own lives to
workpeople, whether through workmen's councils to overlook
matters of discipline and workshop organisation in conjunction
with the employer, or through a democratically elected Parliament directly responsible for nationalised industries, or, if this
should prove feasible, through some form of State-recognised
and State-controlled national guilds,[2] might increase welfare
as a whole, even though they were to leave unchanged, or
actually to damage, economic welfare.

Secondly, non-economic welfare is liable to be modified by
the manner in which income is spent. Of different acts of
consumption that yield equal satisfactions, one may exercise
a debasing, and another an elevating, influence.[3] The reflex
effect upon the quality of people produced by public museums,
or even by municipal baths,[4] is very different from the reflex
effect of equal satisfactions in a public bar. The coarsening
and brutalizing influence of bad housing accommodation is an
incident not less important than the direct dissatisfaction
involved in it. Instances of the same kind could be multiplied.
The point that they would illustrate is obviously of large
practical importance. Imagine, for example, that a statesman

---

[1] Cf. Mazzini, *The Duties of Man*, p. 99.

[2] Cf. *The Meaning of National Guilds*, by Beckhover and Reckitt, *passim*.
" The essence of Labour's demand for responsibility is that it should be recognised
as responsible to the community, not to the capitalist" (p. 100). The goal of
National Guilds " is the control of production by self-governing Guilds of workers
sharing with the State the control of the produce of their labour" (p. 285).
The fact that schemes of industrial reorganisation on these lines are exposed to
serious practical difficulties, which their authors do not as yet seem fully to
have faced, does not render any less admirable the *spirit* of this ideal.

[3] Mr. Hawtrey has criticised my analysis upon the ground that it implicitly
makes equal satisfactions embody equal amounts of welfare, whereas, in fact,
satisfactions are of various degrees of goodness and badness (*The Economic
Problem*, pp. 184-5). There is, however, no difference in substance between
Mr. Hawtrey and myself. We both take account of those variations of quality.
Whether it is better to say, of two equal satisfactions, that one may in itself
contain more good than the other, or to say that in themselves, *qua* satisfactions,
they are equally good, but that their reactions upon the quality of the people
enjoying them may differ in goodness, is chiefly a matter of words. I have substituted in the present text " the quality of people " for my original " people's
characters."   [4] Cf. Darwin, *Municipal Trade*, p. 75.

is considering how far inequality in the distribution of wealth influences welfare as a whole, and not merely in its economic aspects. He will reflect that the satisfaction of some of the desires of the rich, such as gambling excitement or luxurious sensual enjoyment, or perhaps, in Eastern countries, opium-eating, involves reactions on character ethically inferior to those involved in the satisfaction of primary physical needs, to the securing of which the capital and labour controlled by the demand of the rich would, if transferred to the poor, probably be devoted. On the other hand, he will reflect that other satisfactions purchased by the rich—those, for example, connected with literature and art[1]—involve reactions that are ethically superior to those connected with the primary needs, and still more to those derived from excessive indulgence in stimulants. These very real elements in welfare will, indeed, enter into relation with the measuring rod of money, and so be counted in economic welfare, in so far as one group of people devote income to purchasing things *for* other people. When they do this, they are likely to take account of the total effect, and not merely of the effect on the satisfactions of those people—especially if the said people are their own children. For, as Sidgwick acutely observes: "A genuine regard for our neighbour, when not hampered by the tyranny of custom, prompts us to give him what we think really good for him, whereas natural self-regard prompts us to give ourselves what we like."[2] In these special circumstances, therefore, the gap between the effect on economic welfare and the effect on total welfare is partially bridged. Generally, however, it is not so bridged.

§ 9. There is one further consideration, of the great importance of which recent events can leave no doubt. It has to do with the possible conflict, long ago emphasised

---

[1] Thus, Sidgwick observes after a careful discussion: "There seems, there-fore, to be a serious danger that a thorough-going equalisation of wealth among the members of a modern civilised community would have a tendency to check the growth of culture in the community" (*Principles of Political Economy*, p. 523).

[2] *Practical Ethics*, p. 20. Cf. Effertz: "Ce que les intéressés savent généralement mieux que les non-intéressés, ce sont les *moyens* propres à réaliser ce qu'ils croient être leur intérêt. Mais, dans la détermination de l'intérêt le non-intéressé voit généralement plus clair" (*Antagonismes économiques*, pp. 237·8).

by Adam Smith, between opulence and defence. Lack of security against successful hostile attack may involve " dissatisfactions " of a very terrible kind. These things lie outside the economic sphere, but the risk of them may easily be affected by economic policy. It is true, no doubt, that between economic strength and capacity for war there is a certain rough agreement. As Adam Smith wrote : " The nation which, from the annual produce of its domestic industry, from the annual revenue arising out of its lands, labour and consumable stock, has wherewithal to purchase those consumable goods in distant countries, can maintain foreign wars there." [1] But agreement between economic and military strength is ultimate and general, not immediate and detailed. It must, therefore, be clearly recognised that the effect upon economic welfare of the policy which a State adopts towards agriculture, shipping and industries producing war material is often a very subordinate part of its whole effect. Injury to economic welfare may need to be accepted for the sake of defensive strategy. Economically it is probably to the advantage of this country to purchase the greater part of its food supplies from abroad in exchange for manufactured goods, and to keep more than two-thirds of its cultivated land under grass—in which state comparatively little capital and labour is employed upon it and correspondingly little human food produced.[2] In a world of perpetual peace this policy would also probably be advantageous on the whole ; for a small proportion of the population engaged in agriculture does not necessarily imply a small proportion living under rural conditions. But, when account is taken of the possibility that imports may be cut off by blockade in war, that inference need not follow. There can be little doubt that Germany's policy of conserving and developing agriculture for many years at an economic loss enabled her to resist the British blockade in the Great War for a much longer period than would otherwise have been possible ; and, though there are, of course, alternative means

[1] *Wealth of Nations*, p. 333.
[2] Cf. *The Recent Development of German Agriculture* [Cd. 8305], 1916. p. 42 and *passim*.

of defence, such as the establishment of large national grain stores, it is, from a general political point of view, a debatable question whether in this country some form of artificial encouragement should be given to agriculture as a partial insurance against the danger of food difficulties in the event of war. This issue, and the kindred issue concerning materials and industries essential for the conduct of war, cannot be decided by reference to economic considerations alone.

§ 10. The preceding discussion makes it plain that any rigid inference from effects on economic welfare to effects on total welfare is out of the question. In some fields the divergence between the two effects will be insignificant, but in others it will be very wide. Nevertheless, I submit that, in the absence of special knowledge, there is room for a judgment of probability. When we have ascertained the effect of any cause on economic welfare, we may, unless, of course, there is specific evidence to the contrary, regard this effect as *probably* equivalent in direction, though not in magnitude, to the effect on total welfare; and, when we have ascertained that the effect of one cause is more favourable than that of another cause to economic welfare, we may, on the same terms, conclude that the effect of this cause on total welfare is probably more favourable. In short, there is a presumption — what Edgeworth calls an " unverified probability "—that qualitative conclusions about the effect of an economic cause upon economic welfare will hold good also of the effect on total welfare. This presumption is especially strong where experience suggests that the non-economic effects produced are likely to be small. But in all circumstances the burden of proof lies upon those who hold that the presumption should be overruled.

§ 11. The above result suggests *prima facie* that economic science, when it shall have come to full development, is likely to furnish a powerful guide to practice. Against this suggestion there remains, however, one considerable obstacle. When the conclusion set out in the preceding section is admitted to be valid, a question may still be raised as to its practical utility. Granted, it may be said, that the effects produced by economic causes upon economic welfare are probably, in some measure, representative of those produced on total welfare, we have really gained nothing.   For the effects produced upon economic welfare itself cannot, the argument runs, be ascertained beforehand by those partial and limited investigations which alone fall within the scope of economic science.   The reason for this is that the effects upon economic welfare produced by any economic cause are likely to be modified by the non-economic conditions, which, in one form or another, are always present, but which economic science is not adapted to investigate.   The difficulty is stated very clearly by J. S. Mill in his *Logic*.   The study of a *part* of things, he points out, cannot in any circumstances be expected to yield more than approximate results : " Whatever affects, in an appreciable degree, any one element of the social state, affects through it all the other elements. . . . We can never either understand in theory or command in practice the condition of a society in any one respect, without taking into consideration its condition in all other respects.   There is no social phenomenon which is not more or less influenced by every other part of the condition of the same society, and, therefore, by every cause which is influencing any other of the con- temporaneous social phenomena." [1]   In other words, the effects of economic causes are certain to be partially dependent on non-economic circumstances, in such wise that the same cause will produce somewhat different economic effects accord- ing to the general character of, say, the political or religious conditions that prevail.   So far as this kind of dependence exists, it is obvious that causal propositions in economics can only be laid down subject to the condition that things outside the economic sphere either remain constant or, at least, do not vary beyond certain defined limits.   Does this condi- tion destroy the practical utility of our science ?   I hold that, among nations with a stable general culture, like those inhabiting Western Europe, the condition is fulfilled nearly enough to render the results reached by economic inquiry reasonably good approximations to truth.   This is the view taken by Mill.   While fully recognising " the paramount

[1] *Logic*, ii. p. 488.

ascendancy which the general state of civilisation and social progress in any given society must exercise over all the partial and subordinate phenomena," he concludes that the portion of social phenomena, in which the immediately determining causes are principally those that act through the desire for wealth, " do *mainly* depend, at least in the first resort, on one class of circumstances only." He adds that, "even when other circumstances interfere, the ascertainment of the effect due to the one class of circumstances alone is a sufficiently intricate and difficult business to make it expedient to perform it once for all, and then allow for the effect of the modifying circumstances; especially as certain fixed combinations of the former are apt to recur often, in conjunction with ever-varying circumstances of the latter class."[1] I have nothing to add to this statement. If it is accepted, the difficulty discussed in this section need no longer give us pause. It is not necessarily impracticable to ascertain by means of economic science the approximate effects of economic causes upon economic welfare. The bridge that has been built in earlier sections between economic welfare and total welfare need not, therefore, rust unused.

[1] *Logic,* ii. pp. 490-91.

CHAPTER II

DESIRES AND SATISFACTIONS

§ 1. In the preceding chapter economic welfare was taken broadly to consist in that group of satisfactions and dissatisfactions which can be brought into relation with a money measure. We have now to observe that this relation is not a direct one, but is mediated through desires and aversions. That is to say, the money which a person is prepared to offer for a thing measures directly, not the satisfaction he will get from the thing, but the intensity of his desire for it. This distinction, obvious when stated, has been somewhat obscured for English-speaking students by the employment of the term utility—which naturally carries an association with satisfaction—to represent intensity of desire. Thus, when one thing is desired by a person more keenly than another, it is said to possess a greater utility to that person. Several writers have endeavoured to get rid of the confusion which this use of words generates by substituting for " utility " in the above sense some other term, such, for example, as " desirability." The term " desiredness " seems, however, to be preferable, because, since it cannot be taken to have any ethical implication, it is less ambiguous. I shall myself employ that term. The verbal issue is, however, a subordinate one. The substantial point is that we are entitled to use the comparative amounts of money which a person is prepared to offer for two different things as a test of the comparative satisfactions which these things will yield to him, only on condition that the ratio between the intensities of desire that he feels for the two is equal to the ratio between the amounts of satisfaction which their possession will yield to him. This condition, however, is not always fulfilled. By this statement I do not, of course, merely mean that people's expectations as to the satisfaction they will derive from different commodities are often erroneous. The point is that, even apart from this, the condition sometimes breaks down. Thus Sidgwick observes: " I do not judge pleasures [and the same thing obviously holds of satisfactions other than pleasures] to be greater and less exactly in proportion as they exercise more or less influence in stimulating the will to actions tending to sustain or produce them ": [1] and again, " I do not think it ought to be assumed that intensity of immediate gratification is always in proportion to intensity of pre-existing desire." [2] This consideration obviously has great theoretical importance. When it is recollected that all comparisons between different taxes and different monopolies, which proceed by an analysis of their effects upon consumer's surplus, tacitly assume that demand price (the money measure of desire) is also the money measure of satisfaction, it is apparent that it *may* have great practical importance also. The question whether it has in actual fact great practical importance has, therefore, to be examined.

§ 2. In a broad general way we may, I think, safely answer this question in the negative. It is fair to suppose that most commodities, especially those of wide consumption that are required, as articles of food and clothing are, for direct personal use, will be wanted as a means to satisfaction, and will, consequently, be desired with intensities proportioned to the satisfactions they are expected to yield.[3] For the most general purposes of economic analysis, therefore, not much harm is likely to be done by the current practice of regarding money demand price indifferently as the measure of a desire and as the measure of the satisfaction felt when the desired thing is obtained. To this general conclusion, however, there is one very important exception.

§ 3. This exception has to do with people's attitude toward the future. Generally speaking, everybody prefers present pleasures or satisfactions of given magnitude to future pleasures or satisfactions of equal magnitude, even when the latter are

[1] *Methods of Ethics*, p. 126.
[2] *The Ethics of T. H. Green*, etc., p. 340.
[3] Cf. my " Some Remarks on Utility," *Economic Journal*, 1903, p. 58 *et seq*,

perfectly certain to occur. But this preference for present pleasures does not—the idea is self-contradictory—imply that a present pleasure of given magnitude is any *greater* than a future pleasure of the same magnitude. It implies only that our telescopic faculty is defective, and that we, therefore, see future pleasures, as it were, on a diminished scale. That this is the right explanation is proved by the fact that exactly the same diminution is experienced when, apart from our tendency to forget ungratifying incidents, we contemplate the past. Hence the existence of preference for present over equally certain future pleasures does not imply that any economic dissatisfaction would be suffered if future pleasures were substituted at full value for present ones. The non-satisfaction this year of a man's preference to consume this year rather than next year is balanced by the satisfaction of his preference next year to consume next year rather than to have consumed this year. Hence, there is nothing to set against the fact that, if we set out a series of exactly equal satisfactions — *satisfactions*, not objects that yield satisfactions—all of them absolutely certain to occur over a series of years beginning now, the desires which a man will entertain for these several satisfactions will not be equal, but will be represented by a scale of magnitudes continually diminishing as the years to which the satisfactions are allocated become more remote. This reveals a far-reaching economic disharmony. For it implies that people distribute their resources between the present, the near future and the remote future on the basis of a wholly irrational preference. When they have a choice between two satisfactions, they will not necessarily choose the larger of the two, but will often devote themselves to producing or obtaining a small one now in preference to a much larger one some years hence. The inevitable result is that efforts directed towards the remote future are starved relatively to those directed to the near future, while these in turn are starved relatively to efforts directed towards the present. Suppose, for example, that a person's telescopic faculty is such that he discounts future satisfactions, which are perfectly certain to occur, at the rate of 5 per cent per annum. Then, instead of being ready to work for next year, or a year ten years hence, so long as a given increment of effort will yield as much satisfaction as an equal increment devoted to work for the present, he will only work for next year so long as the yield of an increment of effort employed for that year is 1·05 times, and for ten years hence so long as it is $(1·05)^{10}$ times, the yield of an increment employed for the present. It follows that the aggregate amount of economic satisfaction which people in fact enjoy is much less than it would be if their telescopic faculty were not perverted, but equal (certain) satisfactions were desired with equal intensity whatever the period at which they are destined to emerge.

§ 4. This, however, is not all. Since human life is limited, such fruits of work or saving as accrue after a considerable interval are not enjoyed by the person to whose efforts they are due. This means that the satisfaction with which his desire is connected is not his own satisfaction, but the satisfaction of somebody else, possibly an immediate successor whose interest he regards as nearly equivalent to his own, possibly somebody quite remote in blood or in time, about whom he scarcely cares at all. It follows that, even though our desires for equal satisfactions *of our own* occurring at different times were equal, our desire for future satisfaction would often be less intense than for present satisfaction, because it is very likely that the future satisfaction will not be our own. This discrepancy will be more important the more distant is the time at which the source of future satisfaction is likely to come into being; for every addition to the interval increases the chance of death, not merely to oneself, but also to children and near relatives and friends in whom one's interest is likely to be most keen.[1] No doubt,

---

[1] If k be the fraction of importance that I attach to a pound in the hands of my heirs as compared with myself, and $\phi(t)$ the probability that I shall be alive t years from now, a certain pound *to me or my heirs* then attracts me now equally with a certain pound multiplied by $\{\phi(t)+k(1-\phi(t))\}$ *to me* then. This is obviously increased by anything that increases either $\phi(t)$ or k.

If, through an anticipated change of fortune or temperament, one pound after t years is expected to be equivalent to $(1-a)$ times one pound now, a certain $\{\phi(t)+k(1-\phi(t))\}$ pounds of the then prevailing sort to me then attracts me equally with $(1-a)\{\phi(t)+k(1-\phi(t))\}$ pounds of the now prevailing sort to me then. Therefore, a certain pound to my heirs will be as persuasive to call out investment now as the above sum would be if I were certain to live for ever and always to be equally well off and the same in temperament.

this obstacle to investment for distant returns is partly overcome by stock-exchange devices. If £100 invested now is
expected to reappear after 50 years expanded at, say, 5 per
cent compound interest, the man who originally provides the
£100 may be able, after a year, to sell his title in the eventual
fruit for £105; the man who buys from him may be able
similarly to get his capital of £105 back with 5 per cent
interest after one year; and so on. In these circumstances the
fact that any one man would require a higher rate of interest
per annum to induce him to lock up £100 for 50 years than
he would to induce him to lock up the same sum for one year
makes no difference. But, of course, in actual fact this device
is of very narrow application. As regards investments, such
as planting a forest or undertaking drainage development on
one's own estate, which can only be accomplished privately, it
is not applicable at all; and, even when investment is undertaken by a company, investors cannot seriously expect to find
a smooth and continuous market for non-dividend paying
securities.

§ 5. The practical way in which these discrepancies
between desire and satisfaction work themselves out to the
injury of economic welfare is by checking the creation of
new capital and encouraging people to use up existing capital
to such a degree that larger future advantages are sacrificed
for smaller present ones. Always the chief effect is felt
when the interval of time between action and consequence
is long. Thus, of the check to investment, Giffen wrote:
" Probably there are no works more beneficial to a community
in the long run than those, like a tunnel between Ireland
and Great Britain, which open an entirely new means of
communication of strategical as well as of commercial value,
but are not likely to pay the individual enterpriser in any
short period of time." A number of other large undertakings, such as works of afforestation or water supply,
the return to which is distant, are similarly handicapped
by the slackness of desire towards distant satisfactions.[1] This

---

[1] In this connection the following passage from Knoop's *Principles and
Methods of Municipal Trade* is of interest : " To secure an additional supply
of water to a town, ten or more years of continuous work may easily be

same slackness of desire towards the future is also responsible for a tendency to wasteful exploitation of Nature's gifts. Sometimes people will win what they require by methods that destroy, as against the future, much more than they themselves obtain. Over-hasty exploitation of the best coal seams by methods that cover up and render unworkable for ever worse, but still valuable, seams;[1] fishing operations so conducted as to disregard breeding seasons, thus threatening certain species of fish with extinction;[2] farming operations so conducted as to exhaust the fertility of the soil, are all instances in point. There is also waste, in the sense of injury to the sum total of economic satisfaction, when one generation, though not destroying more actual stuff than it itself obtains, uses up for trivial purposes a natural product which is abundant now but which is likely to become scarce and not readily available, even for very important purposes, to future generations. This sort of waste is illustrated when enormous quantities of coal are employed in high-speed vessels in order to shorten in a small degree the time of a journey that is already short. We cut an hour off the time of our passage to New York at the cost of preventing, perhaps, one of our descendants from making the passage at all.

§ 6. In view of this "natural" tendency of people to devote too much of their resources to present service and too little to future service, any artificial interference on the part of Government in favour of that tendency is bound, unless it has compensating advantages on the side of distribution, to diminish economic welfare. Subject to that condition, therefore, all taxes which differentiate against saving, as compared with spending, must diminish economic welfare. Even without

---

required. This means that for several years a large amount of capital will be unproductive, thus seriously affecting the profits of the undertaking and making boards of directors very chary about entering upon any large scheme. . . . It is almost inconceivable that a water company would have undertaken the great schemes by which Manchester draws its supply of water from Lake Thirlmere in Cumberland, a distance of some 96 miles; Liverpool its supply from Lake Vyrnwy in North Wales, a distance of some 78 miles; and Brighton its supply from the Elan Valley in Mid Wales, a distance of some 80 miles" (loc. cit. p. 38).

[1] Cf. Chiozza-Money, The Triumph of Nationalisation, p. 199.
[2] Cf. Sidgwick, Principles of Political Economy, p. 410.

differentiation there will be too little saving: with it there will be much too little saving. Property taxes, where they exist, and death duties, obviously differentiate against saving. The English income tax, though it appears to be neutral, in fact, as is shown elsewhere, also does this.[1] The foregoing analysis shows that there is a *prima facie* case for softening the differential element in these taxes. Proposals, therefore, for exempting saved income from income tax, balancing property taxes by heavy "indirect" taxes upon important objects of expenditure, exempting from local rates improvements contributed during the preceding twenty years, and so on, deserve to be carefully weighed. In the construction of a practical tax-system, however, considerations as to what is "fair" between people of different degrees of wealth and as to what is administratively feasible may compel us to accept arrangements which differentiate against savings in spite of our knowledge that such differentiation is in itself undesirable.[2]

§ 7. Our analysis also suggests that economic welfare could be increased by some rightly chosen degree of differentiation *in favour* of saving. Nobody, of course, holds that the State should force its citizens to act as though so much objective wealth now and in the future were of exactly equal importance. In view of the uncertainty of productive developments, to say nothing of the mortality of nations and eventually of the human race itself, this would not, even in extremest theory, be sound policy. But there is wide agreement that the State should protect the interests of the future *in some degree* against the effects of our irrational discounting and of our preference for ourselves over our descendants. The whole movement for "conservation" in the United States is based on this conviction. It is the clear duty of Government, which is the trustee for unborn generations as well as for its present citizens, to watch over, and, if need be, by legislative enactment, to defend, the exhaustible natural resources of the country from

---

[1] Cf. my *A! Study in Public Finance*, Part II. ch. x.

[2] For example, the case against the imposition of equal taxation upon two men, each of whom spends £450 a year, but the first has an income of £1000 and the second an income of £500 a year is, from the point of view of equity, overwhelming.

rash and reckless spoliation.   How far it should itself, either
out of taxes, or out of State loans, or by the device of guaranteed
interest, press resources into undertakings from which the
business community, if left to itself, would hold aloof, is a
more difficult problem.   Plainly, if we assume adequate competence on the part of governments, there is a valid case
for *some* artificial encouragement to investment, particularly
to investments the return from which will only begin to
appear after the lapse of many years.   It must, however, be
remembered that, so long as people are left free to decide for
themselves how much work they will do, interference, by fiscal
or any other means, with the way in which they employ the
resources that their work yields to them *may* react to diminish
the aggregate amount of this work and so of those resources.
It does not follow, in short, that, because economic welfare
would be increased if a man who now invests, say, one-tenth
of his income, *chose* to invest one-half, *therefore* it would be
increased if he were compelled by legislative decree, or
induced by taxes and bounties, to make this change.

CHAPTER III

THE NATIONAL DIVIDEND

§ 1. GENERALLY speaking, economic causes act upon the economic welfare of any country, not directly, but through the making and using of that objective counterpart of economic welfare which economists call the national dividend or national income. Just as economic welfare is that part of total welfare which can be brought directly or indirectly into relation with a money measure, so the national dividend is that part of the objective income of the community, including, of course, income derived from abroad, which can be measured in money. The two concepts, economic welfare and the national dividend, are thus co-ordinate, in such wise that any description of the content of one of them implies a corresponding description of the content of the other. In the preceding chapter it was shown that the concept of economic welfare is essentially elastic. The same measure of elasticity belongs to the concept of the national dividend. It is only possible to define this concept precisely by introducing an arbitrary line into the continuum presented by nature. It is entirely plain that the national dividend is composed in the last resort of a number of objective services, some of which are embodied in commodities, while others are rendered direct. These things are most conveniently described as goods—whether immediately perishable or durable—and services, it being, of course, understood that a service that has already been counted in the form of the piano or loaf of bread, which it has helped to make, must not be counted again in its own right as a service. It is not, however, entirely plain *which part* of the stream of services, or goods and services, that flows

31

annually into being can usefully be included under the title of the national dividend.   That is the question which has now to be discussed.

§ 2. The answer which first suggests itself is that those goods and services should be included (double-counting, of course, being avoided), and only those, that are actually sold for money.   This plan, it would seem, must place us in the best possible position for making use of the monetary measuring rod.   Unfortunately, however, for the symmetry of this arrangement, some of the services which would be excluded under it are intimately connected, and even interwoven, with some of the included services.   The bought and the unbought kinds do not differ from one another in any fundamental respect, and frequently an unbought service is transformed into a bought one, and *vice versa.*   This leads to a number of violent paradoxes.   Thus, if a man hires a house and furniture belonging to somebody else, the services he obtains from them enter into the national dividend, as we are here provisionally defining it, but, if he receives the house and furniture as a gift and continues to occupy it, they do so no longer.   Again, if a farmer sells the produce of his farm and buys the food he needs for his family in the market, a considerable amount of produce enters into the national dividend which would cease to enter into it if, instead of buying things in the market, he held back part of his own meat and vegetables and consumed them on the farm.   Again, the philanthropic work done by unpaid organisers, Church workers and Sunday school teachers, the scientific work of disinterested experimenters, and the political work of many among the leisured classes, which at present do not enter, or, when there is a nominal payment, enter at much less than their real worth, into the national dividend, would enter into it if those people undertook to pay salaries to one another.   Thus, for example, the Act providing for the payment of members of Parliament increased the national dividend by services valued at some £250,000.   Yet again, the services rendered by women enter into the dividend when they are rendered in exchange for wages, whether in the factory or in the home, but do not enter into it when they are rendered by mothers and wives gratuitously to their own families. Thus, if a man marries his housekeeper or his cook, the national dividend is diminished. These things are paradoxes. It is a paradox also that, when Poor Law or Factory Regulations divert women workers from factory work or paid home-work to unpaid home-work, in attendance on their children, preparation of the family meals, repair of the family clothes, thoughtful expenditure of housekeeping money, and so on, the national dividend, on our definition, suffers a loss against which there is to be set no compensating gain.[1] It is a paradox, lastly, that the frequent desecration of natural beauty through the hunt for coal or gold, or through the more blatant forms of commercial advertisement, must, on our definition, leave the national dividend intact, though, if it had been practicable, as it is in some exceptional circumstances, to make a charge for viewing scenery, it would not have done so.[2]

§ 3. Reflection upon these objections makes it plain that they are of a type that could be urged in some degree against any definition of the national dividend except one that coincided in range with the whole annual flow of goods and services. But to adopt a definition so wide as that would be tantamount to abandoning dependence upon the measuring rod of money. We are bound, therefore, either to dispense altogether with any formal definition or to fall back upon a compromise. The former policy, though there is more to be said for it than is sometimes allowed, would certainly arouse distrust, even though it led to no confusion. The latter, therefore, seems on

---

[1] It would be wrong to infer from the above that the large entry of women into industry during the war was associated with an approximately equal loss of work outside industry. For, first, a great deal of war work was undertaken by women who previously did little work of any kind ; secondly, the place of women who entered industry was taken largely by other women who had previously done little—for example, many mistresses in servant-keeping houses themselves took the place of a servant ; and, thirdly, owing to the absence of husbands and sons at the war, the domestic work, which women would have had to do if they had not gone into industry, would have been much less than in normal times.

[2] The Advertisement Regulation Act, 1907, allows local authorities to frame by-laws designed to prevent open-air advertising from affecting prejudicially the natural beauty of a landscape or the amenities of a public park or pleasure promenade. It is not, we may note in this connection, a decisive argument against underground, and in favour of overhead, systems of tramway power wires that they are more expensive. The London County Council deliberately chose the more expensive underground variety for aesthetic reasons.

the whole to be preferable. The method I propose to adopt is as follows. First, in accordance with the precedent set by Marshall, I shall take, as the standard meaning of the term national dividend, that suggested by the practice of the British Income Tax Commissioners. I, therefore, include everything that people buy with money income, together with the services that a man obtains from a house owned and inhabited by himself. But "the services which a person renders to himself and those which he renders gratuitously to members of his family or friends; the benefits which he derives from using his own personal goods [such as furniture and clothes], or public property such as toll-free bridges, are not reckoned as parts of the national dividend, but are left to be accounted for separately."[1] Secondly, while constructing in this way my standard definition of the national dividend, I reserve full liberty, with proper warning, to use the term in a wider sense on all occasions when the discussion of any problem would be impeded or injured by a pedantic adherence to the standard use. There is, no doubt, a good deal that is unsatisfactory about this compromise. Unfortunately, however, the conditions are such that nothing better appears to be available.

§ 4. The above conclusion does not complete the solution of our problem. Given the general class of things which are *relevant* to the national dividend, a further issue has to be faced. For the dividend may be conceived in two sharply contrasted ways: as the flow of goods and services which is *produced* during the year, or as the flow which passes during the year into the hands of ultimate consumers. Marshall adopts the former of these alternatives. He writes: "The labour and capital of the country, acting on its natural resources, produce annually a certain net aggregate of commodities, material and immaterial, including services of all kinds. This is the true net annual income or revenue of the country, or the national dividend."[2] Naturally, since in every year plant and equipment wear out and decay, what is produced must mean what is produced on the whole when allowance has been made for this process

---

[1] Marshall, *Principles of Economics*, p. 524.
[2] *Ibid.* p. 523.

of attrition. To make this clear, Marshall adds elsewhere: " If we look chiefly at the income of a country, we must allow for the depreciation of the sources from which it is derived." [1] In concrete terms, his conception of the dividend includes an inventory of all the new things that are made, and of all the services not embodied in things that are rendered, accompanied, as a negative element, by an inventory of all the decay and demolition that the stock of capital undergoes. Anyone, on the other hand, who had been so far convinced by Professor Fisher [2] as to hold with him that savings are, in no circumstances, income, would identify the national dividend with those goods and services, and those only, that come into the hands of ultimate consumers. [3] According to this view, Marshall's national dividend represents, not the dividend that actually *is* realised, but the dividend that *would be* realised if the country's capital were maintained and no more than maintained. In a stationary state, where the creation of new machinery and plant in any industry exactly balances, and no more than balances, loss by wear and tear, these two things would be *materially* equivalent. The dividend on either definition would consist simply of the flow of goods and services entering into the hands of ultimate consumers; for all new materials at earlier stages in the productive process that came into factories and shops would be exactly balanced by the corresponding materials that left them in worked-up products; and all newly created machinery and plant would

---

[1] Marshall, *Principles of Economics*, p. 80.

[2] Professor Fisher himself takes the position that the national dividend, or income, consists solely of *services* as received by ultimate consumers, whether from their material or from their human environment. Thus a piano or an overcoat made for me this year is not a part of this year's income, but an addition to capital. Only the services rendered to me during this year by these things are income (*The Nature of Capital and Income*, pp. 104 *et seq.*). This way of looking at the matter is obviously very attractive from a mathematical point of view. But the wide departure which it makes from the ordinary use of language involves disadvantages which seem to outweigh the gain in logical clarity. It is easy to fall into inconsistencies if we refuse to follow Professor Fisher's way; but it is not necessary to do so. So long as we do not do so, the choice of definitions is a matter, not of principle, but of convenience.

[3] For consistency it would be necessary to exempt new houses that are built to be occupied by their owners from the category of income and to place them in that of capital, if a money valuation of their annual rental value is included in income.

exactly take the place, and no more than take the place, of corresponding machinery and plant that became worn out during the year. In practice, however, the industry of a country is hardly ever in this kind of stationary state. Hence it is extremely rare for the two versions of the national dividend to be *materially* equivalent, and it is impossible for them to be *analytically* equivalent. The question how the choice between them should fall is, therefore, an important one.

§ 5. The answer to it, as I conceive the matter, turns upon the purpose for which we intend the conception to be used. If we are interested in the comparative amounts of economic welfare which a community obtains over a long series of years, and are looking for an objective index with which this series of amounts can be suitably correlated, then, no doubt, the conception which I have attributed to Professor Fisher's hypothetical follower is the proper one. It is also much more relevant than the other when we are considering how much a country is able to provide over a limited number of years for the conduct of a war; because, for this purpose, we want to know what is the utmost amount that can be squeezed out and " consumed," and we do not premise that capital must be maintained intact. The major part of this volume, however, is concerned, not with war, but with peace, and not with measurement, but with causation. The general form of our questions will be : " What effect on economic welfare as a whole is produced by such and such a cause operating on the economic circumstances of 1920 ? " Now it is agreed that the cause operates through the dividend, and that direct statements of its effects must refer to the dividend. Let us consider, therefore, the results that follow from the adoption of those two conceptions respectively. On Fisher's follower's plan, we have to set down the difference made by the cause to the dividend, not merely of 1920, but of every year following 1920 ; for, if the cause induces new savings, it is only through a statement covering all subsequent years that its effect on the dividend, as conceived by Fisher's follower, can be properly estimated. Thus, on his showing, if a large new factory is built in 1920, not the capital establishment of that factory, but only the flow of services rendered by it in 1920, should be reckoned in the dividend of 1920; and the aggregate effects of the creation of the factory cannot be measured without reference to the national dividend of a long series of years. On Marshall's plan this inconvenient elaboration is dispensed with. When we have stated the effect produced on the dividend, in his sense, for the year 1920, we have implicitly included the effects, so far as they can be anticipated, on the consumption both of 1920 and of all subsequent years; for these effects are reflected back in the capital establishment provided for the factory. The *immediate* effect on consumption is measured by the alteration in the 1920 dividend as conceived by Fisher's follower. But it is through total consumption, and not through immediate consumption, that economic welfare and economic causes are linked together. Consequently, Marshall's definition of the *national dividend* is likely, on the whole, to prove more useful than the other, and I propose in what follows to adopt it. The entity — also, of course, an important one — which Fisher's follower calls by that name, we may speak of as the *national income of consumption goods*, or, more briefly, *consumption income*.

§ 6. We have thus achieved a definition which, unsatisfactory as it is, is still reasonably precise, of the concrete content of the national dividend. This definition carries with it certain plain implications as to the way in which that dividend must be evaluated. The first and most obvious of these is that, when the value of a finished product is counted, the value of materials employed in making that product must not be counted also. In the *British Census of Production of 1907* this form of double counting was carefully avoided. The Director described his method as follows: The result of deducting the total cost of materials used, and the amount paid to other firms for work given out, from the value of the gross output for any one industry or group of industries is to give a figure which may, for convenience, be called the "net output" of the industry or the group. This figure "expresses completely and without duplication the total amount by which the value (at works) of the products of the industry or the group, taken as a whole, exceeded the value (at works) of the materials purchased from outside, *i.e.* it represents the value added to the materials in the course of manufacture. This sum constitutes for any industry the fund from which wages, salaries, rent, royalties, rates, taxes, depreciation, and all other similar charges, have to be defrayed, as well as profits." [1] When, however, it is desired to evaluate the national dividend as a whole, these allowances are not sufficient. There is no real difference between the flour, which is used up in making bread, and bread-making machinery, which is used up and worn out in the process of effecting the conversion. If adding together the flour and the bread in summing the national dividend involves double counting, so also does adding together the machinery and the bread. " Logically," as Marshall observes, " we ought to deduct the looms which a weaving factory buys as well as its yarn. Again, if the factory itself was reckoned as a product of the building trade, its value should be deducted from the output (over a term of years) of the weaving trade. Similarly with regard to farm buildings. Farm houses ought certainly not to be counted, nor for some purposes any houses used in trade." [2] In a broad general way these considerations can be taken into account by subtracting from the sum of the values of the net products of various industries, as defined in the Census of Production, the value of the annual depreciation, which signifies the annual cost of renewal and repair of all kinds of machinery and plant. [3] Thus, if a particular sort of machinery wears out in ten years —Professor Taussig's estimate for the average life of machinery in a cotton mill [4]—the value of the national dividend over ten years will fall short of the value of the aggregated net product by the value of this machinery. [5] Again,

---

[1] [Cd. 6320], p. 8.

[2] Marshall, *Principles of Economics*, p. 614 *n.*

[3] Cf. Flux, *Statistical Journal*, 1913, p. 559.

[4] *Quarterly Journal of Economics*, 1908, p. 342. The report of the *Census of Production*, 1907, sanctions the view that an average life of ten years may reasonably be assigned to buildings and plant in general (*Report*, p. 35).

[5] In industries where large individual items of assets need replacement at fairly long intervals, it is usual to meet this need by the accumulation of a depreciation fund built up by annual instalments during the life of the wasting asset. For machinery which wears out in about equal quantities every year, Professor Young argues that, provided the renewals and

in so far as any sort of crop wastes the productive powers of the soil, the value of the dividend will fall short of the value of the aggregated net product by the cost of returning to the soil those chemical ingredients that it removes.[1] Yet again, when minerals are dug out of the ground, a deduction should be made equal to the excess of the value which the minerals used during the year had in their original situation—theoretically represented by the royalties paid on their working—over the value which whatever is left of them possesses to the country after they have been used. If "using" means exporting in exchange for imports that are not used as capital, this latter value is zero. If, on the other hand, it means inducing Nature miraculously to transmute the mineral into something possessing greater value than it had in the mine, then, in order to obtain the value of the national dividend from the value of the aggregated net product, we shall need to add, and not to subtract, something. This is sufficient for our present purpose. More delicate issues concerning the precise significance of the notion "maintaining capital intact" are treated in detail in the next chapter.

---

repairs required every year are duly furnished, capital will be maintained intact by that fact alone, and no depreciation fund is necessary (*Quarterly Journal of Economics*, 1914, pp. 630 *et seq.*). It is true that by this method, when the plant has been running for some time, the capital is maintained in any one year at the level at which it stood in the preceding year. But Professor Young himself shows that, in static conditions, when a plant has been established for some time, it will normally be about half worn out (*loc. cit.* p. 632). If half-worn-out plant, that is to say, plant half-way through its normal life—is technically of the same efficiency as new plant, this fact does not injure his conclusion. But, in so far as the efficiency of plant diminishes with age, the case is otherwise. If the capital is to be maintained at the level at which it stood *when first invested*, it is necessary, not merely to provide renewals and repairs as needed, but also to maintain a permanent depreciation fund, to balance the difference between the values of a wholly new plant and of one the constituents of which are, on the average, half-way through their effective life. (Cf. also a discussion between Professor Young and Mr. J. S. Davis under the title "Depreciation and Rate Control" in the *Quarterly Journal of Economics*, Feb. 1915.)

[1] Professor Carver writes of the United States : "Taking the country over, it is probable that, other things equal, if the farmers had been compelled to buy fertilisers to maintain the fertility of their soil without depletion, the whole industry would have become bankrupt. . . . The average farmer had never (up to about 1887) counted the partial exhaustion of the soil as a part of the cost of his crop" (*Sketch of American Agriculture*, p. 70). Against this capital loss, however, must be set the capital gain due to the settlement of the land.

§ 7. It remains to consider the relation between the national dividend as thus evaluated—an addition, of course, being made for the value of income received from abroad—and the money income accruing to the community. On the face of things we should expect these two sums to be substantially equal, just as we should expect a man's receipts and his expenditure (including investments) to be equal. With proper account-keeping this clearly ought to be so. In order that it may be so, however, it is necessary for the money income of the community to be so defined as to exclude all income that is obtained by one person as a gift against which no service entering into the inventory of the national dividend is rendered—all allowances, for example, received by children from their parents. In like manner, if A sells existing property or property rights to B for £1000, the £1000, if already counted as a part of B's income, must not be counted as a part of A's income also. These points are, of course, well understood. But certain further implications are less fully realised. Thus the incomes constituted by old-age pensions and special war pensions must be excluded; though ordinary civil service pensions are properly included, " because these may be said to be equivalent to salaries, and the pension system is only an alternative to paying a higher salary to those rendering existing services and leaving them to look after their own superannuation allowance." [1] There must also be excluded all income received by native creditors of the State in interest on loans that have been employed " unproductively," *i.e.* in such a way that they do not, as loans to build railways would do, themselves lead to the production of services which are sold for money and thus enter into the national dividend as evaluated in money. This means that the income received as interest on war loan must be excluded. Nor is it possible to overthrow this conclusion by suggesting that the money spent on the war has really been " productive," because it indirectly prevented invasion and the destruction of material capital that is now producing goods sold for money ; for whatever product war expenditure may have been responsible for in this way— and a similar argument applies to expenditure on school build-

[1] Stamp, *Wealth and Taxable Capacity*, p. 57.

ings—is already counted in the income earned by the material capital. Yet again, it would seem that income obtained by force or fraud, against which no real service has been rendered, ought not to be counted. There are, furthermore, certain difficulties about payments made to Government. The moneys that governing authorities, whether central or local, receive in net profits on services rendered by them, *e.g.* the profits of the Post Office or of a municipal tramway service, should clearly be counted. What the Treasury receives in income tax or death duties should, on the other hand, clearly not be counted, because this income, which has already been reckoned as such in private hands, is not passed to the Treasury in payment for any services rendered by it, but is merely transferred to it as an agent for the tax-payers. What the Treasury receives in (the now abolished) excess-profit duty and corporation tax, as operated in England, stands, however, on a different footing. It should be counted, because the incomes of companies and individuals were reckoned as what was left *after* these taxes had been paid, so that, if the income represented by them had not been counted when in the hands of the Treasury, it would not have been counted at all.[1] Finally, the main part of what the Treasury receives in customs and excise duties ought, paradoxical as it may seem, to be counted, in spite of the fact that it is already counted when in the hands of the tax-payers and that it is not paid against any service. The reason is that the prices of the taxed articles are pushed up (we may suppose) by nearly the amount of the duties, and that, therefore, unless the aggregate money income of the country is reckoned in such a way that it is pushed up correspondingly, this aggregate money income divided by prices, that is to say, the real income of the country, would necessarily appear to be diminished by the imposition of these duties even though it were in fact the same as before.[2] When the nominal money income of the country has been " corrected " in these various ways, what is left should

---

[1] Cf. Stamp, *Wealth and Taxable Capacity*, pp. 55-6.

[2] The reason why it is only claimed that the main part, not the whole, of what the Treasury receives under this head should be counted as income is (1) that commodity taxes may not always raise prices by their full amount, and (2) that they may indirectly cause production to contract.

approximate fairly closely to the value of the national dividend (inclusive of incomes from abroad) estimated on the plan set out above.[1]

[1] It should be noticed, however, that one paradox still remains uncorrected by the qualifications set out in the text.   If a service, for which hitherto fees have been charged to business men, the fees being of a sort that it is lawful to deduct as a business expense before incomes are reckoned, comes to be provided for and to be paid for by an addition to income tax, the money income of the country is increased, though the real income is unchanged (cf. Stamp, *Wealth and Taxable Capacity*, pp. 52-3).   The only way to get rid of this paradox would be to allow business men to deduct the cost of any services which, *if paid for by fees*, would count as a business expense, whether in fact they are paid for by fees or not.

CHAPTER IV

WHAT IS MEANT BY MAINTAINING CAPITAL INTACT

§ 1. THE issue, deferred from § 6 of the preceding chapter, as to the precise significance of " maintaining capital intact " has now to be taken up. We are debarred by the conventions we have adopted from counting as capital durable goods—other than houses—in consumers' hands, in spite of the fact that, so far as giving employment to labour is concerned, a motor car, for example, belonging to anybody other than an owner-driver, is indistinguishable from one belonging to a hiring establishment. This, however, is a secondary matter. For the present purpose the precise content of capital is immaterial. However we define it, it may be likened to a lake into which a great variety of things, which are the fruit of savings, are continually being projected. These things, having once entered the lake, survive there for various periods, according to their several natures and the fortunes that befall them. Among them are things of long life, like elaborately built factories, things of moderate life, like machinery, and things of very short life, like material designed to be worked up into finished goods for consumption or coal destined to be burned. Length of life in this connection means, of course, length of life *as capital* in the industrial machine functioning as a going concern, not the length of life which a thing would enjoy if nobody interfered with it. Coal, for example, if left alone, will last without change of form for an indefinite number of years ; but, none the less, the " life " enjoyed by coal in the lake of capital, *i.e.* the period covered between its entrance and its exit, is almost always very short. All things that enter the lake eventually pass out of it again. Some of them pass, so to speak, in their own persons, embodied as material in some finished product, as when cotton yarn emerges as a cloth garment. But exits are not always, or indeed generally, made in the form of a passage outward of the actual elements that originally came in. When coal is burnt in the process of smelting iron, which is to be used eventually in making cutlery, it is the cutlery, embodying the "virtue" of the coal, and not the coal itself, which passes in person out of the lake. In like manner it is, of course, the "virtue" of machines that are worn out in making finished goods, and not the machines themselves, which passes out in person. In one form or another, however, whatever enters also leaves. There is then of necessity always a stream flowing out of the lake so long as it has any contents at all, and in practice there is also always a stream flowing into it. Its contents at any moment consist of everything that has flowed into it in the past *minus* anything that has flowed out. It is theoretically possible to make an inventory of them and also to evaluate them from day to day. When we speak, in connection with our definition of the national dividend, of the need for "maintaining capital intact," *something* is implied about the relation between successive inventories or successive evaluations of the contents of the lake we have been describing. It is the task of the present chapter to make clear what precisely that something is.

§ 2. For our present purpose it is plain that maintenance of capital intact does not require that the money valuation of the contents of the lake shall be held constant. There are certain sorts of change in this valuation to which everybody will agree that, in our reckoning of the national dividend, no attention whatever should be paid. Thus, if in consequence of a contraction in the supply of money in any year, money values all round are substantially reduced, the money value of the stock of capital will contract along with the rest: but nobody would suggest that this should be reckoned when the national dividend is being estimated. Again, Marshall has observed: "The value of the capital already involved in improving land or erecting a building; in making a railway or a machine; is the aggregate discounted value of its estimated future net income."[1] This implies that, if the general rate of interest rises, the money value of the stock of capital will, other things remaining equal, be reduced. Such reductions are irrelevant to the magnitude of the national dividend. When the value of particular items in the capital stock falls because people's taste for the things they help to produce has declined or because foreign competitors offer these things at a diminished price, that fall also ought not, I think, to be deemed relevant; and the same conclusion holds when the creation of a new item of capital equipment diminishes the value of an existing item ; e.g. when the construction of an electric lighting plant depreciates a neighbouring gas plant, or when the introduction of a new type of battleship or bootmaking machine renders existing battleships or bootmaking machines obsolete. In fact we may, I think, say quite generally, that all contractions in the money value of any parts of the capital stock that remain physically unaltered are irrelevant to the national dividend ; and that their occurrence is perfectly compatible with the maintenance of capital intact.

§ 3. It might seem at first sight to follow from what has been said that the maintenance of capital intact must mean the maintenance in an unaltered physical state of the inventory of things lying in the capital lake. Plainly, if this inventory is in no way modified, capital is maintained intact in an absolute sense ; and, if some things fall out of the inventory, it is not maintained intact in an absolute sense. But, for the special purpose of this analysis, maintenance of capital intact does not mean maintenance in an absolute sense. *Certain* contractions in the physical stock of capital will have to be held compatible with its maintenance intact, as the phrase is here understood. For, it must always be remembered, our concern is to define the national dividend without parting from the phraseology made familiar by Marshall. Thus, suppose that an earthquake or the onslaught of a hostile nation destroys in one year half this country's accumulated stock of wealth. It would be paradoxical and inconvenient to conclude that our national dividend was thereby automatically rendered negative. We must say rather that the loss is a loss on capital account,

---

[1] *Principles of Economics*, p. 593.

not on income account.   In other words, this sort of loss,
though, of course, it is incompatible with the maintenance of
capital intact in any literal sense, is not relevant to estimates
of the national dividend.   Hence for our purpose maintenance
of capital intact must be *defined* to mean maintenance of it
intact, not absolutely, but only when this particular type of
loss does not occur.

§ 4. It may perhaps be thought that this opens the way
for an endless string of further prevarications; that, for example,
the loss of houses by fire or of ships by storm should be put
on the same footing as the losses just discussed.   That, however, is not so.   All disintegrations of capital goods other
than catastrophic destructions of the type described in the
preceding section are really incidental to the use of them, and
are involved in the production of the dividend.   This is most
obviously true of the ordinary wear and tear which machinery
and plant undergo when carrying out their functions.
Weathering by lapse of time apart from use is in like case;
for a necessary condition of use is subjection to the passage
of time.   Even the accidents of fire and storm are in like
case; for the use of houses implies their subjection to the
risk of fire and the use of ships their subjection to that of
storm.   The national dividend is not truly reckoned until
allowance has been made for the replacement of all these
types of capital loss.   Maintenance of capital intact in our
sense is thus equivalent to maintenance in an absolute sense
save only that provision must not be made against destruction
by " act of God or the King's enemies."

§ 5. We have now reached the conclusion that the
maintenance of capital intact for our purpose requires that
all ordinary physical deteriorations in the capital stock should
be made good.   But what exactly do we mean by making
good ?   When a capital stock deteriorates, *e.g.* through wear
and tear, its material components do not disappear from the
world, but merely become rearranged in a way that renders
them less useful to mankind.   Thus what has really disappeared is a physical arrangement embodying a certain sum
of values, which we may for convenience measure in money.
To make this good there must be added to the capital stock

new arrangements of matter embodying a sum of values equal to this sum. Thus, if a machine becomes worn out and has no value at all, we require to add to the capital stock something whose value is equal to that which the machine, had it remained physically intact, would have *now*. The original cost of the machine, whether in real terms or in money terms, is not relevant. Thus it may have cost a thousand pounds to make; but, if its wearing out reduces its sum of values below what it would otherwise have been, not by £1000 but by £500 or by £1500, the replacing machine must have one or other of these values, not the value of £1000. It follows, *inter alia*, that if any piece of capital stock, *e.g.* the equipment of a steel works, has fallen in value in consequence, say, of intensified foreign competition, and if wear and tear depreciates the equipment 10 per cent per annum, to maintain capital intact we need 10 per cent, not of the original cost of the equipment nor of its present replacement cost, but of its present value. If the foreign competition is so strong or if popular taste has turned away from the product made by the equipment so completely that its value has become nil, physical deterioration in it by wear and tear or lapse of time involves no loss of value, and so calls for no replacement. Maintenance of capital intact for our purpose means then, not replacement of all value losses nor yet replacement of all physical losses (not due to acts of God and the King's enemies), but replacement of such value losses as are caused by physical losses other than the above.

§ 6. It is easy to see that different sorts of capital stock undergo losses of this sort—flow out of the capital lake—at different rates. Working capital—materials, coal and so on—usually only has a few months of life in the lake; and fixed capital a life of a number of years, greater or less according to its nature. Hence the annual amount of replacement that is needed to keep £1's worth of working capital intact is much larger than the amount required in respect of a £1's worth of fixed capital. Professor Mitchell quotes some figures which suggest that in the United States the part of fixed capital represented by " movable equipment "—machinery and so on—engaged in industry and agriculture is about equal to the stock of working capital, each being valued at 9000 million pounds.[1]   If the normal life of movable equipment be put at ten years and that of working capital at one year, this implies that the annual replacement of fixed capital must, to maintain it intact, amount to 900 and the annual replacement of working capital to 9000 millions—ten times as much.   Hence if, in any year, a £100 millions worth of deterioration in fixed capital is made good by adding to the capital stock a new 100 millions worth, not of fixed but of working capital, the value of annual replacement needed in future years to keep the aggregate stock of capital intact will be *pro tanto* increased.   In converse conditions it will be diminished.

§ 7. In conclusion a word may be said about the effect of failure to provide sufficient replacement to maintain capital intact.   Let us suppose that we start from a condition of stability; that continually for a long time past savings at the rate of 2 million £ per day have been required for maintenance, and have in fact been forthcoming.   Something occurs, as a result of which henceforward only 1 million £ will be forthcoming.   It is obvious that the level of the lake must fall. But it will not continue to fall indefinitely.   For, as a result of the decline in the inflow, the outflow also must diminish, since the progressive fall in the stock of capital involves at the same time a progressive fall in the daily wastage.   Presently the outflow will so far decrease that the reduced inflow of 1 million a day suffices to replace it.   The contraction in the capital stock thereupon comes to an end and a new equilibrium is established.   The period of time that will need to elapse before this happens will depend on the proportions existing initially between capital items of various lengths of life and on such changes as may take place in these proportions during the course of the decline.   If the failure to provide replacements is carried to the point that henceforward none whatever are forthcoming, the stock of capital must, of course, eventually disappear altogether.   Items with a short remainder of life will become extinct first; then others and yet others.   The outflowing stream will diminish to a smaller and smaller trickle,

[1] *Business Cycles* (1927), p. 93.

until, with the demise of the longest-lived item, it and the lake from which it came alike go dry. In this event, however, humanity will take no interest, for the demise of the last capital item will certainly have been preceded by that of the " last man."

CHAPTER V

CHANGES IN THE SIZE OF THE NATIONAL DIVIDEND

§ 1. The economic welfare of the country is intimately associated with the size of the national dividend, and changes in economic welfare with changes in the size of the dividend. We are concerned to understand, so far as may be, the nature of these associations. To this end an essential preliminary is to form clear ideas as to what precisely changes in the size of the dividend *mean*. It will be convenient, in the first instance, to postulate that the size of that group whose dividend we are studying remains unchanged.

§ 2. The dividend is an objective thing, consisting in any period of such and such a collection of goods and services that flow into being during the period. Since it is an objective thing, we should naturally wish, if we were able, to define changes in the size of it by reference to some objective physical unit, and without any regard to people's attitude of mind towards the several items contained in it. I do not mean that changes in public tastes would be thought of as incapable of affecting the size of the national dividend. They are obviously capable of affecting it by causing changes in the objective constituents of the dividend. I mean that, *given those objective constituents*, the size of the dividend should depend on them alone, and not at all on the state of people's tastes. This is the point of view which everybody intuitively wishes to take.

§ 3. If the national dividend consisted of one single sort of commodity only, there would be no difficulty about this. Everybody would agree that an increase in the size of the dividend should mean an increase, and a decrease a decrease, in the number of units of this commodity. In like manner, if the dividend consisted of a number of different commodities, but the quantities of all of them always varied in equal proportions, there would be no difficulty. The dividend would at any time consist of a certain number of complex units, each of them made up of so much of each commodity, and increases and decreases in the dividend would mean increases and decreases in the number of these complex units.

§ 4. If the national dividend consisted of a number of different sorts of things, the proportion between which was not fixed, but some pre-established harmony made it impossible for the quantity of any one of them to diminish when the quantity of any other was increasing, we should no longer be able to say that the dividend at any moment consisted of such a number of units and at another moment of such another number of units. But we should still always be able to determine by a physical reference whether the dividend of one moment was greater or less than the dividend of another moment: and this, for many purposes, would be all that anybody would need.

§ 5. In actual life, however, the national dividend consists of a number of different sorts of things, the quantities of some of which are liable to increase at the same time that the quantities of others are decreasing. In these circumstances there is no direct means of determining by a physical reference whether the dividend of one period is greater or less than that of another; and it becomes necessary to seek for a definition along other lines. Plainly the definition chosen must be such that, supposing the dividend consisted of one sort of thing only, we should always be able to say that an increase in the quantity of this thing constituted an increase in the size of the dividend. A definition that did not admit of this would be paradoxical. From this starting-point we are led forward as follows. Considering a single individual whose tastes are taken as fixed, we say that his dividend in period II. is greater than in period I. if the items that are added to it in period II. are items that he *wants more* than the items that are taken away from it in period II. Passing to a group of persons (of given numbers), whose tastes are taken as fixed and among whom the distribution of purchasing power is also taken as fixed, we say that the dividend in period II. is greater than in period I. if the items that are added to it in period II. are items *to conserve which they would be willing to give more money than they would be willing to give to conserve the items that are taken away from it in period II.* This definition is free from ambiguity. However the technique of production has altered, —though it has become more costly to make one thing and less costly to make another, though it has become possible to make some entirely new things and at the same time impossible to make some things that used to be made before,—it can yield one conclusion, and one only, as to the effect on the size of the national dividend of any change in its content that may have taken place. If, then, tastes and the distribution of purchasing power were really fixed, there would be nothing to set against the advantages of this method of definition. It would be the natural and obvious one to adopt.

§ 6. As a matter of fact, however, tastes and the distribution of purchasing power both vary. The consequence of this is that our definition leads in certain circumstances to results which, in appearance at least, are highly paradoxical. Thus in period I. tastes are such and such, and in period II. they are something different; in period I. the dividend is a collection C_1 and in period II. a collection C_2. It may happen both that the group with period I. tastes would give *less* money for the items added in period II. than for the items subtracted in that period, and also that the group (of equal numbers) with period II. tastes would give *more* money for the items added in period II. than for the items subtracted in that period. In this case our definition makes C_2 both less than C_1 and also greater than C_1; which is a violent paradox. The only escape from this is to admit that, in these circumstances, there is no meaning in speaking of an increase or decrease in the national dividend in an absolute sense. The dividend decreases from the point of view of period I. tastes, and increases from the point of view of period II. tastes; and there is nothing more to say.[1] It is

---

[1] An exactly analogous difficulty emerges when we attempt to compare the size of the national dividend, as defined above, in two countries. Thus, if the

easy to see that the same paradox may arise, and the same solution be forced upon us, when the distribution of purchasing power alters between period I. and period II. Here again we can only speak of an increase (or decrease) in the size of the dividend from the point of view of period I. distribution or from the point of view of period II. distribution : we cannot speak of an increase or decrease in any absolute sense.[1]

§ 7. We are thus confronted with the awkward fact that there are likely to be certain changes in the constitution of the national dividend, of which it is not possible to say that they are either increases or decreases in an absolute sense. Plainly there is serious objection to a definition which leads to this result. On the other hand, though it will rarely happen that a modification of the dividend, which constitutes an upward (or downward) change of so much per cent from the point of view of period I., will constitute an equal percentage change from the point of view of period II., if between these two periods tastes or distribution have altered, yet it will, we may reasonably expect, *usually* constitute a change *in the same direction* from

---

German population with German tastes were given the national dividend of England, they might get less economic satisfaction than before ; while, if the English population with English tastes were given the German national dividend, they also might get less economic satisfaction than before. The proposed definition would, in these circumstances, compel us to say both that the English dividend is larger (from the English point of view) than the German dividend, and also that the German dividend is larger (from the German point of view) than the English dividend. It may be added, though the point is not strictly relevant, that differences in comparative tastes between the people of two countries can sometimes, though not always, be detected by statistical methods. For example, Germans before the war would not eat mutton though it was a penny cheaper than pork, while Englishmen ate it readily (Cd. 4032, pp. xlviii and xlix). Again Germans eat rye bread, whereas English people eat white bread. We know that this is not due merely to the fact that rye bread is relatively cheap in Germany and that Germans are poorer than Englishmen, because, if it were cheapness alone that was responsible for the consumption of rye in Germany, there would presumably be a higher consumption of white bread among better-to-do Germans. This, however, is not found. Hence, we may legitimately infer that Germans have a taste for rye bread, as against wheaten bread, different from the English taste.

[1] Cf. Dr. Bowley's observation : "The values included in incomes are values in exchange, which are dependent, not only on the goods or services in question, but also on the whole complex of the income and purchases of the whole of a society. . . . The numerical measurement of total national income is thus dependent on the distribution of income and would alter with it" (*The Measurement of Social Phenomena*, pp. 207-8). Cf. also Stamp, *British Incomes and Property*, pp. 419-20.

the point of view of period II. Most causes, in short, will increase the dividend from both points of view or diminish it from both points of view. Usually, therefore, we can say, without circumlocution or complicated reference to two points of view, that a given cause either has or has not increased the size of the national dividend. The defect in our definition is thus not a fatal defect. Moreover, continued reflection fails to reveal any other definition that is not even more defective. In spite, therefore, of all that has been said, I propose, for the purposes of this volume, to define an increase in the size of the dividend for a group of given numbers as follows. From the point of view of period I. an increase in the size of the dividend is a change in its content such that, *if* tastes in period II. were the same as those prevailing in period I. and *if* the distribution of purchasing power were also the same as prevailed in period I., the group would be willing to give more money to conserve the items added in period II. than they would be willing to give to conserve the items that are taken away in period II. Waiving the distinction, discussed in Chapter II., between desire and the satisfaction that results when a desired thing is obtained, we may state the above definition alternatively thus. From the point of view of period I. an increase in the size of the dividend for a group of given numbers is a change in its content such that, *if* tastes in period II. were the same as those prevailing in period I., and *if* the distribution of purchasing power were also the same as prevailed in period I., the economic satisfaction (as measured in money) due to the items added in period II. is greater than the economic satisfaction (as measured in money) due to the items taken away in period II. From the point of view of period II. an increase in the dividend is defined in exactly analogous ways. From an absolute point of view an increase in the size of the dividend is a change which constitutes an increase from both the above two points of view. When, of two dividends, one is larger from the point of view of one period and the other from that of the other, the two are, from an absolute point of view, incommensurable.

§ 8. Hitherto we have been concerned with groups containing equal numbers. As between groups of different sizes a direct comparison of dividends would be of little service. We may, however, in imagination reduce the numbers—all classes of persons being treated equally—in the larger group in the proportion required to make it equal to the smaller group, and reduce its money income in an equal proportion. The dividend of the group so obtained may then be compared, on the lines of the preceding analysis, with that of the smaller group. The result is roughly a comparison of the *per capita* dividends of the two original groups.

CHAPTER VI

THE MEASUREMENT OF CHANGES IN THE SIZE OF THE
NATIONAL DIVIDEND

§ 1. THE discussion of the preceding chapter has provided us with a *criterion* by which to decide whether the national dividend of one period is larger or smaller than the national dividend of another period from the point of view of one or other of the periods. But to provide a *criterion* of increases and decreases in the size of anything is not to provide a *measure* of these changes. We have now to study the problem of devising an appropriate measure.

§ 2. Our *criterion* of increase from the point of view of any period being that, with the tastes and distribution of that period, the money demand for the things that have been added to the dividend exceeds the money demand for the things taken away from it, it is natural to suggest that we should employ as a *measure* of increase, from the point of view of the period, the proportion in which the aggregate money demand for the things contained in the dividend of that period (in the sense of the amount of money that people would be willing to give rather than do without those things) exceeds the aggregate money demand for the things contained in the dividend of the other period. A measure of this kind would conform exactly to our criterion. We should have two figures, one giving the change from the point of view of the tastes and distribution of period I. and the other that from the point of view of the tastes and distribution of period II. Plainly, given the criterion decided upon in the last chapter, this is the measure that we should adopt if we were able to do so.

§ 3. Unfortunately, however, this type of measure is

altogether impracticable. In the way of it there stands, as a final obstacle, the fact that the aggregate money demand for the things contained in the dividend of any period, in the sense explained above, is an unworkable conception. It involves the money figure that would be obtained by adding together the consumers' surpluses, as measured in money, derived from each several sort of commodity contained in the dividend. As Marshall has shown, however, the task of adding together consumers' surpluses in this way, partly on account of the presence of complementary and rival commodities, presents difficulties which, even if they are capable of being overcome in theory by means of elaborate mathematical formulae, are certainly insuperable in practice.[1] Even apart from these remoter complications, it is evident that no measure of the kind contemplated could be built up which did not embrace among its terms the elasticities of demand for the various elements contained in the dividend, or, more exactly, the forms of the various demand functions that are involved. These data are not, and are not likely, within any reasonable period of time, to become, accessible to us. Any type of measure which involves the use of them must, therefore, be ruled out of court.

§ 4. Continuing along the line of thought which this consideration suggests, we are soon led to the conclusion that the only data which there is any serious hope of organising on a scale adequate to yield a measure of dividend changes are the quantities and prices of various sorts of commodities. There is nothing else available, and, therefore, if we are to construct any measure at all, we *must* use these data. Our problem then becomes : in what way, if at all, is it possible, out of them, to construct a measure that will conform to the definition of changes in the size of the dividend that was reached in the last chapter? An attempt to solve this problem falls naturally into three parts : first, a general inquiry as to what measure would conform most nearly to that definition if all relevant information about quantities and prices were accessible ; secondly, a mathematical inquiry as to what practicable measure built up from the sample information

---

[1] *Principles of Economics*, pp. 131-2, footnote.

about quantities and prices that we can in fact obtain would approximate most closely to the above measure; thirdly, a mixed general and mathematical inquiry as to *how reliable* the practicable measure, as an index of the above measure is likely to be.

§ 5. In attacking the first and most fundamental of these issues we have to admit at once that complete success is unattainable. According to the definition of the last chapter, the national dividend will change in one way from the point of view of a period in which tastes and distribution are of one sort, and in a different way from that of a period in which they are of another sort. In order to conform with this, our measure of change would need to be double, being expressed in one figure from the point of view of the first period, and, if tastes and distribution were different in the two periods, in another figure from the point of view of the second period. A measure built up on quantities and prices only cannot possibly answer to this requirement. For, though we may know the quantities and prices that actually ruled in period I., when tastes and distribution were of sort A, and the quantities and prices that ruled in period II., when tastes and distribution were of sort B, we cannot possibly know either the quantities and prices which would have ruled in period I., if tastes and distribution had then been of sort B, or those which would have ruled in period II., if tastes and distribution had then been of sort A. Hence, the utmost we can hope for is a measure which will be independent of what the state of tastes and distribution actually is in either of the periods to be compared, but which will always increase when the content of the dividend has changed in such a way that economic welfare (as measured in money) would be increased whatever the state of tastes and distribution, provided only that this was the same in both periods. Even if the whole of the data about quantities and prices were accessible to us, it would be impossible to construct a measure, based on these data alone, conforming more closely than this to our definition; and, plainly, this degree of conformity is very incomplete.

§ 6. So much being understood, let us turn to the problem

of constructing from full data a measure—we may call it from henceforth the full-data measure—that will conform as closely as possible to the modest ideal specified in the preceding section. What is required is a measure which will show increases in the size of the dividend whenever its content is changed in such a way that, in terms of the money of either period,[1] for a group of given size with constant tastes and distribution, the money demand for the items that have been added is greater than the money demand for those that have been subtracted;[2] or, in other words, that the economic satisfaction (as measured in money) obtained by the group in the second period is greater than it was in the first period. It is not, of course, required that, if, when the excess of economic satisfaction (as measured in money) is E, our measure shows an increase of 1 per cent, it shall, when the excess of economic satisfaction (as measured in money) is 2 E, show an increase of 2 per cent. This is not only not necessary, but, in the special case of a dividend consisting of one sort of commodity only, it would even lead to paradoxical results. It is required, however, that, when the excess of economic satisfaction (as measured in money) is E, our measure shall show *some* increase, and that, when the excess of economic satisfaction (as measured in money) is more than E, it shall show a greater increase than it does when the excess is E. This is the framework within which our construction must be made. The problem is to discover what construction will best fulfil the purpose that has been specified.[3]

[1] These words are necessary to take account of the fact that, if the aggregate money income of our group be altered, a second period £ will not be the same thing as a first period £.

[2] It is perhaps well to repeat here in symbols what has been stated previously in words, that, the equation of the demand curve for any commodity being $p = \phi(x)$, the money demand for an increment of h units means, not

$$(x+h)\phi(x+h) - x\phi(x)\}, \text{ but } \int_0^{x+h} \phi(x) - \int_0^x \phi(x).$$

[3] Professor Irving Fisher, in his admirable study of *The Making of Index Numbers*, appears to take the view that there is a way of making measures of this sort which is right in an absolute sense, and not merely in the sense that it will yield a measure consonant with the particular purpose which we want the measure to serve. Having examined a great many different sorts of index numbers, he found that, after those suffering from definite defects of a technical sort had been eliminated, the remainder, though formed on widely different plans, gave approximately equivalent results, and concluded: "Humanly

§ 7. In the first of any two periods that we wish to compare any group of given size expends its purchasing power upon one collection of commodities, and in the second on a different collection. Each collection must, of course, be so estimated that the same thing is not counted twice over, that is to say, it must be taken to include direct services rendered to consumers—*e.g.* the services of doctors, finished consumable articles, and a portion of the finished durable machines produced during the year,[1] but not the raw materials or the services of labour that are embodied in these things, and not, of course, " securities." Let us, at this stage, ignore the fact that in one of the collections there may be some newly invented kinds of commodity which are not represented at all in the other. The first collection, which we may call C_1, then embraces x_1, y_1, z_1 . . . units of various commodities; and the second collection, C_2, embraces x_2, y_2, z_2 . . . units of the same commodities. Let the prices per unit of these several commodities be, in the first period, a_1, b_1, c_1, . . . ;

---

speaking, then, an index number is an absolutely accurate instrument " (p. 229). Now, the close consilience of the results reached by different methods undoubtedly suggests to the mind that there exists somewhere an absolutely right result to which they are all approximating. But there is, so far as I can see, no real ground for accepting this metaphysical suggestion. Consider the analogy of a measure designed to ascertain the average height of a group of trees. It is easy to find the arithmetical, the geometrical, or any other average of their heights. In many conditions all ordinary forms of average will work out very nearly the same. But this is no proof that there is stored up in heaven an ideal average height different from these and, in an absolute sense, more accurate or truer than any of them. There is a true arithmetical average, a true geometrical average, a true harmonic average ; but the concept of an archetypal average right in an absolute sense is, as it seems to me, an illusion. When we want to satisfy a given purpose it is proper to ask : Will the arithmetical or the geometrical average best serve our purpose ? If the two averages happen to be nearly the same, we are in the happy position that it does not much matter should we accidentally choose the wrong one. But we cannot properly say more than this. There is some reason to believe, however, that, when Professor Fisher claims that the choice of the formula for a price index number is independent of the purpose to be served, he is using the term purpose in a narrower sense than mine, and would not disagree with what is here said.

[1] This is necessary in order to conform to the definition of the national dividend given in Chapter III. Had we defined the dividend so that it included only what is actually consumed during the year, no machines would come into it. On our definition we ought strictly to include all new machinery and plant over and above what is required to maintain capital intact, *minus* an allowance for that part of the value of this machinery and plant that is used up in producing consumable goods during the year itself.

and, in the second period, a_2, b_2, c_2. . . . Let the aggregate money income of our group, in the first period, be I_1, in the second I_2. The following propositions result:

1. If our group in the second period purchased the several commodities in the same proportion in which it purchased them in the first period, that is to say, if it purchased in both periods a collection of the general form C_1, its purchase of each commodity in the second period would be equal to its purchase of each commodity in the first period multiplied by the fraction

$$\frac{I_2}{I_1} \cdot \frac{x_1 a_1 + y_1 b_1 + z_1 c_1 +}{x_1 a_2 + y_1 b_2 + z_1 c_2 +}.$$

2. If our group in the first period purchased the several commodities in the same proportion in which it purchased them in the second period, that is to say, if it purchased in both periods a collection of the general form C_2, its purchase of each commodity in the second period would be equal to its purchase of each commodity in the first period multiplied by the fraction

$$\frac{I_2}{I_1} \cdot \frac{x_2 a_1 + y_2 b_1 + z_2 c_1 + \dots}{x_2 a_2 + y_2 b_2 + z_2 c_2 + \dots}.$$

On the basis of these propositions, provided that a certain assumption is made, our problem can be partially solved.

§ 8. If in period II. a single man who had been purchasing a collection of the form C_2, i.e. made up of elements in the proportions (x_2, y_2, z_2 . . .), chose instead to purchase a collection of the form C_1, it is certain that his action would leave prices unchanged, so that he could buy the items in his new collection at prices a_2, b_2, c_2, . . . An analogous proposition holds of a single man in period I. who should choose to shift from a collection of form C_1 to one of form C_2. But, when it is the whole of a group, or, if we prefer it, a representative man, who shifts his consumption in this way, it is no longer certain that prices would be unaffected. If the group in period II. shifted from a collection of form C_2 to one of form C_1, it would have to pay, let us suppose, prices a_1', b_1', c_1'. In like manner, if the group in period I. shifted from a collection of form C_1 to one of form C_2, it would have to pay prices a_2', b_2', c_2'. The assumption referred to at the end of the preceding section is that $\{x_1a_1' + y_1b_1' + z_1c_1' + \ldots\}$ is equal to $\{x_1a_1 + y_1b_1 + z_1c_1 + \ldots\}$ and that $\{x_2a_2' + y_2b_2' + z_2c_2' + \ldots\}$ is equal to $\{x_2a_2 + y_2b_2 + z_2c_2 + \ldots\}$. This means that the group in period II. could then, if it chose, buy as much of a C_1 collection, in spite of the shift of prices caused by its decision to do this, as it would have been able to do had that decision caused no shift of prices; and that an analogous proposition holds of the group in period I. If all the commodities concerned were being produced under conditions of constant supply price, the above assumption would conform exactly to the facts. In real life, with a large number of commodities, it is reasonable to suppose that the upward price movements caused by shifts of consumption would roughly balance the downward movements; so that, in general, our assumption will conform approximately to the facts. It is important to remember, however, throughout the following argument, that this assumption is being made.

§ 9. Let us begin with the case in which both the fractions set out in § 7 lie upon the same side of unity; they are either both greater than unity or both less than unity. If they are both greater than unity, this means that our group, if it wishes, can buy more commodities in the second period than in the first, whether its purchases are arranged in the form of collection C_1 or in that of collection C_2. Hence the fact that in the second period it chooses the form C_2 proves that the economic satisfaction (as measured in money) yielded by what it then purchases in the form C_2 is greater than the economic satisfaction (as measured in money) that would be yielded by a collection of the form C_1 larger than the collection of that form which it purchased in the first period.[1] *A fortiori*, therefore, it is greater than the economic satisfaction (as measured in money) that would be yielded by the actual collection of the form C_1 which it purchased in the first period.

[1] This proposition and the results based upon it depend on the condition that our group is *able* to buy at the ruling price the quantity of any commodity which it wishes to buy at that price. When official maximum prices have been fixed, and people's purchases at those prices are restricted, either by a process of rationing or by the fact that at those prices there is not enough of the commodity to satisfy the demand, this condition is, of course, not realised. During the Great War the situation was further complicated by the fact that the legal prices were often departed from—at least in Germany—in practice.

But, since tastes and distribution are unaltered, the economic satisfaction (as measured in money) that would be yielded by the actual collection C_1 in the second period is equal to the economic satisfaction (as measured in money) that was yielded by the actual collection in the first period. Hence, if both our fractions are greater than unity, it necessarily follows that the economic satisfaction (as measured in money) yielded by the collection C_2 bought in the second period is greater than the economic satisfaction (as measured in money) yielded by the collection C_1 bought in the first period. By analogous reasoning it can be shown that, if both the above fractions are less than unity, the converse result holds good. In these circumstances, therefore, either of the two fractions

$$\frac{I_2}{I_1} \cdot \frac{x_1 a_1 + y_1 b_1 + z_1 c_1 \, \cdots}{x_1 a_2 + y_1 b_2 + z_1 c_2 \, \cdots} \quad \text{or} \quad \frac{I_2}{I_1} \cdot \frac{x_2 a_1 + y_2 b_1 + z_2 c_1 + \, \cdots}{x_2 a_2 + y_2 b_2 + z_2 c_2 + \, \cdots},$$

or any expression intermediate between them, will satisfy the condition, set out in § 6, which our measure is required to fulfil as a criterion of changes in the volume of the dividend.

§ 10. In the above circumstances, therefore, the condition we have laid down does not determine the choice of a measure, but merely fixes the limits within which that choice must lie. The width of these limits depends upon the extent to which the two fractions differ from one another. In some conditions there exists between them a relation of approximate equality. Thus, during the later nineteenth century, the dominant factor in the Englishman's increased capacity to obtain almost every important commodity was one and the same, namely, improved transport; for a main part of what improvements in manufacture accomplished was to cheapen means of transport. In other conditions the difference between the two fractions is considerable. Illustrations that would be directly applicable might perhaps be found. I must content myself, however, with one drawn, not from an inter-temporary comparison of two states of the same group, but from a contemporary comparison of the states of two groups. This illustration is only relevant to the present purpose on the unreal assumption that English and German workmen's tastes are the same and that their purchases differ solely on account of differences in

their income and in the prices charged to them. It is
taken from the Board of Trade's Report on the *Cost of Living
in German Towns*. The Report shows that, at the time when
it was made, what an English workman customarily consumed
cost about one-fifth more in Germany than in England, while
what a German workman customarily consumed cost about
one-tenth more in Germany than in England.[1] If, then, the
letters with the suffix 1 be referred to English consumption
and prices, and those with the suffix 2 to German consumption
and prices,

$$\frac{x_1 a_1 + y_1 b_1 + z_1 c_1}{x_1 a_2 + y_1 b_2 + z_1 c_2} = \frac{100}{120}, \text{ and } \frac{x_2 a_1 + y_2 b_1 + z_2 c_1}{x_2 a_2 + y_2 b_2 + z_2 c_2} = \frac{100}{110}.$$

§ 11. Though our condition, in the class of problem so far
considered, only fixes these two limits within which the measure
of dividend changes should lie, considerations of convenience
suggest even here the wisdom of selecting, though it be in
an arbitrary manner, some one among the indefinite number
of possible measures. When we proceed from this class of
problem to another more difficult class, the need for purely
arbitrary choice is narrower in range. It sometimes happens
that one of the above two fractions is greater than unity and
the other less than unity. Then it is clear that both of them
cannot indicate the direction in which the economic satisfaction
(as measured in money) enjoyed by the group has changed.
In the second period, let us suppose, the group's later
income commands a larger amount of the collection of form C_2
than its earlier income commanded; but it commands a smaller
amount of the collection of form C_1 than its earlier income
commanded. In these circumstances common sense suggests
that, if the fraction

$$\frac{I_2}{I_1} \cdot \frac{x_1 a_1 + y_1 b_1 + z_1 c_1 + \ldots}{x_1 a_2 + y_1 b_2 + z_1 c_2 + \ldots}$$

falls short of unity by a large proportion, while the fraction

$$\frac{I_2}{I_1} \cdot \frac{x_2 a_1 + y_2 b_1 + z_2 c_1 + \ldots}{x_2 a_2 + y_2 b_2 + z_2 c_2 + \ldots}$$

exceeds unity only by a small proportion, the economic

[1] [Cd. 4032], pp. vii and xlv.

satisfaction (as measured in money) enjoyed by our group has *probably* diminished; and that, if conditions of an opposite character are realised, it has probably increased. A like inference, it would seem, may be drawn, though with less confidence, when one fraction differs from unity in only a *slightly* greater proportion than the other. If this be so, the economic satisfaction—it will be understood that we are speaking of satisfaction as measured in money—obtained by our group *probably* decreases or increases in the second period according as either

$$\frac{I_2}{I_1} \cdot \frac{x_1a_1 + y_1b_1 + z_1c_1 + \ldots}{x_1a_2 + y_1b_2 + z_1c_2 + \ldots} \times \frac{I_2}{I_1} \cdot \frac{x_2a_1 + y_2b_1 + z_2c_1 + \ldots}{x_2a_2 + y_2b_2 + z_2c_2 + \ldots}$$

or any power of this expression, or any other formula which moves more or less as it does, is greater or less than unity. Any fraction constructed on these lines will, therefore, *probably* satisfy the conditions required of our measure.

§ 12. In former editions of this work the above common-sense view was defended by direct analysis as follows. If

$$\frac{I_2}{I_1} \cdot \frac{x_1a_1 + y_1b_1 + z_1c_1 + \ldots}{x_1a_2 + y_1b_2 + z_1c_2 + \ldots}$$

is less than unity by a large fraction, this means that, were our group to purchase in the second year a collection of the form C_1, its purchases of each item would be less by a large percentage than they were in the first year, and therefore—tastes and distribution being unchanged—it would probably enjoy an amount of satisfaction less than in the first year by a large amount, say by K_1. The fact that, instead of doing this, it purchases in the second year a collection of the form C_2 proves that the satisfaction yielded by its purchase of this collection in the second year does not fall short of that yielded by its purchase of the other collection in the first year by more than K_1. In like manner, if

$$\frac{I_2}{I_1} \cdot \frac{x_2a_1 + y_2b_1 + z_2c_1 + \ldots}{x_2a_2 + y_2b_2 + z_2c_2 + \ldots}$$

is greater than unity by only a small fraction, this means that, were our group to purchase a collection of the form C_2 in the first year, its purchases of each item would be less by only a small percentage than they are in the second year, and—tastes and distribution being unchanged—it would probably enjoy an amount of satisfaction less than in the second year by only a small amount, say K_2. Hence, the satisfaction yielded by the collection actually purchased in the second year does not exceed that yielded by the collection actually purchased in the first year by more than K_2. Since, therefore, in view of the largeness of K_1 relatively to K_2, there are more ways in which the satisfaction from the second year's purchase can be less, than there are ways in which it can be more, than the satisfaction from the first year's purchase, and since, further, the probability of any one of these different ways is *prima facie* equal to that of any other, it is *probable* that the satisfaction from the second year's purchase is less than that from the first year's. This line of reasoning now seems to me to depend on *a priori* probabilities in a manner that is not correct. It is necessary to look at the matter more closely. To this end let us write

q_1 for the quantity of collection C_1 obtainable (and obtained) with the then income in period I. :

q_2 for the quantity of collection C_1 obtainable with the then income in period II. :

r_1 for the quantity of collection C_2 obtainable with the then income in period I. :

r_2 for the quantity of collection C_2 obtainable (and obtained) with the then income in period II. :

and $\phi(q_1)$, $\phi(q_2)$, $F(r_1)$ and $F(r_2)$ for the quantities of satisfaction (as measured in money) associated with these several actual and potential purchases.

We are given that

$$q_1 > q_2 \quad (1)$$
$$r_2 > r_1 \quad (2)$$
$$\frac{q_1}{q_2} > \frac{r_2}{r_1} \quad (3)$$

Then, since q_1 of C_1 is preferred in period I. to r_1 of C_2, we know that $\phi(q_1) > F(r_1)$. In like manner we know that $F(r_2) > \phi(q_2)$. Further, from (1) $\phi(q_1) > \phi(q_2)$; and from (2) $F(r_2) > F(r_1)$.

Write
$$\phi(q_1) = F(r_1) + A$$
$$F(r_2) = \phi(q_2) + B$$
$$\phi(q_1) = \phi(q_2) + H$$
$$F(r_2) = F(r_1) + K$$

Thus A, B, H and K are all positive, and, by simple transposition, $\phi(q_1) - F(r_2) = \frac{1}{2}(A - B + H - K)$. The inequality (3), at all events if the excess of $\frac{q_1}{q_2}$ over $\frac{r_2}{r_1}$ is considerable, permits us to say that *probably* H > K. But we know nothing about the values of A and B. The so-called principle of non-sufficient reason does not entitle us to educe out of this nescience the proposition that *probably* (B − A) < (H − K). It is only, however, with the help of some such proposition that we can infer that $\phi(q_1)$ is *probably* > $F(r_2)$. Hence no general proof of our common-sense view is possible. It is true that, the larger the excess of $\frac{q_1}{q_2}$ above $\frac{r_2}{r_1}$, *the more likely it is* that satisfaction in the second period will be less than satisfaction in the first; but we cannot specify any values for these quantities in respect of which satisfaction in the second period is *more likely than not* to be less than satisfaction in the first. As Mr. Keynes puts it, " We are faced with a problem in probability, for which in any particular case we may have relevant data, but which, in the absence of such data, is simply indeterminate."[1]

§ 13. If this conclusion is correct it follows that, when of the expressions

$$\frac{I_2}{I_1} \cdot \frac{x_1 a_1 + y_1 b_1 + z_1 c_1 + \ldots}{x_1 a_2 + y_1 b_2 + z_1 c_2 + \ldots} \qquad \text{and}$$

$$\frac{I_2}{I_1} \cdot \frac{x_2 a_1 + y_2 b_1 + z_2 c_1 + \ldots}{x_2 a_2 + y_2 b_2 + z_2 c_2 + \ldots} \qquad \text{one is greater and}$$

the other less than unity, there is *no* intermediate expression of which we can say in general terms that the economic satisfaction obtained by our group probably increases or decreases in the second period according as the expression is greater or less than unity. Nevertheless, when both our limiting expressions are on the same side of unity, so that there is no doubt as to whether economic satisfaction, as between the two periods, has increased or diminished, it is practically much more convenient to write down some single expression intermediate between the two limiting expressions rather than both of these. There are an infinite number of intermediate

---

[1] *A Treatise on Money*, vol. i. p. 112.

expressions available. In making our choice among them, since there is no deeper ground of preference, we may, as Mr. Keynes writes, "legitimately be influenced by considerations of algebraical elegance, of arithmetical simplicity, of labour-saving, and of internal consistency between different occasions of using a particular system of short-hand."[1] It is thus, I suggest, proper to make use of the two fundamental tests of technical excellence in price index numbers—for, of course, the measure we are seeking is simply the reciprocal of a price index number multiplied by the proportionate change that has taken place in money incomes —which Professor Irving Fisher has brought into prominence. First, the formula chosen should be such that "it will give the same ratio between one point of comparison and the other point, no matter which of the two is taken as base."[2] If, calculated forward, it shows that in 1910 prices were double what they were in 1900, it must not, as a so-called unweighted arithmetical index number of the Sauerbeck type would do, show, when calculated backwards, that in 1900 prices were something other than half what they were in 1910. Secondly, the formula chosen should obey what Professor Fisher calls the factor-reversal test. "Whenever there is a price of anything exchanged, there is implied a quantity of it exchanged, or produced, or consumed, or otherwise involved, so that the problem of an index number of *prices* implies the twin problem of an index number of quantities. . . . No reason can be given for employing a given formula for one of the two factors which does not apply to the other."[3] Hence, the formula chosen should be such that, assuming the aggregate money values of all the commodities we are studying to have moved between two years from E to $(E + e)$, then, if the formula, as applied to prices, gives an upward movement from P to $(P + p)$ and, as applied to quantities, an upward movement from Q to $(Q + q)$,

$$\left\{ \frac{P + p}{P} \cdot \frac{Q + q}{Q} \right\} \text{ is equal to } \frac{E + e}{E}.$$

Besides conformity with these tests we may also properly

[1] *A Treatise on Money*, vol. i. p. 113.
[2] *The Making of Index Numbers*, p. 64.
[3] *Loc. cit.* pp. 72 and 74.

require in our measure simplicity of structure and convenience of handling. These various considerations taken together point, on the whole, to the formula

$$\frac{I_2}{I_1} \sqrt{\frac{x_1a_1 + y_1b_1 + z_1c_1 + \dots}{x_1a_2 + y_1b_2 + z_1c_2 + \dots} \times \frac{x_2a_1 + y_2b_1 + z_2c_1 + \dots}{x_2a_2 + y_2b_2 + z_2c_2 + \dots}}$$

as the measure of change most satisfactory for our purpose. The portion of this expression to the right of $\frac{I_2}{I_1}$ is the reciprocal of that form of price index number to which Professor Fisher assigns the first prize for general merit, and which he proposes to call "the ideal index number."[1]

§ 14. The formulae discussed so far, alike the limiting formulae and the intermediate formula, have been built up on the tacit assumption that no commodities are included in either of the collections C_1 and C_2, which are not included in both. If, therefore, a commodity is available for purchase in one of any two years but not in the other, the satisfaction yielded by this commodity in the year in which it is purchased is wholly ignored by these measures. So far then as "new commodities" are introduced between two periods which are being compared, the measures are imperfect. This matter is important, because new commodities, in the sense here relevant, embrace, not merely commodities that are new physically, but also old commodities that have become obtainable at new times or places, such as strawberries in December, or the wheat which railways have introduced into parts of India where it was formerly unknown. Obviously, we must not count December strawberries along with ordinary strawberries, and so make inventions for strawberry forcing raise the price of strawberries, but must reckon December strawberries as a new and distinct commodity. Since, however, new commodities seldom play an important part in the consumption of any group till some little while after they are first introduced, the imperfection due to this is not likely to be very serious for comparisons between two years that are fairly close together. We can

[1] *The Making of Index Numbers*, p. 242.

ignore the existence of the new commodities and confine our calculations to the old ones without serious risk of invalidating our results. As between distant years, however, in the later of which a great number of important commodities may be available that did not exist at all in the earlier ones, a measure that ignored new commodities would be almost worthless as a gauge of changes (as defined in the preceding chapter) in the size of the national dividend.[1] Unless, therefore, some way can be found of bringing these things into account, the hope of making comparisons over other than very short intervals must, it would seem, be abandoned. A way out of this impasse is, however, available in the chain method devised by Marshall.[2] On this method, the price level of 1900 is compared with that of 1901 on the basis of the commodities available in both those years, new commodities introduced and old commodities dropped out during 1901 being ignored; the price level of 1901 is then compared with that of 1902, the new commodities of 1901 this time being counted, but those of 1902 ignored; and so on. Thus we may suppose prices in 1901 to be 95 per cent of prices of 1900; those of 1902, 87 per cent of those of 1901; those of 1903, 103 per cent of those of 1902. On this basis we construct a chain, the price level of 1900 being put at 100. With the above figures the chain will be:

$$
\begin{aligned}
&1900 \quad . \quad . \quad 100 \\
&1901 \quad . \quad . \quad 95 \\
&1902 \quad . \quad . \quad 82 \cdot 6 \quad \left(i.e.\ \frac{95 \times 87}{100} \right) \\
&1903 \quad . \quad . \quad 85 \quad \left(i.e.\ \frac{82 \cdot 6 \times 103}{100} \right).
\end{aligned}
$$

When the reciprocals of these price indices, which obviously

---

[1] Similar considerations suggest that the existence of " new commodities," or rather, in this case, different commodities, is a more serious obstacle in the way of comparing two distant than two neighbouring places, because it is much more likely that one of the two distant places (*e.g.* a tropical as against a polar region) than it is that one of the two neighbouring places will purchase commodities that are not known in the other. As between distant places the chain method, about to be described, could theoretically be applied *via* a chain of intermediate places; but practically this method of comparison would probably prove unworkable.

[2] Cf. Marshall, *Contemporary Review*, March 1887, p. 371, etc.

constitute indices of the purchasing power of £1, are put into our measure of the national dividend, we obtain an instrument by which years, too distant from one another to be effectively compared by any direct process, can be compared by a chain of successive stages. It is as though we were unable to construct any measuring rod capable of maintaining its shape if carried more than 100 miles. It would then be impossible to make any direct comparison between the height of the trees in places 1000 miles apart. But, by comparing the trees at the first mile with those at the 100th mile, these with those at the 199th mile, and so on continually, it would be possible to make an indirect comparison.[1] It must, indeed, be conceded that, if the successive individual comparisons embodied in the chain method, each of which admittedly suffers from a small error, are likely for the most part to suffer from errors *in the same direction*, the cumulative error as between distant years may be large. Were people equally likely to forget how to make things now in use as to

---

[1] Professor Fisher does not, as it seems to me, take sufficient account of this aspect of the chain method. If there were no new commodities to be considered, or if new commodities as between distant years were unimportant, I should not quarrel with his position. It would then be true, as he argues, that, in a comparison of 1900 and 1920, our index number should be based directly on the prices and quantities ruling in those two years, and that the prices and quantities ruling in 1910, which, if the chain method were used, would be involved, are irrelevant, and resort to them a source of error. It is easy to see, for example, that, if the position of 1900 as to quantities and prices is exactly repeated in 1920, an index made on the chain method would probably not give, as it ought to do, a number for 1920 equal to that for 1900. (Cf. *The Review of Economic Statistics*, May 1921, p. 110.) But if, say, half the expenditure in 1920 is on commodities that did not exist in 1900, a chain comparison is no longer an inferior substitute for a direct comparison : it is the only sort of comparison that it is possible to make at all. For this reason it seems to me on the whole best that, in constructing a *series* of index numbers, we should employ the chain method, and not the method of calculating a number for each year relative to one (the same) base year. In the absence of new commodities the issue would be balanced, because, whereas the chain method gives perfectly correct results only as between successive years, the other method—except with constant-weight formulae, which are inadmissible on other grounds—gives perfectly correct results only as between the base year and each other year. But the argument from new commodities tips the scale in favour of chain series. Of course, if, having constructed a chain series, we desire a more special comparison between two years (other than successive years) covered by it, and if, as between those years, the "new commodity" trouble happens to be unimportant, it will be well to calculate a new number directly for this purpose instead of using the series number. (For Fisher's view compare *The Making of Index Numbers*, p. 308, etc.)

invent new things, a large cumulative error would be unlikely. But, in fact, we know that the great march of inventive progress is not offset in this way. Hence the errors introduced by the chain method are likely to be predominantly in one direction, in such wise that, if the method, as between two distant years, gives equal purchasing power for the £, it is *probable* that the £ really brings more satisfaction to the representative man of given tastes in the later year that in the earlier. Consequently, if our chain measure in 1900 gave 90 as the index of a £'s purchasing power, and gave 100 as the index in 1920, even though meanwhile a large number of new commodities had been introduced and old commodities abandoned, we might confidently infer that, in the conditions postulated in § 5, the amount of economic satisfaction carried to our group by a £ was larger in 1920 than it had been in 1900. But, if these indices were reversed, we could not infer with equal confidence—indeed, unless the fall of the index were very great, we could not infer with *any* confidence—that the sum of economic satisfaction carried by a £ was *smaller* in 1920 than in 1900.

§ 15. We now turn to the second main problem of this chapter. The formula of § 13 is the one we should select if our choice was completely free. But it cannot be employed in practice because, in order to construct it, a great deal of information would be necessary which is never in fact available. It is, therefore, necessary to construct, from such information as we can obtain, a model, or representative, measure that shall approximate to it as closely as possible. Our full-data measure, apart from its multiplier $\frac{I_2}{I_1}$ representing change of income, is built up of two parts: the reciprocal of the price change of the collection C_1 (containing quantities of different commodities equal to x_1, y_1, z_1, . . .) and the reciprocal of the price change of the collection C_2 (containing quantities equal to x_2, y_2, z_2, . . .). Our approximate measure will, therefore, also be built up of two parts constituting approximations to the price changes of C_1 and of C_2 respectively. By what use of the method of sampling can these approximations best be made ?

§ 16. Whatever be the collection of commodities with which we are concerned, whether it be that purchased at any time by people in general, or by artisans, or by labourers, or by any other body of persons, it is likely to contain commodities drawn from several different groups, the broad characteristics of whose price movements are different. A good sample collection should contain representatives of all the groups with different characteristics that enter into the national dividend, or of that part of it which we are trying to measure.[1] Unfortunately, however, practical considerations make it impossible that this requirement should be satisfied, and even make it necessary that resort should be had to commodities that do not themselves enter into the purchases of ordinary people, but are, like wheat and barley, raw materials of commodities that do. For the range of things whose prices we are able to observe and bring into our sample collection is limited in two directions.

First, except for certain articles of large popular consumption, the retail prices charged to consumers are difficult to ascertain. Giffen once went so far as to say: " Practically it is found that only the prices of leading commodities capable of being dealt with in large wholesale markets can be made use of." This statement must now be qualified, in view of the studies of retail prices of food that have been made by the Board of Trade and the late Ministry of Food, but it still holds good over a considerable field. Even, however, when the difficulty of ascertaining retail prices can be overcome, these prices are unsuitable for comparison over a series of years, because the thing priced is apt to contain a different proportion of the services of the retailer and of the transporter, and, therefore, to be a different thing at one time from what it is at another. " When fresh sea fish could be had only at the seaside, its average price

---

[1] Professor Mitchell writes : " The sluggish movement of manufactured goods and of consumers' commodities in particular, the capricious jumping of farm products, the rapidly increasing dearness of lumber, etc., are all part and parcel of the fluctuations which the price level is actually undergoing. . . . Every restriction in the scope of the data implies a limitation in the significance of the results " (*Bulletin of the U.S.A. Bureau of Labour Statistics*, No. 173, pp. 66-7). This is quite correct as it stands, but it must not be interpreted to imply that both finished products and the raw materials embodied in *those same* finished products should be included.

was low. Now that railways enable it to be sold inland, its average retail price includes much higher charges for distribution than it used to do. The simplest plan for dealing with this difficulty is to take, as a rule, the wholesale price of a thing at its place of production, and to allow full weight to the cheapening of the transport of goods, of persons, and of news as separate and most weighty items."[1]

Secondly, it is very difficult to take account even of the wholesale prices of manufactured articles, because, while still called by the same name, they are continually undergoing changes in character and quality. Stilton cheese, once a double-cream, is now a single-cream cheese. Clarets of different vintages are not equivalent. A third-class seat in a railway carriage is not the same thing now as it was forty years ago. " An average ten-roomed house is, perhaps, twice as large in volume as it used to be ; and a great part of its cost goes for water, gas, and other appliances which were not in the older house."[2] "During the past twelve years, owing to more scientific methods of thawing and freezing, the quality of the foreign mutton sold in this country has steadily improved ; on the other hand, that of foreign beef has gone down, owing to the fact that the supply from North America has practically ceased, and its place has been taken by a poorer quality coming from the Argentine."[3] The same class of difficulty is met with in attempts to evaluate many direct services—the services of doctors, for example, which, as Pareto pointedly observes, absorb more expenditure than the cotton industry[4] —for these, while retaining their name, often vary their nature.

It would thus seem that the principal things available for observation—though it must be admitted that the official Canadian Index Number and more than one index number employed in the United States have attempted a wider survey —are raw materials in the wholesale markets, particularly in the large world markets. These things—apart, of course, from

[1] Cf. Marshall, *Contemporary Review*, March 1887, p. 374.
[2] *Ibid.* p. 375. Cf. also Marshall, *Money, Credit, and Commerce*, p. 33.
[3] Mrs. Wood, *Economic Journal*, 1913, pp. 622-3.
[4] *Cours d'économie politique*, p. 281.

the war—have probably of late years fallen in price relatively to minor articles, in which the cost of transport generally plays a smaller part; they have certainly fallen relatively to personal services; and they have probably risen relatively to manufactured articles, because the actual processes of manufacture have been improving. The probable tendency to mutual compensation in the movements of items omitted from our samples makes the omission a less serious evil than it would otherwise be. But, of course, the approximation to a true measure is *pro tanto* worsened; and it is almost certain, since the value of raw materials is often only a small proportion of the value of finished products, so that a 50 per cent change in the former might involve only a 5 per cent change in the latter, that it will give an exaggerated impression of the fluctuations that occur.

Nor does what has just been said exhaust the list of our disabilities. For the samples wanted to represent the several "collections" is a list, not merely of prices, but of prices multiplied by quantities purchased: and our information about quantities is even more limited than our information about prices. There are very few records of annual output— still less of annual purchases—of commodities produced at home. Quantities of imports are, indeed, recorded, but there are not very many important things that are wholly obtained by importation. The difficulty can, indeed, be turned, for some purposes, by resort to typical budgets of expenditure. These make it possible to get a rough idea of the average purchases of certain principal articles that are made by particular classes of people. But this method can scarcely as yet provide more than rough averages. It will seldom enable us to distinguish between the quantities of various things which are embodied in the collections representative of different years fairly close together.

§ 17. Let us next suppose that these difficulties have been so far overcome that a sample embracing both prices and quantities at all relevant periods is available. The next problem is to determine the way in which the prices ought to be "weighted." At first sight it seems natural that the weights should be proportioned to the quantities of the several commodities that are contained in the collection from which the sample is drawn. But, in theory at all events, it is sometimes possible to improve upon this arrangement. For some of the commodities about which we have information may be connected with some excluded commodities in such a way that their prices generally vary in the same sense. These commodities, being representative of the others as well as of themselves, may properly be given weights in excess of what they are entitled to in their own right. Thus, ideally, if we had statistics for a few commodities, each drawn from a different broad group of commodities with similar characteristics, it would be proper to "weight" the prices of our several sample commodities in proportion, not to their own importance, but to that of the groups which they represent. This, however, is scarcely practicable. There may be certain commodities whose representative character is so obvious that a doctored weight may rightly be given to them, but we shall seldom have enough knowledge to attempt this kind of discrimination. To use our sample as it stands is, in general, the best plan that is practically available.[1] Hence, the full-data measure of the price change of the collection C_1 being

$$\frac{x_1 a_2 + y_1 b_2 + z_1 c_2 + \ldots}{x_1 a_1 + y_1 b_1 + z_1 c_1 + \ldots},$$

the best available approximation to this will be

$$\frac{x_1 a_2 + y_1 b_2 + \ldots}{x_1 a_1 + y_1 b_1 + \ldots},$$

[1] This proposition can be proved by means of the principle of inverse probability. There are more ways in which a sample that will change in a given degree can be drawn from a complete collection which changes in that degree than there are ways in which such a sample could be drawn from a collection that changed in a different degree. Therefore any given sample that has been taken without bias from any collection is more likely to represent that collection correctly as it stands than it would do after being subjected to any kind of doctoring. It must be confessed, however, that the question, whether a commodity whose price has moved very differently from the main part of our sample ought to be included, is a delicate one. The omission of "extreme observations" is sometimes deemed desirable in the calculation of physical measurements. What should be done in this matter depends on whether or not a priori expectations, coupled with the general form of our sample, show that the original distribution, from which the sample is taken, obeys some ascertained law of error. Whether they do this or not will often be hard to decide. It should be added that the practical effect of omitting extreme observations is only likely to be important when the number of commodities included in our sample is small ; and that it is just when this number is small that adequate grounds for exclusion are most difficult to come by.

where the number of terms is limited to the number of articles contained in the sample. It follows that the best approximation to the full-data measure of dividend change set out at the end of § 13 is

$$\frac{I_2}{I_1} \sqrt{\frac{x_1a_1 + y_1b_1 + \ldots}{x_1a_2 + y_1b_2 + \ldots} \times \frac{x_2a_1 + y_2b_1 + \ldots}{x_2a_2 + y_2b_2 + \ldots}}.$$

§ 18. In practice, as has already been hinted, we cannot usually find a reasonable sample set of articles, in regard to which the quantities of the same articles purchased in each of the two periods (or places) we are comparing are known. In these circumstances we may have to content ourselves with a sample in which quantities are given only for one of the years in our comparison. In this case we are forced to truncate our formula and adopt the form

$$\frac{I_2}{I_1} \frac{x_1a_1 + y_1b_1 + \ldots}{x_1a_2 + y_1b_2 + \ldots}.$$

This is the type of formula (inverted) employed by the British Board of Trade in the cost of living index number. Obviously a sample of this truncated sort is inferior to a full sample. But Professor Fisher's investigations show that it does not usually yield results very widely divergent from those given by the full sample. We need not, therefore, attack the very difficult question whether there may not be some other formula founded on the same data that would give a closer approximation to the full sample.

§ 19. It is, however, desirable at this point to make plain the exact relation between the above formula and that implicit in a so-called " unweighted " index number such as Sauerbeck's. In that type of index number a certain year or average of years is taken as base, the prices of all commodities for this base-year or base-period are put at 100, and the prices for other years at the appropriate fractions of 100. If a_1, b_1, c_1, are the actual prices in the base-year, and a_2, b_2, c_2, the actual prices in the other year, the index of a £'s purchasing power for this other year will be

$$\frac{100 + 100 + 100 \ldots}{100\frac{a_2}{a_1} + 100\frac{b_2}{b_1} + 100\frac{c_2}{c_1} \ldots}$$

This is equivalent to the formula given in the preceding section if and only if x_1, y_1, z_1, . . . in that formula have values proportioned to $\dfrac{100}{a_1}$, $\dfrac{100}{b_1}$, $\dfrac{100}{c_1}$, . . . That is to say, the Sauerbeck formula measures the changes that take place in the aggregate price of a collection made up of such quantities of each sort of commodity as would, in the base-year or base-period, have sold for equal multiples of £100. It is extremely improbable that, as a matter of fact, those quantities were the quantities actually sold in the base-year or base-period. Therefore, it is only by an extraordinary accident that a formula constructed on the Sauerbeck plan with any given year or period as base will coincide with a formula modelled on the plan of the preceding section and designed to display the changes that occur in the aggregate price of the collection that was actually sold in the base-year or base-period.

§ 20. To what has just been said an obvious corollary attaches. We have seen that an index number on the Sauerbeck plan is built up with any year or period R as base; it measures changes in the aggregate price of a collection made up of such quantities of each commodity as in the year R would have sold for £100. It follows that, when the base is shifted from the year R_1 to the year R_2, the collection whose aggregate price movements are being measured is, in general, altered. Since, then, a different thing is being measured, it is to be expected that a different result will be attained; and there is no reason why the results should not differ so far that an index number on base R_1 shows a rise in the purchasing power of money, while a similar number (of the Sauerbeck type) on the base R_2 shows a fall. Thus, if we have to do with two commodities only, one of which doubles in price while the other halves, this type of index number will show a 25 per cent rise in the price of the two together if the first year is taken as base and a 20 per cent fall if the second year is taken. An excellent practical illustration of this type of discrepancy is afforded by certain tables in the Board of Trade publications concerning the cost of living in English and German towns respectively. In the Blue-book dealing with England the real wages of

London, the Midlands and Ireland are calculated by means of index numbers, in which London (corresponding in our time index, say, to the year 1890) is taken as base, and the price of consumables and the rents prevailing there are both represented by 100. On this plan, prices of consumables and rents being given weights of 4 and 1 respectively, the Board of Trade found real wages in London to be equal to those of the Midlands, and 3 per cent higher than those of Ireland. If, however, Ireland had been taken as base, the indices of real wages would have been in London 98, in the Midlands 104, in Ireland 100. A similar difficulty emerges in the Blue-book on German towns. The Board of Trade, taking Berlin as base, found real wages higher in that city than in any place save one on their list.[1] " If the North Sea ports, instead of Berlin, had been taken as base, Berlin would have appeared fourth on the list instead of second, and the order of the other districts would have been changed; and, by taking Central Germany as base, even greater changes in the order would have been effected." [2] It is true, no doubt, that *large* discrepancies of this sort are not likely to occur, except when there are large differences, or, as between different times, large fluctuations, in the prices of commodities that are heavily weighted. But that fact, though practically interesting, is not relevant to my present point.

§ 21. It may happen in some circumstances that we have no knowledge of, and no data for guessing, quantities for any of the years we wish to compare, and are, therefore, forced back, for the price index number involved in our measure, on a sample of price relatives alone without any weights at all. In these circumstances the preceding discussions make one thing quite clear. We must not construct our index by combining the price relatives in a simple arithmetical average, after the manner of Sauerbeck. The paradoxes to which that method leads are avoided if either the simple geometric mean—this will not work if the price of any of our commodities is liable to become nothing !—or the median of the price relatives is taken. Professor Fisher has an

---

[1] [Cd. 4032], p. xxxiv.
[2] J. M. Keynes, *Economic Journal*, 1908, p. 473.

interesting discussion of the comparative advantages of these two forms.[1] Both are plainly inferior to the weighted formula of § 18, where the data required for that formula are available.

§ 22. In conclusion we have to consider the *reliability* of the various practicable measures which are available as representatives of the full-data measure. Let us first suppose that we can obtain a sample of the same general form as the full-data measure, quantities as well as prices being available for both (or all) of the periods that we wish to compare. Five general observations may then be made. First, when the sample is drawn from most of the principal sets of commodities included in the full-data collection, which have characteristic price movements, the probable error of our measure will be less than it is when a less representative field is covered. Secondly, when the sample is large, in the sense that the expenditure upon the items included in it comprises a large part of the aggregate expenditure of our group upon the whole collection, the probable error is less than it is when the sample is small. With random sampling in the strict technical sense, the reliability increases as the square root of the number of items contained in the sample. Thirdly, when each of the items constituting the full-data collection absorbs individually a small part of the aggregate expenditure upon that collection, the probable error is less than when some of the items absorb individually a large part of the total expenditure. Fourthly, when the items included in the sample exhibit a small " scatter," the various prices changing as between the years we are comparing in very similar degrees, the probable error is less than it is when the items exhibit a wide scatter. From this consideration it follows that the magnitude of the error to which our measure is liable is greater—apart altogether from the difficulty of " new commodities " referred to in § 14—as between distant years than as between years that are close together. The reason is, as Professor Mitchell, on the basis of a wide survey of facts, has shown, that the distribution of the variations in wholesale prices as between one year and the next is highly

[1] Cf. *The Making of Index Numbers*, p. 211, etc., and p. 260, etc.

concentrated,—more concentrated than the distribution proper to the normal law of error,—but the distribution of variations as between one year and a somewhat distant year is highly scattered. " With some commodities the trend of successive price changes continues distinctly upwards for years at a time; with other commodities there is a constant downward trend; with still others no definite long-period trend appears." [1] Finally, if we are unable to obtain a sample of the same general form as our full-data measure, and have to be content with one of the truncated form described in § 18, our measure will, of course, be less reliable than one of equal range of the better type. If we have to do without quantities altogether, and must use the simple geometric mean or the median of price relatives, the measure will be less reliable still. But, it is important to notice, the damage done to reliability by the use of an inferior index formula, like the damage done by the use of a small sample, is not very great when the scatter of price movements between the years we are comparing is small or moderate, but may be very great when the scatter is large.

[1] *U.S. Bulletin of Labour*, No. 173, p. 23.

CHAPTER VII

ECONOMIC WELFARE AND CHANGES IN THE SIZE OF THE NATIONAL DIVIDEND

§ 1. IT is evident that, provided the dividend accruing to the poor is not diminished, increases in the size of the aggregate national dividend, if they occur in isolation without anything else whatever happening, must involve increases in economic welfare. For, though, no doubt, economic welfare as measured in money, and, therefore, the national dividend as here defined, might be increased and economic welfare in itself—not as measured in money—at the same time diminished, if an addition to the supply of rich men's goods was accompanied by a contraction in the supply of poor men's goods, this sort of double change is ruled out by the proviso that the dividend accruing to the poor shall not be diminished. But it does not follow that every cause, which, while leaving the dividend of the poor unharmed, increases the size of the aggregate dividend, must bring about an increase in economic welfare; because it is possible that a cause which increases the size of the dividend may at the same time produce other effects adverse to economic welfare. It is desirable, therefore, to inquire how far this possibility needs to be reckoned with in practice.

§ 2. Changes in consumption that come about in consequence of an increase in facilities for obtaining some of the items contained in the dividend are liable to bring about changes in taste. But, when any particular kind of commodity becomes more readily available the resultant change of taste is *usually* an enhancement. Thus, when machines are sent out on trial, or articles presented in sample-packets, or pictures exhibited free to the public, the popular desire for these objects tends to be augmented. When public-houses, or lotteries, or libraries are easily accessible, the taste for drink, or gambling, or literature is not merely gratified, but is also stimulated. When cleanliness, or light,[1] or model dwellings, or model plots of agricultural land are set up, though it is only to be seen, and not owned, by the neighbours, the object lesson may still succeed and make plain superiorities hitherto unrecognised.[2] Thus, "free libraries are engines for creating the habitual power of enjoying high-class literature," and a savings bank, if confined to the poor, is an "engine for teaching thrift."[3] In like manner the policy of many German cities, in subsidising theatres and opera-houses and in providing symphony concerts two or three evenings a week at a very small admission fee, is an *educational* policy that bears fruit in increased capacity for enjoyment. It is true that an increase in taste for one thing is generally associated with a decline in taste for any other things that fulfil the same or a similar purpose, *e.g.* wool as against cotton or a new "best type" of motor car as against what used to be the best type, and sometimes with a decline in taste for other quite disconnected means of enjoyment. But it is reasonable, in these circumstances, to hold that the provision made for the new taste is likely to yield *some* excess of satisfaction over that made for the old;

[1] Cf. Walpole's account of the way in which the introduction of street lamps led to an increased demand for illuminants *within* the neighbouring houses (*History of England*, i. 86). An elaborate method of advertising electric light is quoted in Whyte's *Electrical Industry* (p. 57). A company undertakes to instal six lamps in a house free of all charge for a six months' trial, the householder paying only for the current that he uses. After the six months, the company undertakes to remove the whole arrangement if the customer so desires.

[2] Cf. Miss Octavia Hill's practice of insisting on the cleanliness of the *staircases* of her houses, and Sir H. Plunkett's account of the Cork Exhibition, 1902 (*Ireland in the New Century*, pp. 285-7).

[3] Jevons, *Methods of Social Reform*, p. 32. It should be noted, however, that Dr. Marshall believes this order of consideration to have a relatively small range. He writes : "Those demands, which show high elasticity in the long run, show a high elasticity almost at once ; so that, subject to a few exceptions, we may speak of the demand for a commodity as being of high or low elasticity without specifying how far we are looking ahead" (*Principles of Economics*, p. 456).

so that the net result of an increase in facilities for obtaining some of the items contained in the dividend will be to increase economic welfare.

§ 3. The above argument does not, however, go to the root of things. It is relevant to immediate short-period effects rather than to ultimate effects. When a group of people have passed from a state of relative poverty, to which they were accustomed and adapted, to a state of relative wealth, to which they have become adapted, will they really derive more satisfaction from the last state of their environment than they did from the first? With the changed conditions the whole scheme of their desires and habits and expectations will also be changed. If a man who had all his life slept in a soft bed was suddenly compelled to sleep on the ground under the sky, he would suffer greatly; but does a man who has always slept on a soft bed enjoy his nights more than one who has always slept under the sky? Is it certain that a hundred Rolls-Royce cars in a Rolls-Royce world would yield a greater sum of satisfaction than a hundred dog-carts in a world of dog-carts? In the chapter that follows some reasons will be given for doubting whether a substantial reduction in the real consumable income of rich people, provided it were general, would, after time had been allowed for adaptation to it, appreciably diminish their economic welfare. Analogous considerations hold good of an increase in their real consumable income. The point is a very important one. If the *per capita* income of this country were, say, twenty times what it actually is, it may well be that a further increase in it would not ultimately—the population being supposed constant—add anything at all to economic welfare. As things are, however, in view of low level of average real income, we may, I think, safely conclude that an increase in the dividend—apart from the fantastic hypothesis that the whole increase goes to persons already very rich—would carry with it, ultimately and not merely immediately, an increase in economic welfare. The goal of economic betterment is not a mere illusion.[1]

---

[1] Cf. M. Bousquet (*Weltwirtschaftliches Archiv*, Oct. 1929, pp. 174 *et seq.*) for an opposite view. M. Bousquet argues that economic welfare depends on the

§ 4. There is, however, a further point to be considered. The economic welfare of a community consists in the balance of satisfactions derived from the use of the national dividend over the dissatisfactions involved in the making of it. Consequently, when an increase in the national dividend comes about in association with an increase in the quantity of work done to produce it, the question may be raised whether the increase in work done may not involve dissatisfaction in excess of the satisfaction which its product yields. Now, in so far as extra work is called out because, through inventions and so on, new and more advantageous means of employing it have been opened up, there is no fear of this. Nor is there any fear of it if the extra work is called out because obstacles, such as quarrels between employers and employed, which used to prevent people who wanted to work from doing so, have been removed. Nor again is there any fear of it if the extra work is called out because methods of remunerating workpeople, which reward extra work with equivalent extra pay, have been introduced. It is possible, however, that extra work may be called out in other ways than these. Suppose, for example, that the whole community was compelled by law to work for eighteen hours a day, and—which is in fact improbable—that this policy made the national dividend larger. It is practically certain that the satisfaction yielded by the extra product would be enormously less than the dissatisfaction caused by the extra labour. There is here a cause which has increased the size of the national dividend while lessening, and not increasing, the sum of economic welfare. This type of cause is not, in the modern world, practically important, because, apart from military conscription, we have to do with voluntary, not with compulsory, labour. It is, however, conceivable that, even under a voluntary system, something analogous may emerge. From a mistaken view of their own real interest, workpeople may welcome an addition to the hours of labour of a sort which augments the dividend

relation between incomes and needs, and that an increase in income involves, after time for adjustment has been allowed, such an increase of needs that the original relation between income and needs is re-established. Hence, he concludes, the economic welfare of a representative man is a constant, unaffected in the long run by changes in his income.

but damages economic welfare.   Again, under the exploitation of employers, workpeople may be forced to assent to an increase of work as a less evil than reduced earnings.   There are here a number of possible causes of additions to the dividend associated with damage to economic welfare.   Plainly, however, among the general body of causes relevant to our discussion the part they play will be small.   In general, causes which increase the size of the national dividend while involving an increase in work, as well as causes which increase it without involving this, will, the conditions of distribution being assumed, increase economic welfare.

CHAPTER VIII

ECONOMIC WELFARE AND CHANGES IN THE DISTRIBUTION
OF THE NATIONAL DIVIDEND

§ 1. IF income is transferred from rich persons to poor persons the proportion in which different sorts of goods and services are provided will be changed. Expensive luxuries will give place to more necessary articles, rare wines to meat and bread, new machines and factories to clothes and improved small dwellings; and there will be other changes of a like sort.[1]

---

[1] It should be noticed that one of the things to which people will divert consumption, if distribution is altered in favour of the poor, is the quasi-commodity, leisure. It is well established that the high-wage countries and industries are generally also both the short-hour countries and industries and the countries and industries in which the wage-earning work required from women and children in supplement of the family budget is the smallest. The former point is illustrated by some statistics of the wage rate and hours of labour of carpenters in the United States, Great Britain, France, Germany, and Belgium, published in No. 54 of the Bulletin of the U.S. Bureau of Labour (p. 1125). In illustration of the latter point, Sir Sydney Chapman notes the assertion that, whereas the German collier finds only 65·8 per cent of his family's earnings, the wealthier American collier finds 77·5 per cent (*Work and Wages*, i. p. 17). Mr. Rowntree's interesting table for York points, when properly analysed, in the same direction (*Poverty*, p. 171); and Miss Vessellitsky shows that low-paid home-work among women is found principally in those districts, *e.g.* East Anglia, "where the bad conditions of male labour make it almost indispensable for the wife to supplement the husband's earnings," whereas, in districts where men's wages are good, women only work at industry if they themselves can obtain well-paid jobs (*The Home-worker*, p. 4). Again, reference may be made to the familiar correlation found in recent English history between rising wages and falling hours. Yet again, a study of the rates of wages and hours of labour in different districts in England would, I suspect, reveal a correlation of the same type. It does so for the wages and hours statistics of bricklayers as given in the *Abstract of Labour Statistics for 1908* (pp. 42, etc.). These facts are somewhat awkward to fit in to the method of exposition followed in this book, because leisure is not included as a commodity in my definition of the national dividend: and in so far, therefore, as improved distribution causes leisure to be substituted for things, it must involve a decrease in the national dividend. Plainly, however, this sort of decrease should be ignored when we

87

In view of this fact, it is inexact to speak of a change in the distribution of the dividend in favour of, or adverse to, the poor.   There is not a single definitely constituted heap of things coming into being each year and distributed now in one way, now in another.   In fact, there is no such thing as *the* dividend from the point of view of both of two years, and, therefore, there can be no such thing as a change in *its* distribution.

§ 2. This, however, is a point of words rather than of substance.   What I *mean* when I say that the distribution of the dividend has changed in favour of the poor is that, the general productive power of the community being given, poor people are getting more of the things they want at the expense of rich people getting less of the things they want.   It might be thought at first sight that the only way in which this could happen would be through a transference of purchasing power from the rich to the poor.   That, however, is not so. It is possible for the poor to be advantaged and the rich damaged, even though the quantity of purchasing power, *i.e.* of command over productive resources, held by both groups remains unaltered.   This might happen if the technical methods of producing something predominatingly consumed by the poor were improved and at the same time those of producing something predominatingly consumed by the rich were worsened, and if the net result was to leave the size of the national dividend as defined in Chapter V. unchanged. It might also happen if, by a system of rationing or some other device, the rich were forced to transfer their demand away from things which are important to the poor and which are produced under such conditions that diminished demand leads to lowered prices.   *Per contra*—and this point will be seen in Part IV. to be very important practically—the share, both proportionate and absolute of command over the country's productive resources held by the poor may be increased, and yet, if the process by which they acquire this greater share involves an increase in the cost of things that play a large part in their own consumption, they may not really gain.

are considering the effect of changes of distribution on economic welfare ; for the loss of welfare associated with the constriction of production to which they lead is necessarily less than the gain of welfare due to the leisure itself.

Thus a change in distribution favourable to the poor may be brought about otherwise than by a transference of purchasing power, or command over productive resources, to them, and it does not *mean* a transference of these things to them. None the less, this sort of transference is the most important, and may be regarded as the typical, means by which changes in distribution favourable to the poor come about.

§ 3. On this basis it is desired, if possible, to establish some connection between changes in the distribution of the national dividend and changes in economic welfare, corresponding to the connection established in the preceding chapter between changes in the size of the national dividend and changes in economic welfare. In considering this matter we must not forget that the economic welfare enjoyed by anybody in any period depends on the income that he consumes rather than on the income that he receives ; and that, the richer a man is, the smaller proportion of his total income he is likely to consume, so that, if his total income is, say, twenty times as large as that of a poorer man, his consumed income may be only, say, five times as large. Nevertheless, it is evident that any transference of income from a relatively rich man to a relatively poor man of similar temperament, since it enables more intense wants to be satisfied at the expense of less intense wants, must increase the aggregate sum of satisfaction. The old " law of diminishing utility " thus leads securely to the proposition : Any cause which increases the absolute share of real income in the hands of the poor, provided that it does not lead to a contraction in the size of the national dividend from any point of view, will, in general, increase economic welfare.[1] This conclusion is further fortified by another consideration. Mill wrote : " Men do not desire to be *rich*, but to be richer than other men. The avaricious or covetous man would find little or no satisfaction in the

---

[1] The difficult case in which a transference leads to a contraction in the size of the dividend from the point of view of either the pre-change or the post-change period, and not from that of the other, will not be considered here. Henceforward it will be assumed that we have to do with changes in the dividend that are either positive or negative from both the relevant points of view, and, therefore, except for special reasons, we shall speak simply of increases and decreases in the dividend.

possession of any amount of wealth, if he were the poorest amongst all his neighbours or fellow-countrymen."[1] More elaborately, Signor Rignano writes : "As for the needs which vanity creates, they can be satisfied equally well by a small as by a large expenditure of energy. It is only the existence of great riches which makes necessary for such satisfaction a very large, instead of a very small, expenditure. In reality a man's desire to appear 'worth' double what another man is worth, that is to say, to possess goods (jewels, clothes, horses, parks, luxuries, houses, etc.) twice as valuable as those possessed by another man, is satisfied just as fully, if the first has ten things and the second five, as it would be if the first had a hundred and the second fifty."[2] Now the part played by comparative, as distinguished from absolute, income is likely to be small for incomes that only suffice to provide the necessaries and primary comforts of life, but to be large with large incomes. In other words, a larger proportion of the satisfaction yielded by the incomes of rich people comes from their *relative*, rather than from their absolute, amount. This part of it will not be destroyed if the incomes of all rich people are diminished together. The loss of economic welfare suffered by the rich when command over resources is transferred from them to the poor will, therefore, be substantially smaller relatively to the gain of economic welfare to the poor than a consideration of the law of diminishing utility taken by itself suggests.

§ 4. It must be conceded, of course, that, if the rich and the poor were two races with different mental constitutions, such that the rich were inherently capable of securing a greater amount of economic satisfaction from any given income than the poor, the possibility of increasing welfare by this type of change would be seriously doubtful. Furthermore, even without any assumption about inherent racial difference, it may be maintained that a rich man, from the nature of his upbringing and training, is capable of obtaining considerably more satisfaction from a given income —say a thousand pounds—than a poor man would be.

---

[1] Posthumous Essay on Social Freedom, *Oxford and Cambridge Review*, Jan. 1907.

[2] *Di un socialismo in accordo colla dottrina economica liberale*, p. 285.

For, if anybody accustomed to a given standard of living suddenly finds his income enlarged, he is apt to dissipate the extra income in forms of exciting pleasure, which, when their indirect, as well as their direct, effects are taken into account, may even lead to a positive loss of satisfaction. To this argument, however, there is a sufficient answer. It is true that at any given moment the tastes and temperament of persons who have long been poor are more or less adjusted to their environment, and that a sudden and sharp rise of income is likely to be followed by a good deal of foolish expenditure which involves little or no addition to economic welfare. If, however, the higher income is maintained for any length of time, this phase will pass ; whereas, if the increase is gradual or, still better, if it comes about in such a way as not to be directly perceived—through a fall in prices, for example—the period of foolishness need not occur at all. In any case, to contend that the folly of poor persons is so great that a rise of income among them will not promote economic welfare in any degree is to press paradox beyond the point up to which discussion can reasonably be called upon to follow. The true view, as I conceive it, is admirably stated by Messrs. Pringle and Jackson in their special report to the Poor Law Commissioners : "It is in the unskilled and least educated part of the population that drink continues to hold its ground ; as greater regularity of employment and higher wages are achieved by sections of the working-classes, the men rise in respectability and character. That the drink bill is diminishing, while wages are rising throughout the country, is one of the most hopeful indications of progress we possess."[1] The root of the matter is that, even when, under existing conditions, the mental constitution of poor persons is such that an enlarged income will at the moment yield them little benefit, yet, after a time—more especially if the time is long enough to allow a new generation to grow up—the possession of such an income will make possible the development in them, through education and otherwise, of capacities and faculties adapted for the enjoyment of the enlarged income. Thus in the long run differences

---

[1] [Cd. 4795], p. 46.

of temperament and taste between rich and poor are over-come by the very fact of a shifting of income between them. Plainly, therefore, they cannot be used as an· argument to disprove the benefits of a transference.[1]

§ 5. After all, however, general reasoning of the above type, though perhaps necessary to provide formal justification for our thesis, is not necessary to convince us practically that it is valid. For that purpose it is sufficient to reflect on the way in which, in this country, income has in fact been distributed in recent times. There are not sufficient data to enable this to be calculated with any degree of accuracy. On the basis, however, of work done by Dr. Bowley,[2] we may hazard the following rough estimate for the period immediately prior to the war. The 12,000 richest families in the country received about one-fifteenth of the total national income; the richest *fiftieth* of the population received about one-quarter, and the richest *ninth* of the population received nearly one-half of that total income. The remainder of it, a little more than a half, was left to be shared among small independent workers and salary-receivers earning less than £160 a year and practically the whole body of wage-earners. The table below, giving Dr. Bowley's estimate of distribution among a portion of this last group in 1911, carries the matter a little farther.

[1] Similarly, of course, when we are taking a long view, the argument that a reduction in the real income of the rich inflicts a special injury, because it forces them to abandon habits to which they have grown accustomed, loses most of its force.

[2] *Quarterly Journal of Economics*, Feb. 1914, p. 261 ; and *The Division of the Product of Industry before the War*, 1918, pp. 11 and 14.

[TABLE

WEEKLY MONEY WAGES OF ADULT WORKMEN IN ORDINARY
FULL WORK

(INCLUDING VALUATION FOR PAYMENT IN KIND) [1]

Wage.	Number of Men.	Per cent of whole.
Under 15/- . .	320,000 (mainly agriculture)	4
15/- to 20/- . .	640,000	8
20/- to 25/- . .	1,600,000	20
25/- to 30/- . .	1,680,000	21
30/- to 35/- . .	1,680,000	21
35/- to 40/- . .	1,040,000	13
40/- to 45/- . .	560,000	7
45/- and over .	480,000	6

In studying these figures we must, indeed, remember that
in families where the man has a small income the wife and
children are more likely to be earning wages than they are
in families headed by richer men; so that distribution among
families was probably more satisfactory than distribution among
individuals. This, however, is comparatively a small matter.
What the figures cited meant in the concrete is brought out
very clearly in the same author's pre-war study of the conditions
of life in four industrial towns. Together these towns embrace
"about 2150 working-class households and 9720 persons.
Of these households 293 or 13½ per cent, of these persons
1567 or 16 per cent, are living in a condition of primary
poverty," i.e. with incomes so low that, even if expended with
perfect wisdom, they could not have provided an adequate
subsistence. "Out of 3287 children who appear in our tables,
879, or 27 per cent, are living in families which fail to reach
the low standard taken as necessary for healthy existence." [2]
The excess incomes of the richer classes did not, of course,
represent corresponding excess consumption. The dominant part

---

[1] From the *Contemporary Review*, Oct. 1911, p. 1.

[2] *Livelihood and Poverty*, pp. 46-7. The reason for the excess in the
proportion of children in poverty is the twofold one, that poor families are apt
to be larger than others, and that a large family is itself a cause of life in poverty.
Cf. Bowley, *The Measurement of Social Phenomena*, p. 187.

of the annual new investments of the country—before the war perhaps 350 millions—and a large part of the expenses of central and local government—over 200 millions—had to be provided out of them; so that not more than 300 millions annually can have been spent by the rich and moderately well-off on any form of luxury. Moreover, estimates of money income tend to exaggerate the relative real income of wealthy persons, because these persons are often charged higher prices than poor persons pay for the same services. A number of London shops, for example, discriminate against " good addresses," and hotel charges are also often discrimina-tory. It has even been suggested that as much as 25 per cent of the money income of the rich, as spent by them, represents no equivalent in real income.[1] In like manner, estimates of money income sometimes make it appear that the real incomes of poor persons are less than they really are, by ignoring discriminations in their favour. Thus Dr. Bowley points out : " A butcher can perhaps raise his prices to his day customers without much affecting the sale, but not to those in the evening. In this case the working class would suffer a smaller rise than the richer class. This consideration applies especially to the very large volume of purchases made late on Saturday night." But, when all quali-fications have been made, the figures cited above leave no room for doubt that there was before the war, and is still, a substantial excess income in the hands of the richer classes available, in Dr. Bowley's phrase, " for attack " by way of transference.

§ 6. Some study of the post-war distribution of income in Great Britain and Northern Ireland has been made by Dr. Bowley and Sir Josiah Stamp with special reference to the year 1924. From this it appears that the proportion of the total accruing, pre-tax, to the richest classes, i.e. those with incomes in excess of £9400, which roughly corresponds to £5000 at the pre-war price-level, has somewhat diminished.[2] In general these writers conclude as follows. The distribution of income between wage-earners, other earners and unearned

1 Urwick, *Luxury and the Waste of Life*, pp. 87 and 90.
2 *The National Income*, 1924, p. 58.

incomes was changed slightly in favour of the earning classes. Manual workers on the average make slightly increased real earnings, and there have also been transfers for their benefit in insurance schemes and other public expenditure. In addition they have the advantage of a reduction of about one-tenth of the working week. This change can be connected with the reduction in the real income derived from house property and investments bearing fixed rates of interest. The indications are that profits as a whole, reckoned before tax is paid, form nearly the same proportion of total income at the two dates (*i.e.* 1911 and 1924). Within the wage-earning classes women and unskilled workers have received a substantial real advance in wages; the great majority of skilled workers made at least as much (after allowing for the rise of prices) in 1924 as in 1911.[1] That these changes have meant a great deal to the lives of the very poor is well brought out by Dr. Bowley's second investigation, made after the war, into the conditions of the four towns referred to in the preceding section. " Even," he writes, " on the assumption that all the families suffering from unemployment in a particular week nad no adequate resources, and that their unemployment was chronic, the proportion in poverty in 1924 was little more than half that in 1913. If there had been no unemployment the proportion of families in poverty in the towns taken together would have fallen to one-third (3·6 per cent as against 11 per cent), and of persons to little over a quarter (3·5 per cent against 12·6 per cent) of the proportion in 1913."[2] Again: "The proportion of families, in which a man is normally earning, found to be in poverty, was in 1924 only one-fifth of the proportion in 1913, if full employment is assumed; while, if the maximum effect of unemployment is reckoned, it is little over one-half."[3] This large improvement is partly due (to the extent of about one-third of the whole) to a decrease in the average number of children per family;

[1] *The National Income*, 1924, pp. 58-9.

[2] *Has Poverty Diminished*, p. 16. The discrepancies between the percentages given in this passage for 1913 and that given in *Livelihood and Poverty* is apparently due to the fact that in the latter work 480 houses inhabited by the middle and upper classes were excluded from the calculation (cf. *Livelihood and Poverty*, p. 46, footnote).

[3] *Has Poverty Diminished*, p. 21.

but chiefly (to the extent of the remaining two-thirds) to a
rise in the rate of real wages of unskilled labourers. In
spite of this improvement, however, and in spite of the fact that,
"when the full effects of taxation are taken into account, the
real income available for saving or expenditure in the hands
of the rich is definitely less than before the war,"[1] the distribution, not merely of incomes prior to taxation, but of what
is left over after taxes have been taken away, is still very
uneven. It was still true, for example, in 1924, that something like 100 millions a year *net, i.e.* about $2\frac{1}{2}$ per cent of
the total income of the country, was enjoyed by 3000 families.
We must not hesitate, therefore, to conclude that, so long as
the dividend as a whole is not diminished, any increase, within
wide limits, in the real income enjoyed by the poorer classes, at
the expense of an equal decrease in that enjoyed by the richer
classes, is practically certain to involve an addition to economic
welfare.

§ 7. It should be noticed that the conclusion set out above is
not exactly equivalent to the proposition that economic welfare
will be increased by anything that, *ceteris paribus*, renders the
distribution of the national dividend less unequal. If the
community consisted of two members only, it would, indeed,
coincide with this. But, in a community consisting of more
than two members, the meaning of "rendering the distribution of the dividend less unequal" is ambiguous. Pareto
measures inequality of distribution by dividing the logarithm
of the number of incomes in excess of any amount x into the
logarithm of x. This measure is very difficult to apply unless
we accept Pareto's view that, in any given income distribution, the ratio between his two logarithms is approximately
the same for all values of x; and, even so, it is a matter of
dispute whether the reciprocal of his measure,—which, of
course, would indicate less equality when the measure itself
indicates greater equality,—is not to be preferred to that
measure.[2] Among other measures of inequality the most

---

[1] *The National Income*, 1924, p. 59. It must, of course, be held in mind
that a large part of the heavy taxation of rich persons goes to pay interest on
war loan held by rich persons.
[2] Cf. Gini, *Variabilità e mutabilità*, p. 72.

familiar is the mean square deviation from the mean. With that criterion it can be proved that, assuming similarity of temperament among the members of the community, a diminution in the inequality of distribution *probably*, though not necessarily, increases the aggregate sum of satisfaction.[1]

[1] If A be the mean income, n the number of incomes, and a_1, a_2 . . . deviations from the mean, aggregate satisfaction, on our assumption,

$$= nf(A) + (a_1 + a_2 + \ldots)f' + \frac{1}{2!}(a_1{}^2 + a_2{}^2 + \ldots)f'' + \frac{1}{3!}(a_1{}^3 + a_2{}^3 + \ldots)f''' + \ldots$$

But we know that $\{a_1 + a_2 + \ldots\} = 0$.

We know nothing to suggest whether the sum of the terms beyond the third is positive or negative. But it is certain that $\frac{1}{2}\{a_1{}^2 + a_2{}^2 + \ldots\}f''$ is negative. If, therefore, the fourth and following terms are small relatively to the third term, it is certain, and in general it is probable, that aggregate satisfaction is larger, the smaller is $(a_1{}^2 + a_2{}^2 + \ldots)$. This latter sum, of course, varies in the same sense as the mean square deviation or standard deviation $\sqrt{\dfrac{\Sigma a^2}{n}}$. Dr. Dalton, in the course of an interesting article on " The Measurement of the Inequality of Incomes," has shown that, in a community where many incomes diverge widely from the average, the probability which the above argument establishes is only of a low order (*Economic Journal*, Sept. 1920, p. 355).

CHAPTER IX

§ 1. In the two preceding chapters nothing was said about the possible reactions which the changes we have been contemplating may have on the numbers of the population. This omission must now be remedied. To the broad conclusions which were reached relating respectively to the size and distribution of the national dividend, it may be objected that an increase in the income enjoyed by any group causes its numbers to increase until income per head is again reduced to its old amount, and, therefore, that it leads to no lasting benefit. In practice this argument is most often used about the effects of an increase in the income of manual workers; and it is, of course, much more plausible in this field than in any other. It will, therefore, be enough to examine this aspect of it. I shall consider it first from the point of view of the whole world, or of a single country imagined, for the purposes of the argument, to be isolated, and afterwards shall inquire how far the results achieved need to be modified for a single country constituting one among the associated family of modern nations. In the argument to be developed under these two heads it must be understood that the additions to the income of wage-earners that we have in mind do not include additions brought about by the offer, on behalf of the State, of deliberate and overt bounties upon the acquisition of large families. Under the old Poor Law in the United Kingdom bounties were, in effect, given; our present income-tax law acts in a slight degree in the same sense; and in a law passed in France[1]

---

[1] Cf. *Economic Journal*, Dec. 1913, p. 641.

shortly before the war a similar policy was adopted. This class of addition to the income of the poor has, of course, a tendency to augment population, and, in some practical problems, the point is of importance. For the present, however, we are concerned with additions that do not offer a special differential inducement to the begetting of children.

§ 2. If we provisionally ignore the deeper-seated reactions which increased income may exert upon wants and tastes, our discussion virtually resolves itself into an inquiry into the validity of the celebrated "iron law of wages." According to this "law," expanding numbers continually press the earnings of the workpeople down to "subsistence level," thus making it impossible for their real income *per head* in any circumstances to increase. It should be noted in passing that, even if there really were such a law, the proposition that better fortune for the workers increases economic welfare would not be definitely disproved. For it might still be urged that, provided the average working family attains in the whole period of life any surplus of satisfaction over dissatisfaction, an increase of numbers implies by itself an addition to economic welfare.[1] But, for my present purpose, there is no need to press this doubtful point. Population does not tend to expand in such a manner as to hold down income per head to a predetermined "subsistence level." It is true, no doubt, that the direct and immediate result of an increase in the dividend accruing to any group is likely to be *some* increase of population. It is well known that the English marriage rate was negatively correlated with wheat prices in the earlier part of the nineteenth century and was positively correlated with exports, clearing-house returns

---

[1] But cf. Sidgwick's observation : "It seems at least highly doubtful whether a mere increase in the number of human beings living as an average unskilled labourer lives in England can be regarded as involving a material increase in the quantum of human happiness " (*Principles of Political Economy*, p. 522, note). A population, which, in given conditions, maximises this quantum, seems to have a much better claim to be called the *optimum* population than a population which maximises *real income per head*. The practice, which has gained a certain currency, of using the term in this latter sense is, therefore, unfortunate.

and so on in the latter part:[1] and that the rate of mortality falls with growing wealth, and *vice versa*. But it is contrary to experience to assert that increased income stimulates population to so large an extent that the individual earnings of workpeople are brought down again to the level they occupied before the improvement. There are two ways in which the manual workers can use their increased claims over material things, namely, to increase their numbers and to increase their standard of comfort. The distinction between these two ways is well illustrated by the following contrasted passages from Malthus's *Principles of Political Economy*. On the one hand, he found that the greater wealth resulting from the introduction of the potato into Ireland in the eighteenth century was "spent almost exclusively in the maintenance of large and frequent families." On the other hand, when the price of corn in England fell between 1660 and 1720, a considerable portion of the workpeople's "increased real wages was expended in a marked improvement of the quality of the food consumed and a decided elevation in the standard of their comforts and conveniences."[2] It is not possible to prophesy *a priori* the proportion in which increased resources will be devoted to these two uses. The proportion will vary at different times and in different places. Leroy-Beaulieu, for example, suggests that the population use has been predominantly followed in recent times in Belgium and Germany, and the standard-of-comfort use in other European countries.[3] But—and this is the point—it is practically certain that the population use will not be allowed to absorb the *whole* fruits of increased command over nature.

§ 3. The preceding argument, as was indicated at the outset, leaves out of account the deeper-seated reactions that may be set up by expanded earnings. An important

---

[1] Cf. Pareto, *Cours d'économie politique*, pp. 88 *et seq.* Cf. also Marshall, *Principles of Economics*, pp. 189-90.

[2] *Principles of Political Economy*, pp. 252 and 254. Mr. Wright, commenting on the fall in the birth rate in the later nineteenth century, suggests that increased command over nature is more likely to be taken out in an improved standard of comfort when it manifests itself in a fall of prices than when it manifests itself in higher money wages ; for people do not readily see behind money (*Population*, p. 117).   [3] *La Répartition des richesses*, p. 439.

school of writers, headed by Professor Brentano, admits that the direct and immediate effect of enhanced material prosperity in any class will, in general, be to increase the marriage rate and, therewith, the birth rate. They maintain, however, that the enhanced prosperity will, in the long run, bring about the development of a higher spiritual and cultural level, in which more forethought is exercised about children and more satisfactions rival to that of having children come to the front. Hence, they urge, in the long run an increase in the income of any class is likely to lead to no increase at all, but actually to a decrease, in their birth rate and their numbers.[1] Thus Professor Brentano declares that a permanent improvement in wealth and culture, " as a comparison of different ranks, as well as of the same ranks and the same people at different stages of development, has shown us, results in a diminution of births. . . . As prosperity increases, so do the pleasures which compete with marriage, while the feeling towards children takes on a new character of refinement, and both these facts tend to diminish the desire to beget and to bear children." [2] Those persons, for instance, who have something to leave to their children are more affected by the fact that, if their family is large, what is left at their death must be divided into a number of small parts, than those who have nothing to leave and act apart from economic motives. Detailed confirmation of this view is afforded by Dr. Heron's statistical study of London in 1906. In certain selected districts he found the correlation co-efficients between the number of births per 100 wives and various indices of social status. The indices chosen were the proportion of occupied males engaged in professional occupations, the number of female domestic servants per 100 families, the number of general labourers per 1000 males, the proportion of the population living more than two in a room, and the number of paupers and of lunatics per 1000 of the population. A low index of prosperity and a high birth rate were found to go together.

---

[1] Cf. Mombert, *Archiv für Socialwissenschaft*, vol. xxxiv. p. 817. Cf. also Aftalion, *Les Crises périodiques de surproduction*, vol. i. pp. 208-9.

[2] *Economic Journal*, 1910, p. 385.

Against this result there had to be set the fact that a low index of prosperity was also accompanied by a high rate of infant mortality. Investigation, however, showed that the excess of mortality was not sufficient to balance the excess of births; and the conclusion emerged, that "the wives in the districts of least prosperity and culture (and, of course, these poor wives were married to poor husbands) have the largest families."[1] Furthermore, a comparison between the conditions of 1851 and 1901 brought out the startling fact "that the intensity of this relationship has almost doubled in the last fifty years."[2] Heron's results have been amply confirmed by later investigations over a wider field. Thus Mr. Yule writes : " At the present date (1920) there is no doubt that marriage fertility is, on the whole, broadly speaking, graduated continuously from a very low figure for the upper and professional classes to a very much higher figure for unskilled labour."[3] In like manner Dr. Stevenson, as the result of an elaborate study, concludes : " The difference in fertility between the social classes is small from marriages contracted before 1861, and rapidly increases to a maximum for those of 1891–96. The slight subsequent approximation between the classes may be apparent rather than real. The difference in fertility between the social classes is, broadly speaking, a new phenomenon."[4] Up till the middle of last century, though the upper classes, whose full earning capacity develops later than that of manual workers, tended to marry later, and so to have somewhat fewer children, this tendency was nearly balanced by the lower mortality among them.

---

[1] The Relation of Fertility in Man to Social Status, pp. 15 and 19. M. Bertillon has shown that, in general, a high birth rate and a high death rate are correlated (La Dépopulation de la France, pp. 66 et seq.). This correlation is partly due to the fact that the death of children induces parents to get more, and partly to the fact that a high birth rate often means many children born in poor circumstances and so likely to die. Thus, Dr. Newsholme suggests that the observed correlation " is probably due in great part to the fact that large families are common among the poorest classes, and these classes are specially exposed to influences producing excessive infant mortality " (Second Report on Infant Mortality [Cd. 6909], p. 57). A similar conclusion as regards the North of England is reached in Elderton's Report on the English Birth-rate, Part I.

[2] The Relation of Fertility in Man to Social Status, pp. 15 and 19.

[3] The Fall in the Birth-rate, p. 31.

[4] Journal of the Royal Statistical Society, 1920, p. 431.

Their fertility after marriage was not much less, and the survival rate among them only a little lower. Now, in consequence of the relatively large fall in their fertility, the survival rate among them is very much lower.[1] The inferences suggested by these statistical facts are, indeed, less firmly based than they appear to be at first sight. The correlation between high prosperity and low birth rate may be partly due to the fact that a man with a small family is in a better position to accumulate a fortune, and that between rich districts and low birth rate may be partly due to the accumulation of domestic servants and other dependants—a particularly infertile class—in these districts.[2] Moreover, a part of the correlation between wealth and small families is probably due to the fact that physiologically infertile stocks, having their property divided among fewer persons on inheritance, tend, on the average, to be more than ordinarily rich.[3]   But these considerations, important as they are, do not, there is reason to believe, completely account for the observed facts.   What has been said of the deeper-seated reactions of prosperity appreciably strengthens our conclusion that an improvement in the fortunes of the poor is not likely, in an isolated community, to cancel itself by causing a large expansion of population.

§ 4. When account is taken of the fact that, in the modern world, no country is isolated from the rest, the issue

---

[1] Cf. *Journal of the Royal Statistical Society*, 1920, p. 417.

[2] Cf. Leroy-Beaulieu's argument: " Il se trouve dans les quartiers riches une plus forte proportion de ménages âgés, de gens retraités, de domestiques, classe particulièrement stérile, et personnes qui ne passent qu'une partie de l'année à la ville ; la natalité enregistrée doit donc y être plus faible, sans qu'on puisse rien en inférer.   On qualifie le XVIᵉ arrondissement qui compte 135,000 habitants comme un arrondissement riche et le VIIIᵉ également qui, de son côte, compte 104,000 habitants.   Or, il est manifeste que les gens vraiment riches ne représentent pas la dixième partie, peut-être pas même la vingtième partie, de la population de ces arrondissements dits riches ; les gens opulents ne se comptent pas, même à Paris, par centaines de mille ; le gros de la population de ces arrondissements est composé de domestiques, de concierges, de petits boutiquiers et d'ouvriers d'élite.   Les conclusions que l'on tire de la natalité dans les quartiers dits riches de Paris sont donc sans valeur " (*La Question de la population*, p. 399).

[3] Cf. Darwin, " Eugenics in Relation to Economics and Statistics," *Journal of the Royal Statistical Society*, 1919, p. 7.

becomes less plain.   Of course, if the real income of the manual
working class anywhere is increased because the average level
of capacity among that class has been raised, no inducement
is thereby offered to immigration from elsewhere.   But, if
their real income is increased through some discovery, or
invention, or stroke of policy that improves the economic
position of one country considerably more than it improves
that of others, an inducement is offered.   The same thing
happens if legislative or other measures bring about a transference of income from the richer to the poorer members of
some one community—provided, of course, that poor persons
who have immigrated are not excluded from the benefits of
these measures.[1]   These considerations are very important ;
for they show that many causes tending to increase the real
income per head of the wage-earners in a single country will
ultimately exercise a smaller influence in that direction than
they appear likely to do at first sight.   It should not be
forgotten, however, that that very immigration, which lessens
their effect at the point of primary impact, involves indirectly
an improvement in the fortunes of labour elsewhere.   Hence,
in any event, the beneficial influence of the changed conditions
is not destroyed, but is merely spread over a wider area.   In
the country primarily affected *some* addition to economic
welfare is necessarily secured.

§ 5. The above discussion disproves the suggestion that
the beneficial effect on economic welfare of an increase in
the real income of wage-earners will be neutralised by an
expansion of population.   It does not, however, disprove
the suggestion that the beneficial effect on economic welfare
of transferences of income from the rich to the poor will
be so neutralised.   For, in order to that result, it is not necessary that the gain of economic welfare to the poor should
be destroyed—only that it should be made smaller than
the loss of economic welfare to the rich.   It cannot be denied
that this *might* happen.   But, in a country where the distri-

---

[1] The inducement to immigration offered by old-age pensions might be kept
very small by a rule requiring previous residence of, say, 20 years as a condition
of qualification ; for a far-off benefit affects action but slightly, the more so if,
as in this case, the possibility of death makes it uncertain as well as distant.

bution of wealth is as uneven as it is in the United Kingdom, and where, therefore, there are many high incomes which could be largely cut down with very little injury to economic welfare, the chance that it *will* happen may reasonably be regarded as small.

CHAPTER X

THE NATIONAL DIVIDEND AND THE QUALITY OF THE PEOPLE

§ 1. THE general conclusions of Chapters VII.-VIII. might, until quite recently, have been stated as they are there stated, without evoking quarrel or dispute. But of late years a great advance has occurred in biological knowledge. In former times economists had, indeed, to take some account of the reactions of economic causes upon the quantity of the population, and upon its quality so far as that was determined by environment : but questions about the reaction of economic causes upon the quality of the population, as determined by fundamental biological attributes, were not raised. Now, the situation is different. Biometricians and Mendelians alike have turned their attention to sociology, and are insisting upon the fundamental importance for our science of a proper understanding of the laws of heredity. Economists, it is said, in discussing, as I have done, the direct effect of the state of the national dividend upon welfare, are wasting their energies. The direct effect is of no significance; it is only the indirect effect on the size of the families of good and bad stocks respectively that really matters. For every form of welfare depends ultimately on something much more fundamental than economic arrangements, namely, the general forces governing biological selection. I have intentionally stated these claims in a somewhat indefinite form, because I am anxious to investigate the problem thus raised in a constructive rather than in a critical spirit. I shall endeavour, in the following sections, to indicate, as precisely as possible, how far the recent advance in biological knowledge really affects our science.

To this end, I shall distinguish, first, certain results of that knowledge, which, though of great value, are not strictly relevant to economics; secondly, the general claim that the method of economic study indicated in the preceding chapters is rendered by the new knowledge trivial and unimportant; and, thirdly, certain points, in respect of which the new knowledge comes directly into contact with the problems I have undertaken to investigate, and makes it necessary to qualify the conclusions that have been reached.

§ 2. By far the most important contribution of modern biological study to sociology is the assurance, which it affords, of the definite heritable character of certain inborn defects. Whatever view be taken of the physiological mechanism of inheritance, the practical result is the same. We know that persons with congenital defects are likely, if they marry, to hand down a defective organisation to some of their children. We do not possess this definite knowledge with regard to general desirable qualities, particularly on the mental side. Bateson issued a wise caution when he wrote : " Whereas our experience of what constitutes the extremes of unfitness is fairly reliable and definite, we have little to guide us in estimating the qualities for which society has or may have a use, or the numerical proportions in which they may be required. . . . There is as yet nothing in the descent of the higher mental qualities to suggest that they follow any simple system of transmission. It is likely that both they and the more marked developments of physical powers result rather from the coincidence of numerous factors than from the possession of any one genetic element." [1] Again, Mr. and Mrs. Whetham rightly observe that desirable qualities, such as ability, moral character, good health, physical strength and grace, beauty and charm, " are, from the point of view of heredity, essentially different from some of the bad qualities hitherto considered, in that they depend on the conjunction of a great many factors. Such a conjunction must be very hard to trace in the hereditary process, where possibly each character may descend independently, or different characters

[1] *Mendel's Principles of Heredity*, p. 305.

may be linked together, or be incompatible, in far more complicated ways than we have traced in the qualities of plants and animals. Our present knowledge is quite insufficient to enable us to predict how a complex combination of factors, making up the personality of an able or charming man or woman, will reappear in their offspring."[1] We are, in fact, in this region, surrounded by so much ignorance that the utmost caution is essential. Doncaster well observed: " In this direction empirical rules and common sense must still be followed, until the time shall come when science can speak with no uncertain voice."[2] More recently, the late Sir Francis Galton lent the weight of his authority to this opinion: " Enough is already known to those who have studied the question to leave no doubt in their minds about the general results, but not enough is quantitatively known to justify legislative or other action, except in extreme cases."[3] It is well not to forget that Beethoven's father was an habitual drunkard and that his mother died of consumption.[4] About definite defects our ignorance is much less profound. These *are* the extreme cases of which Galton was thinking. Not a few medical men have long been urging that authoritatively to prevent propagation among those afflicted with imbecility, idiocy, syphilis, or tuberculosis would mean cutting off at its source a long stream of defective humanity. This matter is especially urgent among the mentally defective, on account of the exceptionally high rate at which, if left to themselves, they tend to produce children. Thus, before the Royal Commission on the Feeble-Minded, " Dr. Tredgold, an especially experienced witness, pointed out that the average number of children in the families which now use the public elementary schools is about four ; whereas, in the degenerate families, whose children are passed over to the special schools, there is an average of 7·3 children, not including those still-born."[5] Further-

---

[1] *The Family and the Nation*, p. 74.
[2] *Independent Review*, May 1906, p. 183.
[3] *Probability the Basis of Eugenics*, p. 29.
[4] Cf. Bateson, Presidential Address to the British Association, *Nature*, Aug. 1914, p. 677.
[5] *The Family and the Nation*, p. 71.

more, feeble-minded women often begin child-bearing at an exceptionally early age; and it must be remembered that, even if the size of families is unaffected, early marriage is not a matter of indifference; for, when the normal age of marriage in any group is reduced, " generations succeed one another with greater rapidity," so that the proportion of the whole population embraced among the descendants of the original members of that group is increased.[1] The mentally defective are not, however, the only class among which propagation might with advantage be restrained. Some writers suggest that certain forms of criminality and certain qualities conducive to pauperism might be eradicated from the race in the same way. Professor Karl Pearson makes a suggestion, which, if correct, strengthens considerably the probability that this sort of policy would reach its goal. He thinks that imperfections of quite different kinds are correlated, and that " there is something akin to germinal degeneracy, which may show itself in different defects of the same organ or in defects of different organs." [2] Bateson, to the same practical, though not to the same theoretical, effect, speaks of the existence of " indications that, in the extreme cases, unfitness is comparatively definite in its genetic causation, and can, not unfrequently, be recognised as due to the presence of a simple genetic factor." [3] In sum, as the last-quoted writer states, there is little doubt that " some serious physical and mental defects, almost certainly also some morbid diatheses, and some of the forms of vice and criminality could be eradicated if society so determined." [4] This is a conclusion of extreme importance. It is one, too,

---

[1] Haycraft, *Darwinism and Race Progress*, p. 144.

[2] *The Scope and Importance of National Eugenics*, p. 38.

[3] *Mendel's Principles of Heredity*, p. 305.

[4] *Ibid.* p. 305. It is, however, important to remember that a bad *recessive* quality cannot be eliminated merely by preventing propagation among persons who manifest it ; for it will also be borne in the germ-plasm of a number of apparently normal persons. Feeble-mindedness appears to be a recessive quality (cf. Gates, *Heredity and Eugenics*, p. 159). Calculation shows that, if 3 per cent of a population now is feeble-minded, it would require 250 generations (*i.e.* about 8000 years) to reduce the proportion to 1 in 100,000 by merely segregating or sterilising those who show the characteristics. To distinguish and to prevent propagation among those apparently normal persons who bear feeble-mindedness as a recessive quality would, however, be a task far beyond our present powers (cf. *ibid.* p. 173).

that seems *prima facie* susceptible, without great difficulty, of some measure of practical application. Occasions frequently arise when tainted persons, whether on account of crime or of dementia, are compulsorily passed into governmental institutions. When this happens, propagation might be prevented, after careful inquiry had been made, either by permanent segregation, or possibly, as is authorised by law in certain American States, by surgical means.[1] The knowledge we possess seems clearly sufficient to warrant us in taking some cautious steps in this direction. There can be no doubt that such a policy would redound both to the general and to the economic welfare of the community. For this conclusion, and for the great step forward which it is hoped may follow from it, we are indebted to modern biology. The conclusion, however, is outside the sphere of economics, and does not in any way disturb the results that were attained in the preceding chapters.

§ 3. I pass, therefore, to something of whose relevance at all events there can be no doubt, the view, namely, that biological science proves all such inquiries as we are pursuing here to be trivial and misdirected. Put broadly, the charge is this. Economic changes, such as alterations in the size, composition, or distribution of the national dividend, affect environment only; and environment is of no importance, because improvements in it cannot react on the quality of the children born to those who enjoy the improvements. This view was crystallised by Professor Punnett, when he declared that hygiene, education and so on are but " fleeting palliatives at best, which, in postponing, but augment the difficulties they profess to solve. . . . Permanent progress is a question of breeding rather than of pedagogics ; a matter of gametes, not of training." [2] Mr. Lock [3] is even more emphatic in the same sense. The opinions of these writers on the practical side are substantially in agreement with those of Professor Karl Pearson. The scientific foundation on which all such views rest is,

---

[1] The standard work on this subject is *Eugenical Sterilisation in the United States*, by Dr. H. H. Laughlin, 1922.

[2] *Mendelism* (second edition), pp. 80-81.

[3] Cf. *Recent Progress in the Study of Variation, Heredity and Evolution*, by R. H. Lock.

of course, the thesis that acquired characters, which arise out of the influence of environment, are not inherited. It is held, at least as regards the more complicated multicellular organisms, that the germ-cells, which will ultimately form the offspring of a living being, are distinct at the outset from those which will form the body of that being. Thus, Mr. Wilson writes : " It is a reversal of the true point of view to regard inheritance as taking place from the body of the parent to that of the child. The child inherits from the parent *germ-cell*, not from the parent body, and the germ-cell owes its characteristics, not to the body which bears it, but to its descent from a pre-existing germ-cell of the same kind. Thus, the body is, as it were, an offshoot from the germ-cell. As far as inheritance is concerned, the body is merely the carrier of the germ-cells, which are held in trust for coming generations." [1] Doncaster takes up substantially the same position : " In the earlier theories of heredity it was assumed that the germ-cells were produced by the body, and that they must, therefore, be supposed either to contain samples of all parts of it, or at least some kind of units derived from those parts and able to cause their development in the next generation. Gradually, as the study of heredity and of the actual origin of the germ-cells has progressed, biologists have given up this view in favour of a belief in germinal continuity, that is, that the germ - substance is derived from previous germ-substance, the body being a kind of offshoot from it. The child is, thus, like its parent, not because it is produced from the parent, but because both child and parent are produced from the same stock of germ-plasm." [2] If this view be sound, it follows that those definite characteristics of an organism, whose appearance is determined by the presence of definite structures or substances in the germ-cells, cannot be directly affected by any quality " acquired " by an ancestor. It is only characteristics of an indefinite quantitative kind, such as may be supposed to arise from the intercommunication of the germ-cells with the other cells of

---

[1] Wilson, *The Cell in Development and Inheritance*, p. 13 ; quoted by R. H. Lock, *Variation, Heredity and Evolution*, p. 68.
[2] *Heredity*, p. 124.

the body and the reception of fluid or easily soluble substances from them, that can be affected in this way.   The characteristics thus reserved are not, of course, wholly without significance.   The question whether the submission of germ-cells to a poisonous environment reacts permanently upon the descendants of those cells does not seem to be a closed one.   Professor J. A. Thomson writes : " There is a great difference between a poisoning of the germ-cells along with the body and the influencing them in a manner so specific that they can, when they develop, reproduce the particular parental modification." [1]   The germ-cells do not lead " a charmed life, uninfluenced by any of the accidents or incidents of the daily life of the body which is their bearer." [2]   On the contrary, there is some evidence that, not only direct poisons like alcohol, but even injuries to the parent, may, by reacting on the nutrition of the germ-cells, cause general weakness and resultant bad properties in the offspring, though how far *the offspring of their offspring* would be affected is doubtful.   But the general opinion among biologists appears to be that the effect of the acquired characteristics of one generation upon the quality of the succeeding generation is, at all events, very small compared with the effect of the inborn characteristics of the one generation.[3]   "Education is to man what manure is to the pea.   The educated are in themselves the better for it, but their experience will alter not one jot the irrevocable nature of their offspring." [4]   In like manner " neglect, poverty, and parental ignorance, serious as their results are, (do not) possess any marked hereditary effect." [5]

This biological thesis, which, since it is dominant among experts, an outsider has no title to dispute, is, as I have said, the scientific foundation of the view that economic circumstances, because they are environmental, are not, from a long - period standpoint, of any real importance.   The

[1] J. A. Thomson, *Heredity*, p. 198.
[2] *Ibid.* p. 204.
[3] Lock, *Variation and Heredity*, pp. 69-71.
[4] Punnett, *Mendelism*, p. 81.
[5] Eichholz, "Evidence to the Committee on Physical Deterioration," Report, p. 14.   Dr. Eichholz's view appears to be formed *a posteriori*, and not to be an inference from general biological principles.

biological premise I accept. To the sociological conclusion, however, I demur. Mr. Sidney Webb has uttered a genial protest against a too exclusive attention to the biological aspect of social problems. "After all," he writes, "it would not be of much use to have all babies born from good stocks, if, generation after generation, they were made to grow up into bad men and women. A world of well-born but physically and morally perverted adults is not attractive." [1] My criticism, however, goes deeper than this. Professor Punnett and his fellow-workers would accept Mr. Webb's plea. They freely grant that environing circumstances can affect the persons immediately subjected to them, but they, nevertheless, hold that these circumstances are unimportant, because, not being able to influence the inborn quality of succeeding generations, they cannot produce any lasting result. My reply is that the environment of one generation *can* produce a lasting result, because it can affect the environment of future generations. Environments, in short, as well as people, have children. Though education and so forth cannot influence new births in the physical world, they can influence them in the world of ideas; [2] and ideas, once

[1] *Eugenics Review*, November 1910, p. 236.

[2] An interesting comparison can be made between the process of evolution in these two worlds. In both we find three elements, the *occurrence of*, *propagation of*, and *conflict between*, mutations.

In both worlds the *kind* of mutations that occur appear to be fortuitous, and cannot be controlled, though in both it is sometimes suggested that the tendency to mutate is encouraged by large changes in, and particular kinds of, environment. For example, Rae suggested, as conditions favourable to the emergence of inventions, general upheavals, such as wars or migrations, and the adoption in any art of a new material—such as steel in building—either for lack of the old material or through the possession of a specially effective new one, and he maintained that the stable agricultural districts rarely yield inventions (*The Sociological Theory of Capital*, pp. 172-3). In both worlds again, with every increase of *variability*, the chance that a "good" mutation will occur is increased. Hence, *ceteris paribus*, environments that make for variability are a means to good. Thus, of local governments Marshall writes: "All power of variation that is consistent with order and economy of administration is an almost unmixed good. The prospects of progress are increased by the multiplicity of parallel experiments and the intercommunion of ideas between many people, each of whom has some opportunity of testing practically the value of his own suggestions" (*Memorandum to the Royal Commission on Local Taxation*, p. 123 ; cf. also Booth, *Industry*, v. p. 86 ; and Hobhouse, *Democracy and Reaction*, pp. 121-3).

The *propagation* of mutations, on the other hand, does not proceed in the same way among ideas as among organisms. Among the latter the fertility of

produced or once accepted by a particular generation, whether or not they can be materialised into mechanical inventions, may not only remodel from its very base the environment which succeeding generations enjoy,[1] but may also pave the way for further advance. For, whereas each new man must begin where his last ancestor began, each new invention begins where its last ancestor left off.[2] In this way a permanent or, rather, a progressive change of environment is brought about, and, since environment is admittedly able to exert an important influence on persons actually subjected to it, such a change may produce enduring consequences. Among animals, indeed, and among the primitive races of men this point is not important. For there what the members of one generation have wrought in the field of ideas is not easily communicated to their successors. "The human race, when widely scattered and incapable of intercommunication, makes the same discovery a hundred times. Its efforts and its triumphs are annihilated with the death of the individual, or of the last member of the family in which the invention has been passed on by oral tradition."[3] But among civilised men the arts of writing and of printing have rendered thought viable through time, and have thus extended to each generation power to mould and remodel the ideal environment of its successors. Tarde grasped

---

the mutated members that survive is not, but among the former it is, affected by their adaptation or otherwise to successful struggle. Animals that are failures and those that are successes are equally likely, if they survive, to have offspring. But, among ideas, those that fail are likely to be barren and those that succeed to be prolific.

Still more marked is the difference between the character of the *struggle* that takes place between mutated members in the two groups. In the physical world the process is negative—the failures are cut off. In the world of ideas it is positive—successful ideas are adopted and imitated. One consequence of this is that, in general, a successful experiment diffuses itself much more rapidly than a successful "sport."

[1] This consideration affords a powerful argument for the expenditure of State funds upon training the girls of the present generation to become competent mothers and housewives, because, if only one generation were so taught, a family tradition would very probably become established, and the knowledge given in the first instance at public cost would propagate itself through successive generations without any further cost to anybody. (Cf. Report of the Interdepartmental Committee on Physical Deterioration, p. 42.)

[2] Cf. Fiske, *Invention*, p. 253.

[3] Majewski, *La Science de la civilisation*, p. 228.

this point when he wrote: "To facilitate further production is the principal virtue of capital, as that term ought to be understood. But in what is it inherent? In commodities or in particular kinds of commodities? Nay, rather in those fortunate experiments of which the memory has been preserved. Capital is tradition or social memory. It is to societies what heredity or vital memory,—enigmatical term, —is to living beings. As for the products that have been saved and stored up to facilitate the construction of new copies of the models conceived by inventors, they are to these models, which are the true social germs, what the cotyledon, a mere store of food, is to the embryo."[1] Bacon had already exclaimed: "The introduction of new inventions seemeth to be the very chief of all human actions. The benefits of new inventions may extend to all mankind universally, but the good of political activities can respect but some particular country of men: these latter do not perdure above a few ages, the former for ever." Marshall writes in the same spirit: "The world's material wealth would quickly be replaced if it were destroyed, but the ideas by which it was made were retained. If, however, the ideas were lost, but not the material wealth, then that would dwindle and the world would go back to poverty. And most of our knowledge of mere facts could quickly be recovered if it were lost, but the constructive ideas of thought remained; while, if the ideas perished, the world would enter again on the Dark Ages."[2] Nor is even this a full account of the matter. As Marshall observes in another place: "Any change that awards to the workers of one generation better earnings, together with better opportunities of developing their best qualities, will increase the material and moral advantages which they have the power to offer to their children; while, by increasing their own intelligence, wisdom and forethought, such a change will also, to some extent, increase their willingness to sacrifice their own pleasures for the well-being of their children."[3] Those children, in turn, being themselves rendered

---

[1] *La Logique sociale*, p. 352.
[2] *Principles of Economics*, p. 780.
[3] *Ibid.* p. 563.

stronger and more intelligent, will be able, when they grow up, to offer a better environment—and under the term environment I include the physical circumstances of the mother before, and immediately after, child-birth [1]—to their children, and so on.   The effect goes on piling itself up. Changes in ancestral environment start forces, which modify continuously and cumulatively the conditions of succeeding environments, and, through them, the human qualities for which current environment is in part responsible.   Hence, Professor Punnett's assertion is unduly sweeping.[2]   Progress, not merely permanent but growing, *can* be brought about by causes with which breeding and gametes have nothing to do.   Nor, indeed, must we rest content with the word *can*. There is strong reason for holding that the enormous development in the *mental* equipment of mankind, which has taken place during historic times, has not been associated with any significant germinal change.   With growing density of population the machinery of thought has been developed through contact and co-operation among persons of not substantially greater germinal endowment than was possessed by earlier generations.   " This is the paradox of the population problem. Change among species in a state of nature is based upon germinal change alone ; change among our pre-human ancestors was equally a matter of change in the quality of population ; but the explanation of the most outstanding fact in recent history broadly viewed (*i.e.* the great acceleration of progress in knowledge and power) is to be sought in a change in quantity, rather than in quality, of population." [3]   We conclude, then, that there is no fundamental difference of the kind sometimes supposed between causes operating on acquired, and causes operating on inborn, qualities.   The two are of co-ordinate importance ; and the students of neither have a right to belittle the work of those who study the other.

[1] The importance of this point is illustrated by the observation of the London Education Committee of 1905, that the children born in a year when infant mortality is low have more than average physique, and *vice versa*.   (Cf. Wells, *New Worlds for Old*, p. 216.)

[2] In later editions of his book Professor Punnett's argument is stated in a less sweeping form and does not conflict with what has been said above.   (Cf. *Mendelism*, third edition, p. 167.)

[3] Carr-Saunders, *The Population Problem*, p. 481.

§ 4. I proceed now to the third of the topics indicated for discussion in the first section of this chapter, namely, the extent to which new biological knowledge makes it necessary for us to qualify the conclusions laid down in Chapters VII. and VIII. These conclusions, it will be remembered, were to the effect that, other things being equal, (1) an increase in the size of national dividend—provided that it is not brought about by the exercise of undue pressure upon workpeople,—and (2) a change in the distribution of the dividend favourable to the poor, would be likely to increase economic welfare and, through economic welfare, general welfare. Against these conclusions the biologically trained critic urges an important caution. May it not be, he asks, that advance along the first of these lines, by checking the free play of natural selection and enabling feeble children to survive, will set up a cumulative influence making for national weakness; and that advance along the second line, by differentiating in favour of inferior stocks, will have a similar evil effect? Is there not ground for fear that the brightness of the stream of progress is deceptive, that it bears along, as it flows, seeds of disaster, and that the changes we have pronounced to be productive of welfare are, at the best, of doubtful import? The two parts of this thesis must now be examined in turn.

§ 5. The danger to national strength that results from a growth of wealth in general has been emphasised by many writers. In a softened environment children of feeble constitution, who, in harder circumstances, would have died, are enabled to survive and themselves to have children.[1] It has even been suggested that in this fact may lie the secret of the eventual decay of nations and of aristocracies which have attained great wealth. There are, indeed, mitigating circumstances, which may be urged in extenuation of this view. First, according to the most recent biological opinion, the survival of weakly children, if their weakness is, as it were, accidental, and not due to inherited defect, is not ultimately harmful to the stock, because the children of the weakly children are quite likely to be strong. Secondly,

[1] Cf. Haycraft, *Darwinism and Race Progress*, p. 58.

weakness in infancy is not necessarily a good index of essential inborn weakness; and Mr. Yule, after reviewing the available statistics by mathematical methods, is led to suggest that, perhaps, " the mortality of infancy is selective only as regards the special dangers of infancy, and its influence scarcely extends beyond the second year of life, whilst the weakening effect of a sickly infancy is of greater duration." [1] These mitigating circumstances somewhat limit, though they may well fail to overthrow, the thesis that growth in wealth, unaccompanied by any safeguard, is likely to deteriorate the inherent quality of the race. There is also available a further mitigating circumstance, which is less fundamental, though not less important. For, even if the inherent quality of the race is somewhat injured, it does not follow that the finished products, which contain, of course, at once inherent and environmental qualities, are so injured. If increased wealth removes influences that make for the elimination of the unfit, it also removes influences that make for the weakening of the fit. The total effect of this twofold action may well be beneficial rather than injurious. That this is in fact so is suggested by an important report published by the Local Government Board on the relation of infantile mortality to general mortality. In that report Dr. Newsholme directly combats the view that improvements making for a reduction of infant mortality, by enabling more weaklings to survive, must be inimical to the average health of the population. He finds, on the contrary, " that the counties having high infant mortalities continue, in general, to suffer somewhat excessively throughout the first twenty years of human life, and that counties having low infantile mortalities continue to have relatively low death-rates in the first twenty years of life, though the superiority is not so great at the later as at the earlier ages. . . . It is fair to assume, in accordance with general experience, that the amount of sickness varies approximately with the number of deaths; and there can be no reasonable doubt that, in the counties having a high infant death-rate, there is—apart from migration—more sickness and a lower

[1] [Cd. 5263], p. 82 (1909–10).

standard of health in youth and in adult life than in counties in which the toll of infant mortality is less."[1]   Dr. Newsholme's argument is, indeed, open to the reply that ascertained differences between the several counties in infantile death-rate and later death-rate may *both* be due to differences in the quality of the inhabitants of the several counties.   The argument, therefore, fails to prove that the direct beneficial effect of better environments due to greater wealth outweighs the indirect injurious effect of the impediment they place in the way of natural selection.   It may be that the injurious effect is really the stronger, but that it is masked in the statistics because it is exercised upon persons who are *ab initio* of better physique—as is, indeed, suggested by their ability to earn more and so to live in better conditions—than the average.   This criticism lessens the force of Dr. Newsholme's statistical argument.[2]   Still the directly observed fact that good environment removes influences tending to weaken the fit remains.   In company with the considerations set out earlier in this section, that fact militates against the view that a growing dividend and the improvements that naturally accompany it carry seeds of future weakness, and so ultimately make against, rather than in favour of, economic welfare.   In any event, the danger that they may have this effect can be readily and completely counteracted, if the policy of segregating the unfit, advocated in the second section, is adopted.   As Professor Thomson points out, no biological evil can result from the preservation of weaklings, provided that they are not allowed to have children.[3]   There is, therefore, no need to surrender our conclusion that causes, which make for an expansion of the dividend, in general make for economic and, through economic, for aggregate, welfare.

§ 6. The danger to national strength and efficiency through an improvement in the distribution of the dividend

---

[1] Report for 1909–10 [Cd. 5263], p. 17.

[2] Dr. Newsholme's argument was severely criticised—partly under a misapprehension of its purpose—by Professor Karl Pearson in his Cavendish lecture, 1912, p. 13.   Dr. Newsholme replied in his second (1913) report [Cd. 6909], pp. 46-52.

[3] *Heredity*, p. 528.

might seem *a priori* to be very important. For improved distribution is likely to modify the proportion in which future generations are born from the richer and poorer classes respectively. If, therefore, the poorer classes comprise less efficient stocks than the richer classes—if, in fact, economic status is anything of an index of inborn quality—improved distribution must modify the general level of inborn quality, and so, in the long run, must react with cumulative force upon the magnitude of the national dividend. Now I do not agree with those who hold that poverty and inborn inefficiency are obviously and certainly correlated. Extreme poverty is, no doubt, often the result of feckless character, physical infirmity, and other "bad" qualities of finished persons. But these themselves are generally correlated with bad environment; and it is ridiculous to treat as unworthy of argument the suggestion that the "bad" qualities are mainly the result, not of bad original properties, but of bad original environment.[1] Nevertheless, though it is not self-evident, it is, I think, probable, that a considerable measure of correlation exists between poverty and "bad" original properties. For among the relatively rich there are always a number of persons who have risen from a poor environment, which their fellows, who have remained poor, shared with them in childhood; and this sort of movement is probably becoming more marked, as opportunities of education and so forth are being brought more within the reach of the poorer classes. In like manner, of course, among the poor are some persons who have fallen from a

---

[1] This class of difficulty is experienced in many statistical investigations of social problems. For example, an interesting inquiry into the inheritance of ability, as indicated by the Oxford class lists and the school lists of Harrow and Charterhouse, was published some years ago by Mr. Schuster. But the value of his results is in some measure—it is not possible to say in *what* measure—impaired by the fact that the possession of able parents is apt to be correlated with the reception of a good formal, and, still more, informal, education. Mr. Schuster argues (p. 23) that the error due to this circumstance is not likely to be large. (Cf. also Karl Pearson, *Biometrika*, vol. iii. p. 156.) M. Nicefero, on the other hand, in his study of *Les Classes pauvres*, lays stress on the effects of environment in promoting the physical and psychical inferiority of these classes; but he does not seem to justify by evidence his conclusion that "tous les facteurs—en dernière analyse—plongent leur racine bien plus dans le milieu économique de la société moderne que dans la structure même de l'individu" (p. 332).

superior environment. Among the original properties of *these* relatively rich there are presumably qualities making for efficiency, which account for their rise ; while, among the original properties of *these* relatively poor, there are, presumably, qualities of an opposite kind.[1] Hence, it is probably true that causes affecting the comparative rate of child-bearing among the relatively rich and the relatively poor respectively affect the comparative rate among those with " better " and " worse " original properties (from the point of view of efficiency) in the same direction. If it were true that increased prosperity in a poor class involved a higher rate of reproduction, it would follow that an improved distribution of the dividend would increase the number and, therewith, the proportion, of children born from parents of stock other than the best. Since, however, as is notorious, propagation among the lowest class of all is practically untrammelled by economic considerations, an increase in fortune to the poor as a whole could only increase the number of children born to sections of the poorer classes other than the worst. It would not, therefore, necessarily follow that the average quality of the population as a whole would be lowered. It is not, however, necessary to stop at this point. Professor Brentano's investigations, which were previously noticed, have suggested that increased prosperity in a class tends, on the whole, to diminish rather than to increase the reproduction rate of that class, and reason has been shown for believing that this tendency is not fully offset by accompanying improvements in the mortality rate.[2] Hence, it would seem, an improvement in the distribution of the dividend may be expected actually to diminish the proportion of children born from inferior stocks. In

---

[1] Pareto ignores these considerations when he argues (*Systèmes socialistes*, p. 13 *et seq.*) that an increase in the relative number of children born to the rich must make for national deterioration because, since the children of the rich are subjected to a less severe struggle than those of the poor, feeble children, who would die if born to the poor, will, if born to the rich, survive and, in turn, have feeble children. In view of the facts noted in the text, this circumstance should be regarded merely as a counteracting force, mitigating, but not destroying, the beneficial consequences likely to result from a relative increase in the fertility of the rich.

[2] Cf. *ante*, Chapter IX. § 3.

short, this biological consideration, so far from reversing the conclusion of Chapter VIII., that improved distribution makes for economic and general welfare, lends, in present conditions, some support to that conclusion. The results of that chapter, along with those of Chapter VII., therefore, remain intact.

CHAPTER XI

IN the preceding chapters it has been shown that economic welfare is liable to be affected in an important degree (1) through the size of the national dividend and (2) through the way in which it is distributed among the members of the community. If causes affecting the size of the dividend had no influence on its distribution, and causes affecting its distribution no influence on its size, the remaining stages of our inquiry would be simple. Each of these groups of causes would be examined in turn separately. As a fact, however, the same causes will often act along both of these channels, with the result that an entirely satisfactory method of exposition is difficult to devise. After weighing up the comparative advantages of different courses I propose to proceed as follows. In Parts II. and III., I shall study the way in which economic welfare is affected by certain causes that operate upon it through the size of the dividend. I do not propose to examine all the causes that might properly be brought under review in this connection. Inventions and discoveries, the opening up of extensive sources of foreign demand, improvements in the technique of marketing, and the growth of accumulated capital will scarcely be discussed at all. Part II. will be concerned with the way in which the productive resources of the community, looked at generally, are distributed among different uses, and Part III. with the organisation of labour in various aspects. These discussions having been completed, Part IV. is devoted to an inquiry as to how far in actual fact causes that affect economic welfare in one sense through the size of the dividend are liable to affect it in a different sense through the distribution of the dividend, and to a study of the problems that arise when this sort of disharmony is manifested.

PART II

THE SIZE OF THE NATIONAL DIVIDEND
AND THE DISTRIBUTION OF RESOURCES
AMONG DIFFERENT USES

CHAPTER I

INTRODUCTORY

§ 1. In this Part we are concerned with causes that increase or diminish the size of the national dividend by acting on the way in which the productive resources of no matter what kind belonging to the country are distributed among different uses or occupations. Throughout this discussion, except when the contrary is expressly stated, the fact that some resources are generally unemployed against the will of the owners is ignored. This does not affect the substance of the argument, while it simplifies its exposition. The purpose of this introductory chapter is to indicate the general scope of the problem before us.

§ 2. Certain optimistic followers of the classical economists have suggested that the "free play of self-interest," if only Government refrains from interference, will automatically cause the land, capital and labour of any country to be so distributed as to yield a larger output and, therefore, more economic welfare than could be attained by any arrangement other than that which comes about "naturally." Even Adam Smith himself, while making an exception in favour of State action in "erecting and maintaining certain public works and certain public institutions, which it can never be for the interests of any individual, or small number of individuals, to erect and maintain," lays it down that "any system which endeavours, either by extraordinary encouragements to draw towards a particular species of industry a greater share of the capital of the society than what would naturally go to it; or by extraordinary restraints to force from a particular species of industry some share of the capital which would otherwise be employed in it . . . retards, instead of accelerating, the progress of the society towards real wealth and greatness, and diminishes, instead of increasing, the real value of the annual produce of its land and labour." [1] It would, of course, be unreasonable to interpret this passage in any abstract or universal sense. Adam Smith had in mind the actual world as he knew it, with an organised system of civilised government and contract law. He would not have quarrelled with the dictum of a later economist that "the activities of man are expended along two routes, the first being directed to the production or transformation of economic goods, the second to the appropriation of goods produced by others." [2] Activities devoted to appropriation obviously do not promote production, and production would be promoted if they were diverted into the channels of industry. We must, therefore, understand him to assume the existence of laws designed, and, in the main, competent, to prevent acts of *mere* appropriation, such as those perpetrated by highwaymen and card-sharpers. The free play of self-interest is conceived by him to be "confined to certain directions by our general social institutions, especially the Family, Property, and the territorial State." [3] More generally, when one man obtains goods from another man, he is conceived to obtain them by the process, not of seizure, but of exchange in an open market, where the bargainers on both sides are reasonably competent and reasonably cognisant of the conditions. There is ground, however, for believing that even Adam Smith had not realised fully the extent to which the System of Natural Liberty needs to be qualified and guarded by special laws, before it will promote the most productive employment of a country's resources. It has been said by a recent writer that "the working of self-interest is generally beneficent, not because of some natural coincidence between the self-interest of each and the good of all, but because human institutions are arranged so as to compel self-interest to work in directions in which it

---

[1] *Wealth of Nations*, Book iv. chapter ix., third paragraph from the end.
[2] Pareto, *Manuale di economia politica*, pp. 444-5.
[3] Cannan, *The History of Local Rates*, p. 176. Cf. also Carver, *Essays in Social Justice*, p. 109.

will be beneficent."[1]   Thus, though it is, apart from any
institutions, to the interest of each individual that all
individuals, including himself, should refrain from thieving
rather than that all should thieve, it would not be to the
interest of any one that he personally should refrain from
thieving, unless *either*, by so doing, he could induce others to
follow his example—which he could not do—*or* there was a
law or other sanction imposing penalties for theft.   This kind
of coercive legal device for directing self-interest into social
channels is well illustrated by the limitations which some
civilised States impose upon the absolute powers of owners
of property—such limitations as the Bavarian rule forbidding
owners of forests to exclude pedestrians from their land, the
French and American rules restraining a man from setting
fire to his own house, and the practice prevalent in all
countries of expropriating private owners where their expropria-
tion is urgently required in the general interest.[2]   It is
further illustrated by the attitude of the law of modern
nations towards types of contract—gambling debts, contracts
in restraint of trade, agreements for contracting-out of certain
legal obligations—which are deemed contrary to public policy
and are, therefore, treated by the courts as void.[3]   This adjustment of institutions to the end of directing self-interest into
beneficial channels has been carried out in considerable detail.
But even in the most advanced States there are failures and
imperfections.   We are not here concerned with those deficiencies of organisation which sometimes cause higher non-
economic interests to be sacrificed to less important economic
interests.   Over and above these, there are many obstacles
that prevent a community's resources from being distributed
among different uses or occupations in the most effective
way.   The study of these constitutes our present problem.
That study involves some difficult analysis.   But its purpose
is essentially practical.   It seeks to bring into clearer light
some of the ways in which it now is, or eventually may become,
feasible for governments to control the play of economic

---

[1] Cannan, *Economic Review*, July 1913, p. 333.
[2] Cf. Ely, *Property and Contract*, pp. 61 and 150.
[3] *Ibid.* pp. 616 and 731.

forces in such wise as to promote the economic welfare, and, through that, the total welfare, of their citizens as a whole.[1]

[1] Cf. Marshall's observation: "Much remains to be done, by a careful collection of the statistics of demand and supply and a scientific interpretation of their results, in order to discover what are the limits of the work that society can with advantage do towards turning the economic actions of individuals into those channels in which they will add the most to the sum total of happiness" (*Principles of Economics*, p. 475).

CHAPTER II

§ 1. CONCERNED as we are with the national dividend as
a continuing flow, we naturally understand by the resources
directed to making it, not a stock of resources, but a
similarly continuing flow; and we conceive the distribution
of these resources among different uses or places on the
analogy, not of a stagnant pond divided into a number of
sections, but rather of a river divided into a number of
streams. This conception involves, no doubt, many difficulties
in connection both with the varying durability of the
equipment employed in different industries and with the
dynamic, or changing, tendencies of industry as a whole.
In spite of these difficulties, however, the general idea is
exact enough for the present purpose. That purpose is
to provide a suitable definition for the concepts which
are fundamental throughout this Part, namely, *the value of
marginal private* and *the value of the marginal social net
product*. The essential point is that these too must be conceived as flows—as the result *per year* of the employment
per year of the marginal increment of some given quantity
of resources. On this basis we may proceed to work out our
definition.

§ 2. For complete accuracy it is necessary to distinguish
between two senses in which the term marginal increment of
resources may be employed. It may be conceived either as
being added, so to speak, from outside, thus constituting a net
addition to the sum total of resources in existence, or as being
transferred to the particular use or place we are studying

from some other use or place.   If the effect on production in
a particular use or place of adding an increment of resources
is independent of the quantity of resources employed elsewhere,
the net products of these two sorts of marginal increment will
be the same.   It often happens, however, that this condition
of independence is not satisfied.   Thus, as will be shown more
fully in a later chapter, the nth unit of resources employed
in a particular firm will yield different quantities of produce
according as the quantity of resources employed in other
firms in the same industry is larger or smaller.   The net
products derived from marginal increments of resources, interpreted in the above two ways, might perhaps be distinguished as additive marginal net products and substitutive
marginal net products.   In general, however, the net products
derived from the two sorts of marginal increment of resources
in any use or place are not likely to differ sensibly from one
another, and for most purposes they may be treated as equivalent.

§ 3. Waiving, then, this point, we have next to define more
precisely what is meant when we speak of the marginal net
product of the resources employed in any use or place as *the
result of* the marginal increment of resources employed there.
This is tantamount to saying that the marginal net product
of a given quantity of resources is equal to the difference
that would be' made to the total product of these resources
by adding to or subtracting from them a small increment.
This, however, is not by itself sufficient.   For the addition
or subtraction of a small increment can be accomplished in
several different ways with correspondingly different results.
We are here concerned with a particular way.   For us the
marginal net product of any flow of resources employed in any
use or place is equal to the difference between the aggregate
flow of product for which that flow of resources, *when appropriately organised*, is responsible and the aggregate flow of product for which a flow of resources differing from that flow
by a small (marginal) increment, *when appropriately organised*,
would be responsible.   In this statement the phrase *when
appropriately organised* is essential.   If we were thinking
of marginal net product in the sense of the difference

between the products of two adjacent *quantities* of resources, we should normally imagine the resources to be organised suitably to one of these quantities and, therefore, not to the other. Since, however, our interest is in the difference between the products of two adjacent *flows* of resources, it is natural to conceive each of the two flows as organised in the manner most appropriate to itself. This is the conception we need. It is excellently illustrated by Professor J. B. Clark. The marginal increment of capital invested in a railway corporation is in reality, he writes, "a difference between two kinds of plant for carrying goods and passengers. One of these is the railroad as it stands, with all its equipment brought up to the highest pitch of perfection that is possible with the present resources. The other is the road built and equipped as it would have been if the resources had been by one degree less. A difference in all-round quality between an actual and a possible railroad is in reality the final increment of capital now used by the actual corporation. The product of that last unit of capital is the difference between what the road actually produces and what it would have produced if it had been made one degree poorer." [1]

§ 4. One further point must be made clear. The marginal net product of a factor of production is the difference that would be made to the aggregate product by withdrawing *any* (small) unit of the factor. The marginal unit is thus not any particular unit. Still less is it the worst unit in existence —the most incompetent workman who is employed at all— as some writers have supposed ! It is *any* (small) unit out of the aggregate of units, *all exactly alike*, into which we imagine this aggregate to be divided. Though, however, the marginal unit is thus *any* unit, it is not any unit *however placed*. On the contrary, it is any unit *conceived as placed at the margin*. The significance of this is best understood with the help of an illustration. To withdraw a man attending a new machine or working in an easy place in any industry and to do nothing else would, of course, affect aggregate output more seriously than to withdraw a man attending an obsolete machine or

---

[1] *The Distribution of Wealth*, p. 250. I have substituted "produced" for "earned" in the sentence quoted above.

working in a difficult place would do. The marginal net product of work in that industry is then the difference that would be made to aggregate output by withdrawing for a day any (similar) man and redistributing, if necessary, the men that are left in such wise that the machine consequently left unattended or place of work left unfilled is the least productive machine or place of work of which use has hitherto been made.

§ 5. So much being understood, we have next to distinguish precisely between the two varieties of marginal net product which I have named respectively *social* and *private*. The marginal social net product is the total net product of physical things or objective services due to the marginal increment of resources in any given use or place, no matter to whom any part of this product may accrue. It might happen, for example, as will be explained more fully in a later chapter, that costs are thrown upon people not directly concerned, through, say, uncompensated damage done to surrounding woods by sparks from railway engines. All such effects must be included—some of them will be positive, others negative elements—in reckoning up the social net product of the marginal increment of any volume of resources turned into any use or place. Again an increase in the quantity of resources employed by one firm in an industry may give rise to external economies in the industry as a whole and so lessen the real costs involved in the production by other firms, of a given output. Everything of this kind must be counted in. For some purposes it is desirable to count in also indirect effects induced in people's tastes and in their capacity to derive satisfaction from their purchases and possessions. Our principal objective, however, is the national dividend and changes in it as defined in Part I. Chapters III. and V. Therefore psychical consequences are excluded, and the marginal social net product of any given volume of resources is taken, except when special notice to the contrary is given, to consist of physical elements and objective services only. The marginal private net product is that part of the total net product of physical things or objective services due to the marginal increment of resources in any given use or place which accrues in the first instance—

i.e. prior to sale—to the person responsible for investing resources there.   In some conditions this is equal to, in some it is greater than, in others it is less than the marginal social net product.

§ 6. The *value* of the marginal social net product of any quantity of resources employed in any use or place is simply the sum of money which the marginal social net product is worth in the market.   In like manner the value of the marginal private net product is the sum of money which the marginal private net product is worth in the market.   Thus, when the marginal social net product and the marginal private net product are identical and the person responsible for the investment sells what accrues to him, the value of both sorts of marginal net product in respect of a given volume of resources is equal to the increment of product multiplied by the price per unit at which the product is sold when that volume of resources is being employed in producing it.[1]   For example, the two sorts of marginal net product per year of a million units of resources invested in weaving being assumed to be identical, the value of both is equal to the number of bales of cloth by which the output of a million *plus* a small increment, say a million and one, exceeds the output of a million units, multiplied by the money value of a bale of cloth when this output is being produced.[2]   This, it should be observed in passing, is different from, and must by no means be confused with, the excess—if there is an excess—of the money value of the whole product when a million and one units of resources are being employed over the money value of the whole product when a million units are being employed.

---

[1] This definition tacitly assumes that the realised price is equal to the (marginal) demand price.   If government limitation of price causes it to be temporarily less than this, the value of the marginal net product will need to be interpreted as the marginal (physical) net product multiplied by the marginal demand price, and the marginal demand price in these conditions will not be equal to the actual selling price.

[2] Cf. Marshall, *Principles of Economics*, p. 847.   It will be noticed by the careful reader that, even when the *additive* marginal net product and the *substitutive* marginal net product are equal, the *value* of the marginal net product will be different according as marginal net product is interpreted as additive and as substitutive marginal net product.   The difference will, however, in general, be of the second order of smalls.

CHAPTER III

THE VALUES OF MARGINAL SOCIAL NET PRODUCTS AND
THE SIZE OF THE NATIONAL DIVIDEND

§ 1. LET us suppose that a given quantity of productive
resources is being employed, that there are no costs of movement between different occupations and places, and that conditions are such that only one arrangement of resources will
make the values of marginal social net products everywhere
equal.[1] On these suppositions it is easy to show that this
arrangement of resources will make the national dividend
larger than it would be under any other arrangement. This
follows from the definition of changes in the size of the
national dividend given in Part I. Chapter V. The value of
the marginal social net product of resources in any use is the
money measure of the satisfaction which the marginal increment
of resources in that use is yielding. Whenever, therefore, the
value of the marginal social net product of resources is less
in any one use than it is in any other, the money measure of
satisfaction in the aggregate can be increased by transferring
resources from the use where the value of the marginal social
net product is smaller to the use where it is larger. It follows
that, since, *ex hypothesi*, there is only one arrangement of
resources that will make the values of the marginal social
net products equal in all uses, this arrangement is necessarily
the one that makes the national dividend, as here defined, a
maximum.[2]

[1] The considerations developed in Part III. Chapter IX. § 2 are here provisionally ignored.

[2] A minor point should be noticed in passing. In occupations in which *no*
resources are employed, the value of the marginal net product of resources will,
in general, be smaller than it is in occupations where *some* resources are employed.

§ 2. This conclusion may be extended to show that, when complete equality among the values of marginal social net products is wanting, a diminution in the degree of inequality that exists among them is likely to benefit the national dividend. This result cannot, however, be set down without explanation. If the uses in which resources are employed were only two in number, its meaning would be perfectly clear and its validity undoubted.   In fact, however, these uses are very numerous. This circumstance gives rise to a difficulty, which has already been referred to in another connection.[1]   The meaning of the concept of greater or less equality among a large number of values is ambiguous.   Are we to measure the degree of equality by the mean deviation from the average value, or by the standard deviation, or by the " probable error," or by some other statistical measure ?   If we use the standard deviation as our criterion, reasoning akin to that of the footnote on p. 97 shows that a decrease in the degree of inequality subsisting among the values of marginal social net products in different uses will *probably* lead to an increase in the national dividend.   But it is not certain to do this unless the decrease of inequality is brought about by a group of (one or more) changes of individual values, *each one of which taken by itself* tends to decrease inequality.   Thus, if the distribution of resources is so altered that a number of values of marginal social net products which are below the average are all increased, or if a number which are above the average are all diminished, it is certain that the dividend will be increased.   But, if a cause comes into play, which, while decreasing the degree of inequality among the values of marginal social net products on the whole, yet increases *some* values that are above the average and diminishes *some* that are below it, this is not certain. This type of difficulty is not, however, of great practical

---

This circumstance clearly does not imply the existence of inequality among the values of marginal net products in any sense incompatible with the maximisation of the national dividend.   But, if it should anywhere happen that the value of the marginal net product of resources in an occupation where no resources are employed is larger than it is in occupations where some resources are employed, —*e.g.* a profitable venture which for some reason people have failed to exploit,— *that* inequality would be an effective inequality and would be incompatible with the maximisation of the dividend.

[1] Cf. *ante*, Part I. Chapter VIII. § 7.

importance, because the obstacles to equality with which
we have to deal are, for the most part, general obstacles,
and operate in the same sense at nearly all points where
they operate at all.

§ 3. Let us next take account of the fact that in real life
costs are often involved in moving resources from one place
or occupation to another, and let us inquire in what, if any,
respects this fact makes it necessary to modify the conclusions
set out above. The kernel of the matter can be displayed
as follows. Suppose that between two points A and B the
movement of a unit of resources can be effected at a capital
cost equivalent to an annual charge of n shillings for
every year during which a unit that is moved continues in
productive work in its new home. In these circumstances the
national dividend will be increased by the movement of resources
from A to B, so long as the annual value of the marginal
social net product at B exceeds that at A by more than n
shillings; and it will be injured by any movement of resources
which occurs after the excess of the value of the marginal
social net product at B has been reduced below n shillings. If
the initial distribution of resources between A and B is such
that the value of the marginal social net product at B exceeds
(or falls short of) the value of the marginal social net product
at A by any number of shillings less than n, say by $(n - h)$
shillings, the existing arrangement—that under which the
values of the marginal social net products at the two points
differ by $(n - h)$ shillings—is the best arrangement, not indeed
absolutely, since, if there were no costs, a better arrangement
would be possible,[1] but *relatively to the fact of the initial distribution and the existing costs of movement.* It is not, be it noted,
the best arrangement relatively to the existing costs of movement alone. We cannot say that, when the costs of movement
are equivalent to n shillings, the national dividend is best
served by a distribution under which the values of the marginal
social net products at A and B differ by such and such a defined
number of shillings. The only accurate statement is : when the
costs of movement between A and B are equivalent to n shillings,
the national dividend is best served by the maintenance of

[1] Cf. *post*, Ch. V. § 6.

the existing distribution, whatever that may be, provided that this distribution does not involve a divergence in the values of marginal social net products greater than n shillings; and, if the existing distribution does involve a divergence greater than n shillings, by a new distribution brought about by the transference of sufficient resources to bring the divergence down to n shillings.

§ 4. The results set out in the two preceding sections rest upon the assumption that there is only one arrangement of resources which makes the values of marginal social net products everywhere equal—or as nearly equal as, in view of costs of movement, it is to the interest of the national dividend that they should be made. This assumption would be justified if the value of the marginal social net product of resources employed in each several use was always smaller, the greater the volume of resources employed there. There are, however, two sets of conditions in which this is not so. First, the employment of additional resources in the production of a commodity may, after a time, enable improved methods of organisation to be developed. This means that decreasing supply price[1] prevails, in such wise that the marginal (physical) net product of a greater quantity of resources exceeds the marginal (physical) net product of a smaller quantity: and, whenever this happens, it is *possible*, though, of course, it is not *necessary*, that the value of the marginal social net product of several different quantities of resources that might be engaged in producing the commodity will be the same. Secondly, the employment of additional resources in the production of a commodity may, after a time, lead to an increase in the price per unit offered by consumers of any given quantity of it. For their taste for it may be lastingly enhanced—obvious examples are afforded by the taste for music and tobacco— through experience of it. When this happens the value per unit of a larger product will (after an appropriate interval of time) be greater than the value per unit of a smaller product. It follows that, even for commodities whose production is not subject to conditions of decreasing supply price in the sense defined above, there *may* be, though, of course,

[1] For a study of this concept cf. *post*, Chapter XI.

there need not be, several different quantities of invested resources, the values of whose marginal social net products are the same.[1] Hence, the conclusions set out above require to be restated in a modified form. Allowance being made for costs of movement, it is true that the dividend cannot reach the maximum attainable amount *unless* the values of the marginal social net products of resources in all uses are equal. For, if they are not equal, the dividend can always be increased by a transference of resources from the margin of some uses to the margin of others. But, when the values of the marginal social net products in all uses are equal, the dividend *need not* attain an unequivocal maximum. For, if several arrangements are possible, all of which make the values of the marginal social net products equal, each of these arrangements does, indeed, imply what may be called a *relative maximum* for the dividend; but only one of these maxima is the unequivocal, or absolute, maximum. All of the relative maxima are, as it were, the tops of hills higher than the surrounding country, but only one of them is the highest hill-top of all. Furthermore, it is not necessary that all positions of relative maximum should represent larger dividends than all positions which are not maxima. On the contrary, a scheme of distribution approximating to that which yields the absolute maximum, but not itself fulfilling the condition of equal marginal yields, would probably imply a larger dividend than most of the schemes which do fulfil this condition and so constitute relative maxima of a minor character. A point *near* the summit of the highest hill may be higher than any summit except the highest itself.

---

[1] If equality of the values of marginal net products is attained when 1000 units of resources are devoted to the production of a particular thing, and also, *because of decreasing supply price*, when 5000 units are so devoted, the national dividend is necessarily larger under the latter arrangement. If equality is attained with 1000 units and also, *because of reactions upon tastes*, with 5000 units, both economic welfare and the national dividend, from the point of view of the period in which the 5000 units are operating, are necessarily larger under the latter arrangement. But the national dividend, from the point of view of the other period, may be smaller under the 5000 units arrangement. In these circumstances, the definition of p. 54 compels us to conclude that, from an absolute point of view, the dividends under the two arrangements are incommensurable.

§ 5. These considerations show that, even though the values of marginal social net products were everywhere equal or differed only in ways "justified" by the costs of movement, there might still be scope for State action designed to increase the magnitude of the national dividend and augment economic welfare.   Benefit might be secured by a *temporary* bounty (or temporary protection) so arranged as to jerk the industrial system out of its present poise at a position of relative maximum, and induce it to settle down again at the position of absolute maximum—the highest hill-top of all.   This is the analytical basis of the argument for the *temporary* protection, or other encouragement, of infant industries ; and, if the right infants are selected, the right amount of protection accorded, and this protection removed again at the right time, the argument is perfectly valid.   Benefit might also be secured by a *permanent* bounty at a different rate from that contemplated above, so arranged as to force the industrial system from the summit of the hill-top on which it is found to any position, that overtops its present site, on the slope of a higher hill.   The conditions in which bounties are likely to have this effect, rather than that of shifting the economic system to a different position on the hill that it is on already, are somewhat special.   But it can be proved that, in certain states of demand and supply, *some* rates of bounty *must* have this effect.[1]

[1] The shapes of the demand and supply curves and the size of the bounty must be such that, when the demand curve is raised by the bounty, it does not cut the supply curve at any point corresponding to its former point of intersection, but does cut it at a point corresponding to a point of stable equilibrium further to the right than this.   This condition can readily be depicted in a diagram.

CHAPTER IV

§ 1. THE rate of return per unit in money obtained from any
quantity of any kind of productive resource in any use is, in
general, equal to the value of the marginal private net product
of that quantity of that kind of resource there. As between
different occupations and places, therefore, the relation between
rates of return is the same as the relation between values of
marginal private net products; so that equality or inequality
among rates of return is the same thing as equality or inequality among values of marginal private net products. In
this and the four following chapters I shall, for convenience,
sometimes use the term of rate of returns—or, more loosely,
returns—in place of the longer synonym.

§ 2. Anybody who has control of any quantity of any
form of productive resource will try so to distribute it among
various uses that it brings him the largest possible money
receipts. If he thinks that, apart from cost of carriage and
so on, he can get more money by transferring a unit from any
one use to any other, he will do so. It follows that the free
play of self-interest, so far as it is not hampered by ignorance,
tends, in the absence of costs of movement, so to distribute
resources among different uses and places as to render rates
of return everywhere equal. By an easy extension of the
argument it can be shown that, where there *are* costs of
movement, the free play of self-interest, again so far as it is
not hampered by ignorance, tends, not to bring about equality
in rates of return, but to prevent any divergences from equality
in excess of those that, relatively to the fact that there

142

are costs of movement, allow the sum total of returns to attain a maximum.

§ 3. It follows that, if private and social net products everywhere coincide, the free play of self-interest, so far as it is not hampered by ignorance, will tend to bring about such a distribution of resources among different uses and places as will raise the national dividend and, with it, the sum of economic welfare to *a* maximum.[1] The distinctions drawn in the last sections of the preceding chapter show, indeed, that several maxima are possible, so that the one which self-interest tends to bring about need not be the highest maximum attainable. This, however, is a secondary matter. The essential point for our present purpose is that, when marginal private net products and marginal social net products coincide, any obstacles that obstruct the free play of self-interest will, in general, damage the national dividend. In real life, of course, marginal private and marginal social net products frequently do not coincide. In Chapters V.-VIII. this fact will be left out of account: but in later chapters, particularly Chapters IX.-XI., the consequences that follow from it will be fully examined.

---

[1] The conception of the free play of self-interest must, of course, for this purpose, be taken to exclude monopoly action. Cf. *post*, Chapters XIV.-XVII.

CHAPTER V

§ 1. THE purpose of this chapter is to study the way in which the size of the national dividend will be affected by a reduction of the obstacles to the movement of productive resources that are set up by ignorance and costs of movement. It is legitimate for this purpose to ignore differences between marginal social net products and marginal private net products; for, though particular obstacles to movement may prevent equality between the values of marginal private net products in such wise as to promote equality between the values of marginal social net products, there is no reason to suppose that obstacles to movement in general act in this way. It is proper to regard divergences between social and private net products as one factor making for inequality in the values of marginal social net products, and obstacles to movement as a second factor superimposed upon this; so that to weaken the force of either factor may be expected, in general, to promote *pro tanto* the equality that is desired. Assuming this, I shall, for simplicity of diction, in this and the following chapter, speak of marginal net product without any adjective.

§ 2. If the total quantity of productive resources at work be taken as given, it would seem at first sight that a reduction effected without expense in either sort of obstacle must necessarily make the rates of return in different uses and places, that is to say, the values of marginal net products, less unequal, and, consequently, must make the dividend larger. In reality, however, things are not so simple as this. The fact that obstacles to free movement comprise both costs of movement and imperfections of knowledge complicates the situation; for we have to contemplate reductions of costs while knowledge is still imperfect and improvement of knowledge while costs remain.

§ 3. It is plain that, if people think that a larger return can be obtained by sending resources away from A for employment at B, a diminution in costs will cause resources to be sent, which, as a matter of fact, would have been more productive if left where they were. It is thus certainly *possible* that a reduction of costs in actual life may render the values of marginal net products more unequal, and so lessen the national dividend. In the appended footnote, however, it is shown by a technical argument that this is, on the whole, unlikely.[1]

§ 4. There is a different kind of complication when costs of movement remain unchanged but knowledge is improved. This improvement need not lead to an increase in equality

[1] The proof is as follows. Let people's judgment concerning the value of the marginal net product of resources invested at B be correct, but let their estimate of the corresponding value at A differ from fact by a defined quantity k. Let the costs of movement between A and B be equated to an annual sum spread over the period during which the unit of resources that has moved may be expected to find profit in staying in its new place. This annual sum is not necessarily the same in respect of movements from A to B and movements from B to A. Transport, for example, "acts more easily down than up hill or stream [and] . . . the barrier of language acts more strongly from England to Germany than *vice versa*" (Macgregor, *Industrial Combination*, p. 24). For the present purpose, however, we may ignore this complication and represent costs in either direction by an annual sum equal to n. Construct a figure in which positive values are marked off to the right of O and negative values to the left. Mark off OM equal to k; and MQ, MP on either side of M each equal to n. It is then evident that the excess of the value of the marginal net product of resources at B over that at A—let this excess be known as h—is indeterminate and may lie anywhere between a value OQ, which may be either positive or negative, and a value OP which may also be either positive or negative. A diminution in the value of n is represented by movements on the part of the two points P and Q towards M. So long as the values

$$\overset{\text{M}}{\underset{\dot{P} \quad \cdot \quad \dot{Q} \quad \dot{O}}{}}$$

$$\overset{\text{M}}{\underset{\dot{P} \qquad \dot{O} \quad \dot{Q}}{}}$$

of k and n are such that P and Q lie on opposite sides of O, it is obvious that these movements make impossible the largest positive and the largest negative values of h that were possible before, and have no other effect. When, however, P and Q lie on the same side of O—in which case, of course, all possible values of h are of the same sign—they make impossible both the largest values of h that were possible before and also the smallest values. This double change seems equally likely to increase or to diminish the value of h. Hence, if it

among the values of marginal net products. For suppose the conditions to be such that, if perfect knowledge prevailed, the value of the marginal net product of resources at one point A would exceed the corresponding value at another point B by one shilling, and that the cost of moving a unit of resources from B to A would just balance this advantage. But, in fact, let us further suppose, knowledge is imperfect; people believe the value of the marginal net product at A to be higher than it really is; they therefore send more resources from B to A than they would do if better informed; and, therefore, the excess of the value of the marginal net product at A over that at B stands at less than n shillings. In these circumstances the growth of a more correct judgment would evidently *increase* the degree of inequality prevailing between the values of the marginal net products of resources at A and B. At the same time, however, it would evidently also increase the size of the national dividend. A reduction effected without expense in the obstacles set up by ignorance will thus always increase the national dividend; though it will not always do it by promoting equality among the values of marginal net products.

§ 5. At this point, however, we are brought up against a serious difficulty. Hitherto the total quantity of resources at work has been taken as given. In fact, however, the elimination or reduction of obstacles to the movement of productive resources may modify the quantity of these resources that come into action. We have, therefore, to ask whether the quantity of resources at work will ever be reduced, as a consequence of obstacles being removed, in such a way that the national dividend is made smaller and not larger than

---

were the fact that the points P and Q always lay on the same side of O, we could not infer that diminutions of the value of n would be likely to affect the value of h either way. In fact, however, it must often happen that P and Q lie on opposite sides of O. When account is taken of these cases as well as of the others, we can infer that, over the mass of many cases, diminutions in the value of n are likely to reduce the value of h. In other words, diminutions in the costs of movement are likely, in general, to make the values of the marginal net products of resources at A and B less unequal. Furthermore, it is evident that, when the distances MP and MQ are given, the probability that P and Q will both lie on the same side of O and, therefore, the probability that a diminution in the distances MP and MQ will be associated with an increase in the value of h, is smaller the smaller is the value of k.

before. That this result may be possible is suggested by an argument of Cournot's, in which he shows that, when "communication is opened between two markets, previously separated by a barrier, the total quantity produced of any commodity, which now begins to be exported from one market and imported to the other, will not necessarily be increased."[1] The increase in the output of the (hitherto) cheaper market will not, in some conditions, be as large as the decrease in that of the (hitherto) dearer market. By analogy it would seem that the opening up of communication between occupations and places hitherto separate might cause the aggregate quantity of labour at work, or of capital created, to be reduced; and the reduction might, in some circumstances, suffice to cause a reduction in the size of the national dividend in spite of the fact that part of the labour or capital still left would be operating under more favourable conditions than before. We must, I think, admit that, as a result of the opening up of communication, the amount of labour at work or of capital created may be reduced. I have difficulty, however, in imagining conditions in which the national dividend, as I have conceived it, could be diminished. For why should anybody choose more leisure than before unless the new conditions had given him a bigger aggregate income from work than before; and why should any one choose to save less than before unless the new conditions had given him a bigger aggregate income from savings than before? It may be that a full analysis would reveal possibilities in this matter that I have failed to see; but the possibilities are certainly remote. There can be no doubt that, in a broad general way, the conclusions reached in the preceding sections on the assumption that the quantity of resources at work is given are also valid when that assumption is removed.

§ 6. It remains to clear up an important issue. This has to do with the effect of State bounties designed to lessen ignorance or to reduce the costs of movement.[2] A cheapening of knowledge and movement to individuals, brought about

---

[1] Cf. Cournot, *Mathematical Theory of Wealth*, ch. xi., and Edgeworth, "Theory of International Values," *Economic Journal*, 1894, p. 625.

[2] Cf. *post*, Part III. Ch. IX. §§ 11-14.

by the transference of a part of the cost of these things to
the State, is quite a different thing and works quite differently
from a cheapening brought about by a real fall in cost. The
two sorts of cheapening have the same tendency to promote—
apart from the exceptional cases noticed above—increased
equality among the values of marginal net products at different
points.   But, when the cheapening is due to transference, the
resultant increase of equality is an increase beyond what,
relatively to existing conditions, is most advantageous. *Prima
facie* this sort of cheapening, though it will generally make
the values of marginal net products more equal, is likely to
injure the national dividend.[1]

---

[1] To obviate misunderstanding two modifying considerations should be
added.   First, the presumption just established against the grant of a bounty
to the industry of promoting mobility is merely a special case of the general
presumption against the grant of a bounty to any industry.   It may,
therefore, be overthrown if there is special reason to believe that, in the
absence of a bounty, investment in the industry in question would not be
carried so far as is desirable.   Secondly, when the State takes over the work
of providing either information or the means of movement, and elects for
any reason to sell the result of its efforts either for nothing or below cost
price, we have, in general, to do, not merely with the grant of a bounty
on these things, but at the same time with a real cheapening due to the
introduction of large-scale methods.   Even, therefore, though the bounty
element in the new arrangement were proved to be injurious, it might still
happen that that arrangement as a whole was beneficial.

CHAPTER VI

§ 1. IN the present chapter I shall study in some detail the obstructive influence of ignorance. A flowing stream of resources is continually coming into being and struggling, so far as unavoidable costs of movement allow of this, to distribute itself away from points of relatively low returns towards points of relatively high returns. Success in this struggle is interfered with by imperfect knowledge on the part of those in whose hands the power to direct the various branches of the stream resides. To obtain an idea of the scale of the damage which results from this cause, it is desirable to study briefly certain aspects of modern business finance.

§ 2. First, it must be observed that the returns, which are important as a guide to the right distribution of resources, are those that are accruing in different uses from resources turned into them at each successive moment. The quotient obtained by dividing the net income of a business by the sum of all the money investment made in it in the past would, in a stationary state, afford a true measure of the returns to current investment there. But in actual conditions the measure thus obtained will often be hopelessly misleading. For example, a man may have put £100,000 into a factory for making some particular thing, and the factory may have been destroyed by fire or may have become worthless through obsolescence. An investment of £10,000 now might have just yielded him a return of £2000, or 20 per cent on the new investment, but the return on the total investment will appear as £2000 on £110,000, or less than 2 per cent. This sort of difficulty could hardly fail to obscure relevant facts however excellently business accounts were drawn up and however fully they were published.

§ 3. The next thing that calls for comment is the general character of the accounts as they actually are. In businesses conducted by private firms no statement of profits is made public. In businesses conducted by joint stock companies a certain amount of publicity is enforced by law. But stock-watering and other devices are often used to conceal from outsiders the rate of return that is obtained on the capital actually invested, so that, even when this would afford a reasonable guide to the return on current investment, and, therefore, to future prospects, the way is blocked to anybody other than a specialist. The difficulty is still further enhanced by the fact that the prospects which it is necessary to forecast refer, not to immediate returns only, but to returns spread over a considerable period. It is evident that, as regards these returns, even correct knowledge of the immediate past gives but imperfect guidance. In view of these facts, it might seem that, in existing conditions, ignorance will almost entirely inhibit the tendency towards equality among the returns to resources flowing at any time into different uses. Such a view, however, would be unduly pessimistic. "Though it may be difficult," Marshall writes, "to read the lessons of an individual trader's experience, those of a whole trade can never be completely hidden, and cannot be hidden at all for long. Although one cannot tell whether the tide is rising or falling by merely watching half-a-dozen waves breaking on the seashore, yet a very little patience settles the question ; and there is a general agreement among business men that the average rate of profits in a trade cannot rise or fall much without general attention being attracted to the change before long. And though it may sometimes be a more difficult task for a business man than for a skilled labourer to find out whether he could improve his prospects by changing his trade, yet the business man has great opportunities for discovering whatever can be found out about the present and future of other trades ; and, if he should wish to change his trade, he will generally be able to do so more easily than the skilled workman could." [1] In short, though individual firms may successfully conceal their position, industries as wholes can hardly do so. Ignorance as to the comparative returns to be got by using resources to start new businesses in different occupations may be very great among the general public, but it is probably much less important than it appears to be at first sight among those persons by whose agency the flow of resources is, in the main, directed. Nevertheless, there is clearly room for improvement in the matter of business publicity,[2] and, if such improvement were made, ignorance would be lessened, equality in the values of marginal net products promoted, and the size of the national dividend consequently increased.

§ 4. I turn next to the relation between ignorance and the quality of the persons by whom the employment of resources is controlled. In a primitive community investment is carried on almost exclusively by entrepreneurs actually engaged in the various industries and devoting to the conduct of them resources belonging to themselves. Their quality alone is relevant to our problem; and it is obvious that the range of error in the forecasts that are made is likely to be larger or smaller according as able men are or are not content to adopt business as a career. In the modern world a very large part of the investment made in industry still comes from the people actually engaged in particular businesses, who reinvest their profits in them or obtain funds from partners or friends of their own who are fully conversant with all relevant circumstances. It has been suggested that methods of this sort, lying outside the organisation of the money market proper, are employed to direct more than half the total stream of new home investment.[3] In addition, however, to these methods, the modern world also has resort to others. A very important part of industry is financed from resources belonging to a great number of other people besides those who actually manage businesses. These other people include, on the one

[1] *Principles of Economics*, p. 608.
[2] Cf. Layton, *Capital and Labour*, ch. iv.
[3] Lavington, *The English Capital Market*, p. 281.

hand, professional financiers, company promoters or promoting syndicates, and, on the other hand, moneyed people among the general public, whom these promoters induce to invest in their ventures. " The promoter's special province," writes Professor Mitchell, " is to find and bring to the attention of investors new opportunities for making money, new natural resources to be exploited, new processes to be developed, new products to be manufactured, new organisations of existing business enterprises to be arranged, etc. But the promoter is seldom more than an explorer who points out the way for fresh advances of the army of industry. . . . There are always being launched more schemes than can be financed with the available funds. In rejecting some and accepting others of these schemes, the men of money are taking a very influential, though not a very conspicuous, part in determining how labour shall be employed, what products shall be used, and what localities built up." [1] In modern industry, then, the direction of a large part of the community's investment is in the joint control of professional financiers interested in company promotion and of the moneyed part of the general public. What is to be said about the capacity and business judgment of this complex directing agency ?

§ 5. The comparative capacity for detecting good new openings for enterprise of the professional financier and of the ordinary business man—the entrepreneur investor of former days—is not difficult to determine. First, the professional financier is a specialist in this particular work, whereas to the ordinary business man an opportunity for undertaking it would come, if at all, only at rare intervals. Clearly the specialist is likely to make better forecasts than the general practitioner. Secondly, the international character which the development of the means of communication has in recent times given to many industries has made the advantage enjoyed by the specialist much greater than it used to be when a knowledge of *local* conditions, such as an intelligent business man would naturally possess, afforded a sufficient basis for a good forecast. Lastly, the fact of specialisation gives freer play to the selective agency of bankruptcy, in eliminating persons who undertake

[1] Mitchell, *Business Cycles*, pp. 34-5.

to choose openings for new enterprises and cannot choose well. When the functions of financier and manufacturer are rolled together in one man, the man may flourish through his manufacturing skill—good business tactics—despite of incompetent business strategy. When the two functions are separated, anybody who undertakes the one in which he is incompetent relatively to other people is apt to lose his money and be driven from the field. Furthermore, the efficiency of this natural selection is augmented by the fact that a professional financier undertakes a great number of transactions, and that, therefore, the element of chance plays a small part, and the element of efficiency a large part, in the result. Hence there can be no doubt that the advent into any industry of professional financiers means the advent of persons better able than those immediately concerned in the industry to forecast future conditions. Against this has to be set the fact that the great bulk of those members of the general public, who ultimately supply the funds for the enterprises that professional financiers have organised, are much less capable than ordinary business men of forecasting future conditions. If promoters always looked for the openings most profitable on the whole, as distinguished from those that can be so manipulated as to become most profitable to themselves, this ignorance on the part of people who follow their lead would not, perhaps, greatly matter. Unfortunately, however, it is often to the interest, and it is usually in the power, of the professionals, by spreading false information and in other ways, deliberately to pervert the forecasts of their untutored colleagues. It is this fact that makes the net effect of the modern system upon the distribution of the community's investments among openings of varying merit somewhat doubtful. The prospect of advantage is probably increased when, as in Germany before the war, the flotation of new companies on the basis of shares of extremely low nominal value is forbidden by law; for then a certain number of the poorer and, perhaps, more ignorant persons, who might be easily tricked, are driven away.[1] Again, any legislative enactment,

---

[1] In Germany shares were, in no case, permitted of a lower denomination than £10, and they were not usually permitted of a lower denomination than

capable of being enforced, that checks the fraudulent exploitation of incompetent investors by dishonest professionals tends *pro tanto* to diminish the range of error to which the general mass of operative forecasts made in the community is liable. "The public regulation of the prospectuses of new companies, legislation supported by efficient administration against fraudulent promotion, more rigid requirements on the part of the stock exchanges regarding the securities admitted to official lists, and more efficient agencies for giving information to investors fall under this head."[1]

§ 6. A more fundamental remedy is introduced when the work of promotion itself is kept in the hands of bankers—whose reputation, of course, depends upon the *permanent* success of the business undertakings that they have founded. This is done in Germany. Big German banks retain a staff of technical experts to investigate and report upon any industrial ventures that may be proposed, decide, after elaborate inquiries, which ventures to promote and, in short, constitute themselves a financial general staff to industry. The contrast with the English system is well pointed out in the following passage : "The English joint stock companies (*i.e.* the banks), conforming to the theory, have abstained in a *direct* way from flotations and the underwriting business, as well as from bourse speculation. But this very fact causes another great evil, namely, that the banks have never shown any interest in the newly founded companies or in the securities issued by these companies, while it is a distinct advantage of the German system that the German banks, even if only in the interest of their own issue credit, have been keeping a continuous watch over the development of the companies which they founded."[2] No doubt, this practice of banks acting as promoters involves great risks and absolutely requires that their capital resources shall be, as they are in Germany,[3] very much larger relatively to

---

£50. (Cf. Schuster, *The Principles of German Civil Law*, p. 44.) In 1924 the minimum denomination was reduced to £1 (20 marks), and the usual denomination to £5 (100 marks).

[1] Cf. Mitchell, *Business Cycles*, p. 585.

[2] Riesser, *The German Great Banks*, p. 555.

[3] The general practice of the English banks is to supply "banking facilities," that is to say advances, whether by discount of bills or otherwise,

their liabilities than is usual among English banks; for otherwise losses sustained in the promotion business, or even the temporary "solidification" of funds locked up in this business, might render the banks unable to meet their obligations to their depositors. Moreover, it must be remembered that the position of this country as the banking centre of the world, and, until recently, the principal free market for gold, would make the locking up of bank resources in long ventures more dangerous than in other countries. I make no suggestion, therefore, that the general policy hitherto pursued by British banks has been other than well advised. Nevertheless, there can be no doubt that, when conditions are such as to allow banks safely to undertake the work of promotion, a real advantage results. They are more likely than are certain types of private financiers to look out for openings which really are sound, as distinguished from openings which can be made for a short time to appear sound. It is, indeed, possible that, in some circumstances, where the rival interests of different nationalities are affected, powerful banking institutions operating along these lines may be made the instruments of a *political* movement, and may allow their conduct to be swayed by other than economic considerations. But this aspect of the matter is unsuited for discussion here.

§ 7. It is not, however, only by acting as promoting agents that bankers can help to direct resources into

---

that have a short currency only, and not "financial facilities," *i.e.* advances with a long currency. It is sometimes claimed that this practice handicaps those British industries in which opportunities may arise for the profitable expansion of plant at short notice,—to make possible, for example, their acceptance of some large order which might throw open for them the entry into some new market; for the raising of fresh capital by an issue of shares or debentures necessarily takes time. It is also sometimes claimed that our banking practice makes it difficult for British traders to make their way in those foreign markets where purchasers are accustomed to expect very long credits. It was with a view to meeting these complaints that Lord Farringdon's Committee on Financial Facilities (1916) recommended that an institution should be established with a large capital, not undertaking ordinary deposit banking, but prepared to provide financial facilities both for the development of industries at home and, where necessary, for the conduct of foreign trade. This recommendation was acted upon, and an institution of the kind contemplated—the British Trade Corporation—was granted a Charter in April 1917.

productive channels. It is true that ordinary bankers in their loans to traders, whether made directly or through bill-brokers, are concerned only with the safety of the debt. The judgment that they make about the capacity of would-be borrowers to meet their obligations involves, when acceptable security is offered, no judgment as to the comparative profitableness of the undertakings into which different would-be borrowers will put the money they succeed in raising. But, when bankers are required to make loans to persons who are not in a position to offer full banking security, they are compelled to assume a more important rôle. They cannot lend on a mere promise to pay, but are bound, in their own interest, to make elaborate inquiry both as to the trustworthiness of the borrower and also as to the purpose to which he proposes to devote the proceeds of the loan. Speaking of the peasant borrowers of India, Sir Theodore Morison writes : " It is useless, however amiable, to believe that the ryot is only thirsting for capital in order to invest it at once in the improvement and development of his estate." [1] Again, in the Report on the working of the Co-operative Credit Societies Act in Burma, issued in 1907, it is urged that "in Burma borrowing is mostly due to habit and want of forethought, and not to necessity ; that the capital really required to finance cultivation (apart from luxury) is very much less than what is generally supposed, and that mere provision of cheap money, through co-operative societies or otherwise, tends, owing to the existing state of public feeling, to induce waste of income rather than thrift ; and, lastly, that in Burma very special care will be necessary to see that the societies are managed in such a way that the prevention of waste and inculcation of thrift are effectively impressed on the members' minds." [2] The recognised machinery for exercising this type of control and supervision is provided by People's Banks, such as the Raiffeisen Banks in Germany and their Italian counterparts. These banks evoke the necessary knowledge by a double process. First, the persons brought together as members

---

[1] *The Industrial Organisation of an Indian Province*, p. 110.
[2] Report, p. 15.

of the Bank, and, therefore, as potential borrowers, are gathered from a small area only, in such wise that the controlling committee can easily obtain intimate personal information concerning all of them. Only those persons are allowed to become members, of whose probity and general good character the committee have satisfied themselves. In some banks—in the Italian Banchi Popolari, for instance— the committee draw up, *ab initio* and independently of any particular application, a list of the sums which, in their opinion, may safely be lent to the various members.[1] This list is afterwards used as a basis for loans, just as the lists of the communal *bureaux de bienfaisance* in France are used as a basis for the grant of Poor Relief. Secondly, the grant of a loan is often made conditional on its being employed for a specified purpose, and subject to certain rights of supervision reserved for the lender. Thus, whereas in most land-banks (where material security is taken) " the proceeds of mortgages may be used as the borrower pleases, *e.g.* in paying off loans, in portioning younger sons, etc.," in the Raiffeisen Banks careful inquiry is undertaken into the purpose for which the loan is required, and provision is made for its recall should the borrower divert it from that purpose.[2] The general tendency of this arrangement is to lessen the number of investments made under the impulse of ignorance in undertakings that yield an abnormally low return, and so indirectly to augment the national dividend.

[1] Cf. Wolff, *People's Banks*, p. 154.
[2] For an account of Raiffeisen and kindred Banks, cf. Fay, *Co-operation at Home and Abroad*, Part I.

CHAPTER VII

HINDRANCES TO EQUALITY OF RETURNS DUE TO IMPERFECT
DIVISIBILITY OF THE UNITS IN TERMS OF WHICH
TRANSACTIONS ARE CONDUCTED

§ 1. ALONGSIDE of imperfect knowledge, as discussed in the preceding chapter, stands the cost of movement. Some part of this cost is, of course, represented by the payments that have to be made to various agents in the capital market, promoters, financing syndicates, investment trusts, solicitors, bankers, and others, who, in varying degrees according to the nature of the investment concerned, help in the work of transporting capital from its places of origin to its places of employment.[1] But there is also a less obvious and more peculiar part of the cost of movement, of which some more detailed study is desirable. A pure mathematical treatment of economic problems always assumes that, when there is opportunity anywhere for the profitable employment of given quantities of the several factors of production, each factor can be received there in units that are indefinitely small and are capable of being separated completely from units of any other factor. In so far as this assumption is not warranted, it is readily seen that the tendency to equality of returns will be imperfectly realised. For, on the one hand, if an enterprise is only financed, in respect of any one factor, by means of units, each of which has the value of £1000, it may well be that, though the transference of £1000 worth of the factor to or from elsewhere could not, when equilibrium is established, bring about an increased aggregate return, the transference

---

[1] For an excellent account of these agencies cf. Lavington, *The English Capital Market*, ch. xviii.

of a sum less than £1000 could, if it were permitted, do this. In short, when the units, in terms of which transactions are made, are not indefinitely small, the tendency to equality of returns in all uses degrades into a tendency to limitation of inequality—a limitation the extent of which is diminished with every increase in the size of the units. On the other hand, if an enterprise is only financed, in respect of any two factors, by means of units which combine factor A and factor B in a definite proportion, it may well be that, though the transference of one of these complex combined units to or from elsewhere could not, when equilibrium is established, bring about an increased aggregate return, the transference in isolation of some quantity of either of the two factors might have this effect. Hence, when the units, in terms of which transactions are made, are compounded of fixed proportions of two or more factors, the tendency to equality of returns in all uses again degrades into a tendency to limitation of inequality. It follows that largeness and complexity in the units in terms of which transactions are made act in the same way as costs of movement. In general they obstruct the tendency of self-interest to make the returns obtainable by each several factor of production equal in all uses.

§ 2. At one time it may have been true that the units in which capital transactions were made were noticeably large. Of recent years, however, the size of those units has been greatly reduced in two ways. Of these one is obvious, the other relatively obscure. The obvious way is the diminution in the value of individual deposits which banks will accept—the Savings Bank, for example, allows pennies to be deposited separately—and a similar, though less extensive, diminution in the value of the individual shares issued by companies.[1] The more obscure way depends upon the fact that a unit of capital is a two-dimensional entity. A man can reduce the quantity of capital which he provides, not only by altering the number of pounds that he lends over a defined time, but also by altering the

---

[1] It must be remembered, as was indicated in § 5 of the preceding chapter, that this tendency is not without incidental disadvantages.

time over which he lends a defined number of pounds.
Reduction in the time-extension of the units in which capital
is borrowed is of great importance in practice, because,
whereas most enterprises require funds for a long period,
many lenders are only willing to cut themselves off in-
exorably from their resources for a short period. There
have been evolved in the modern world two devices through
which the required reduction in time-extension has been
effected. The first of these is the actual acceptance of loans
for short terms by entrepreneurs, in dependence partly on the
elasticity of the wants of their enterprise, and partly on the
chance of opportunities for reborrowing elsewhere. The
second is the organisation of the Stock Exchange, by resort
to which the funded debts of enterprises can be transferred,
—a device which is, from the lender's point of view, the
next stage to permission to recall his loan from the enterprise
itself. These two devices have fairly distinct spheres. To
rely too largely on short loans is felt to be dangerous. " In
proportion as enterprises depend upon short-time credits
rather than upon paid-up capital or permanent loans
are they in danger of failure in times of stress " [1]—through
inability to renew the credits. There has, therefore, grown
up a rough general understanding that short-time paper
is an unsuitable means of raising money for things like new
equipment, from which the turn-over is necessarily slow ; it
should be used only to finance expenditure on materials
and labour employed in making commodities that are likely
to be sold before the maturity of the paper.[2] This distinction
between the two devices is not, however, important for the
present purpose. Both of the devices are essentially similar,
for both depend on the general probability that the willingness of the aggregate community to lend will be less variable
than that of a representative individual. In consequence of
this, on the one hand, a company, by discounting bills through
banks, borrows part of its capital for a series of short terms
from different people, thus enabling any one of them to lend
for a few months only. On the other hand, a man, who makes

---

[1] Burton, *Financial Crisis*, p. 263.
[2] Cf. Meade, *Corporation Finance*, p. 231.

savings for a "treat" or to meet an accident, instead of storing what he expects to want, invests it in long-time securities, in reliance on the organisation of the Stock Exchange to enable him to realise his capital at need. These devices are not perfect. In times of stress the discounting of new bills may prove very difficult and costly, and the realisation of capital by the sale of shares may not be possible except at heavy loss. They have availed, however, to bring about a large and important reduction in the time-extension of the units in terms of which capital transactions are conducted. As regards labour transactions, it is plain enough that the units are fairly small. Hence, in the modern world, apart from certain special problems of land transfer that cannot conveniently be discussed here, the only department in which largeness in the units of transactions obstructs the tendency of self-interest to bring about equality of returns in different occupations would seem to be that of employing power. The average wielder of employing power cannot be regarded as indefinitely small, as compared with the aggregate quantity of employing power that is in action in any use. This fact brings it about that the returns to employing power in different uses are checked from approaching very closely towards equality; and, hence, that the national dividend is rendered smaller than it would be if employing power were more fully divisible.

§ 3. Let us next consider complexity, or compound character, in the units in terms of which transactions are made. Here, as before, it is capital which calls for the greatest amount of discussion. For capital, as ordinarily conceived in business, is not a pure elementary factor of production. In the concrete, of course, it appears in the form either of plant and equipment or of a system of connections called goodwill. But this concrete capital is always made up of a combination, in varying proportions, of two factors, namely, waiting and uncertainty-bearing.[1] Under primitive

---

[1] The nature of the service of "waiting" has been much misunderstood. Sometimes it has been supposed to consist in the provision of money, sometimes in the provision of time, and, on both suppositions, it has been argued that no contribution whatever is made by it to the dividend. Neither supposition is correct. "Waiting" simply means postponing consumption which a person

conditions, if an enterprise was undertaken by more than one person, it was practically necessary for *each* of the several contributors to furnish waiting and uncertainty-bearing in the proportions in which these factors were required in the aggregate. They would, in effect, pool their capital, taking upon each £ lent an equal measure of uncertainty-bearing. They would be partners, or, if we wish to suppose them in the enjoyment of limited liability, joint shareholders in a company whose capital consisted entirely of ordinary shares. In modern times, however, this is no longer necessary. An enterprise that requires, say, x units of waiting *plus* y units of uncertainty-bearing, need no longer obtain from each subscriber of one unit of waiting $\frac{y}{x}$ units of uncertainty-bearing also. By the device of guarantees its demand can be separated into two streams, in such wise that waiting alone is drawn from one set of people and uncertainty-bearing alone from another set. Guarantees may assume a great variety of forms. They are given to industrialists by insurance companies, which undertake, for a consideration, that the industrialists' earnings shall be unaffected by fire or accident. They are given by Exchange Banks, such as those which, in India before 1893, bought importers' and exporters' bills at the time of their bargain, and so, for a

---

has power to enjoy immediately, thus allowing resources, which might have been destroyed, to assume the form of productive instruments and to act as "harness, by which natural powers are guided so as to assist mankind in his efforts" (Flux, *Principles of Economics*, p. 89). The unit of "waiting" is, therefore, the use of a given quantity of resources—for example, labour or machinery—for a given time. Thus, to take Professor Carver's example, if a manufacturer buys one ton of coal a day on each day of the year and buys each day's supply one day ahead, the waiting he supplies during that year is one ton of coal for one year—a year-ton of coal (*Distribution of Wealth*, p. 253). In more general terms, we may say that the unit of waiting is a year-value-unit, or, in the simpler, if less accurate, language of Dr. Cassel, a year-pound. The graver difficulties involved in the conception of uncertainty-bearing are discussed in Appendix I. A caution may be added against the common view that the amount of capital accumulated in any year is necessarily equal to the amount of "savings" made in it. This is not so even when savings are interpreted to mean net savings, thus eliminating the savings of one man that are lent to increase the consumption of another, and when temporary accumulations of *unused* claims upon services in the form of bank-money are ignored ; for many savings which are meant to become capital in fact fail of their purpose through misdirection into wasteful uses.

price, insured them against loss (or gain) from any fluctuations in the exchange which might occur in the interval between the bargain and the realisation of the bills. Where industrialists have to do with staple goods, for which grading permits the establishment of future markets, they are given, for the more general risks of business, by speculators. For a miller or cotton merchant, undertaking an order to supply flour or cotton goods, can buy the speculator's promise to provide him with his raw material in the future for a stipulated sum, irrespective of the price which may then prevail in the market. Like guarantees are given to a banker preparing to discount a bill for an industrial enterprise, when a second banker, or a bill-broker, or some independent person, consents to accept, or endorse, the bill, or, as is usual with "cash credits" in Scotland, to stand surety for the original borrower.[1] They are given to a Central Bank, when a People's Bank, working, either on unlimited liability or with a subscribed capital of guarantee, in effect borrows money on behalf of its local clients.[2] They are given finally to a banker or other lender when a borrower obtains a loan from him by a deposit of "collateral" security. By far the most effective form of security consists in government scrip and the share certificates of industrial enterprises. For the deposit of these, unlike the deposit of chattel security, involves no present loss to the depositor, while their ultimate assumption, unlike the foreclosure of a mortgage, threatens no difficulty to the person in whose favour the deposit has

[1] The essence of the guarantee given by the acceptor's signature is the same whether the bill is drawn in respect of goods received, or is an accommodation bill endorsed by an accepting-house, which lends its name for a consideration. The variety of accommodation bills known as "pig-on-bacon," where the acceptor is a branch of the drawing house under an *alias*, is, of course, different, because these bills, in effect, bear only one name ; and the same thing is substantially true when the fortunes of the endorsing house and the original borrower are so closely interwoven that the failure of the one would almost certainly involve the failure of the other.

[2] The controversy between the advocates of limited and unlimited liability has sometimes been keen. In the ordinary banks and in the Schulze-Delitzsch People's Banks limited liability is the universal rule. On the other hand, in the People's Banks of Italy and originally, before their absorption by the Imperial Federation, in the Raiffeisen Banks of Germany (except that the law insists on some *small* shares) the method of unlimited liability was adopted, for the reason that the poor people, for whom the banks were designed, would find difficulty in becoming shareholders to any substantial extent.

been made. Furthermore, the "continuous market" provided for securities by the Stock Exchanges of the world safeguards the holders of them against the danger of slumps in value so sudden and large as those to which persons holding, as collateral, the title-deeds of parcels of real estate are liable.[1] In recent times, partly in consequence of the supersession of partnerships by joint stock companies,[2] the proportion of national wealth represented by stocks and shares, and, therefore, available as collateral security, has enormously increased. According to Schmoller's estimate of a few years before the war, whereas 100 years ago only a very small proportion of any country's wealth was in this form, to-day in Germany 17 per cent—Riesser says 33 per cent—and in England 40 per cent, of it is covered by paper counterparts.[3] According to Mr. Watkins's investigations, 77 per cent of the capital value owned by residents in the United Kingdom, on which estate duty was levied in 1902–3, was "personalty," and, out of personalty, 70 per cent was paper property.[4] As a natural consequence the area over which the device of guarantees can be employed, and, therefore, the segregation of waiting from uncertainty-bearing brought about, has been greatly extended.

§ 4. This device is not, however, the only method by which modern ingenuity has broken up the complex unit of capital into its component parts. It enables waiting to be separated from uncertainty-bearing. But uncertainty-bearing is itself not a single simple thing. To expose a £ to an even chance of becoming 21s. or 19s. is a different thing from exposing it to an even chance of becoming 39s. 10d. or 2d. There are, in short, a great number of different schemes of uncertainty, which different people are ready to shoulder. Over against these there are a great number of different schemes of uncertainty which the undertaking of various business enterprises involves. It is evident that what is offered can be adjusted to what is wanted more satisfactorily when any given demand of industry can be

---

[1] Cf. Brace, *The Value of Organized Speculation*, p. 142.
[2] Cf. Fisher, *The Rate of Interest*, p. 208.
[3] Quoted by Watkins, *The Growth of Large Fortunes*, p. 42.
[4] *Ibid.* pp. 48-9.

met by combining together a number of different schemes that individually do not fit with it. This can now be done. When enterprises, for which capital had to be provided by several people, were worked on the partnership plan, all those concerned submitted the resources invested by them to the same scheme of uncertainty. Consequently, unless a sufficient number of people could be found ready to undertake that particular scheme of uncertainty, profitable enterprises were liable to be hung up. In the modern world this difficulty has been, in great part, overcome by the device, which joint stock companies now invariably adopt, of raising capital by means of different grades of security. Instead of an arrangement, under which every pound invested in an enterprise is submitted to the same scheme of uncertainty, we have systems of capitalisation combining debentures, cumulative preference shares, non-cumulative preference shares, ordinary shares and, sometimes, further special sub-varieties. Each of these classes of security represents a different scheme, or sort, of uncertainty-bearing. This specialisation of shares into a number of different classes has the same kind of effect in facilitating the distribution of resources in the way most advantageous to the national dividend as the simpler specialisation into two grades, one involving some uncertainty and the other involving none.

§ 5. There is yet one more form of specialisation. Hitherto we have tacitly assumed that a given type of holding in a company will always remain what it was when it was first taken up. In fact, however, this is not so : for, as a company becomes established, holdings, that at first involved much uncertainty-bearing, often cease to do so. The modern system of industrial finance enables adjustment to be made to this fact, so that shares of companies are, in general, held by one set of people while the companies are new, and by a different set of people when they become established. Thus, when an important " proposition " is floated, the funds are provided in the first instance by a contributing syndicate—or are guaranteed by an underwriting syndicate—consisting of persons who are willing to risk large losses in the hope of large gains, but are not prepared to lock up their capital for long. The syndicate in its early stages may succeed in disposing of many shares to speculators on margins and others, who are similarly willing to provide uncertainty-bearing but not waiting;[1] and these, in turn, after a short "flutter," may sell again to others like unto themselves. At a later stage, when trial has shown what the concern is really like, and so has greatly reduced the element of uncertainty-bearing involved in taking up its shares, the "investing public," those who are anxious to furnish waiting without much alloy, come into the field and purchase the shares. In this way providers of uncertainty-bearing and providers of waiting are both afforded an opportunity of playing the parts for which they are respectively fitted.

§ 6. The broad result of these modern developments has been to break up into simple and convenient parts the compound units in terms of which it was formerly necessary for capital transactions to be conducted. In transactions affecting labour and land—apart from the fact, to be examined in Part III., that the family must sometimes be taken as the unit of migration—there has never been any great complexity in the units. In the field of "enterprise" complexity still rules, in so far as employing power can only find an engagement if it brings with it a certain amount of capital. But the advent of salaried managers, working on behalf of joint stock companies, has done much to break down the complex unit here also. In general, therefore, we may conclude that, in the modern world, complexity in the structure of the units in which transactions are conducted is not an important hindrance to adjustments making for equality of returns in different occupations.

---

[1] For details cf. Meade, *Corporation Finance*, pp. 153-7.

CHAPTER VIII

HINDRANCES TO EQUALITY OF RETURNS DUE TO RELATIVE VARIATIONS OF DEMAND IN DIFFERENT OCCUPATIONS AND PLACES

§ 1. WE have now to introduce a new conception, that of the relative variations of demand in different parts of the industrial field. If the amount of any sort of productive resource demanded at a given price at all points collectively is constant, and the amounts demanded at the several points individually are variable, the relative variation of demand between two periods, say, between two successive years, may be measured by the sum of the excesses of the amounts demanded in the second year, at those points where there are excesses, over the amounts demanded in the previous year at the same points. If the demand for the productive resource at all points collectively is not constant, this variation may be measured, either by the sum of the excesses of the amounts demanded in the second year over the amounts demanded in the previous year at the same points, or by the sum of the deficiencies of the amounts so demanded over the corresponding amounts of the previous year, *according as the one or the other of these sums is the smaller.*

§ 2. On the basis of this description, it can readily be shown that the influence of impediments to movement, in causing departures from equality of returns, is, in general, greater, the greater are the relative variations of demand in the sense just explained. For let attention be concentrated upon those impediments, which are not adequate to prevent returns from being equalised in " the long run," but suffice to prevent the movements required to equalise them immediately.

If the various parts of the industrial field are fluctuating relatively to one another, impediments of this order will keep returns *always* unequal. Mill's illustration from wave movements on the ocean is wholly apposite. Under the influence of gravity, there is a constant tendency to equality of level in all parts ; but, since, after any disturbance, this tendency takes time to assert itself, and since, before the necessary time has elapsed, some fresh disturbance is always introduced, equality of level does not in fact ever occur. It is evident that the average amount of inequality of level depends in part on the magnitude of these disturbances. It is, similarly, evident that the average degree of inequality of returns depends in part, in respect of any system of impediments to movement, upon the size of the relative variations which the demands for productive resources at different points in the industrial field undergo. It is the task of the present chapter to distinguish the principal influences upon which the magnitude of these relative variations in different circumstances depends.

§ 3. First, it is plain, in so far as the demands for the services of productive resources in different occupations and places are affected by independent causes, anything that promotes variations in any particular occupation or place is likely to enhance the relative variations of demand as a whole. Thus all the factors affecting particular industries, which we shall be studying for a different purpose in Chapter XX. of Part III., are also relevant here.

§ 4. Secondly, when the demands for a commodity that is being produced in several centres fluctuate as between the centres, anything that prevents variations of demand for the commodity from being reflected in variations of demand for productive resources lessens the relative variations of demand for these resources. The practice followed by some firms of giving out work on commission in times of over-pressure to other firms in the same industry that are temporarily slack has this effect. When the firms engaged in an industry combine into a single concern, this device can, of course, be carried further. Orders, at whatever point they originate, can be spread among the members of the combination in such wise that there are no relative variations in the several demands for resources to meet these orders.

§ 5. Thirdly, there are sometimes at work causes which bring about definite transfers of demand from one group of occupations to another. The most obvious of these are seasonal changes in climatic conditions; in the summer, for example, people want less gas for lighting but more petrol for motoring than they do in the winter. Shiftings of taste, under the influence of fashion, from one class of luxury article to another are on the same plane. Yet again, even when every individual's tastes remain unaltered, the transfer of income from people with one set of tastes to people with another set involves a transfer of demand from the products favoured by the first class to those favoured by the second. Thus an improvement in the incomes of the poor at the expense of the rich would cause the demand for poor men's goods to grow, and that for rich men's to contract: and this change would be reflected in the demands for productive resources to make the two sorts of goods.

§ 6. Fourthly, there are at work certain general causes, which affect the demand for productive resources in a large number of occupations in the same sense, but in different degrees. Thus the psychical, monetary and other factors that underlie what are commonly called cyclical fluctuations in industry involve, for reasons which I have endeavoured to explain elsewhere,[1] much more violent swings in the demand for instrumental goods than in that for the general run of consumption goods. This, of course, means that demands for productive resources to produce these two sorts of goods fluctuate relatively to one another. Any policy, therefore, that succeeded in mitigating the swing of cyclical industrial fluctuations, would, incidentally, also lessen the *relative* variations in the demands of different industries.

§ 7. If we suppose ourselves starting from a position of equilibrium and imagine *any* relative variation of demand to occur as between two occupations, until the appropriate transfer of productive resources has taken place the national dividend must fall below its maximum. But, nevertheless, it

---

[1] Cf. my *Industrial Fluctuations*, Part I. chapter ix.

is for some purposes important to distinguish between relative variations in which the demands in both occupations have moved in the same direction and relative variations in which one demand has risen and the other fallen. *Where wage earners maintain rigid rates of wages in the face of falling demand*, it will be possible for those displaced from a depressed industry to find employment in an expanded one, but not possible for them to find employment in one which, though less depressed, is itself depressed in some degree. To eliminate obstacles to movement—provided that the expense of doing this were not too great—would, therefore, help the national dividend in the first case, but would have no effect upon it in the second.

§ 8. In conclusion it should be noted that relative variations in the demand for productive resources, whether between places or between occupations, may be expected to have different effects according as they take place rapidly or slowly. If one occupation or place declines slowly while another expands slowly, adjustment may be made to the new conditions without it being necessary for any actual transfer of resources to take place between them. All that need happen is that in the declining occupation or place, capital, as it wears out, and workpeople, as they retire or die, are not fully replaced; while newly created capital and young men and women coming to industrial age are turned into the expanding place or occupation to the extent required to fit the enlarged demand. In these conditions, no actual transfer of capital or labour being required, obstacles in the way of transfer do no harm to the national dividend. When, however, relative variations of demand take place rapidly, adjustment cannot be fully made in the way described, and, if it is to be made, actual transfers must take place. Here, therefore, obstacles to movement necessarily injure the dividend, and the elimination of them (if this could be accomplished without too great cost) would benefit it. Where exactly the line between " gradual " and " rapid " relative variations lies from the standpoint of this discussion, depends on the rates at which, in the occupations and places concerned, capital equipment normally decays and the labour force normally requires replacement. As will be observed presently in another connection, the proportion of the annual flow to total stock is, in general, much larger among women workers than among men workers.[1]

---

[1] Cf. *post*, Part III. Chapter IX. § 6.

CHAPTER IX

§ 1. IN general industrialists are interested, not in the social, but only in the private, net product of their operations. Subject to what was said in Chapter V. about costs of movement, self-interest will tend to bring about equality in the values of the marginal private net products of resources invested in different ways. But it will not tend to bring about equality in the values of the marginal social net products except when marginal private net product and marginal social net product are identical. When there is a divergence between these two sorts of marginal net products, self-interest will not, therefore, tend to make the national dividend a maximum ; and, consequently, certain specific acts of interference with normal economic processes may be expected, not to diminish, but to increase the dividend. It thus becomes important to inquire in what conditions the values of the social net product and the private net product of any given (r^{th}) increment of investment in an industry are liable to diverge from one another in either direction. There are certain general sorts of divergence that are found even under conditions of simple competition, certain additional sorts that may be introduced under conditions of monopolistic competition, and yet others that may be introduced under conditions of bilateral monopoly.

§ 2. If there existed only one type of productive resource, say, labour of a given quality, this statement of the issues would be complete. It would also be complete if several types of productive resources existed, but they were everywhere and in all circumstances combined together in exactly the same

proportions.   In real life there are a number of different types
of resource and they are combined in various proportions, not
only in different industries, but in the same industry in
respect of different quantities of output.   Hence the expression
" the rth increment of investment in an industry," which was
employed in the preceding section, calls for further elucidation.
In a given industry y units of output are produced as a result
of the joint operations of a, b and c (physical) units of three
types of productive resource, or factors of production.   When
the output of the industry is increased to $(y + \Delta y)$, the
quantities of the several factors become a', b' and c'.   There
being no reason to suppose that $\dfrac{a' - a}{a}$, $\dfrac{b' - b}{b}$ and $\dfrac{c' - c}{c}$ will
be equal, it is impossible to describe unambiguously the change
in the quantities of productive resources taken collectively
that has led to a given change in the output of the commodity.
If, therefore, the rth increment of investment is to have a
precise meaning, it must be interpreted as the rth (physical)
increment of some one sort of productive resource (*e.g.* labour
of a given quality) *plus* whatever additions to the quantities
of the other sorts *properly go with* that increment.   These
quantities are perfectly definite, being determined by the
condition that, in respect of any given quantity of output, the
various factors of production must be combined in such wise as
to make their aggregate money cost a minimum.[1]   The above
definition appears at first sight objectionable, because under it
the rth " unit " of investment is, in general, of different physical
constitution from the $(r + h)^{th}$ " unit."   This objection would,
of course, be fatal if we were concerned to compare the net
products of different increments or units of investment.   But
in fact we are concerned to compare two sorts of net product
—social and private as yielded by *given increments of investment.*   For this purpose the relation in which different incre-

---

[1] Thus, let y be the output of the commodity in question, and a, b, c the
(physical) quantities of the several factors of production combined in making it.
Then $y = F(a,b,c)$. Let $f_1(a)$, $f_2(b)$ and $f_3(c)$ be the prices of these factors.
Then, in respect of any quantity of output, the quantities of the several factors
are determined by the equations

$$\frac{1}{f_1(a)} \cdot \frac{\partial F(a,b,c)}{\partial a} = \frac{1}{f_2(b)} \cdot \frac{\partial F(a,b,c)}{\partial b} = \frac{1}{f_3(c)} \cdot \frac{\partial F(a,b,c)}{\partial c}.$$

ments, or different " units," stand to one another is irrelevant. Our definition simply removes an ambiguity, and enables us to proceed unhampered with the line of analysis outlined in the preceding section.

§ 3. The source of the general divergences between the values of marginal social and marginal private net product that occur under simple competition is the fact that, in some occupations, a part of the product of a unit of resources consists of something, which, instead of coming in the first instance to the person who invests the unit, comes instead, in the first instance (*i.e.* prior to sale if sale takes place), as a positive or negative item, to other people. These other people may fall into any one of three principal groups : (1) the owners of durable instruments of production, of which the investor is a tenant ; (2) persons who are not producers of the commodity in which the investor is investing ; (3) persons who are producers of this commodity. The divergences between the values of social and private net product that are liable to arise in respect of this last class of persons will be discussed separately in Chapter XI. In the present chapter attention is confined to the other two classes of divergence.

§ 4. Let us consider first the class connected with the separation between tenancy and ownership of certain durable instruments of production. The extent to which the actual owners of durable instruments leave the work of maintaining and improving them to temporary occupiers varies, of course, in different industries, and is largely determined by considerations of technical convenience. It also depends in part upon tradition and custom, and is further liable to vary in different places with the comparative wealth of the owners and the occupiers. It appears, for example, that in Ireland, owing to the poverty of many landlords, the kinds of expenditure on land which they leave wholly to their tenants are more numerous than in England.[1] Details thus vary, but there can be no doubt that over a wide field some part of the investment designed to improve durable instruments of production is often made by persons other than their owners. Whenever this happens, some divergence between

---

[1] Cf. Bonn, *Modern Ireland*, p. 63.

the private and the social net product of this investment is liable to occur, and is larger or smaller in extent according to the terms of the contract between lessor and lessee. These terms we have now to consider.

§ 5. The social net product of an assigned dose of investment being given, the private net product will fall short of it by an especially large amount under a system which merely provides for the return of the instrument to the owner at the end of the lease in the condition in which the instrument then happens to be. Under this arrangement the private net product of any r^{th} increment of investment falls short of the social net product by nearly the whole of the deferred benefit which would be conferred upon the instrument. It need not fall short of it by quite the whole of this deferred benefit, because a tenant, who is known to leave hired instruments in good condition, is likely to obtain them more easily and on better terms than one who is known not to do this. So far, careful tenancy yields an element of private, as well as of social, net product. Since, however, separate contracts are often made at considerable intervals of time, this qualification is not especially important. Passing it over, therefore, we notice that, since the effects of investment in improving and maintaining instruments generally exhaust themselves after a while, the contraction of private net product below social net product, which the form of tenancy just described brings about, is not likely to be considerable in the earlier years of a long lease. In the later years of such a lease, however, and during the whole period of a short lease, it may be very considerable. Indeed, it is often found that, towards the close of his tenancy, a farmer, in the natural and undisguised endeavour to get back as much of his capital as possible, takes so much out of the land that, for some years afterwards, the yield is markedly reduced.[1]

§ 6. The form of tenancy just described is illustrated by that primitive type of contract between landlord and tenant, in which nothing is said about the condition of the land at the end of the lease. But it is by no means

[1] Cf. Nicholson, *Principles of Economics*, vol. i. p. 418.

confined to this type of contract. Another very important
field in which it is present is that of "concessions" to gas
companies, electric lighting companies and so forth. An
arrangement, under which the plant of a concessionaire
company passes ultimately, without compensation, into the
hands of the town chartering it, corresponds exactly to the
system of land leases without provision for compensation for
tenants' improvements. Such an arrangement at one time
governed the Berlin Tramways. The Company's charter
provided that, "at the end of the contract, all property of the
road located in the city streets, including poles, wires, any
waiting-rooms built on city property, and patents, come into the
possession of the city without charge." [1] From the present
point of view, this system is similar to that of the British
Tramways Act of 1870 and Electric Lighting Act of 1881,
which provided for the taking over of the company's plant
"upon terms of paying the then value (exclusive of any allowance for past or future profits of the undertaking, or any
compensation for compulsory sale or other consideration whatever)." For the "reproduction cost," which value in this
sense seems to represent, of a concern established many years
back might be expected to fall far short of its value as a going
concern. It follows that, under the German and English plans
alike, the terminating franchise system must, unless some plan
is adopted to obviate that result,[2] reduce the private net product
of investments, alike in the original plant and in later extensions, below their social net product, thus causing them to be
carried less far than the best interests of the national dividend require. Furthermore, it is obvious that the restrictive

---

[1] Beamish, *Municipal Problems*, p. 565.

[2] Of course, the English plan is not so severe as the German in respect of
investments in plant made near the end of the lease; for, presumably, for a
short time the cost of manufacturing such plant will remain fairly constant.
But for investments designed to create goodwill, and, through this, future
business, it is exactly similar. Thus, after the agreement of 1905, by
which the Post Office undertook to buy up in 1911 such part of the National
Telephone Company's plant as proved suitable, at the cost of replacement, the
Chairman of the Company stated that "the Company would not attempt to
build up business that would require nursing as well as time to develop; it
would confine itself to operations that from the start would pay interest and all
other proper charges" (H. Meyer, *Public Ownership and the Telephones*, p. 309).
A device for getting over the difficulty considered in the text was embodied in

influence will be most marked towards the close of the concession period. In view of this fact, M. Colson recommends a
policy, under which negotiations for the renewal of concession
charters would be taken up some 15 or 20 years before these
charters are due to expire.[1]

§ 7. The deficiency of the private, as compared with the
social, net product of any r^{th} increment of investment, which
arises in connection with what I have called the primitive type
of tenancy contracts, can be mitigated in various degrees
by compensation schemes. These may conveniently be
illustrated from the recent history of land tenure. Arrangements can be made for compensating tenants, when they
leave their holdings, for whatever injury or benefit they may
have caused to the land. Negative compensation for injury
is practically everywhere provided for in the terms of the
leases. In its simplest form it consists in monetary
penalties for failure on the part of tenants to return their
land to the owner in "tenantable repair." These penalties
may be made operative directly, through an explicit legal
contract; or they may be made operative indirectly, by a
rule forbidding the tenant to depart from the local customs
of husbandry; or, again, they may be made operative through
a modification in this rule concerning local customs, so
arranged as to free enterprising tenants from the burden
which the rule in its simple form imposes, without sacrificing
the purpose of the rule. Thus, under the Agricultural

---

the contract extending the franchise of the Berlin Tramway Company to 1919.
This contract provided, *inter alia* : "If, during the life of the contract, the city
authorities require extensions within the city limits, which are not specified in
the contract, the company must build as much as 93 miles, double track being
counted as single. But the company should receive from the city one-third of
the cost of construction of all lines ordered between Jan. 1, 1902, and Jan. 1,
1907 ; and one-half of the cost on all lines ordered between Jan. 1, 1908, and Jan.
1, 1914. For all lines ordered after that the city must pay the full costs of construction, or a full allowance towards the cost of operation, as determined by
later agreement. The overhead trolley was to be employed at first, except where
the city demanded storage batteries ; but, if any other motor system should later
prove practicable and in the judgment of the city authorities should appear more
suitable, the company may introduce it ; and, if the city authorities request,
the company must introduce it. If increased cost accrue to the company
thereby, due allowance being made for benefits obtained from the new system,
the city must indemnify the company" (Beamish, *Municipal Problems*, p. 563).
[1] Cf. Colson, *Cours d'économie politique*, vol. vi. p. 419.

Holdings Act, 1906, a tenant may depart from local custom, or even from a contract, as to cropping arable land, provided that he shall make "suitable and adequate provision to protect the holding from injury or deterioration"—except in the year before the expiration of the contract of tenancy. If the tenant's action under this section does injure the holding, the landlord is entitled to recover damages and to obtain, if necessary, an injunction against the continuance of the tenant's conduct. Positive compensation was of somewhat later growth. Rules about it were at first a matter of voluntary arrangement in the yearly leases made by landlords. Mr. Taylor quotes a Yorkshire lease, in which the landlord covenants to allow the tenant "what two different persons shall deem reasonable," in payment for the capital put into the land in the course of ordinary farming operations during the last two years of the lease.[1] Gradually compensation schemes have been given a legal status. Something in this direction was done in Ireland under the Act of 1870—the need for it being specially great in a country where the English custom, under which the landlord provides the buildings and permanent improvements, seldom applied.[2] In 1875 an Act laying down conditions for compensating the outgoing tenant in England and Wales was passed, but contracting-out was permitted. In 1883 a new Act, the Agricultural Holdings Act, was passed, in which contracting-out was forbidden. This Act distinguished between improvements for which the landlord's consent was necessary and those for which it was not necessary.[3] Scotland is now under a similar Act. It has largely superseded the old long leases, and these are now practically being modified out of existence.[4] In the detailed drafting of all Acts of this class difficulty is caused by the fact that some "improvements" do not add to the enduring value of the estate the equivalent of their cost of production. If the compensation for these improvements is based upon their cost, the private net product is raised above the social net product. In practice this danger

---

[1] Cf. Taylor, *Agricultural Economics*, p. 305.
[2] Cf. Smith-Gordon and Staples, *Rural Reconstruction in Ireland*, p. 20.
[3] Cf. Taylor, *Agricultural Economics*, pp. 313 *et seq*
[4] Cf. Taylor, *ibid.* p. 320.

is largely overcome by the rejection of initial cost as a basis of compensation value, coupled with the requirement of the landlord's consent to some kinds of improvement. Under the Town Tenants (Ireland) Act, 1906, for example, when a tenant proposes to make an improvement he must give notice to the landlord, and, if the latter objects, the question, whether the improvement is reasonable and will add to the letting value of the holding, is determined by the County Court. The British Landlord and Tenant Act (1927) contains a similar provision for compensation for improvements and goodwill on the termination of tenancies of business premises. But even on this plan the private net product may be slightly in excess. In order that private and social net product may coalesce, the value of an improvement, for compensation purposes, should in strictness be estimated subject to the fact that, at interchanges of tenants, the land may stand for a time unlet, and that during this time the improvement is not likely to yield its full annual value. If this is not done, it will pay a tenant to press investment slightly—very slightly—further than it will pay either the landlord or society to have it pressed; and hence, where, as in market-gardening, improvements can be made without the landlord's consent, it will check landlords from letting land. It is, thus, theoretically an error in the Agricultural Holdings Act of 1906, that it defines the compensation, which an outgoing tenant may claim for improvements, as "such sum as fairly represents the value of the improvements to an incoming tenant." The standard ought to be "the value to the landlord." But, when, as is usual, improvements exhaust themselves in a few years, the practical effect of this slight error is negligible, and does not cause the private and social net products of any r^{th} increment of investment to diverge appreciably.

§ 8. These compensation arrangements, as so far considered, possess one obvious weakness, which generally impedes the adjustment they are designed to effect between private and social net product. It is true that a tenant can claim compensation for improvements on quitting. But he knows that the rent may be raised against him on the strength of his improvements, and his compensation claim does not come into force unless he takes the extreme step of giving up his farm.   Hence the private net product of investment is still contracted below the social net product.   This result is partially mitigated under the Agricultural Holdings Act of 1906— somewhat strengthened in 1920—where it is provided that: " When the landlord, without good and sufficient cause, and for reasons inconsistent with good estate management, terminates a tenancy by notice to quit," or when the tenant leaves in consequence of a proved demand for increased rent consequent upon tenants' improvements, the tenant may claim, not merely compensation for the improvements, but also " compensation for the loss or expense directly attributable to his quitting the holding," in connection with the sale or removal of household goods, implements of husbandry, and so forth.   The above remedy is, however, defective in several respects.   In the first place, since a tenant quitting his holding under the conditions contemplated obtains no compensation for the loss of " good-will " or the non-monetary inconveniences of a change of home, he will still be very unwilling to leave, and the landlord will still possess a powerful weapon with which to force him to consent to an increase of rent.   In the second place, notice to quit on account of sale is not held to be " incompatible with good estate management."   Consequently, when the land farmed by a sitting tenant is sold by one landlord to another, the tenant, if he leaves, obtains no secondary compensation of the kind just described.   He will, therefore, be even more unwilling to leave.   Should he elect, however, to rent the farm under the new landlord, he " is liable to the rent on any improvement which he has executed, without receiving any compensation." [1]   It is probably a recognition of this danger that has given rise to the growing demand among farmers for legislation permitting them, when the landlord wishes to sell,

---

[1] *Report of the Committee on Tenant Farmers* [Cd. 6030], p. 6.   Notice given to a sitting tenant on the ground that his land is wanted for building is also " not incompatible with good husbandry " and carries no secondary compensation. There would plainly be danger in the grant of such compensation here, since it would encourage the investment of resources in agricultural improvements at the cost of a *more than equivalent* social injury in postponing the use for building of land that has become ripe for it.

to purchase their holdings on the basis of the old rent. A provision for secondary compensation on disturbance similar to that of the Agricultural Holdings Act is contained in the Town Tenants (Ireland) Act, 1906. Here, under the circumstances specified, compensation may also be claimed for "goodwill." But even with this provision it is apparent that the adjustment secured cannot be more than partial.[1]

§ 9. In view of these imperfections in compensation arrangements, it is often contended, in effect, that for a really adequate adjustment, not merely compensation for tenants vacating their holdings, but legal security of tenure, coupled with the legal prohibition of renting tenants' improvements, is required. Of course, in some circumstances the state of things which this policy is designed to bring about is attained without any legislative intervention. In Belgium, for example, it is substantially established everywhere by the force of custom:[2] and, no doubt, many English landlords conduct the management of their estates in a like spirit. It is plain, however, that the willingness of landlords to refrain from using economic power for their own advantage, when the use of this power is permitted by law, cannot always be assumed; indeed, if it could be assumed, the whole elaborate development of compensation laws, which we have been discussing, would have been unnecessary. We are thus led forward to a consideration of the policy of legally enforced security of tenure *plus* "fair rents." In the way of this policy there are two principal difficulties. In the first place, the security of tenure that is granted cannot be absolute; for, if it were, considerable economic waste might sometimes result. It would appear, therefore, that security must be conditional upon reasonably good farming. Furthermore, it must be "conditional upon the land not being required in the public

---

[1] The argument for compensation, it should be noted, is not that it would benefit the tenant. Professor Nicholson is right when he observes "that compensation for improvements will not benefit the tenant so much as is generally supposed, because the privilege itself will have a pecuniary value; that is to say, a landlord will demand, and the tenant can afford to give, a higher rent in proportion. Under the old improving leases, as they were called, the rent was low because ultimately the permanent improvements were to go to the landlord " (*Principles of Economics*, vol. i. p. 322). Cf. Morison's account of Indian arrangements (*The Industrial Organisation of an Indian Province*, pp. 154-5). [2] Cf. Rowntree, *Land and Labour*, p. 129.

interest, whether for small holdings, allotments, labourers'
cottages, urban development, the working of minerals, or the
making of water-courses, roads and sanitary works.   When it
is required for any of these purposes the Land Court should
have the power to terminate the tenancy, while ensuring
adequate compensation to the tenant."[1]   The precise drafting
of appropriate conditions is not likely to prove altogether easy.
In the second place, security of tenure being plainly illusory
if the landlord can force the tenant to give notice by arbitrary
increases of rent, it is necessary that fair rents be somehow
enforced.   This cannot be done by a mere prohibition of *any*
increases of rent, for in some circumstances an increase would
be fair.   There would be no justice, for example, in taking from
the landlord and giving to the tenant the benefit of an addition
to the value of the land brought about by some general change
in agricultural prices wholly independent of the tenant's action.
Hence this policy seems to involve the setting up of a tribunal
to fix rents, or, at all events, to settle disputes about rents,
when invoked for that purpose.   Were the Land Court, or
whatever the body set up may be, omniscient and all-wise,
there would, indeed, be no objection to this.   But, in view of
the necessary imperfection of all human institutions, there is
some danger that a tenant may be tempted deliberately to let
down the value of his holding in the hope of obtaining a
reduced rent.   Under the Irish system of judicial rents, a
defence against this abuse was nominally provided in the form
of permission to the Courts to refuse revision.   But this
remedy was not utilised in practice.   Very often "not productivity, but production, and more especially the evidences of
production in the fifteenth year, were the determining factors"
in rent revision.[2]   Professor Bonn illustrates the result thus:
"Two brothers divided a farm into two shares of equal values
—the good husbandman got a rent reduction from the Courts
of $7\frac{1}{2}$ per cent, the bad got one of $17\frac{1}{2}$ per cent."[3]   It is not,
therefore, by any means obvious that the policy of fixity of
tenure and judicial rents will really bring marginal private net

[1] *Land Enquiry Report*, p. 378.
[2] Smith-Gordon and Staples, *Rural Reconstruction in Ireland*, p. 24.
[3] Bonn, *Modern Ireland*, p. 113.

product and marginal social net product more closely together than they are brought by simple compensation laws. The gap between the two marginal net products can only be completely closed if the person who owns the land and the person who makes investments in it are the same. But this arrangement is frequently uneconomic in other ways. For, especially if the farmers are small men, they are likely, as owners, to find much difficulty in raising the capital required for those larger improvements, which, under the English land-system, it is now usual for the landlord to undertake. It is beyond the scope of this volume to attempt a detailed discussion of the controversial topics thus opened up. What has been said, however, will suffice to illustrate one type of discrepancy between marginal private net product and marginal social net product, that is liable to arise in occupations where resources have to be invested in durable instruments by persons who do not own the instruments.

§ 10. I now turn to the second class of divergence between social and private net product which was distinguished in § 3. Here the essence of the matter is that one person A, in the course of rendering some service, for which payment is made, to a second person B, incidentally also renders services or disservices to other persons (not producers of like services), of such a sort that payment cannot be exacted from the benefited parties or compensation enforced on behalf of the injured parties. If we were to be pedantically loyal to the definition of the national dividend given in Chapter III. of Part I., it would be necessary to distinguish further between industries in which the uncompensated benefit or burden respectively is and is not one that can be readily brought into relation with the measuring rod of money. This distinction, however, would be of formal rather than of real importance, and would obscure rather than illuminate the main issues. I shall, therefore, in the examples I am about to give, deliberately pass it over.

Among these examples we may set out first a number of instances in which marginal private net product falls short of marginal social net product, because incidental services are performed to third parties from whom it is technically difficult to exact payment. Thus, as Sidgwick observes, " it may easily happen that the benefits of a well-placed lighthouse must be largely enjoyed by ships on which no toll could be conveniently levied." [1]   Again, uncompensated services are rendered when resources are invested in private parks in cities ; for these, even though the public is not admitted to them, improve the air of the neighbourhood. The same thing is true—though here allowance should be made for a detriment elsewhere—of resources invested in roads and tramways that increase the value of the adjoining land—except, indeed, where a special betterment rate, corresponding to the improvements they enjoy, is levied on the owners of this land. It is true, in like manner, of resources devoted to afforestation, since the beneficial effect on climate often extends beyond the borders of the estates owned by the person responsible for the forest. It is true also of resources invested in lamps erected at the doors of private houses, for these necessarily throw light also on the streets.[2]   It is true of resources devoted to the prevention of smoke from factory chimneys :[3] for this smoke in large towns inflicts a heavy uncharged loss on the community, in injury to buildings and vegetables, expenses for washing clothes and cleaning rooms, expenses for the provision of extra artificial light, and in many other ways.[4]   Lastly and

[1] *Principles of Political Economy*, p. 406.

[2] Cf. Smart, *Studies in Economics*, p. 314.

[3] It has been said that in London, owing to the smoke, there is only 12 per cent as much sunlight as is astronomically possible, and that one fog in five is directly caused by smoke alone, while all the fogs are befouled and prolonged by it (J. W. Graham, *The Destruction of Daylight*, pp. 6 and 24). It would seem that mere ignorance and inertia prevent the adoption of smoke-preventing appliances in many instances where, through the addition they would make to the efficiency of fuel, they would be directly profitable to the users. The general interest, however, requires that these devices should be employed beyond the point at which they " pay." There seems no doubt that, by means of mechanical stokers, hot-air blasts and other arrangements, factory chimneys can be made practically smokeless. Noxious fumes from alkali works are suppressed by the law more vigorously than smoke (*ibid.* p. 126).

[4] Thus the Interim Report of the Departmental Committee on smoke and Noxious Vapours Abatement 1920 contains the following passages :

" 17. *Actual economic loss Due to Coal Smoke.*—It is impossible to arrive at any complete and exact statistical statement of the amount of damage occasioned to the whole community by smoke. We may, however, quote the following investigations.

" A report on an exhaustive investigation conducted by an expert Committee

most important of all, it is true of resources devoted alike to the fundamental problems of scientific research, out of which, in unexpected ways, discoveries of high practical utility often grow, and also to the perfecting of inventions and improvements in industrial processes. These latter are often of such a nature that they can neither be patented nor kept secret, and, therefore, the whole of the extra reward, which they at first bring to their inventor, is very quickly transferred from him to the general public in the form of reduced prices. The patent laws aim, in effect, at bringing marginal private net product and marginal social net product more closely together. By offering the prospect of reward for certain types of invention they do not, indeed, appreciably stimulate inventive activity, which is, for the most part, spontaneous, but they do direct it into channels of general usefulness.[1]

Corresponding to the above investments in which marginal private net product falls short of marginal social net product, there are a number of others, in which, owing to the technical difficulty of enforcing compensation for incidental disservices, marginal private net product is greater than marginal social net product. Thus, incidental uncharged disservices are rendered to third parties when the game-preserving activities of one occupier involve the overrunning of a neighbouring occupier's land by rabbits—unless, indeed, the two occupiers stand in the relation of landlord and tenant, so that compensation is given in an adjustment of the rent. They are rendered, again, when the owner of a site in a residential quarter of a city builds a factory there and so destroys a great

of engineers, architects, and scientists in 1912 in Pittsburgh, U.S.A., estimated the cost of the smoke nuisance to Pittsburgh at approximately £4 per head of the population per annum.

"18. A valuable investigation was made in 1918 by the Manchester Air Pollution Advisory Board into the comparative cost of household washing in Manchester—a smoky town—as compared with Harrogate—a clean town. The investigator obtained 100 properly comparable statements for Manchester and Harrogate respectively as to the cost of the weekly washing in working-class houses. These showed an extra cost in Manchester of 7½d. a week per household for fuel and washing material. The total loss for the whole city, taking the extra cost of fuel and washing materials alone, disregarding the extra labour involved, and assuming no greater loss for middle-class than for working-class households (a considerable under-statement), works out at over £290,000 a year for a population of three quarters of a million."

[1] Cf. Taussig, *Inventors and Money Makers*, p. 51.

part of the amenities of the neighbouring sites; or, in a less
degree, when he uses his site in such a way as to spoil
the lighting of the houses opposite:[1] or when he invests
resources in erecting buildings in a crowded centre, which,
by contracting the air space and the playing-room of the
neighbourhood, tend to injure the health and efficiency of the
families living there.   Yet again, third parties—this time
the public in general—suffer incidental uncharged disservices
from resources invested in the running of motor cars that wear
out the surface of the roads.   The case is similar—the
conditions of public taste being assumed—with resources
devoted to the production and sale of intoxicants.   To enable
the social net product to be inferred from the private net
product of the marginal pound invested in this form of
production, the investment should, as Mr. Bernard Shaw
observes, be debited with the extra costs in policemen and
prisons which it indirectly makes necessary.[2]   Exactly similar
considerations hold good in some measure of foreign investment in general.   For, if foreigners can obtain some of the
exports they need from us by selling promises, they will not
have to send so many goods; which implies that the ratio of
interchange between our exports and our imports will become
slightly less favourable to us.   For certain sorts of foreign
investments more serious reactions come into account.   Thus,
when the indirect effect of an increment of investment made
abroad, or of the diplomatic manœuvres employed in securing
the concession for it, is an actual war or preparations to
guard against war, the cost of these things ought to be
deducted from any interest that the increment yields before
its net contribution to the national dividend is calculated.
When this is done, the marginal social net product even of
investments, which, as may often happen in countries where
highly profitable openings are still unworked and hard bargains
can be driven with corrupt officials, yield a very high return
to the investors, may easily turn out to be negative.   Yet

---

[1] In Germany the town-planning schemes of most cities render anti-social
action of this kind impossible ; but in America individual site-owners appear to
be entirely free, and in England to be largely free, to do what they will with
their land.   (Cf. Howe, *European Cities at Work*, pp. 46, 95 and 346.)
[2] *The Common Sense of Municipal Trading*, pp. 19-20.

again, when the investment consists in a loan to a foreign
government and makes it possible for that government to
engage in a war which otherwise would not have taken place,
the indirect loss which Englishmen in general suffer, in consequence of the world impoverishment caused by the war,
should be debited against the interest which English financiers
receive. Here, too, the marginal social net product may well
be negative. Perhaps, however, the crowning illustration of
this order of excess of private over social net product is afforded
by the work done by women in factories, particularly during
the periods immediately preceding and succeeding confinement;
for there can be no doubt that this work often carries with it,
besides the earnings of the women themselves, grave injury to
the health of their children.[1] The reality of this evil is not
disproved by the low, even negative, correlation which sometimes
is found to exist between the factory work of mothers and the
rate of infantile mortality. For in districts where women's
work of this kind prevails there is presumably—and this is
the cause of the women's work—great poverty. This poverty,
which is obviously injurious to children's health, is likely,
other things being equal, to be greater than elsewhere in
families where the mother declines factory work, and it may
be that the evil of the extra poverty is greater than that
of the factory work.[2] This consideration explains the
statistical facts that are known. They, therefore, militate in
no way against the view that, *other things equal*, the factory
work of mothers is injurious. All that they tend to show
is that prohibition of such work should be accompanied

---

[1] Cf. Hutchins, *Economic Journal*, 1908, p. 227.

[2] Cf. Newsholme, *Second Report on Infant and Child Mortality* [Cd. 6909],
p. 56. Similar considerations to the above hold good of night work by boys.
The *Departmental Committee on Night Employment* did not, indeed, obtain any
strong evidence that this work injures the boys' health. But they found that
it reacts injuriously on their efficiency in another way, *i.e.* by practically precluding them from going on with their education in continuation classes and so
forth. The *theory* of our factory laws appears to be that boys between 14 and 18
should only be permitted to work at night upon continuous processes of such a kind
that great loss would result if they did not do so. The *practice* of these laws,
however, permits them to be employed at night on unnecessary non-continuous
processes which are carried out in the same factory as continuous processes.
Consequently, the Committee recommend that in future " such permits should
be granted in terms of processes, and not of premises, factories, or parts of
factories without reference to processes " ([Cd. 6503], p. 17).

by relief to those families whom the prohibition renders necessitous.[1]

§ 11. At this point it is desirable to call attention to a somewhat specious fallacy. Some writers unaccustomed to mathematical analysis have imagined that, when improved methods of producing some commodities are introduced, the value of the marginal social net product of the resources invested in developing these methods is less than the value of the marginal private net product, because there is not included in the latter any allowance for the depreciation which the improvement causes in the value of existing plant; and, as they hold, in order to arrive at the value of the marginal social net product, such allowance ought to be included.[2] If this view were correct, reason would be shown for attempts to make the authorisation of railways dependent on the railway companies compensating existing canals, for refusals to license motor omnibuses in the interests of municipal tramways, and for the placing of hindrances in the way of electric lighting enterprises in order to conserve the contribution made to the rates by municipal gas companies. But in fact the view is not correct. The marginal social net product of resources devoted to *improved methods of producing a given commodity* is not, in general, different from the marginal private net product; for whatever loss the old producers suffer through a reduction in the price of their products is balanced by the gain which the reduction confers upon the purchasers of these products. This is obvious if, after the new investment has been made, the old

---

[1] Cf. *Annual Report of the Local Government Board*, 1909–10, p. 57. The suggestion that the injurious consequences of the factory work of mothers can be done away with, if the factory worker gets some unmarried woman to look after her home in factory hours, is mistaken, because it ignores the fact that a woman's work has a special personal value in respect of her own children. In Birmingham this fact seems to be recognised, for, after a little experience of the bad results of putting their children out to "mind," married women are apt, it was said before the war, to leave the factory and take to home work. (Cf. Cadbury, *Women's Work*, p. 175.)

[2] For example, J. A. Hobson, *Sociological Review*, July 1911, p. 197, and *Gold, Prices and Wages*, pp. 107-8. Even Sidgwick might be suspected of countenancing the argument set out in the text (cf. *Principles of Political Economy*, p. 408). It does not seem to have been noticed that this argument, if valid, would justify the State in prohibiting the use of new machinery that dispenses with the services of skilled mechanics until the generation of mechanics possessing that skill has been depleted by death.

machines continue to produce the same output as before at reduced prices. If the production of the old machines is diminished on account of the change, it seems at first sight doubtful. Reflection, however, makes it plain that no unit formerly produced by the old machinery will be supplanted by one produced by the new machinery, except when the new machinery can produce it at a *total cost* smaller than the *prime cost* that would have been involved in its production with the old machinery : except, that is to say, when it can produce it at a price so low that the old machinery would have earned nothing by producing it at that price. This implies that every unit taken over by the new machinery from the old is sold to the public at a price *reduced* by as much as the whole of the net receipts, after discharging prime costs, which the old machinery would have obtained from it if it had produced that unit. It is thus proved that there is no loss to the owners of the old machines, in respect of any unit of their former output, that is not offset by an equivalent gain to consumers. It follows that to count the loss to these owners, in respect of any unit taken over from them by the new machinery, as a part of the social cost of producing that unit would be incorrect.

An attempt to avoid this conclusion may, indeed, still be made. It may be granted that, so far as direct effects are concerned, ordinary commercial policy, under which investment in improved processes is not restrained by consideration for the earnings of other people's established plant, stands vindicated. There remain, however, indirect effects. If expensive plant is liable to have its earnings reduced at short notice by new inventions, will not the building of such plant be hindered ? Would not the introduction of improved processes on the whole be stimulated, if they were in some way guaranteed against too rapid obsolescence through the competition of processes yet further improved ? The direct answer to this question is, undoubtedly, yes. On the other side, however, has to be set the fact that the policy proposed would retain inferior methods in use when superior methods were available. Whether gain or loss on the whole would result from these two influences in combination, is a question to which it seems difficult to give any confident answer. But this impotent conclusion is not the last word. The argument so far has assumed that the rapidity with which improvements are invented is independent of the rapidity of their practical adoption; and it is on the basis of that assumption that our comparison of rival policies fails to attain a definite result. As a matter of fact, however, improvements are much more likely to be made at any time, if the best methods previously discovered are being employed and, therefore, watched in actual operation, than if they are being held up in the interest of established plant. Hence the holding-up policy indirectly delays, not merely the adoption of improvements that have been invented, but also the invention of new improvements. This circumstance almost certainly turns the balance. The policy proper to ordinary competitive industry is, therefore, in general and on the whole, of greater social advantage than the rival policy. It is not to the interest of the community that business men, contemplating the introduction of improved methods, should take account of the loss which forward action on their part threatens to other business men. The example of some municipalities in postponing the erection of electric-lighting plant till their gas plant is worn out is not one that should be imitated, nor one that can be successfully defended by reference to the distinction between social and private net products. The danger that beneficial advances may be checked by unwise resistance on the part of interested municipal councils is recognised in this country in the rules empowering the central authority to override attempts at local vetoes against private electrical enterprise. The policy followed by the Board of Trade is illustrated by the following extract from their report on the Ardrossan, Saltcoats and District Electric Lighting Order of 1910 : " As the policy of the Board has been to hold that objection on the grounds of competition with a gas undertaking, even when belonging to a local authority, is not sufficient reason to justify them in refusing to grant an Electric Lighting Order, the Board decided to dispense with the consent of the Corporation of Ardrossan." [1]

§ 12. So far we have considered only those divergences

[1] Cf. Knoop, *Principles and Methods of Municipal Trading*, p. 35.

between private and social net products that come about through
the existence of uncompensated services and uncharged disservices, the general conditions of popular taste being tacitly
assumed to remain unchanged. This is in accordance with
the definition of social net product given in Chapter II. § 5.
As was there indicated, however, it is, for some purposes,
desirable to adopt a wider definition. When this is done, we
observe that a further element of divergence between social
and private net products, important to economic welfare
though not to the actual substance of the national dividend,
may emerge in the form of uncompensated or uncharged
effects upon the *satisfaction that consumers derive from the
consumption of things other than the one directly affected.*
For the fact that some people are now able to consume
the new commodity may set up a psychological reaction
in other people, directly changing the amount of satisfaction
that they get from their consumption of the old commodity.
It is conceivable that the reaction may lead to an *increase*
in the satisfaction they obtain from this commodity, since
it may please them to make use of a thing just because it
is superseded and more or less archaic. But, in general, the
reaction will be in the other direction. For, in some measure,
people's affection for the best quality of anything is due simply
to the fact that it is the best quality ; and, when a new best,
superior to the old best, is created, that element of value in
the old best is destroyed. Thus, if an improved form of motor
car is invented, an enthusiast who desires above all "the very
latest thing" will, for the future, derive scarcely any satisfaction from a car, the possession of which, before this new invention, afforded him intense pleasure. In these circumstances
the marginal social net product of resources invested in producing the improved type is somewhat smaller than the
marginal private net product.[1] It is *possible* that the introduction of electric lighting into a town may, in some very slight
degree, bring about this sort of psychological reaction in regard

[1] It should be noticed that the argument of the text may be applicable even
where the product formerly consumed is wholly superseded by the new rival,
and where, therefore, nobody is actually deriving diminished satisfaction from
the old product : for it may be that complete supersession would not have come
about unless people's desire for the old product had been reduced by the psycho-

to gas: and this possibility may provide a real defence, supplementary to the fallacious defence described in the preceding section, for the policy of municipalities in delaying the introduction of electricity. This valid defence, however, is almost certainly inadequate. The arguments actually employed in support of the view that municipalities should not permit competition with their gas plant are those described in the preceding section. They are, in general, independent of any reference to psychological reactions, and are, therefore, like the arguments which persons interested in canals brought against the authorisation of the early railways, wholly fallacious.

§ 13. It is plain that divergences between private and social net product of the kinds we have so far been considering cannot, like divergences due to tenancy laws, be mitigated by a modification of the contractual relation between any two contracting parties, because the divergence arises out of a service or disservice rendered to persons other than the contracting parties. It is, however, possible for the State, if it so chooses, to remove the divergence in any field by "extraordinary encouragements" or "extraordinary restraints" upon investments in that field. The most obvious forms which these encouragements and restraints may assume are, of course, those of bounties and taxes. Broad illustrations of the policy of intervention in both its negative and positive aspects are easily provided.

The private net product of any unit of investment is unduly large relatively to the social net product in the businesses of producing and distributing alcoholic drinks. Consequently, in nearly all countries, special taxes are placed upon these businesses. Marshall was in favour of treating in the same way resources devoted to the erection of buildings in crowded areas. He suggested, to a witness before the Royal Com-

---

logical reaction we have been contemplating. Furthermore, the preceding argument shows that inventions *may* actually diminish aggregate economic welfare ; for they may cause labour to be withdrawn from other forms of productive service to make a new variety of some article to supersede an old one, whereas, if there had been no invention, the old one would have continued in use and would have yielded as much economic satisfaction as the new one yields now. This is true, broadly speaking, of inventions of new weapons of war, so far as these are known to all nations, because it is of no advantage to one country to have improved armaments if its rivals have them also.

mission on Labour, "that every person putting up a house in a district that has got as closely populated as is good should be compelled to contribute towards providing free playgrounds."[1]   The principle is susceptible of general application.   It is employed, though in a very incomplete and partial manner, in the British levy of a petrol duty and a motor-car licence tax upon the users of motor cars, the proceeds of which are devoted to the service of the roads.[2]   It is employed again in an ingenious way in the National Insurance Act.   When the sickness rate in any district is exceptionally high, provision is made for throwing the consequent abnormal expenses upon employers, local authorities or water companies, if the high rate can be shown to be due to neglect or carelessness on the part of any of these bodies.   Some writers have thought that it might be employed in the form of a discriminating tax upon income derived from foreign investments.   But, since the element of disadvantage described in § 10 only belongs to some of these investments and not to others, this arrangement would not be a satisfactory one.   Moreover, foreign investment is already penalised to a considerable extent both by general ignorance of foreign conditions and by the fact that income earned abroad is frequently subjected to foreign income tax as well as to British income tax.

The private net product of any unit of investment is unduly small in industries, such as agriculture, which are supposed to yield the indirect service of developing citizens suitable for military training.   Partly for this reason agriculture in Germany was accorded the indirect bounty of protection.   A more extreme form of bounty, in which a governmental authority provides *all* the funds required, is given upon such services as the planning of towns, police administration, and, sometimes, the clearing of slum areas.   This type of bounty is also not

---

[1] *Royal Commission on Labour*, Q. 8665.

[2] The application of the principle is incomplete, because the revenue from these taxes, administered through the Road Board, must be devoted, "not to the ordinary road maintenance at all, however onerous it might be, but exclusively to the execution of new and specific road improvements" (Webb, *The King's Highway*, p. 250).   Thus, in the main, the motorist does not pay for the damage he does to the ordinary roads, but obtains in return for his payment an additional service useful to him rather than to the general public.

H

infrequently given upon the work of spreading information
about improved processes of production in occupations where,
owing to lack of appreciation on the part of potential
beneficiaries, it would be difficult to collect a fee for undertaking that task. Thus the Canadian Government has
established a system, " by means of which any farmer can
make inquiry, without even the cost of postage, about any
matter relating to his business " ; [1] and the Department of
the Interior also sometimes provides, for a time, actual
instruction in farming.[2] Many Governments adopt the same
principle in respect of information about Labour, by providing
the services of Exchanges free of charge. In the United
Kingdom the various Agricultural Organisation Societies are
voluntary organisations, providing a kindred type of bounty
at their subscribers' expense. An important part of their
purpose is, in Sir Horace Plunkett's words, to bring freely
" to the help of those whose life is passed in the quiet of the
field the experience, which belongs to wider opportunities of
observation and a larger acquaintance with commercial and
industrial affairs." [3] The Development Act of 1909, with
its provision for grants towards scientific research, instruction,
and experiment in agricultural science, follows the same lines.

It should be added that sometimes, when the inter-
relations of the various private persons affected are highly
complex, the Government may find it necessary to exercise
some means of authoritative control in addition to providing
a bounty. Thus it is coming to be recognised as an axiom
of government that, in every town, power must be held by
some authority to limit the quantity of building permitted
to a given area, to restrict the height to which houses may
be carried, — for the erection of barrack dwellings may
cause great overcrowding of area even though there is no
overcrowding of rooms,[4]—and generally to control the building

---

[1] Mavor, *Report on the Canadian North-West*, p. 36.

[2] *Ibid.* p. 78.

[3] C. Webb, *Industrial Co-operation*, p. 149.

[4] Mr. Dawson believes that this type of overcrowding prevails to a considerable extent in German towns. He writes : " The excessive width of the streets,
insisted on by cast-iron regulations, adds greatly to the cost of house-building,
and in order to recoup himself, and make the most of his profits, the builder
begins to extend his house vertically instead of horizontally " (*Municipal Life*

activities of individuals. It is as idle to expect a well-planned town to result from the independent activities of isolated speculators as it would be to expect a satisfactory picture to result if each separate square inch were painted by an independent artist. No " invisible hand " can be relied on to produce a good arrangement of the whole from a combination of separate treatments of the parts. It is, therefore, necessary that an authority of wider reach should intervene and should tackle the collective problems of beauty, of air and of light, as those other collective problems of gas and water have been tackled. Hence, shortly before the war, there came into being, on the pattern of long previous German practice, Mr. Burns's extremely important town-planning Act. In this Act, for the first time, control over individual buildings, from the standpoint, not of individual structure, but of the structure of the town as a whole, was definitely conferred upon those town councils that are willing to accept the powers offered to them. Part II. of the Act begins : " A town-planning scheme may be made in accordance with the provisions of this Part of the Act as respects any land which is in course of development, or appears likely to be used for building purposes, with the general object of securing proper sanitary conditions, amenity, and convenience in connection with the laying out and use of the land, and of any neighbouring lands." The scheme may be worked out, as is the custom in Germany, many years in advance of actual building, thus laying down beforehand the lines of future development. Furthermore, it may, if desired, be extended to include land on which buildings have already been put up, and may provide " for the demolition or alteration of any buildings thereon, so far as may be necessary for carrying the scheme into effect." Finally, where local authorities are remiss in preparing a plan on their own initiative, power is given to the appropriate department of the central Government to order them to take action. There is ground for hope, however, that, so soon as people

---

and Government in Germany, pp. 163-4). Hence German municipalities now often control the height of buildings, providing a scale of permitted heights which decreases on passing from the centre to the outlying parts of a town.

become thoroughly familiarised with town-planning, local patriotism and inter-local emulation will make resort to pressure from above less and less necessary.

§ 14. So far we have been concerned with forms of divergence between social and private net products that are liable to occur even under conditions of simple competition. Where conditions of monopolistic competition [1]—competition, that is to say, between several sellers each producing a considerable proportion of the aggregate output—are present, the way is opened up for a new kind of investment. This consists in competitive advertisement directed to the sole purpose of transferring the demand for a given commodity from one source of supply to another.[2] There is, indeed, little opportunity for this as regards goods of a kind whose quality is uniform and, as with salt, lumber or grain, can be easily tested ; but, where quality cannot be easily tested, and especially where goods are sold in small quantities, which can readily be put into distinctive packages for the use of retail customers, there is plenty of opportunity.[3] Not all advertisement is, of course, strictly competitive. Some advertisement, on the contrary, fulfils a social purpose, in informing people of the existence of articles adapted to their tastes. Indeed, it has been said " that advertising is a necessary consequence of sale by description," and represents merely a segregated part of the complex work formerly done by those middlemen who exhibited, as well as sold, their goods.[4] Without it many useful articles, such as new machines, or useful services, such as that of life insurance, might not be brought at all to the notice of potential purchasers who have a real need for them. Furthermore, some advertisement serves to develop an entirely new set of wants on the part of consumers, the satisfaction of which involves a real addition to social well-being; and the development of which on a large scale at the same time enables the commodity that satisfies them to be produced on

---

[1] Cf. *post*, Part II. Ch. XV.

[2] Under simple competition, there is no purpose in this advertisement, because, *ex hypothesi*, the market will take, at the market price, as much as any one small seller wants to sell. Practically monopolistic competition comprises all forms of imperfect competition.

[3] Cf. Jenks and Clark, *The Trust Problem*, pp. 26-7.

[4] Cf. Shaw, *Quarterly Journal of Economics*, 1912, p. 743.

a large scale and, therefore, cheaply.[1]   Under this head it is possible to make out a case in favour of the peculiar system of advertisement arranged on behalf of the general body of its currant growers (without the mention of individual names) by the Greek Government :[2] though, of course, the development of a taste for currants is probably in part at the expense of the taste for something else.   It is not, however, necessary to my purpose to attempt an estimate of the proportion which strictly competitive advertisement bears to advertisement in the aggregate—an aggregate the cost of which has been put, for the United Kingdom, at eighty million pounds, and, for the world, at six hundred million pounds per annum.[3]   That a considerable part of the advertisement of the modern world is strictly competitive is plain.[4]   This is true alike of the more obvious forms, such as pictorial displays, newspaper paragraphs,[5] travellers, salesmen, and so on; and of the more subtle forms, such as a large exhibit of jewellery in the shop window, the according of credit, with the consequential expenditure on book-keeping and on the collection of recalcitrant debts, expenditure in keeping shops open at hours inconvenient and costly to the sellers, and other such forms.   It is plain that, up to a point, investment of this type, in so far as it retains, or gains, for the investor "a place in the sun," yields, like expenditure upon national armaments, a considerable private net product.   A curve, representing the private net products yielded by successive increments of it, would indicate positive values for a long distance.   What relation does this curve bear to the corresponding curve representing the social net products of successive increments ?

[1] Cf. the discussion of "constructive" and "combative" advertisements in Marshall's *Industry and Trade*, pp. 304-7.

[2] Cf. Goodall, *Advertizing*, p. 49.   [3] *Ibid.* p. 2.

[4] It should be observed that this type of advertisement, which aims in effect at diverting custom from a rival to oneself, may be pressed to lengths that the laws of modern States will not tolerate.   Thus in some European States certain definite false statements about awards alleged to have been won at exhibitions or about an exceptional offer of bankrupt stock, direct disparagement of a rival's character or produce, and attempts to pass off one's own goods as the goods of a well-known house are punishable offences. (Cf. Davies, *Trust Laws and Unfair Competition*, ch. x.)

[5] Of course the "resources" invested in these things are measured by the actual capital and labour involved in the production of the paragraphs, not by a monopoly charge—if such is made—exacted for them by the newspaper concerned.

First, it may happen that the net result of the expenditures made by the various rivals in conflict with each other is to bring about an alliance between them. If this happens, the expenditures induced by a state of monopolistic competition are responsible for the evolution of simple monopoly. It does not seem possible to determine in a general way the comparative effects on output that will be produced by simple monopoly and by monopolistic competition. Consequently no general statement can be made as to whether the curve representing the social net products of successive increments of investment will indicate positive values over any part of its course.

Secondly, it may happen that the expenditures on advertisement made by competing monopolists will simply neutralise one another, and leave the industrial position exactly as it would have been if neither had expended anything. For, clearly, if each of two rivals makes equal efforts to attract the favour of the public away from the other, the total result is the same as it would have been if neither had made any effort at all. This point was set in a very clear light in Mr. Butterworth's Memorandum to the Board of Trade Railway Conference in 1908. He pointed out that, under competitive arrangements, the officers of rival companies spend a great part of their time and energy in " scheming how to secure traffic for their own line, instead of in devising how best to combine economy with efficiency of working. At present much of the time and energy of the more highly-paid officials of a railway company is taken up with work in which the trading community has no interest, and which is only rendered necessary in the interest of the shareholders whom they serve by the keen competition which exists between companies." [1] In these circumstances the curve representing the social net products of successive increments of investment will indicate negative values throughout.

Thirdly, it may happen that the expenditures lead simply to the substitution in a market of goods made by one firm for the same quantity of equivalent goods made by another firm. If we suppose production, both under A's auspices and under B's,

_____

[1]. [Cd. 4677], p. 27.

to obey the law of constant supply price, and to involve equal cost per unit, it is clearly a matter of indifference to the community as a whole from which of these two producers the public buys. In other words, all units of resources expended by either producer in building up goodwill as against the other have a social net product equal to zero. If conditions are such that a diminution in the aggregate cost of production of the commodity would be brought about by the transference of some of the orders from B to A, some units of resources employed by A to abstract orders from B would yield a positive social net product, while all units of resources employed by B to abstract orders from A would yield a negative social net product. If we suppose the more efficient and the less efficient firms to expend resources in these hostilities in about equal measure, in such wise that their efforts cancel one another and leave things much as they would have been had the efforts of both been removed, it is obvious that the social net product of any compound unit of these efforts taken as a whole is, again, zero. There is, however, some slight ground for believing that firms of low productive efficiency tend to indulge in advertisement to a greater extent than their productively more efficient rivals. For, clearly, they have greater inducements to expenditure on devices, such as special packages, designed to obviate comparison of the bulk of commodity offered by them and by other producers at a given price. This consideration suggests that the curve representing the social net products of successive increments of investment is likely to indicate negative values throughout.

The discussion of the preceding paragraphs makes it plain that, speaking generally, the social net product of any r^{th} increment of resources invested in competitive advertisement is exceedingly unlikely to be as large as the private net product. The consequent waste might be diminished by special undertakings among competitors not to advertise, such as hold good among barristers, doctors and members of the London Stock Exchange. Failing this, the evil might be attacked by the State through the taxation, or prohibition, of competitive advertisements — if these could be distinguished from advertisements which are not strictly competitive. It could be removed altogether if conditions of monopolistic competition were destroyed.

§ 15. We now turn to conditions of bilateral monopoly, that is to say, conditions under which the relations between individual buyers and sellers are not rigidly fixed by a surrounding market. The presence of bilateral monopoly in this sense implies an element of theoretical indeterminateness, and, therefore, opens up the way for the employment of activities and resources in efforts to modify the ratio of exchange in favour of one or other of the "monopolists." The nature of the indeterminateness present is different according as the monopolists are, as it were, solidified units, such as single individuals and joint-stock companies, or representative units, such as Trade Unions or Employers' Federations, whose officials negotiate to establish a rate of pay, but whose individual members, when this rate is established, are still free at will to continue or to abandon business. This distinction is, for some purposes, important and ought not to be ignored.[1] It does not, however, bear directly upon our present inquiry. For, whatever the nature of the indeterminateness, it is plain that activities and resources devoted to manipulating the ratio of exchange may yield a positive private net product ; but they cannot—even the earliest dose of them cannot—yield a positive social net product, and they may in some conditions yield a negative social net product.[2] The activities here contemplated consist chiefly— for physical force exercised in direct plunder does not operate through exchange—in the brain work of " bargaining " proper and in the practice of one or other of two sorts of deception. These latter are, first, deception as to the physical nature of a thing offered for sale, and, secondly, deception as to the

---

[1] With solidified units the *settlement locus*—*i.e.* the range of possible bargains—lies along the contract curve, and with representative units along portions of the two reciprocal demand (or supply) curves. For a technical discussion of this and connected points cf. my paper "Equilibrium under Bilateral Monopoly" (*Economic Journal*, Jan. 1908, pp. 205 *et seq.*) ; also my *Principles and Methods of Industrial Peace*, Appendix A.

[2] It will be understood that net product here means net product of dividend. It is not, of course, denied that, if a poor man outbargains a rich one, there is a positive net product of economic satisfaction, and, if a rich man outbargains a poor one, a corresponding negative net product of satisfaction.

future yield that it is reasonable to expect from a thing offered for sale, when the physical nature of that thing has been correctly described.

§ 16. Of bargaining proper there is little that need be said. It is obvious that intelligence and resources devoted to this purpose, whether on one side or on the other, and whether successful or unsuccessful, yield no net product to the community as a whole. According to Professor Carver, a considerable part of the energies of business men is devoted to, and a considerable part of their earnings arise out of, activities of this kind.[1] These activities are wasted. They contribute to private, but not to social, net product. But this conclusion does not exhaust the subject. It is often pointed out that, where their clients, be they customers or workpeople, can be squeezed, employers tend to expend their energy in accomplishing this, rather than in improving the organisation of their factories. When they act thus, the social net product even of the earliest dose of resources devoted to bargaining may be, not merely zero, but negative. Whenever that happens, no tax that yields a revenue, though it may effect an improvement, can provide a complete remedy. For that absolute prohibition is required. But absolute prohibition of bargaining is hardly feasible except where prices and conditions of sale are imposed upon private industry by some organ of State authority.[2]

§ 17. Deception as to the physical nature of a thing offered for sale is practised through false weights and measures, adulteration and misnaming of goods, and dishonest advertisement. Before the days of co-operation "the back streets of the manufacturing towns swarmed with small shops, in which the worst of everything was sold, with unchecked measures and unproved weights."[3] To a less degree similar practices still prevail. There is little temptation to adopt them in marketing "production goods," where the buyers are large industrial concerns, like railway companies, which

[1] Cf. *American Economic Association*, 1909, p. 51.

[2] The legislation of many States concerning private labour exchanges is relevant here. For an account of this legislation, cf. Becker and Bernhardt, *Gesetzliche Regelung der Arbeitsvermittelung*.

[3] Aves, *Co-operative Industry*, p. 16.

possess elaborately organised testing departments. But, in selling " consumption goods "—particularly semi-mysterious consumption goods like patent medicines—to poor and ignorant buyers, and even in selling production goods to less skilled buyers, such as farmers, there is still some temptation. It is always profitable for sellers to " offer commodities which seem, rather than are, useful, if the difference between seeming and reality is likely to escape notice." [1] Deception as to the future yield, which it is reasonable to expect from a thing offered for sale, is practised, in the main, by unscrupulous financiers selling stocks and shares. Among the methods employed are the manipulation of dividend payments, " matched orders," the deliberate publication of false information,[2] and — a practice less clearly over the border line of fairness—the deliberate withholding of relevant information.[3] It is evident that, up to a point, activities devoted to either of these forms of deception bring about a positive private net product, but not a positive social net product. Furthermore, they often lead to enhanced purchases and, therefore, enhanced production of the thing about which deception has been practised. Hence they divert to the

---

[1] Sidgwick, *Principles of Political Economy*, p. 416.

[2] For a lurid account of some of these methods *vide* Lawson, *Frenzied Finance, passim*, and for an analysis of the protective devices embodied in the celebrated German law of 1884, *vide* Schuster, " The Promotion of Companies and the Valuation of their Assets according to German Law," *Economic Journal*, 1900, p. 1 *et seq.* It should be observed that the device of " matched orders " may be made difficult by a rule forbidding offers and bids for large amounts of stock on the terms " all or none." For, when such a rule exists, there is more chance that a seller or buyer operating a matched order may be forced unwillingly to make a deal with some one other than his confidant. (Cf. Brace, *The Value of Organised Speculation*, p. 241.)

[3] It is interesting to observe that, whereas the law often, and public opinion generally, condemns a seller who withholds relevant information, a buyer who acts in this way is generally commended for his " good bargain." Thus to pick up a piece of valuable oak furniture in an out-of-the-way cottage for much less than it is worth is thought by some to be creditable; and nobody maintains that the Rothschild, who founded the fortunes of his house by buying government stock on the strength of his early knowledge of the battle of Waterloo, was bound in honour to make that information public before acting on it. The reason for this distinction probably is that the possessor of an article is presumed to have full opportunity of knowing its real value, and, if he fails to do this, becomes, for his carelessness, legitimate prey. A director of a company who bought up shares in that company on the strength of knowledge gained in the Board room, and so not available to the shareholders generally, would be universally condemned.

production of this thing resources that would otherwise have been devoted to investments yielding the normal marginal return. Therefore, when this indirect consequence is taken into account, the social net product even of the earliest dose of resources devoted to deception, is, in general, not zero but negative. If the thing in question is something the production of which involves no expenditure of resources, like the fictitious situations created by fraudulent registry offices, the social net product does not, indeed, sink below zero, for extra production of these imaginary entities involves no withdrawal of resources from elsewhere. As a rule, however, the social net product of any dose of resources invested in a deceptive activity is negative. Consequently, as with bargaining, no tax that yields a revenue, though it may effect an improvement, can provide a complete remedy, and absolute prohibition of the activity is required. Attempts to establish such prohibition have been made, on the one side, in various laws concerning false weights and measures and the adulteration of foods, and, on the other side, in various laws—laws, which to be effective, must be enforceable at the instance, not of the damaged party, but of public inspectors or commissioners [1]—designed to control and regulate the practice of company promotion. In other fields the evil can be met in a more direct way by the establishment of Purchasers' Associations, in which the interests of the sellers and the buyers are unified.[2]

[1] Cf. Van Hise, *Concentration and Control*, pp. 76-9.
[2] Cf. *post* Part II. Ch. XIX.

CHAPTER X

MARGINAL PRIVATE AND SOCIAL NET PRODUCTS IN RELATION TO INDUSTRIAL FORMS

§ 1. In the preceding chapter we were engaged in a study of the differences between the marginal social net product and the marginal private net product of resources devoted to various occupations or industries. It is now necessary to conduct an analogous inquiry about resources devoted to various forms of economic organisation within the several occupations or industries. Marshall long ago observed: "As a general rule the law of substitution—which is nothing more than a special and limited application of the law of the survival of the fittest— tends to make one method of industrial organisation supplant another when it offers a direct and immediate service at a lower price. The indirect and ultimate services, which either will render, have, as a general rule, little or no weight in the balance."[1] These indirect services constitute the difference between the social net product and the private net product of a unit of resources invested in any form of economic organisation. Our present task is to distinguish the principal fields in which they play an important part.

§ 2. One very important indirect service is rendered by the general economic organisation of a country in so far as, in addition to fulfilling its function as an instrument of production, it also acts, in greater or less degree, as a training ground of business capacities. In order that it may do this effectively, the size of business units must be so graded that persons possessed of good native endowments can learn the principles of enterprise in some small and simple concern, and thereafter

[1] *Principles of Economics*, p. 597.

can gradually move upwards, as their capacity improves with practice, to larger and more difficult posts. The point may be put in this way. When the separate steps in the agricultural or industrial ladder are large, it is difficult for a man adapted, if adequate practice is obtained, for life at one stage, but standing by some accident at another stage, to move to his proper place. Thus—to take a hypothetical example—if agriculture or industry were worked exclusively in large units consisting of one or two large entrepreneurs assisted by a number of mere labourers, any capacity for management and direction that might be born among people in the labouring class would have no opportunity for use or development. Many persons endowed with native capacity would thus be compelled to be watchers only and not doers. But, as Jevons has well taught, it is doing, and not watching, that trains. "A few specimens probed thoroughly," he wrote, "teach more than thousands glanced at through a glass case. The whole British Museum accordingly will not teach a youth as much as he will learn by collecting a few fossils or a few minerals, *in situ* if possible, and taking them home to examine and read and think about."[1] The point was put even more forcibly by Marshall in his address to the Co-operative Society in 1885: "It is a better training in seamanship to sail a fishing-boat than to watch a three-masted ship, the tops of whose masts alone appear above the horizon."[2] Thus it would seem that, in the absence of a proper ladder, a great deal of the business capacity born among the working classes must run to waste. If, however, industry or agriculture is organised by way of units of many different sizes, a workman possessing mental power beyond what is normal to his class can, without great difficulty, himself become the entrepreneur of a small establishment, and gradually advance, educating his powers the while, higher up the ladder that is provided for him.

§ 3. This train of thought suggests that, in a community organised on the general lines of a modern industrial State, associations of workers combined together in small co-partner-

---

[1] *Methods of Social Reform*, p. 61.
[2] *Loc. cit.* p. 17.

ship workshops constitute an industrial form, investment in which is likely to yield a marginal social net product considerably in excess of the marginal private net product. For such workshops provide the first stage of the ladder that is needed to lift upwards the great fund of capacity for management that is almost certainly lying latent among the manual labouring classes. They furnish, as it were, a first school in which this capacity can be developed, and, in so doing, contribute for the service of the community, not merely boots and shoes, but well-trained, competent men, by whose work the national dividend will afterwards be augmented. Much the same thing holds good of the analogous workers' businesses in agriculture. Gardens and small allotments near their cottages for workmen in regular employment elsewhere, large allotments for workmen occasionally taking odd jobs elsewhere, and small holdings for those who devote themselves entirely to work on these holdings, provide in combination a complete ladder from the status of labourer to that of independent farmer. This ladder yields a product of human capacity over and above its immediate product of crops. That element of social net product, however, does not accrue to those persons by whom the size of agricultural holdings is regulated, and is not included in the marginal private net product of the resources invested in them. This is enough to establish a *prima facie* case for the " artificial encouragement," by State action or by private philanthropy, of Workers' Associations and of various grades of allotments and small holdings. Such encouragement is given to Workers' Associations, in England by the support of Retail Co-operative Societies, and in France and Italy by the grant of special facilities for tendering on Government work. The movement for developing allotments and small holdings has also, in this country, received governmental help.

§ 4. The same line of thought, looked at from the other side, suggests that the marginal social net product of activities devoted to bringing about any widespread "trustification" of industry is likely to be smaller than the marginal private net product. For large combinations—this does not apply to those Kartels whose members remain separate and independent on the productive side—by lessening the opportunities for training in the entrepreneur function, tend to prevent the level of business ability from rising as high as it might otherwise do. "The development of a high order of undertaking genius in the few seems to depend upon a wide range of undertaking experience in the many." With the main part of industry organised into million dollar combines, the ladder connecting different stages of managing ability would be gravely damaged. Nor would the opportunity for obtaining positions as managers of departments in a giant concern go far to make up for this; for, apart from the limited degree of independent initiative which the management of a department, as compared with the control of a business, necessarily involves, departments will not vary in size so widely, or reach so low down in the scale, as private businesses may do. In his address to the Royal Economic Society in 1908, Marshall called attention to the educative possibilities of small businesses, illustrating his thesis from the present organisation of the milk trade. He pointed out that, so far as the working of industries by the State—and the same thing, of course, applies to the working of them by large commercial combinations—does away with this sort of educative ladder, the mere proof that it was *immediately* more economical than private management would not suffice to show that it was more economical on the whole.[1] This is the same thing as saying that the marginal social net product is less than the marginal private net product. The practical inference, so far as the present argument goes, is plain. Though in the special emergency of the Great War, when immediate output was absolutely essential and had to be won even though the future suffered, the State might rightly intervene to *enforce* various forms of combination that would not have come about without it, yet in normal times of peace it should always hesitate before encouraging, and should

---

[1] We may notice that, when, as in such a country as India, the narrowness of the markets and other causes prevent the development of any large-scale industries, the top end of the industrial ladder is cut off, and there is a difficulty, analogous to the difficulty discussed in the text, about the provision of an adequate training-ground for the higher forms of business ability. (Cf. Morison, *The Industrial Organisation of an Indian Province*, p. 186.)

perhaps in some instances impede, any threatened excess in the growth of giant businesses, whether these are publicly or privately owned. What has been said above, however, obviously does not exhaust the considerations relevant to this problem. Further discussion of it will be found in Chapters XIV. and XXI.

§ 5. Considerations of the same general character as the above are relevant to certain developments in the method and practice of standardised production.[1] It has long been known that, by specialisation to a limited number of standard forms, great economy of cost and increase of output can be achieved. This economy, furthermore, is not confined to the point at which standardisation is first applied; for, if one industry agrees to standardise its product, the industries which make machines and tools for making that product are in turn enabled to standardise theirs. The Standards Committee of the Engineering Trade of this country has done much work in drawing up, for screws, nuts, certain motor parts and various other things, standard specifications which have been adopted throughout the engineering industry of the country generally. The experience of the Great War, in which military equipment and munitions had necessarily to be of uniform patterns, brought out more clearly than before the enormous scope for direct economies which, partly by making possible the employment of relatively unskilled labour, standardisation of product is able, in favourable circumstances, to create. The urgent need for immediate large output at a minimum of cost even led to standardisation, under Government authority, of such things as ships and boots. The essence of the matter is that the standardisation of certain products over the whole of an industry, by enabling the firms that make them, and the other firms that make tools for making them, to specialise more closely than would otherwise be possible, leads immediately to an enormously increased output of these products. This increased output we may call, if we will, the private net product of the method of standardisation. If, however, attention is concen-

---

[1] In *Industry and Trade*, Bk. ii., chapters ii. and iii., Marshall, after distinguishing between standards *particular* to an individual producer and standards that are *general* to the greater part of an industry, has much interesting discussion of modern developments in standardisation.

trated exclusively upon this, the net advantages of the method will sometimes be greatly exaggerated. For standardisation almost inevitably checks the development of new patterns, new processes and new ideas. It is all very well to make rules for revising periodically the standard specifications. This is not an adequate remedy, because the real danger of standardisation is, not so much that it will prevent the adoption of new things when their superiority has been recognised, but that it will greatly lessen the inducement to manufacturers to devise and try new things. For in normal industry the profit which a man gets out of an improvement is chiefly won in the period when he is ahead of his competitors, before the improvement is adopted generally. With a rigid system of standardisation nobody would be able to be ahead of anybody else or to introduce a new pattern till the whole trade did so. The whole line, in short, must advance together; and this means that no part of it has any great inducement to advance at all. Other things being equal, the marginal social net product of effort devoted towards standardising processes falls short of the marginal private net product, in so far as it indirectly checks inventions and improvements and so lessens productive powers in the future. Obviously the gap thus indicated is not equally wide for all commodities. It is difficult to believe, for example, that the establishment of standard sizes and standard forms for such things as screws and nuts is likely to prevent the development of any important improvement. In these simple things there is little or no room for improvement. But with complex manufactures the position is altogether different. Even in the course of the Great War, when large output was of overwhelming importance, it would have been madness to standardise the production of aeroplanes ; the opening for discovery and for the development of better types was so wide. In many other finished manufactures it is impossible to feel any confidence that the final form has already been evolved. There is, therefore, always the danger that, by standardisation, we shall augment enormously the production of the good at the cost of never attaining to the better. In any action that the State may take to foster standardisation for the sake of the immediate and direct stimulus which it gives to output this danger must be carefully borne in mind.

§ 6. Yet again, the analysis here developed is applicable to certain aspects of that method of business organisation that has come to be known as "scientific management." The general characteristics of that system are well known. Elaborate study of the various operations to be performed is undertaken by trained experts, who analyse these operations into their separate elements, and, on the basis of this analysis, coupled with careful observation of the methods actually followed by a number of good workmen, construct, by combination, an ideal method superior to any yet in vogue. The kind of improvement to which this process leads is illustrated by the results of Mr. Gilbraith's investigation of the problem of laying bricks. He "studied the best height for the mortar box and brick pile, and then designed a scaffold, with a table on it, upon which all of the materials are placed, so as to keep the bricks, the mortar, the man, and the wall in their proper relative positions. These scaffolds are adjusted, as the wall grows in height, for all of the bricklayers, by a labourer especially detailed for this purpose, and by this means the bricklayer is saved the exertion of stooping down to the level of his feet for each brick and each trowelful of mortar and then straightening up again. Think of the waste of effort that has gone on through all these years, with each bricklayer lowering his body, weighing, say, 150 pounds, down two feet and raising it up again every time a brick (weighing about 5 pounds) is laid in the wall! And this each bricklayer did about one thousand times a day."[1] This device is, however, merely one example of what scientific management endeavours to achieve in general. The central conception involved in it is that of handing over the task of planning methods to trained experts, and then explaining to the workmen in elaborate detail what it is they have to do, including even the pauses and rest periods that they should take between successive operations and movements. "The work of every workman is fully planned out by the management at least one day in advance, and each man receives in most cases complete written instructions, describing in detail

[1] Taylor, *The Principles of Scientific Management*, p. 78.

the task which he is to accomplish, as well as the means to be used in doing the work. And the work planned in advance in this way constitutes a task which is to be solved, as explained above, not by the workman alone, but in almost all cases by the joint effort of the workman and the management. This task specifies, not only what is to be done, but how it is to be done and the exact time allowed for doing it."[1] The work of teaching the workmen how to do it, and of seeing that they properly understand and carry out their instructions, is entrusted to a new class of officials known as "functional foremen." These officials, working in conjunction with the accounting officer, can ascertain at once how far the costs of any particular workman's output exceed the proper costs laid down beforehand, and can then concentrate attention and instruction at any point where there is *prima facie* reason to hope for improvement.[2] Now it is perfectly plain that this type of industrial organisation is likely to yield large immediate economies, and that the careful teaching involved in it must *up to a point* yield much permanent good. It is a paradox that, "though in the athletic world instructors exist to teach boxers how to balance themselves and use their arms, and cricket professionals are constantly at work improving the efficiency of batsmen and bowlers, and coaches are a necessity to teach a boat's crew collectively and individually how and when to move their bodies and hands, yet in the industrial world the value of teaching operatives how to earn their livelihood is hardly yet recognised."[3] Nevertheless, there is real danger lest this new-found science should be pushed too far. Carried to excessive lengths it *may*, from a long period point of view, defeat its own ends. First, it is not proper to assume that there is only one best method of doing a thing independent of the psychological and physical qualities of the individual doing it. There may be several first-class methods, some more fitted to bring out the best in one man, another more

---

[1] Taylor, *The Principles of Scientific Management*, p. 39.

[2] Cf. Emerson, *Efficiency*, ch. vii. Mr. Dicksee draws some instructive comparisons between these methods and the various forms of drill practised among soldiers. (*Business Methods and the War*, Lecture 2.)

[3] Health of Munition Workers Committee, *Interim Report*, p. **77.**

suited to another man.[1] Secondly, so far as the operations of the individual workman are reduced to a mechanical plan, the original source from which the directing authority derived its standard methods—namely, a combination of the best points in the *varied* individual methods of different workmen—would be dried up. Overt suggestions from workpeople for improvements in method would also, perhaps, be rendered less probable. No doubt, this loss could be partly atoned for by the employment of scientific experts specially charged with the task of experimenting in new methods. But, after all, these are available under ordinary systems of works' management and cannot, therefore, be regarded as a peculiar asset of the Taylor system, to be set against its peculiar failings. Nor is it only in respect of specific suggestions and devices that injury may be indirectly wrought by this system. There is grave reason to fear lest the *general* initiative and independent activity of workpeople may be injured by their complete subordination to the detailed control of functional foremen, much as the *general* initiative of soldiers is injured by the grinding of an over-rigid and mechanical military system. By the removal of opportunities for the exercise of initiative, capacity for initiative may be destroyed, and the quality of the labouring force may in this way be subtly lowered. In so far as this happens, the marginal social net product of resources invested in the development and application of scientific management falls short of the marginal private net product. Unless the State or philanthropy intervenes, there is a danger that this method of industrial organisation may be carried further and applied more widely than the interest of the national dividend—not to speak of the more general interest of society—when viewed as a whole, demands.

[1] Cf. Miers, *Mind and Work*, p. 192.

CHAPTER XI

INCREASING AND DECREASING SUPPLY PRICE

§ 1. In Chapter IX. § 3 attention was drawn to a type of divergence between private and social net product additional to the two types that were studied in that chapter. This type of divergence arises when a part of the effect of employing a unit of resources in any occupation consists of something, which, instead of coming in the first instance to the person who invests the unit, comes instead, in the first instance, to other persons engaged in the occupation. To simplify the study of these divergences I shall imagine that there exists an archetypal industry, in which the values of the marginal private net product and of the marginal social net product of investment are *both* equal to one another and *also* stand at a sort of central level representative of industries in general.[1] In any actual industry conducted under conditions of simple competition—that is to say, conditions such that each seller produces as much as he can at the ruling market price, and does not restrict his output in the hope of causing that price to rise—investment and output must be carried to a point at which the value of the marginal private net product of investment there conforms to the central value. It follows that the value of the marginal social net product of investment in the industry can only diverge from this central value if and in so far as it diverges from the value of the marginal private net product. The present

---

[1] It is not necessary to suppose that this central value is actually attained in any industry ; it is rather to be conceived as the level which would be attained under conditions of simple competition in an industry of constant supply price.

chapter is concerned exclusively with conditions of simple competition.

§ 2. Let us place ourselves in imagination in a country where the flow of resources coming annually into being has to be distributed regularly among a variety of occupations. It is assumed that, when any given quantity of resources is devoted to a given occupation, the concrete form assumed by these resources—their distribution, for example, into many or few individual firms and so forth—is the most economical form available (from the standpoint of the period of time relevant to our problem) for that quantity of new resources; and that, when a slightly greater quantity is devoted to the occupation, the concrete form assumed is the most economical form available (from the same standpoint) for that quantity. When this assumption is made, it is plain that, if one unit is added to the resources *of any given sort*[1] that normally flow into any one occupation, that unit will yield the same net product as each of the other units in the flow. All the units are interchangeable in this sense. But, none the less, the presence of an extra unit may alter the output of the other units, in such wise that the addition made to aggregate output is either more or less than proportionate to the difference made to the quantity of resources invested. In so far as the other units belong to the investor of the given unit and the difference made to the output of the other units comes in the first instance to him, it enters into the private net product as well as into the social net product of the extra unit. But, in so far as the other units belong to people other than the investor of the given unit, the difference made to the output of these units enters into the social net product, but not into the private net product of the given unit. The two sorts of marginal net product in the particular industry, and hence their values, therefore, differ. Since then investment under competitive conditions is carried to the point at which the value of the marginal private net product of the resources placed there is equal to the central value, the value of the

---

[1] In view of the definition of an increment of investment given in Chapter IX. § 2, we must not speak of units being added to *the* resources without qualification that flow into an occupation.

social net product in that industry must diverge from the central value ; and the national dividend is not maximised.[1]

§ 3. This statement has now to be brought into connection with the familiar economic concept of increasing, constant and diminishing returns, or, as some prefer to say, decreasing, constant and increasing costs. As a preliminary it will be convenient to provide ourselves with an appropriate terminology. The expressions cited above. used in the present connection,[2] are designed to describe certain relations between the output of a commodity and the expenses, measured in money, that are incurred in producing it. Diminishing and increasing returns mean diminishing and increasing yields of commodity per unit of money expenses as the output of the commodity increases ; increasing and decreasing costs mean increasing and decreasing money expenses per unit of the commodity as the output increases. The two sets of terms are thus,

[1] In an industry, for whose product the demand has an elasticity equal to unity, the amount of resources devoted to production will obviously be the same whether, the social net product of any r^{th} increment of investment being given, this social net product of that increment is equal to or greater than the private net product. Therefore, when there is an excess of social over private net product in respect of the marginal unit of resources invested, the effect of the existence of this excess, in conditions of competition, is that consumers obtain for nothing exactly this excess : and the effect of there being an excess of (the given) social above private net product in respect of the other units of invested resources is that they obtain for nothing the aggregate of all these excesses. In industries, however, in which the elasticity of demand is not equal to unity, the existence of an excess of (the given) social above private net product of various quantities of investment causes the quantity of investment made to be different from what it would otherwise have been. This implies that the effect on the consumers' material estate, due to the existence of an excess of social over private net product in respect of the unit of investment which is marginal when there is such an excess, is not simply the amount of that excess. In like manner the effect on their material estate of the sum of all the excesses of the units of resources that are in fact employed is not simply the sum of those excesses. It follows, of course, that the effect on their satisfaction (as expressed in money) is not measured, as it is in the case of unitary demand elasticity, by the excess of their aggregate demand price for the quantity of product they do secure over their aggregate demand price for the quantity that they would have secured had (the given) social net product throughout been equal to private net product. These considerations render it inappropriate, except when the elasticity of demand is unitary, to speak of the excess of marginal social net product over marginal private net product as equivalent, in conditions of competition, to what "accrues" to the consumer in consequence of there being such an excess. For this reason I have in the present text modified the phraseology employed in the corresponding passages of the third edition.

[2] For another use cf. *post*, Part IV. Ch. III.

so to speak, reciprocals of one another.   Both alike, however,
are open to an objection.   It is not clear, on the face of
things, whether the returns per unit of money expenses, or
expenses per unit of returns, to which they refer, are average
or marginal returns or expenses; and, when diminishing
returns (or increasing costs) hold for some amounts of output
and increasing returns (or decreasing costs) for other amounts,
there must, it would seem, be certain amounts in respect of
which marginal returns are increasing (or marginal expenses
decreasing) while average returns are decreasing (or average
expenses increasing), and *vice versa*.   It is, therefore, best, as
I think, to surrender both the above forms of expression,
and to distinguish industries according as they conform to
conditions of *increasing, constant or decreasing supply price.*
It will be shown in Appendix III. that, in competitive
industries, the supply price of any quantity of output is
equal both to the marginal expenses and to the average
expenses of what I call the equilibrium firm engaged in the
industry; and that it is a concept free from ambiguity.
That discussion need not be repeated here.   For the reader
not interested in refinements of analysis it is sufficient to
say that my laws of increasing, constant and decreasing
supply price correspond, for practical purposes, to what are
ordinarily known as the laws of diminishing, constant and increasing returns, or increasing, constant and decreasing costs.[1]
It is, of course, with long-period or "normal," not with any
form of short-period supply price, that we here have to do.

§ 4. The relations which these laws express between
variations in supply price and variations in output are not
necessarily the relations which do subsist between these
things in history, but the relations which would subsist
subject to the condition *other things being equal.*   In real
life, with the general advance of knowledge, new methods of

---

[1] Professor Cannan has objected to the use of the term "law" in connection
with diminishing and increasing returns as defined above, on the ground that,
whereas in some industries diminishing, and in others increasing, returns
prevail, a scientific law is a statement that holds true in all, and not only in
some, circumstances (*Wealth*, p. 70).   It might be answered that in fact this
is only true of the most general laws of physics.   Biologists, for example,
regularly speak of Mendel's law of inheritance, without any implication that
all inheritance obeys this law.   But in any event the point is a verbal one.

production are being continually introduced and new technical appliances invented. Some of these changes are due to factors which would operate *even though the scale of output of the industry remained constant.* Others are the result of the changes in the scale of output, being called out in response to changes in demand. Of course, in practice, it may often be impossible to say whether a particular invention in, say, the process of steel manufacture is or is not due to changes in the scale of output. Logically, however, the distinction is quite clear. For the present purpose changes not due to changes in the scale of output are definitely ruled out of consideration. Therefore an industry may display continually falling supply price through a long series of years, and yet may not be operating under conditions of decreasing supply price [1] as understood here. In like manner, when, for example, the coal seams of a country are being gradually worked out, an industry may display continually rising supply and yet may not be operating under conditions of increasing supply price.[2] An industry is said to conform to increasing, constant or decreasing supply price, when, apart from changes in technique or other inventions not due to changes in the scale of output, increase of output would be associated, as the case may be, with increasing, constant or decreasing supply prices.

§ 5. Attention must next be called to a distinction, which, for the present purpose, is fundamental. When we speak without qualification of laws of increasing, constant or decreasing supply price, we have in view the relation between variations in the output of a commodity and variations in the supply price per unit *from the standpoint of the industry producing the commodity.* These variations are not always or necessarily the same as the variations in the supply price per unit of the commodity *from the standpoint of the community.* Consider an industry which purchases from others factors of production only. When, with a given measure of increase

---

[1] Geometrically the continuous fall in costs would be represented by a lowering of the whole supply curve.

[2] In this case the extent to which the seams are worked out at any time is, of course, a result of the scale of output that ruled in the past ; but this leaves my distinction intact.

in the output of anything, the money expenses per unit of output incurred by the equilibrium firm increase, because for each unit of output it has to buy, at the same price as before, greater quantities of one or another factor, the two sorts of variation are identical. But, when the expenses per unit increase because it has to pay for the factors of production which it employs a higher money price, the extra payment that it makes is offset by an equal and opposite extra payment which the owners of the several factors of production receive. From the point of view of the community as a whole no extra expense per unit of output is incurred. In like manner, when the expenses per unit to the equilibrium firm in an industry decrease because it pays for the factors it employs a lower money price, from the point of view of the community as a whole there is no saving of expenses per unit of output. This matter is examined in more detail in Appendix III. We say, then, that an industry conforms to the law of increasing, constant or decreasing supply price *simpliciter*, when it so conforms from the standpoint of the industry under review, *i.e.* when the variations in supply price, calculated without any allowance for the transfer elements distinguished above, that are associated with increases of output, are positive, nil or negative respectively. We say that it conforms to the law of increasing, constant or decreasing supply price from the standpoint of the community, when these variations, corrected so as to eliminate transfer elements, are positive, nil or negative.[1]

[1] This conception, though mathematically simple, needs to be handled carefully when translated into ordinary language. An industry conforms to conditions of decreasing, constant or increasing supply price *simpliciter* according as the rate of increase, from the standpoint of the industry, of the supply price (associated with increasing output) is negative, nil or positive : it conforms to conditions of decreasing, constant or increasing supply price from the standpoint of the community according as the rate of increase from the standpoint of the community is negative, nil or positive. The rate of increase from the standpoint of the industry of the supply price is a differential, the integral of which is the supply price. The rate of increase from the standpoint of the community of the supply price is also a differential, but the integral which corresponds to it has no real significance. *The rate of change from the standpoint of the community in the supply price* does *not* mean *the rate of change in the supply price from the standpoint of the community.* There is no separate supply price from the standpoint of the community : there is only one supply price from all standpoints.

§ 6. Conditions of decreasing supply price *from the stand-point of the community* are clearly possible in a material as well as in a formal sense. For, when the scale of an industry increases, this change often leads to changes in the internal structure and methods of working of the firms engaged in it, or in the proportions in which the several factors of production are employed, of a kind which would lower the cost of production per unit, even though the prices per unit of all the factors of production employed were unaltered. Thus many writers have called attention to the fact that, when an industry is on a small scale, the firms belonging to it all engage in producing a number of different types or varieties of their commodity. They are, more or less, firms of all work. There is not a sufficiently wide or assured market to allow of close specialisation. As, however, the general demand grows, it becomes more and more worth while for firms to specialise on particular types. Thus Sir Sydney Chapman has observed that the relatively large scale of the cotton industry in England is associated, not only with specialisation between the processes of spinning and weaving, but with further specialisation between firms spinning fine counts and those spinning coarse counts. In contrast to this : " The range of work undertaken by the typical factory in Germany is far greater than that undertaken by the typical factory in England. Hence naturally the skill of the operatives is less in Germany ; more time is wasted and factory organisation is less perfect."[1] The increased specialisation of its component firms made possible by an enlargement in an industry as a whole often involves a large reduction in costs. This reduction might, so far as pure theory goes, be accompanied by no change, or even by a decrease, in the size of the typical firm. In practice it is likely to be accompanied by some increase in this size. Thus Marshall writes : " An increase in the aggregate volume of the production of anything will generally increase the size, and, therefore, the internal economies possessed by (such) a representative firm."[2] This, however, is a secondary consideration. The essential point is that an increase in the scale to

[1] *Work and Wages*, vol. i. p. 166.
[2] *Principles of Economics*, p. 318.

which an industry is producing frequently alters—in general diminishes—the average (and marginal) costs of the equilibrium firm contained in it, whether or not it also alters its size. There is, then, no difficulty in seeing that the law of decreasing supply price from the standpoint of the community is not merely formally possible, but is likely to be followed in practice by many manufacturing industries.

§ 7. Conditions of increasing supply price *from the standpoint of the community* are, however, in different case. We consider, as before, an industry which purchases for its own use factors of production, but no other ingredients. At the worst the equilibrium firm is in a position to maintain its original scale of output: and it will, in fact, do this unless some other scale now makes possible a lower cost per unit of output. Hence, in order that the law of increasing supply price from the standpoint of the community may prevail, conditions must be such that a mere increase in the output of the industry as a whole would cause the average expenses of the equilibrium firm —which are equal, as is shown in Appendix III., to the supply price of the industry—to increase, even though that firm continued to produce exactly the same output as before and paid exactly the same prices for the factors of production employed by it. It is *possible*, no doubt, that diseconomies of this character— injuries to the efficiency of old firms brought about by the mere existence of new ones—may occur. But their occurrence is, on the face of things, highly improbable; and that they should occur in sufficient measure to outweigh the factors, described in the preceding section, that make for decreasing supply price is more improbable still. In general, therefore, we may conclude that an industry, whose purchases embrace only factors of production, cannot conform to the law of increasing supply price from the standpoint of the community, *i.e.* when variations in supply price are expressed in such a way that transfer elements are eliminated.

§ 8. When an industry, besides purchasing ultimate factors of production, purchases also materials, machinery and so on, the matter is less simple. The price variations in these things, if such occur, do not now necessarily represent only transfer expenditure. They do not do so, for example, when an increase in the size of the cotton industry enables textile machinery to be produced with more help from specialisation and standardisation, and, therefore, more cheaply. The fall in price of textile machinery brought about in this way when the cotton industry expands is relevant to the law of supply price in that industry, not merely from the standpoint of the industry, but also from that of the community. Since, however, what is sold to one industry, other than factors of production, must be the product of another industry, it follows from the discussion of the preceding section that an increase in the output (and, therefore, in the demand for materials and machinery) in a given industry cannot involve an increase in the price of the things it buys, except by causing an increase in the price of the factors of production that make them. Therefore, in this complex case, no less than in the simpler one, conditions of increasing supply price from the standpoint of the community are excluded. From the cosmopolitan point of view they are excluded absolutely. From the point of view of a particular country purchasing materials from abroad they may, however, be present. For, though, if the price of imported materials rises as a consequence of an increase in the scale of the given industry, this can only be because a transfer is made to the owners of the factors that help to make them, these owners belong to other countries, and, therefore, so far as the one country is concerned, the transfer does not cancel itself.

§ 9. We may now return to the argument of § 2. In that argument, it will have been noticed, no reference was made to the prices of the several factors of production that are at work. Quantities of resources in a physical sense were related directly to quantities of output, so what was said was complete. Now, provided that (small) variations in output in a given industry do not involve variations in the prices of any factor of production, variations in the quantities of the several factors employed may, with propriety, be measured by the variations in the amount of money which is expended by the industry in purchasing them for its use. In these conditions the argument of § 2 can be translated into an inverse form thus. The marginal private net product of the equilibrium firm is equal to the average net product of the equilibrium firm per unit cost; and is thus the reciprocal of the supply price of the product. The marginal social net product, on the other hand, is the reciprocal of the marginal supply price of the product to the industry, *i.e.* of the difference made to the total money expenses of the industry by adding a small increment of output. Hence to say that the marginal private net product of investment in any industry is greater (or less) than the marginal social net product is the same thing as to say that the supply price is less (or greater) than the marginal supply price to the industry. This fact, taken in conjunction with the argument of Appendix III. §§ 16-17, implies that in a many-firm industry the value of the marginal private net product of any quantity of investment is greater than, equal to or less than the value of the marginal social net product, according as the industry conforms to conditions of increasing, constant or decreasing supply price from the standpoint of the industry—which in the conditions supposed is the same as the standpoint of the community. When, in a competitive industry, variations in output involve variations in the price of some of the factors of production employed, so that the rates of change in supply price, regarded from the two standpoints, differ, an extension of the above argument shows that the value of the marginal private net product of investment is greater than, equal to or less than the value of the marginal social net product according as the industry conforms to conditions of increasing, constant or decreasing supply price from the standpoint, not of the industry, but of the community.[1]

§ 10. It remains to inquire in this last case what, if any, light can be thrown on the relation between the values of the marginal social and marginal private net products, if we know of an industry merely that it conforms to one or other of the laws of increasing, constant or decreasing supply price *simpliciter* (*i.e.* from the standpoint of the industry). The conclusions that flow from the preceding analysis are then as follows: First, it is on the face of things very improbable that an increase in the output of any commodity will cause a *fall* in

[1] Cf. Appendix III. § 17.

the aggregate money price that would have to be expended to secure the same quantities of all the factors collectively as were employed before the increase.[1] Therefore, when conditions of decreasing supply price *simpliciter* rule, conditions of decreasing supply price from the standpoint of the community must, *in general*, also rule, and, therefore, under competitive conditions, the marginal private net product of investment in the industry will, in general, fall short of the marginal social net product. When, however, conditions of increasing supply price *simpliciter* rule, it need not happen that conditions of increasing supply price from the standpoint of the community also rule : indeed, except in the special circumstances described in § 8, this cannot happen. Therefore the law of increasing supply price *simpliciter* does not imply that, under competitive conditions, the marginal private net product of investment in the industry exceeds the marginal social net product ; on the contrary it may fall short of it. Hence, while, with rare exceptions, simple competition always causes too little investment to be made in industries of decreasing supply price (*simpliciter*), it does not always, or even generally, cause too much to be made in industries of increasing supply price (*simpliciter*). On the contrary, in a number of those industries it may cause too little investment to be made. British agriculture, for example, though obviously conforming to conditions of increasing supply price (*simpliciter*), may well be an industry of decreasing supply price from the standpoint of the community, and as such, in danger of suffering from a shortage of investment.

§ 11. If the amount of investment in any industry was carried exactly to the point at which the value of the marginal social net product there is equal to the central value of

---

[1] It is not, it should be understood, impossible that this should happen. For example, if an industry employed only a small proportion of the total supplies of two factors of production and nearly the whole supply of a third, and if an increase in the scale of output caused new methods to be introduced which led to an absolute decrease in the amount of this third factor that was wanted, the prices of the first two factors would be practically unchanged, while that of the third would fall substantially. As a result *a* units of the first plus *b* units of the second plus *c* units of the third might cost less money than before. Plainly, however, such a combination of circumstances is not likely to occur.

marginal social net products, the national dividend, so far as
that industry is concerned, would be maximised. Disregarding
the possibility of multiple maximum positions, I propose, for
convenience, to call the investment that would then be made
in the industry the ideal investment and the output that would
be obtained the ideal output. Under conditions of simple
competition, if in any industry the value of the marginal social
net product of investment is greater than the value of the
marginal private net product, this implies that the output
obtained is less than the ideal output: if the value of the
marginal social net product is less than the value of the
marginal private net product, this implies that the output
obtained is greater than the ideal output. It follows that, under
conditions of simple competition, for every industry in which the
value of the marginal social net product is greater than that of
the marginal private net product, there will be certain rates of
bounty, the granting of which by the State would modify
output in such a way as to make the value of the marginal
social net product there more nearly equal to the value of the
marginal social net product of resources in general, thus—
provided that the funds for the bounty can be raised by a mere
transfer that does not inflict any indirect injury on production—
increasing the size of the national dividend and the sum of
economic welfare ; and there will be one rate of bounty, the
granting of which would have the *optimum* effect in this
respect. In like manner, for every industry in which the
value of the marginal social net product is less than that of
the marginal private net product, there will be certain rates
of tax, the imposition of which by the State would increase
the size of the national dividend and increase economic
welfare ; and one rate of tax, which would have the *optimum*
effect in this respect. These conclusions, taken in conjunction
with what has been said in the preceding paragraphs, create
a presumption in favour of State bounties to industries in
which conditions of decreasing supply price *simpliciter* are
operating, and of State taxes upon industries in which conditions of increasing supply price from the standpoint of the
community are operating. They do *not*, of course, create a
presumption in favour of fiscal interference with industries

selected at haphazard or operated through rates of bounty or tax so selected. It is true that particular drugs consumed in particular quantities at particular times may cure diseases; but it is no less true that the consumption of drugs in general in a miscellaneous manner is highly injurious to health.

§ 12. Moreover, it may be well to make explicit a further consideration. When it was urged above that in certain industries a wrong amount of resources is being invested because the value of the marginal social net product there differs from the value of the marginal private net product, it was tacitly assumed that in the main body of industries these two values are equal, and, therefore, that there is scope for increasing the national dividend by shifting resources between the particular industry under review and this body of industries. If in all industries the values of marginal social and marginal private net product differed to exactly the same extent, the *optimum* distribution of resources would always be attained, and there would be, on these lines, no case for fiscal interference. It would still be possible, however, to defend a system of bounties to industries in general, the funds for which should be collected by some kind of lump-sum taxation, by arguing that the sum total of effort and waiting devoted to industry could be increased with advantage to economic welfare. Moreover, even when attention is confined to the distribution of resources among the several industries, what has been said does not imply that the mere prevalence in all industries of some degree of decreasing supply price from the standpoint of the community would rule out fiscal interference. It would still be possible—at all events in theory—to increase the national dividend by shifting resources from industries in which the law of decreasing supply price acted only weakly to industries in which it acted strongly.

§ 13. For completeness — though strictly this matter lies outside our formal limits—attention may be called, in parenthesis, to a type of reaction analogous to that discussed in § 12 of Chapter IX. The investment of an increment of resources in an industry, besides yielding a product to the purchasers, not reflected in the investor's profit, by altering costs of production, may yield a further

I

product of a like kind by altering the amount of satisfaction which the purchasers derive from a given quantity of their purchases. This form of indirect product may be either positive or negative. Among commodities, the desire for which is partly a desire to possess what other people possess, the creation of the 1000th unit adds to aggregate satisfaction more satisfaction than it carries itself, because it makes every unit of the commodity more common. Top-hats are examples. Among commodities, the desire for which is partly a desire to possess what other people do not possess, the creation of the 1000th unit adds to aggregate satisfaction less satisfaction than it carries itself, because it makes every unit of the commodity more common. Diamonds are examples.[1] Among industries whose products are desired for their own sake, and not as means to any form of distinction, the creation of the 1000th unit adds to aggregate satisfaction exactly as much satisfaction as it carries itself. On the basis of this analysis, inferences analogous to those set out in § 11 are easily obtained. For every industry, the desire for whose products is enhanced if they become less common, there must be certain rates of tax, the levy of which on the industry would increase economic welfare; and for every industry, the desire for whose products is enhanced if they become more common, there must be certain rates of bounty, the imposition of which would produce a like effect. But there is reason to believe that the great bulk of ordinary commodities consumed by the mass of the population are desired almost entirely for their own sake, and not as a means to any form of distinction. The sphere of usefulness that could belong, even under a perfectly wise and perfectly virtuous Government, to these fiscal devices is, therefore, probably smaller than it might appear to be at first sight.

§ 14. These results, like the companion results which

---

[1] It should be added that, when commonness or rareness is an element in the esteem in which a person holds a thing, it is often not general commonness or general rareness alone, but, in many instances, both commonness among one set of people and also rareness among another set. As Mr. McDougall writes of the followers of fashion: "Each victim is moved not only by the prestige of those whom he imitates but also by the desire to be different from the mass who have not yet adopted the fashion" (*Social Psychology*, p. 336). This aspect of the matter cannot, however, be pursued here.

will be established presently in connection with monopoly, are results in pure theory. Attempts to develop and expand them are sometimes frowned upon on the ground that they cannot be applied to practice. For, it is argued, though we may be able to say that the size of the national dividend and the sum of economic welfare would be increased by granting bounties to industries falling into one category and by imposing taxes upon those falling into another category, we are not able to say to which of our categories the various actual industries of real life belong. In other words, it is maintained that the economic boxes and sub-boxes, labelled increasing, constant and decreasing supply price (whether *simpliciter* or from the standpoint of the community) and so on, are *empty* boxes and, therefore, useless except as toys. This conclusion does not, however, appear to be well grounded. Even though we should be for ever unable to fill these boxes and sub-boxes, the labour involved in studying them would not be thrown away. By means of it we are enabled to see, for example, what conditions are implicitly assumed when it is stated that the imposition of a tax or the introduction of monopolistic policy will have such and such consequences. We are thus put in a position to detect and expose sophistical dogmatism. It is better to know exactly what facts are required to make the answering of a question possible, even though those facts are unattainable, than to rest in a fog of vague and credulous opinion. But this is not all. Difficult as it must necessarily be to classify industries into the categories which analysis has distinguished, we need not yet conclude that it is impossible. Statistical technique, by itself, in spite of the growing volume and improving quality of the material available, will not enable us to accomplish this; for statistics refer only to the past. But able business men with a detailed realistic knowledge of the conditions of their several industries should be able to provide economists with the raw material for rough probable judgments. Economists unaided cannot fill their empty boxes because they lack the necessary realistic knowledge; and business men unaided cannot fill them because they do not know where or what the boxes are. With collaboration,

however, it is not unreasonable to hope that some measure of
success may eventually be achieved.   At least the effort is
worth making.   It is premature, in impatience at the present
shortage of straw, to scrap our brickmaking machinery.   It
is the better part to advertise abroad the urgent need for
straw, and to call for students to produce it.[1]

[1] Cf. a paper by Dr. Clapham on " Empty Economic Boxes " in the *Economic
Journal* for September 1922, and a reply by the present writer in the December
issue of the same journal.

CHAPTER XII

§ 1. THE preceding discussion seems at first sight to prove that, apart from divergences between private and social net product, State interference, designed to modify in any way the working of free competition, is bound to injure the national dividend; for this competition left to itself will continually push resources from points of lower productivity (in terms of economic satisfaction as measured in money) to points of higher productivity, thus tending always away from less favourable, and towards more favourable, arrangements of the community's resources. We have now to confront this general presumption with the extensive policy of price regulation which was followed by the British, as by most other Governments, during the course of the great European War. I propose first to give a general account of that policy and then to inquire how far, if at all, the experience gained should modify the conclusions reached in preceding chapters.

§ 2. Broadly put, the position was as follows. The war caused in two ways a great shortage in certain things. On the one hand, for munition articles, army clothes and so forth, there was an enormous new Government demand much in excess of normal supplies. On the other hand, for various articles of ordinary civilian use, the contraction of available tonnage and the withdrawal of labour for the army and munition work caused supplies to fall much below the normal. The shortage brought about in one or other of these ways put it in the power of persons who happened to hold stocks of short commodities, or to be able to produce them quickly, to charge for them prices very much higher than usual. When

229

the shortage was due to increased Government demand, the
scale of business done by these persons being as large as, or
larger than, before, the high prices that they were enabled
to charge necessarily yielded them abnormally large profits.
When it was due to contraction of supply (*e.g.* through the
withdrawal of labour or other obstacles to output), the gain
from high prices *might* be cancelled by loss due to lessened
sales; so that abnormally large profits were not obtained.
For a great number of things, however, the conditions of
demand are such that a shortage of, say, 10 per cent in the
supply causes the price offered by purchasers to rise by much
more than 10 per cent. For the sellers of articles of this
class the shortage, even when it was due to a supply contraction, often meant abnormal profits. Of course, some of these
abnormal profits were more apparent than real, for, if prices
all round are doubled, a doubling of money profits will only
enable a man to get the same amount of things as before.
Very often, however, the money profits were enhanced very
much more than in proportion to the rise in general prices.
Wherever this happened, certain specially favoured persons
were benefiting greatly as a direct consequence of the war.
This state of things naturally caused resentment, and suggested
State interference.

§ 3. This interference might follow either of two principal
lines. On the one hand, fortunately situated sellers might be
allowed to charge such prices as the market would bear, thus
collecting abnormal profits in the first instance; but, thereafter, be deprived of the bulk of these for the benefit of the
Exchequer by a high excess profits tax. On the other hand,
the prices they were allowed to charge might be limited by
authority to rates at which it was estimated that abnormal
profits would not accrue to them. Apart from points of
technique and administration, the choice between these two
plans makes no difference to the fortunately situated seller.
But it does make a difference to the people who happen to
need the particular goods or services that he sells. For,
whereas under the maximum price plan they are left untouched, under the excess profits plan a special levy is, in
effect, placed upon them for the benefit of the general taxpayers.

It follows that, where the taxpayers themselves, through the Government, are the principal buyers, or where the public are buyers more or less in the proportion in which they are taxpayers, it does not greatly matter which of the two plans is chosen. But where, as with all the staple articles of food, poor people play a much larger part, compared with rich people, as buyers of an article which is short than they play as taxpayers, it does greatly matter. For, if the State were to adopt the excess profits plan in preference to the maximum prices plan, it would be relieving the well-to-do of a large block of taxation, and throwing it, by a roundabout and semi-secret process, upon the shoulders of the poor. Whatever might be thought of the desirability of exacting a larger contribution to the expenses of the war from relatively poor persons, it was obvious that a device of that kind would never be tolerated. Consequently, over a large part of the field, the excess profits plan could not practically be made the *main* engine for preventing fortunately situated sellers from making fortunes out of the war. Resort had of necessity to be had to the plan of maximum prices.

§ 4. In the actual working out of that plan, a great number of difficulties emerged, which it will be well to set out in order. The first of these was the difficulty of definition. The same name often covers a great variety of different qualities of article, which it may be extremely hard to disentangle in any formal schedule. When this condition prevails it is impossible to exercise control over prices by general rules, and it becomes necessary to fall back upon the cumbrous device of individual appraisement. Thus, under the Raw Cocoa Order of March 1918, it was laid down that no raw cocoa might be sold except at "a fair value," this fair value being determined by a person authorised by the Food Controller to determine the grade of the various lots of cocoa. A similar plan was adopted at the end of 1917 for controlling the prices of cattle and sheep sold by live weight at market. Obviously, however, this plan could not be employed on a large scale, owing to the vast amount of labour that it involves. Consequently, in general, some modification of it was essential, and some general classification of grades had, in spite of the openings for evasion that this permits, to be, in one way or another, relied upon.

A second difficulty, when the problem of *defining* grades of quality was overcome, resulted from the mere fact that grades were often very numerous. The task of fixing prices directly for a great variety of these might well be more than any authority, at all events in the earlier stages of its operation, was prepared to enter upon. When there were only a few grades, it was comparatively easy, with the help of advice from experts, to do this; but, when there were a great many, it was thought better to rely, not on a schedule of maximum prices, but on a general Order determining the relations between the prices that might be charged in the future and those that had been charged in the past. An example of this plan was the Order of the Ministry of Munitions, issued in August 1916, by which sellers of machine tools were forbidden, except with the sanction of the Minister, henceforward to charge prices higher than they were charging in July 1915.

An analogous difficulty had to be faced when a commodity, about the grading of which, perhaps, there was no need to trouble, was produced under different conditions in a number of different localities, in such wise that a single maximum price would not treat different producers fairly. Here, too, inability to construct a schedule as varied as the circumstances required forced the controlling authority to fall back on the plan of fixing, not future prices themselves, but the relation between future prices and past prices. Thus, in May 1917, an Order was issued that no imported soft wood should be sold at prices above those that ruled *in each several locality* in the week ending 31st January 1917. This Order was subsequently modified as regards imports from Scandinavia; but with that we are not concerned.

So far it has been tacitly assumed that the maximum price aimed at for any one commodity of a given grade is a single price. For some commodities, however, no one uniform price ruling throughout the year is adapted to the conditions of their production and sale, and a series of maxima is needed. Plainly, a series is more difficult to determine

correctly than a single price. Consequently, here again the
controlling authority was driven to the method of regulating
the *relation* between future and past prices. Thus, in July
1917, it was ordered that the wholesale price of milk per
imperial gallon should not henceforward anywhere exceed
by more than 6½d. the price charged in the corresponding
month a year before, and that the retail price per imperial
quart should not exceed this corresponding price by more
than 2d.   The same plan was followed in the Price of Coal
(Limitation) Act of 1915, which decreed that no colliery
company should charge a price exceeding by more than 4s.
(afterwards raised to 6s. 6d.) the price charged on a similar
sale at a similar date in 1913–14.

Plainly, all these indirect and roundabout methods of
control left the way open for evasion and were likely
to prove difficult to enforce.   Consequently, controlling
authorities, as they got a better grip and better knowledge
of the conditions of various industries, tried to step forward
to the more precise method of maximum price schedules.
More and more this became the predominant plan. The
producers' and wholesalers' prices of most of the more
important articles of food came to be fixed directly by
schedule, as were also the prices of most of the commodities
controlled by the Ministry of Munitions. For most things
it was found sufficient to set up a single schedule. But
sometimes different producers' prices were fixed for different
parts of the country. For hay, for example, Scotland was
given one price, England another. Sometimes, too, a series
of schedules were set up to apply to different parts of the
year. For potatoes the Order of February 1917 fixed one
price up till March 31st, and another higher price after that
date ; and for peas and beans an Order of May 1917 fixed
three prices, diminishing in amount, for sales in June, July
and later months. Similarly for wheat, oats and barley, to
be harvested in the United Kingdom, the Food Controller,
in August 1917, fixed a series of prices rising gradually
in each successive two months from November 1917 on to
June 1918. A later Order fixing maximum milk prices
made a similar differentiation between different parts of the

year. It is plain that the direct establishment of maximum prices is, if the appropriate prices can once be worked out satisfactorily, likely to prove much more effective than any roundabout plan.

So far we have only taken account of industries so simply organised that the producers sell a finished product direct, without any intermediary, to ultimate consumers. In most industries, however, there are several stages between the original material or service and the finished product in consumers' hands. This fact gives rise to further problems. The conditions of demand for any finished product being given, when an artificial price is fixed for any material or service used in the course of making and selling it, the price of the finished product need not be lowered correspondingly, but it is in the power of other persons in a line between the provider of this material or service and the finished product to add on to their charges the equivalent of whatever has been knocked off the charges of the regulated sellers. Thus, if the price of coal at the pit-mouth were reduced by State action, and nothing else were done, the only effect might be that dealers in coal could buy more cheaply while retaining the old price of sale. Again, if the price of cattle were forced down, and nothing else done, retail prices might remain unaltered, while butchers and meat dealers gained enormously. Yet again, if freight-rates on imported materials were kept artificially low by Government action, the various people who use these materials in their industries might get the whole benefit. Nor is it merely *possible* that this *might* happen. In general it *would* happen, except in so far as the people, on whom a power of exaction was thus conferred, deliberately from patriotic motives, or from fear of popular resentment, decided to forgo their advantage. In order to prevent this, the fixing of maximum prices at the earlier stages of production had to be coupled with control over the profits which manufacturers or dealers at a later stage may make by adding further charges on to these prices. One way in which this control was exercised was by limiting the *percentage* addition that might be made by any seller in the line. In May 1917, for example, it was decreed that no timber from Russia should be sold at an advance of more than 10 per cent on the purchase price; and in September 1917 a schedule of prices for fish was fixed as between fish-curers and wholesale dealers, and other sellers (with the exception of retailers) were prohibited from adding more than 10 per cent on to the scheduled prices. More usually it was not the *percentage*, but the *amount*, of addition that was limited. Thus, under the Cheese Order of August 1917, first-hand prices of various sorts of British-made cheese were fixed as from the maker, and it was provided that no dealer other than the maker should add on to them more than the actual charge for transport *plus*, in general, 6s. per cwt. In October it was provided further that retailers should not add on to the prices actually paid by them more than $2\frac{1}{2}$d. per lb. In the same month the prices of the various sorts of leather were regulated on the same general plan. In like manner the price of horse and poultry mixture was controlled, in November 1917, by an Order forbidding the maker to charge a price exceeding the cost to him of his ingredients by more than £1 : 10s. per ton ; and the amount that other sellers might add on was limited to 1s. per cwt. on sales of 6 cwt. and more, 3s. per cwt. on sales of from 3 to 6 cwt., and so on. In meat a variant on this plan was adopted, in the first instance, on account of difficulties due to the custom among retailers of obtaining different proportions of their profit from the sale of different joints. In an Order of September 1917 it was laid down that no person shall in any fortnight sell meat by retail at such prices as cause the aggregate price received by him to exceed actual costs to him by more than a prescribed percentage (20 per cent or $2\frac{1}{2}$d. per lb., whichever shall be less). In August 1917 a rule on similar lines was laid down for retailers of bacon and hams.

It is evident that plans of this kind for controlling the charges to be made at the later stages of a commodity's progress to the consumer suffer from the same sort of disadvantage that roundabout attempts to control producers' charges suffer from. They are liable to evasion. Consequently, the controlling authorities sought, as they became more masters of their work, to evolve some more satisfactory

arrangement.   One stage in this evolution is illustrated by
the Butter Prices Order of August 1917.   In that Order
it was laid down that retailers should not add to the price of
butter sold by them more than $2\frac{1}{2}$d. per lb. above the actual
cost of it to them; but it was provided further that local
Food Control Committees *might* prescribe a scale of maximum
retail prices in accordance with the general directions of the
Order (which includes rules about maker's, importer's and
wholesaler's prices), although conformity with that scale
should not relieve any retailer from the obligation not to
add on more than $2\frac{1}{2}$d. per lb.   A slightly more advanced
stage is illustrated by the plan adopted for regulating the
retail prices of coal.   The general principle was laid down
that retailers should not add on to their own purchase price
more than 1s. per ton over and above the costs of actual
handling and dealing with the coal (including office expenses
apart from the trader's own salary).   But this principle was
not left, as it were, in the air.   It was provided that local
authorities, after consultation and inquiry, should work it out
and apply it in the form of a definite list of retail prices
applicable to their district.   Yet a further stage is reached
when the controlling authority itself fixes lists of maximum
prices at more than one point on the way from production
to consumption.   The Potato Order of September 1917
was of this type.   Maximum prices were fixed for growers;
wholesale dealers were forbidden to sell in any week at prices
that yielded them more than 7s. 6d. a ton beyond their
total costs on all purchases of potatoes—costs which varied
with the transport conditions of different districts; and an
elaborate scale of retail prices was fixed, which related the
permitted price per lb. to the price per cwt., including price
of transport, that the retailer had actually paid for different
classes of potatoes.   The final stage is reached when definite
schedules are fixed throughout—for producer, wholesaler and
retailer equally—by the controlling authority itself.   This was
the arrangement to which the Ministry of Food steadily
progressed.   It was definitely attained in regard to British
onions, most sorts of fish, beef and mutton, fruit for jam and
jam, peas and beans, and hay, oats and wheat straw.   Lest,

through imperfect knowledge, the special circumstances of particular districts should have been neglected in the construction of these scales, a safeguard was sometimes provided in the form of a rule empowering local Food Committees, with the sanction of the Food Controller, to vary the maxima in their district. This provision was introduced into the Order of January 1918 fixing maximum prices for rabbits. In like manner it was provided in an Order of September 1917, that, where the Food Controller or a local Food Committee was satisfied that, by reason of some exceptional circumstance, flour or bread could not be sold by *retail* at the official maximum price "so as to yield a reasonable profit," a licence might be issued, either for the whole or for a part of any Committee's area, permitting higher prices to be charged. The Order of January 1918, fixing a schedule of maximum prices for most kinds of fish, was made subject, as regards *retail* prices, to similar local revision, as was also the Milk Prices Order of March 1918. A like power of varying local retail prices, with the sanction of the Food Controller, was accorded to the local Food Committees under the Potato Prices Order of September 1917.

Hitherto attention has been confined to commodities that come into the consumer's hands in much the same form as that in which they leave the hands of producers. Further complications are introduced when we have to do with raw materials that are worked up into elaborately finished articles. Here, owing to the various parts which the raw material plays in different types and grades of finished goods, it is not generally possible to fix schedules of prices beyond the raw material. Consequently, for two important articles, boots and clothes, an ingenious roundabout plan was adopted. An attempt was made to induce or compel manufacturers to devote a considerable part of their plant to making "standard articles" to be sold at prices calculated on a basis of conversion costs, in the hope that the competition of these articles in the market would indirectly keep down the price that it was profitable to charge for similar articles that were not standardised. In boots, manufacturers were ordered to devote one-third of that part of their plant which was engaged on civilian work to making "standard boots." In clothes, no fixed proportion of plant was forced into making standard goods, but manufacturers were tempted to take up this kind of work by relatively favourable treatment in the matter of the quota of raw wool allowed to them. In cotton goods, though the price of raw cotton was artificially controlled, no corresponding control of the finished commodity was attempted, the argument being that cotton manufacturers were sufficiently burdened by having to provide a special levy to pay benefit to workpeople thrown out of work by the reduction in the number of spindles and looms that might be operated.

§ 5. The foregoing account of the difficulties encountered and the expedients employed in the exercise of price control suggests a question of some theoretical interest. It is plain enough that, in the earlier stages of control, practical considerations make it necessary to begin at the producer's, rather than the retailer's, end; for the local differentiations needed in a retail schedule are generally much more serious and require much more knowledge to allow of their being fairly made. As has been shown, however, as the controlling authority became more expert and got a better grip on its industries, it tended to make price schedules all along the line from the producer to the final seller. Thus, in the end, retail maximum prices often were fixed. The point in doubt is whether, when this has all been arranged, there is any real need to continue the earlier stages of control. Will not maximum retail prices be reflected back all along the line, and so automatically stop "profiteering" at earlier stages? The view that this will be so seems to have guided the work of some of the Ministry of Food's controls. For example, the prices of turnips and swedes were regulated by a rule that *nobody* might sell them for more than 1½d. per lb., and the price of chocolates and sweets by a rule that *nobody* might sell them for more than 3d. per oz. and 2d. per oz. respectively. In general, however, it was thought better to maintain price schedules at the earlier stages, separate from, and adjusted to, the retail maxima. In a world of pure competition it does not appear that this would really have been necessary. If the retail maxima were rightly arranged, everybody in line would automatically be forced to charge prices that yielded them about the ordinary rate of profits. The artificial restriction upon retail price would act in exactly the same way as a fall in the public demand for the commodity sufficient to counteract the shortage of supply. It is probable, however, that this adjustment would not, in real life, be made without a certain amount of friction, and that some of the traders affected might be in a position to exercise quasi-monopolistic pressure against particular shopkeepers or others who happened to be mainly dependent on them. Consequently, when schedules of maximum prices for the earlier stages had already been worked out, to drop them, in the hope that the retailers' schedules subsequently superimposed would by themselves achieve the whole of the ends desired, would probably have been unwise.

§ 6. We have now to consider the broad analytical problem which these expedients of war time suggest. What *exactly* is to be said of the relation between the kind of price regulation that was then attempted and the size of the national dividend? The great upheaval of the war had caused the existing distribution of resources to be uneconomic, in the sense that the value of the marginal net product (social and private alike) of those employed in making certain specially scarce articles was abnormally high. Apart from outside interference abnormal values of marginal net products mean abnormal returns to the investor; and these abnormal returns tend to draw resources from occupations of relatively low productivity to those occupations of greater productivity in which they rule. When prices are cut down by law, the value of the marginal net product of any given quantity of resources in any occupation is, indeed, necessarily cut down also, because we have defined this value as the marginal physical net product multiplied by the realised price. Plainly, however, this definition tacitly assumes the realised price to be identical with the demand price. When these two are artificially divorced, our definition must be changed. The values of the marginal net products of resources, which it is to the interest of the national dividend to make equal everywhere, consist in the marginal physical net products multiplied by the demand prices. When this is understood, it is evident that an artificial reduction of price, while lowering returns in the industry affected by it, leaves the true value of the marginal net product of any quantity of resources invested there unchanged. The desirability, from the standpoint of the national dividend, of a transference of resources is thus unaltered, while the principal influence tending to bring it about is weakened. To put the same point in more general terms, any external limitation imposed on the price of an article produced under competitive conditions (*i.e.* otherwise than by a monopolist) must lessen the inducement that people have to make that article. Normally it is just through high prices and high profits that a shortage of anything corrects itself. The prospect of exceptional gain directs free resources into the industry which makes the thing that is short. Cut off this prospect, and that increase of supply, which the interest of the national dividend demands, will be checked, and checked more severely the greater is the cut made from the " natural " price.

§ 7. In the special circumstances of the Great War this injurious tendency of price limitation was largely counteracted by other influences. For the State itself, in many departments of industry, took over the task of allocating resources among different occupations. It built up munition works, controlled shipbuilding, and urged on agricultural production by the promise of land, tractors, and labour drawn from the Army. Thus, though price regulation might weaken the directive force normally exercised by economic motives, the task of direction was taken over by another and more powerful agency. No doubt, had prices in any occupation been artificially pushed down so low that profits to the " representative " firm fell actually below the ordinary money level, capital and labour would have gone elsewhere in spite of government pressure. But, of course, prices were not artificially pushed down to this extent in any occupation. On the contrary, complaint was often made that they were left high enough to yield abnormally large profits, not merely to firms that could fairly be regarded as " representative," but even to those very weak and inefficient firms which, in the ordinary course, would have been making losses and decaying out of business.[1] On the

---

[1] It might have proved practicable to fix prices at a considerably lower level if the good and bad firms had been formed into a kind of pool, and the objective

whole, therefore, we may conclude that, as things were, in view of the abnormal activity of the State, and, it should be added, of the effectiveness of appeals to patriotism, price control in the peculiar circumstances of the war probably caused very little damage to the volume of the national dividend.

§ 8. It would, however, be a great error to infer from this that a general permanent policy of control, designed to prevent groups of producers from reaping abnormal profit on occasions when the conditions of the market give them power to do so, would be equally innocuous. People, in choosing their investments, take account of these ups and downs, and, so far as their judgment is correct, place their resources in such a way that, on the average and on the whole, the marginal yield works out about equally in different occupations. In these circumstances it is obvious that any general State policy of cutting down prices in any industry below the competitive level, on occasions when the conditions of demand and supply would enable that industry to obtain exceptional profits, must, in effect, penalise it as compared with stable industries. For, if, in a hilly district where the average level of peaks and valleys is the same as it is on a plateau, the tops of the peaks are removed, the average level there will, of course, be reduced below that of the plateau. The discouraging effect of this differential action cannot be made good by any direct manipulation of production by the State. For here we have to do, not merely with a tendency for free resources to go elsewhere *at the time* when the régime of price control is at work, but with a tendency that operates continually and checks the general flow of resources that would otherwise seek investment in building up the permanent equipment of the threatened industry. If, for example, this country adopted a general policy of forbidding farmers to charge high prices when they have power to do

---

sought been normal profits for the pool as a whole. Professor Taussig has pointed out that, before an arrangement of this kind could be worked, very serious administrative difficulties would have to be overcome and an elaborate system of detailed costings set up (*Quarterly Journal of Economics*, Feb. 1919). Besides this technical objection, there is the further more general objection that efficient management in individual firms would be very greatly discouraged, since it would reap very little reward.

so on account of a bad world harvest, this would check investment in British agriculture ; because people expect bad world
harvests from time to time and look to high prices then to set
against low prices in bumper years.   While, therefore, on the
one hand, our analysis does not imply that the policy of price
limitation adopted in the abnormal circumstances of the war
worked injury to the national dividend, on the other hand,
the experience of the war gives no ground for doubting that
a general permanent policy of price limitation, in non-
monopolised industries, would produce this effect.   This conclusion is, of course, subject to the considerations set out in
the preceding chapter.   It is subject, too, to the qualification
that, if maximum prices are fixed so high as to leave all
ordinary sales unaffected and merely to protect an occasional
weak purchaser from exploitation by unscrupulous dealers,
they will not interfere with the way in which resources
are distributed between different uses, and will not, therefore,
injure the national dividend.   Moreover, if State interference
to prevent any group of producers from making excessive
earnings in good times were balanced by interference to
prevent them from making abnormally low earnings in bad
times, the net result, though it would necessarily involve a
redistribution of their production between good times and bad,
would not necessarily involve a contraction in the aggregate
amount of their production.

CHAPTER XIII

STATE REGULATION OF SUPPLIES

§ 1. It is not only in the matter of prices that the war afforded examples of Government interference with competitive industry. Extensive interference also took place with the free distribution of commodities among different industries, different firms within the same industry, and different ultimate consumers. This interference had to be undertaken in order to get over difficulties to which the price regulations described in the preceding chapter gave rise. For, when prices in competitive industries are artificially reduced below the level that they tend naturally to assume, the ordinary market influences regulating the distribution of commodities between different purchasers are thrown out of gear. When there are no price restrictions, at any price everybody buys for every purpose as much of a thing as, at that price, he wants, and this process exhausts the whole supply. But, when, *in competitive industries*, prices are artificially kept down, the sum of the demands of all purchasers for all purposes is greater, and may be much greater, than the supply. In the United States, where the wheat for the whole year comes from the national harvest, the result of price limitation unaccompanied by rationing was that everybody got all he wanted in the earlier part of the harvest year and had to fall back on substitutes in the later part.[1] There was, in short, a bad distribution through time. For most commodities, however production as well as consumption is continuous. Thus, at no time can everybody get all he wants, but there is a

[1] Cf. Supplement to *American Economic Review*, March 1919, p. 244.

continuous shortage. Distribution becomes, if nothing is done, the sport of accident, influence, and ability to stand for a long time without fainting in a queue. There is no reason to expect that the distribution reached through these agencies will be, in any sense, a good distribution. Consequently, when, during the course of the war, the policy of controlling prices was adopted, it was, in general, found necessary to control distribution also, and, with that object, to establish some criterion for fixing the shares available for different purchasers. It was not, indeed, only where prices were regulated that supplies to individuals were controlled. In some instances, where there was no price regulation, they were controlled in order to prevent private persons from absorbing for their own use an undue quantity of things and services urgently needed by the Government for war. Here the control limited aggregate private consumption and did not merely regulate the distribution of an aggregate already limited. The technical problems involved are, however, the same whether control of supplies is or is not associated with the fixing of maximum prices.

§ 2. When the commodity dealt with was a material that could be employed for several alternative purposes, the obvious criterion was relative urgency, from the point of view of national war service, of these several purposes. The simplest method of applying this criterion was to make rules cutting off the supply of material from the least urgent uses either in part or altogether, thus leaving more available for more urgent uses. Examples of this method were :

(1) The imposition of Treasury restrictions upon the investment of new capital abroad and, in a less degree, in civilian home industries.

(2) The enunciation of a rule that no building costing more than £500, and no building whatever containing structural steel, should be put up without a licence.

(3) The reduction of railway service for all forms of civilian, as distinguished from military, use.

(4) The prohibition of the use of petrol for pleasure.

(5) The withdrawal of materials, etc., from the less important tramways and light railways to others of greater national importance.

(6) The regulation of the use of horses in towns and on farms and the control of road transport generally.

(7) The prohibition of the use of paper for newspaper contents bills, and, under certain conditions, for traders' circulars, and the abolition of " Returns."

(8) The prohibition by the Timber Supplies Department against packing various articles in wooden cases and crates.

(9) The prohibition of the use of electricity for lighting shop fronts, and the order restricting the hours during which hotel and restaurant dining-rooms might use artificial light or theatres might remain open.

This method is entirely negative : the least urgent uses are ruled out, either by a general order, or by making a licence —refused to the least urgent uses—a condition of action.

§ 3. Obviously, devices of this character are of limited application. They take no account of the fact that uses other than the least urgent are not all of equal urgency. Consequently, if the material or labour available is insufficient for all the uses that are left when the least urgent uses have been cut off, it becomes necessary to arrange for some system of priority among those that are left. The simplest way in which this was attempted was as follows. The material was left in private hands, but a system of Priority Certificates was instituted, which only permitted sales to would-be buyers with certificates of lower urgency after those with certificates of higher urgency had been satisfied. Government work had the first grade of certificate, work of special national import- ance (e.g. export work deemed valuable for protecting the foreign exchanges) the next, and so on in successive stages. Iron and steel products were dealt with on this plan, and quarry stone and other road material on less elaborate, but substantially equivalent, lines. When the proportion of the available commodity that is needed for Government war work or other especially urgent need is very large, the plan of priority certificates by itself is not always safe. The Government may get less than it needs. To meet this risk it is tempted itself, either by purchase or requisition, to become an owner (or hirer) of so much of the commodity as is of specially urgent need. It may then hand over to firms engaged on Government work, or other specially urgent work, the supplies that are required for that work; but, even so, it will need to distribute the surplus on some system of priority to other firms. This plan was followed in a rough general way with imported leather and flax and with a number of metals.

§ 4. The application in these different forms of the criterion of comparative urgency among competing uses presented very considerable difficulties during the war. These difficulties, however, were necessarily much less than those which would have to be overcome if a similar criterion had to be applied to normal conditions of peace. For the comparative urgency of different uses in war time depends on the contribution which they severally make to national war efficiency. This provides a definite standard to which to work. It is obvious that food and munitions and the support of the armed forces must take precedence over every-thing else ; and, though, as the rivalry between the demands of munitions and of ships for steel made plain, it is difficult, still it is not impossible, by conferences between representatives of the various Ministries, to work out a fairly satisfactory scheme of priorities. The reason for this is that everything is subordinated to a single relatively simple end. Under a régime of established peace—apart, of course, from possible " key " industries, for which the natural method of assistance is bounties or a tariff, and not the allocation of material—there is no single end of this kind. We have no longer to deal with the Government's wants for war service, but with the wants of an immense and varied population for necessaries, comforts and luxuries. In war time it is clearly more important to bring steel into the country than it is to bring paper, and to manufacture army baking ovens than private kitchen ranges. But in peace time simple propositions of this kind cannot be laid down. Those things ought to be made which are most wanted and will yield the greatest. sum of satisfaction. But the Government cannot possibly decide what these things are; and, even if it could decide what they are at one moment, before its decision had been put into effect conditions would very probably be changed, and they would have become something entirely different. It is not easy to see how this obstacle to a permanent policy of rationing materials among the several industries of the country could be satisfactorily overcome.

§ 5. To allocate materials to different uses according to the comparative national urgency of these uses was not a complete solution of the war problem. Within each grade of use purchases are sought by a number of rival firms anxious to work up the material into the finished product. Normally price would have established itself at such a level that each firm obtained the quantity of material which, at that price, it desired. With restricted prices it is necessary to provide an alternative basis for distribution among these firms, as well as among the different categories of urgency. The basis adopted by the British Government was that of comparative pre-war purchases. It is illustrated by—

(a) The regulation of the Cotton Control Board (1918), limiting the proportion of machinery that any firm might keep at work on American cotton ;

(b) The condition imposed on importers by the Paper Control, that they should supply their customers (i.e. manufacturers) in the same proportions as in 1916–17.

In highly organised trades, like the cotton industry, there was no technical difficulty in applying regulations on these lines. But in many of the metal trades a special organisation had to be created for the purpose. It is clear that this basis of allocation could not be employed in connection with any policy designed to last for more than a short period. For an arrangement, which tended to maintain the various firms engaged in an industry always in the same relative position as they occupied in an arbitrarily chosen year, would constitute a quite intolerable obstacle to efficiency and progress.

§ 6. When the prices of finished products as well as of their raw materials were limited by regulation, a problem exactly analogous to the above had to be faced as regards distribution among ultimate consumers. To organise a plausible basis for this is only practicable in connection with commodities in wide, regular and continuous consumption. The basis aimed at here was, not comparative pre-war purchases, but an estimate of comparative current need. For coal, gas and electricity an objective measure of this was sought in the number and size of rooms and the number of inhabitants in different people's houses. For food products, while some differentiation was attempted by means of supplementary rations to soldiers, sailors, heavy workers, invalids and children, in the main the knot was cut by assuming the needs of the general body of all the civil population to be equal, and rationing all alike. This sort of distributional arrangement is fundamentally different from the other two kinds. The passage from war to peace does not destroy or render violently unsuitable the criterion adopted for it. Plainly, however, in peace, as indeed in war also, its necessarily rough and arbitrary character constitutes a very serious objection to it. " The proportion in which families of equal means use the different ' necessaries of life ' are very different. In ordinary times they distribute their expenditure among the different necessaries in the manner which seems best, some getting more bread, some more meat and milk, and so on. By equal rationing all this variety is done away with; each household is given the same amount per head of each commodity; allowance for age, sex, occupation and other things can only be introduced with difficulty."[1] There can be little doubt that British Food Rationing during the war, in spite of this disability, led to a much more satisfactory result than would have been attained from the scramble—a scramble in which rich people would have been able to exercise various sorts of pull upon tradesmen—that must have resulted had food prices been limited but distribution left to take care of itself. In peace time, however, when presumably the alternative to rationing would be less intolerable, the inconvenience and inequalities attaching to it have correspondingly greater weight.

§ 7. If we are content to regard the various arrangements which I have been describing as merely supplementary to price restrictions already decided upon, it is plain that, though

[1] Cannan, *Economic Journal*, Dec. 1917, p. 468.

they may affect the size of the national dividend, as it were, at the second remove—if, for example, they grant priority to steel for making machinery rather than motor-cars—they cannot affect it directly or fundamentally. They modify the way in which certain elements in the dividend are shared out, but not the quantities of the elements contained in it. These are modified by the price regulations in the way that was explained in the preceding chapter. They are not modified further by any distributional supplements to those regulations. Consequently, from the standpoint of the present Part, no further analysis is required; though in Part IV., where the distributional relations of rich and poor are examined, something more will have to be said about the rationing of food.

CHAPTER XIV

THE CONDITIONS OF MONOPOLISATION

§ 1. WE may now return to the main argument. In Chapter XI. we supposed self-interest to act along the route of simple competition. We showed that in these circumstances, apart from divergences of the types discussed in Chapter IX., the value of the marginal private net product of resources in any industry tends to equality with the central value of marginal net products in general, and inquired in what circumstances the value of the marginal social net product of resources in the given industry would diverge from the value of the marginal private net product there. We have now to consider other routes along which self-interest may act. As has already been observed, an essential note of "simple competition" is that the supply of each seller constitutes so small a part of the aggregate supply of the market that he is content to "accept market prices without trying, of set purpose, to modify them." [1] When any seller's output constitutes a substantial part of the whole, there is scope for various sorts of monopolistic action ; and, when any sort of monopolistic action is present, self-interest does not tend to evolve an output such that the value of the marginal private net product of resources devoted to its production is equal to that yielded by resources employed elsewhere. In future chapters I shall examine monopolistic action in detail. Before that is done, however, convenience suggests that some study should be made of the conditions which determine the appearance of monopolistic power.

§ 2. First, other things being equal, circumstances, which,

[1] Pareto, *Cours d'économie politique*, i. p. 20.

when the aggregate scale of an industry is given, make it structurally economical for the typical individual establishment to be large, *pro tanto* increase the likelihood that a single *seller* will market a considerable part of the aggregate output of his industry; for such circumstances necessarily increase the probability that a single *establishment* will market a considerable part of that output. Whether any single establishment will, in fact, become big enough, relatively to the whole of an industry, to procure an element of monopolistic power, depends on the general characteristics of the various industries concerned. Such an event is more than usually likely in industries that produce fancy goods liable to become "specialities." For in these industries there often exist, within the broad general market, minor markets, to a certain extent non-competitive among themselves ; and, when this is so, a single establishment may supply a considerable proportion of its own minor market without itself being of very great size absolutely. In a few peculiar industries, among those concerned with staple goods and services, it may also well be that the prospect of internal economies will lead to the evolution of single establishments large enough to control a predominant part of the whole output of the industry. One of the most notable instances of this is afforded by the industry of railway transportation along any assigned route. In view of the great engineering cost of preparing a suitable way, it will, obviously, be much less expensive to have one or, at most, a few railways providing the whole of the transport service between any two assigned points than to have this service undertaken by a great number of railways, each performing an insignificant proportion of the whole service. Similar remarks hold good of the industries of furnishing water, gas, electricity, or tramway service to a town. The existence of many separate establishments involves a large number of main pipes, wires and rails. But the whole business of any ordinary district can be worked with a very small number of these mains. Therefore the existence of many separate establishments implies the investment of a great quantity of capital in mains that are only employed up to a very small proportion of their capacity. There is an obvious economy in avoiding such investment. This economy is the *ultimate* reason for the tendency, which appears strongly in the class of industry just discussed, for individual establishments to furnish a large proportion of the total supply. The truth is partly veiled by the fact that the *immediate* reason is, in general, unwillingness, on the part of national and local government authorities, to allow the right of eminent domain to be invoked, or the streets to be disturbed, on more occasions, or by more people, than is absolutely necessary. It is, however, the extra expense of such procedure that lies behind this unwillingness on the part of the authorities. In the general body of industries concerned with staple goods and services the conditions peculiar to railways and their allied industries are not reproduced. Internal economies reach their limit at different points in different kinds of industry, at one point in the cotton industry, at another in the iron and steel industry; generally at a less advanced stage where the part played by labour relatively to capital is large and at a more advanced stage where it is small; but always long before the individual establishment has grown to any appreciable fraction of the whole industry of which it is a part.[1] When this happens, internal economies evidently cannot be responsible for monopolistic power.

§ 3. Secondly, other things being equal, circumstances, which, when the aggregate scale of an industry and the size of the typical individual establishment are given, make it structurally economical for the typical individual unit of business management—a number of establishments, for example, controlled by one authority—to be large, *pro tanto* increase the likelihood that a single seller will market a considerable part of the aggregate output of his industry. This proposition has, in recent times, become of predominant importance, and it is, therefore, necessary to examine carefully the various structural

---

[1] Cf. Van Hise's account of the development of various important industries in the United States (*Concentration and Control*, pp. 42 *et seq.*) and Sir Sydney Chapman's discussion of the normal size of individual factories in the cotton industry (*Journal of the Royal Statistical Society,* April 1914, p. 513).

economies, for which large scale control may, in different situations, be responsible.

Much has been made by some writers of the fact that, when a number of parallel establishments are grouped under a single head, the different plants can be thoroughly specialised to particular grades of work; and of the other kindred fact that the orders in any place can be met from the plant nearest to that place, and that, thus, cross freights are saved. That the economies resulting from close specialisation upon particular articles or even particular processes may, in some circumstances, be very great has been abundantly proved in the British engineering industry during the war. But it does not appear that a single control over many separate establishments is essential in order to secure these economies. Even though the different establishments were to remain separate, it might be expected, when once their great importance is realised, that the industrial organism would tend, under the sway of ordinary economic motives, to evolve them. In the paper industry of the United States, for example, each mill confines itself as a rule to the manufacture of some one quality of paper;[1] and in the Lancashire cotton industry, not only are fine spinning, coarse spinning, and weaving localised separately, but individual firms frequently specialise on a narrow range of counts for spinning.[2] The same thing is true of the economies obtainable from the utilisation of by-products. Nor does it appear that those economies in respect of marketing, which some writers ascribe to large-scale control, are a dominating factor making for combination. For, " if a manufacturer is purchasing raw material, there is generally a market price for it which all must pay, and which any one can obtain it for, so long as he buys the customary minimum quantity; while, if what he requires is a partly manufactured article, purchases amounting in value to hundreds of pounds per annum, accompanied by prompt payment, can generally be made at the cheapest possible rate. The sole advantage enjoyed by the largest concerns in the purchase of raw materials seems to me to lie in the possibility of occasionally

---

[1] Cf. Chapman, *Work and Wages*, vol. i. p. 237.
[2] Cf. Marshall, *Industry and Trade*, p. 601.

clearing the market of raw materials or of a surplus output of partly manufactured stuff, by some purchase quite out of the power of a smaller concern to compass. Such an operation, however, partakes of the nature of a speculation, and the profit, when gained, is hardly to be called a cheapening of the cost of production, if only for the reason that the opportunity for such a special purchase cannot be relied upon to occur very often, and, when it does occur, is perhaps as likely to result in a loss as in a gain."[1] Nor, again, should much importance be attached to those advantages of large-scale management which have been summarised as "concentration of office work, provision of central warehouse for goods, centralisation of insurance and banking, establishment of a uniform system of accounts, enabling easy comparison to be made of the working of branches, institution of a uniform system of costing and of a central sales agency,"[2] and so forth. For these economies are scarcely practicable under the lower types of price-fixing Kartel, which are common in Germany, and, even in fusions and holding companies,[3] they are very soon outweighed by the immense difficulty of finding people competent properly to manage very large businesses.

There are, however, certain structural economies of large-scale management which are of a different order and have a wider reach. First, greater size, implying, as it does, greater wealth, makes it possible and profitable to spend more money on experiment. The Committee on Scientific and Industrial Research report: "Our experience up to the present leads us, indeed, to think that the small scale on which most British industrial firms have been planned is one of the principal

---

[1] Hobson, *The Industrial System*, p. 187, quoted from W. R. Hamilton, *The Cost of Production in Relation to Increasing Output.*

[2] McCrosty, *Economic Journal*, Sept. 1902, p. 359.

[3] Dr. Liefmann writes: "Einige Trusts, so der Zucker- und Spiritustrust, bildeten sich zu *einer einzigen Gesellschaft* um, also im Wege der vollständigen Verschmelzung, der Fusion, d.h. die betreffenden Unternehmungen gehen alle in einer einzigen derart auf, dass sie als besondere wirtschaftliche Organisation aufhören zu existieren. Die meisten aber nahmen in neuester Zeit nach verschiedenen Versuchen die Form der sogenannten *Holding Company*, einer *Kontrollgesellschaft*, wie wir es nennen können, an, d.h. die Gesellschaft erwarb alle oder doch die Mehrheit der Aktien sämtlicher zum Trust gehörender Einzelgesellschaften" (*Kartelle und Trusts*, p. 114).

impediments in the way of the organisation of research with
a view to the conduct of those long and complicated investigations which are necessary for the solution of the fundamental
problems lying at the basis of our staple industries." [1]   This is
obviously a very important matter ; though it is not clear why
a number of small firms should not, while retaining full
independence in other respects, agree to collaborate in
promoting research.   Secondly, the union into one of what
would have been many firms means that, instead of each
wielding only the secret processes discovered by itself, each
can wield the secrets of all ; and in some circumstances this
may involve large savings.   Thirdly, a business combining
many establishments is, in general, in contact with a number
of different markets, in which the fluctuations of demand are,
in some measure, independent.   It is, therefore, in a position
so to adjust things that the output of each of its component
establishments shall vary through a narrower range than it
would do if the several components were under separate
control.   But, if an establishment produces an average output
A made up of $(A + a)$ units one year and $(A - a)$ the next,
its costs are bound to be less than if it produces the same
average output made up of $(A + 2a)$ units one year and
$(A - 2a)$ units the next ; for in the latter case it must have
a capital equipment adequate to a " peak load " of $(A + 2a)$
units instead of the one of $(A + a)$ units.   That this is an
important matter is illustrated by the eagerness of co-operative
societies—creameries and so on—to assure themselves of the
" loyalty " of their members, and of Shipping Companies to
" tie " their customers to them by deferred rebates or in other
ways.[2]   Furthermore, even though, apart from combination,
the sum of the ranges of variation in the output of the
component establishments were already reduced to a minimum,
i.e. to equality with the range of variation in aggregate output, combination might still lead to economies, by enabling
the bulk of the plant to be run steadily, and reserving,
after the pattern of the Sugar Trust, one specially adapted
plant to adjust its output to the fluctuations in aggregate

---

[1] *Report*, p. 25. Cf. Marshall, *Industry and Trade*, p. 24, footnote.
[2] Cf. *post*, Part II. Chap. XIX. § 4.

demand.[1]   Fourthly, since it is much easier to forecast the
incidence of various sorts of good and ill fortunes upon the
aggregate of a number of separate concerns than it is to forecast
the incidence upon each one individually, the operation of a
business combining many establishments involves in the
aggregate less uncertainty-bearing than the operation of its
parts would involve if they were separated.   The general
economy resulting from this fact may manifest itself in the
greater facility with which loans can be obtained, or in the
lower price that has to be paid for them, or in the smaller
proportionate reserve fund that the concern needs to keep for
equalising dividends, or in other ways.   The essential point
is that the general economy, however it manifests itself, is
necessarily there.   The larger the unit of individual control,
the larger is this economy.   After a point, indeed, its growth,
as the unit grows, becomes exceedingly slow.   But, until the
unit has reached a very large size, it grows rapidly, and
constitutes a powerful force making for larger units—
though, no doubt, among commodities suitable for grading, a
speculative market may be developed, and may enable small
concerns, through the practice of hedging, to put themselves,
for *some* sorts of uncertainty, on a level with large concerns.[2]
One further point may be mentioned.   In certain special
industries large-scale control not only achieves a direct economy
by lessening the uncertainty-bearing that is involved in given
fluctuations in the individual fortunes of different firms ; it
also achieves an indirect economy by reducing the probability
that fluctuations will occur.   It does this in occupations
where public confidence is important, and where largeness
of capital resource is calculated to create confidence.   This
condition is fulfilled in banking—the more so since publicity
of bankers' accounts has become common.   The reason that
banks differ in this respect from other concerns is, of course,
that their customers are their creditors, and not, as in most
trades, their debtors.[3]

[1] Cf. Jenks and Clark, *The Trust Problem*, p. 43.
[2] Cf. Brace, *The Value of Organised Speculation*, p. 210.
[3] For a very full study of the subject-matter of §§ 2-3, cf. Marshall, *Industry and Trade*, Bk. ii. chaps. iii.-iv.

§ 4. So far we have considered exclusively what I have called *structural* economies. There is also another sort of economy that, in certain circumstances, favours the growth of large-scale management. So long as an industry is occupied by a number of establishments separately controlled, expenditure is likely to be incurred by all in defending their market against the others. A large part of the expenditure upon advertisements and travellers is, as was indicated in Chapter IX., of this character. But when, instead of a number of competing firms, there appear, in any section of an industry, a number of firms under a single authority, a great part of this expenditure can, as was also indicated in that chapter, be dispensed with. A and B being united, it is no longer to the interest of either to spend money in persuading people, whether through travelling salesmen or in other ways, to prefer the one to the other. It was stated, in regard to railways, before the Board of Trade Conference of 1908: "It is well known that railway companies find it necessary to spend large sums of money in canvassing against one another, and, if competition were removed by judicious amalgamation, the greater part of this money could be saved." [1] This economy is, of course, liable to be largest where, apart from unification, "competitive" advertisement would be largest, namely, not in staple industries providing easily recognised standard articles, but in various sorts of "fancy" trades.[2]

§ 5. Let us next suppose that the size of the individual firm and the size of the individual unit of control in an industry have been adjusted to the structural and other economies obtainable, and that the units evolved in this way are not large enough to exercise any element of monopolistic power. It is then clear that monopolistic power will

---

[1] *Railway Conference*, p. 26.

[2] The suggestion, that combination enables savings to be made in respect of the number or quality of travelling salesmen and so on, is not upset by the fact that, in some instances, after the formation of a combination, the aggregate annual wages paid to salesmen have increased. For the increase was probably due to attempts on the part of the combination to extend its market into fields which were not formerly occupied by any of its constituent members, or in which the business accessible to *single* firms was not enough to make it worth while for any of them to have salesmen there.

K

not be called into being incidentally, as a by-product of developments that take place without reference to it. But there still remains, as an influence tending to produce it the direct expectation of the gains to which it may lead When promoters have reason to believe that amateur speculators will expect a particular monopoly to prove more profitable than it really will do, this fact promises extra gains to those who form amalgamated companies, because it enables them to unload their shares at inflated values.[1] Apart from this special consideration, however, we may lay it down that the magnitude of the gains obtainable from monopolisation depends, the conditions of supply being given, on the elasticity of the demand — *i.e.* the fraction obtained by dividing a (*small*) percentage change in price into the associated percentage change in quantity purchased—for relevant quantities of the commodity concerned.[2] The less elastic the demand, the greater, *ceteris paribus*, are the probable gains. Incidentally, it may be observed, this circumstance, coupled with that noted in the next paragraph, makes it profitable for a monopolist to extend his control over products that compete

---

[1] The following passage from Mr. J. M. Clark's *The Economics of Overhead Costs* is interesting in this connection. " How great are the economies of combination ? So far as horizontal combination goes, the most definite quantitative evidence is afforded by Dewing's study of thirty-five combinations, all of which merged at least five concerns which had formerly competed and all of which had had a ten-year history before 1914, when the disturbances due to the world-war made further comparisons irrelevant. He finds that the promoters of these combinations prophesied sufficient savings to increase their net earnings, on the average, about 43 per cent above their previous level. This average included only serious estimates, taking no account of what were obviously sheer exhibitions of rosy imagination. The outcome told another story, however, for the net earnings of the first year after consolidation averaged about 15 per cent less than the previous earnings of the constituent parts, while the result for the ten years following combination was still worse ; about 18 per cent less than the previous earnings of the constituent parts, without allowing for the fact that considerable amounts of new capital were invested during the ten-year period " (*loc. cit.* pp. 146-7).

[2] If x is the quantity purchased and $\phi(x)$ the demand price per unit, the elasticity of demand is represented by $\dfrac{\phi(x)}{x\,\phi'(x)}$. If this is equal to unity for all values of x, the demand curve is a rectangular hyperbola. The verbal definition of the text is an approximate translation of the above technical definition, so long as the term *small* contained in it is emphasised. But, of course, a 50 per cent fall in price must be accompanied, if the elasticity of demand is to be equal to unity, by a 100 per cent rise in consumption. It will be understood, of course, that, when we speak of the gains from

with his own; for example, for the "Big Five" meat-packers of the United States to absorb both (*a*) non-American meat and (*b*) non-meat foods.[1] The principal conditions of highly inelastic demand have now to be set out.

The first condition is that the commodity shall be of a kind for which it is not easy to find convenient substitutes. The demand for mutton is made comparatively elastic by the existence of beef, the demand for oil by the existence of gas, and the demand for the service of trams by the existence of omnibuses. In like manner, the demand for the service of transport by rail is probably more elastic in England than in continental America, because "the long broken coast-line of England and the great number of ports" render the competition of water carriage exceedingly powerful;[2] and the demand for the services of any particular line of railway is, in general, fairly elastic, even where no water competition exists, in consequence of the indirect competition of lines running to other markets.[3] From another field a good example of the point I am now considering is furnished by Jevons, in his book on the *Coal Question*: "When the Government of the Two Sicilies placed an exorbitant tax on sulphur, Italy having, as it was thought, a monopoly of native sulphur, our manufacturers soon had resort to the distillation of iron pyrites or sulphide of iron."[4] As regards the kinds of commodity for which it is likely that substitutes can be employed little of general interest can be said. It should be observed, however, that the products of a district, or a country, whose efforts are directed

---

monopolisation depending on *the* elasticity of demand, there is a tacit implication that the elasticities as defined above, at the several points on the relevant range of the demand curve, do not greatly differ from one another. Mr. Dalton has suggested (*The Inequality of Incomes* p. 192 *et seq.*) that, when the price of anything increases by any finite percentage, the term "arc elasticity" should be used to represent this percentage change divided into the corresponding percentage change of quantity. But, since there would generally be a different arc elasticity for every different amount of price change from a given starting point, this new term might, in unpractised hands, easily lead to confusion.

[1] Cf. *Report of the Federal Trade Commission, 1919, on the Meat-packing Industry*, pp. 86 and 89.

[2] Cf. Macpherson, *Transportation in Europe*, p. 231.

[3] Cf. Johnson, *American Railway Transportation*, pp. 267-8.

[4] *The Coal Question*, p. 135.

to leadership in quality as distinguished from quantity, are less exposed to the competition of substitutes than other products. For example, the prime qualities of beef and mutton in Great Britain have not been affected by the development of the American and Australian trade to nearly the same extent as the inferior qualities.[1] It is, therefore, a commercially important fact that English manufacturers enjoy a very marked leadership of quality in wall-papers, fine textiles and cables, whereas in the electrical and chemical industries they are in a decidedly inferior position.[2] Obviously, from the present point of view, we must include among the substitutes for any commodity produced by a seller exercising monopolistic power the same commodity produced by other sellers. The larger, therefore, is the proportion of the total output of product that a seller exercising monopolistic power provides in any market, the less elastic the demand for his services will be. Inelasticity of demand for monopoly goods is, therefore, promoted in industries where importation from rival sources is hindered by high transport charges, high tariffs, or international agreements providing for the division of the field between the combined producers of different countries. Furthermore, in order that the elasticity of demand may be affected by substitutes, it is not necessary that the rival source of supply should be actually existing. In some industries manufacture by people who are normally purchasers is itself a possible rival source of supply. Thus the Committee on Home Work observe: "Unless the price at which these articles (baby linen and ladies' blouses and underclothing) are sold to the wives and daughters of the better-paid working men and small middle-class people is low, those who would otherwise be purchasers will buy the materials and make the articles at home." The same remark seems to apply to laundry-work and charing. The poor housewife has the power, if reason offers, to do these things for herself. Consequently, the demand for the services of specialists at such tasks is exceptionally elastic.[3] For example, it has been

---

[1] Cf. Besse, *L'Agriculture en Angleterre*, pp. 45 and 85.
[2] Cf. Levy, *Monopole, Kartelle und Trusts*, pp. 227, 229, 237.
[3] Cf. Chapman, *Unemployment in Lancashire*, p. 87.

remarked of Birmingham: " The washerwomen are among the first to suffer in any period of trade depression, for, as the first economy in bad times is to do your own washing, the tiny laundry with a very local connection is soon emptied."[1]

The second condition, making for inelasticity of demand is that a commodity shall give rise to only a small proportion of the total cost of any further commodities in the production of which it may be employed. The reason, of course, is that, when this proportion is small, a large percentage rise in the price of the commodity, with which we are concerned, involves only a small percentage rise in the price of these further commodities, and, therefore, only a small percentage contraction of consumption. Dr. Levy suggests that this condition makes the demand for the ordinary raw materials of industry highly inelastic.[2] A similar line of thought brings out the fact that the elasticity of the demand for commodities at wholesale will be smaller, the larger is the proportionate part played by retailing and transport expenses in the cost of the commodities to consumers.

The third condition is that the further commodities, if any, in whose production our commodity is employed, shall be such that substitutes cannot easily be found for them. Thus the raw materials of the building trade should be subject, other things being equal, to a less elastic demand than those of the engineering trade, because foreign machines can compete with English machines much more easily than foreign houses can compete with English houses.[3]

The fourth condition is that the other commodities or services which co-operate with our commodity in the making of a finished product shall be easily " squeezable," or, in technical language, shall have an inelastic supply schedule.

---

[1] Cadbury, *Women's Work*, p. 172. It may be added that, from a short-period point of view, the elasticity of the demand for new production of certain durable goods is made greater than it would otherwise be by the fact that half-worn-out garments and other such things are possible substitutes for new ones. (Cf. Chapman, *The Lancashire Cotton Industry*, p. 120.)

[2] *Monopole, Kartelle und Trusts*, p. 280.

[3] It should be noticed, however, that, though houses as wholes cannot be imported, it is becoming always easier to import *parts* of them. The imports of wrought stone, marble and joinery doubled between 1890 and 1902 ; whereas from the provinces to London the "imports" of these things have increased still more largely (Dearle, *The London Building Trades*, p. 52).

All these four conditions, which Marshall has distinguished, refer directly to the nature of people's *desire* for different commodities. There is yet another condition, dependent on the fact that the demand schedule derived from a given desire schedule for any commodity is only identical in form with the desire schedule, provided that the proportion of people's incomes spent on the commodity is so small that variations in the quantity of their purchase make no appreciable difference to the "marginal utility" of money to them. When this condition is not realised, the following considerations become relevant. Suppose that there is only one sort of commodity in the world, and that it is impossible to store money. Then, whatever the form of people's desire schedule for this commodity, their demand schedule is necessarily such that the same sum will be spent on it whatever the amount of it available; in other words, the elasticity of demand, in respect of all possible amounts of consumption, is necessarily equal to unity. From this we may generalise as follows: Given the elasticity of the desire for any commodity, the elasticity of the demand for it will diverge from this elasticity to a greater extent, and will approach more closely towards unity, the larger is the proportionate part of people's income that is normally spent on this commodity. Thus, the demand for commodities which absorb a large part of people's incomes cannot be either so inelastic or so elastic as it is possible for the demand for commodities which only absorb a small part of their incomes to be.[1]

§ 6. The preceding considerations suggest that units of control adequate to exercise monopolistic power will often be found, even though neither structural economies nor advertisement economies dictate their formation. The tendency towards this result is opposed by the difficulty and cost involved in bringing about agreements among competing sellers. This difficulty and cost depend upon the following general circumstances. First, combination is easier when the number of sellers is small than when it is large; for small numbers both facilitate the actual process of negotiation and diminish the chance that some party to an agreement will subsequently violate it. An attempt to form a Kartel in the German

---

[1] Cf. Birck, *Theory of Marginal Values*, pp. 133-4.

match trade in 1883 is reported by Liefmann to have failed because no less than 245 separate producers had to be consulted.[1]   Secondly, combination is easier when the various producers live fairly close to one another, and so can come together easily, than when they are widely scattered.   The reason why combination prevails in the German coal industry, and not in the English, is partly that, in Germany, the production of coal is localised, and not spread over a number of different districts, as it is in this country.[2]   A similar reason probably accounts, in great measure, for the excess of combination that appears among sellers in general, as compared with buyers in general ; for, it may be observed, at auctions, where buyers also are closely assembled, combination among them is not infrequent.   Thirdly, combination is easier when the products of the various firms are simple, of constant quality, not adjusted to individual tastes, and, therefore, capable of being intelligently and more or less precisely defined.   Marshall wrote : " It is almost impossible to arrange a uniform price list for carpets or curtain stuffs into which wool of different qualities, cotton, jute and other materials are worked in varying proportions and with incessant changes in fabric as well as in pattern.   There is no room for cartellisation of such things as biscuits, or ladies' hats, in which versatility is demanded as well as high quality." [3] One writer suggests that a reason why English firms are combined to a less extent than foreign firms is that they concern themselves, as a rule, with the higher qualities, and the more specialised kinds, of commodities, rather than with " mass goods " ; [4] and another, in like manner, attributes the greater ease with which Coke Kartels are formed in Germany, as against Coal Kartels, to the greater uniformity of quality generally found in coke.[5]   Fourthly, combination is easier when the tradition and habit of the country is favourable, than when it is unfavourable, to joint action in general.   When employers have been accustomed to act together in Chambers

[1] *Unternehmeverbände*, p. 57.
[2] Cf. Levy, *Monopole, Kartelle und Trusts*, p. 172.
[3] *Industry and Trade*, p. 549.
[4] Levy, *Monopole, Kartelle und Trusts*, p. 187.
[5] Walker, *Combinations in the German Coal Industry*, p. 43.

of Commerce, in agreements as to discounts and rebates, or in negotiations with unions of workpeople, the friction to be overcome in making a price agreement is evidently less than it would be if they came together for the first time for that purpose. Thus: "The Association—such as the Merchants' Association of New York—has, indeed, no monopoly power, but it is, nevertheless, of very great importance, owing to its socialising effects and its tendency to prepare the way for a stronger organisation, the combination or pool."[1]   In like manner, the New Zealand arbitration law "forces employers into unions, for only thus can they defend themselves under the Act, and these naturally evolve into organisations for restricting competition."[2]   Yet again, there can be no doubt that the various forms of joint action which British engineering firms, for example, were compelled to take during the Great War must have done much to smooth the way for future combination. Perhaps the opposing friction is also somewhat smaller when the producers concerned are companies than it is when they are private firms, in whose operations the sense of personal importance plays a larger part.

§ 7. The preceding section has tacitly implied that, where the gain from unification exceeds the cost and trouble involved, unification will, in fact, occur. This implication, however, is not warranted. It does not necessarily follow that, because an opportunity for agreement advantageous to all parties exists, an agreement will in fact be made. The reason is that mutual jealousy may cause A and B to leave the melon of common gain uncut, rather than that either should allow the other to obtain what he considers a share unduly large relatively to his own. Shall "participation" be proportional to the capacity of the several combining firms, or to their average product during recent years, or to the amount of the investment that has been made in plant and goodwill, or to some other quantity? "One manufacturer has patents and special machinery, which have cost him a great deal of money, and by which he sets much store. He will not enter the proposed combination unless these costs are made up to

---

[1] Robinson, *American Economic Association*, 1904, p. 126.
[2] V. S. Clark, *United States Bulletin of Labour*, No. 43, p. 1251.

him. Another manufacturer may have a large productive capacity, fifty nail machines, for example. He may have been unable to find a market for the output of more than half his machines, but in the combination, he contends, all his capacity will become available. He, therefore, insists that productive capacity should be the basis on which the allotment of shares in the trust should be made. A third man, by the excellence of his equipment and the energy of his methods, has been able to run his plant at its full capacity, while his competitor, with a larger productive capacity but a less favourable location or a less capable body of subordinates, has operated only half time. The successful manufacturer contends that average sales should be the basis of allotment." [1] Disputes on these lines may easily prevent agreement if direct negotiation between the different firms is attempted. It should, however, be noticed that they can, in great part, be obviated, and that the difficulty of combination can be correspondingly reduced, when an amalgamation is effected gradually by the process of absorption (exemplified among English banks), or when a company promoter, undertaking to buy up and consolidate a number of competing concerns, negotiates terms separately with each of them, without stating into what arrangements he has entered with the others.

[1] Meade, *Corporation Finance*, p. 36.

CHAPTER XV

MONOPOLISTIC COMPETITION

§ 1. A CONDITION of monopolistic competition exists when each of two or more sellers supplies a considerable part of the market with which they are connected. In these circumstances it can be shown that there is no tendency for them to devote to the industry in which they are employed that amount of resources which I have called the ideal investment, namely, that amount which will make the value of the marginal social net product there equal to the central value of marginal social net products in general.[1] A demonstration of this proposition, possible differences between social and private net product of the type examined in Chapter IX. being ignored, can be given in ordinary language as follows.

§ 2. Let us first ignore all forms of action which aim, by sacrifice in the present, at obtaining an advantage against rivals in the future. We have, then, to do with the pure problem of "multiple monopoly." This problem assumes its simplest form when two monopolists only are supposed to be present; and, in this form, it has been much discussed among mathematical economists. Cournot decided, as is well known, that the resources devoted to production under duopoly are a determinate quantity, lying somewhere between the quantities that would have been so devoted under simple competition and under simple monopoly respectively. Edgeworth, on the other hand, in an elaborate critique, maintained that the quantity is indeterminate. In more recent discussions there is apparent some measure of return towards Cournot. If, it is held, each of two monopolists, in regulating his action,

[1] Cf. *ante*, pp. 223-4.

assumes that the other will not alter his *output* in consequence of what he does, the quantity of resources devoted to production by the two together is determinate at the amount calculated by Cournot. If each monopolist assumes that the other will not alter his *price* in consequence of what he does, then, in a perfect market, the quantity of resources devoted to production by the two together is determinate at the amount proper to simple competition ; in an imperfect market—that is to say, a market in which some of the buyers have a *preference* for one monopolist over the other—this quantity is determinate at an amount less than that proper to simple competition, and falling short of it more largely the more imperfect the market is.[1] More generally, if each seller makes and holds to *any* definite assumption about the conduct of the other, it would seem that the quantity of resources devoted to production by both together is determinate at some amount not greater than that proper to simple competition, and not less, in a perfect market than the Cournot amount, in an imperfect market than the amount proper to simple monopoly. In real life, however, it is, I suggest, very unlikely that either seller will hold any consistent view about his rival's state of mind. His judgment will be variable and uncertain. As in a game of chess each player will act on some forecast of the other's reply ; but the forecast he acts on may, according to his mood and his reading of that opponent's psychology, be one thing or another thing. Hence, as it seems to me, we may properly say that the aggregate amount of resources to be devoted to production is indeterminate in the sense that from a mere knowledge of the demand conditions and of the cost conditions affecting the two monopolists—whether the cost conditions are independent or inter-linked—we cannot foretell what it will be. The range of indeterminateness extends over a distance which is larger in a perfect than it is in an imperfect market, and in either sort of market is diminished as the number of monopolists is increased above two. In no case can the aggregate investment be greater than the quantity proper to simple competition. We have learned, however, from Chapter XI. that, except in industries in which imported

---

[1] G. Hotelling, "Stability in Competition," *Economic Journal*, March 1929.

materials subject to increasing supply price are employed, this last quantity cannot be greater than the ideal investment. It follows that, except in these industries, the investment which is forthcoming under multiple monopoly cannot be greater than the ideal investment. It may, however, easily be, and, in view of what has been said, in general seems likely to be, substantially less than this.

§ 3. Hitherto we have specifically excluded the effects of price warfare designed to secure future gains by driving a rival from the field or exacting favourable terms of agreement from him. The indeterminateness just described exists under monopolistic competition, even though neither of the monopolists "hopes to ruin the other by cut-throat prices."[1] In many instances of monopolistic competition, however, price warfare —or cut-throat competition—does, in fact, take place. It consists in the practice of selling at a loss in order to inflict injury on a rival. It must be distinguished carefully from the practice of reducing prices down to, or towards, prime cost, which frequently occurs in periods of depression. This latter practice may involve large reductions of price below the "normal," and it is certain to do this when demand is variable and prime cost is small relatively to supplementary cost; but it does not involve "selling at a loss" in the strict sense. Cut-throat competition proper occurs only when the sale price of any quantity of commodity stands below the short-period supply price of that quantity. When it occurs, the range of possible aggregate investment no longer has, as an upper limit, the quantity proper to simple competition, but is liable to exceed this quantity to an extent determined by the opinion entertained by each of the combatants about the staying power of his opponent and by other strategical considerations. There is, obviously, no tendency for it to approximate to the ideal investment; but we can no longer say, as we could when cut-throat competition was ignored, that it is likely to be less than the ideal investment.

[1] Edgeworth, *Giornale degli economisti*, November 1897, p. 405.

CHAPTER XVI

SIMPLE MONOPOLY

§ 1. A CONDITION of simple monopoly exists when a single seller only is exercising monopolistic power—whether or not there are other sellers in the market who accept the price fixed by this seller—and when, allowance being made for cost of carriage and so forth, the same price rules throughout the whole of his market. In order that the effects of simple monopoly, as distinguished from simple competition, may be made clear, we must, of course, presume that the economies and technique of production are the same under both.[1] The fact that in real life they are often not the same gives rise to further problems, which will be discussed in Chapter XXI. Simple monopoly works out in two different ways, according as, on the one hand, the entry to the industry is so far restricted that no resources are drawn into it other than those actually finding employment in it, or, on the other hand, entry to the industry is free. I shall study first industries of restricted entry.

§ 2. In Chapter XI. it was shown that, in the absence of divergences between social and private net product of the

---

[1] Thus, if y be the aggregate output of an industry and x the output of a firm of typical size, then, writing $F(x, y)$ for the total cost of its output to this firm, we have x determined by the equation $\dfrac{\partial}{\partial x}\left\{\dfrac{F(x, y)}{x}\right\} = 0$. We must *not* suppose monopoly to come about because the introduction of a new technique has changed F into ψ, in such wise that, for a given value of y, $\dfrac{\partial}{\partial x}\left\{\dfrac{\psi(x, y)}{x}\right\} = 0$ gives a larger value of x than $\dfrac{\partial}{\partial x}\left\{\dfrac{F(x, y)}{x}\right\} = 0$ does, thus reducing the number of firms in that industry, and so making the formation of a price agreement easier. We must suppose F to be the same under both systems.

types discussed in Chapter IX., simple competition makes actual output less than ideal output in industries subject to decreasing supply price from the standpoint of the community; equal to ideal output in industries of constant supply price in this sense; and greater than ideal output in industries of increasing supply price in this sense. When simple monopoly prevails, it is to the interest of the monopolist so to regulate his output as to make the excess of his aggregate receipts over his aggregate costs (including earnings of management and so forth) as large as possible. It follows that under simple monopoly output will always, other things being equal, be less than it would have been under simple competition. Hence in industries of decreasing supply price from the standpoint of the community the substitution of simple monopoly for simple competition will cause actual output, which is now below ideal output, to fall further below it: in industries of constant supply price in this sense, it will cause actual output, which is now equal to ideal output, to fall below ideal output; in industries of increasing supply price in this sense, it will cause actual output, which is now above ideal output, to contract, and it *may* cause it to contract in a measure that brings it closer to ideal output than it has been hitherto. The conditions in which it will do this can be determined mathematically, but, unless unusual assumptions are introduced, they cannot be stated in simple terms. This, however, does not greatly matter. For in practice simple monopoly is much more likely to be introduced into industries of decreasing supply price from the standpoint of the industry, which, as was shown in Chapter XI., *in general* implies decreasing supply price from the standpoint of the community, than into other industries; and hence there is no uncertainty about the result.

§ 3. When monopolistic power is exercised by a combination of sellers through the agency of a price-agreement, the restrictive influence upon investment may be enhanced in an indirect way by a further circumstance. It is not practicable to make an agreement touching more than one or two roughly defined grades of service. Consequently, since an adapted charge cannot be made for them, the intermediate grades tend to disappear, even though numerous purchasers—some of whom, as things are, buy nothing—would have bought these grades, if they had been obtainable at a proportionate charge. Therefore resources, which, under a perfectly constructed monopoly agreement, would have been devoted to the production of these grades, are excluded by the imperfect character of actual agreements. This effect is chiefly found among railway and shipping companies, which are bound by freight-rate conventions but compete in the frequency, speed and comfort of their trains or ships.[1] Thus first-class rapid vessels may be employed to carry things for which they are quite unnecessary, because agreements preclude the offer of lower rates if slower and cheaper vessels are used;[2] and so forth. The misdirection of resources that arises in this way is additional to the misdirection due to a simple exercise of monopolistic power.

§ 4. Some qualification of the above results is necessary in industries where temporary low prices may lead to the development of new demands. For, when a prospect of this kind exists, particularly if conditions of decreasing supply price rule and if the current rate of interest on investments is low, it may pay a monopolist to accept low prices for a time, even though to do so involves production at a loss, for the sake of the future gain; whereas it would not pay any one among a large number of competing sellers to do this, since only a very small proportion of the future gain resulting from his action would accrue to himself. It is important, however, to observe that the creation of a new demand, which may thus sometimes be credited to monopoly, is only a social gain when the demand is really new, and not when it is merely a substitute for some other demand which is at the same time destroyed. It is not, for example, a social gain if a railway company, by temporary low prices, " develops the traffic " from one district at the expense of destroying the traffic from another equally well-situated district; and it is not a social gain if, by a like

---

[1] The agreements, short of pooling, between railways sometimes embrace agreements as to speed ; those between the members of some, but not all, shipping conferences, agreements as to the relative number of sailings permitted to the various members (*Royal Commission on Shipping Rings, Report*, p. 23).

[2] *Royal Commission on Shipping Rings, Report*, p. 108.

policy, some ring of traders causes people, who used to obtain a given measure of satisfaction from crinolines and no satisfaction from hobble-skirts, to obtain the like given measure of satisfaction from hobble-skirts and no satisfaction from crinolines. This consideration suggests that the transitional advantage of simple monopoly, that has just been set out, is not generally very important in comparison with the long-period disadvantages previously explained.

§ 5. There should be added a further consideration of some importance. It was shown in Part II. Ch. III. § 11 that to hold back new inventions and so on in order to keep up the value of existing forms of equipment *in general* inflicts more damage on the public than the benefits it confers on the owners of the equipment, and it was shown further that under simple competition there is no tendency for this kind of hold-up to occur. Under monopoly, on the other hand, there always is such a tendency; for the private monopolist is interested in the gain to him that monopoly implies, but not in the associated loss of consumers' satisfaction. It was recognised in the chapter cited that, when the introduction of new models of finished goods lessens the satisfaction which owners get from existing models, there is a substantial set-off to the gains of " progress," so that this tendency of private monopoly need not always be anti-social. But, when it is a question of new instruments and processes for making finished goods, there can be no such set-off, and hold-up policies must be socially injurious. The point is of great practical interest in view of the rapidity with which new inventions and minor improvements of method are normally made. This is illustrated by the fact that in the United States, over industry in general, twice as much is, it is estimated, normally written down against obsolescence as against depreciation;[1] and by the further fact that, out of 200 representative firms questioned for the President's Survey, 43·6 require new equipment to return its cost in two years : 64·1 per cent in three years or less.[2]

§ 6. In the discussion so far we have assumed the entry to industries, in which simple monopoly prevails, to be so

---

[1] *Changes in the Structure of World Economics since the War*, p. 158.
[2] *Recent Economic Changes*, p. 139.

far obstructed or restricted that no resources are drawn into them other than those actually finding employment there. As a rule this condition is fulfilled, because, when it is not fulfilled, the trouble of forming monopolistic agreements will seldom be worth undertaking.   Still, monopolistic agreements without restriction of entry are sometimes made.   It is easy to show that, under these agreements, the national dividend suffers more than it would do if the same monopolistic price policy prevailed in conjunction with restriction of entry to the industry.   For, broadly speaking, what happens is this.   The marginal social net product of resources actually finding employment in the monopolised industry is the same as it would be under a system of restricted entry. But, besides these resources, other resources have been drawn away from employment elsewhere and have become attached to the industry.   These extra resources will either be all idle themselves, or will make a corresponding quantity of resources already in the industry idle.   The dividend, therefore, will be reduced below what it would have been under a system of restricted entry, by the difference between the productivity of that quantity of resources which it pays to set to work in the monopolised industry and the productivity of that quantity for which the receipts of the industry would suffice to provide normal earnings.   This consideration does not, of course, prove that restriction of entry to an industry, in which monopoly prevails, is socially desirable ; for it may well happen that free entry would compel the monopolist to change his policy, and to adopt one approximately equivalent to that dictated by competition. It only proves that restriction is advantageous in those— probably exceptional — monopolies where the removal of restriction cannot affect price policy.[1]

---

[1] Attention may be called here to a peculiar case. Suppose the same process to yield two joint products, one of which is controlled monopolistically but the other is not. Then, as shown above, if entry to the industry can be restricted, simple monopoly will make the outputs of both products less than they would be under simple competition. The whole of the non-monopolised joint product that is produced will be sold, but, provided that the demand for the monopolised product has an elasticity less than unity, and that, in respect of the most profitable scale of output, the demand price for the non-monopolised product exceeds the supply price of the process that produces both products, a

part of the monopolised product will be thrown away. If entry to the industry is not restricted, more resources will flow into it than would so flow under simple competition. On the assumption that these are actually set to work and not left standing idle, this will mean that, in the above conditions, the output and sale of the non-monopolised joint product is larger than it would have been under simple competition. It is *possible*, though improbable, that, as a net result, there may be evolved a larger sum of consumers' surplus than simple competition would allow.

CHAPTER XVII

DISCRIMINATING MONOPOLY

§ 1. Up to this point we have supposed that monopolisation, when it occurs, will be of the simple form which does not involve discrimination of prices as between different customers. We have now to observe that this variety of monopolisation is not the only possible sort. Discriminating power will sometimes exist alongside of monopolistic power, and, when it does, the results are affected. It is, therefore, important to determine the circumstances in which, and the degree to which, monopolists are able to exercise, and find advantage in exercising, this power.

§ 2. The conditions are most favourable to discrimination, that is to say, discrimination will yield most advantage to the monopolist, when the demand price for any unit of a commodity is independent of the price of sale of every other unit. This implies that it is impossible for any one unit to take the place of any other unit, and this, in turn, implies two things. The first of these is that no unit of the commodity sold in one market can be transferred to another market. The second is that no unit of demand, proper to one market, can be transferred to another market. The former sort of transference needs no description, but the latter is somewhat subtle. It would occur if the promulgation of different rates for transporting coal originating in A and coal originating in B enabled the more favoured district to increase its production of coal, and, therefore, its demand for carriage, at the expense of the less favoured district. In order that the conditions most favourable to discrimination may prevail, this sort of transferability, as well as the other, must be excluded. Under the monopolistic arrangements practicable in real life the above kinds of transferability are absent or present in varying degrees. I propose to set out a series of examples under each of the heads just distinguished.

§ 3. Units of commodity are entirely non-transferable when the commodity in question consists of services applied directly by the sellers to the persons of their customers, such as the services of medical men, barristers, teachers, dentists, hotelkeepers and so forth. A medical man's offer to charge any one set of persons less than any other set cannot lead to the one set becoming middlemen for the services which the other set desire. Services applied directly by the seller to commodities handed to them for treatment, such as the service of transporting different articles, are also entirely non-transferable. A railway's offer to charge one price for a ton-mile of transport service to copper merchants and a lower price to coal merchants cannot lead to any middleman device, because it is physically impossible to convert copper into coal for the purpose of transport and afterwards to reconvert it. A slightly, but only slightly, lower degree of non-transferability exists among services that are normally rendered in physical connection with the private dwellings of purchasers. Gas and water supplied to private houses are instances in point. Here transference is not entirely excluded, because it is *possible*, at sufficient cost of money and trouble, to detach the commodities from the distributing plant along which they are brought and to carry them elsewhere. Lesser degrees of non-transferability exist among commodities whose transference is obstructed merely by high costs of transportation or by tariff charges. The degree of non-transferability in these circumstances may, evidently, be large or small, according as the distance, or the rate of customs duty, that separates two markets between which discrimination is attempted is large or small. In like manner, various degrees of non-transferability can be brought about artificially by enforcing upon purchasers contracts that penalise re-sales. For example, in the Ruhr coal district, the (pre-war) agreement made by the syndicate with industrial purchasers provided " that re-sale to railways, gas works, brick works or lime-kilns, or any reshipment from the original point of destination, shall be penalised by an addition of 3 marks per ton to the selling price."[1] If no agreement of this kind, no cost of carriage, and no tariff exist, complete transferability will prevail.

§ 4. Units of demand are almost completely non-transferable from one market to another, when the commodity concerned is something ready for final consumption, and when the markets, between which discrimination is to be made, are distinguished according to the wealth of the purchasers. It is clear, for instance, that the willingness of doctors to charge less to poor people than to rich people does not lead to any rich people, for the sake of cheap doctoring, becoming poor. In like manner, the provision of the service of transport at different rates to coal merchants and to copper merchants does not lead to any copper merchants, for the sake of the cheap transportation, becoming coal merchants. No doubt, in both these examples some slight transference *may* be achieved through successful fraud, such as a pretence on the part of rich people that they belong to the poorer group, and the smuggling of copper in the guise of coal; but this kind of thing is of no practical importance. It is interesting to note that sellers often attempt artificially to create the above type of non-transferability by attaching to different grades of their product trade marks, special brands, special types of packing and so on—all incidents designed to prevent possible purchasers of the grades that are highly priced relatively to the cost of production from becoming, instead, purchasers of the grades that are sold at a lower rate of profit.[2] A smaller degree of non-transferability exists between the markets for hotel accommodation in the season and out of the season; for heavy discrimination might cause a considerable number of people to change the time of their

---

[1] Walker, *Combination in the German Coal Industry*, p. 274.

[2] It must be added, however, that, though trade marks are sometimes mere devices for creating monopoly power, there is, nevertheless, a valid reason for protecting them against infringement by legal enactments, because " an inducement is thereby given to make satisfactory articles and to continue making them." (Cf. Taussig, *American Economic Review Supplement*, vol. vi., 1916, p. 177.)

holiday.   A still smaller degree of non-transferability exists between the markets for railway transport from A to B, which are provided respectively by traders in A wishing to send a given commodity direct to B, and by traders in C wishing to send this commodity to B through A.   For a large difference in the rates charged would cause production, that would normally occur at the less favoured, to take place instead at the more favoured, point.   Perfect transferability exists when the markets are distinguished by some badge, the attachment of which involves no cost, as, for example, if railways charged one fare to passengers carrying pencils and another fare to passengers without pencils.   The immediate effect of this discrimination would be to transfer *all* demands from the less to the more favoured market, and discrimination would yield *no* advantage to the monopolist.

§ 5.   When a degree of non-transferability, of commodity units on the one hand or of demand units on the other hand, sufficient to make discrimination profitable, is present, the relation between the monopolistic seller and each buyer is, strictly, one of bilateral monopoly.   The terms of the contract that will emerge between them is, therefore, theoretically indeterminate and subject to the play of that " bargaining " whose social effects were analysed at the end of Chapter IX. When a railway company is arranging terms with a few large shippers, the indeterminate element may have considerable importance.   Usually, however, where discrimination is of practical interest, the opposed parties are, not a single large seller and a few large buyers, but a single large seller and a great number of relatively small buyers.   The loss of an individual customer's purchase means so much less to the monopolistic seller than to any one of the many monopolistic purchasers that, apart from combination among purchasers, all of them will almost certainly accept the monopolistic seller's price.   They will recognise that it is useless to stand out in the hope of bluffing a concession, and will buy what is offered, so long as the terms demanded from them leave to them *any* consumers' surplus.   In what follows I assume that the customers act in this way.   So assuming, we may distinguish three degrees of discriminating power, which a monopolist may conceivably wield. A first degree would involve the charge of a different price against all the different units of commodity, in such wise that the price exacted for each was equal to the demand price for it, and no consumers' surplus was left to the buyers. A second degree would obtain if a monopolist were able to make n separate prices, in such wise that all units with a demand price greater than x were sold at a price x, all with a demand price less than x and greater than y at a price y, and so on. A third degree would obtain if the monopolist were able to distinguish among his customers n different groups, separated from one another more or less by some practicable mark, and could charge a separate monopoly price to the members of each group. This degree, it will be noticed, differs fundamentally from either of the preceding degrees, in that it may involve the refusal to satisfy, in one market, demands represented by demand prices in excess of some of those which, in another market, are satisfied.

§ 6. These three degrees of discriminating power, though all theoretically possible, are not, from a practical point of view, of equal importance. On the contrary, in real life the third degree only is found. No doubt, we can imagine conditions in which discrimination even of the first degree could be achieved. If all consumers had exactly similar demand schedules,[1] it could be achieved by the simple device of refusing to sell in packets of less than the quantity which each consumer required per unit of time, and fixing the price per packet at such a rate as to make it worth the consumer's while, but only just worth his while, to purchase the packet. Thus, if every demander would give for a hundredth physical unit of commodity, when he already has ninety-nine units, the sum of one shilling, but would prefer to give 300 shillings for a hundred units rather than have no units at all, the monopolist may make his unit of sale one hundred physical units and charge for this unit of sale a price of 300 shillings. If there is no combination

---

[1] A person's demand schedule for any commodity is the list of different quantities of that commodity that he would purchase at different price levels. Cf. Marshall, *Principles of Economics*, p. 96.

among the buyers, the number of units sold will then
be the same as would have been sold at a price of
one shilling per physical unit, and, in effect, the physical
units satisfying demands of different keenness will have
been sold at different prices. But this method of discrimination, whether in a complete or a partial form, is
scarcely ever practicable, because the individual demand
schedules, of which the market demand schedule is made
up, are, as a rule, very far indeed from being similar. For
this reason an analysis of the method is of academic interest
only.[1] Apart from this method, discrimination of the first
degree might still conceivably be established by detailed
separate bargaining with every separate customer. But that
method would involve enormous cost and trouble. Furthermore, since it implies separate bargains with individuals,
it opens the way, not only to error, but also to the perversion
of agents through bribery. These considerations are, in
general, sufficient to make monopolists themselves unwilling
to adopt the method; and, even if they were not thus
unwilling, it would be hardly possible for the State, in view
of the large opportunities for " unfair " competition which
the method affords, to leave their hands free. " Whatever
financial advantage there may be in charging against each
act of transport a rate adapted to its individual circumstances,
the arbitrary nature of a system of rates arranged on this
plan implies so much uncertainty and lends itself to such
serious abuses, that we are compelled to condemn it." [2] Thus
a powerful influence is always at work persuading or compelling monopolists to act on general rules, with published

---

[1] For such an analysis, cf. my paper " Monopoly and Consumers' Surplus,"
Economic Journal, September 1904.

[2] Colson, *Cours d'économie politique*, vol. vi. p. 211. Special opportunities
for injurious discrimination of this sort exist when a railway company is
itself a large producer of some commodity, say coal, which it also transports
for rival producers. To prevent the obvious abuses to which this state of things
may lead, the "commodity clause" of the Hepburn Act passed in 1906 in the
United States made it unlawful for any railway to engage in interstate
transport of any commodity which had been mined or manufactured by itself.
The law does not, however, prevent a railway from transporting a commodity
produced by a company in which it holds a majority of the shares, and it can,
therefore, be evaded without great difficulty. (Cf. Jones, *The Anthracite Coal
Combination*, pp. 190 *et seq.*)

tariffs, guarded, as effectively as may be, against the under-mining influence of unpublished rebates. This means that they cannot, except in extraordinary circumstances, introduce either the first or the second degree of discrimination, and that the third degree is of chief practical importance.

§ 7. Monopoly *plus* discrimination of the third degree is not a determinate conception. It is theoretically possible to divide any market in an indefinitely large number of different ways, of which some would be more, and others less, advantageous to the monopolist. If the monopolist had an absolutely free hand in the matter, the division he would choose would be such that the lowest demand price in sub-market A exceeded the highest demand price in sub-market B, and so on throughout. If the aggregate demand of the markets collectively had an elasticity greater than unity throughout, the resulting system would be identical with that proper to the second degree of discrimination, for the lowest demand price in each group would also be the price calculated to yield maximum monopoly revenue from that group. If the aggregate demand had not an elasticity greater than unity throughout, the maximising price in some groups would be greater than the lowest demand price in those groups, and the system would, therefore, be different from the above. In any event the separation of markets, in such wise that the lowest demand price in the first exceeds the highest demand price in the second, and so on, would obviously be better, from the monopolist's point of view, than any other kind of separation. But in practice the monopolist's freedom of action is limited by the need, already referred to, of acting on general rules. This consideration makes it necessary that he shall choose, for his sub-markets, groups that are distinguishable from one another by some readily recognisable mark. More-over, since a hostile public opinion might lead to legislative intervention, his choice must not be such as to outrage the popular sense of justice. Thus, he will not distinguish and bring together entirely new groups, but will make use of distinctions already given in nature. Nor is this all. For in some circumstances the condition of non-transferability holds good, not generally, but only as between certain markets, which are constituted independently of the monopolist's volition. Thus, the existence of an import tariff or of high transport charges on imports to all parts of his country's frontier—a condition easiest to realise when that country is an island—may make it possible for a seller to charge a lower price for his goods abroad than at home without the risk of inviting the return and resale of his exports. Clearly, therefore, a monopolist cannot hope to find a series of sub-markets that conforms to his ideal altogether, but he may find one in which only a comparatively small number of the demand prices embraced in the first sub-market are lower than the highest demand price of the second sub-market, and so on throughout all the sub-markets.

§ 8. I now pass to an analysis of consequences, and, as in the preceding chapter, I shall begin with monopolised industries to which entry can be restricted. The analysis, to be complete, would need to take account of the fact that, in real life, the demand of one purchaser for any r^{th} unit of a commodity is sometimes, in part, dependent upon the price at which this commodity is being sold to other purchasers.[1] When markets are interdependent in this way, the issue is complicated, but the broad results, though rendered less certain, are not, it would appear, substantially altered. Consequently in the following pages I shall assume that the quantity demanded in each sub-market depends only on the price ruling in that sub-market. This procedure enables resort to be had to the same general method that has been pursued hitherto.

§ 9. As already explained, practical interest centres upon monopoly *plus* discrimination of the third degree. But, before studying this, we may, with advantage, glance at the simpler problem presented by the two higher forms of discrimination. It is easily seen that, *in industries in which the rates of change in supply price from the standpoint of the industry are identical with the rates of change from the standpoint of the community*, under monopoly *plus* discrimination of the first degree, it will always pay the monopolist to make the ideal amount of investment and to produce the ideal output. This implies that, under conditions of constant supply price, monopoly *plus* discrimination of the first degree will make

[1] Cf. *ante*, Part II. Ch. XI. § 13.

the national dividend the same as simple competition would have made it. Under conditions of decreasing and of increasing supply price it will always improve on the result of simple competition. The extent to which it improves on it will be measured by the extent to which the output proper to simple competition differs from the ideal output. This is evidently greater, the more elastic is the demand for the commodity produced by the industry and the more markedly the conditions of the industry depart in either direction from those of constant supply price. Finally, it should be observed that, when conditions of decreasing supply price prevail, monopoly *plus* discrimination of the first degree *may* increase the size of the national dividend in a more special way. It *may* bring about a considerable amount of socially desirable investment in an industry, in which, under a régime of simple competition, it would not have been to anybody's interest to make any investment at all. It is shown in Appendix III. that this result is most likely to be realised (1) if, other things being equal, supply price decreases sharply, in such wise that a small increase of output involves a large fall in supply price per unit, and (2) if, other things being equal, the demand for the commodity or service is elastic till fairly low price levels have been reached.[1]

§ 10. In industries where the rates of change of supply price from the standpoint of the industry and of the community are not identical, matters are slightly more complicated. As was implied in Chapter XI. §§ 6-8, we are entitled to presume that the rate of change from the standpoint of the community will, in general, be a larger negative or a smaller positive quantity than the rate from the other standpoint. It can be inferred that the output proper to discriminating monopoly of the first degree will be less than the ideal output. In industries of decreasing supply price from the standpoint of the industry, it will be greater than the output proper to simple competition, and, therefore, nearer than that output to the ideal output. In industries of increasing supply price from the standpoint of the industry, it will be less than the output proper to simple competition. But the output proper to simple competition *may* in this case be greater than the ideal output. It is,

[1] Cf. Appendix III. § 26.

therefore, possible that the output proper to discriminating monopoly of the first degree may be further than the output proper to simple competition from the ideal output. Since, however, as was observed in Chapter XVI. § 2, monopolistic action is chiefly to be expected in industries of decreasing supply price, this possibility is of small importance.

§ 11. It is readily seen that the effects of monopoly *plus* discrimination of the second degree approximate towards those of monopoly *plus* discrimination of the first degree, as the number of different prices, which it is possible for the monopolist to charge, increases; just as the area of a polygon inscribed in a circle approximates to the area of the circle as the number of its sides increases. Let us call the output proper to discrimination of the first degree, that is to say, the ideal output, a. Then monopoly of the second degree would lead to an output less than a, but approaching more nearly towards it the larger is the number of the different price groups which the monopolist is able to distinguish; and the value of the marginal social net product of resources invested in our industry would, in like manner, approach more nearly towards equality with the value of the marginal social net products in general, the larger is this number.

§ 12. The study of monopoly *plus* discrimination of the third degree is more complicated than that of either of the two higher forms. In the discussion of these we have been able to make use of a simple relation between the aggregate output which comes about in various circumstances and the output which I have called the ideal output. According as actual output exceeds, falls short of, or is equal to the ideal output, we could conclude that the value of the marginal social net product of resources invested in our industry falls short of, exceeds, or is equal to the value of the marginal social net product of resources in general. But, under monopoly *plus* discrimination of the third degree, the relation between actual output and ideal output no longer suffices for a criterion. The reason is that, when a demand represented by a demand price p is satisfied, it is not necessary, as it has been necessary so far, that all the demands represented by demand prices greater than p shall have been satisfied.

On the contrary, the monopolist may, in one market, be satisfying all demands represented by demand prices higher than p, while, in another market, he is refusing to satisfy any demands whose demand prices fall short of $(p + h)$. It follows that the resources invested in the industry fall into a number of different parts, in each of which the value of the marginal social net product is different. Consequently, we have no longer to ask how the value of the marginal social net product of resources invested *in the industry* is related to the value of the marginal social net product of resources in general, but how the various values of marginal social net products of resources invested to cater for *each of the several markets of the industry* are related to that standard. Our ideal output ceases to be a single output of the whole industry, and becomes a number of separate outputs sold in separate markets. A given output of the whole industry may be broken up in different ways among these markets, and the system of values of marginal social net products will be different according to the way in which it is, in fact, broken up. Hence a study of the effect which monopoly *plus* discrimination of the third degree produces upon output is only a first step to a study of the effect which it produces, as compared with that which simple monopoly and simple competition respectively produce, upon the relation between the values of marginal social net products in different parts of the industrial field. Nevertheless, it is well that such a study should be made. To facilitate it, let us suppose that the demands for the product of an industry can be broken up into two markets A and B, between which price discrimination is feasible; and let us ask, first, whether output under discriminating monopoly of the third degree will be absolutely greater or smaller than output under simple monopoly and simple competition respectively.

§ 13. To compare the output proper to discriminating monopoly of the third degree with that proper to simple monopoly, we may conveniently distinguish three principal cases. First, let the conditions be such that, under simple monopoly, some of the commodity, in which we are interested, would be consumed in both A and B. In these conditions there is no adequate ground for expecting either that output under discriminating monopoly of the third degree will exceed, or that it will fall short of, output under simple monopoly; if the curves of demand and supply are straight lines, the two outputs will be equal.[1]   Secondly, let the conditions be such that, under simple monopoly, some of the commodity would have been consumed in A, but none in B.   In these conditions it is impossible that the introduction of discriminating power should lead to diminished output.   On the contrary, if there is any substantial demand in B, it must lead to increased output.   The amount of the increase will be specially great if the demand in B is elastic, and if the commodity obeys the law of decreasing supply price (*simpliciter*).   These conditions are often fulfilled among Kartels selling regularly at specially low rates in markets, foreign and other, where they are exposed to competition.   An interesting practical inference is that, if a commodity, whose production obeys the law of decreasing supply price, is monopolised, it is to the interest of the consumers in the producing country that the Government should allow the monopolist to make sales abroad at lower prices than at home, rather than that, while still permitting monopoly, it should forbid this discrimination.   This inference cannot be upset by reference to the more advanced industries that use the commodity as a raw material, because the sales abroad, being at market prices there, —prices which the monopolistic exports cannot in ordinary circumstances sensibly affect—do not enable foreign users to get it appreciably more cheaply than they could before.   Finally, let the conditions be such that, under simple monopoly, none of the commodity would have been consumed in either A or B.   In these conditions it is obviously impossible that the introduction of discriminating power should lead to diminished output.   It is possible that it may lead to increased output. The condition for this is the same as the condition, mentioned in the next paragraph, that enables discriminating monopoly of the third degree to yield some output, though simple competition would yield none.

§ 14.   We have now to compare the output proper to

[1] Cf. Appendix III. § 28.

discriminating monopoly of the third degree with that proper to simple competition. Under conditions of constant and of increasing supply price it is obviously impossible for discriminating monopoly of any degree to make output greater than it would be under simple competition. Discriminating monopoly of the third degree must make it smaller than it would be under that system. When, however, conditions of decreasing supply price prevail, the question is more complex. It has been proved in an earlier section that, in that event, monopoly *plus* discrimination of the first degree must raise output above the quantity proper to simple competition. Furthermore, it is evident that discrimination of the third degree approximates towards discrimination of the first degree as the number of markets into which demands can be divided approximate towards the number of units for which any demand exists. Hence it follows that, under decreasing supply price, monopoly *plus* discrimination of the third degree *may* raise output above the competitive amount, and is more likely to do this the more numerous are the markets between which discrimination can be made. Sometimes, but not, of course, so frequently as with discrimination of the first degree, discriminating monopoly of the third degree will evolve some output where simple competition would have evolved none. In view, however, of the limitation, which practical considerations impose, alike upon the number of markets that can be formed, and upon the monopolist's freedom to make up the several markets in the way most advantageous to him, it appears, on the whole, exceedingly improbable that, in an industry selected at random, monopoly *plus* discrimination of the third degree will yield an output as large as would be yielded by simple competition.

§ 15. In the preceding paragraphs we have compared *the absolute amount* of output under discriminating monopoly of the third degree with the absolute amount under simple monopoly and simple competition respectively. The next step is to compare the measure of approximation towards the ideal output that is attained under these different systems. What has been said enables us to conclude broadly that, whatever law of supply price prevails, discriminating monopoly of the third degree is likely to yield an output nearer to the ideal output than simple monopoly yields; but that it is not likely to yield an output nearer to it than simple competition yields. When, however, the conditions are such that (1) there is an ideal output (other than a zero output), (2) simple competition yields no output, and (3) discriminating monopoly of the third degree yields some output, this output *must* be nearer to the ideal output than the zero output of simple competition.

§ 16. I now return to the considerations suggested in § 12. It was there pointed out that the measure of correspondence between the actual aggregate output of an industry and the ideal output is not, when discriminating monopoly of the third degree is in question, the decisive index that it is in other circumstances. Suppose, for example, that discriminating monopoly of this degree brings about an output closer to the ideal output than either simple monopoly or simple competition would bring about. We cannot infer from this that the value of the marginal social net product of resources employed in the industry is brought nearer to the value of marginal social net products in general. For there is no longer any such thing as the value of the marginal social net product of resources employed in the industry. There are different values of marginal social net product in different portions of the industry. The value of the marginal social net product of resources that serve the needs of low-priced markets is smaller than the value of the marginal social net product of those that serve high-priced markets. Hence, even when, in any industry, discriminating monopoly makes aggregate output more nearly conformable to ideal output than simple monopoly or simple competition would do, it does not follow that it will involve greater equality between the values of marginal social net products over industry as a whole. Nor need we stop at this negative result. It can be shown, further, that the establishment in any industry of a given output associated with discriminating prices is likely to conduce less towards equality among the values of marginal social net products as a whole than the establishment of the same output associated with uniform prices. For let the value of the marginal social net product of resources in general be P; and let the quantity of resources invested in our industry be such that, if the product is sold at the same price in all markets, the value of the marginal social net product of the resources employed to supply each of them will be equal to p. Then, if this same quantity of resources is invested in the industry, but the product is sold at a higher price in some markets than in others, the value of the marginal social net product of the resources utilised for the higher-priced markets will be greater than p, and that of the resources utilised for the lower-priced markets will be less than p. This implies that the mean square deviation (our measure of inequality) of these various values from P is likely to be greater than it would have been if all of them had stood at p. Hence the probability that discriminating monopoly of the third degree will be more favourable to equality among the values of marginal social net products than simple monopoly or simple competition is less than the probability that it will be more favourable than they are to the production of the ideal output. The probability that it will be more favourable than they are to the national dividend is, therefore, also less than that probability.

§ 17. So far we have supposed that discriminating monopoly is coupled with power to restrict the entry to the monopolised industry. When this condition is not satisfied, reasoning analogous to that employed at the close of the preceding chapter is applicable. Resources tend to be attracted into the industry till the point is reached at which the expectation of earnings there is equal to that ruling elsewhere. So long as monopoly prices are maintained, this means that a considerable part of the resources so attracted is standing idle and is yielding no net product whatever. It is evident, therefore, that the national dividend suffers more from discriminating monopoly without restriction of entry than it does from discriminating monopoly *plus* restriction of entry. But, as with simple monopoly, so also here, it may, nevertheless, be desirable that restriction should be forbidden, because, when it is absent, there is a better chance that the entrenchments of monopolistic power will ultimately be broken down.

L

CHAPTER XVIII

THE SPECIAL PROBLEM OF RAILWAY RATES

§ 1. THE discussion of the preceding chapter has necessarily been somewhat abstract. It has, however, practical applications of very great importance in connection with the problem of arranging the charges to be made for such things as water, gas, and electricity, when these commodities are supplied to different groups of consumers or for different purposes. Still greater interest attaches to it in connection with the rates chargeable by railway companies. Considerable controversy has taken place between those who hold that these rates should be based on " the cost of service principle " and those who would base them on the " value of service principle." [1] The " cost of service principle " is, in effect, the simple competition discussed in Chapter XI. : " the value of service principle " is discriminating monopoly of the third degree. In the light of what has been said, the issue between them can be clearly set out ; and it will, in the present chapter, be examined. We have no concern with the circumstance, explained in Chapter XVI., that, in certain conditions, a railway with power to discriminate may find it profitable, *as a temporary measure*, to charge exceptionally low rates for transport between certain places or for certain selected commodities, with a view to building up a new demand ; nor yet with the related circumstance that this policy, if the demand is really a new one, and not merely a substitute for another that has been supplanted, may be

[1] It is interesting to note that the problem of how retail shops should distribute their charges for the act of retailing over the various commodities that they sell is very closely analogous to the problem of railway charges. Among retail shops, however, there is the additional complication that a retailer is sometimes able to obtain a general advertisement for his shop by selling particular well-known goods practically free of retailer's profit.

more advantageous to economic welfare, if not to the national dividend,[1] than anything which simple competition—unless it were modified by a system of State bounties—could evolve. These matters call for no further investigation here. Leaving them aside, I propose to exhibit the meaning, in concrete form, of the cost of service principle—or simple competition—and of the value of service principle—or discriminating monopoly of the third degree,—and to compare their respective consequences.

§ 2. It is generally agreed that, except in so far as the transport services sold to one set of purchasers are "supplied jointly" with those sold to another set, simple competition would tend to bring about a system of uniform rates per ton-mile for similar services.[2] For these services the level of the uniform rate would be such that the demand price and the supply price would coincide; and, when the service of railway transport was sold in conjunction with some other service, such as cartage or packing, an appropriate addition would be made to the charge. This general analysis can be briefly developed as follows.

First, the actual level of the uniform mileage rate, to which simple competition would lead on any particular railway, will depend on the circumstances and position of the railway. *Ceteris paribus*, a specially high rate would be appropriate if the route lay through districts where, as with mountain railways, the engineering costs of making a line are specially great, or where the traffic is very irregular from

---

[1] Cf. *ante*, Part II. Chapter III. § 4, footnote.

[2] It is, indeed, sometimes maintained that this will only happen if "simple competition" is defined to include complete transferability of the things that are sold among customers, and it is pointed out that competition, apart from this condition, has proved compatible with discriminating charges for services sold to different sets of persons by shipping companies and by retailers; different sorts of cargoes are carried at different rates, and the absolute charge for retailing work is different in regard to different articles. (Cf. G. P. Watkins, "The Theory of Differential Rates," *Quarterly Journal of Economics*, 1916, pp. 693-5.) Reflection, however, shows that, when competition really prevails, seller A must always endeavour to undersell seller B by offering to serve B's better-paying customers at a rate slightly less than B is charging, and that this process must eventually level all rates. The explanation of the discriminations cited above is, not the absence of complete transferability, but the fact that custom and tacit understandings introduce an element of monopolistic action.

one time to another ;[1] because, in these conditions, the supply prices of all quantities of transportation along the route are specially high. In like manner, *ceteris paribus*, a specially high rate would be appropriate if the route lay through sparsely populated regions where little traffic can be obtained, or through regions where the configuration of the country renders water transport a readily available substitute for land transport for certain classes of commodities between the terminals ; because, in these conditions, the demand schedule is specially low, and the supply conforms to conditions of decreasing supply price ; the expenses involved in building and working a railway adapted for a small amount of traffic being proportionately greater than those involved in the production of transport service on a large scale. It is, no doubt, in recognition of these considerations that the *maxima*, imposed in the British parliamentary freight classification, are made different for different lines, though the classification itself is, of course, the same for all of them.

Secondly, departures from the uniform mileage rate would occur under simple competition, in so far as buyers of a ton-mile of transportation require, along with this, other incidental services involving expense. The adjustments needed are exactly analogous to the adjustments made in the price of plain cotton cloth delivered c.i.f. to buyers who live at different distances from the seat of manufacture. Thus rates should be comparatively low for the transport of any class of goods, when the method of packing adopted is convenient to the railway. It is more costly, other things being equal, to carry small consignments than large. " Small consignments mean to a railway three distinct sources of serious additional expense : separate collection and delivery; separate handling, invoicing, accounting, etc., at the terminal stations ; and bad loading in the railway waggons."[2] It is, therefore, proper that, in the British parliamentary classification, goods, which are placed in class A—the cheapest class—when loaded in lots of 4 tons, are raised to class B when despatched in loads of between 2 and 4

---

[1] Cf. Williams, *Economics of Railway Transport*, p. 212.
[2] Acworth, *Elements of Railway Economics*, p. 120.

tons, and to class C when despatched in loads of less than 2 tons. On a like principle, it is proper that English railway companies should voluntarily make arrangements, under which certain goods are put into a class lower than the parliamentary classification requires, on condition that they are loaded in certain quantities or packed in certain ways. Further, when the method of packing is given, it is proper that rates per ton should vary with conditions that affect the cost of handling, such as bulk, fragility, liquidity, explosiveness, structure and so on; and also with the speed and regularity of the service required.[1] This point is clearly brought out in one of the decisions of the United States Railway Commissioners. They declared: "Relatively higher rates on strawberries appear to be justified by the exceptional character of the service connected with their transportation. This exceptional service is necessitated by the highly perishable character of the traffic, requiring refrigeration *en route*, rapid transit, specially provided trains, and prompt delivery at destination. There is also involved in this service extra trouble in handling at receiving and delivering points, the ' drilling' of cars in a train, reduction of length of trains to secure celerity of movement, partially loaded cars, the return of cars empty, and, perhaps, other similar incidentals." [2] Finally, it is proper that the rate for carrying from A to B goods that are to go forward to C on the same line should, in general, be less than the rate for so carrying goods destined for consumption at B. In so far as terminal charges are paid for in the rate, this is obvious, because, on the former class of goods, terminal charges at B are saved altogether. Even apart from terminals, however, the journey from A to B, as a part of a longer journey, is less costly than the same journey undertaken as an isolated whole. The reason is that, roughly speaking, the interval of idleness for engines and plant, following upon any journey, involves a cost properly attributable to that journey, and the length of the interval does not vary with the length of the journey which it follows. Thus, "long hauls get more mileage out of

---

[1] Cf. Haines, *Restrictive Railway Legislation*, p. 148.
[2] *Quarterly Journal of Economics*, November 1910, p. 47.

engines, waggons, train-staff, etc., than a number of short hauls, necessarily with waits between; engines and waggons are better loaded, and the line is more continuously utilised." [1] This consideration points to some form of tapering rate for the service of carriage, apart from terminal charges. The English (pre-war) classification of merchandise rates accepts this. It provides for one maximum ton-mile rate for the first 20 miles, a lower maximum for the next 30 miles, a still lower one for the next 50 miles, and the lowest of all for further distances. This scale does not include terminal charges, which are fixed independently of distance. [2]

Thirdly, attention must be called to the fact that services, though physically similar, are not necessarily similar in respect of cost when they are rendered at different times or seasons of the year. This consideration is in practice chiefly important as regards the supply of electricity. In order that it may be possible to provide the current required at "the peak of the load," a large quantity of equipment must be erected additional to what would be required if there were no hours or seasons of exceptional demand. Let us suppose that during one-fifth of the time 2 million units per hour are wanted and during the rest of the time $1\frac{1}{2}$ million units, and that, in consequence, the equipment costs $\frac{4}{5}$ times what it would have done had $1\frac{1}{2}$ million units been required always. Then the real cost of the peak-load current, so far as it depends on cost of equipment, can be calculated as follows: the equipment cost of producing the units needed in the aggregate of off-peak times is $\frac{4}{5}$ times $\frac{3}{4}$ths (i.e. $\frac{3}{5}$ths) of the total equipment cost, and the equipment cost of producing the units needed in peak times is $\frac{1}{5}$ times $\frac{3}{4}$ths of the total equipment cost, plus the whole of $\frac{1}{4}$ of that cost, i.e. $\frac{2}{5}$ths of the whole. That is, the cost of providing 2 million units at the peak is equal to $\frac{2}{3}$rds that of providing 6 million units off the peak: or, in other words, the equipment cost (apart from prime cost) of peak-load service is twice as much per unit as the equipment cost of normal service. This shows that simple competition, or the cost of service principle, involves

---

[1] Acworth, *Elements of Railway Economics*, footnote, pp. 122-3.
[2] Cf. Marriott, *The Fixing of Rates and Fares*, p. 21.

different charges for electricity supplied at different times. The same thing obviously holds good of telephone service and cable service—not to speak of hotel and lodging-house service in places that cater specially for seasonal visitors. In industries, the product of which can be stored in slack times, and where, therefore, the equipment can be adjusted to produce continuously the average output demanded, these differences should not exceed the cost and the loss of interest involved in storage. Railways, however, at least in the matter of passenger transport, are directly akin to electricity concerns, in that they provide a service which must be produced at the time that it is supplied. Consequently, the cost of service principle would seem to warrant higher fares for travel at busy seasons and at busy hours of the day than are charged at other times. Differential charges of this character are not, of course, exactly adjusted. Indeed, as a matter of fact, it so happens that, for other reasons, it is just for the most crowded parts of the day and week that the cheapest tickets (workmen's tickets and week-end tickets) are issued. In a concealed form, however, differential charges of this type do exist: for, when a man travelling as a straphanger in the London Tube at 5 o'clock in the evening pays the same absolute price as he does when travelling in comfort at 3 o'clock, he is paying that price for a different and much inferior service. There is just as real a differentiation as there would be if he travelled in equal comfort on both journeys and paid a considerably higher fare at the crowded time.

Lastly, the cost of service principle in some conditions leads logically to lower charges to people whose purchases are continuous than to those who buy intermittently. One reason for this is that a man taking continuous service cannot contribute to the peakiness of a peak load, whereas one taking intermittent service is likely, in some degree, to do this. Hence, if it is impracticable to charge differential rates directly as between peak and off-peak service, this may sometimes be attempted indirectly by differentiation between continuous and intermittent services. The device is an imperfect one, because a consumer, whose demand is intermittent but wholly off-peak, involves less cost than one whose demand is continuous. In practice this type of differentiation is found only in industries where special equipment has to be laid down to enable the service to be supplied to the various customers severally. Obviously, if this equipment is used rarely, a greater sum will have to be charged for each act of service than if it is used frequently. If desired, adjustment can be made by exacting a lump charge, or an annual rent, for the installation of the equipment and, thereafter, charging the same rate to everybody per unit of service obtained through it. This is, broadly, the plan in vogue with telephones. When, however, for any reason this plan is not followed, and the whole charge is levied through the price of the service, the cost of service principle necessarily leads to overt differentiation against customers whose individual load factor is small. But this consideration has no direct application to railway rates, since, apart from special sidings for which direct charges are made, railways do not provide equipment specialised to the service of particular customers.

§ 3. The results so far obtained are only valid in so far as transport services sold to different groups of purchasers are not jointly supplied. If they are jointly supplied, simple competition, or the cost of service principle, would no longer imply that, subject to the reservations of the preceding section, all ton-miles of transportation must be sold at the same price. It would not imply this any more than it implies that a pound of beef and a pound of hides must be sold at the same price. For, when two or more commodities or services are the joint result of a single process, in such wise that one of them cannot be provided without facilitating the provision of the other, simple competition evolves, not identical prices per pound (or other unit) of the various products, but prices so adjusted to demand that the whole output of all of them is carried off. Thus, if the transport of two commodities A and B, or the transport of commodity A for two purposes X and Y, were joint products, simple competition might well evolve for them different rates per ton-mile. It is, therefore, of great importance to determine how far the various services provided by railway companies are in fact joint products in the sense defined above.

§ 4. Many writers of authority maintain that joint costs play a dominant part in the industry of railway transportation. They believe that the transport of coal and the transport of copper along a railway from any point A to any point B are essentially and fundamentally joint products ; and that the same thing is true of the transport from A to B of commodities to be consumed at B and the transport from A to B of commodities to be carried forward to C. This argument is developed by Professor Taussig as follows. First, he observes : " Whenever a very large fixed plant is used, not for a single purpose, but for varied purposes, the influence of joint cost asserts itself." [1] Further : " The labour which built the railway—or, to put the same thing in other words, the capital which is sunk in it—seems equally to aid in carrying on every item of traffic. . . . Not only the fixed capital of a railway, but a very large part, in fact much the largest part, of the operating expenses, represents outlay, not separate for each item of traffic, but common to the whole of it or to great groups of it." [2] The existence of a large mass of common supplementary costs is not, in Professor Taussig's view, by itself sufficient to bring joint supply into action. For that it is essential that the plant be used for *varied purposes*. Thus he writes : " Where a large plant is used for producing one homogeneous commodity —say steel rails or plain cotton cloth—the peculiar effects of joint cost cannot, of course, appear." [3] Further, he is willing to admit that the transport of tons of different things and the transport of the same thing for different purposes from A to B do constitute, *in one sense*, a single homogeneous commodity, on precisely the same footing as plain cotton cloth. The fact that some " carrying of tons " is sold to copper merchants and some to coal merchants does not imply that two different services are being provided, any more than the fact that some plain cotton cloth is sold to one purchaser

[1] *Principles of Economics*, vol. i. p. 221. Cf. also vol. ii. p. 369.
[2] Taussig, "Theory of Railway Rates," in Ripley's *Railway Problems*, pp. 128-9.
[3] *Principles of Economics*, vol. i. p. 221.

and some is sold to another implies that two different commodities are being provided. He holds, however, that these different transports, though homogeneous in one sense, are not homogeneous " in the sense important for the purpose in hand—namely as regards *the conditions of demand.*" [1] Thus his essential contention is that, when a commodity, in the production of which supplementary general costs play a large part, is supplied, not to different people in a single unified market, but in a number of separated markets, the provision to one market is supplied jointly with the provision to the other markets, in such wise that simple competition might be expected to evolve a system of divergent prices.

Now, whether or not the term joint products should be used of services related in the way that Professor Taussig is contemplating is, of course, a verbal question : but whether these services are joint products *in such wise that simple competition might be expected to evolve a system of divergent prices* is a real question. In my view, the conjunction of large common supplementary costs with separation between the markets to which their yield is supplied does not make railway services joint products in this—the only significant—sense. In order that they may be joint products, it is further necessary, not merely that additional investment in plant and so on may be used alternatively to facilitate the supply to either market, but that such additional investment cannot be used to facilitate the supply to one market without facilitating the supply to the other. The point may be illustrated as follows. When cotton goods are provided for two distinct and isolated markets, the costs of furnishing these different markets are, in great part, *common* : for they consist, to a large extent, of the supplementary expenses of the cotton industry, which cannot be allocated specifically to the goods destined for the different markets. A given addition to investment does not, however, necessarily add anything to the output available for *each* of the two markets. If, before it occurred, the first market received x units of cotton and the second y units, after it has occurred the extra cotton may be divided between them, or it may go wholly to the first, or wholly to the

---

[1] *Quarterly Journal of Economics*, 1913, p. 381.

second. When, however, cotton fibre and cotton seed are provided for two distinct and isolated markets by one and the same process, a given addition to investment does necessarily add something to the output available for each of the two markets. In the latter case it is easily seen that simple competition will, in general, lead to divergent prices. In the former case, however, it will not do this. For, if there are a number of competing sellers supplying transportation, or anything else, to several markets with separate demand schedules, and if the price in one of these markets is higher than in another, it is necessarily to the interest of each individual seller to transfer his offer of service from the lower-priced market to the higher-priced market; and this process must tend ultimately to bring the prices in the different markets to a uniform level. This result, *when conditions of simple competition prevail*, obviously holds good independently of the question whether or not the commodity or service under discussion is one in the production of which supplementary costs are large relatively to prime costs. Hence Professor Taussig's argument cannot be accepted. Joint supply, in the sense in which we are here using the term, does not prevail in the industry of railway transport in that fundamental and general way that he supposes it to do.[1]

[1] On the general subject of the relation of the concept of joint costs to railway service, cf. a discussion between Professor Taussig and the present writer in the *Quarterly Journal of Economics* for May and August 1913. Two further points should be added.

First, it is sometimes maintained that the concept of joint costs, in the sense assigned to it in the text, is applicable where only one sort of commodity is produced, provided that the units of process, by which the commodity is made, are large relatively to the units of commodity. When, for instance, the marginal unit of process produces 100 units of product, it may be argued that 100 units must yield a price sufficient to remunerate one unit of process, but that it is immaterial to the suppliers by what combination of individual prices the aggregate price of 100 units is made up. This suggestion, however, *when stated in the above general form*, ignores the fact that 100 units of product can be removed, not only by abstracting one unit from the fruit of each of a hundred units of process, but also by abolishing one unit of process, and that, under free competition, if any units of product were refused a price as high as $\frac{1}{100}$th part of the supply price of a unit of process, this latter method of abstraction would naturally be employed. This shows that physically identical products, yielded by the same process at the same time, are not, *in general*, joint products in any sense, even though the marginal unit of the process of production is large. But this reply is not relevant, and the concept of joint supply cannot be ruled out, when the number of units of process that are actually being provided

§ 5. At the same time it should be clearly recognised that, in the services rendered by railway companies, joint supply does play *some* part. This is conspicuously true as between transportation from A to B and transportation in the reverse direction from B to A. The organisation of a railway, like that of a steamship company, requires that vehicles running from A to B shall subsequently return from B to A. The addition of a million pounds to the expenditure on moving vehicles necessarily increases both the number of movements of vehicles from A to B and the number of movements from B to A. This implies true jointness. It follows that a competitive system of railway or shipping rates would not, in general, make the vehicle charges the same for journeys from A to B and from B to A, but the direction, for which the demand was higher, would be charged a higher rate. This is, of course, the reason why outward

---

is the minimum number that it is practicable to provide so long as any are provided. In these circumstances there is nothing incompatible with the analysis of the text in regarding the resultant units of product as jointly supplied. The costs of constructing through any region the least expensive railway that it is possible to construct at all are joint costs of all the various items of service rendered by the railway. It is possible by following this line of analysis to reach the results obtained by the different line of analysis to be followed in § 8. In the special problem of the least expensive railway that it is possible to construct at all, the two lines are equally admissible. (Cf. *Quarterly Journal of Economics*, August 1913, p. 688.) Since, however, analysis by way of joint supply is only applicable in a single and peculiar type of problem, whereas analysis by way of discriminating monopoly, to be adopted in the text, is applicable to all problems, the latter method should be given preference.

Secondly, the concept of joint supply can, if desired, be applied to the same services rendered at different times by the same fixed plant. Thus the services of railways for night travelling and day travelling may be called joint, and different rates advocated on that ground. This consideration is especially important with electricity rates. It justifies differentiation of a form designed to carry off nearly equal supplies throughout the day or year. The same result can be obtained on a different route if we regard the services supplied at the two times as being the same service but subject to varying demands. The point of distinction, as against a railway carrying different things *at the same time*, is that the railway can be adjusted to carry any quantity of things, so that to carry A does not involve power to carry B ; but a railway fitted to carry A in the day cannot be provided except in a form that gives power to carry A also at night. The distinction would, of course, lose most of its significance if the capital equipment were expected to maintain its full value over a *defined period of use* and not over a defined period of time ; for then less night use now would make possible more day use later on. But in fact plant largely wears out *through time* independently of use ; *e.g.* rails and ties deteriorate with weather (cf. Watkins, *Electrical Rates*, p. 203), and also tend to become obsolete.

freights from England are generally low, relatively to inward freights, for commodities of similar value. Our imports being largely food and raw materials, and our exports, apart from coal, mainly finished manufactures, the former naturally make a greater demand for shipping accommodation. If it were not for our coal exports, the disparity would be much greater than it is. There is a similar relation in the transport of goods—though not of passengers—between eastward and westward travel in the United States; because "those who supply the world with food and raw materials dispose of much more tonnage than they purchase."[1] This element of jointness is, however, of comparatively small importance. Contrary to the general opinion of writers on railway economics, the services provided by railway companies are, in the main, not jointly supplied. Hence, the conclusion emerges that, subject to the reservations set out in § 2, simple competition would, in general, evolve a system of equal ton-mileage rates for all commodities, whatever their character, and whether they are to be consumed at B or be sent on from B for some further part of a "long haul."

§ 6. The meaning in concrete form of "the value of service principle," or monopoly *plus* discrimination of the third degree, is more complicated. It was shown in the last chapter that a monopolist adopting this principle will divide the total market served by him into a number of minor markets, by discriminating between which he may make his aggregate advantage as large as possible. It was shown, further, that the kind of division best calculated to promote this end is one under which the separate markets are arranged, so far as practical considerations allow, in such a way that each higher-priced market contains as few demands as possible with a demand price lower than the highest demand price contained in the next market. When once the minor markets have been separated, the determination of the rates to be charged

---

[1] Cf. Johnson, *American Railway Transportation*, p. 138. It should be noticed that, whereas there is little jointness as between first and third class passenger service on railways, there is probably a considerable element of such jointness as between first and third class service on ships; because the structure of a ship necessarily involves the provision at the same time of more and of less comfortable parts of the vessel.

in them presents no analytical difficulty, and can be expressed in a simple mathematical formula.[1]   It is not, indeed, true, as is sometimes supposed, that the relative rates charged to different markets will depend, if this plan is adopted, simply upon the comparative elasticities (in respect of some unspecified amount of output) of the demands of these markets, nor yet that they will depend simply upon the comparative demand prices (also in respect of some unspecified amount of output) ruling in these markets.   The true determinant is the whole body of conditions represented in the complete demand schedules of the different markets.[2]   Still, though the determinant is, in general, complex, when once the constitution of the different markets has been settled, it is precise.   The real difficulty lies in the choice, limited, as it is, by practical conditions, which a railway company has to make between various possible systems of minor markets. The search for the most advantageous system—from the company's point of view—has evolved, in practice, elaborate schemes of classification both for passenger traffic and for goods traffic.   To show the application of the value of service principle in practice, some description of these schemes is required.

In passenger traffic railway companies find the value of service principle most nearly satisfied by a classification based, in the main, on the relative wealth of different groups of persons, the presumption being that most of the demands for the transport of richer people yield demand prices higher than most of the demands for the transport of poorer people.

---

[1] Thus, let $\phi_1(x_1)$, $(\phi_2)x_2$ . . . represent the demand prices in n separate markets, and $f(x)$ the supply price.

The prices proper to the separate markets under monopoly *plus* discrimination of the third degree are given by the values of $\phi_1(x_1)$, $\phi_2(x_2)$, . . . that satisfy n equations of the form :

$$\frac{\partial}{\partial x_r}[x_r\{\phi_r(x_r) - x_r f(x_1 + x_2 + \ . \ . \ .)\}] = 0.$$

These n equations are sufficient to determine the n unknowns.

[2] Where the curves representing the demand schedules are straight lines, this complex determinant dissolves into a simple one, namely, the comparative demand prices of those units which are most keenly demanded in each of the several markets.   Under these conditions, if conditions of constant supply price prevail, the monopoly price proper to each market can be shown to be equal to one half of the difference between the supply price and the demand price of the unit that is most keenly demanded there.

Since it is impracticable to make a classification founded directly on differences of wealth, various indices or badges, generally associated with varying degrees of wealth, are employed. Thus, in the United States, certain railways make specially low rates for immigrants—lower than those required from native Americans,—even though the latter are willing to travel in immigrant cars.[1] In certain colonies there is a discriminating rate according to the *colour* of the traveller; black men, who are supposed, in general, to be less well-to-do, being charged lower fares than white men.[2] Again, in England, and still more markedly in Belgium,[3] railway companies charge specially low rates for workmen's tickets. This procedure is exactly analogous to that of those London shopkeepers who charge to customers with "good addresses" prices different from those charged to others, and of the Cambridge boatmen who used to charge a collective customer of five persons 5s. for the hire of a boat for an afternoon, while to a single person they would let the same boat for one shilling. A classification based on indices of wealth alone is, however, somewhat crude, since people of the same wealth will desire a given journey with very different intensities on different occasions. In recognition of this fact railway companies have constructed a variety of cross-groupings, based on such incidents as the degree of comfort or of speed with which, or the hour at which, journeys are undertaken, or the presumed purpose which these journeys serve. Thus the fares for first-class accommodation, or for conveyance by certain express trains, are made to exceed those for inferior accommodation or lower speed by more than the difference in the cost of providing these different sorts of service;[4] and specially low fares are sometimes charged for journeys made in the early morning.[5] In like manner, attempts are made to separate holiday journeys, of pre-

---

[1] *Quarterly Journal of Economics*, November 1910, p. 38.
[2] Cf. Colson, *Cours d'économie politique*, vol. vi. p. 230.
[3] Cf. Rowntree, *Land and Labour*, p. 289.
[4] M. Colson suggests that a plan, under which all trains should take third class passengers, the fast trains charging a supplement, would be superior to the present Continental plan, under which a passenger, who wishes to travel fast, has to pay the whole difference between third and second class fare.
[5] Cf. Mahaim, *Les Abonnements d'ouvriers*, p. 12.

sumed low demand, from necessary business journeys, by the supply, on special terms, of tourist, week-end and excursion tickets.

In goods traffic railway companies find the value of service principle most nearly satisfied by a classification based, in the main, upon the relative value of the different commodities claiming transport, the presumption being that most of the demands for the transport of a more valuable group of goods yield demand prices higher than most of the demands for the transport of a less valuable group. The reason for this presumption is as follows. The demand price for the transport of any n^{th} unit of any commodity from A to B is measured by the excess of the price of that commodity in B over its price in A, which would prevail if the said n^{th} unit were not transported. But, on any law of distribution, the probable difference between the prices of any article in A and B respectively, which would arise if these two places were not connected by the assigned act of transport, is greater, the greater is the absolute price that would prevail in either of them; just as the probable difference in the heights of poplars in A and B is greater than the probable difference in the heights of cabbages. There is no reason to expect that the percentage difference will be greater for valuable than for cheap commodities, but there is reason to expect that the absolute difference will be greater. A study of the details of the classification adopted for British railways under the Railway Rates and Charges Act shows that, in the main, the value of the commodities concerned was taken as a basis. Broadly speaking, the lower the position of any class in the list, the cheaper are the goods that it contains.[1] In like manner, several of the decisions of the United States Railway Commissioners have been founded on the proposition that less expensive articles ought not to be put in a higher class than more expensive articles—chair materials than finished chairs, raisins than dried fruits, and so on.[2]

Sometimes it is practically inconvenient for a company

---

[1] Cf. Marriott, *The Fixing of Rates and Fares*, p. 27 *et seq.*, for these lists.
[2] Cf. *Quarterly Journal of Economics*, November 1910, pp. 13, 15 and 29.

or a regulating authority to group goods directly in accordance with their value. When this is so, a like result can be obtained indirectly by grouping them according to indices whose differences are likely to correspond to differences of value. Thus, since the valuable qualities of any commodity are generally packed better than the cheap qualities, rates are sometimes made to vary with the elaboration of the packing employed. For example, in France, where good wines are generally packed " en barriques de 220 à 230 litres " and common wines " en demi-muids de 650 à 700 litres ou en wagons-réservoirs,"[1] wines in " barriques " are charged on a higher scale.

It must be added that, as with passenger service, so also with goods service, a classification based exclusively on the value of the commodities transported is necessarily somewhat crude. In consequence of this, cross-groupings based upon other incidents have also been employed. Thus, within each group of commodities of given value transported from A to B, a subdivision may be made between those which B can easily make for itself, or obtain elsewhere than from A, and those which it cannot so make or obtain ; and a higher rate may be charged to the latter group. Again, within a homogeneous group made up of units of the same commodity, sub-groups are constructed. For example, vegetables imported from Germany to England during the weeks before the English crop is ready used to be charged more than vegetables imported from Germany to England after this crop had appeared ; and the same thing is true of vegetables sent from the south to the north of France.[2] Sometimes, again, an attempt is made to charge different rates for the transport of the same thing according to the use to which it is to be put—bricks for building, paving bricks and fire bricks being put in different classes. It should be observed, however, that the United States Interstate Commerce Commission has declined to recognise the validity of a classification on this basis.[3] More important is the subdivision according

---

[1] Colson, *Cours d'économie politique*, vol. vi. p. 227.
[2] Cf. *ibid.* p. 227.
[3] Ripley, *Railroads, Rates and Regulation*, p. 318.

to ultimate place of destination. Thus commodities sent from A to B, to be consumed at B, are placed in a different group, and charged, for that act of transport, a different rate from commodities sent from A to B to be forwarded from B to C. The reason is that different parts of the world do not differ in nature in proportion as they differ in distance. There is not much ground for expecting *a priori* that the cost of producing a given commodity in B will differ from the cost in A to a greater extent if A is 500, than if it is 100, miles away. Consequently the demand for any r^{th} mile's worth of carriage is probably less in long transports of goods than in short transports. This consideration applies with especial force to articles of food and raw material, which are physically adapted to growth over a wide range of temperature and climate. But it has some relation to all sorts of goods and is, no doubt, partly responsible for the systems of tapering rates for goods,—but not for passengers,— that prevail in England, France and Germany.[1] The case for discriminating rates is, however, much stronger, when A is connected with C by direct water transport, as well as by a railway from A to B *plus* either more railway or water from B to C. In these circumstances the demand price of *many* units of transportation from A to B, of any commodity to be consumed at B, is likely to be much higher than the demand price of *any* unit of transportation from A to B, of the same commodity to be carried on from B to C. Grouping in accordance with this fact is responsible for the occurrence of rates from Cheshire to London, for goods imported through Liverpool, much below the rates for corresponding goods originating in Cheshire. On the same principle, "special rates have been granted by the Prussian State Railways for the conveyance of grain traffic from Russia to oversea countries (Sweden, Norway, England, etc.), and the rate per ton per kilometre from the frontier to the German harbours, Königsberg, Danzig, etc., is lower than the charge for German grain between the same points. . . . It was pointed out that this specially low rate was granted with the object of securing the traffic to the Prussian

[1] Cf. Marriott, *The Fixing of Rates and Fares*, p. 43.

railways, as it need not necessarily pass over the Prussian lines, but could go via Riga, Reval and Libau, and would have done so without this reduction in the rates."[1]

§ 7. We are now in a position to compare the principle of cost of service and the principle of value of service from the point of view of the national dividend. It is well known that, in common opinion, the determination of railway rates by the value of service principle, or, in the alternative phrase, by what the traffic will bear, is unquestionably superior to its rival. The popular view, however, as I understand it, rests, in the main, upon two confusions. The first of these starts from the assumption that the transport of copper and the transport of coal, and the transport from A to B when further transport respectively is, and is not, required, are joint products. This assumption was shown to be unwarranted in § 4. It proceeds by means of the further assumption that to charge for joint products rates adapted to comparative marginal demands is to charge in accordance with the value of service principle. This assumption is no less unwarranted than the other. A moment's reflection shows that to charge for joint products in this way would be to follow the guidance of the cost of service principle, or— what is another name for the same thing—of simple competition. The second confusion is an *ignoratio elenchi*. Arguments are advanced to prove that the value of service principle, in the proper sense of discriminating monopoly, is superior to simple monopoly. Thus it is pointed out that, when the conditions are such that the rate most advantageous to himself which the monopolist can make, subject to the condition that equal rates shall be charged for the transport of copper and of coal, will cause him to stop transporting coal altogether while continuing to transport copper at a high rate, the national dividend could be increased by permission to discriminate between the two rates.[2] Such an argument, it is obvious, though valid in its own field, is wholly irrelevant to the question whether discriminating monopoly of the third degree is superior, not to simple monopoly, but to simple

---

[1] *Report of the Railway Conference*, 1909, p. 99.
[2] Cf. *ante*, Part II. Chapter XVII. § 13.

competition. When these confusions are swept away, the issue between the value of service principle and the cost of service principle in railway rates is seen to constitute a special case of the general issue, set out in the preceding chapter, between the said discriminating monopoly of the third degree and the said simple competition.

§ 8. The result of the discussion on that issue was that simple competition is, in general, the more advantageous. There emerged, however, one set of conditions, in which the advantage lies with its rival. These conditions are that, while no uniform price can be found which will cover the expenses of producing *any* quantity of output, a system of discriminating prices is practicable, which will make *some* output profitable. They have been illustrated by Principal Hadley, with special reference to discriminations between the charges for carriage from A to B that are made for goods going to B for consumption at B and for goods going to B for further transport to C. "Suppose," he writes, "it is a question whether a road can be built through a country district, lying between two large cities, which have the benefit of water communication, while the intervening district has not." To meet water competition, the charge for carriage from one extreme A to an intermediate point B must be low for goods to be carried forward to the other extreme C; so low that, if it were applied to all carriage from A to B, it would make the working of this part of the road unprofitable. But the demand for carriage from A to B, in respect of goods to be retained at B, is so small that this alone cannot support the road, no matter how low or how high the rates are made. "In other words, in order to live at all, the road must secure two different things—the high rates for its local traffic, and the large traffic of the through points, which can only be attracted by low rates. If they are to have the road, they must have discrimination."[1] An exactly analogous argument can be constructed in favour of discriminations in the ton-

---

[1] *Railroad Transportation*, p. 115. It may conceivably be objected to the construction of a railway in these circumstances that it will injure the rival industry of water carriage to an extent that will offset the advantages to which it leads. This objection can, however, be shown to be inapplicable, so long as the railway as a whole pays its way. Cf. *ante*, Part II. Chapter IX. § 11.

mile rates that are charged on different commodities, when the conditions are such that, apart from discrimination, there would be no quantity of transportation units, the proceeds of whose sale would cover their expenses of production. On the same principle, it may be argued that in some circumstances a roundabout line should be permitted to charge abnormally low rates between its terminal points, with the effect of preventing the development of a direct line between these points; for conditions may be such that, apart from this arrangement, no roundabout line could be profitably built, and so centres which it might serve would suffer. I have no quarrel with the proposition that these conditions *may* occur in practice. Principal Hadley and his followers, however, not content with demonstrating that they are possible, implicitly add, without argument, that they are typical of the whole railway world, and suppose themselves, therefore, to have proved that the value of service principle ought to be followed in the determination of all railway rates. Such an unargued inference is, plainly, illegitimate. A careful inquiry is necessary concerning the range over which conditions of a sort to justify the value of service principle are likely to extend in practice.

§ 9. From an analytical point of view, the situation is simple. As explained in the preceding chapter, in order that monopoly *plus* discrimination of the first degree may create an output where simple competition fails to do so—I take the simplest case, in which the demand in one market is independent of the price in the other—certain relations, which were there described, between the general conditions of demand and of supply must exist. The conditions enabling monopoly *plus* discrimination of the third degree to lead to this result are less precise. Circumstances, in which discrimination of the first degree would only just succeed, will not, in general, enable discrimination of the third degree to succeed. We may conclude, roughly, however, that discrimination of the third degree will have a good chance of succeeding—a chance that is better, the more numerous are the markets between which discrimination is made, and the more satisfactory, from the monopolist's standpoint, is their constitution—when the conditions are such that discrimination of the first degree would succeed with a wide margin. Our problem is to determine how far this state of things is likely to occur in practice.

First: it has been shown that the likelihood of this is greatest in forms of investment in which the law of decreasing supply price acts strongly.[1] Among railways there is ground for believing that, at all events until considerable development has been reached, this condition is generally satisfied. The reason is that the fixed plant of a railway cannot, in practice, be so made as to be capable of effecting less than a certain considerable minimum of transportation. The aggregate costs of arranging for rail transport for one ounce per week are very nearly as great as those of arranging for the transport of many thousand tons. For the same heavy expenditure must be undertaken for surveying and legal charges, bridging valleys and torrents, tunnelling through rock, erecting stations and platforms, and so on. This implies that the law decreasing supply price acts strongly till a large investment has been made, and afterwards less strongly. So far, therefore, conditions in which discriminating monopoly would prove superior to simple competition are more likely to occur in railway service than in some other industries.

Secondly, it has been shown that the likelihood of discriminating monopoly yielding some output when simple competition yields none is greatest in forms of investment where the demand for the product is elastic.[2] In railway service, when once rates have been brought down to a moderate level, there is reason to believe that a small reduction of rates would call out a large increase of demand, not only from commodities that might otherwise have been transported by some other agency, but also from commodities that otherwise would not have been transported at all. In other words, there is reason to believe that the demand is, in general, elastic. Here, too, then, it may be said that railway service is more apt to yield conditions suitable for discriminating monopoly than some other industries.

Granted, however, both that the law of decreasing supply price acts strongly until considerable density of traffic has been

---

[1] Cf. *ante*, Part II. Chapter XVII. § 9, and Appendix III. § 26.
[2] *Ibid.*

attained, and that the demand for the service of railway transport is elastic, these conditions alone are by no means sufficient to ensure that discriminating monopoly would evolve some output, while simple competition would fail to do this. It is necessary, further, that the actual levels of demand price and supply price for a small quantity of service—more generally, the demand schedule and the supply schedule as a whole—shall be related in a particular way. Clearly, if the demand price for a small quantity is greater than the supply price, some output will be evolved under simple competition, and, therefore, the conditions we have in view do not arise. Clearly, again, if the demand price for a small quantity is very much less than the supply price, it is unlikely that any output will be evolved either under simple competition or under discriminating monopoly, and, therefore, again these conditions do not arise. In order that they may arise, a sort of intermediate position must, it would seem, be established. Thus, on the one hand, the district affected must not be too busy and thickly populated; on the other hand, it must not be too little busy and sparsely populated. There is a certain intermediate range of activity and population that is needed. This range, compared with the total range of possibility, is naturally not extensive. Hence the probability that the conditions necessary to make discriminating monopoly more advantageous to the national dividend than simple competition will be present in any railway selected at random at any time seems *a priori* to be very small. There are, indeed, many *dicta* of practical experts which suggest that they have in fact a wide range. But, as Edgeworth, who lays stress upon this point, recognises, "the testimony of high authorities would, no doubt, carry even greater weight if it should be repeated with a full recognition of the *a priori* improbability" to which it is opposed.[1]

§ 10. It must be observed, however, that, as population and aggregate wealth in any country expand, the demand schedule for railway service, along any assigned route, gradually rises. Hence, though, at any moment selected

[1] *Economic Journal*, 1913, p. 223.

at random, it is improbable that the conditions affecting
any route, selected at random, are such that a railway rate
system based on the value of service principle would be
more advantageous to the dividend than one based on the
" cost of service principle," it is not improbable that any
route, selected at random, will *pass through a period* during
which the conditions are of this kind. Such conditions tend
to emerge when one point in the growth of wealth and
population has been reached, and to disappear when another
somewhat later point has been reached. If the cost of
service principle ruled universally, and if no State bounties
were given, certain lines would not be built till the arrival
of the latter point—when there is hope of " building up "
a demand by experience of supply, this point need not, of
course, be such that the railway pays at the moment—
despite the fact that they could have been built, with
advantage to the community, on the arrival of the earlier
point. The inference is that discrimination, or the value
of service principle, should be adopted when any route is
in the intermediate stage between these two stages, and that
this principle should give place to simple competition, or the
cost of service principle, as soon as population has grown
and demand has risen sufficiently to lift it out of that
stage.[1] The period proper to the value of service principle
would seem, in most ordinary lines, to be a comparatively
brief one.[2]

---

[1] Mr. Bickerdike (*Economic Journal*, March 1911, p. 148) and Mr. Clark
(*Bulletin of American Economic Association*, September 1911, p. 479) argue, in
effect, that the transition from the one system to the other should occur, not
when rising demand lifts the railway in question out of the stage just described,
but when, if ever, it rises so high as to impinge on that point of the supply
curve at which a negative slope passes into a positive one. There is not, in
my opinion, any adequate ground for this view.

[2] It is possible to maintain, on lines similar to the above, that, after a
railway has been built, and has reached the stage of profitable working on the
cost of service principle, another stage will presently arrive, at which a return
to the value of service principle would enable a second track to be laid down
with advantage to the community, though, under a rate system based on the
cost of service principle, such an extension would not as yet be profitable to
the company. This argument justifies the establishment of a system of
discriminating rates, *to be applied to traffic carried on the new track only* ; and
a modification of it justifies the establishment of such a system, to be applied
exclusively to traffic carried in any *additional* train or truck which, apart from
discrimination, it is just not worth while to run. In practice, however, it is

§ 11. Even this limited application of the principle is only warranted on the assumption that there is no third way between the pure value of service principle and the pure cost of service principle. In fact, however, there is a third way. The cost of service principle may be maintained and the State may give a bounty. Plainly, with the help of a bounty exactly the same effect in speeding up the building of a railroad could be accomplished under the cost of service principle as would be accomplished under the value of service principle without a bounty. The community as a whole would be providing out of taxes the necessary profit for the railway, which, on the other plan, would come from the charges made to the people who buy the most highly charged freight service. Since the building of the railway is in the general interest, it would seem, on the whole, to be fairer that the taxpayers, and not a special class of traders—or rather, in the end, the consumers of these traders' products—should provide these funds. In view of the practical awkwardness of changing from a discriminating to a non-discriminating system of rates when the intermediate stage described in the preceding paragraph is passed, the plan of giving a bounty for a time and withdrawing it when it is no longer needed is also superior from the side of administrative convenience. If, on account of the indirect advantages of cheap railway transport in facilitating the division of labour between different parts of the country, making possible the development of large-scale localised industries, and, through the improved communication of markets, lessening local price fluctuations—all changes which, in one way or another, benefit production—it is held that the railway industry is one to which a general bounty should be accorded permanently, it is obvious that a second instrument for doing what bounties can do by themselves is not required and that no place is left for the value of service principle.

§ 12. Of the relative advantages of the cost of service principle, or prices proper to simple competition, and the

---

impossible to apply the value of service principle in this limited way. If it is introduced for the traffic proper to the second track or the extra truck, it must, in real life, be introduced for all the traffic carried on the line. The argument set out above does not justify this.

value of service principle, or prices proper to discriminating monopoly, this is all that need be said. There is, however, yet another possible arrangement. Control might be exercised in such a way that a railway company should only secure competitive or normal profits on the whole, but these profits might be obtained by a combination of some charges below cost with others above cost, just as a doctor's profits are obtained by a combination of low prices to poor patients and high prices to rich patients. In one field of railway service there is a plain *prima facie* case for an arrangement of this kind. Great social advantage can be derived from the provision of cheap workmen's tickets: for in favourable circumstances this makes it possible for workpeople to live in the country, though working in towns, and thus to bring up their children in healthy surroundings.[1] Such provision can be ensured if railway companies (whose earnings are supposed to be kept down by regulation to a normal competitive level) are compelled to make it, and are allowed to recoup themselves by "monopolistic" charges upon other traffic. Plainly, however, exactly the same result can be achieved if the reimbursement required for the railway companies is provided out of the national revenue. There seems to be no good reason for throwing this burden upon persons who make use of the service of railways rather than upon the general body of taxpayers. For, though it may well be that railway service is a suitable object through which to impose a tax on these persons, we can hardly suppose that the extent to which they ought to be taxed through this object exactly corresponds to the amount of funds required for the bounty to poor purchasers of railway service. There is still less reason for allowing discriminated rates, determined, not in the purchasers' interest,

---

[1] In Belgium the system of cheap workmen's tickets, which has been carried to great perfection, seems to act in this way. (Cf. Rowntree, *Land and Labour*, p. 108.) Dr. Mahaim offers some confirmation of the view that it acts so in the fact that Belgium is a land of "large towns" rather than of "great cities," a much larger proportion of the population living in communes of from 5000 to 20,000 inhabitants in that country than in France or Germany (*Les Abonnements d'ouvriers*, p. 149). At the same time, Dr. Mahaim admits that the cheap tickets have also an adverse effect. "On commence par aller à la ville ou à l'usine en revenant tous les soirs ou tous les samedis chez soi ; puis on s'habitue peu à peu au nouveau milieu, et l'on finit par s'y implanter" (*ibid.* p. 143). In fact the cheap tickets "apprennent le chemin de l'émigration."

but at the choice of the railway companies themselves. Hence this system of discriminated charges coupled with regulated profits cannot, on the whole, be justified. We are thus left with the cost of service principle, modified at need, sometimes by general bounties, sometimes by bounties on particular services deliberately sold for less than cost price.

§ 13. One last point remains. To apply this cost of service principle accurately involves, as was shown in § 2, a number of delicate adjustments. For the principle leads, not to a single price for everybody, but to prices that vary with the incidental costs attaching to each service and with the time at which it is furnished in relation to the peak of the load. To provide for these adjustments in practice is often a very difficult matter involving costly technique and account-keeping. It is, therefore, always a question how near to the ideal it is desirable to approach ; at what point the advantage of getting closer is outweighed by the complications, inconveniences and expense involved in doing so. In the early days of the telephone service the desire for simplicity and ease in rate making led to a system in which flat rates were charged for the use of instruments, without any reference whatever to the number of calls made; and water rates are even yet often based, not on any measurement of the supply that is actually taken, but on an estimate of what is likely to be taken, derived from the rental of the houses served. For electricity, while ingenious meters have been devised, which not only record the supply taken, but also weight more heavily the part of it which is taken in the peak hours, nevertheless the high cost of any sort of meter still causes the service of small houses to be charged in many districts on a flat unmetered rate. In like manner, though for the transport of parcels it has been thought worth while to take account, in the charges made, of those differences in the cost of service which arise out of differences of weight, for the transport of letters this is not done : and for neither parcels nor letters are charges adjusted to the distance (within the British Empire) over which they have to be conveyed. On similar grounds of simplicity and cheapness, a railway administration, which had decided to base its rating system upon the cost of service principle, must, nevertheless, ignore, within considerable limits, differences in the weight of luggage which different passengers carry. This class of consideration shows that there is not necessarily any departure from the spirit of the cost of service principle when a railway administration elects to utilise a system of zone tariffs. A street railway system obviously must do this; for the mere fact that there is no coin smaller than a farthing makes it physically impossible to fix different fares for every different distance of journey. So long as the zones are narrow, zone tariffs on ordinary railways have an equally good defence. If, however, the zones are made broad, the cost of service principle is deliberately violated. A system under which the rates are the same for all places in broad zones involves substantial differentiation in favour of firms situated far from their markets, as against firms situated nearer to them. In effect, it confers upon them a kind of bounty at the expense of their rivals. It can, indeed, be shown that differentiation in favour of one source of supply as against another source may, in certain circumstances and if introduced in a certain manner, be advantageous to the national dividend. The sort of differentiation that results from the zone system is, however, random differentiation, not specially designed to favour a carefully chosen list of selected firms. It is, thus, on the average, like differentiation in favour of one set against another set of *similar* firms. This sort of differentiation causes the production (including transport) of some part of the commodity concerned to be carried out at greater real cost than is necessary; for the marginal real costs of producing anything in the distant source and bringing it to the market must necessarily be greater than the marginal real costs of producing it in the nearer source and bringing it to the market.[1] It is possible to maintain that the direct loss resulting from this may be balanced by the effect of the zone system in scattering the producing firms belonging to an industry, and so making combination, with the opportunity which this gives for anti-social monopolistic action, more difficult.[2] But this

---

[1] Cf. *Quarterly Journal of Economics*, February 1911, pp. 292-3, 297-8 and 300 : also *Departmental Committee on Railway Rates*, p. 10.

[2] Cf. *Quarterly Journal of Economics*, May 1911, pp. 493-5.

argument does not appear to have great force. It is not, in itself, desirable to check the formation of large productive units, since such units introduce economies. As will be argued presently, it would seem a better policy to attack the evil consequences of monopolistic action, which combination threatens, directly, rather than indirectly by attempts to discourage unification.[1]

[1] Cf. *post*, Part II. Chapter XXI. § **2.**

CHAPTER XIX

PURCHASERS' ASSOCIATIONS

§ 1. THE results of the preceding chapters make it plain that, in many industries, neither simple competition, nor monopolistic competition, nor simple monopoly, nor discriminating monopoly will make the value of the marginal social net product there equal to the value of marginal social net products generally, and, therefore, that they will not maximise either the national dividend or economic welfare. It will have been noticed, however, that the systems so far investigated have all been systems under which goods are produced by one set of people and sold to another set. The failures of adjustment, to which they lead, have, therefore, all been dependent on this fact. Hence the question naturally arises: Could not these failures be eliminated by the device of voluntary groups of purchasers undertaking for themselves the supply of the goods and services they need?

§ 2. Now, the essence of a Purchasers' Association, whether it is formed of the consumers of finished goods or of producers who will utilise their purchases in further production, is that its policy is directed to maximise aggregate purchaser's benefit *minus* aggregate costs. It must, therefore, call out just that quantity of output, which, except where others besides the purchasers of the commodity are affected by its production, will make the value of the marginal social net product of resources devoted to it equal to the value of the marginal social net product of resources in general. That is to say, other things being equal, it must eliminate, in great measure, the disharmonies belonging alike to monopoly and to simple competition. This

318

preliminary abstract statement does not, however, solve our problem. It is not enough to know that, *if other things are equal*, Purchasers' Associations will advantage the national dividend. Before we can infer anything from this about the effect of these Associations in actual life, we need to inquire how they compare with ordinary commercial businesses in crude economic efficiency; for it is clear that any advantages, which a Purchasers' Association may possess in price policy, and, therefore, in respect of the distribution of resources among different occupations, are liable to be out-weighed if it is inefficient on the productive side.

§ 3. As a prelude to this task, it is desirable to guard against certain confusions. First and most obviously, we need to rule out all appeals to the superior efficiency, in certain fields, of Purchasers' Associations, as compared with the members of these Associations operating as isolated individuals. It is easy to point to services, which many persons need in small individual lots, but which can be produced much more economically in large lots. A good example is the service of marketing agricultural products of variable quality produced in small quantities by small farmers. For economical selling requires careful grading of qualities and a fairly continuous supply of each grade; and small farmers, who attempt individually to market their butter or their eggs, are not operating on a large enough scale to meet these requirements satisfactorily. Thus Mr. Rider Haggard writes of Denmark: "In 1882 what was called 'peasant butter' fetched 33 per cent less than first-class butter made on the big farms, but in 1894 the co-operative butter, which, of course, for the most part comes from the peasant farms, took more medals and prizes than that from the great farms, and what used to be called second and third class butter ceased to exist as a Danish commodity of commerce."[1] The fact, however, that, for this kind of reason, the manufacture of butter, the curing of bacon, and the marketing of eggs "afford a splendid opening for the application of co-operative principles," is irrelevant to the present issue, since these things also afford a splendid opening for the

[1] *Rural Denmark*, pp. 195-6.

application of commercial principles.[1] It is true that a Purchasers' Association can work in this field much more cheaply than a single small farmer; but, exactly the same thing is true of an ordinary commercial firm, undertaking to sell the service of marketing to these farmers. Two examples are given by Sir R. H. Rew. "One is the French butter trade. This has been built up by the merchants in Normandy and Brittany—some of whom are Englishmen—who purchase the butter at the local markets from the individual farmers, and work it up in their blending houses. Another instance is the poultry trade in the Heathfield district of Sussex. There the system is that the fatteners, or 'higglers' as they are termed, purchase and collect the chickens from those who rear them; they are then duly fattened, killed, and prepared for market, and again collected by the carrier or railway agent, by whom they are forwarded to London and other markets. Both these are instances of complete organisation without co-operation."[2] Secondly, we must refrain from stressing unduly the history of English Co-operative Stores. The reason is that, when the device of Purchasers' Associations was introduced into retail trading, it is very doubtful if the rival method was fairly represented. Partly in consequence of the imperfect competition between different shops, not all the economies that were available had been taken up.[3] Even from their own point of view, "retailers

---

[1] In like manner, the charge that the development of Purchasers' Associations on the part of groups of persons other than ultimate consumers may make possible monopolistic action against these consumers is irrelevant; for, so also may the development of commercial firms.

[2] Rew, *An Agricultural Faggot*, p. 120.

[3] Care must be taken, however, not to treat as waste in the work of retailing those costs that are necessarily involved in the kind of retailing that the public chooses to ask for. "Imagine that every one intending to buy a pair of shoes or a suit of clothes was called on to send notice of his proposed purchase a week or two in advance, to give a preliminary account of the thing wanted, and then to accept an appointment for a stated place or time at which the purchases must be made. It is easy to see how the work of retailing could be systematised, how the selling force would be kept constantly employed, how stocks would be kept to the minimum. As things now stand, we pay heavily for the privilege of freedom in the use of our time, for vacillation and choice, for the maintenance of a stock and a staff adequate for all tastes and all emergencies. It is common to speak of the waste of competition; much of it is in reality the waste necessarily involved in liberty" (Taussig, *American Economic Review*, vol. vi. No. 1 Supplement, 1916, p. 182).

as a body kept far more shops than was necessary, spent far too much trouble and money in attracting a few customers, and then in taking care that those few customers paid them in the long run—the very long run—for those goods which they had bought on credit, or, in other words, had borrowed; and for all this they had to charge. . . . Retail trade was the one accessible business—Marshall was probably not thinking of house-keeping and domestic cooking as a business—in which there were great economies to be effected." [1] This view of the matter is fortified by Pareto's observation, that retail shops were easily ousted by the competition, not only of *sociétés co-opératives*, but also of *les grands magasins* [2]—to which should be added, in England, the very important multiple shops. A comparison between retail trading, as it stood when our consumers' stores came into being, and these stores cannot, therefore, be accepted as a conclusive test of the relative merits of the industrial forms they represent. It is like a comparison between a member of one race whom there is some reason to suspect of being less healthy than the average of his compatriots and a thoroughly sound member of another. No great weight, therefore, can be attached to historical examples, and we are driven forward to an analytical study. [3]

§ 4. In attempting, from this point of view, to estimate the economic efficiency of Purchasers' Associations, we may observe, first, that these Associations are, in structure, a form of Joint Stock Company. Like any other Joint Stock Company, a Purchasers' Association is owned by shareholders, and is controlled by a manager under the supervision of a committee elected from among the shareholders. The alternatives to it are the private business and the ordinary commercial company. In attempting to compare its economic efficiency with theirs, we naturally look to the organisation

---

[1] Marshall, *Inaugural Address to the Co-operative Congress*, 1889, p. 8.

[2] Cf. *Cours d'économie politique*, p. 274.

[3] It should be added that, *even if other things were equal*, the payment of a dividend by a co-operative society trading at the same price as another concern would not prove greater efficiency of management; for, if, as is common, the society proceeded to a greater extent on a system of cash sales, the dividend would *pro tanto* be simply payment to purchasers of interest on their earlier discharge of indebtedness.

M

of the management. Under this head the Purchasers' Association and the commercial company alike are inferior to the private business, just in so far as Boards of officials lack the opportunities for quick action and the stimulus of personal possession belonging to the private business.[1] But the Purchasers' Association is likely, in some degree, to make up for this deficiency through the ardour instilled into the manager and the committee by the fact that they are engaged in a service suited to evoke public spirit. The Purchasers' Association may, in fact, utilise the altruistic motives, alongside of the egoistic, as a spur to industrial efficiency. Against this consideration, however, there has to be set a second. In so far as Purchasers' Associations consist of poor persons, unaccustomed to large business, there is a danger that they may grudge adequate freedom to their managers and may discourage them by illiberal treatment in the matter of salaries. Furthermore, their committee-men are drawn from a more limited area, and are apt to possess less business experience than the directors of commercial companies. These conflicting influences will, of course, have different weights in different circumstances.

Secondly, when any section of a country's industry is given over to monopolistic competition, ordinary commercial businesses are bound to engage in much wasteful expenditure on advertising, in the manner described in Chapter IX. § 14. In this respect Purchasers' Associations are in a much more favourable position. When the services they provide consist of such things as the purchase of agricultural feeding stuffs or manures, or the work of wholesale trading, they are practically assured, without any direct effort on their part, of the whole demand of their members. When they provide the service of packing eggs, or curing bacon, or converting milk and cream into cheese and butter, their members may, indeed, sometimes be tempted by an offer of better terms to go elsewhere, but it is

[1] In the United States, where the President of a company often holds a very large individual interest, it appears that he sometimes acts on behalf of the company, just as a private owner would do. "Generally speaking, the President of an American Corporation acts just as freely and energetically on behalf of his company as he would on his own behalf" (Knoop, *American Business Enterprise*, p. 26). He only consults the directors when he wishes to do so.

possible for the Societies, by making "loyalty," within limits, a condition of membership, in great measure to restrain such action without resort to advertisement. When they provide the service of retailing or of granting credit, the enforcement of loyalty by rule is, indeed, impracticable, and is not attempted ; but even here loyalty will in fact be largely maintained through the members' sense of proprietary interest in their own shop. Among non-members, no doubt, when it is desired to extend the range of any Association's business, advertisement of one sort or another may be necessary. The Purchasers' Association, however, has a considerable advantage over an ordinary Joint Stock Company, because it is able to offer to those who join it, not only cheap goods, but also a certain sense of part ownership in an important corporate institution. Such advertisement as it does undertake, therefore, is likely to prove more effective, and less of it is needed to achieve a given result. By so much its efficiency is, *ceteris paribus*, greater than that of its rivals.

Thirdly, there is another way, besides the saving of advertisement costs, in which "loyalty" makes for economy. As was pointed out in Chapter XIV. § 3, it enables the work of a co-operative concern to be conducted steadily without those large fluctuations, to which private concerns are often subject and the presence of which inevitably involves cost. Thus the rule insisting upon loyalty as a condition of membership of co-operative bacon factories and creameries enables these establishments to count on a constant supply of raw material with greater confidence than private firms can do ;[1] and, in like manner, the practice of the English and Scotch

---

[1] In the Danish co-operative bacon factories loyalty is generally enforced by a provision to the effect that members shall deliver all their saleable pigs (with certain specified exceptions) to the factory for a period of seven years, unless in the meantime they remove from the district (Rew, *An Agricultural Faggot*, pp. 123-4). In like manner many Irish dairying societies provide that " any member who shall supply milk to any creamery other than that owned by the society for the space of three years from the date of his admission to membership, without the consent in writing of the Committee, shall forfeit his shares together with all the money credited thereon " (*Report on Co-operative Societies* [Cd. 6045], 1912, p. xxxix). It will be noticed that in these classes of societies—and it is only in them that loyalty is enforced in the rules—the use of a considerable plant makes the maintenance of a steady demand a more important influence in eliminating cost than it would be in, say, an agricultural purchasing society.

Wholesale Societies and of local Retail Associations, in concentrating the constant part of their demand upon their own productive departments and throwing the variable part upon outside traders, greatly lessens the fluctuations to which these productive departments are exposed.   No doubt, the economies which co-operative concerns secure in this way have, from a national point of view, to be balanced against any diseconomies that may be caused to outside concerns by increased fluctuations thrown upon them ; and so are not a net gain to the nation.   To the co-operative concerns themselves, however, they are a net gain.   Moreover, in so far as the aggregate demand or supply of a market is constant, and fluctuations in the parts are due to other causes than fluctuations in the whole, the introduction of steadiness in one part cannot increase, but necessarily diminishes, the fluctuations of other parts.   Hence it is probable that a considerable part of the economies which co-operative concerns derive from loyalty represent a net increase in efficiency for the community as a whole as well as for themselves.

Fourthly, the relation that is set up between the various members of a Co-operative Society greatly facilitates the dissemination among them of knowledge about the best methods of production.   Thus Sir Horace Plunkett observes of the work of the Irish Department of Agriculture : " It was only where the farmers were organised in properly representative societies that many of the lessons the Department had to teach could effectually reach the farming classes, or that many of the agricultural experiments intended for their guidance could be profitably carried out." [1]   The root of the matter is reached by Mr. Fay when he writes : " Both the co-operative society and the firm are trading bodies, and they will not pay the farmers more than their milk is worth.   But, whereas the firm's remedy is to punish the farmer by the payment of low prices, the society's remedy is to educate him so that he may command high ones." [2]

Fifthly, when in any field of industry there is an element of bilateral monopoly, ordinary commercial businesses and their customers, respectively, are driven to expend energy, if not

---

[1] *Ireland in the New Century*, p. 241.
[2] *Co-operation at Home and Abroad*, p. 164.

money, after the manner described in Chapter IX. §§ 15-17, in attempts to get the better of one another. Where a Purchasers' Association exists, this class of expenditure is likely to be reduced. In co-operative retail stores, as Marshall has observed, the proprietors, since they are also the customers, have no inducement to adulterate their goods, and costly precautions to prevent such adulteration are, therefore, unnecessary.[1] The gain is no less clear in societies providing for their members the services of insurance and the retailing of loans. The insurance contract is conditional on some event happening to the buyer; the loan contract is conditional on the buyer's promise to repay. In the one case the buyer may gain at the seller's expense by simulating, or even by voluntarily bringing about, the event provided against; in the other he may gain by deliberately breaking, or by so acting as to render himself unable to perform, his promise. Now, it is, of course, true that individual buyers are able to gain by this class of conduct, not only when the relation of identity between buyers and sellers collectively does not exist, but also when it does exist. The point, however, is this. Under the Joint Stock form of industrial organisation the fraudulent or quasi-fraudulent conduct of one buyer does not matter to the other buyers, and can, therefore, only be guarded against by an elaborate and continuous system of inspection. Under the Purchasers' Association form, however, the other buyers are directly injured by such conduct, and are, therefore, interested to prevent it. If, then, the Purchasers' Association consists of neighbours, all will, incidentally and in the course of the ordinary conduct of life, constitute themselves voluntary and unpaid inspectors of each. In this way small local Purchasers' Associations for the supply of insurance or the retailing of loans are, in effect, free from a substantial part, not merely of the nominal, but also of the real, costs that Joint Stock Companies attempting to furnish these services would be compelled to bear. In so far as people are less willing—apart altogether from the prospect of success—to try to defraud a Mutual Association than a commercial company, the gain under this head is increased.

§ 5. The various advantages that have been enumerated above

---

[1] Cf. Inaugural Address to the Co-operative Congress, 1889, p. 7.

suggest that there is a wide field over which Purchasers' Associations are likely to prove at least as efficient as any other form of business organisation: and in many important departments of industry they have proved their fitness by prosperous survival. This is true of the so-called supply associations often formed by farmers—associations, that is to say, which supply to their members the service of marketing from manufacturing firms such things as manure, seeds and agricultural machinery. It is true of the agricultural selling societies, which provide such services as the sorting, grading, selling and packing of eggs or of butter. It is true of the Co-operative Creameries, which play so important a part in Denmark and in Ireland, and whose services include a manufacturing as well as a marketing operation. Last but not least, it is true of that widespread organisation based on consumers' stores, which provides for the retailing, wholesaling, and sometimes even the manufacturing, of staple household goods (including houses themselves) for large agglomerations of working people with fixed homes.

§ 6. Even, however, in departments of work where experience gives good hope of efficiency and success, it does not follow that Purchasers' Associations will always come into being. Very poor people may lack the initiative and understanding needed to form one. Where the population is migratory, attempts are especially unlikely to be made — a circumstance which explains why co-operative stores " have seemed to shun capital and seafaring towns." Better-to-do persons, while fully competent to develop Purchasers' Associations, if they had the wish, may, in fact, not have the wish. With commodities on which they only spend a very small part of their income at rare intervals—commodities that are luxuries to the main body of purchasers—the possible savings may be too small to be worth while. Or again, even when they are worth while, it may be possible to get an equivalent advantage in some other less troublesome way. British tenant farmers, for example, with their traditional right to appeal to the squire in times of difficulty for a reduction of rent, are slow to overcome their native individualism for the (to them) relatively small advantages of co-operation with their neighbours. No doubt, encouragement may be given to them by State action. Thus in Canada "in 1897 the Dominion Department of Agriculture established a system by means of which loans were made to farmers who undertook to organise themselves into Butter and Cheese Manufacturing Associations and to send their produce to Co-operative Creameries equipped by means of the loans. The Department undertook to organise the management of these creameries, and to manufacture and sell the butter for a fixed charge of four cents (2d.) per lb., an additional charge of one cent per lb. being made for the amortisation of the loans."[1] But this device is obviously of limited scope. Moreover, there are a number of very important sorts of work to which the Purchasers' Association form of organisation is not well suited. Whenever a large speculative element is present, whenever, in other words, much uncertainty has to be borne, this factor of production will not be readily forthcoming from organised purchasers. For, if capital has to be ventured at a hazard, the people who venture it will expect to exercise control, and to harvest the profits, more or less in proportion to their venture. Associations that raise capital at fixed interest and distribute surplus in accordance, not with investment, but with purchases, do not enable them to do this. The graded machinery of debentures, preference shares and ordinary shares furnished by Joint Stock Companies is much more satisfactory. In risky undertakings, therefore, Purchasers' Associations will not work. Nor will they work as regards commodities and services for which economy demands centralised production, but of which the purchasers are spread over wide areas and make their purchases at irregular intervals. The idea, for instance, that the services now rendered by the cotton industry could be provided satisfactorily by any arrangement of Purchasers' Associations is plainly fantastic. "In many cases the users or consumers of the service do not form a practicable constituency, apart from that of themselves as citizens, which could control the administration. The national railway service could hardly be governed by the votes of the incoherent mob of passengers who pour out of the termini of our great cities; or the characteristic municipal services by any other membership

---

[1] Mavor, *Report on the Canadian North-West*, p. 44.

than that of all the municipal electors."[1] We conclude, therefore, that, though the Purchasers' Association, as a means of overcoming the evils of ordinary competitive and ordinary monopolistic industry, has, undoubtedly, an important part to play, the field open to it is limited in extent, and the study of further remedies is, therefore, still required.[2]

[1] Webb, *A Constitution for the Socialistic Commonwealth*, p. 252.

[2] For a full discussion of the various forms of co-operative activity, *vide* Fay, *Co-operation at Home and Abroad.* I am also indebted to Mr. Fay for useful criticism and suggestion in connection with this chapter.

CHAPTER XX

§ 1. Over the large field of industry, where voluntary Purchasers' Associations are not an adequate means of overcoming those failures in industrial adjustment which occur under the more ordinary business forms, the question arises whether the magnitude of the national dividend might not be increased by some kind of public intervention, either by the exercise of control over concerns left in private hands or by direct public management. In the present chapter we are concerned, not with the comparative merits of these two sorts of intervention, but with the broadest aspects of intervention generally.

§ 2. It is natural at first sight to look for light on this question from the experience of the war. The urgent national need for enlarged supplies of munitions, home - grown food, ships, and certain other articles, led to extensive State intervention in production. National productive establishments were set up, and private establishments were controlled and sometimes accorded special grants to enable them to expand their operations; while the Board of Agriculture took powers to encourage, and, if need be, to compel, increased cultivation of land, and also provided a number of facilities in the way of soldiers' and prisoners' labour and specially imported machinery to assist farmers. A study of what was accomplished under these and other heads would, indeed, be of great interest. But it would not really do much to help our present inquiry. The difference between war and peace conditions is too great. In those four years of strain the underlying motive of the main part of the Government's industrial action was to force capital, enterprise and labour, forthwith and at no matter what cost, into the production of particular urgently needed things. Nobody denies that, when there is a shortage of anything relatively to the demand for it, this fact by itself always tends to stimulate people to direct their efforts towards producing that thing rather than other things. But this reaction is usually a slow one; and in the Great War the essential requirement was always speed. The principal purpose of government assistance and coercion was to secure this; to surmount at once by direct attack obstacles that, in the ordinary course, could only be turned by a slow and gradual movement. The need for such action was, of course, intensified in industries where the Government itself, by artificially keeping down prices, had removed what would normally have been the main stimulus to private efforts after increased production. With the end of the war all this has been changed. The problem of national economy is no longer to effect an instantaneous transformation from one scheme of production to another, but to maintain permanently the best scheme. To show that Government is fit (or unfit) to accomplish the former of these tasks is not to show that it is fit (or unfit) to accomplish the latter. Moreover, the scheme of production called for in the Great War involved an enormous output of things of uniform types for the direct use of Government itself. To show that Government is fit (or unfit) to control or operate industries devoted to a scheme of this kind is not to show that it is fit (or unfit) to control or operate industries devoted to the more variegated scheme called for in normal times. Yet again, in the Great War, the various controls set up by Government were necessarily improvised in a great hurry in a time of abnormal difficulty and pressure. No evidence that intervention in these conditions was wasteful or ineffective could prove that it would display the same defects in the more favourable conditions of normal life. For these reasons war experience can afford very little real guidance, and our problem must be attacked by other means.

§ 3. For some persons the obvious approach towards it is blocked by the supposition that certain industries, those, namely, that make use of the right of eminent domain, such as railway service (national and street), gas-lighting, electricity supply, water supply and so forth, are, for that reason, suitable for public intervention, while other industries, because they do not make use of the right of eminent domain, are not suitable. This supposition is erroneous. It is true that the exercise of eminent domain practically implies monopoly, since neither State nor municipal authorities are at all likely to allow double parallel interference with streets and highways. But this circumstance only puts these public utility services into the general class of monopolistic services : it does not render them different, in any essential respect, from services that have come into that class—like the oil and tobacco industries in America—in quite other ways. Thus eminent domain is in no way a condition precedent either to governmental management or to governmental control through a licence. Public slaughter-houses, licensed premises for the sale of intoxicants, and the system of licensed cabs in London are practical illustrations of this fact. The broad question of policy is different according as we are concerned with mono-polistic or with non-monopolistic industries ; it is different again, within monopolistic industries, according as dis-criminating prices are, or are not, practicable ; but it is the same, *ceteris paribus*, whether the industry concerned does or does not require to exercise the right of eminent domain. No doubt, as will appear presently, undertakings at the start of which this right has to be exercised, since they necessarily come into contact with the public authorities in their first beginnings, and, therefore, can be brought under control at once before any vested interests have grown up, can be subjected to public intervention much more easily than others. This distinction of practice is very important, but it is not, and should not be treated as, a distinction of principle.

§ 4. In any industry, where there is reason to believe that the free play of self-interest will cause an amount of re-sources to be invested different from the amount that is re-quired in the best interest of the national dividend, there is a *prima facie* case for public intervention. The case, however, cannot become more than a *prima facie* one, until we have considered the qualifications, which governmental agencies may be expected to possess for intervening advantageously. It is not sufficient to contrast the imperfect adjustments of unfettered private enterprise with the best adjustment that economists in their studies can imagine. For we cannot expect that any public authority will attain, or will even whole-heartedly seek, that ideal. Such authorities are liable alike to ignorance, to sectional pressure and to personal corruption by private interest. A loud-voiced part of their constituents, if organised for votes, may easily outweigh the whole. This objection to public intervention in industry applies both to intervention through control of private companies and to intervention through direct public operation. On the one side, companies, particularly when there is continuing regulation, may employ corruption, not only in the getting of their franchise, but also in the execution of it. "Regulation does not end with the formulation and adoption of a satisfactory contract, itself a considerable task. . . . As with a constitution, a statute, or a charter, so with a franchise. It has been proved that such an agreement is not self-enforcing, but must be fought for, through a term of years, as vigorously as at the time of formulation and adoption. A hostile, lax, or ignorant city council, or even a State legislature, may vary the terms of the agreement in such a manner as totally to destroy or seriously to impair its value."[1] For this the companies maintain a *continuing lobby*. "It is from them that the politicians get their campaign funds."[2] This evil has a cumulative effect; for it checks the entry of upright men into government, and so makes the corrupting influence more free. On the other side, when public authorities themselves work enterprises, the possibilities of corruption are changed only in form. "The new undertakings proposed by the municipalisers would lead to dealings to the extent of many million dollars with tradesmen, builders, architects, etc., to the increase, by hundreds, of

---

[1] *Municipal and Private Operation of Public Utilities* (Report to the National Civic Federation, U.S.A.), vol. i. p. 39.

[2] Bemis, *Municipal Monopolies*, p. 174.

important offices, and to the employment of tens of thousands of additional public servants. Party leaders would have their proportion of increased patronage. Every public official is a potential opportunity for some form of self-interest arrayed against the common interest." [1]

§ 5. The force of this argument for non-interference by public authorities is, clearly, not the same at all times and places ; for any given kind of public authority will vary, alike in efficiency and in sense of public duty, with the general tone of the time. Thus, during the past century in England, there has been " a vast increase in the probity, the strength, the unselfishness, and the resources of government. . . . And the people are now able to rule their rulers, and to check class abuse of power and privilege, in a way which was impossible before the days of general education and a general surplus of energy over that required for earning a living." [2] This important fact implies that there is now a greater likelihood that any given piece of interference, by any given public authority, will prove beneficial than there was in former times. Nor is this all. Besides improvement in the working of existing forms of public authority, we have also to reckon with the invention of improved forms. This point may be put thus. The principal disadvantages of municipal and national representative assemblies, as organs for the control or the operation of business, are four in number. First, in the United Kingdom—though this statement is hardly true of Germany—these bodies are primarily chosen for purposes quite other than that of intervention in industry. Consequently, there is little reason to expect in their members any special competence for such a task. Secondly, the fluctuating make-up of a national government or of a town council is a serious handicap. Sir W. Preece wrote : " I have the experience of electric lighting in my mind. Large municipalities overcome the difficulty by forming small and strong committees and selecting the same chairman, and thus maintain a kind of continuity of policy. Small corporations start with very large committees ; they

---

[1] *Municipal and Private Operation of Public Utilities*, vol. i. p. 429.
[2] Marshall, " Economic Chivalry," *Economic Journal*, 1907, pp. 18-19.

are constantly changing, and the result is that you find, sometimes inability to agree upon the system to be used, sometimes inability to agree upon the means to be employed to
conduct the service; and it is incessant trouble and
squabble."[1] Moreover, this incident of fluctuating membership may lead to action based on short views—views
bounded by the next election, not extending to the permanent
interests of the community. Thirdly, the areas, to which
public authorities are normally allocated, are determined by
non-commercial considerations, and, consequently, are often
likely to prove unsuitable for any form of intervention with
the working of an industry. It is well known, for example,
that attempts, on the part of some municipalities to regulate,
and of others to operate, the service of street-traction and the
supply of electrical power have suffered greatly from the
fact that these services, since the development of modern
inventions, can be organised most economically on a scale
much in excess of the requirements of any one municipality.
Finally, as indicated above, regular governmental agencies,
in so far as they are elective bodies, are liable to
injurious forms of electoral pressure. These four disadvantages are all serious. But all of them can be, in great
measure, obviated. The first, second and fourth are practically
done away with under a system of municipal government
such as prevails in Germany, where the burgomasters and
aldermen, corresponding to the English chairmen of committees, are whole-time paid experts with practically permanent
tenure of office. All four disadvantages can be overcome,
perhaps even more effectively, by the recently developed
device of Commissions or *ad hoc* Boards, that is to say, bodies of
men appointed for the express purpose of industrial operation
or control. An example of a Commission for operation is
afforded by the Railway Department of New South Wales
or the Port of London Authority in this country, and one of a
Commission for control by the Interstate Railway Commission
of the United States. The members of such Commissions can be
specially chosen for their fitness for their task, their appointment can be for long periods, the area allotted to them can

[1] H. Meyer, *Municipal Ownership in Great Britain*, p. 258.

be suitably adjusted, and their terms of appointment can be such as to free them, in the main, from electoral pressure. The system of Commissions or *ad hoc* Boards also, in great part, escapes a further important objection to intervention in industry by such bodies as municipal councils. This objection, as stated by Major Darwin, is that such intervention " lessens the time which these bodies can devote to their primary and essential duties, and, by increasing the unwillingness of busy men to devote their time to public affairs, it lowers the average administrative capacity of the Local Authorities." [1] When industries are operated or controlled by special public Commissions, this objection is inapplicable. The broad result is that modern developments in the structure and methods of governmental agencies have fitted these agencies for beneficial intervention in industry under conditions which would not have justified intervention in earlier times.

[1] Darwin, *Municipal Trade*, 102.

CHAPTER XXI

§ 1. In the course of Chapters IX., X. and XI., reference was frequently made to devices, by which the State could interfere, where self-interest, acting through simple competition, failed to make the national dividend as large as it might be made. Apart from governmental operation of industries into which the right amount of resources would not otherwise be turned, and apart also from penal legislation in extreme cases, these devices were fiscal in character and consisted in the concession of bounties or the imposition of taxes. Where self-interest works, not through simple competition, but through monopoly, fiscal intervention evidently ceases to be effective. A bounty might, indeed, be so contrived as to prevent restrictions of output below what is socially desirable, but only at the cost of enabling the monopolist to add to his already excessive profits a large ransom from the State. In the present chapter, therefore, I propose to consider what methods are available under conditions of monopoly. For simplicity of exposition, I shall ignore the qualifications set out in Chapter XI. and proceed as though simple competition might still be believed, as it was believed by some of the more rigid followers of the classical economists, to make the national dividend a maximum. The State, then, contemplating a monopoly or the possibility of a monopoly in some industry, may be supposed to contrast the dividend under it with the dividend under simple competition. Its problem will be, not to make things perfect, but to make them as good as they would be if monopolistic power were not at work.

§ 2. In industries where monopolistic power is liable to be introduced through the development of combinations, it is open to the State, if it chooses, to aim at preventing monopoly power from arising, or, if it has arisen, at destroying it. The original Federal Anti-Trust Law (1890) of the United States, commonly known as the Sherman Act, was overtly directed against actions " in restraint of trade or commerce among the several States," but was interpreted in the earlier decisions of the Supreme Court as an Act banning all combinations large enough to possess a substantial element of monopolistic power. Thus Justice Harlan's judgment in the Northern Securities Case, 1904, asserted that " to vitiate a combination, such as the Act of Congress condemns, it need not be shown that the combination in fact results, or will result, in a total suppression of trade or in a complete monopoly, but it is only essential to show that by its necessary operation it tends to restrain interstate or international trade or commerce, or tends to create a monopoly in such trade or commerce and to deprive the public of the advantages that flow from free competition." [1]   The Clayton Law of 1914, while making no further provision as regards combinations that had already been formed, follows the line of this interpretation as regards the formation of new combinations in the future. It lays it down, not only that no person shall be a director of more than one large bank or large corporation, but also that no corporation shall acquire—acquirements already made are not affected—the whole or part of the stock of any other corporation, when the effect of such acquisition may be substantially to lessen competition, or to restrain commerce in any section of the community, or to tend to the creation of a monopoly in any line of commerce. This general policy—trust prohibition and trust breaking— seems, however, to be open to three serious objections.

First, it is a policy exceedingly difficult to enforce in an effective manner. The legislature and the courts may succeed in getting rid of certain forms of combination, but the result will often be merely the appearance of other forms—possibly of forms, which, as would happen if an

[1] Jenks and Clark, *The Trust Problem*, p. 295.

informal price-fixing agreement took the place of a complete amalgamation, sacrifice the merits, without getting rid of the demerits, of those which preceded them. The declaration of the Supreme Court of the United States, that the granting of a power of attorney to common trustees by a number of companies was *ultra vires*, led, in some industries, to the purchase of a majority of stock in each of the companies by the said trustees, and, in others, to the substitution of a holding company for a trust. Governmental attacks on holding companies can easily be met either by complete consolidation, if this is not also made illegal, or by dissolution into separate companies, each subject to the same controlling interest. The Austrian law against Kartels likely to injure the revenue abolished Kartels possessed of a central office; but only with the result of substituting informal understandings. The British Committee on Railway Agreements and Amalgamations (1911) summed up the situation thus: "While Parliament may enact that this must be done and that must be prohibited, past experience shows that even Parliament appears to be powerless to prevent two parties, either by agreement or without formal agreement, from abstaining from a course of action, namely, active competition, that neither party desires to take. Parliament can, of course, refuse to sanction Bills authorising the amalgamation or working union of two or more railway companies, and may provide that certain classes of agreement shall be invalid or even illegal. But it cannot prevent railway companies [and, of course, the same thing is true of industrial companies] coming to understandings with each other to adopt a common course of action, or to cease from active competition."[1] The recent policy of the United States Government and Courts, in forcing the dissolution of monopolistic companies into their constituent parts and providing at the same time various regulations to prevent these from becoming subject to a common control, may, indeed, for a time be more effective, and, even though it does not succeed in stimulating real competition among men formerly colleagues, yet may, by its harassing

[1] *Departmental Committee on Railway Agreements and Amalgamations,* 1911, p. 18.

effect, make the task of forming new combinations less attractive. It was stated, for example, by Professor Durand in 1914, that no new combinations had been formed since the Government began to bring suits under the Sherman Act.[1] This, however, is no longer true. In the Memorandum on American Combinations furnished by the Board of Trade to the Committee on Industry and Trade in 1927, the following conclusion is reached. " Only a very partial success has been achieved in preventing the growth of combination or the lessening of competition. The experience of the administration of the Sherman Act between 1890 and 1914 seems to have been repeated. When one form of combination is attacked and declared illegal, the lawyers advising the corporation evolve a new form, which, even if an objection by the Federal Trade Commission is eventually upheld, takes a considerable period to upset." [2] Thus it may still be claimed, as the teaching of experience as a whole, that laws aimed directly at "maintaining competition" have very small prospect of succeeding in their purpose.

There is a second serious objection to this policy. The root idea lying behind it is that competition implies a condition of things in which the value of the marginal social net product of investment in the businesses affected is about equal to the value of the marginal social net product elsewhere. But, passing by the qualifications to this view set out in Chapters IX. and XI., we have to note that the competition, from which the above good result may be expected, is " simple competition," whereas the competition, to which laws against combination lead, will very probably be monopolistic competition, namely, competition among a *few* competitors. With railway combinations this result is certain; for the number of railways plying between any two given centres is necessarily very small. With industrial combinations the issue at first sight seems more doubtful, since there is no such necessary limitation in the number of industrial concerns of any given type. When,

---

[1] Cf. *American Economic Review Supplement*, March 1914, p. 176. For a full account of American Anti-Trust Laws and Cases, cf. Davies, *Trust Laws and Unfair Competition.*

[2] *Factors in Industrial and Commercial Efficiency*, 1927, p. 107.

however, we reflect that combinations can rarely be organised except in industries where, as a matter of fact, the number of leading firms is small, the force of this objection is much reduced. Among industrial combinations, as well as among railway combinations, dissolution is much more likely to lead to monopolistic than to simple competition. It has been shown, however, in Chapter XV., that monopolistic competition does not tend to bring about an output of such a magnitude that the value of the marginal social net product of investment in the industry affected is equal to that prevailing elsewhere. On the contrary, the output is indeterminate. When the competitors hope to destroy or to absorb one another, we may get "cut-throat competition," under which production is carried so far as to involve absolute loss; and the chance of this is made greater by the desire of one giant business to win even a barren victory over another. In short, even if the conditions were such that laws for "maintaining competition" could really prevent combination, they would still be unable to secure the establishment of competition in that sense in which alone it can be expected to evolve the level of prices and the rate of output which is most advantageous from the standpoint of the national dividend.

Even now, however, the case against the policy we are considering is not exhausted. There remains a third objection. Combination is not the parent of monopoly only, but also, very often, of incidental benefits. Thus, as was observed in Chapter XIV., a combination, which is large relatively to the market in which it trades, has more inducement than a small single seller to adopt a policy of developing demand among potential customers, since it may reckon on receiving a larger proportion of the gain resulting from any investments which it may make with this object. In addition to this, a large combination will often enjoy certain economies of production, which, if the Government were to adopt a policy of maintaining active competition, would fail to emerge. No doubt, some of those forms of Kartel agreement, under which a proportion of the market is guaranteed to the several members, since they tend to conserve weak firms, which competition would "naturally" destroy, not only fail to yield economies, but actually yield diseconomies.[1] It should be observed, however, that pooling agreements do not necessarily act in this way. The British Committee on Trusts (1919), for example, reports that in a great many associations there is an arrangement under which firms, on producing less than their quota, receive from the pool 5 per cent in value upon the amount of their deficiency. It was urged by some witnesses that this arrangement had the effect of driving weak firms out of the industry by the economical method of pensioning, instead of the more costly method of fighting them.[2] Against this, indeed, we have to set the fact that the money to provide the pensions has to be obtained by some kind of tax on firms that exceed their quota—a necessary discouragement to them. Moreover, some forms of pool, by making the profits of each member severally depend on the efficiency of all collectively, may lead to relaxed energy and enterprise. But, on the other hand, in all combinations that involve any measure of common management, savings of the kind referred to in Chapter XIV. are bound to accrue in greater or less degree.[3] In a peculiar industry like the telephones, where the actual thing supplied to A is improved if B draws his supply from the same agency, the advantage is especially great. It may also be considerable in more ordinary industries. *Inter alia*, weak or badly situated plants are apt to be shut down

---

[1] Cf. Walker, *Combinations in the German Coal Industry*, p. 322. Mr. Walker points out, however, that this tendency, at all events in the Ruhr Kartel, is smaller than appears at first sight, since the large mines, by sinking more shafts and by buying up small mines, can increase their "participation" (*ibid.* p. 94). Morgenroth, in his *Exportpolitik der Kartelle*, emphasises this point in regard to Kartels generally. He points out further that the anti-economic effects of Kartels are mitigated by their tendency to lead to the development of "mixed works," which refuse to admit any limitation in their output of raw stuff to be worked up in their own further products. Thus among these important mixed works the selective influence of competition is not restrained by agreements (*loc. cit.* p. 72).

[2] Report of the Committee on Trusts, 1919, p. 3.

[3] Cf. Liefmann's statement : " Verschiedene grosse Unternehmungen erwarben nämlich diese kleinen Zechen nur um ihrer Beteiligungsziffer im Syndikat willen, legten sie aber dann still und förderten deren Absatzquote auf ihren eigenen Schächten billiger. War dies auch natürlich für die betroffenen Arbeiter und Gemeinden sehr nachteilig, so ist doch zu berücksichtigen, dass diese kleinen Zechen bei freier Konkurrenz längst zugrunde gegangen wären. Höchstens kann man sagen, dass dann die Still-legung und die Entlassung der Arbeiter sich weniger plötzlich vollzogen hätte und länger voraussehbar gewesen wäre " (*Kartelle und Trusts*, pp. 61-2).

much more quickly than they would be under competition; while, among those that remain, the purposive force of "comparative cost accounting" may be expected to stimulate the energy of managers more strongly than the blind force of market rivalry could ever do.[1]

We must, indeed, be on our guard against exaggerating the importance of these economies. For, if by combination we mean existing combinations, it is necessary to recollect that, since the magnitude of the unit of control is determined by monopolistic considerations as well as by considerations of structural and other economies, this unit is often larger than the unit of maximum efficiency. If we mean only such combinations as it would be profitable to form *de novo*, were the exercise of monopolistic power wholly excluded, combination will, indeed, evolve the unit of maximum *immediate* efficiency, but that unit will very likely prove too large when ultimate indirect effects, as well as immediate effects, are taken into account. For this there are two reasons. The first is that a producer controlling the main part of any industry, in considering the wisdom of adopting any mechanical improvement, is tempted to take account, not merely of the direct positive yield to be expected from capital invested in that improvement, but also of the indirect negative yield in lessening the returns to his existing plant. But, if he does this, he will, as was shown on pp. 190-92, be holding back from improvements which it is to the interest of the national dividend that he should adopt. A monopoly makes no proper use—at all events is under temptation to make insufficient use—of that invaluable agent of progress, the scrap heap.[2] The second reason is that indicated in Chapter X., namely, that large combinations, by lessening the opportunities for training in the entrepreneur function, which are available when men who have done well in one company can be passed on to more responsible work in another, and by weakening the stimulus to keenness and efficiency, which is afforded by the rivalry of

---

[1] Cf. Macgregor, *Industrial Combination*, p. 34. This device rules prominently in the United States Steel Corporation (Van Hise, *Concentration and Control*, p. 136). An elaborate account of it is given by Jenks in the *U.S.A. Bulletin of Labour*, 1900, p. 675.

[2] Clark, *The Control of Trusts* (revised edition), p. 14.

competing concerns, tend indirectly to prevent the average level of business ability from rising as high as it might otherwise do.

The qualifications which these considerations suggest are of great importance. They tell strongly against the claim made by Professor Clark, when he writes: " A nearly ideal condition would be that in which, in every department of industry, there should be one great corporation, working without friction and with enormous economy, and *compelled to give to the public the full benefit of that economy.*" [1] Nevertheless, there can be little doubt that, *in some circumstances*, the combination of competing institutions into "Trusts" and consolidations that dominate the market does involve, even from a long-period point of view, considerable net economies. [2] These economies *may* be so great that the favourable effect produced by them on the output of the monopolised commodity exceeds the unfavourable effect produced on this output by the exercise of monopolistic power. Attempts to determine, by a comparison of prices, or of " margins " between prices and the cost of materials, before and after the formation of any combination, whether or not this has actually been so, are inevitably baffled by our inability to allow for changes in manufacturing methods and in the utilisation of by-products, or to gauge accurately the—probably abnormal—price conditions that ruled immediately before the combination was formed. [3] Analysis, however, enables us to say that combination is likely, on the whole, to diminish the output of the commodity affected by it and to raise its price, unless the associated economies are

---

[1] *The Control of Trusts*, p. 29.

[2] Professor Durand argues in favour of a policy of trust-breaking that, in general, the business units evolved apart from combination would be large enough to secure practically all the structural and other economies of production available to trusts (*Quarterly Journal of Economics*, 1914, p. 677 *et seq.*). It should be observed, however, that, even if this were true, the policy of trust-breaking would not be shown to be superior to one of depriving trusts of monopolistic power : for *both* policies would then lead to the establishment of business units of a size yielding maximum efficiency. In fact, however, it is plainly not true in all industries ; and, when it is not true, trust-breaking leads to the establishment of units too small to yield maximum efficiency.

[3] For these reasons the admirable price studies in Jenks's *Trust Problem* are hardly adequate to support the favourable judgment as to the effect of combinations that he rests on them.

so large that, had they been introduced without monopolisation, they would have raised output to about double its former amount.[1] Economies so large as this are improbable, and I do not, therefore, claim that to prevent combination in any department of industry would often make the output of that department smaller than it might have been. But—and this is the essential point—the effect of combination on the output of the commodity affected by it is not the same thing as its effect on the national dividend. For suppose combination to bring about economies which enable the same output as before to be produced by the use of half the former quantity of productive resources, and suppose that, in consequence of monopolistic action, no more than this output is in fact produced. The released productive resources will not, in general, be idle, but will be occupied in adding to the output of other commodities. Hence, in this case, the output of no commodity is diminished and the output of some commodities is increased, which obviously implies that the size of the national dividend is increased. It follows that to prevent combination would sometimes injure the dividend, even though it enabled the output of the commodity immediately affected to be larger than it would have been. This point need not, however, be laboured further. For it is in any event certain that to prevent combination, when combination carries with it any net economies, must be more injurious to the dividend than to allow combination and to prevent the exercise of monopolistic power.

§ 3. A second line of policy which it is open to the State to pursue is as follows. Instead of endeavouring, by obstructing combination, to prevent industrial concerns from becoming possessed of monopolistic power, it may seek, by conserving *potential* rather than actual competition, to make it to their interest to leave that power unexercised ; the idea, of course, being that, if they expect new competitors to come into the field, should output be restricted and prices be raised high enough to yield abnormal profits, they will have no inducement to charge more than " reasonable " prices. The policy,

---

[1] This proposition is exactly true on the hypothesis that the curves of demand and supply are straight lines.

to which this line of thought leads, is that of penalising the use of "clubbing" devices, whose repute might otherwise drive potential competitors away.   Among these devices the two principal are cut-throat competition, as described in Chapter XV., and various forms of boycott, namely, the exercise of pressure upon third parties not to purchase services from, or sell services to, a rival seller on terms as favourable as they would have offered to him if left to themselves.[1]

§ 4.   It is obvious that the weapon of cut-throat competition, or, as it is sometimes called, "destructive dumping," when practised by a business already large enough to monopolise any department of industry, must prove overwhelmingly powerful against newcomers.   The monopolist necessarily possesses immense resources, and these can be poured out, in almost unlimited quantities, for the destruction of a new, and presumably much less wealthy, intruder.   This is especially clear when a monopolist, dealing in many markets or in many lines of goods, has to do with a competitor dealing only in a few; for in these conditions the competitor can be destroyed by a cut, made either openly or through a bogus independent company,[2] that affects only a small part of the monopolist's business.   An extreme example of this kind of cut is given in the statement of certain opponents of the Standard Oil Trust, "that persons are engaged to follow the waggons of competitors to learn who their customers are, and that then they make lower offers to those customers; and it is still further asserted that at times the employés in the offices of rivals are bribed to disclose their business to the Standard Oil Company."[3]   It is needless to emphasise

[1] The weapon of boycott can also be used to force upon retailers an agreement to maintain the prices of particular goods sold by them at a level dictated by the manufacturers of the goods.   It would seem that manufacturers do not wish quality-articles to be sold too cheap to consumers, lest they should "lose caste" with them.   But probably their main motive is the knowledge that, if the goods are made into "leaders," on which the retailers make scarcely any direct profit, and which serve merely to advertise other wares, the retailers will tend not to push their sale (Taussig, *American Economic Review*, vol. vi. No. 1 Supplement, 1916, pp. 172-3).

[2] This method is alleged to have been practised by the Standard Oil Company.   The object, of course, is to obviate a clamour from customers in other markets for a similar cut on their purchases.   (Cf. Davies, *Trust Laws and Unfair Competition*, p. 319.)

[3] *U.S.A. Industrial Commission*, I. i. p. 20.

the immense power of this weapon. "After two or three attempts to compete with Jay Gould's telegraph line from New York to Philadelphia had been frustrated by a lowering of rates to a merely nominal price, the notoriety of this terrible weapon sufficed to check further attempts at competition."[1]

§ 5. The weapon of boycott has a narrower range than that of cut-throat competition. It is worked through a refusal to deal, except on specially onerous terms, with any one who also deals elsewhere. When the worsened terms attached by a dominating seller to dealings with himself are more injurious to the client than the loss of that client's other dealings, the monopolist can force the client to boycott his rivals. In order that he may be able to do this, the goods or services that he offers for sale must be rendered, by nature or by art, non-transferable;[2] for it is impossible to hurt a customer by refusing to sell to him, if he is able to purchase through a middleman the goods which are refused to him by the monopolist. Hence, when nature does not cause non-transferability, there must be stringent conditions about re-sales in the contracts between the monopolist and any intermediary agents, if such there are, who intervene between him and the ultimate consumers. But non-transferability is not sufficient by itself. It is necessary, further, that the rival producer's possible supply *to one recalcitrant consumer* at current prices shall be very small. Usually, of course, though any one seller's output is likely to be small relatively to the total consumption of the market, it is many times as large as that of any representative single consumer. Where this is so, recalcitrant consumers can successfully counter a refusal to sell on the part of the monopolist by purchasing all that they want from outside competitors and leaving to non-recalcitrants the whole output of the monopolist. This consideration is not, however, entirely fatal to the weapon of boycott, because in many industries, though by no means in all,[3] producers deal with their customers

---

[1] Hobson, *Evolution of Modern Capitalism*, p. 219.

[2] Cf. my paper, "Monopoly and Consumers' Surplus," *Economic Journal*, September 1904, p. 392.

[3] Thus Jenks (*U.S.A. Bulletin of Labour*, 1900, p. 679) states that "about half the combinations reporting sell direct to consumers."

indirectly through wholesalers or further manufacturers or transporters, who purchase individually a considerable mass of products. When intermediaries of this kind are present, effective boycott may become practicable.

First, a boycott can be forced when the commodities or services supplied by the monopolist consist, not in a single kind of good, but in several goods, and when, among these several goods, there are one or more for which the demand is very urgent, and of which the monopolist has, through patents or reputation (*e.g.* brands of tobacco) or otherwise, exclusive control. A good example is furnished by the boot and shoe trade, in which certain firms control important patents. The patented machines are not sold, but are let out on lease, under "conditions which debar manufacturers from employing these machines save and except in conjunction with other machines supplied by the same controlling owners . . . one of the conditions being that the latest machines must not be used for goods which have, in any other process of manufacturing, been touched by machines supplied by other makers."[1] This kind of boycott is also illustrated by the "factors' agreement," which makers of popular proprietary goods sometimes secure from retailers.

Secondly, a boycott can be forced where it is important for purchasers—here, as before, the purchasers are, in general, manufacturers—to be able to get the service that they need immediately the need arises, and where an ordinary supplier, though producing much more service in the aggregate than any single purchaser wants, may not be producing more than such a purchaser wants at some definite single moment. This condition is realised in the transport of goods which are so perishable, or for which the demand is so instant, that transport, to be of use, must be available at the moment when it is asked for. It is in the transport by sea of goods of this kind that the method of boycott has been most fully elaborated.

---

[1] *Times*, 8th February 1903. Cf. Appendix to the Report of the (British) Committee on Trusts, 1919, p. 27. Action of this kind is directly prohibited in Australia under the Patents Act of 1903. (Cf. Davies, *Trust Laws and Unfair Competition*, p. 247.) The British Patents Act of 1907 permits it only provided that the lessee is given an opportunity of hiring the patented machine without the tying clauses on "reasonable," though not, of course, equal terms.

The transport of goods, which are in fairly steady demand and which have no need of speedy delivery, can be arranged for by purchasers, if they wish, wholly through tramp steamers; but the transport of urgent goods cannot be so arranged for, because tramps and small lines cannot guarantee regular sailings.[1] Hence it comes to be practicable for shipping rings to force a boycott against independent lines. They usually accomplish this through " deferred rebates." [2] Of these there are two degrees. When the Royal Commission on Shipping Rings published their report (1909), in the West

[1] Cf. *Royal Commission on Shipping Rings*, 1909, Report, p. 13. The Commissioners suggest that it is for this reason that the deferred rebate system is not applied to our outward trade in coal or to the greater part of our inward trade, which consists of rough goods, but only to those cargoes for which a regular service of high-class steamers is essential. (Cf. *ibid.* p. 77.)

[2] This method was described by the Royal Commissioners on Shipping Rings, 1909, thus : "The Companies issue a notice or circular to shippers informing them that, if at the end of a certain period (usually four or six months) they have not shipped goods by any vessels other than those despatched by members of the Conference, they will be credited with a sum equivalent to a certain part (usually 10 per cent) of the aggregate freights paid on their shipments during that period, and that this sum will be paid over to them, if at the end of a further period (usually four or six months) they have continued to confine their shipments to vessels belonging to members of the Conference. The sum so paid is known as a deferred rebate. Thus in the South African trade at the present day the amount of the rebate payable is 5 per cent of the freight paid by the shipper. The rebates are calculated in respect of two six-monthly periods ending with the 30th June and 31st December respectively, but their payment to the shipper is not due until a further period of six months has elapsed ; that is to say, that, as to shipments made between the 1st January and the following 30th June, the rebates are payable on the 1st January following, and, as to shipments made between the 1st July and the 31st December, the rebates are payable on the following 1st July. It follows that in this instance the payment of the rebate on any particular item of cargo is withheld by the shipowners for at least six months and that, in the case of cargo shipped on the 1st January or 1st July, it is withheld for a period of twelve months. If during any period a shipper sends any quantity of goods, however small, by a vessel other than those despatched by the Conference Lines, he becomes disentitled to rebates on any of his shipments by Conference vessels during that period and the preceding one " (Report, pp. 9-10). Since the issue of the Royal Commission's Report a new method of tying shippers, known as the agreement system, has come into operation. When South African legislation in 1911 " forced the liner companies trading with South Africa to relinquish the rebate system, an agreement was drawn up after negotiations between the South African Trade Association and the South African Shipping Conference. . . . The shippers who sign agree to give their active support to the regular lines in the Conference. In return the lines undertake to maintain regular berth sailings at advertised dates, the ships to sail full or not full, and to provide sufficient tonnage for the ordinary requirements of the trade ; and, further, to maintain stability of freights, which are definitely prescribed in the agreement, and equality of rates to large and small shippers alike " (*Report of the Imperial Shipping Committee*, 1923, Cmd. 1802, pp. 20-21).

African Shipping Conference and in all the Conferences engaged in the trade with India and the Far East, the rebates were paid to exporting merchants only, on condition that these merchants had not been interested in any shipment by rival carriers, but there was no requirement that the forwarding agent, through whom the merchant might have acted, should have dealt exclusively with the Conference in respect of the goods of his other clients.[1] In the South American Conferences, however, " the form of claim for rebates has, in the case of goods shipped through a forwarding agent, to be signed by such agent as well as by the principal, and, if the forwarding agent has not conformed to the conditions of the rebate circular in all his shipments for all his clients, claims to rebates are invalidated." [2]

Thirdly, a boycott can be forced when the intermediary, whom a monopolist wishes to use as his instrument, is, not a manufacturer or a wholesaler purchasing that rival's goods, but a railway company conveying them. When an alternative route for his own goods is available, the monopolist, by threatening the railway with the withdrawal of his custom, is sometimes in a position to compel it to charge differential rates against his rival. In a boycott engineered by the Oil Trust it is even asserted that the railways were compelled to hand over a part of the extra charges levied on their rivals to the executive of the Trust.[3] When the boycotting concern actually owns the agency of transport, its power in this matter is, of course, still greater.[4] A boycott of this kind

---

[1] *Royal Commission on Shipping Rings*, Report, pp. 29-30.

[2] *Ibid.* p. 30. The decision of the House of Lords in the Mogul Steamship Co. case, 1892, was to the effect that the party injured by an arrangement of this kind had no ground of action for damages, but it did not, it would seem, necessarily imply that the combination against which action was brought was itself lawful (Davies, *Trust Laws and Unfair Competition*, p. 234). In a similar case in the German Imperial Court (1901), an injunction against discrimination was granted (*ibid.* p. 262).

[3] Cf. *The Great Oil Octopus*, p. 40 ; Ripley, *Railroads, Rates and Regulation*, p. 200.

[4] The same thing is true when the boycotting concern owns, as the Big Five meat-packers do, stockyards and cold-storage warehouses which their rivals must use and in respect of which they can make discriminating charges against them. The Federal Trade Commission, in their report on the meat-packing industry in 1919, urged that, to obviate this, the State should itself acquire these stockyards and cold-storage plants.

may also be operated through banks, pressure being exerted upon them to refuse loans to a rival producer.

§ 6. Attempts to prevent the use of cut-throat competition, *i.e.* destructive dumping, by legal enactment are confronted with the difficulty of evasion. The American Industrial Commission recommended that "cutting prices in any locality below those which prevail generally, for the purpose of destroying local competition," should be made an offence. Any person damaged was to have the right to sue for penalties, and officers were required to prosecute offenders.[1] It is plain, however, that, even when it is possible, as it is with public service corporations, to insist that tariff rates shall be regularly published, evasion may be practised through unpublished discounts and rebates to particular customers; nor, since discovery is unlikely, will the enactment of heavy penalties against breaches of the law necessarily secure obedience thereto.[2] Where destructive dumping is threatened, not by public service corporations, but by industrialists engaged in the manufacture of many commodities at different places, the enforcement of regular published rates is impracticable. Hence the problem confronting the legislator demands the unravelling of still more tangled knots. Where the form of destructive dumping which is employed is that of price-cutting limited to the local market of a particular competitor or group of competitors, the offence is at least definite, though, especially when worked through a bogus independent company, it may be extraordinarily difficult to detect. Against destructive dumping of this kind *operated by foreigners* the Governments of Canada (1904) and South Africa (1914) have endeavoured to guard their citizens by anti-dumping legislation, providing that, when goods are exported to them at prices, which, exclusive of freight charges and so on, are substantially below

---

[1] *United States Industrial Commission*, vol. xviii. p. 154.

[2] It is instructive to read in M. Colson's great work (*Cours d'économie politique*, vol. vi. p. 398) that abusive discriminations "semblent être devenus bien plus rares en Angleterre qu'en Amérique, bien que l'Administration y ait des pouvoirs beaucoup moins étendus et que les pénalités y soient moins sévères, parce que l'entente entre Compagnies y est admise par la loi ; au contraire en Amérique, les pouvoirs publics s'efforcent d'empêcher les accords qui mettraient fin à la concurrence, cause essentielle des inégalités de traitement, et par suite ne sont pas arrivés, jusqu'ici, à déraciner celles-ci."

the contemporary prices ruling at home, these goods shall be subjected to a special import duty equivalent to the difference between the home and foreign prices.[1]   This legislation, however, hits, not merely destructive dumping in the sense here defined, but also (1) the clearing of surplus stock on a foreign market at less than home prices in periods of depression and (2) the permanent selling abroad at the world price, by a foreign monopolistic producer, of goods for which at home he is able to charge monopoly prices.   The policy of discouraging the former of these two practices is one whose merits are open to debate, but clearly there is nothing to be said for discouraging the second—except, indeed, the least tenable of the things that can be said in favour of all-round protection.   The United States Government, wishing to direct its legislative blows against destructive dumping exclusively, included in the Federal Revenue Act of 1916 the following modified version of the Canadian anti-dumping law.   In Section 801 of the Act it is enacted: "That it shall be unlawful, for any person importing or assisting in importing any articles from any foreign country into the United States, commonly and systematically to import, sell or cause to be imported or sold such articles within the United States at a price substantially less than the actual market value or wholesale price of such articles, at the time of exporting to the United States, in the principal market of the country of their production, or of other foreign countries to which they are commonly exported, after adding to such market value or wholesale price freight, duty and other charges and expenses necessarily incident to the importation and sale thereof in the United States.   Provided, that such act or acts be done with the intent of destroying or injuring an industry in the United States or of preventing the establishment of an industry in the United States or of

---

[1] For these laws cf. Davies, *Trust Laws and Unfair Competition*, pp. 550-51. Australia (1906) has a more complicated law which condemns dumping in the Canadian sense, along with certain other forms of importation, under the general head of unfair competition, and meets it with a penalty, not a special duty.   Cf. for a general discussion of anti-dumping legislation, Viner, *Dumping* (1923), ch. xi.-xiv.   For the most recent facts cf. *Memorandum on the Legislation of Different States for the Prevention of Dumping*, Economic and Financial Section of the League of Nations, C.E., 1.7.1927.

restraining or monopolising any part of the trade or commerce in such articles in the United States." Offences against this clause were penalised, not, as in Canada, by a special duty, but by a fine. Under the Emergency Tariff Act of 1921 and the final Act of 1922 the reference to intention was omitted, and the imposition of a special duty was authorised whenever an efficiently conducted industry of the United States was being, or was likely to be, injured by importation at less than the price ruling in the principal home market of the exporting country *plus* f.o.b. costs. In the United Kingdom the Safeguarding of Industries Act 1921 provided for the imposition of special duties on goods that are being imported from any foreign country and sold in the United Kingdom at a price, *inclusive of freight charges*, less than 95 per cent of the wholesale price at the works charged to consumers in that country; provided that, by reason of the importation, employment in any industry in the United Kingdom is being, or is likely to be, seriously affected. An Act of the same general character was passed in Australia in 1921, though under that Act discretion is allowed to the Executive to refrain from action if it so chooses. We need not concern ourselves here with the difficult problems which legislation of this kind provides for the officials charged with ascertaining the relevant facts— including, as these did under the Federal Revenue Act of 1916, the motive actuating foreign sellers—and for those who have to detect and prevent the evasive use of nominally independent agents, on whose account goods may be imported at full price, thereafter to be sold at less than was paid for them. The main point for our present purpose is that, when, as in the conditions which this legislation contemplates, destructive dumping is attempted by inter-local price discriminations, the task of preventing it is *relatively* easy, because there is something definite to go on. When, however, as often happens in domestic trade, we have to do with cuts made on *all* sales of a particular line of goods, the offence is not definite; for, clearly, not all cuts are destructive dumping, and it is difficult to distinguish among them the innocent from the guilty. One authoritative writer proposes as a test that, "if the price of the particular grade of goods were first put down and then put up again, and if rivals were crushed in the interval, this would be evidence that the purpose of the cut was illegitimate." [1] Such a test has been attempted in the American Mann-Elkins Railway Law of 1910, which provides that, "when a railway reduces rates between competitive points, it shall not be permitted to increase the rates on the cessation of the competition, unless it can satisfy the Commission that the conditions are changed otherwise than by the mere elimination of water competition." [2] There is a similar provision in the American Shipping Act of 1916 as regards shipping charges in interstate trade. But this test cannot be pushed very vigorously ; for, if it were, any firm, which lowered prices in a time of depression or for purposes of experiment, might find itself precluded from afterwards raising them again, should any other firm in the same line meanwhile have failed.

Similar difficulties stand in the way of effective legislation against boycotts. It is true that such legislation has been widely attempted. The United States (under the Clayton Law), Australia and New Zealand all prohibit, under penalty, any person from making the act of sale, or the terms of sale, of anything conditional on the buyer not using or dealing in the goods of any competitor. On similar lines the United States Federal Revenue Law of September 1916 " imposes a double duty upon goods imported under agreement that the importer or others shall use those goods exclusively." [3] Yet again, the American Shipping Act of 1916 makes deferred rebates illegal. It is obvious, however, that, when the condition or agreement is made between a manufacturer and a dealer, both of whom profit by it, the difficulty of preventing evasion must be very great. When the boycott is worked, not through a wholesaler, but through a railway company, the difficulty is still

---

[1] Clark, *The Control of Trusts*, p. 69.

[2] *Economist*, 25th Jan. 1910, p. 1412. Cf. Ripley, *Railroads, Rates and Regulation*, p. 566.

[3] The English Patents and Designs Amendment Act of 1907 prohibits exclusive dealing contracts of this kind, unless the seller, lessor or licensee proves that, when the contract was made, his competitors had the option of obtaining the patented goods on reasonable terms without the exclusive condition (Davies, *Trust Laws and Unfair Competition*, p. 539).

N

greater.   American law has long endeavoured to prevent railway discriminations favourable to the large Trusts.   But : "A
partisan of the Trust said to me : ' The Pennsylvania Railroad
could not refuse the cars of a competitor of the Standard Oil
Company, but nothing could hinder it from side-tracking
them.' " [1]   " A consignment note acknowledges the receipt of
70 barrels of flour ; 65 only are shipped, and the railway company pays damages for the loss of the five non-existent
barrels."   Except when long notice of alterations is required
by law, rates may be changed suddenly, secret notice being
given to the favoured shipper and no information to others ;
and so forth.   It is true that the Attorney-General of the
United States declared in 1903, after the passing of the
Elkins law : " The giving and taking of railroad rebates is now
prohibited by a law capable of effective enforcement against
corporations as well as against individuals." [2]   This view, however, appears to have been unduly optimistic.   The Interstate
Commerce Commission reported, as to the conditions in 1908,
that many shippers still enjoy illegal advantages.   " Thus
the rebate, as an evil in transportation, even since amendment
of the law in 1906–10, while under control, is still far from
being eradicated.   Favouritism lurks in every covert, assuming
almost every hue and form.   Practices, which outwardly appear
to be necessary and legitimate, have been shown to conceal
special favours of a substantial sort." [3]   The boycott engineered
through railway companies thus dies hard.   It is said, however,
that, in the United States, the Transportation Act of 1920,
which created a system of Federal supervision over railways,
has finally put an end to it.[4]

These considerations make it clear that a policy of legal
prohibition against the exercise of clubbing methods cannot
easily be rendered proof against evasion.   It should not be
forgotten, however, that laws, which *could* be evaded if people
took sufficient pains, as a matter of fact are often not evaded.
For the mere passage of a law reacts on public opinion and

---

[1] Quoted by Ely, *Monopolies and Trusts*, p. 97.
[2] *Economist*, 28th Feb. 1903.
[3] Ripley, *Railroads, Rates and Regulation*, p. 209.
[4] P. de Roussiers, *Cartels and Trusts and their Development* (Economic and
Financial Section of the League of Nations, 1927, II. 21), p. 9.

throws on the side of the practice upheld by law the strong forces of respectability and inertia. Hence we may reasonably expect that laws of this character, if carefully prepared, would, at all events, partially succeed in their immediate purpose. It is, therefore, of great interest to observe that Section 5 of the United States Federal Trade Commission Act of 1914 declares " that unfair methods of competitive commerce are hereby declared unlawful," and establishes a Federal Trade Commission to take proceedings to enforce this declaration whenever it appears to it to be in the public interest to do so. Section 14 of the Clayton Act provides further that, whenever a corporation violates any of the penal provisions of any of the anti-trust laws, " such violation shall be deemed to be also that of the individual directors, officers, or agents of such corporation as shall have authorised, ordered, or done any of the acts constituting in whole or in part such violation." Upon conviction any director, officer or agent is subject to a fine not exceeding 5000 dollars, or to imprisonment not exceeding one year, or to both, in the discretion of the Court.

§ 7. Granted that clubbing methods can be, in some measure, prevented, we turn to the further question, how far their prevention would avail to maintain potential competition. Professor Clark appears to hold that it would avail completely for this purpose. " In so far," he writes, " as legitimate rivalry in production is concerned, it is safe enough to build a new mill." In reality, however, even when clubbing methods are excluded, other obstacles to the full maintenance of competition are still present. First, when the unit firm normal to any industry is very large, the heavy capital expenditure required to start a new firm will check the ardour of aspirants. Furthermore, it should be noticed, in this connection, that in many industries the size of the normal unit firm has recently been increasing. For example, the output of the English paper industry between 1841 and 1903 rose from 43,000 to 773,080 tons, but the number of firms fell from 500 to 282;[1] and a like development has taken place in the raw iron industry. Secondly, the inducement

[1] Levy, *Monopole, Kartelle und Trusts*, p. 197.

to new competitors to spring up is smaller, the greater are
the productive economies which concentration on the part of
the monopolistic seller has involved. For, if great economy has
been brought about by concentration, a potential competitor
will know that the monopolistic seller, by simply abandoning
some of his monopoly revenue, can, without suffering any
positive loss, easily undersell him. Thirdly, the obstacles
in the way of new competition are further enlarged, when
a policy of secrecy as to costs and profits makes it difficult for
outsiders to guess at what rate the monopolistic seller *could*
sell, if he were to content himself with the normal gains of
competitive industry. Fourthly, a combination, by extensive
advertising or a distinctive trade mark, may have established
a sort of monopoly of reputation, which it would require heavy
advertising expenditure on the part of any would-be rival to
break down. It may, indeed, be suggested that, even so, the
combination would be kept in check by fear of a rival concern
being started with a view to forcing the combination to buy it
out. But there is less in this than there might appear to be
at first sight. For, if a rival did succeed in this policy, the
increase in the combination's capital might well be so large
that the rate of profit available per unit of capital would
turn out too small to make the venture worth the rival's
while.[1] This consideration would, of course, tend strongly to
hold him back. Thus attempts to maintain potential competition by preventing the employment of clubbing devices
can at best be only partially successful, and are, therefore,
very imperfect means of restraining bodies that possess monopolistic power from making use of that power. This is true
even of industry proper. In some departments of production—
roughly those covered by public utility concerns—the evident
wastefulness of competition makes it practically certain that
the public authorities will not permit it, and so exempts
monopolists from any check which the fear of it might otherwise exercise upon them.

§ 8. The inadequacy, as a method of control, of preventing
combination, which means maintaining actual competition,
and of anti-clubbing legislation, which means maintaining

[1] Cf. Jenks and Clark, *The Trust Problem*, pp. 69-70.

potential competition, leads forward naturally to the suggestion of direct methods. The position, which is relevant to industrial, no less than to railway, monopolies, is well put by the Departmental Committee on Railway Agreements and Amalgamations (1911) with special reference to the latter class. They write : " To sum up, we are strongly of opinion that, in so far as protection is required from any of the consequences which may be associated with railway co-operation, such protection should, in the main, be afforded by general legislation dealing with the consequences as such, independently of whether they occur as the result of agreement or not. Such a method would afford a much more extensive protection than the regulation of agreements. It would protect the public in the case of understandings as well as agreements. . . . It would not tend to introduce a confusing distinction between what a company might reasonably do under an agreement and what it might reasonably do if no agreement existed." [1] If this method could be employed with perfect accuracy, there would, of course, be no need for *any* accompanying indirect methods of the kind we have so far been discussing. In practice, however, the policy of dealing directly with the consequences of monopolistic power is, as will presently appear, exposed to very great difficulties. Furthermore, since in most forms it must almost necessarily work on the basis of some standard of reasonable earnings, deduced from the circumstances of other industries in which competition is available, these difficulties would become enormous, if attempts to maintain potential competition were abandoned altogether and resort had universally to direct methods. Consequently, it would seem that the policy of maintaining potential competition should be pursued everywhere vigorously, and that direct methods of dealing with the consequences should be employed, not instead of, but in addition to it.

§ 9. At first sight it seems obvious that direct dealing with the consequences of monopolistic power means, and can only mean, some kind of direct interference on the part of the public authority. In the main, of course, this

---

[1] *Report of the Departmental Committee on Railway Agreements and Amalgamations*, p. 21.

is what it does mean. But it is of some theoretical interest to note a possible alternative line of policy which was advocated, as regards shipping, by the Royal Commission on Shipping Rings. The Commission recommended, in effect, that the State should encourage the formation, over against a monopolistic seller, of a combination of buyers possessing also monopolistic powers. It was hoped that the combination of buyers might be able to neutralise attempts on the part of the seller to charge monopoly prices. This plan was advocated as a partial remedy for the evils that have arisen out of the conference system. Analytically, the plan is a weak one, because what the creation of the second monopolist does is, not to bring prices to the natural, or competitive, point, but to render them indeterminate over a considerable range, within which that point lies. No doubt, the position of the purchasers is made better than it would be if combination among them were absent; and there is reason to hope that prices and output will approach more nearly to what, from the standpoint of the national dividend, is desirable than they would do under those conditions. But the chance that the bargain between the two combinations will lie in the near neighbourhood of that proper to simple competition is not very large. This difficulty would exist even though the monopoly created to stand against the sellers were a monopoly of ultimate consumers. In practice, however, ultimate consumers are scarcely ever in a position to combine in this way. The only persons who can so combine are middlemen between the ultimate consumers and the monopolistic seller,—middlemen who are not particularly concerned to fight for the consumers' interests.[1] If they combine, the goods in which they deal will have to pass through the hands of two monopolistic combinations, instead of one, before they reach the ultimate consumers. The effect upon the price which those people will then have to pay is economically indeterminate. The price may be less than it would have been if the middlemen had not combined, but it may, on the other hand, be greater. In any event, it and, with it, the quantity of service accessible to the

[1] Cf. Marshall, *Industry and Trade*, p. 625.

ultimate consumers, are likely to be exceedingly unstable.[1] These considerations show that there is a serious flaw in the Commissioners' policy.[2]

§ 10. Interference on the part of the public authority does not necessarily mean orders about the terms of sale. It may well be that anti-social practices by powerful corporations might be substantially restrained by publicity alone. An important part of the task assigned to the Federal Trade Commission of the United States is to make investigations and to publish reports. The British *Committee on Trusts* (1919) recommended that the Board of Trade should obtain and publish in an annual report information about the development of organisations having for their purpose the regulation of prices or output so far as they tended to the creation of monopolies or to the restraint of trade; and should investigate complaints regarding the action of such organisations. Powers would, of course, need to be taken to compel the officers of the organisations affected to produce their books and to answer questions. The fear of an adverse report issued by an investigating body in which public opinion had confidence might often turn the scale against gross abuses of monopoly power. There is, in short, little doubt that the weapon of publicity can accomplish something of importance : but it can hardly accomplish all that is required.

§ 11. We turn, therefore, to interference by the public authority with the terms of sale—a method which *may* be necessary even in industrial enterprises, when the "remedies" considered so far prove inadequate, and which, apart from public operation, is certainly necessary in public utility concerns. Analytically, the problem may be stated as follows. Assuming that the output proper to simple competition (allowing, of course, for any economies in production which a combination may have introduced) is also the output most advantageous to the national dividend, we need so to regulate things that that output will be forthcoming. In industries operating under

---

[1] Cf. Marshall, *Principles of Economics*, Bk. v. ch. xiv. § 9.

[2] The Imperial Shipping Committee 1923, while endorsing that policy, observe that (so far as shipping is concerned) "only two bodies of importance formed on the lines recommended by the Commission and since its appointment have come to their notice" (Cmd. 1802, p. 23).

conditions of increasing supply price, this type of regulation cannot be accomplished by the machinery of price control alone. For, if the price be fixed by the State at the level proper to competitive conditions, *i.e.* at such a level that, if competitive conditions prevailed, the output would be adjusted to yield normal profits, it will pay a monopolist to produce less than this output. By reducing output he will, under conditions of increasing supply price, also diminish the supply price, thus obtaining a monopoly gain measured by the difference between the regulated selling price multiplied by the output and the supply price multiplied by the output. It will be to his interest to control his output in such a way as to make this monopoly gain as large as possible. According to the form of the demand and supply schedules, the resultant output may be greater or less than it would have been under unregulated monopoly ; but, in any event, it is certain to be less than the output proper to competition, at which the Government is aiming. This difficulty, however, is only present in industries operating under conditions of the increasing supply price. When constant supply price or decreasing supply price prevails, it will not pay a monopolist, when price is fixed at the competitive level, to reduce output below the competitive output; for he would not secure any diminution in his costs by doing this. Consequently, if the Government can succeed in fixing prices at the competitive level, it will also indirectly secure competitive output.[1] As a matter of practice, concerns (whether industrial combinations or public utility corporations), which it is necessary to regulate because they tend towards monopoly, are rarely of a kind which we should expect to be subject to increasing supply price. In the main, therefore, control means control over price.

§ 12. When this has been said, there inevitably comes to mind the sort of control over price which was exercised during the Great War, and some account of which was given in Chapter XII. It is very important, however, to realise that what we are now concerned with is fundamentally different from that. In controlling monopoly, it is required to prevent the monopolist from charging high prices, because, by so doing, he will

[1] Cf. Appendix III. § 23.

reduce output below the level at which he could put it with normal profits to himself. As explained above, under conditions of constant supply price or decreasing supply price, the fixing of maximum prices at the rate corresponding to the "competitive" output will in fact cause that output to be forthcoming. There is no question of the maximum price being associated with an output for which the demand price that the public are prepared to pay exceeds that price.[1] But in the war problem, as was clearly brought out in Chapter XII., the whole point of intervention was to fix a maximum price below the demand price that the public would be prepared, at need, to pay for such quantity of the commodity as was forthcoming. This is the reason why, at the maximum price, there was always a greater quantity demanded than could be supplied, and why, therefore, it was necessary to prevent accidental inequities in distribution by rationing all consumers to purchases smaller than many of them would have wished to make. This, too, is the reason why it was not sufficient to fix prices as from the producer only. Because the demand price was bigger than the price which the Government wished to allow, to have limited, e.g., shipping freights, without also limiting the price of the things brought in at the limited freights, would merely have enabled the intermediaries between the ship and the consumer to take the whole benefit for themselves. It was necessary, therefore, not merely to fix maximum prices to the original producer, but also to fix maximum additions that might be put on to these prices by the various persons through whose hands (whether as further manufacturers or as retailers) the controlled commodities would afterwards pass. In the regulation of monopoly charges there is, of course, no need for any of these secondary arrangements.

§ 13. We may now proceed to investigate this form of price control directly. One way in which it may be exercised is, as it were, negative. It may take the form of general provisions against " unreasonable " conduct, leaving the definition of what is, in fact, unreasonable to the decision of a

---

[1] In technical language, the limitation of monopoly prices moves the exchange index along the demand curve towards the right ; the limitation of competitive prices pushes the exchange index below the demand curve.

Commission or of the Courts. This way was, in substance, followed, for proposed *changes* of rates, in the work of the English Railway Commissioners prior to 1921, and of the American Railway Commissioners prior to the passage of the Hepburn law. The Commissioners had to decide whether any proposed increase of rates was reasonable, and to permit or forbid it accordingly. Thus their task was *comparatively light.* They had not to regulate all prices always, but only to intervene against specially unreasonable prices ; and, furthermore, the knowledge of their existence was likely to serve indirectly as a check against the setting-up of unreasonable prices.[1] The negative way is also followed in certain franchises, which permit municipalities to take over the business of a licensed corporation *at a proper price*—an ambiguous phrase—should the corporation fail to " operate and develop it in compliance with reasonable public requirements."[2] It is followed again in the Canadian Industrial Combines Investigation Act (1910). Provision is made for determining whether, with regard to any article, on the subject of which complaint has been made, "there exists any combine to promote unduly the advantage of the manufacturers or dealers at the expense of the consumers by fixing the price higher than is proper "; and, if the charge is established, penalties are provided. In New Zealand the Act of 1910 applies the same test. " Any person commits an offence, who, either as principal or agent, sells or supplies, or offers for sale or supply, any goods at a price which is unreasonably high, if that price has been in any manner, directly or indirectly, determined, controlled, or influenced by any commercial trust, of which that person or his principal (if any) is or has been a member." The Russian Criminal Code of 1903 had a similar proviso : " A merchant or manufacturer, who increases the price of victuals or other articles of prime necessity in an extraordinary degree in accord with other merchants or manufacturers dealing in the same articles, shall be punished with imprisonment." [3]   In all these

---

[1] Cf. Van Hise, *Concentration and Control*, p. 261.

[2] National Civic Federation, *Municipal and Private Operation of Public Utilities*, vol. i. p. 41.

[3] The text of these laws is printed in Appendix G to Jenks and Clark, *The Trust Problem.*

rules excessive prices are forbidden, but no attempt is made actually to fix prices by decree. The other, positive, way, in which control may be exercised, consists in the authoritative determination of definite maximum rates of charge or minimum provision of service. This way is illustrated by the terms of the charters usually accorded to companies operating public utility services under lease from city governments and by the power, conferred on the Interstate Commerce Commission by the Hepburn law of 1906, to "determine and prescribe" maximum rates for railway, telephone, and other services of communication.

§ 14. Whether the negative or the positive way of regulation is followed, some sort of sanction to make the law effective must be provided. This can be done in a variety of ways. Sometimes the penalty for breach is a direct money fine. Sometimes, in protected countries, for example in Brazil,[1] it consists in the withdrawal of duties on competing foreign goods. The Canadian Industrial Combines Investigation Act of 1910 provides for both sorts of penalty. If a statutory Commission "finds that there is a Combine, the Government may either lower or repeal the duties, and, in addition, impose a fine of 1000 dollars a day on those who continue in their evil courses after the judgment of the Board has been officially published."[2] Another interesting form of sanction is provided, as against the owners of vessels which violate any of the American anti-trust laws, by a clause in the Panama Canal Act of 1912 forbidding the use of the canal to their ships.[3] Sometimes the sanction consists in the threat of governmental competition. Thus, in connection with the 1892 agreement, by which the Post-Office took over the National Telephone Company's trunk lines, the Chancellor of the Exchequer hinted that the State, while securing its right to compete, would not be likely to exercise that right if the Company acted reasonably.[4] Sometimes, again, the sanction consists in the threat of State purchase, on terms either fixed beforehand or to be decided by arbitration, of the whole

---

[1] Cf. Davies, *Trust Laws and Unfair Competition*, p. 294.

[2] *Economist*, March 26, 1910, p. 665. Cf. *Annals of the American Academy,* July 1912, p. 152.

[3] Cf. Johnson and Huebner, *Principles of Ocean Transportation*, p. 386.

[4] H. Meyer, *Public Ownership and the Telephones*, pp. 56, 199.

of the plant of the regulated business. Sometimes, finally,—
and this, in effect, is what seems to be contemplated under the
authoritative interpretation of the Sherman Act, as given by
the United States Supreme Court in the Standard Oil Case
(1911)—combinations, whose price (and other) policy is found
to be reasonable, may be left undisturbed, but combinations
which use their power to the injury of the public may be
dissolved by order of the Court.[1]

§ 15. Though, however, many sanctions, some of them
of great force, are available when breaches of the law
are detected, it is necessary to add that, whether the
negative or the positive method of control is adopted,
it is exceedingly difficult to prevent people from escaping
these sanctions by evasion. Thus in the pre-war period our
railway companies, in effect, raised their rates without applying for the consent of the railway commissioners. Charges
for rent of sidings and so forth were created; the
number of articles which the companies refuse to carry
at owner's risk, unless packed to their satisfaction, was
increased; rebates were withdrawn; and other such devices
were employed.[2] But the kind of evasion which it is hardest
to deal with is that which meets price regulation by manipulating quality. To prevent this it is essential to couple
with rules about maximum price further rules about minimum quality. But in some things, such as the comfort and
punctuality of a tramway service, or the sanitary condition of
slaughter-houses and sewers, it is difficult to *define* a minimum
of quality. When there are a number of different grades of
quality, all of which have to be distinguished from one another
and subjected to a separate maximum price—different grades,
even of simple things like tea, and, still more, of complicated
things like hats—the difficulty of effective definition is
enormous. It is easy to sell a lower-grade thing at a higher-
grade price. In other things, such as water supply, gas
supply, milk supply and house accommodation, where tests
of quality are available to give a basis for definition, it may

[1] Cf. the judgment of Chief-Justice White, laying down in this case what
has now become known as "the rule of reason" in interpreting the Act (quoted
by Jenks and Clark, *The Trust Problem*, p. 299).

[2] Cf. *Railway Conference Report*, p. 57.

be difficult to *detect* departures from the stipulated minimum. Something can, no doubt, be done by an elaborate system of inspection, like that developed in support of the Adulteration of Food and Drugs Act, but the openings for evasion are, in any event, likely to be considerable.

§ 16. Even, however, if this difficulty could be completely overcome, the most formidable obstacle in the way of direct control would still remain. It is necessary to determine what prices shall be regarded as unreasonable, and, when the positive method of fixing maxima is adopted, what the maxima shall be. As was explained at the beginning of this chapter, the goal aimed at is the competitive price, *i.e.* the price which would have been arrived at if other things had been the same but the output had been that proper to simple competition instead of that proper to monopoly. In what way is this price to be ascertained by the controlling authority ? It is conceivable that some reader, thinking loosely upon recent experience, may claim that competitive prices could be determined directly from the recorded expenses of converting the raw material used into finished goods. Plainly, however, in order to get the *full* conversion costs, we need to know how much should be added to the cost of material and labour for the share due, for the article we are studying, to the standing charges of the business. Given a decision about that, we can, indeed, by conversion cost accounting—the technique of which was greatly developed during the war—determine the proper price for any particular product or group of joint products ;[1] but to proceed in the reverse direction is impossible. The calculation of conversion costs is a necessary step towards any practical scheme of price regulation. But it is a subordinate step.

§ 17. It seems clear that our problem can only be solved by some reference to a " normal " rate of return on investment. We know that, had the investment proper to competition been made, a price, which, on the then profitable output, would

---

[1] With joint products, of course, it is impossible to isolate separate costs of production, and the "proper" price for each of them will depend on the comparative demands for them severally as well as upon their cost of production jointly : a fact which still further complicates the task of any would-be price-fixer.

have yielded a normal return on this investment, would be the price we require. Unfortunately, however, the investment that actually has been made is not likely to be equal to that proper to competition. If the monopoly has been started *ab initio*, so to speak, it will be less than that proper to competition, and, if the monopoly is a result of a combination of unduly numerous concerns engaged in cut-throat competition, it will be greater than this. Clearly then the price we require is not the price that, with the output profitable in respect of the actual investment, would yield a normal return, unless it so happens that that price is equal to the price which would have yielded a normal return on the amount of investment proper to competition, had that amount been provided. This condition implies that the commodity with whose production we are concerned is one that, from a long period point of view, is produced under conditions of constant supply price. With a monopoly that has been started *ab initio*, if the commodity is produced under conditions of increasing supply price, the price that yields a normal return on actual investment will be too low; if it is produced under conditions of decreasing supply price, too high. In fact, as has already been observed, there is little likelihood of commodities subject to increasing supply price coming under monopolistic control. If then we calculate our " proper price," for control purposes, by reckoning what price would yield a normal return were the output most profitable at that price produced,[1] the figure we reach will, with a monopoly that has been started *ab initio*, probably be somewhat too high. With a monopoly that is the aftermath of excessive investment and cut-throat competition, it will, on the other hand, probably be too low. There is not, however, so far as I can see, any other way in which a figure can be calculated at all.[2]

[1] The careful reader will have noticed that, should the equipment possessed by the monopolist be larger than that proper to competition, it will not in fact be possible, at a price determined as above, to find a market for the whole of the output that it would be profitable to produce at that price. This fact, however, does not in any way impair the analysis of the text.

[2] The difficulty dealt with in the above section, which in earlier editions I had not noticed, was brought out in an illuminating article on "Control of Investment versus Control of Return" by Professor Knight in the *Quarterly Journal of Economics* for February 1930.

§ 18. If then, *faute de mieux*, we decide to make use of this way, it becomes necessary to determine what rate of profit, in any particular enterprise, the price of whose product has to be regulated, may rightly be considered normal. At first sight it might be thought that this issue can be settled fairly easily. Will not normal profit be such profit that, when allowance is made for earnings of management (as in joint stock companies is done automatically), what is left provides interest at the ordinary rate on the capital of the concern? This plausible suggestion is, however, easily shown to be very far from adequate. Let us, to begin with, suppose that the ordinary rate of interest really does correspond in all businesses to normal profits. We have still to determine what the capital is on which this ordinary rate is to be paid. Clearly we cannot interpret it as the market value of the concern, because, the market value of a business being simply the present value of its anticipated earnings, these earnings *must* yield the ordinary rate of interest on it, allowing for the particular risks involved, whatever sum they amount to. Indeed, if we were to take existing market value as our basis, since this depends on what people believe that the system of rate regulation will be, we should come perilously near to circular reasoning. Capital value, therefore, for rate control purposes, is something quite different from capital value for, say, taxation purposes. It must mean, in some sense, that capital which has in fact been invested in the business in the past. But this is not at all easy to calculate. When the sums of money invested in any concern include commission paid to a promoter for accomplishing a fusion, the advantage of which is expected to consist in the power to exact monopoly charges from the public, this commission ought not, it would seem, to be counted, except in so far as the fusion has also brought about increased productive efficiency. That this is an exceedingly important point becomes apparent when we learn that, according to high officials in some of the industrial combinations of the United States, " the cost of organisation, including the pay of the promoter and financier, amounts often to from 20 to 40 per cent of the total amount of stock issued."[1]

[1] Jenks and Clark, *The Trust Problem*, p. 90.

The same difficulty has to be faced as regards that part of the capital expenditure which has been employed in buying up existing concerns at a price enhanced by the hope that combination will make monopolistic action practicable. Apart from these difficult items, what we want to ascertain is the original capital expenditure, whether employed in physical construction, parliamentary costs, the purchase of patent rights or the upbuilding of a connection by advertisement, together with such later expenditure, in excess of the repairs and renewals required to keep the original capital intact, as has not been taken out again in earnings, allowance being made for the different dates of the various investments.[1] For new businesses, to be established in the future, it would be easy enough to secure by law that information about all these items should be made available. But for businesses already long established it may be impossible to get this information. For example, similar expenditures on good‑will and so forth, which one concern may have charged to capital, another will have treated as current expenditure, in such a way that it cannot practically be distinguished. In view of these difficulties some roundabout way of approximating to the truth may have to be employed. Obviously the nominal capital is quite useless for this purpose. It may have been watered and manipulated in ways that completely disguise the real facts. The market value of the capital we have already shown to be inappropriate. It is usual, therefore, to make use either of the estimated " cost of reproduction " of the concern's plant—which may be very misleading if the relevant prices have changed substantially since the original investment was made—or of a value ascertained by direct physical valuation of the plant—the amount of which will, of course, depend on the principles in accordance with which the valuation is made— ; and then to make some more or less arbitrary allowance for costs of promotion, investments to build up good-will, patent rights, and so on. These *data* are not wanted for themselves, but are supposed to enable a rough estimate to be made of the actual capital investment, when this is not directly ascer-

[1] Cf. Heilman, " Principles of Public Utility Valuation," *Quarterly Journal of Economics*, Feb. 1914, pp. 281-90.

tainable. To develop the difficulties of this process is outside my present purpose.[1]

§ 19. There remains a more fundamental complication. Up to this point it has been tacitly assumed that the capital invested in any concern is properly and unambiguously represented by the money invested in it. In actual fact, however, a real investment of 1000 days' labour may be measured by £200 if it happens to be made in one year, and by £400 or, in conceivable circumstances, by £400,000 if it happens to be made in another. In periods during which currencies are violently unstable, as in Russia and Germany after the war, this sort of difficulty inevitably becomes prominent. It is plain that real investment, and not money investment, is the fundamental thing, and that, therefore, in strictness, when general prices have changed, money investments ought, for our present purpose, to be written up or down so as to allow for this fact. This means revising all the records of past years and multiplying the money investment of each year by the ratio between the index number of general prices for that year and for the present time. In view of the acknowledged imperfections of existing index numbers, a device of this kind could hardly hope to win sufficient acceptance to make it practicable. When, as often happens, a substantial part of the investment in a concern has been made in the form of bonds or debentures, on which a fixed money interest is contracted for whatever happens to prices, it is open to a further serious objection. To allow a doubled gross money return to offset a doubling of prices would involve compensating the stockholders for the bondholders' losses as well as for their own and leaving the bondholders to bear their fate unaided.[2] None the less, to ignore altogether large and rapid changes in general prices, such as have resulted from the Great War, would be to accept and act upon a serious falsification of the facts. These considerations, taken in conjunction with those set out in the preceding paragraph, suffice to show that to determine what the capital of a concern

---

[1] Cf. Barker, *Public Utility Rates*, chapters v. and vi.

[2] Cf. Bauer, "Fair Value for Effective Rate Control," *American Economic Review*, December 1924, pp. 664-6.

is,'on which "ordinary" interest is to be allowed, is not an easy task.

§ 20. But this is not all. It is not true that the normal "competitive" profits of any enterprise are the profits that would yield the "ordinary" rate of interest on the capital that has actually been invested in that enterprise. For the establishment of different enterprises involves both different degrees of risk and different initial periods of development, during which no return at all is likely to be obtained; and appropriate compensation under these heads must be made to those investors—the only ones with whom the State can deal —whose enterprises turn out successfully, and who, therefore, must be paid enough to balance the losses of those who have failed.[1] This circumstance need not, indeed, be responsible for large practical difficulties in industries in which production has attained more or less of a routine character, but in all industries in an experimental stage it is of dominant import-ance.[2] Furthermore, even if there were no risks, we could not regard as proper prices which would yield the ordinary rate of interest in all circumstances, but only prices which would yield that rate, if the management, and, indeed, the actual organisation of the original investment also, were conducted with "ordinary" ability; and this is a vague and difficult con-ception. As Professor Taussig pertinently observes : "Every one knows that fortunes are made in industries strictly com-petitive, and are to be ascribed to unusual business capacity. . . . When a monopoly or quasi-monopoly secures high returns, how are we to separate the part attributable to monopoly from the part attributable to excellence in management ? "[3] To allow the same rate of return to companies which invest their

[1] Cf. Greene, *Corporation Finance*, p. 134.

[2] If a concern has been taken over by a company after the first stage of speculative adventure has been successfully passed, the purchase price will probably include a large sum above cost. This may be a fair remuneration for the risk taken and uncertainty borne. But clearly, after it has been paid, to allow the new company to reap profits which are both adjusted to the risks of the occupa-tion and also calculated upon a capital which includes the above sum, would be to compel the public to reward it for risk-taking for which it has not been re-sponsible, and recompense for which has already been made. For an excellent general discussion of good-will cf. Leake, *Good-will, its nature and how to value it*.

[3] *American Economy Review Supplement*, March 1913, p. 132.

capital wastefully as to those which invest it well plainly makes against economical production. Incidentally, if there were two competing combinations to be dealt with, it would logically require forcing the better managed one to charge lower prices than the other, an arrangement which would not only have awkward consequences at the moment but would effectively discourage good management. In this connection it should be noted that to extend combination further, so long as extension involves economies, is a form of good management, and a form that would be discouraged if prices were so regulated that no advantage were allowed to accrue to those who had brought it about. Finally, when a plant has been built to fit an expected future demand much in excess of the present demand, it would plainly be unreasonable to sanction rates high enough to yield a full return on the whole investment before that future demand has developed.[1] In view of these complications, and of the necessary limitations of its knowledge—for, as a rule, the controllers are bound to be much behind the controlled in technical experience—a public authority is almost certain either to exact too easy terms from the concerns it is seeking to control, and so to leave them with the power of simple monopoly, or to exact too hard terms, and so, though not permitting monopoly exaction to them, nevertheless to prevent the development of their industry to the point proper to simple competition. The British Tramways Act of 1870 appears to have failed in the latter way, and to have been responsible for prolonged delay in the development of electric traction in this country.

§ 21. It is evident that the difficulties, which are involved in determining what scale of return should be regarded as normal in any particular productive enterprise, complicate alike the negative way of control, under which the Legislature simply condemns unreasonable prices, leaving the Courts to decide whether any given price scheme is in fact unreasonable, and the positive way, which lays down definite price maxima. Plainly, however, they complicate the positive way more seriously than the other. An ordinary industrial concern produces a great number of different varieties of goods, the raw materials

---

[1] Cf. Hartman, *Fair Values*, p. 130 *et seq.*

for which are continually altering in cost, and the distinctive character of the finished product continually being modified. For any outside authority to draw up a schedule of permitted charges for a concern of this sort would be a hopeless task. On the other hand, for a trained Commission or judicial body, equipped, like the American Federal Trade Commission, to make full inquiries, it would not be impossible to decide in a broad way whether, taking one product with another and one time with another, some selected large combination—the Standard Oil Company, the United Steel Corporation, or another—was charging prices calculated to yield to it more than the return deemed in the circumstances to be reasonable. For industrial concerns in normal times no attempt has ever been made to go beyond this negative way, and it does not seem, at all events in the present condition of economic knowledge and governmental competence, that any such attempt either can, or should, be made. Imperfect as the results to be hoped for from the negative way are, they are better than would be got from a blundering struggle after the other. In public utility concerns, on the other hand, the excess difficulty of the positive over the negative way is slight. As a general rule, the service provided by these concerns is single and relatively simple—gas, water, electricity, transport of passengers. Not many separate prices —railway freight rates are, of course, a very important exception—have, therefore, to be fixed. Further, the demand is generally unaffected by fashion, and equipment plays so large a part in the cost that changes in the price of raw material do not very greatly matter. Finally, even if these things were otherwise, the nature of the goods sold and the convenience of customers make it very desirable that the prices charged should not undergo frequent change. In these concerns, therefore, the positive way of control by fixing maximum prices has generally been adopted.

§ 22. When this is done, it becomes imperative to seek out the best means of guarding against the two opposite sorts of error, undue laxness and undue harshness, to which, as was shown in § 20, all forms of regulation are in practice inclined. For this purpose one device sometimes recommended is to put up the licence to operate certain public utility services to a kind of auction. This plan allows the persons most interested themselves to present estimates of terms which they would reckon profitable. It has been described thus : " According to the best plan now in vogue, the City sells the franchise for constructing the works to the company, which bids to furnish water at the lowest rates under definitely specified conditions, the franchise being sometimes perpetual, but often granting to the City at some future date an option for the purchase of the works." Since, however, in many cities, the companies capable of making tenders will be very few in number, and since, furthermore, their own estimates must be largely tentative, the adoption of this device is not incompatible with large errors. The likelihood of error is made greater by the fact that the conditions of most industries are continually changing, in such wise that the scheme of price-regulation, which is proper at one time, necessarily becomes improper at another.

§ 23. A further effort at limiting the range of error can be made through arrangements under which the regulations imposed are submitted to periodical revision. Franchises "cannot be fixed, or justly fixed, for all time, owing to rapidly changing conditions."[1] With the growth of improvements and so on, it may well happen that a maximum price designed to imitate competitive conditions will, after a while, stand above the price that an unrestricted monopolist would find it profitable to charge, and will, therefore, be altogether ineffective. "The public should retain in all cases an interest in the growth and profits of the future."[2] A provision for periodic revision in a franchise may, however, by creating uncertainty, restrict investment in the industry concerned to an extent that is injurious to the national dividend. Further, if the revision is to occur at fixed intervals, it may tempt companies, shortly before the close of one of these intervals, to hold back important developments till after the revision has taken place, lest a large part of their fruits

---

[1] Bemis, *Municipal Monopolies*, p. 32.
[2] *Municipal and Private Operation of Public Utilities*, vol. i. p. 24.

should be taken away in the form of lowered prices;[1] and this difficulty cannot be wholly overcome by clauses stipulating for the introduction of such technical improvements as are, from time to time, invented elsewhere. One way of meeting these dangers is to hedge round the revising body with conditions designed to defend the company's interest. For example, the Railway Act of 1844 provided that, if dividends exceeded 10 per cent on the paid-up capital after twenty-one years from the sanctioning of the lines, the Lords of the Treasury might revise tolls, fares, etc., on the condition that they guaranteed a 10 per cent dividend for the next twenty-one years. Another way is to make the revision period so far distant from the date at which an undertaking is initiated that the effect upon investment due to the anticipation of it will be very small. It is evident that, just in so far as either of these lines of defence is adopted, the efficacy of revision, as a means of lessening the gap between actual regulation and ideal regulation, is diminished. But, if regulation is to be attempted at all, the retention by the State of revising powers in some form is absolutely essential. It would seem that this could be provided for without imposing a serious check either on investment or on enterprise, if the principles on which the revision would proceed were clearly laid down and understood. The revisers might be instructed at each revision period to fix a price—or, when they have to do with joint products, several adjusted prices— sufficiently high to continue to the company a fair rate on their total real investment, account being taken of the fact that the capital turned into it in the first instance was probably subject to great risk, while that added subsequently needs a less reward under this head. They might be instructed further, in deciding what constitutes a fair return, to consider generally the quality of management that has been displayed, fixing prices to yield higher returns when the management has been good than when it has been indifferent or bad. No doubt, the technical difficulty of this kind of revision would be exceedingly great, but it

---

[1] Cf. Whitten, *Regulation of Public Service Companies in Great Britain*, p. 224.

would not be nearly so great as that of the initial regulation. It is not unreasonable to suppose that a class of official might eventually be evolved whose decision on such matters, when founded on adequate comparative statistics, would at once deserve and command the confidence of would-be investors. Such investors would have the consolation of knowing that, while, on the one hand, the price of their product was liable to enforced reduction, on the other hand, if costs of material and labour went against them, it might be raised in their favour.

§ 24. Yet another device designed to limit the range of error remains. In all ordinary industries many variations in the costs of material and so forth occur *within* the successive revision periods. If the guidance of simple competition is to be followed, such variations should be accompanied by variations in the prices charged to consumers. No doubt, where, as in railway service, the technical inconvenience of constantly changing prices would be very great, it may, on the whole, be best not to follow this guidance for short-period movements ; but such cases are probably rare. Attempts are sometimes made by controlling authorities to organise the required price variations by some sort of self-adjusting arrangement. A crude method, which has been applied to some gas companies in this country, is to fix a *maximum* dividend. If the competence of the management remains constant, this implies that, when costs fall beyond a certain point, the prices charged to consumers must also fall. This method, however, has the grave disadvantage that it is likely, so soon as it becomes operative, to cut away the normal motives for skill and care in management and for avoidance of waste. A less crude method is to lay down a standard of earnings, always to allow prices to be charged high enough to yield this standard, and to provide further that, when this standard is passed, a defined proportion of the balance shall be used to reduce prices, while the remainder is left to augment earnings. In the South Metropolitan Gas Company's Act of 1920 there is an arrangement of this kind, three-quarters of whatever balance there may be over standard earnings being allotted to consumers. Railway rates in this country are now governed on a somewhat similar plan. The Railways Act, 1921, lays down for each amalgamated company a *standard income*, based on the earnings of 1913 with allowances for new investments, and so forth. If experience shows that the rates of charge fixed by the Rates Tribunal yield, or could, with efficient and economical management, have yielded, an income greater than the standard income, the Rates Tribunal are instructed to reduce the rates of charge " so as to effect the reduction of the net income of the company in subsequent years to an extent equivalent to 80 per cent of such excess "; and, if the net income actually yielded turns out to be less than the standard income together with appropriate allowances for new capital, the tribunal shall increase the rates of charge to bring it up to this amount, provided that the deficiency is not due to lack of efficiency or economy in the management. Plainly, under this arrangement the discouragement to skill and economy will be smaller than it would be under a maximum dividend plan *after* the maximum has been reached; but, in view of the extreme difficulty that any tribunal must find in adjudicating as to efficiency and economy in management, it is bound to be greater than it would be under that plan *before* the maximum has been reached. Yet a third method is that of connecting changes in the dividend paid to share-holders during any licence period with changes in selling price by means of a sliding scale. Illustrations of this method are furnished in a number of English Acts of Parliament dealing with gas companies. One pre-war Act, for example, fixed a standard price of 3s. 9d. per thousand cubic feet, and provided that, for every penny put on or off that price, the company might, when there are reductions, and must, when there were increases, move the dividend up or down a quarter per cent. Another illustration is furnished by the Act governing the Lancashire Power Company, which furnishes electricity in bulk. This Act " provides for a dividend of 8 per cent and an additional 1·25 per cent reduction in price for every 0·25 per cent increase of dividend above 8 per cent, in respect of every 5 per cent charged below the maximum price allowed by the Act." [1]   Sliding scales of this kind—

---

[1] H. Meyer, *Municipal Ownership in Great Britain*, p. 281.

which, if they are to be effective, must, of course, be combined with Government control over the issue of new capital by the companies concerned—are, like sliding scales of wages, not substitutes for, but complements to, a system of periodic revision of the licence terms; for, if they were treated as permanent arrangements, all improvements and discoveries that reduced cost of production, whether made by the concerns themselves or by others, would steadily and continuously enhance profits.   They are not easily organised for new companies, because the appropriate standards of price and dividend cannot be determined till some experience has been gained of the working of a concern.   But it is feasible, and before the war it was the practice of the Board of Trade in dealing with gas companies, to fix a simple maximum price at first and to reserve power to substitute a sliding scale after the lapse of a certain interval.[1]   These scale arrangements, like the other methods discussed above, are open to the [objection that they push prices up, not only when the costs of raw materials and labour rise, but equally when the profits of a company are reduced by incompetent management. In spite, however, of these difficulties, sliding scales—and the same thing may be said of the standard earnings plan —may be expected, when carefully constructed, to make possible a nearer approach to the system of prices proper to simple competition than would be possible under any plan that, over the intervals between revision periods, fixed prices rigidly.   Moreover, the danger of discouraging competent management may be met to some extent by provisions, such as those embodied in the British railway law, under which the controlling authority is allowed to veto an increase of charges when falling earnings appear to be the result, not of natural causes, but of incompetence.

§ 25. It should be added that arrangements of the kind I have been describing, though they may make fair provision for adjusting charges within the revision periods to variations in the cost of raw materials, and so forth, are extremely ill-fitted to cope with variations in demand; for, whereas, if simple

[1] Cf. Whitten, *Regulation of Public Service Companies in Great Britain*, p. 129.

competition is to be followed, upward movements of demand —we are here, of course, only concerned with short-period fluctuations—should be associated with upward movements of price, under these arrangements they will be associated with downward movements of price. Demand variations, moreover, may be very important, and may call for large associated price variations. With given demand variations, the extent of these should be especially great in industries where the part played by supplementary costs—which are not reduced proportionately when output is reduced—is large relatively to the part played by prime costs: and supplementary costs are, in fact, very important in the generality of industries. It might be possible to take account of variations in demand, as well as of variations in cost, by a scale system that should link up permitted changes in price with changes in the volume of service supplied, instead of with changes in earnings. So far as I am aware, however, no self-acting system of this kind is as yet anywhere in operation.

§ 26. There remains another difficulty of a different order. The main part of what has been said so far has tacitly assumed that, in framing our control policy, we start with a clear table. For industrial monopolies that come into being after the general lines of our policy have been fixed, and for public utility corporations upon which conditions are imposed at the time when the original franchise is granted, this is, of course, true. But, in so far as we have to do with monopolistic concerns over which at present control is either not exercised at all or exercised in a very imperfect manner, the case is different. To bring these concerns now under a system of price regulation of the type that we are contemplating would, in many instances, involve a large reduction in their income and in the capital value of their shares. So far as original shareholders or persons who have inherited from them are concerned, this does not greatly matter. The fact that these persons have made abnormal profits in the past is no reason why they should be allowed to do so in the future. But the position is different with recent purchasers of shares, whose purchase price has been regulated by the conditions ruling before control, or the strict form of control here contemplated, was seriously thought about. Such persons may perhaps be getting now, say 8 per cent on their money, and control may knock this down to 5 per cent, reducing the value of their capital by one-third or even one-half. To make regulations that will strike with cruel severity on arbitrarily selected groups of perfectly innocent persons is not a thing to be lightly undertaken. There are limits to the right of the State to ride rough-shod over legitimate expectations. And yet to refrain from control that ought to be imposed, because we neglected our duty in not imposing it before, is to enslave ourselves to past mistakes. Surrender to the " widows and orphans " argument means, in substance, abandonment of reform. No perfect solution of this conflict can be hoped for. But it would seem a reasonable compromise, and one adequately careful of vested interests, to provide that, when the sudden introduction of a full measure of price control on the principles indicated above would greatly depress values, this control should only be introduced after an interval of notice, and then by gradual steps.

§ 27. Even, however, if this somewhat special difficulty be left out of account, the preceding general review makes it evident that, under any form of State control over private monopoly—and it should be noticed that, though the examples cited have to do only with special kinds of private monopoly, the argument refers to all kinds—a considerable gap between the ideal and the actual is likely to remain. The method of control, whether positive or negative, is, in short, an exceedingly imperfect means of approximating industry towards the price level and output proper to simple competition. Moreover, it is apt to prove a costly method. As Professor Durand observes : " Government regulation of prices and profits of private concerns always involves a large element of waste, of duplication of energy and cost. It means that two sets of persons are concerning themselves with the same work. The managers and employees of the corporation must study cost accounting and conditions of demand in determining price policy. The officers and employees of the Government must follow and do it all over again. Moreover, the fact that these two sets of persons have different motives in approaching their work means friction and litigation, and these spell further expense. To superimpose a vast governmental machinery upon the vast machinery of private business is an extravagance, which should be avoided if it is possible to do so." [1] This consideration is one that ought not to be ignored. The expense involved in public supervision should be debited against the system of private enterprise in monopolistic industries before the real efficiency of this system is brought into comparison with the rival system of public enterprise.

[1] *Quarterly Journal of Economics*, 1914, pp. 674-5 ; and *The Trust Problem*, p. 57.

CHAPTER XXII

§ 1. In earlier chapters of this book it has been shown that private enterprise left to itself, even when it operates under conditions of simple competition, often leads to a distribution of resources less favourable to the national dividend than some other possible distributions. In some occupations the value of the marginal private net product of the resources employed is less than the value of the marginal social net product, with the result that too little is invested; in other industries the value of the marginal private net product is the larger, and too much is invested; in yet others the exercise of monopoly power contracts output, and investment falls much below what the public interest requires. When competition rules and social and private net product at the margin diverge, it is theoretically possible to put matters right by the imposition of a tax or the grant of a subsidy; when monopoly rules, it is theoretically possible to render it innocuous by the regulation of price,—in conjunction, in some circumstances, with the regulation of output. The preceding discussion, however, has made it plain that to counter the bias of private interest in these ways must prove in practice an extraordinarily difficult task, and one which cannot be carried through completely. Hence the question arises whether, other things being equal, it would not be better for public authorities themselves to operate certain classes of undertaking instead of trying to control their operation by private enterprise.

§ 2. It must be clearly understood that the issue here raised concerns public operation, not public ownership.

Public ownership by itself, and apart from any distributional change that may have come about if the ownership has been acquired without the payment of full compensation, means very little. Suppose, for example, that a municipality raises a loan of a million pounds in order to establish an electric supply works, interest to be paid at 5 per cent and the principal to be paid off in fifty years through a sinking fund. The legal position will be that the municipality owns the works from the moment they are built, subject to what is, in effect, a mortgage to the fundholders. If a private syndicate had put up money, built the works, and loaned them to the municipality on terms involving exactly the same charges to the municipality and providing for the works to pass into its possession after fifty years, the syndicate would, during those fifty years, be the owner. But, granted that the municipality was free to do what it chose with the works, whether by altering them or adding to them, the real position would be exactly the same on this as on the other plan. The distinction between public ownership and private ownership would be a mere technicality of no practical effect. In like manner, if a public authority lends a million pounds to a private concern at 5 per cent perpetual interest to enable it to build an electric works, the real position is exactly the same as if it built the works itself and let them to a private concern at a perpetual interest of equal amount: but under the former plan the private concern, and under the latter the public body, is technically owner. There is a difference in form, but identity in substance. Between public operation and private operation, on the other hand, there is always and necessarily a fundamental difference of substance.

§ 3. In view of the many technical difficulties, to which attention has been called in the preceding chapter, in the way of the effective exercise of public control over private industry, the case for public operation, at all events in industries with a tendency towards monopoly, is, from the point of view of a right distribution of national resources among different occupations, a very strong one. It remains very strong in spite of the fact that, as is alleged to have happened with Government railways in certain democratically governed States, it may be perverted to satisfy local and sectional, or even personal, ends;[1] for this danger has been substantially lessened by the invention of extra-parliamentary "commissions," as described in Chapter XX., for working public enterprises. But the comparative effect of public control and public operation upon the right distribution of national resources among different occupations is not the only thing we have to consider in making our choice between them. Other things besides this are involved, just as other things were involved in our comparison between voluntary Purchasers' Associations and ordinary commercial businesses. We are not entitled to assume without argument that the economies of production will be the same under public operation and private operation. It may be that public operation is less economical than private operation, even when private firms are subject to public control. If this is so, the disadvantages of public operation as regards economical production have to be balanced against its advantages as regards the distribution of resources among different occupations. Hence, before any real answer to our question can be attempted, it is necessary to undertake some comparison of public with private operation from the standpoint of productive efficiency.

§ 4. It will be well at the outset to clear out of the way two arguments drawn from the experience of the war, which are based on a loose use of the term efficiency and are not really relevant.

First, it has been argued as follows: " If the individualist principle is the right thing, then it was manifestly absurd in war time to do what the Government did, for example in taking over the railways. If divided railway control was efficient, why interfere with it; why not carry on as usual? What was there in the way of moving trains and men that was not the proper business of railway companies, and why, then, were they 'interfered with'? If it becomes obviously necessary to mobilise railways in war to move some hundreds of thousands or millions of men, why is it not necessary to mobilise railways in peace to move to the best advantage nearly three hundred million tons of coal in a year—the

[1] Cf. Acworth, *State Railway Ownership*, p. 103.

coal which is the very life-blood of British industry ? " [1] This reasoning assumes that the State took over the railways in war time in order to render them technically more efficient. In fact it took them over in order to ensure that the Government should have full command over their lines and equipment, and should not have to do without services it needed on account of conflicting claims from private persons. Normally railways, like all other concerns that sell their output for money, allocate that output in accordance with the effective monetary demand of their various customers. In war time it was obviously necessary to scrap effective monetary demand as the directing factor in the distribution of railway services among rival customers. The fact that this was done with general agreement is no proof that any one considered railways to be technically less efficient, i.e. to require a greater real cost to obtain a given result, under private than under public management.

Secondly, an analogous argument has been built up to prove that the establishment of national munition factories enabled the Government to obtain its supplies enormously more cheaply than it could have done, and was in fact doing, from private firms. But the circumstances of the war were such that the private sellers of munitions, faced with an unlimited Government demand, were able to exact prices very greatly in excess of their own cost of production. Such a state of affairs does, indeed, provide a strong argument for national action, but the fact that a national shell-works can produce shells at a less cost than the price that a private works can force the Government to pay is no proof that it is technically more efficient. Technical efficiency concerns real costs of production, not sale prices fixed under conditions of shortage or conditions of monopoly. I do not here raise the question whether, in fact, cost of production was less in Government than in private shell factories. Whether it was so or not, it certainly cannot be proved to have been so by a comparison of the costs of production in Government factories with the selling price of private factories. This argument, like the preceding, therefore, falls to the ground.

[1] Chiozza Money, *The Triumph of Nationalization*, pp. 86-7.

§ 5. Another negative proposition of a general character may be set down. This is that attempts to conduct such a comparison by reference to statistics are foredoomed to failure. No doubt, if it could be shown that, *other conditions being the same*, a given output was, in general, obtained at greater, or at less, real cost under public than under private management, genuine evidence about the relative efficiency of the two forms of organisation would be obtained. But in real life this is impracticable. In the first place, the quality of services, which are called by the same name, varies enormously in different places, and it is almost impossible properly to allow for these variations. " Our street cars," say the Reporters of the American Civic Federation, " run faster, carry more strap passengers, and kill and injure more people than the street cars, public or private, of any other country. Our people seem to like this, but the English would not." [1] How can differences of this sort possibly be taken into account ? Again, the conditions of production in different places are utterly different. " In Syracuse (U.S.A.) the water flows to the city by gravity; in Indianapolis it must be pumped." [2] " To compare a private corporation within the limits of a great city, where an immense supply is furnished, and where special conditions of non-interference with adjoining property rights are to be met, with some municipal plant in a suburban town, upon a basis of the relative amount of supplies and labour required per unit of electrical energy, would obviously be unfair to both contestants. Nor is it possible to compare in this manner two lighting-stations having approximately the same yearly output, and which are similarly located with reference to adjoining interests, but are situated, the one in the North and the other in the South, for the reason that the daily period of service will vary in these two localities on account of variation in the hours of darkness. For the same reason we cannot compare the summer service of one station with the winter service of another, even though we should attempt to reduce them both to a common basis by obtaining the amount of human effort employed per unit of electrical

[1] *Municipal and Private Operation of Public Utilities*, vol. i. p. 287.
[2] *Ibid.* vol. i. p. 21.

energy." [1] In short, arguments from statistics, even apart
from the pitfalls with which unwary inquirers are confronted
in the interpretation of municipal accounts,[2] are, in this
field, almost entirely valueless. This remark is of general
application. But, in view of the exceptional psychological
conditions of war time and the temporary use by government
of a large number of able men normally engaged in private
business, as well as of the fact that the commodities produced
in government factories during the war were for State use
and not for the market, it has very special relevance to
arguments drawn from the experiences of the war period.

§ 6. Statistical evidence being thus inadequate, it is
necessary to proceed—again as in our study of voluntary
Purchasers' Associations—by way of general considerations.
Let us begin by comparing public operation with *uncontrolled*
private operation. There is general agreement that, when
conditions are such as to allow of small scale production by
private businesses, the personal interest of the head of the
business in its success provides a stimulus to efficiency that is
lacking in both joint stock private concerns and in public
concerns. Over a large field of industry, however, the
practical choice is, not between private businesses and
public concerns, but between joint stock companies and public
concerns. Here the initiative, freedom and interest of the
captain of industry working his own comparatively small
business cannot be had in any event. The issue is a different
and more evenly balanced one. The discussion of it may
well be started with an observation of the Committee of
the American Civic Federation : " There are no particular
reasons why the financial results from private or public
operation should be different if the conditions are the same." [3]
The reason for this remark, of course, is that, whether a
service is provided by a private company or by a public
governmental authority, the actual running of the business
must be similar. An expert staff must be appointed, controlled in a general way, in the one case by a committee of

---

[1] Bemis, *Municipal Monopolies*, pp. 289-90.

[2] Cf., *inter alia*, Knoop, *Principles and Methods of Municipal Trading*,
chap. v.

[3] *Municipal and Private Operation of Public Utilities*, vol. i. p. 23.

directors chosen by the shareholders, in the other case by a committee, a commission, a council, a ministerial department, or an *ad hoc* body like the Port of London Authority, to represent the public. Managing power, as a whole, may be conceived as distributed among electors, directors—or committee, or whatever the controlling authority is—and staff. There seem no general *a priori* grounds for holding, without reference to the special nature of the controlling organisations evolved under them, that either public or private management is likely to prove technically the more efficient.

§ 7. In some matters of slight, but not negligible, importance experience suggests that the public authority has an advantage. This advantage is analogous to one found in productive co-operation. It is that, for a given sum of money, a more efficient engineer or manager can be obtained than will be forthcoming under private management, for the reason that the position of a public servant is at once attractive in itself and also makes appeal to altruistic motives; or, alternatively, that an engineer or manager of given efficiency can be obtained for a smaller sum of money. This advantage, it must be clearly understood, is a real advantage, and not a kind of bounty obtained at the expense of the engineer or manager; for there is created a new value in the extra satisfaction which the said engineer or manager derives from the fact of serving the public. The difference between what a man of given ability would have been willing to work for in a private company and what he does work for in a State department is, in effect, extra product due to the adoption of the public form of industrial organisation. This difference is not, of course, equivalent to the difference between the earnings of the head of a State department and those of the head of a private business, because in the earnings of the latter there is generally included a return for " waiting " and " uncertainty-bearing,"—services which in the public departments are provided by the tax-payer. It is fallacious to take the excess of the income of an American railway king over that of the administrator of the Prussian State railways in pre-war days as a measure of the comparative wastefulness of private enterprise. Still there is, *pro tanto*, an advantage on the side of public operation in the fact that good technical experts under it cost less.

§ 8. A more important matter is the business capacity of the authority above the technical managers which determines general policy. In municipal undertakings this authority is generally a committee of the town council—a body whose members are elected for their political, rather than for their commercial, qualifications, and are also more liable than the directors of a company to lose their seats at short intervals. There is the further difficulty that the employees of a municipal enterprise may play an important part in electing councillors. This may lead some councillors to interfere for political reasons with the disciplinary and other discretionary powers of the higher officials. It has even been suggested that in some towns city engineers have been hindered by the council from introducing labour-saving devices, by which the employment of some of the councillors' electors would be threatened.[1]

In national undertakings run by a government department the higher authority is a body of civil servants technically subordinate to a political head responsible to Parliament. Through this political head, pressure of various sorts, some of it probably anti-social in character, can be exercised on the running of the undertaking. But, even if this does not happen, the civil service organisation, no doubt excellent for the purposes for which it is primarily designed, is apt to cramp efficiency. When important decisions have to be taken there is a tradition of method in government offices that makes for delay, hesitancy and immobility.[2] Thus Mr. Justice

---

[1] *Municipal and Private Operation of Public Utilities,* vol. i. p. 23.

[2] Mr. Hawtrey writes : "Substitute a functionary for an independent trader, and he finds himself precluded from doing anything which he cannot explain and defend if called upon, to his official superior. . . . The practical judgment is partly sub-conscious, and, in so far as it is conscious, its mental processes are not *linguistic.* To express in language even the decision itself is an effort ; to express the grounds on which it is taken would often be a formidable exercise in both psychology and literary composition. . . . There is a tendency for any official hierarchy to be limited to those decisions that can be readily communicated in language from one functionary to another. . . . An enlightened bureaucracy would try by every available means to escape from this paralysing limitation, and to devolve and decentralise whenever possible. But the limitation is inherent in the system and cannot be avoided altogether" (*The Economic Problem,* pp. 339-40).

Sankey, in his report on the coal mining industry, speaks of "the present Civil Service system of selection and promotion by length of service, of grades of servants, of minuting copies and reports from one servant to another, and of salaries and pensions." In pure routine work this system may do no harm, but, when enterprise and quick decisions are necessary, it cannot fail to prove hampering both in the choice of the most suitable man for a given work and in the actual carrying on of work. It should be noted that this consideration is very much less important in concerns producing exclusively, as, in war time especially, certain concerns do, for government; for work of this kind must be done on order, and there is no scope for that forecasting of the market in which government departments are commonly supposed to be inferior to private businesses or joint stock companies. Thus Professor Lehfeldt has well observed: "Anyone—government, company or individual—who can take over the whole output of a factory may well be justified in setting one up for himself; but the ordinary factory has to sell its products and to find customers: that is quite a different matter." [1] In this connection the early history of telegraphic communication is interesting. The semaphore system of optical telegraphy invented at the end of the eighteenth century was taken up by the French Government for military use, confined to that use, and worked by the government exclusively. In 1845 the French Government, in a like spirit and for a like purpose, started an electric telegraph. "The public authorities felt a need of their own, and, finding no one else to supply it for them, set to work to supply it for themselves. . . . Public ownership of telegraphs in the beginning was not, strictly speaking, a manifestation of the spirit of business enterprise. It was simply a branch of the public administration, forced upon the government by the lack of private enterprise." [2] When an industry is chiefly engaged in producing things for the consumption of the general public, the call for prevision and constructive speculation is, of course, much greater, and, therefore, the defects of civil service methods correspondingly more marked.

---

[1] *Economics in the Light of War*, p. 26.
[2] Holcombe, *Public Ownership of Telephones on the Continent of Europe*, p. 21.

It is coming, however, more and more to be realised that the public operation of national undertakings does not necessarily imply that these undertakings are run by a government department organised on civil service principles. The Port of London Authority is a special authority working quite differently from a government department. Canada has created the Canadian National Railways Company, with the government as the only shareholder, but with business directors appointed like ordinary directors and endowed with complete freedom of management.[1] The proposals of the Sankey Commission also aimed at setting up an authority for coal mining, which, though national, should nevertheless be run in the main on non-bureaucratic and non-political lines. Consumers' representatives were to be associated with the management, as is already done in the national telephone service of Switzerland.[2] A comparison of a body of this type with the directorate of a joint stock company might well work out more favourably than a comparison of, say, the body ruling the Post Office with such a directorate. Plainly, it is impossible to generalise on this matter of business competence, apart from a knowledge of the detailed organisation under which it is proposed that particular public undertakings should be run.

§ 9. So far governmental operation has been set against *uncontrolled* private or joint stock operation. In practice, however, as has already been made clear, where public operation is a live issue, the alternative is *controlled* private or joint stock operation. Control must hamper that initiative which is the chief merit of private enterprise, and the extent to which it hampers it will be greater the more far-reaching is the control. If it goes so far as to settle the things to be produced and the method of production, it will hamper initiative greatly. If, on the other hand, it does not extend beyond fixing a maximum price with a liberal margin, or even

---

[1] Acworth, *State Railway Ownership*, p. 12. The directors are, however, only appointed for one year, and it is, therefore, in the power of the government at any time to make the management, in effect, political by choosing directors subservient to itself.

[2] Cf. Holcombe, *Public Ownership of Telephones on the Continent of Europe*, p. 252.

fixing a sliding scale of profits and prices in combination, as under some gas company charters, it will, of course, hamper initiative much less. It is, thus, not possible to compare the technical efficiency of government operation and of controlled private operation in general terms, because controlled private operation may mean any one of a great number of different things—just, indeed, as, on the showing of preceding sections, government operation itself may also do. The only broad inference to which we are entitled is that, as between government operation and controlled private operation, a comparison of technical efficiency is likely to be somewhat more favourable to government operation than it would be as against uncontrolled private operation.

§ 10. This somewhat impotent conclusion does not, however, exhaust the discussion. There remain three important groups of considerations which, when we look beyond mere technical competence, tend to suggest that public operation is likely—not, of course, always, but as a general rule—to be inferior, from the standpoint of the dividend, to public control. The first of these has to do with the fact that, not only different producers within the same industry, but also different producers in apparently disconnected industries, are often, in reality, rivals. No doubt, an industry can be imagined which is monopolistic in the widest possible sense, in such wise that not only are there no competing firms within it, but also there are no competing industries outside it. There is some reason to believe that the service of supplying a modern city with water is monopolistic in this sense. It would be possible, by combining together a number of industries that are now separate, to create other monopolies of the same sort. For example, the various means of communication, such as omnibuses, trams, motor cars and carriages, might all conceivably be brought together under one hand. The same thing might conceivably be done with all the means of providing artificial light or all the means of providing power. But such arrangements are quite out of relation to actual facts. As things are at present, I should doubt if any industry, except that of water supply, can properly be regarded as monopolistic in the wide sense here taken. Now, the interest of the national dividend requires that, where a number of establishments, whether in the same industry or in different industries, are competing for the supply of some public need, that one which can supply it most efficiently shall oust the others. But, when any enterprise is operated by a public authority, it is likely to be maintained by artificial support, even though it is less efficient than its rivals. The reason is that persons in control of such an enterprise, being naturally anxious to make that enterprise a success, tend to identify the good of the whole with the good of their own department. Hence a government authority embarked on a business is almost certain, if it prove commercially weak, to employ unfair weapons from its non-commercial armoury, the use of which will maintain it more or less permanently in being, despite the fact that its productive methods are more costly than those of its rivals. These unfair methods are of two sorts, according as they are directed primarily to defend the government enterprise or to obstruct its competitors.

Defensive non-commercial methods consist, in the main, in the conscious or unconscious practice of devices for securing a differential bounty from the general public. A government authority, which is engaged partly in business and partly in rendering general unremunerated services, may charge expenses that really belong to the business against the other part of its work. A very glaring example is the practice of the London County Council in writing down the value of land purchased for workmen's dwellings to the value which it has, not in the general market, but as ear-marked for this particular purpose. Again, municipal tramway accounts may be given a false appearance of prosperity by the device of charging expenditure upon roads, which is properly attributable to them, to the general road account.[1] A like device is adopted in a milder form when a municipality fails to set aside a special fund to balance the advantage it possesses over private enterprise in being able to borrow money on easier terms. "A municipality can float bonds at a lower rate of interest than a private company, since the whole assessable

---

[1] *Municipal and Private Operation of Public Utilities*, vol. i. p. 469.

property of the town is generally liable for the payment of interest and principal, while the company can give security only on the works."[1] This ability on the part of a municipality is thus due, in the main, simply to the fact that it is able to force upon the ratepayers an obligation to pay its bondholders even if the enterprise fails, while a private company has, by the offer of higher pay, to obtain debenture holders who are prepared, in the event of failure, to lose their money. Except in so far as the fear of failure, and, therefore, the extra compensation asked for by debenture holders, is due to public ignorance of facts which are more readily ascertainable in connection with municipalities than with companies[2]—to that extent municipal operation effects a small real saving—the social cost of the municipality's cheap loan is the same as that of the company's relatively dear loan. If the two enterprises are to compete fairly, the municipality ought to transfer to the rates the bulk of its gain from better credit, before balancing the accounts of its business. If it does not do this, it is, in effect, assisting that business by a contribution from the general public. In so far as the lower terms on which it can engage managers and engineers are due to the fact that the shouldering of risks by the ratepayers safeguards them against the possibility of their employers going bankrupt, it is doing the same thing a second time, unless it transfers the gain made under this head also to the rates. Of course, if a municipally managed undertaking, *on account of superior efficiency*, is less likely to make a loss than a corresponding private concern, there is a real gain. But, since, in any event, there is the gilt-edged guarantee of the ratepayers, that gain is not reflected in the better terms on which the municipality can borrow.

Aggressive non-commercial methods are made possible by the fact that public authorities, besides operating their own

[1] Bemis, *Municipal Monopolies*, p. 45.

[2] The advantage available for municipal enterprise, thus hinted at, turns upon the fact that, when people invest in any undertaking through an intermediary, they always face the possibility that this intermediary may prove to be dishonest and unwilling to fulfil his obligations. The uncertainty-bearing undertaken in this way is a real element in the cost of production. When the State is the intermediary, its honesty and financial strength are, in general, so well known that this element is practically eliminated.

enterprises, are often also endowed with powers of control over other enterprises. When they are in this position, there is a grave danger that the public authorities may be tempted to use their powers of control in such a way as to obstruct and injure rivals. An Education Authority, for example, which both runs schools of its own and makes regulations for the running of rival schools, is under strong temptation. So is an authority which at once builds houses and frames building bye-laws; and so also are municipalities operating gas-lighting or tramways and controlling electric-lighting or motor omnibuses. Among the methods of aggression open to them perhaps the simplest is that of making the conditions about sinking funds, under which their own establishments work, more favourable than the conditions about purchase at the end of the lease, which are imposed upon private companies. A public authority, which provides a sinking fund to extinguish the capital debt of its enterprise, as well as a fund to cover depreciation and obsolescence, is, in effect, taxing its present citizens for the benefit of posterity.[1] In like manner, a public authority, which confers a franchise on a private company upon condition that the company's plant shall pass to itself at the end of the lease, either free of charge or at "cost of replacement," is imposing a similar tax. It is readily seen that the terms of sinking funds and franchises respectively *can* be so arranged that the burden under the sinking fund is the smaller, and, therefore, that private operation suffers, as against the rival system, a differential injury.

There are, however, grosser forms of aggression than the above. It is notorious that those municipalities which operated their own gas-plant vigorously obstructed, by the exercise of their veto and in other ways, the development of electric-lighting companies. Again: "Since 1898 the desire to protect the local municipal electric light plants has been permitted to impede the spread of the so-called electricity-in-bulk generating and distributing companies."[2] In like manner,

---

[1] The Board of Agriculture has made a new departure in not requiring the County Councils to charge small holders, who hire land from them, rents high enough to provide this kind of sinking fund.—[Cd. 4245], p. 12.

[2] H. Meyer, *Public Ownership and the Telephones*, p. 351.

the central government, in order to protect its telegraph monopoly, has placed administrative obstacles in the way of other means of electrical communication. In 1884 the Postmaster-General declined to allow the National Telephone Company to receive or deliver a written message at any of its offices, and, in defending this course, said: " It would make, I am afraid, a serious hole in the telegraph revenue, if written messages were allowed to be sent."[1] In like manner, in Norway, when (in 1881) a company sought a licence to establish a long-distance telephone between Drammen and Christiania, the Government made it a condition that the company should guarantee to make good " all losses occasioned to its (the Government's) telegraph lines between the two cities "; and similar compensations were required of other telephone promoters.[2] Finally, in the charter granted to the Marconi Wireless Company in 1906, permitting the transmission of wireless messages between the United Kingdom and North America, it was specially provided that permission would not be granted for messages to or from any European country except Italy, the purpose being to safeguard the interests of the cables owned by the British and Continental governments.[3]

The use of defensive and aggressive weapons of an " unfair " uncommercial character by public authorities operating enterprises brings it about, as already explained, that an enterprise run by them is often maintained in existence, despite the fact that the end served by it would be served more cheaply by a rival enterprise. It is necessary to note, in conclusion, that the use of these methods tends to extrude economically superior rivals even more effectively than it appears to do at first sight. For it acts, not only directly, but also indirectly through anticipation. It not only drives out of the market existing competitors, but checks the entry of new ones. When a man contemplating a philanthropic enterprise is given to understand that, should his experiment succeed, a public authority will enter the field he has proved fruitful, he

---

[1] H. Meyer, *Public Ownership and the Telephones*, p. 18.

[2] Cf. Holcombe, *Public Ownership of Telephones on the Continent of Europe*, pp. 375 and 377.

[3] H. Meyer, *Public Ownership and the Telephones*, pp. 341-2.

does—or should—rejoice. But, when a man engaged in a business enterprise is given to understand this, the end he is pursuing is not, like the philanthropist's, furthered. It is, on the contrary, thwarted, and his energies are, therefore, diverted from the undertaking. An effect of this kind is claimed to have resulted from municipal experiments in house-building. These considerations, when they have relevance, evidently strengthen the probability that the operation of industries by public authorities will be injurious to productive efficiency; and they are bound to have some degree of relevance except in industries that are monopolistic in the widest possible sense.

§ 11. I pass to a second consideration. This has to do with the fact that the working of any industrial enterprise involves some degree of uncertainty. As will be explained at length in Appendix I., the exposing of money to uncertainty is a definite factor of production, which makes output larger than it would become without it. In the long run willingness to expose £100 to an equal chance of becoming £160 or of becoming £50 is bound to increase the national dividend. If willingness to expose money to uncertainty on the part of people in control of industry is "artificially" restricted, enterprise and adventure that make for industrial progress, and, therewith, for production, will be hampered. Furthermore, the injury thus wrought is very much larger than appears at first sight. For, since any experiment with an untried process *may* fail, a diminished willingness to expose money to uncertainty implies a restriction of experiment, and, hence, a diminution in the inducement to enterprising persons to make useful inventions. No doubt, there is reason to believe that, with the growing dependence of industry upon non-commercial science, this consideration has become less important than it used to be. Dr. Mertz has well observed: "The great inventions of former ages were made in countries whose practical life, industry and commerce were most advanced; but the great inventions of the last fifty years in chemistry, electricity and the science of heat have been made in the scientific laboratory; the former were stimulated by practical wants; the latter themselves produced new functional requirements, and created new spheres of labour, industry and commerce."[1] It still remains true, however, that, though the fundamental discoveries are often non-commercial, yet the application of them through "inventions," in the earlier stages before the inventions have been proved by experience, generally requires a commercial stimulus. Anything which restricts unduly willingness to make ventures in any industry must still, therefore, threaten heavy loss. The point I have to urge is that a public body engaged in industrial operations is *likely* to restrict unduly this willingness.

The defence of this proposition rests on the following reasons. First, public authorities recognise that hostility to government on the part of the people is an evil, and they also recognise that an unsuccessful State speculation, " if it involves repudiation or oppressive taxation for years to come, produces a popular revulsion and deep-seated distrust of government itself in all its branches." Secondly, the persons at any time in control of a public authority, when that authority is dependent on the party system, cannot but know that "failure would give their political opponents too good an opportunity to ride into power."[2] Thirdly, these persons are partly able to perceive that, if people are *compelled* to expose resources to uncertainty in proportion to the rateable value of their houses, more real sacrifice will be involved than if the same aggregate of resources to be exposed to the same scheme of uncertainty were obtained, by way of voluntary contributions, in proportion to the attractive force exercised upon the several contributors by the prospective profits. Finally, and this is really the most fundamental point, if inventors must appeal to government officials, they are confronted, as it were, with the average daring of the community, whereas, if they are free to appeal to private enterprise, they can select a group of supporters from persons above this average. As Leroy Beaulieu well wrote : " A man of initiative will always find, among the forty million inhabitants of a country, *some* audacious persons who will believe in him, will follow him, will make their fortunes with him or will ruin themselves with him. He would waste

---

[1] Mertz, *History of European Thought*, vol. i. p. 92.
[2] H. Meyer, *Public Ownership and the Telephones in Great Britain*, p. 349.

his time in trying to convince those hierarchical bureaus which are the heavy and necessary thought-organs and action-organs of a State."[1] It follows that, in general, while the hope of gain operates more strongly on private enterprise than on the public authority, the fear of loss operates more strongly on the public authority. Of course, this is not true in war time. Then, as recent experience has shown, governments will authorise experiments in new types of destructive apparatus regardless of cost. But the fact that it is not true in war time is no argument against its truth in times of peace. Just as experience shows it to be untrue in war, so also it shows it to be true in normal conditions. Public authorities are, in general, less willing than private concerns to take risks, or, to put it technically, to provide the factor uncertainty-bearing. A good illustration of this tendency is afforded by the conduct of the British Government in regard to the working of the telephone trunk lines after they had been taken over by the Post Office in 1892. "The Treasury compelled the Post Office to adopt the policy of refusing to make any extensions of doubtful prospect, unless private persons, or the local authority interested, should guarantee 'a specific revenue per year, fixed with reference to the estimated cost of working and maintaining a given mileage of trunk-line wire.'"[2] The opinion of Sir George Gibb may be cited in evidence that this proceeding is representative of the general attitude of public authorities. He wrote: "Whatever may be thought as to the respective merits of private and public ownership, it cannot be denied that private enterprise does take more risk than any government is likely to do except under pressure of military necessities."[3] Marshall brings out very clearly the effect upon inventions implied in this unwillingness of public bodies to bear uncertainty: "It is notorious that, though departments of central and municipal governments employ many thousands of highly-paid servants in engineering and other progressive industries, very few inventions of any importance are made by them; and nearly all of these few are the work of men like

---

[1] L'État moderne, pp. 55, 208.
[2] H. Meyer, Public Ownership and the Telephones in Great Britain, p. 65.
[3] Railway Nationalisation, p. 9.

Sir W. H. Preece, who had been thoroughly trained in free enterprise before they entered Government service. Government creates scarcely anything. . . . A Government could print a good edition of Shakespeare's works, but it could not have got them written. . . . The carcase of municipal electric works belongs to the officials, the genius belongs to free enterprise."[1] Again, the Reporter of the American Civic Federation writes: " The Assistant Secretary of the Board of Trade, Mr. Pelham, told the Committee [of the Civic Federation] that they did not encourage the trying of new inventions, or the trying of systems in any way experimental, by municipalities. They waited for these to be proven out by private companies. Progress is all with the companies."[2] Moreover, at present, the comparatively small number of undertakings which are operated by public authorities stand in a *milieu* where private enterprise is dominant, and where most of the constituents of governing persons are working under private enterprise. In these circumstances public enterprise may be keyed up to a degree of daring which it would not attain if, instead of being the exception, it became the rule.[3]

Now, it is evident that the effect of a restriction of the willingness to take risks, and, therewith, of the stimulus to invention, upon the economies of production will vary in importance in different industries, according to the extent of the speculative element involved in them. Hence it follows that the relative inefficiency of public operation, as compared with private operation, is very large in highly speculative undertakings, and dwindles to nothing in respect of those where the speculative element is practically non-existent. This idea is sometimes crystallised in an attempt to group industries into two divisions, the speculative and the non-speculative, after the manner in which trustees distinguish between speculative securities and investment securities. This grouping, it is sometimes suggested, can be adequately worked out by setting on the one side new industries in an experimental stage, and on the other industries that are

[1] *Economic Journal*, 1907, pp. 21-2. Cf. also Ryan, *Distributive Justice*, p. 165.
[2] *Municipal and Private Operation of Public Utilities*, vol. i. p. 437.
[3] Cf. Aftalion, *Les Fondements du Socialisme*, pp. 233-4.

already tried and known. Thus a recent writer has put in the former category " airship construction, wireless telegraphy, ornamental and luxury trades, the production of single special machines and special transport arrangements, the erection of big and difficult buildings and the like," and in the latter " coal mines, the manufacture of steel, cement, locomotives, telephones, electric cables, motors, and so forth." [1] Again, Sir George Gibb distinguishes, from this point of view, the railway industry at an early, and at a mature, age. " As regards the age of construction, at all events, England has derived incalculable benefit from the fact that the railway system has been made by private enterprise. But the problem of working the railway system after it has been constructed is, I admit, essentially different from the problem of securing its construction." [2] In like manner, Professor Commons, writing in 1904, while he approved of the establishment of city electric-lighting plants at that time, considered that " those cities which entered upon municipal electric lighting eight or ten years ago are open to criticism." " Private parties," he holds, " should be encouraged to push forward in all the untrod fields." [3] The distinction thus insisted on has, no doubt, considerable importance. Two points, however, should be noticed. First, an industry, which is old-established at one place, may need new construction at another, and the conditions of construction there may be such that a large speculative element remains. For example, though the industry of water supply is an old one, different towns have to be supplied from sources situated so differently, and along routes of such varying character, that little guidance for one town can be drawn from the experience of others. Secondly, no industry is likely to be so far established that experimentation—which involves speculation—as to improved methods is undesirable. In some measure all industries, in which possibilities of development remain, demand readiness to take risks if further inventions are to be made, and are, therefore, liable to be hampered by anything that obstructs this readiness. It would, therefore, be an error to

---

[1] Strobel, *Socialisation in Theory and Practice*, p. 281.
[2] *Railway Nationalisation*, p. 11.
[3] Bemis, *Municipal Monopolies*, p. 56.

suppose that the relatively uneconomic character of public operation, due to the circumstances discussed in this section, is significant only for new industries. It probably has some appreciable significance in regard to nearly all industries, though, of course, its importance is greatest in regard to those in an experimental stage.

§ 12. I pass to a third consideration. The relative inferiority of public operation, due to the interference which it causes with the most economical combination of the different factors of production—for that is, in effect, what obstacles in the way of people's readiness to take risks, or to brave uncertainty, implies—is paralleled, in many industries, by a further inferiority due to interference with the most economical size of business unit. Practically speaking, public undertakings can only be operated by groups of people united into some form of political organisation. But it is highly improbable that the areas of control most economical for the working of any industry will correspond in size with the areas covered by the public authorities existing in a modern State, since these are set up with regard to quite other considerations than the efficient running of industries. Consequently, in general, it must happen either that special public authorities are created for the express purpose of running certain industries or that the size of the units of control in these industries is altered to fit the scope of existing public authorities. For very large enterprises having a scope midway between that of the central government and that of the relevant local authority, experience shows that special public bodies, adapted to this scope, can be, and have been, created. We are familiar, for example, with the various harbour trusts and dock trusts, with the London Water Board and the Port of London Authority. Another device is that of joint boards of management representing two or more local authorities. "In England and Wales, during the year 1907–8, there were twenty-five joint boards or committees for the supply of water, two for the supply of water and gas, and one for the supply of electricity and the management of a tramway undertaking." [1] Though, however, for very

---

[1] Knoop, *Principles and Methods of Municipal Trading*, p. 117. As Prof. Knoop further points out, it not infrequently happens that a municipality enters into

large businesses, the creation of special public bodies is admittedly a practicable policy, it is not always likely to be adopted. The danger, that, under public operation, local authorities inadequate in area will become the agents of that operation, is especially great in industries originally adapted to the area covered by these agents, but afterwards fitted, as a result of new inventions, for larger areas. In former times the areas of management most suitable for the industries of water supply, gas lighting and electric power supply were approximately coincident with the several municipal areas. But, since the advent of certain modern discoveries, the areas, which might be expected to prove economically most efficient, are often much larger than municipal areas. Thus, "with horse traction the limit of each local authority was, roughly, the limit of commercial working. With electric traction the parish became a mere item in a comprehensive system, which might extend over a whole county." [1] Again, with the improvement in methods of distribution for electricity in bulk, the most economical area for the supply of electricity has come to extend over thousands of square miles. Even in the supply of water, now that the needs of large towns are satisfied by the tapping of distant lakes, there may be economy in a joint organisation for supplying a number of towns along the route that the pipes must follow. Indeed, it would seem that gas lighting is the only one of the public utility industries for which the most economical area of management at the present time does not exceed the municipal area. These changes in the area proper to management have not, however, in general, been followed by the transference of the public utility industries to new public authorities created ad hoc; for the task of ousting the municipalities is opposed by an immense amount of friction, and is, therefore, little likely to be successfully undertaken. Hence, in practice, public operation often implies that industries, whose most economical area of management is intermediate between the areas representative of the central authority and of local authorities respectively,

---

an arrangement with smaller authorities to extend its tramway, water, or gas system beyond its own boundaries so as to include adjacent areas also.

[1] Porter, *Dangers of Municipal Ownership*, p. 245.

will, in fact, be worked by local authorities; and this, of course, implies a reduction of the unit of management below what is economically best.[1] In enterprises whose most economical area of management is smaller than that covered by the smallest existing type of public authority, the creation of new authorities for the special purpose of running them cannot even be said to be practicable. If such industries are to be taken over by any public authority, this authority can hardly be other than one of the authorities that already exist for other purposes. Consequently, in these industries public operation, not merely in general, but practically always, implies the introduction of a scale of management larger than is economically most efficient.

§ 13. Now, if it were the fact that under private enterprise all industries would always evolve the most economical unit of management, it would follow that public operation could not, in this respect, be superior, and would, in general, be greatly inferior, to private operation. In industries normally conducted under conditions of simple competition, such as the industries of baking, milk-supply, house-building or farming, we may fairly presume that private enterprise will, for the most part, evolve the most efficient size of unit. But, where any element of monopoly is present, we may by no means presume this. The most economical unit may be prevented from realising itself through friction, or through the hindrance imposed by popular dislike of large amalgamations, or in other ways. The probability that it will be so prevented is especially great in an industry whose normal condition is, not that of simple monopoly, but that of monopolistic competition. Here, as was pointed out in Chapter IX., there are large wastes due to competitive advertisement and so forth, which

[1] It may be objected that the alternative to municipal operation is usually municipal control, and that this control, when the area of the municipality is too small, may render private undertakings as inefficient as municipal undertakings would be. But it is easier to transfer control than it is to transfer operation to an authority of wider scope than the municipalities. The British Light Railways Act of 1906 establishes such a wider authority in the shape of the Light Railway Commissioners. (Cf. H. Meyer, *Municipal Ownership in Great Britain*, p. 69.) Again : " When, as in Massachusetts, it is not uncommon for a street railway company to operate franchises from ten, and, in one case, from nineteen different towns, independent municipal control is out of the question. The State railroad commission is the recognition in law of this condition of fact " (Rowe, *Annals of the American Academy*, 1900, p. 19).

centralisation under a single management might remove. Of railways, for example, Sir George Gibb wrote some years ago: "Each railway company works for its own route. The result is that unnecessary mileage is run, and train loads are lessened. . . . If those responsible for the handling and carriage of railway traffic could work with a single eye to economical results, and in all cases forward traffic by the routes which yielded the best working results, great economies could undoubtedly be effected."[1] This statement was borne out by the experience of the joint working of British railways during the war ; though it must be remembered that the character of war-time traffic, with its large train loads of munitions and troops, was exceptionally favourable to economical working. Like economies are sometimes obtainable from the combination, not of different firms engaged in the same occupation, but of different occupations. There is probably an economy in the co-ordination under one hand of the various industries that utilise the public streets. "Water mains may be laid before streets are paved, thus saving the damage and expense of tearing up good pavement to lay water pipes."[2] In like manner, it may well be held that important economies would result if the work of treating disease could be brought, by means of a State medical service, into direct connection with the work of preventing disease that is now undertaken by the Public Health authorities. Though, therefore, indirect evil consequences of the kind discussed in Chapter X. § 4 may emerge, and though also certain vertical combinations, e.g. between a particular coal-mine and a particular ironworks, that would yield structural economies, may be impeded, it is at least possible that, in enterprises of this sort, public operation, instead of hindering, might actually foster the growth of the most economical unit of management.[3]

§ 14. So far of generalities. When the practical issue is

---

[1] *Railway Nationalisation*, p. 21.
[2] Bemis, *Municipal Monopolies*, p. 46.
[3] This conclusion is not, of course, upset by the fact that, as shown in the recent Act for grouping British railways, it is *possible* for the State to further an expansion of the unit of management in an industry, while leaving that industry in private hands.

raised whether a particular class of enterprise could, with greater advantage to the national dividend, be publicly controlled or publicly operated, it will be necessary, in order to reach a satisfactory conclusion, to take into account both the comparative effects which the two forms of management are likely to have on productive efficiency and the comparative ease with which whatever regulation the public interest may require can be applied under them. In industries closely associated with the public health, where reliable quality is essential and where inspection cannot easily be made thorough, public operation may be desirable, even though the probable alternative is competitive, and not monopolistic, production. Thus there is much to be said for the public provision of slaughter-houses, to which, as in Germany, all butchers are compelled to resort, and for the public provision of milk for the use of young children. The Reporters to the American Civic Federation are of opinion that "undertakings in which the sanitary motive largely enters should be operated by the public." [1] On the other hand, industries, in which the typical producing unit is small, and private firms, rather than joint stock companies, are dominant, are hardly ever suitable for management by public authorities. Apart from a few special exceptions, the proposal for public operation is a live one only in industries in which the typical producing unit is large, and which, therefore, tend towards monopoly. The case for it, as against the case for public control, is strongest in industries which have been reduced more or less to routine and in which there is comparatively little scope for daring adventure. It is relatively weak in industries which are to an important extent rival to other privately operated industries, or in which the normal unit of management covers an area widely different from that covered by existing public authorities. Whether any particular monopolistic industry should be publicly operated or publicly controlled cannot be determined in a general way. Before a decision between these alternative methods is arrived at, a detailed investigation of the industry must be made, and this should be supplemented by an impartial estimate of the quality of the particular

---

[1] *Municipal and Private Operation of Public Utilities*, vol. i. p. 23.

public authority whose action is involved, as well as of the probable effect of new tasks upon its efficiency for the purpose of its primary non-industrial duties.

§ 15. If, on the strength of the foregoing or other considerations, it is decided that an industry already in existence and operated by private persons shall be taken over by public authority, it is necessary to settle the terms on which this shall be done. Let us, for simplicity, suppose the conditions to be such that under public operation the technical efficiency of production will be unaltered. Public operation is desired because, without it, a monopolistic or partially monopolistic concern is able to force up prices against the public and so to check the development of the industry under its command. If, in these circumstances, a public authority buys up the concern *at its market value*, it will have either itself to charge the same price for its services as the private company was charging, or else to operate the concern at a loss. In other words, if it buys the concern at its market value, the proprietors will have made the public *buy* their right to make monopolistic exactions; for the market value will, of course, be, in part, the result of people's belief in their possession of that right. It is natural, therefore, to say that the price paid ought not to be the market value as it actually is, but the market value as it would be if this anti-social right were eliminated. But here the considerations set out at the end of the last chapter give us pause. Some concession must, it would seem, be made in the interests of recent purchasers who have acquired shares in the concern in good faith at the high existing values. How large this concession should be cannot, of course, be laid down in general terms. In each separate instance a detailed review will have to be made of all relevant circumstances, including " legitimate expectations " that have been created, and on this foundation common sense must be invoked to furnish a " reasonable " compromise. When the purchase price is settled, payment will, of course, in general be made by an issue of government, or municipal, or " public authority " (*e.g.* Port of London Authority) stock bearing fixed interest, and not by an actual transfer of cash.

§ 16. This question of the purchase price leads on to

a very important consideration, with which this Part may suitably close. At first sight it might seem that, if the public has to pay the full market value for a monopolistic concern, which is charging exorbitant prices for its products, no national advantage can possibly result. The monopolist simply takes in a lump sum what otherwise he would have got in an annual tribute. This way of looking at the matter is, however, mistaken. The evil of monopoly is not merely, or even mainly, that it enables one set of people to mulct another set. It is that it causes resources to be held back from a form of investment in which the value of the marginal social net product is larger than it is elsewhere, and thereby contracts the national dividend. To do away with this monopolistic policy will increase the size of the national dividend and augment economic welfare, in spite of the fact that, in order to do away with it, one part of the community has to pay a fine to another part. For this reason it is greatly preferable that the government should pay the ransom demanded by the monopolist, write off part of the purchase price, and then operate the concern on terms that would have yielded normal returns if no ransom had been necessary, than that it should allow the private monopolist to continue, by exorbitant charges, to hold back production and check the flow of resources into the enterprise. It is true that, if it does this, the government will have to borrow the purchase price from the public, and, subsequently, to levy taxation to provide interest upon it, and that the amount of this taxation will be roughly equivalent to the exaction which the monopolist would otherwise have made. We may presume, however, that the taxes imposed will either be direct, or, if indirect, will be spread over several commodities, and, therefore, will not shift industrial effort out of its normal channels nearly so far as the monopolist's exaction would have done. This consideration must not, of course, be allowed to make those persons who have to bargain on the public's behalf unduly pliant to the pressure of interested sellers. But it is, none the less, an important consideration. When the vested interests of new shareholders in monopolistic concerns make the government unwilling to force prices down to the proper level through a policy of control, it constitutes a very powerful argument for a policy of purchase. If purchase is made, the natural consequence would be for the government to operate the industry itself. But, if, for any reason, it does not wish to do this, and prefers to sell or lease it to private persons, on terms which involve a money loss to itself but provide for the establishment of a proper price level, it will still have eliminated the evil of monopolistic restriction of output and indirectly benefited the national dividend.

PART III

THE NATIONAL DIVIDEND AND LABOUR

CHAPTER I

WHEN labour and equipment in the whole or any part of an industry are rendered idle by a strike or lock-out, the national dividend must suffer in a way that injures economic welfare. Furthermore, the loss of output for which these disputes are responsible often extends much beyond the industry directly affected. This is well illustrated by the fact that, during the coal strike of March 1912, the general percentage of unemployment over the whole body of trade unionists in the United Kingdom was no less than 11 per cent, as against an average level for March during the ten years 1903–12 of $5\frac{1}{2}$ per cent; while in the strike of 1921, which, it must be remembered, occurred in a period of marked industrial depression, the corresponding percentage was as high as 23 per cent. The reason for this is that a stoppage of work in an important industry checks activity in other industries in two ways. On the one hand, by impoverishing the people actually involved in the stoppage, it lessens the demand for the goods the other industries make; on the other hand, if the industry in which the stoppage has occurred is one that furnishes a commodity or service largely used in the conduct of other industries, it lessens the supply to them of raw material or equipment for their work. Naturally not all strikes and lock-outs produce this secondary effect in equal measure. The larger the range they cover and the more fundamental the commodities or services they supply, the more marked is their influence. Coal and transport service, for example, are basal goods essential to practically all industries, and a miners' or a railway servants' strike will, therefore, produce a much larger indirect effect

than a cotton-workers' strike of the same extent and duration.
But, in some degree, all stoppages of work inflict an indirect
injury upon the national dividend by the reactions they set up
in other industries, in addition to the direct injury that they
carry in themselves. It is true, no doubt, that the net contraction of output consequent upon industrial disputes is
generally smaller than the immediate contraction; for a stoppage of work at one place may lead both to more work at
the same time in rival establishments and to more work at
a later time (in fulfilling delayed orders) in the establishments
where the stoppage has occurred. It must be admitted also
that, on some occasions, the direct damage caused by strikes
and lock-outs is partly compensated by the stimulus indirectly
given to improvements in machinery and in the organisation
of work. Mr. Nasmyth, in his evidence before the Trades
Union Commission of 1868, laid very great stress upon this.
" I believe," he said, " that, if there were a debtor and creditor
account made up of strikes and lock-outs with the interests
of society, up to a certain point they would be found to have
been a benefit. Such has been the stimulus applied to
ingenuity by the intolerable annoyance resulting from strikes
and lock-outs, that it has developed more than anything those
wonderful improvements in automaton machinery that produce
you a window-frame or the piston-rod of a steam-engine of
such an accuracy as would make Euclid's mouth water to
look at. These things are pouring in in quantities as the
result of the stimulus given to ingenuity through the annoyance of strikes. It is not being coaxed on by some grand
reward in the distance, but I think a kick from behind is
sometimes as useful as a gentle leading forward in front." [1]
These reflex effects of conflict are, no doubt, important. But
it would be paradoxical to maintain that the reaction of the
industrial organism against the evils threatening it ordinarily
outweigh those evils themselves. By adapting itself to

---

[1] *Minutes of Evidence*, p. 71. Clifford (*Agricultural Lock-out*, p. 179)
describes the way in which farmers were stimulated by the 1874 dispute to
improve their organisation, and to do the same work as before with fewer men.
In like manner, the great anthracite coal strike in the United States in 1902
led to the invention of economical methods of utilising other fuels, which continued to be employed after normal conditions had returned.

injurious changes of environment it can, indeed, lessen, but it cannot altogether abolish, the damage to which it is exposed. An excellent parallel is afforded by the effects of a blockade instituted by one State against the ports of another. The immediate effect both upon the blockaded State and upon neutrals is an obvious, and sometimes a considerable, injury. By altering the direction and character of their trade they may reduce the extent of their losses. It is even conceivable that the search for new trade openings may lead to the discovery of one, *which otherwise would not have been found*, and which is possessed of advantages great enough to outweigh all the evils of the blockade period. Any such result is, however, extraordinarily improbable, and nobody, on the strength of it, would dream of suggesting that blockades in general are likely to do the world more good than harm. So with industrial disputes. It is conceivable that one of them may stir to action some otherwise mute, inglorious inventor ; but it is immensely unlikely that it will, at best, do more than slightly antedate the discovery that he makes. On a broad view, the hypothetical gain is altogether outweighed by the certain loss of production in the industries directly affected and in related industries, the raw material of which is cut off, or the product of which cannot be worked up into its final stage. Moreover, there may be lasting injury to the workpeople, in industrial careers interrupted, a load of debt contracted to meet a temporary emergency, and permanent damage to their children's health through the enforced period of insufficient nourishment. The extent of these evils varies, of course, partly with the degree to which the commodity whose production is stopped is consumed by the poorer classes, and partly with its importance for life, health, security and order. But, in any event, the aggregate damage with which industrial disputes threaten the national dividend is very grave. It has been pertinently asked : " Would any Board of Managers attempt to run a railway or start an electric-lighting plant, or operate a mill or factory, or send a liner to sea, with a mechanical equipment which was certain to break down periodically and lie in inevitable idleness until repairs could be patched up ? And yet that is almost an absolute analogy to the state of labour conditions throughout nearly the whole range of such enterprises."[1]   Anything that makes it less likely that these break-downs will occur is bound to prove of substantial benefit to the national dividend.   Hence the eagerness of social reformers to build up and fortify the machinery of industrial peace.   They recognise, indeed, that in the work of pacification constitutions and agreements cannot accomplish much.   In industrial, as in international negotiations, perfection of machinery counts for far less than good faith and good will.   Care must, therefore, be taken not to stress unduly matters of mere technique.   Nevertheless, the type of machinery employed is certain to have some effect, and may have a considerable effect, both directly and also by its reflex influence on the general attitude which employers and employees take to one another.   It is, therefore, important to the present purpose to examine the principal problems which have to be faced in building up machinery, through whose aid it is hoped that industrial peace may be preserved.

[1] Goring, *Engineering Magazine*, vol. xx. p. 922.

CHAPTER II

§ 1. A NECESSARY preliminary to analysis is some classification of differences. The classification which naturally suggests itself in the first instance is one based upon the character of the matters in dispute. Such a classification yields two divisions, each in turn containing further subdivisions. The divisions comprise respectively differences about "the fraction of wages" and differences about "the demarcation of function." Differences about the fraction of wages may be subdivided into :

(1) Those connected with the reward of labour, generally raising an issue as to the money rate of wage, but sometimes touching such matters as workshop fines or the amount of special allowances, whether in money or in kind ;

(2) Those connected with the doing and bearing of the employees, generally involving the question of hours.

Differences as to demarcation of function include, besides the well-known, but relatively unimportant, "demarcation disputes" between kindred trades, all quarrels arising out of claims by the workpeople to a larger share in the work of management. They generally relate to :

(1) The way in which work is apportioned between different classes of workmen and machine tools ; or

(2) The sources from which the employer draws his workpeople ; or

(3) The voice allowed to workpeople in the settlement of working conditions.

The second of these subdivisions includes all questions concerning discrimination against, preference to, or exclusive employment of, trade unionists.

§ 2. For many purposes the above classification is the most convenient to follow. But for the task of constructing machinery for preserving industrial peace it is not of serious value, because in practice the design of the machinery never turns upon distinctions between wages differences, differences about hours, or differences about the demarcation of work. We have, therefore, to seek some classification better adapted to the purpose in hand. In this search we are driven to follow two lines of thought, neither of which affords exact or sharp distinctions, but both of which, as will presently appear, somehow run together and yield a compound classification. They turn, respectively, upon the degree of self-sufficiency enjoyed by the parties to the difference and upon the extent of the theoretical ground which they have in common.

§ 3. Under the former of these two heads the determining factor is the relation between the bodies which control negotiations and those which are directly affected by their result. Both the employers and the workpeople implicated may be entirely independent, or both may be subordinate branches of larger organisations; or the employers may be independent and the workpeople a branch; or the employers a branch and the workpeople independent. This distinction is, however, somewhat blurred in practice, because to be a branch of a wider organisation is not the same thing as to have no control over negotiations affecting one's own interests. The extent to which local organisations are subordinated in this matter to national unions varies greatly in different times and places. They may be left entirely free; they may be free to make, but not to denounce, agreements; they may be offered advice or deprived of strike pay; or they may be mere branches, compelled to carry out the instructions of the central executive. Consequently, in this form of classification, no sharp dividing lines can be drawn.

§ 4. The same remark applies to the latter of the two forms distinguished above. In every industrial difference there is *some* common ground between the parties. Even when they diverge most widely, both sides agree that the decision ought to be " just." Sometimes the full limit of agreement is expressed by this phrase. A case in point is the coal strike of 1893, in which the employers understood by justice payment according to efficiency, and the work-people, in a vague way, payment according to needs. The common basis is wider when it is agreed, whether formally or informally, that justice, rightly interpreted, is the doctrine that the wage level should move in the same general direction as some accepted external index. This stage is often reached when the wages of a small group of workmen are in question; for it is generally recognised that these ought not, as a rule, to move very differently from the average wage level of other men in the neighbourhood engaged in similar employment. It is also reached with regard to the wages of larger groups, when the doctrine is accepted that, other things being equal, wages ought, in some sense, to follow prices. Thus, throughout the series of arbitrations in the North of England iron trade studied by Mr. Price, " there is a general agreement that the basis of award is to be primarily the relation of wages to selling price."[1] The common ground here, however, is merely that wages shall rise when prices rise and fall when prices fall. The question of what proportion should hold between the two movements, or what change on the one side " corresponds " to a given change on the other, is left unanswered. A further stage is reached when the exact proportion that the wage change ought to bear to a given change in the index is agreed upon. This is done where employers and employed, in any locality or firm, accept, as in the spinning industry, the average efficiency wage of the trade or district as their own standard, or when wage is related to price by a definite sliding scale. Here the common ground, so far as principle is concerned, is complete, and differences between the parties can only arise upon matters of fact.

§ 5. The discussion of the two preceding sections shows that no sharp divisions are to be found along either of the lines of classification which have been discussed. This, how-ever, is not the last word upon the matter. It may still be necessary, here as elsewhere, for the student with a practical

[1] L. L. Price, *Industrial Peace*, p. 62.

P

end in view to depart somewhat from the majestic continuity
of Nature, and to erect an arbitrary landmark of his own.
Such a landmark may be made out of the common division
of industrial differences into " those which concern the interpretation of the existing terms of employment," and "those
which have to do with the general terms of future employment." [1]   This distinction is analogous to one familiar to the
theory of jurisprudence.   "The settlement of such general
questions may be likened to an act of legislation; the interpretation and application of the general contract may be
likened to a judicial act." [2]   The place assigned to any particular difference is made to turn primarily upon the question
whether or not it is governed by a formal agreement between
the parties.   All differences which arise when there is an
agreement are called "interpretation differences," and are
distinguished from "those which arise out of proposals for
the terms of engagement or contract of service to subsist for
a future period." [3]   Furthermore, these differences are often
identical with those which superior organisations undertake
to settle on behalf of their local branches; they "are for
the most part limited to particular establishments, of little
importance and often purely personal"; [4] dealing, it may
be, with controversies of fact concerning quantity, or quality,
or the more precise definition of the mutually accepted pattern
of quality itself.   "General questions," on the other hand, are,
for the most part, equivalent to those in which independent
organisations are directly concerned; they are "frequently
of wide interest, affect large bodies of men, and are the
most general cause of strikes and lock-outs on a large scale." [5]
Of course it is not maintained that interpretation differences
in the above sense are *necessarily* of minor importance.   Not
only, as with judge-made law, may the act of interpretation
slide insensibly into that of alteration, but also what is called
interpretation may cover as wide a field, and raise questions
quite as fundamental, as those treated in the general agreement.   For example, there is no difference in this respect

---

[1] *U.S.A. Industrial Commission*, xvii. p. lxxv.   [2] *Ibid.* p. lxxvi.
[3] *Royal Commission on Labour, Report*, p. 49.
[4] *Ibid.* p. 49.   [5] *Ibid.* p. 49.

between the question how many pounds a ton of coal is to be taken to contain, or how much "topping" the men must put upon a car-load, and the question what the wage per ton or car-load ought to be. Moreover, it sometimes happens that general questions are deliberately submitted for discussion on what are apparently interpretation references. For example, in the pottery boom of 1871, it was arranged that, for each branch of the trade, an individual case should be selected for arbitration, and that the whole branch should act in accordance with the award.[1] On subsequent occasions exactly the same result was achieved by general arbitrations of the ordinary type. Similarly, it is not maintained that differences as to the terms of a future contract, to be made otherwise than by the interpretation of some overshadowing agreement, must *necessarily* affect large bodies of men. Where the local branches of ill-organised trades have to negotiate new contracts for themselves without reference to such an agreement, the number of men affected by any difference which may arise must be small. Nevertheless, the sentences quoted above from the American Industrial Commission and the British Royal Commission on Labour represent the facts sufficiently well to provide the basis of a rough practical classification.

[1] Cf. Owen, *Potteries*, p. 142.

CHAPTER III

VOLUNTARY ARRANGEMENTS FOR CONCILIATION AND ARBITRATION

§ 1. It is well known that, as industries become better organised and the associations of employers and employed grow more powerful, differences about matters other than general questions are more and more likely to be adjusted. It is not in the interest of powerful organisations to fight about a little thing, and it is generally, though not, of course, always, in their power to control small bodies of their members. Various arrangements—the most perfect, perhaps, is the famous system of "professional experts" in the Lancashire cotton industry—are made for the prompt and effective solution of minor difficulties. We need not pause to examine them. The real problems to be faced are found in connection with those broad general questions, of the successful treatment of which by purely voluntary means the United Kingdom may fairly claim to provide the classical example.

§ 2. In any study of the comparative advantages of different types of machinery devoted to this end, the first question to decide is whether it is better to rest content with a simple agreement—which must, of course, be subject to renewal or denunciation from time to time—to employ defined conciliatory processes when a conflict is threatened or to set up and maintain permanently in being some regularly constituted organ of negotiation. Upon the right answer to this question there is a fairly general consensus of opinion. Unless there is some machinery already established, it will be necessary to appoint negotiators at a moment of heated controversy, and the attempt to do this may not only involve delay

but also afford opportunity for obstruction and friction.   More
generally, as Professor Foxwell observed many years ago : " The
fact is that, where human beings are concerned, where personal
relations should be formed, and where moral forces are at work,
a certain permanence of conditions seems to be essential.   The
altruistic and social feelings, which are the very cement of
the social fabric, and enormously lessen the irksomeness of
effort and the friction of industry, seem to require time for
their development, and frequently cannot exert their full
strength unless they are embodied in the symbol of an organisation." [1]   No doubt, when the Associations upon both sides
are exceptionally strong and the relations between them exceptionally satisfactory, this consideration loses much of its
importance.   In general, however, there can be no doubt that
the prospects of peace will be substantially improved by the
establishment of permanent Boards containing representatives
of employers and employed meeting together regularly.   They
will be still further improved if these Boards are entrusted, as
was contemplated under the Whitley Scheme for national, district, and local industrial councils in each principal industry,
not merely with the settlement of differences, but with
general collaboration in determining conditions of work,
methods of remuneration, technical education, industrial research, improvement of processes, and so forth.   For, working
jointly at these broad problems, the representatives of employers and employed will come to regard themselves more
as partners and less as hostile bargainers, and, consequently,
when differences between them do arise, not only will the
general atmosphere of discussion be a good one, but also both
sides will have at the back of their minds a feeling that
extreme action must at all costs be avoided, lest it destroy an
organisation proved capable of much valuable work in their
common interest.

§ 3. The constitution of the Boards or Councils has
next to be considered.   The essential point is that the
representatives of either side, and particularly of the workmen,
should have the confidence of their clients.   The mechanism
by which this can best be secured varies somewhat according

[1] *The Claims of Labour*, p. 190.

to the character of the two organisations. In some of the
Boards in the Iron and Steel industry, and in the Railway
Conciliation Board under the agreement of 1914, representatives are appointed by a vote of the employers and employed
connected with separate firms or districts. When, however,
the Associations are strong, this device is not necessary. The
confidence of the rank and file in the Board can be obtained
without it. The important thing is that the chief Association
officials should have confidence in it. If they are convinced,
the loyalty of the rest is as well assured as it can be ; if they
are not convinced, the authority of the Board is worthless.
Consequently, though delegates from different works may still
attend to supply information, the Board ought, essentially, to
represent the Associations themselves. The old forms, where
they exist, may be retained, and new Boards may be started,
whose forms are copied from the old. But the representatives must always be controlled by the officials of the Associations, and, in many instances, may also, with advantage, be
appointed by them.

§ 4. The next point has reference to procedure. The
fact that " general questions " are important, and bear directly
upon the permanent interests of all concerned, makes the discussion of them, both on the Board itself and among those
who will be bound by its decisions, peculiarly delicate. Consequently, even when the relations between the parties are
good, it is important that everything which might engender
irritation should be excluded from the machinery of industrial
peace.

From this principle the most obvious inference is that
technicalities and lawyers should not be admitted before the
Board. Such a policy—apart altogether from the saving
in cost and time—tends to reduce to a minimum the appearance, and hence, indirectly, the reality, of opposition between
the parties. There is less of a struggle for victory, and,
therefore, less fear of the introduction of " matters of sentiment." In the practice of the chief English Boards and in
the report of the Labour Commission the policy of excluding
legal representatives, and the legal forms which may be
expected to accompany them, is fully recognised. Finally,

the conciliatory, as distinguished from the litigious, character of negotiations is often still further emphasised by an arrangement, in accordance with which the chairman (a representative employer) and vice-chairman (a representative workman) sit side by side at the Board, thus securing opportunities for conference at critical points in the discussion.[1]

A second inference is that the Board should not be allowed to pronounce upon any matter by the vote of a bare majority. When the solidarity of both of the two sides is complete, there is, of course, little prospect that any vote will be given which is not either unanimous or equally divided. But, when organisation is less perfect, there is always the possibility of defection on the part of one or two representatives of either party. To allow the result of the discussion to be determined by such an incident is to court grave danger. So much dissatisfaction might be aroused that the whole conciliatory machinery would be immediately overturned. It is true that these difficulties do not seem to have been experienced in this country, and that, in a number of instances, the rules provide for a bare majority vote, subject, of course, to the condition that, if equal numbers of employers and employed happen to be present, only equal numbers shall have the opportunity of voting. In the United States, however, where, owing to the weakness of the Unions, there is a greater probability of cross-voting, things have worked out differently. Thus, Mr. Durand, Secretary of the Industrial Commission, asserted, both that the bare majority method will not work, and also that decision by unanimous agreement had become the ordinary practice.[2]

Thirdly and lastly, it will not, as a rule, be desirable for the meetings of the Board to be conducted, like those of the American interstate bituminous coal conferences, in public. It may, indeed, be held that such a system has educative advantages; but, on the other hand, the policy of deliberation *in camera*, which is usual in England, may be expected to

---

[1] As in the Midland Iron and Steel Board (Ashley, *British Industries*, p. 57).

[2] *Industrial Conciliation Conference*, p. 43. It may, perhaps, be suggested that a decision by a large majority, *e.g.* seven-eighths of those present, would be a still better plan, as it would eliminate the possibility of obstructive tactics on the part of a single faddist.

conduce better both to frankness in the discussion itself and also to uncomplaining acceptance of the decision reached.

§ 5. We have next to compare mere agreements to submit differences to conciliation with those under which provision is also made for arbitration in the last resort. The relative merits of the two plans have long been the subject of vigorous controversy. A number of authorities argue in favour of the former, and the Lancashire cotton trade, the British engineering industry, and most of " the important systems of collective bargaining in the United States "[1] follow their views in practice. Other authorities, on the contrary, agree with Mr. Crompton that all conciliation agreements should contain a clause providing for " some power in reserve by which resource to strikes may be avoided,"[2] and are, in turn, followed by certain of the best-developed English industries. Thus, in important conciliation schemes in the coal-mining, iron-mining, and boot and shoe industries provision has been made, in one way or another, for reference to arbitration.

Before entering upon the merits of the issue as between the two methods, we may note a preliminary matter upon which the champions of both views are agreed. Everybody admits that, in differences so important as " general questions," a settlement by arbitration will almost always stir up *considerably* more irritation and bad feeling than a settlement by mutual agreement on a Conciliation Board. Consequently, resort to it should never take place except when it is absolutely necessary. Conciliation should be developed and arbitration reduced to a minimum. In the United Kingdom it may safely be said that there is no trade in which the relations between employers and employed are so good that this proposition fails. In the United States the right line of policy is still clearer ; for there, as was strongly urged twenty years ago, to allow the conditions under which they shall work to be determined by an outsider is " peculiarly obnoxious to the workmen," and they will never agree to it till conferences have failed and no other resort

---

[1] *U.S.A. Industrial Commission*, xvii. p. c.
[2] *Industrial Conciliation*, p. 134.

is left.[1]   Hence, in general questions, even when there is an arbitration agreement in reserve, it is well to enforce delay, in the hope that the greater coolness of an adjourned discussion may bring about a settlement.   The Federated Districts Coal Board realises this so fully that, when they fail to agree, a second meeting is held, of which twenty-one days' notice must be given.   At this meeting the neutral chairman is present, but he only exercises his casting vote after another effort has been made to bring about a settlement acceptable to both sides.

Granted, however, that arbitration is a *pis aller*, the question still remains whether provision should be made for recourse to it in the last resort.   The argument in favour of incorporating a clause to this effect in industrial agreements is drawn from the obvious direct advantages derivable therefrom.   In the absence of such a provision, differences may entail strikes and lock-outs, with all the material loss and mutual irritation which these involve: and, even if a *modus vivendi* upon the immediate issue be found, we can never be certain that the controversy will pass away without incidentally destroying the established conciliatory system.[2]   If, however, the means of securing an arbitrator are provided beforehand, both sides have guarded themselves, in a calm moment, against a possible future access of passion and excitement.   Their policy is similar to that of a person who, unable to trust his will to be sober, goes voluntarily into an inebriate home.   The *vis inertiae* is thrown upon the side of peace, since there is no escape from an amicable solution except the strong step of withdrawal from the Board.

The opposing argument depends upon certain indirect disadvantages, to which the inclusion of an arbitration clause is said to lead.   In the first place, the representatives of the two sides will not make so serious an effort to agree. They may hesitate to offer concessions lest, in the subsequent arbitration, their suggestions should be used against

---

[1] Cf. Aldrich, *U.S. Federation of Labour*, 1898, p. 253. .
[2] This result came about in the federated coal district in 1896 (MacPherson, *U.S.A. Bulletin of Labour*, 1900, p. 478).

them;[1] or, in loyalty to their constituents, they may "feel obliged to win, if possible, through the odd man." In the second place, the possibility of gain, unbalanced by the danger of a stoppage of work, will tend to breed speculative differences. If these things happen, though one or two strikes will be prevented, the number of differences, which reach the stage of arbitration, will be so far increased that a large amount of friction is generated, and, as a result, before very long the whole arrangement breaks down. This danger is, indeed, comparatively slight when the parties are on good terms with one another and are educated up to a proper appreciation of their own ultimate interests. It can also be obviated, in some degree, by a rule enabling the arbitrators, at their discretion, to order the defeated side to pay the whole cost of an arbitration, thus checking speculative appeals. It cannot, however, be eliminated altogether.

Between these two conflicting sets of arguments no general *a priori* decision can be made. Until we know the temper of the parties in each particular industry, their affection or otherwise for a "policy of pin-pricks," the strength of their organisations, the power of the leaders over the men, and the probability that an award will be obeyed, it is impossible to judge whether a provision for arbitration in the event of conciliation failing can safely be put into an industrial agreement. In some circumstances a third way may be the best. A number of conciliation agreements among, for example, the iron-founders of the north-east coast, the Leicester dyeing trade and the Scotch coal trade, while not containing a regular arbitration clause, have, nevertheless, provided for arbitration by "mutual consent," if, when the time arrives, both parties desire it. Of course an intractable difference is more likely to end in a strike under this system than under one backed by an arbitration clause. But this result is indecisive so long as we are unable to gauge the chances, under the two systems respectively, that the stage

---

[1] Cf. the discussion in the boot and shoe trade conference previous to arbitration in 1893. The employers were careful to insist that the concessions they proposed were not to be taken as prejudicing their case in the event of arbitration becoming necessary. Cf. also Mr. V. S. Clark's Report on Labour Conditions in New Zealand, *U.S.A. Bulletin of Labour*, No. 49, pp. 1192-3.

of intractability will be reached. Plainly, however, when the conditions are such that the arbitration clause can be inserted without danger of indirect ill-consequences, the direct advantages that follow from it leave no doubt that it ought to be adopted.

§ 6. When it is adopted, the constitution of the arbitrating authority has to be determined. We have to inquire into the qualities of the persons of whom it should be composed, the number of these persons and the best method of appointing them. These points may conveniently be examined in the order in which they have just been stated.

The qualities most needed for a successful panel are obviously a reputation for impartiality and a reputation for competence. These requirements in combination are, however, not easily satisfied. Persons, whether employers or workpeople, who have been brought up in a trade are inclined to believe that nobody without a " practical knowledge " of it can possibly form an intelligent judgment upon its problems. The natural inference is that the rule of the Midland Iron and Steel Board,[1] which required the independent chairman to be personally connected with the industry, should be followed. Since, however, practical knowledge is scarcely found except among employers or workpeople who have been, or are, actually engaged in the calling, it will rarely happen that a practical expert is available whom *both* sides believe to be unbiassed. It would seem, therefore, that the demand for "practical knowledge" will, in general, have to be abandoned. This can be done the more readily because, as a matter of fact, the decision of broad disputes on such matters as wages and hours calls chiefly " for a *general* economic knowledge of the industry concerned, and, inasmuch as all industries are connected, an acquaintance with the condition of the whole national trade."[2] When technical knowledge is needed, this can be provided by associating with the arbitrator assessors representing both sides, whose business it is to give him whatever help he requires, and not to take part in the decision. Even so, however, the field of selection for the arbitrator will

---

[1] *Industrial Commission*, xvii. p. 500.

[2] Schultze-Gaevernitz, *Social Peace*, p. 165.

be limited. Employers, for example, will not be enthusiastic over a politician in the House of Commons, because workpeople's votes are worth winning, while workpeople are apt to think that any member of the professional classes must, from the very nature of his life and upbringing, be unconsciously biassed in favour of capital. Hence, though a judge or a member of the House of Lords may satisfy the employers, the workpeople's ideal arbitrator can hardly be other than one of themselves. Unless, therefore, there happens to be available some one like Sir David Dale or Lord Askwith, personally known to, and trusted by, both sides, the choice can hardly be other than a compromise.[1] In these circumstances, the best way out of the difficulty may often lie in the selection of some man of outstanding eminence, whose conscious motives, at all events, whatever may be said of his subconscious ones, are above suspicion. Such a man, moreover, if, like the late Lord James of Hereford or Sir Edward Fry, he serves in the same way without payment frequently, may gradually win for himself a large measure of respect and confidence throughout the industrial community. Another solution may be found in the governmental manufacture of professional arbitrators. Something in this direction was attempted when an official panel of arbitrators was set up by the Board of Trade. The establishment of a standing Industrial Court under the Act of 1919 is a further step on the same lines.

What has just been said implicitly determines the number of persons by whom the arbitration panel should be constituted. Eminent outsiders are not likely to be obtained in groups. If their services are to be secured at all, it is practically necessary that the panel shall consist of a single man— very likely the man who also serves as neutral chairman to the Conciliation Board. This, however, is not the only argument against a compound tribunal. Reasoning of a general character shows that, even when practicable, such an arrangement is to be deprecated. The compound body in its most

---

[1] Even Sir David Dale, though entirely trusted by the leaders of the employees, seems on one occasion to have been suspected by some of the rank and file, who knew him less well. (Cf. Price, *Industrial Peace*, p. 50.)

attractive form comprises one representative of each side, together with an umpire, selected either by these representatives or by their principals, to be referred to in the event of disagreement. The argument in favour of it is that the two representatives may possibly agree. On one occasion Messrs. Mundella and Williams succeeded in doing this, and, in a miners' strike on the Loire, M. Jaurès and the employers' representative followed their example. A decision reached in this way is likely to command a higher degree of confidence than one imposed upon the parties by a single arbitrator. On the other hand, agreement between the representatives is improbable, and the real decision will generally rest with the umpire. When that happens, a compound tribunal resembles an elaborate machine, two-thirds of which is ornament. Nor is this all. So often as a division of opinion emerges in this type of tribunal the authority of its decisions is weakened. It is true that the division can be concealed by devices like that once adopted in a Staffordshire potteries' agreement. " The award when given in such general arbitration shall be signed by the umpire and the arbitrators, and shall be issued as their joint award, signified by their individual signatures thereto, and nothing shall be divulged by any of them, or appear on the face of such award, to signify whether the umpire and arbitrators are unanimous in their decision, or whether it is only the award of the majority of them." [1] It may, however, be questioned whether makeshifts of this kind are really of much avail. For it is highly probable that, in spite of, or, perhaps, partly because of, them, the Board will be *thought* to have disagreed, and this is the important point. Except, therefore, when the opinion of the parties tends strongly in favour of multiplicity, it seems clear that the panel had best be a single man.

Thirdly, we have to consider the method of an arbitrator's appointment. There are several different ways in which he may be chosen. [2] Perhaps the most satisfactory is

---

[1] *Strikes and Lock-outs*, 1892, p. 217. There was the same rule for the National Arbitration Board, agreed upon in 1901 between the American Newspaper Publishers' Association and the International Typographical Union (*Industrial Commission*, xvii. p. 367).

[2] The Window Glass Cutters' League of North America has the following interesting method of selection : " If the arbitrators cannot agree on the referee,

that of the Durham Wages Board, where he is elected at the first Board meeting of each year. Annual election of this kind, while not incompatible with prolonged tenure of office, avoids some of the dangers involved in a permanent or very long appointment. For great friction might arise if one side came to consider the arbitrator at once irremovable and biassed in favour of their opponents. Furthermore, election at fixed periods is superior to election *ad hoc*, because an arbitrator is most likely to command confidence if he is chosen by agreement of both sides, and he will seldom be so chosen if his election is deferred until after a difference has arisen. When, in spite of these considerations, an *ad hoc* appointment is preferred, the most obvious arrangement is that the parties should first try to agree on an arbitrator, and, if unsuccessful, should accept one nominated by an impartial outsider. There is, however, a danger that they may try, *and fail*, to agree on the very man who is afterwards imposed on them from without, or that they may have urged against some other suggested name reasons which hold equally against him. It is, therefore, more satisfactory for them to nominate an impartial person, such as the Speaker of the House of Commons, whose duty it shall be to appoint an arbitrator when requested to do so, no name having previously been discussed by the Conciliation Board.

§ 7. The next point to notice is relevant both to arrangements in which there is, and to arrangements in which there is not, provision for arbitration in the last resort. On the whole it seems unwise, *if it can be helped*, to allow anything in the nature of a referendum from the appointed negotiators to the main body of either employers or employed. The ill-informed popular discussion, which would necessarily follow, could hardly fail to stir up irritation and water the seeds of conflict. When the Conciliation Board cannot agree, and when there is not provision for arbitration, it might, indeed, appear at first sight as though an appeal from the

---

then each arbitrator shall write two names of disinterested parties, not in any way connected with the glass business, on slips of paper, all names shall be put into a bag, and the first name drawn out shall be the person selected as the referee " (Rule 18, *ibid.* p. 365).

representatives to their constituents is worth trying as a forlorn hope to prevent war. Practically, however, such a provision will often do more harm than good. If the men's representatives—it is on the men's side only that the question of a referendum has any practical importance—think a point worth fighting for, their constituents are perfectly certain to be at least as bellicose as they. If the representatives do not think it worth fighting for, were there no referendum, they would arrange it; if there is a referendum, they may be weak enough to shift the responsibility, and the men may elect to fight. Moreover, the employers will probably limit their attempts at conciliation when failure to agree means to them, not the absolute certainty of a strike, but only a probability, the extreme greatness of which optimism may lead them to minimise.[1] Hence the chance of an agreement being reached, so far from being augmented, is actually reduced. When there is provision for arbitration, an intermediate reference to the Board's constituents after the failure of conciliation is at least equally dangerous. For, again, the men are practically certain to support their leaders when these are bellicose, and it will hardly conduce to calmness or good feeling should they vote in a body against the very terms which an arbitrator afterwards finds it his duty to award. The off-chance of avoiding arbitration is a worse argument for the referendum than the off-chance of avoiding a strike.

What has been said against this policy, in controversies about which the Conciliation Board has failed to agree, has, of course, still greater force in those where it has succeeded. If there is no arbitration clause, a referendum, in these circumstances, might not improbably substitute war for peace. If, on the other hand, there is such a clause, the referendum would be futile, since an arbitrator, called in through the refusal of either side to endorse the Board's decision, is

---

[1] This argument is more strong, but the preceding one is considerably less so, when the referendum is on the plan of that provided for in the rules of the American Amalgamated Association of Iron, Steel and Tin Workers. Here, when a conference between employers and employed fails to agree, "it requires two-thirds of all the members of the organisation voting to insist upon the demands which have given rise to the disagreement" (*Industrial Commission*, xvii. p. 340).

practically bound to reiterate that decision, if not still further to stiffen it in opposition to the dissatisfied party.

These results are, of course, subject to the general caution that what appears to be ideally best is not always practically possible. When the men's organisation is weak or the authority of their leaders slight, acceptance by referendum may sometimes be the only form in which acceptance for a decision can be secured at all. In a Grimsby fishing dispute in 1902 the officials of the Gasworkers' Union even found it necessary to take a ballot as to whether a decision promulgated, not by a conciliation committee, but by a regularly appointed Board of Trade arbitrator applied for by both sides, should or should not be accepted. These difficulties must be clearly recognised. They do not, however, interfere with our conclusion that a referendum from negotiators to their constituents should be avoided whenever this is possible.

§ 8. Finally there is the question of guarantees—whether for the observance of agreements entered into directly by the parties, or for the acceptance of the award of an arbitrator to whom they have agreed to submit the dispute. In some agreements each party gives a guarantee in the form of a money deposit subject to forfeit. Thus, after the great strike of 1895, the National Associations in the English boot and shoe trade agreed to place £1000 each with trustees, part of which would be forfeited should either be "deemed to have broken an agreement, award or decision"; while, "if any provision of this agreement, or if an award, agreement or decision is broken by any manufacturer or body of workmen belonging to the Federation or National Union, and the Federation or National Union fail within ten days either to induce such members to comply with the agreement, decision or award, or to expel them from the organisation, the Federation or the National Union shall be deemed to have broken the agreement, award or decision,"[1] and shall, thereupon, become

---

[1] Provision 9 of the Agreement *Report on Collective Agreements* [Cd. 5366], 1910, p. 231. When the Union failed to expel the London strikers in 1899, Lord James of Hereford awarded £300 damages from the Union's deposit to the employers (*ibid.* p. 505). Evasion of the fine by refusal to replace money withdrawn under it can be met by a rule that, in this event, the whole of the deposit shall be forfeited. When the agreement was renewed in 1909, the phrase providing for expulsion from the organisation was deleted.

liable to forfeit some or all of their deposit. No doubt, when there is uncertainty as to the power of an association to maintain discipline among its members, its ability to show recalcitrant members that their conduct is causing it to be fined would do something to strengthen its position against them. Apart, however, from this consideration—and in strong Unions it is not an important one—the value of monetary guarantees is doubtful. The Report of the Industrial Council (1912) on the advantages and disadvantages involved is as follows : " Considerable diversity of opinion appears to exist in regard to the efficacy of a monetary guarantee. If the fund is intended to be one out of which a penalty is payable equivalent to the amount of damage suffered, it is clear that, in order to provide for a case involving a large number of persons, the sum of money which it would be necessary to deposit would be such that many of the smaller organisations would be unable to set aside so large a proportion of their funds, or to obtain money for such a purpose. If, on the other hand, the penalty to be paid is merely in the nature of a fine, it does not appear that the adoption of the principle adds much to the restraining influence which is already exercised by the moral obligation to observe agreements. . . . We are of opinion, therefore, that the general adoption of the system of monetary guarantees, in the form of a deposit of money, cannot be regarded as constituting a practicable and efficient means of ensuring the fulfilment of agreements. At the same time, when monetary guarantees are voluntarily offered, we see no objection to their adoption." [1] This conclusion will probably command general assent.

[1] *Loc. cit.* p. 11.

CHAPTER IV

§ 1. THE experience of the United Kingdom and of the United States affords abundant proof that purely voluntary arrangements entered into by employers and workpeople, when worked in a friendly spirit, can do a great deal towards promoting industrial peace. But these arrangements are not adequate to prevent strikes or lock-outs in all circumstances. Purely conciliatory schemes may be broken into by war even during the period of their currency ; and schemes in which provision is made for arbitration may fail to be renewed when this period comes to an end. On occasions of this kind, when voluntary machinery within an industry is lacking or threatens to prove inadequate, something further is necessary if industrial war is to be averted. The solution which naturally suggests itself is that of friendly mediation. In behalf of this the general argument is strong and straightforward. When once a difference has become accentuated, and, still more, when it has developed into an open conflict, both sides are apt to be striving for the " mastery," as well as for the particular object in dispute. They stand to lose dignity as well as money, and, consequently, their obstinacy will be much greater than the material point alone can justify. Not only is this, as a matter of fact, so, but it is frequently known to be so by the parties themselves. They will often have considered some matter worth the *chance* of a rupture, but not worth the certainty of one. Hence, when the rupture actually arrives, all that may be needed is some device for facilitating withdrawal, without undue loss of dignity, from a position assumed for purposes of bluff. Even if, in the earlier stages of a conflict, no way out seems acceptable, a point is sure to be reached sooner or later when one party will be willing to yield, if it can "save its face" in doing so. Hence the opportunity for the "good offices" of a mediator. His appearance on the scene makes prominent the fact, apt to be lost sight of in the heat of controversy, that the general public, as well as the parties directly concerned, have an interest in peace. The mere suggestion from him that a conference should be held may, in some circumstances, of itself suffice to bring about a settlement; and, where it falls short of this large measure of success, tact and a genial luncheon party may still indirectly advance the prospects of peace.[1] For, in the presence of a mediator, the element of "proper pride" and "courage never to submit or yield" is eliminated by the suggestion that reconciliation is made as a favour to a friend, and not as a concession to an adversary. Furthermore, even when good offices do not effect an actual settlement, they may secure that a difference shall be resolved by arbitration instead of by industrial war. Perhaps the most effective way in which a mediator can forward this result is by helping the disputants in the difficult task of finding some mutually acceptable person to decide between them. In this matter the assistance of the British Board of Trade, before its duties were taken over by the Ministry of Labour, used frequently to be invoked.

§ 2. Since there is, thus, scope for mediatorial intervention, it becomes important to examine the different institutions through which it may be made to work. There are three kinds of mediators—the eminent outsider, the non-governmental Board, and the Board connected with some part of the governmental system of the country. These are not mutually incompatible, but can advantageously be used to supplement one another. The great advantage of the first is that the intervention of men like Bishop Westcott,[2] Lord Rosebery,[3] Lord James,[4] Mr. Asquith,[5] or the Prime Minister

---

[1] Cf. Mr. and Mrs. Webb's opinion of the efficacy of Lord Rosebery's luncheon party in conciliating the parties in the coal dispute of 1893 (*Industrial Democracy*, p. 242).

[2] The Durham Coal Strike, 1892.   [3] The Federation Coal Strike, 1893.

[4] The Clyde and Belfast Engineering Dispute, 1895.

[5] The London Cab Strike.

of the day, of itself tends somewhat to smooth the course
of events by flattering the disputants with a sense of their
own importance. The ordinary Board of Mediation, whether
voluntary or official, has not, as a rule, such distinguished
names to conjure with, and is, so far, inferior. Hence for
a certain class of disputes the eminent outsider cannot be
dispensed with.

§ 3. The usefulness of the non-governmental Board is less
generally admitted. It has, indeed, the advantage over the
eminent outsider that, not being constituted *ad hoc*, it is more
readily brought into play, and has a better chance of making
its voice heard in that breathing space before a strike or lock-
out actually begins, when mediation is most likely to succeed.
It has been urged, however, that, whereas in this country a
great number of mediatorial Boards have been set up by the
Chambers of Commerce and Trades Councils of different towns,
none of them, except the London Board, has produced the
slightest effect. In short, according to this argument, the
system of non-governmental Boards has been tried and found
by experience to be worthless. The evidence adduced, however, is inadequate to support so sweeping a conclusion. The
Boards which have failed are exclusively *municipal* Boards, and,
with labour organised as it is in England, the conduct even of
purely local differences is not likely to be left altogether to
the men on the spot. May it not, then, be fairly urged that
the failure of these Boards was due, not to their non-governmental character, but to the narrowness of the area which
they covered, and does not the comparative success of the
London Board add weight to this suggestion ? If, however,
the facts can be thus explained, they do not warrant us in
supposing that local non-governmental Boards would fail if
tried on the less completely unionised soil of the Continent.
Still less do they prove that a non-governmental *national*
Board is doomed to failure. Indeed, a Board of this kind,
under the name of the Industrial Department of the National
Civic Federation, has had considerable success in the United
States.

§ 4. Nevertheless, though it would be a mistake to ignore
the possibilities of non-governmental Boards, it is plain that

there are certain advantages inaccessible to them, but readily available to Boards attached to the governmental machinery of the country. In the first place, the latter possess exceptional facilities—facilities second only to those enjoyed by voluntary Conciliation Boards in particular industries—for ascertaining the existence of differences at the earliest possible moment. For administrative officials can be required to supply them with immediate information whenever a strike or lock-out occurs or is seriously threatened. In the second place, they have greater intellectual and financial resources, and are likely to be more liberal in the use of them. Thus it is probable that the trained ability which the Ministry of Labour—as once the Board of Trade—can command has a good deal to do with the preference displayed for it, as against local Boards, by the parties to disputes covering a small area. Lastly, when, as on the plan adopted in England, the emissaries employed are sent out directly from a central State department, instead of being, as in France, mere local officials endowed with mediatorial powers, they are likely to wield a modicum of reputation which may help them considerably in their work. Consequently, it is not surprising to find that in recent times the work of mediation in industrial disputes has been taken over in great part by machinery attached to some organ of government. In some countries the offer of mediation may only be made on the request of one or other of the parties to a difference. Thus a Belgian law of 1887 authorised the establishment locally of councils of industry and labour with sections representing different industries, and provided : " Whenever circumstances appear to demand it, at the request of either party, the governor of the province, the mayor of the commune, or the president of the section for the industry in which the dispute occurs must convene that section, which is to endeavour, by conciliation, to arrange a settlement." [1] More frequently, however, mediation is authorised at the discretion of the public authority, whether it is asked for by a party to the difference or not. This is the arrangement under the French law of 1892 and under the English Conciliation Act of 1896. The latter Act provides : " When a difference exists, or is apprehended,

[1] *Bulletin of U.S.A. Bureau of Labour*, No. 60, p. 421.

between an employer or any class of employers and workmen, the Board of Trade may, if they think fit, exercise all or any of the following powers, namely : (1) inquire into the causes and circumstances of the difference ; (2) take such steps as to the Board may seem expedient for the purpose of enabling the parties to the difference to meet together, by themselves or their representatives, under the presidency of a chairman mutually agreed upon or nominated by the Board of Trade or by some other person or body, with a view to the amicable settlement of differences ; (3) on the application of employers or workmen interested, and after taking into consideration the existence and adequacy of the means available for conciliation in the district or trade and the circumstances of the case, appoint a person or persons to act as conciliator or as a board of conciliators." The Ministry of Labour, fortified with the Industrial Courts Act of 1919, has inherited these powers from the Board of Trade. Experience shows that mediation, skilfully and sympathetically conducted along these lines, can often bring about the adjustment of differences that might otherwise very probably have led to a stoppage of work.

§ 5. Thus we may conclude generally that eminent outsiders, non-governmental Boards and official agencies of mediation are all valuable in their spheres. It must not, however, be forgotten that they are also dangerous. As an indirect consequence of their presence, the development of peace-promoting machinery within separate industries — a more effective solvent of differences than "good offices" are ever likely to be—may be checked. To prevent this result, discretion on the part of the intervening body is essential. It should never arrogate to itself the claim to more than a transitory usefulness, and should carefully encourage—as the British Board of Trade, under the Act of 1896, and its successor, the Ministry of Labour, have always aimed at doing—the formation of mutual Boards in the industries with which it is brought into contact.

CHAPTER V

§ 1. JUST as differences may prove too hard for voluntary conciliation schemes, so too they may defy the efforts of mediators. The possibility, or rather, except in the developed industries of countries which have reached a high stage of industrial peace, the frequent occurrence of these intractable controversies makes it necessary to inquire whether, and how far, resort should be had to the coercive powers of the State. Intervention of this kind may take place in four principal ways. Of these the simplest and mildest merely makes provision for disputants to enter the net of compulsory adjudication whenever both of them wish to do so. Examples are fairly numerous. In New South Wales the Industrial Arbitration Act of 1901 empowered any industrial union to make an agreement relatively to any industrial matter with another union or with an employer, which, "if made for a specified term not exceeding three years, and, if a copy be filed with the registrar, will be binding on the parties thereto and on every person while he is a member of any union which is a party to the agreement"; and declares "that any such agreement, as between the parties bound by the same, shall have the same effect, and may be enforced in the same way, as an award of the Court of Arbitration."[1] The New Zealand law makes industrial agreements enforceable in the same way as awards of the national Court of Arbitration. Mr. Mundella's abortive English Act of 1872, the Massachusetts provision that, when both parties refer a difference to the State Board, the decision automatically becomes binding,

[1] *Labour Gazette*, Feb. 1902, p. 39.

and the Federal Railway Act of 1898, enabling interstate
carriers voluntarily to establish Arbitration Boards with compulsory powers,[1] were similar in character and intention.
The English law has proved a dead letter, and was repealed
in 1896, but those of Massachusetts and New Zealand have
had a considerable measure of success.

In opposition to this arrangement it may be urged, first,
that, when once arbitration has been agreed upon, a sense of
what is fair and a wholesome respect for public opinion
already afford an adequate guarantee that awards will be
obeyed; secondly, that the introduction of a legal sanction
would so far destroy the honourable one—the payment of the
penalty being felt to condone the offence[2]—that the *net*
sanction would be no stronger than before; and thirdly, that,
through the association in the popular mind of the idea of
compulsion with that of arbitration, "resort to [Conciliation
Boards] for their various purposes would be made less freely
than at present."[3] It may be replied, however, that, at the
worst, since non-coercive arbitration would still be open to
those who preferred it, there is little reason to believe that
differences, which, save for the change, would have been
settled peaceably, will now involve a conflict. Furthermore, the effect of coercive sanctions, in checking resort even
to those Courts which wield them, is much slighter than is
generally supposed. In some circumstances their influence
would actually tend in the opposite direction. In differences
where each party considered itself, and knew that the other
party considered itself, the stronger, there might be no settlement, procurable under a system of weak sanctions, from
which one or other of them would not think it worth while
to break away. Consequently, arbitration might be declined
from dislike to the risk of these ineffective sanctions. If,
however, the sanctions offered were strong, the position would
be different. A series of possible settlements would be

---

[1] *U.S.A. Industrial Commission*, vol. xvii. p. 423.

[2] Cf. *The Report of the Industrial Council on Industrial Agreements*,
1912, p. 7.

[3] *Royal Commission on Labour*, Report, p. 99. Of course, universal compulsion to accept awards, unaccompanied by universal compulsion of reference,
would have this effect in a far more marked degree.

opened up, which, when awarded, could not be profitably violated by either side, and the risk of which both would be willing to incur, since the extra loss involved in failure would be balanced by an extra gain in success. Finally, the power to invoke legal sanctions may strengthen the hands of the leaders of either organisation against their discontented followers. This consideration is especially important where, as in the United States, the direct control of Union executives over individual members is comparatively slight. It is not, however, to be ignored even in this country, for, though, in our greater Unions, breaches of award in defiance of the central authority are rare, among the low-skilled industries they are fairly common. On the whole, therefore, the case seems to be made out for some system under which opportunities for referring differences to a Court with coercive powers is given to those who desire to avail themselves of it.

§ 2. The second way in which the State may intervene is by enabling organisations of employers and employed to invoke government aid in extending to the whole of a trade in a district or country an agreement that has been entered into by associations representing the main body of employers and workpeople engaged in it. In South Australia an Act of 1910 provides that, in trades where there are no Wages Boards, three-fifths of the employers and of the employed may make an agreement and require the government to promulgate it, so that it becomes binding upon the whole trade. The English Munitions Act of 1917 contained a substantially similar provision. The principal argument in favour of legislation of this kind is that, in the absence of it, agreements entered into by the great majority of those engaged in an industry are liable to be disrupted by the competition of a few " bad " employers. For often an employer or group of employers would lose nothing by paying better wages or working shorter hours, provided that all their competitors did the same, but would lose a great deal by doing this, and would, consequently, refuse to do it, if that condition was not fulfilled. Thus it has been stated that " one of the provoking causes of the second and disastrous transport strike in London was the withdrawal of a firm of carters from an agreement which it had signed, in order to compete with the other firms by paying a lower scale of wages than they did."[1] On the other side, however, several considerations of weight may be advanced. In the first place, State action of the kind contemplated would dangerously facilitate the formation of rings and alliances to the detriment of consumers. Secondly, there would sometimes be very great practical difficulty in determining the lengths to which extension should be carried. For the similarity between the products of different districts in an industry is often more apparent than real, and, when this is so, the maintenance of a parallel movement between the rates prevailing in them might work against peace rather than in favour of it. This difficulty may be illustrated from certain voluntary arrangements which have prevailed at one time or another in this country. Thus in 1874 a combined scale was constructed for the iron trade of the Midlands and the North of England. In the North, however, iron rails were still the chief product, while in the Midlands manufacturers were already engaged in producing bars, plates and angles. For the former the market was falling, but it was rising for the latter, with the result that the employers of the North were compelled, at the first adjustment under the scale, to raise wages by 3d., although the price of their own chief ware was falling. Consequently, the scale collapsed within the year. Similarly, there existed for some time in many parts of Lancashire an understanding that the wages of cotton-spinners should rise and fall with advances and reductions in the Oldham district. But " the increasing specialisation of districts, with respect to the yarns produced in them, was instrumental in rendering unworkable an arrangement which had at least been possible, if not desirable, some time before. What had been one market for yarns, roughly speaking, became many markets; and the prices for different ranges and qualities of yarn beginning to move more independently, rendered any sliding arrangements between the lists unsatisfactory."[2] It is true, no doubt, that a policy of extension does not absolutely exclude adjustment

---

[1] Ramsay MacDonald, *The Social Unrest*, p. 109.
[2] Chapman, *Economic Journal*, 1899, p. 598.

to the varying conditions of different districts. But it can hardly be doubted that the task of making these adjustments would often demand greater elasticity in the extensions than the patience and wisdom of the officials concerned are competent to provide. Thirdly, it may be urged that, where the workpeople's organisation is powerful, extension by authority is superfluous, because private enterprise is sufficient to ensure it. The employers are anxious to have recalcitrant competitors brought into line, and the workpeople are no less anxious to help them. Hence, " Trade Unions assist employers' associations to coerce employers into submission to an agreement which they have not signed," and " collective bargaining thus extends over a much larger field than Trade Unionism." [1] The United States Industrial Commission found, for example, that in Illinois the United Mine Workers' Society is expected to strike or threaten to strike in order to bring recalcitrant employers to terms, and that in practice it is generally successful in securing this result.[2] This last consideration, however, is obviously not relevant to industries in which the workpeople's organisation is weak. On the whole, in spite of the possible risks to consumers and of the practical difficulties set out above, and in spite also of the danger that " the extension of the benefits of organisation to the unorganised may tend to perpetuate the class of non-union hangers-on of labour and unfederated hangers-on of capitalists, men who reap the benefit of organisation but refuse to pay their share," [3] it would seem that opinion in this country is not now unfavourably disposed towards this strictly limited form of coercive intervention in industrial disputes. Definite support was given to it in the Report of the Industrial Council (1912), subject to the condition that the Board of Trade should not entertain any application for the extension of an agreement, unless such application was received from both the parties to the agreement. In the Coal Mining Industry Act of 1920 it is provided that recommendations made by District Committees, by Area Boards,

---

[1] Gilman, *Methods of Industrial Peace*, pp. 116-17.
[2] Cf. *Industrial Commission*, vol. xvii. p. 329.
[3] Cole, *The World of Labour*, p. 314.

or by the National Board shall be made compulsory on persons engaged in the industry, if the Board of Trade so directs: and in the Corn Production Act (Repeal) of 1921—superseded three years later by the establishment of a system of Agricultural Wages Boards—the decisions of the voluntary conciliation committees as to minimum wage rates might, if a committee so desired, be made enforceable at law throughout their districts after confirmation by the Board of Agriculture.

§ 3. The third way of State intervention is by laws compelling industrial differences to be referred to some tribunal before any strike or lock-out in the industries covered by the law is permitted. This system is best illustrated by the Canadian Industrial Disputes Investigation Act of 1907. That Act has been imitated in South Africa and elsewhere, and served as model for a United States enactment, covering disputes extending over several States, passed in 1925.[1] In January 1925, after eighteen years of operation, it was declared *ultra vires* by the Judicial Committee of the Privy Council, on the ground that it infringed the rights of the provincial governments. In consequence of this ruling an amending Act was passed, which somewhat restricted its range but left its substance unchanged.[2] The Act is not of general application, but refers exclusively to certain industries in which there is reason to believe that a stoppage of work would prove exceptionally injurious to the community as a whole. The industries covered are mining, transportation, all forms of railway service, the supply of electricity and other motive power, the working of steamships, the telegraph and telephone services, gas supply and water supply. Practically speaking, the Act comes into play in these industries whenever a stoppage of work is seriously threatened, and it cannot be successfully evaded by a joint refusal of both parties to invoke it. The principal provisions are as follows. Thirty days' notice must be given of any proposed change in the terms of contract between employers and employed. If the proposed change is resisted by the other side, a strike or lock-out in reference to it is prohibited,

[1] Cf. Mond, *Industry and Politics*, p. 131.
[2] Cf. *A Survey of Industrial Relations* by the Committee on Industry and Trade, 1926, pp. 355 *et seq.*

under penalties, until the dispute has been investigated by a Board appointed by public authority and until this Board has made a report, together with recommendations as to the proper terms of settlement, for publication by the Minister of Labour. When the report has been published, there is no obligation upon either party to accept its recommendations, and a stoppage of work may legally take place. But, until the report is published, a stoppage is prohibited by law and renders any individual taking part in it liable to a fine ; for employers engaging in a lock-out, of from 100 to 1000 dollars per day ; for workpeople engaging in a strike, of from 10 to 50 dollars per day.

This law, it will be noticed, has three distinct aspects. First, it goes a long way towards ensuring serious discussion between the parties—this is practically involved in the Board's investigations—and an attempt to settle their differences under the guidance, and with the help, of an impartial authority. Secondly, it gives full power to a tribunal appointed by the government " to investigate the matter in dispute, with similar powers in regard to witnesses, production of documents and inspection as are vested in a court of record in civil cases, with a view, if conciliation fails, to recommendations being made as to what are believed to be fair terms."[1] Thirdly, it makes a stoppage of work unlawful until the investigation of the difference has been completed and a report presented. It has been held by competent authorities who have studied the working of the law that the first of these aspects is, in practice, the most valuable. The Reporter to the United States Bureau of Labour writes : " The principal service of the Board is in bringing the parties to the controversy together for an amicable discussion and in guiding the negotiations to a voluntary settlement."[2] He adds : " The Government in appointing Boards, and the most successful Boards in conducting proceedings, have interpreted the Act as a statute for conciliation by informal methods, looking towards a voluntary agreement between the parties as its object."[3] In like manner, Lord (then Sir George) Askwith, in his Report to the British Board

---

[1] Report by Sir George Askwith [Cd. 6603], p. 17.
[2] *United States Bulletin of Labour*, No. 86, 1910, p. 17.   [3] *Ibid.* No. 76, p. 666.

of Trade in 1913, expressed the opinion "that the forwarding of the spirit and intent of conciliation is the more valuable portion of the Canadian Act."[1] None the less, the provision for the promulgation at need of an authoritative report and recommendations may also, on occasions, yield good results. It is true that in trifling disputes, in which the general public takes small interest, little pressure from public opinion can be evoked, and that in all disputes, when once the passion of conflict has been aroused, even strong pressure may be ignored. But, when the issue is one which seriously affects the whole community, by threatening to disorganise, e.g., the railway service or the coal supply, public opinion is a force which must at least be reckoned with; and it is interesting to observe that, on a number of occasions, when one or other of the parties at first refused to accept the recommendations of the Board and a strike or lock-out took place, the dispute was ultimately settled substantially on the basis of the Board's proposals. The third aspect of the law, that which makes a strike or lock-out unlawful until after the Board has reported, is the one about which the most serious doubts have been expressed. There is the objection that, given determined opposition, it may prove impracticable to enforce the law;[2] and the objection that the success of a strike often depends upon its suddenness, so that any enforced delay necessarily handicaps the workpeople. These objections are undoubtedly substantial, though there are some industries, e.g. the transport industries, in which the strike weapon is not appreciably weakened by delay in resort to it. On the other side, stress is laid upon the fact that, when once industrial war has broken out, the issue chiefly in dispute is apt to be lost in a fight for mastery, which only exhaustion can end, and that, therefore, even though the law should often fail to prevent an outbreak, the chance that it will sometimes succeed, and so obviate

[1] [Cd. 6603], p. 17.

[2] In Canada there have, in fact, been numerous illegal stoppages of work and very few attempts to enforce penalties for them. The Deputy Minister of Labour has stated publicly : " It has not been the policy of successive Ministers under whose authority the statute has been administered to undertake the enforcement of the provision."—*United States Bulletin of Labour*, No. 233, 1918, p. 139. Cf. also Report of the Delegation to inquire into industrial conditions in Canada and the U.S.A. [Cmd. 2833], p. 80.

grave injury to the community, constitutes for it an adequate defence. Plainly on this issue no decision of a general kind is possible. What ought, in fact, to be done depends chiefly on what workpeople and employers think ought to be done, and are, therefore, prepared to support. It is, however, now generally agreed that an Act on the Canadian model, without penal clauses against strikes and lock-outs prior to the promulgation of the Board's recommendations, and accompanied, so far as possible, by safeguards to prevent injurious reactions upon the development of voluntary schemes of conciliation and arbitration, is, in Lord Askwith's words, "suitable and practicable for this country." Part II. of the Industrial Court Act of 1919 in effect constitutes such an Act. It empowers the Minister of Labour, when a dispute either exists or is apprehended, to appoint a court of inquiry, armed with the power to compel evidence on oath, whose business it shall be to make an impartial report on the merits of the dispute—a report which the Minister, if he thinks fit, may make public. At present it could not safely include the critical penal clause. But there is much to be said for that clause ; and, if the League of Nations proves its ability to enforce delay in the outbreak of political war, public opinion may presently become ready to accept a similar restraint upon the outbreak of industrial war.

§ 4. The fourth and last way of State intervention is what is commonly and loosely known as compulsory arbitration. Under the Canadian Act, if the parties remain intractable alike to efforts at conciliation and to the suasion of opinion, strikes and lock-outs can ultimately take place without any infringement of the law. It was left to the Australasian colonies to initiate a type of legislation under which, not only does a publicly appointed Board recommend terms for the settlement of differences, but the terms so recommended are legally binding and a strike or lock-out against them is a punishable offence. This type of legislation, when fully developed, closes that loop-hole for a stoppage of work which the Canadian law leaves open. Generally speaking, some effort is made not unduly to discourage settlement by discussion and conciliation, but the principal stress is laid on preventing resort to a strike or lock-out in those difficult conflicts where less heroic expedients have failed. In New Zealand, indeed, a loop-hole is still left. For the compulsory arbitration law of that colony applies only to unions of workpeople registered under the arbitration law, other workpeople being governed, under an Amendment of 1913, by a variant of the Canadian type of law.[1] But in the corresponding laws of New South Wales (prior to the relaxing amendment of 1918) and Western Australia there is no such reservation, and the same remark holds true of the Commonwealth law relating to differences that extend over more than one State. In all these laws the arbitration awards are "sanctioned" by a money fine. In New Zealand individual employers and unions of workpeople who break the law are liable to a penalty of £500, and, if a union of workpeople fails to pay, its individual members are each held liable to a fine of £10, which may be collected through a writ of attachment of wages. Western Australia, like New Zealand, relies wholly on money penalties, but the New South Wales law provides also for the imprisonment of persons who fail to pay their fines, and the Commonwealth law awards imprisonment, without the option of a fine, for a second offence. In 1923 Germany introduced what is in effect compulsory arbitration at the discretion of the government. Conciliation committees are constituted with power to intervene in industrial disputes either at the request of one of the parties or on their own initiative. "If the Board does not succeed in securing agreement between the parties, it may put forward a proposed award, which, if accepted, shall have the force of a written collective agreement. If the proposed award is not accepted by both parties, it may be declared binding if its provisions appear just and reasonable, taking into account the interests of both parties, or if its application is desirable for economic and social reasons; the conciliator of the region, or in some cases the Federal Minister, is the competent authority for

[1] This Amendment admits that a strike may be legal if (1) the strikers are not working under an award or industrial agreement or decide by secret ballot that the award no longer binds them, and (2) give fourteen days' notice to the Minister of Labour of their intention to begin a strike (*Economic Journal*, 1921, p. 309).

declaring an award binding."[1] An important dispute in the Ruhr coal-field in 1927 was settled by resort to this provision. In 1926 Italy passed a general law for compulsory arbitration in industrial disputes, with fines and imprisonment as sanctions against recusants.[2] It is obvious, of course, that no legal prohibition and no provision of penalties can ensure that the prohibited action will *never* be performed. No surprise need, therefore, be caused by the circumstance that, in the Australasian colonies, in spite of their coercive laws, stoppages of work on account of industrial disputes have, in fact, occurred. This is only to be expected. The advocates of compulsory arbitration do not deny it. Nor are they blind to the practical difficulties that may be presented by collusive evasions of the law or by determined refusals to pay fines. Their claim is, not that these laws can create a " country without strikes," but that, by invoking a pressure more direct and potent than that of unorganised opinion, upon which alone the Canadian law in the last resort relies, they can render stoppages of work less frequent than they would otherwise be. How far this claim has been made good in the experience of New Zealand and the Australian States is a controversial question, which could only be answered satisfactorily after prolonged study on the spot. But, from the practical standpoint of English statesmen at the present time, that study is not necessary. It is common ground that legislation, to which the opinion of large masses of the population is strongly opposed, is likely to prove at once difficult to enforce and injurious to that general respect for law which it is to the interest of every community to maintain. Mr. Pember Reeves, the author of the New Zealand law, has himself declared that " to attempt to force such a statute upon an unwilling people would be foredoomed to disaster."[3] In England—and the same thing would seem to be true of the United States—compulsory arbitration, as distinguished from the system of Trade Boards in badly organised industries, is at present looked upon by employers and employed alike with very great distrust. To introduce it at a single stride in

---

[1] *Minimum Wage-fixing Machinery*, International Labour Office (1927), p. 56.
[2] *Ibid.* pp. 85-7.   [3] *State Experiments in Australia*, p. 168.

Q

the face of this general sentiment would be both impracticable and unwise. Public opinion may, no doubt, change and, at a future time, welcome what it now rejects, but at present, whatever may be thought of its abstract merits, compulsory arbitration in the United Kingdom is not practical politics in any department of industry. The partial resort that was had to it during the war does not suggest that it affords a satisfactory method of avoiding strikes—during the thirty-three months that the Munitions of War Acts were in force they were violated by some 1,500,000 workmen [1]—; and in normal times, when the pressure of national need is slighter, it would probably meet with still less acceptance and, therefore, with still less success.[2]

[1] Cf. Montgomery, *British and Continental Labour Policy*, p. 345.
[2] Cf. *The Report on Conciliation and Arbitration*, to the Ministry of Reconstruction [Cd. 9099], 1918, Par. 2.

CHAPTER VI

AN ANALYTICAL VIEW OF INDUSTRIAL PEACE

§ 1. WHAT has been said in the preceding chapters will serve well enough for the rough purposes of practice. But it is interesting to the economist to probe somewhat deeper, and to set out some of the broader issues that have been raised in a different guise. From an analytical point of view differences between a workmen's union and an employers' association are analogous to differences between two nations. When the differences concern such things as the general conditions of work, the methods of wage payment, the hours of labour and the demarcation of work, the analogy is close. But, when they concern wages, there is an important distinction. Issues between governments usually do not, but issues about wages always do, refer to a *rate of interchange* between two things, the quantities to be exchanged being left unspecified.[1] In negotiations of this character the one party does not always benefit himself by forcing the other to accept more and more unpalatable terms. On the contrary, after a point, any further raising of the rate against an opponent will bring about such a reduction in the quantity of the thing which he is prepared to buy that, to put it paradoxically, the victor is made actually worse off by getting better terms. Thus, when the bargain is about a rate, there will be certain upper and lower limits outside of which it will not pay either party to go, whereas, when the bargain is about a thing, there are no such limits.

§ 2. When, both on the side of workpeople and on that of employers, competition works with perfect freedom, the

[1] Cf. *ante*, Part II. Chapter IX. § 14.

result of a bargain about the rate of wages is determinate at a single definite rate, which is settled by the conditions of reciprocal demand. If any worker asks for more than this from any employer, that employer will refuse to engage him and will take somebody else, and, if any employer offers any less than this to any workman, that workman will refuse to work for him and will go to somebody else. Where, however, wage rates are settled, not by the action of free competition, but by bargaining between a workmen's association on one side and an employers' association on the other, the rate of wage is no longer determinate at a single point. There is, on the contrary, a *range of indeterminateness*. The workmen's association will prefer to the competitive rate something higher than that rate, and the employers' association something lower. In view of the fact that a rise in the rate will lessen the amount of employment obtainable, there will be a certain maximum rate above which the workpeople's association will not wish to go, and, in view of the fact that a reduction in the rate will lessen the amount of labour obtainable, there will be a certain minimum rate below which the employers' association will not wish to go. *The range of indeterminateness* is constituted by all the rates enclosed within these two limits. Let us suppose that they are 40s. and 30s. respectively. From any rate lying outside this range it is to the interest of both sides to depart in the same direction. It is, therefore, impossible for a settlement to be reached with any wage rate outside that range. If there is any settlement it must fall at some point within it. The extent of the range will be larger the less elastic is the demand for labour by the employers, and the less elastic is the demand for jobs with these employers by the workpeople.

§ 3. In considering their policy, the workpeople's association will reflect that, if they elect to fight a battle about wages, the fight will cost them so much and the terms obtained at the end of the fight are likely to be such and such. Weighing up these things, they will determine on a certain minimum wage which it is worth while, if necessary, to accept rather than fight. This will be, as it were, their *sticking point*. If they think that a fight would cost them a great deal and that they would get bad terms at the end, this sticking point will be low. It may be a good deal lower than the 30s., which we have supposed to be the lower limit of the range of indeterminateness. On the other hand, if they think that a fight would cost them very little (or, still more, if they think that the actual process of it would benefit them), and that they would get good terms at the end, their sticking point will be high. It may be as high as, but cannot be higher than, the 40s., which is the upper end of the range of indeterminateness. Thus the workpeople's sticking point may, according to circumstances, be any wage less than 40s. By similar reasoning it can be shown that the employers' sticking point may, according to circumstances, be any wage greater than 30s. When the workpeople's sticking point is lower than the employers' sticking point, the range of wages between the two sticking points constitutes, subject to a qualification to be introduced presently, the *range of practicable bargains*. Thus, if the workpeople would take 32s. rather than fight and the employers would pay 37s. rather than fight, this range is made up of all rates between 32s. and 37s. When, however, the workpeople's sticking point is above the employers' sticking point, when, for example, the workpeople would go as low as 35s., but no lower, rather than fight, and the employers would go as high as 33s., but no higher, rather than fight, there is no range of practicable bargains; and it is impossible for the issue between the two sides to be settled without a fight.

§ 4. If both sides have the same expectations as to the way in which a fight would end and as to the wage rate that would be established in consequence of it, and if each side believes that the process of the fight would involve some positive cost to it, the workpeople's sticking point *must* be below the employers' sticking point, and there *must*, therefore, be some range of practicable bargains. If, however, the workpeople expect a fight to yield a higher wage rate than the employers do, this is not necessary, even though each side expects the fight to involve some positive cost: and, if one side expects the fight to be actually of benefit to it,—to involve, as it were, negative cost—it is not necessary, even though workpeople and employers both anticipate the same result to the fight.

§ 5. It should be added in this connection that negative cost is by no means, as might perhaps be thought at first sight, a mere mathematical figment. On the side of the employers it may easily be looked for if their commodity is one the demand for which is highly inelastic, and if, at the time of the conflict, they have large accumulated stocks in hand. Thus it is sometimes alleged that coal-owners are enabled by a conflict " to clear their stocks at famine prices, while postponing the fulfilment of their contracts under strike clauses." [1] They may also anticipate negative costs if they have reason to believe that, by precipitating a conflict in times of bad trade, they can insure themselves against being hampered by one when trade improves.[2] On the side of the workpeople, negative cost is, in the early stages of industrial organisation, fairly common. For in that period what the men are really aiming at is, not the concession of a higher wage, but respect for their Trade Union and consequent increased readiness to deal fairly with them in the future. Or again, the real purpose of the conflict may be to solidify the trade union itself and to attract non-unionists to its ranks. So far as conflicts are undertaken for objects of this kind, the advantage anticipated from the acquisition of those objects needs to be subtracted from the anticipated material losses of the dispute, and, when so subtracted, may leave a net negative result. In these circumstances the men may elect to fight, even though they expect both to be beaten and to be subjected to great suffering in the process. Negative costs are, however, exceptional. As a general rule both sides expect that the actual conduct of a conflict will involve them in loss.

§ 6. The qualification forecasted in § 3 has now to be introduced. Since the workpeople's sticking point may be anything below the highest point in the range of indeterminateness, it may be below the lowest point in that range. In like manner, the employers' sticking point may be above the highest point in that range. Thus, with a range of indeter-

---

[1] *Political Science Quarterly*, vol. xii. p. 426.

[2] Cf. Chapman, *The Lancashire Cotton Industry*, p. 211.

minateness between 30s. or 40s., we might have the workpeople's sticking point at 25s. and the employers' sticking
point at 48s. In these circumstances the range of practicable
bargains will not extend to the two sticking points: for no
bargain is practicable that lies outside the range of indeterminateness. Though one side may be willing to concede
such a wage rather than fight, the other side will not be
willing to accept it. Consequently, any wage rate above the
workpeople's sticking point and any wage rate below the
employers' sticking point, which lies outside the range of
indeterminateness, is wholly ineffective. *The range of practicable bargains*, that is the series of wage rates which both
parties would prefer to a fight, is constituted by the wage
rates (if any) which both lie above the workpeople's sticking
point and below the employers' sticking point and also fall
within the range of indeterminateness. This explanation is
essential to the practical inferences to which we now pass.

§ 7. The extent of the range of indeterminateness is determined, as was pointed out in § 2, by the elasticities of the
reciprocal demands of the two parties. From the present point
of view, therefore, it may be taken as fixed. The range of
practicable bargains cannot, in any circumstances, be extended
beyond the limits so determined. *Within these limits* it is increased by anything that moves the workpeople's sticking point
downwards or the employers' sticking point upwards. The
workpeople's sticking point is moved down by anything that
increases the cost which they look to suffer in a conflict;
and the employers' sticking point is moved up by anything
that increases the cost which they look to suffer in
it. An increase in the strength of the workpeople's association alone will probably both lower the anticipated cost
to them and increase it to employers. Hence it will probably raise both sticking points; but it is impossible to
say whether it will widen the gap between them. An
increase in the strength of the employers' association alone
will, in like manner, lower both sticking points. In practice,
since the development of one rival association is almost
certain to lead to the development of the other also, the
most likely form of increase of strength is an increase on both

sides, leading to an increase in the cost anticipated by both. This will mean a lowering of the workpeople's sticking point accompanied by a rise of the employers'. Within the limits set by the range of indeterminateness it will, therefore, extend the range of practicable bargains in both directions, provided that such range already exists, and it may bring such a range into being if none exists. This tendency is exhibited in international, as well as in industrial, negotiations. If the adjustment of some political difference by war means adjustment by a world war embracing powerful alliances on both sides, the enormous probable cost of a fight makes it certain that, unless the stake at issue is, or is thought to be, immensely important, some range of practicable bargains will be available. In like manner, when the organisations of workpeople and employers in some industry are extended to embrace the whole country instead of being merely local, so that a strike or lock-out, if it occurred, would be national in its scope, an issue affecting, say, the wages payable in some small district, for which, before, it may be, no range of practicable bargains was available, is likely no longer to prove intractable. Broadly speaking, as things are to-day, with the great strength which nations and industrial associations alike possess, we may safely conclude that, for nearly all minor matters and interpretation differences, a wide range of practicable bargains will be available. There will always be an enormous number of ways of settling, say, the political status of an obscure African village, or the exact application to a particular pit of a general wage agreement between coal-owners and coal-miners, any one of which would be very much more advantageous to both parties than a conflict could possibly be. When the matter in dispute is an important one, such as the possession of a large and rich territory or the determination of the general standard of wages in an industry, it is not, of course, equally certain that a range of practicable bargains will exist.

§ 8. When two nations, or two associations, representing employers and employed respectively, have entered into an agreement not to fight but to settle differences by arbitration, there is created a real cost, partly moral and partly material (through the probable loss of outside support), to either of them if it breaks the agreement. This is additional to the direct cost which conflict would involve whether there had been an arbitration agreement or not. Thus the setting up of such an agreement increases the cost of war to both parties, and so, within the limits set by the range of indeterminateness, tends to bring into being, and, if it is already in being, to widen, a range of practicable bargains. Workers, who, apart from the agreement, would have fought rather than accept 32s., may, in view of the agreement, keep at work though only 31s. is awarded; and employers, who would have locked out against a 35s. demand, may now go to 36s.

§ 9. When arbitration is voluntary, entrance into it means to each party, in the circumstances contemplated above, the risk of having to accept a rate less favourable to itself than the worst rate it would have accepted without fighting if it had not entered into arbitration. This consideration will not prevent the parties from entering into it if each thinks that the risk of loss, which it assumes by doing so, will be roughly balanced by a corresponding chance of gain. But it is not certain that there will be a balance of this kind. If, for instance, the lower end of the range of practicable bargains is already lying at the lower end of the range of indeterminateness, the introduction of an arbitration agreement cannot extend the range of practicable bargains in a sense favourable to employers, while it may extend it in a sense adverse to them. In these circumstances they will be disinclined for arbitration agreements. The same thing is true of workpeople in the converse case. When, however, conditions are such that entrance into an arbitration agreement leaves both ends of the range of practicable bargains within the range of indeterminateness, the chances of gain and loss resulting from it are likely to balance for both sides, and, consequently, both sides will often be willing to enter into it in spite of the danger of losing more by it than they would look to have lost by war.

§ 10. But this does not exhaust the matter. If it were feasible to construct a voluntary arbitration agreement in such a way as to preclude the arbitrator from making an award outside that range of practicable bargains, which is established by general conditions coupled with the fact of the agreement, there would, indeed, be nothing more to be said. But it is very hard to include a provision of this kind in any workable scheme. Even when arbitration is proposed in respect of a single existing dispute, the parties can hardly give their case away so far as to reveal to the arbitrator beforehand what their respective sticking points are, and bind him not to go outside them. When it is a question of a general arbitration treaty to cover future disputes not yet in being, the difficulty is still greater. If, however, no provision of this kind is included, each disputant will fear that the arbitrator may award terms so unfavourable to him that, in spite of the agreement, he will feel compelled to fight against them, and so make a net loss of his honour. For this danger the knowledge that his opponent may be placed in a similar position by an award of an opposite character is no compensation. Consequently, both sides will tend to confine arbitration agreements to types of dispute, in which, in their judgment, it is practically certain that arbitrators will not give awards falling beyond their respective sticking points. Thus, in international treaties, States have often reserved from arbitration " vital interests " and " questions of national honour "; and in several plans for the League of Nations a distinction was drawn between "justiciable" disputes, to be submitted to a Court whose awards the League would enforce, and non-justiciable disputes, which should go to a Council empowered only to make non-binding recommendations. Similarly in industrial affairs, while employers and workpeople are generally ready to arbitrate minor matters or interpretation differences, they often hesitate to deal in this way with the general question of wage rates.

§ 11. This unwillingness of the parties to enter voluntarily into far-reaching arbitration agreements has been an important factor in determining State authorities to intervene. Compulsory reference of disputes to a body entitled to recommend, but not to enforce, an award, as under the Canadian Industrial Disputes Investigation Act, tends, subject to the conditions which have been enumerated, to widen the range of practicable bargains, because a hostile public opinion adds to the cost of fighting against any settlement which has been recommended by an impartial public authority. It *may*, therefore, in some instances create a range where none would otherwise exist. The Canadian system is exactly parallel to the arrangement under which international disputes are to be submitted to the Council of the League before war about them is permitted by the League of Nations. Laws which provide, not only that disputes must be submitted to arbitration, but also that the arbitrator's award must be accepted on pain of legal penalties, since they make battle more costly and success in it less probable to a recalcitrant party, will act still more forcibly to create and to extend in both directions the range of practicable bargains.

§ 12. We have now to make clear the bearing of these results upon the prospects of industrial peace. It has already been shown that, when there is no range of practicable bargains, a settlement without conflict is impossible. But it would be wrong to infer that, when there is such a range, a peaceful settlement *must* occur. This is by no means so. The existence of a range of practicable bargains implies that there are a number of possible adjustments, whether it be of territory or of wages or of anything else, any one of which both disputants would prefer to accept rather than engage in conflict. Each of them, however, naturally wishes to obtain the best terms that he can, and is also, though this is not necessary to the analysis, almost certainly ignorant of how far the other would yield rather than fight. Thus, we may suppose that a Trade Union has decided to fight rather than to accept a wage below 30s., and the corresponding Employers' Association to fight rather than pay more than 35s. There is then a range of practicable bargains including all rates between 30s. and 35s. But, even though the workmen know that 35s. is the sticking point of the employers, and the employers know that 30s. is the sticking point of the workmen, there is still a conflict of will as to the precise point within the range, 30s. to 35s., at which the wage shall be put. Each side tries to push the other to his limit. The employers may think that, if they say firmly enough, " not a penny more than 31s.," the workmen will give way; the workmen may think that, if they insist unfalteringly on 34s., the employers will give way. In the result, both sides, equally the victims of unsuccessful bluff, may find themselves in a fight over an issue which both know is not worth it. In the circumstances the chance that conflict will be avoided is clearly greater, the more cordial are the general relations between workpeople and employers and the better is the machinery available for bringing about friendly negotiations. Thus, when a regular Conciliation Board is ready to hand or, failing that, when a mutually acceptable mediator is prepared to intervene, the prospect of a peaceful settlement is, so far, improved. When an arbitrator is available in the last resort, it is improved still further. For, when once an award is given that falls within the range of practicable bargains, it will not pay either side to fight rather than accept this award. One or other of them may, indeed, think it worth while to bluff in the hope of modifying the award by later negotiation. But, the award having, as it will have,—particularly when the arbitration has been entered upon voluntarily— moral force behind it, is not likely to be resisted up to the point of war, unless it lies beyond the sticking point of one party, that is to say, outside the range of practicable bargains. The wider, however, is the range of practicable bargains, the greater is the chance that an arbitrator will succeed in placing his award somewhere upon it. It follows that, when settlements are arbitrated, the chances of a peaceful adjustment are greater where the range of practicable bargains is wide than where it is narrow. This conclusion, however, does not follow when settlements are negotiated. On the contrary, since, the wider the range of practicable bargains, the greater are the opportunities for bluff by both sides, the opposite conclusion seems more easily defensible.

§ 13. From the general course of this discussion it is easily seen that the need for arbitrators does not, as is sometimes supposed, arise solely out of the ignorance of the parties to a dispute, and that their function is not ",simply to find out what the price would naturally have tended to become." [1] Dr. Schultze-Gaevernitz, who enunciates this view, suggests that " the determination of relative strength, which is the function of a contest, could be equally well performed by an exercise of the intelligence, just as we test the pressure of

[1] Schultze-Gaevernitz, *Social Peace*, p. 192.

steam by a special gauge instead of finding it out by the bursting of the boiler."[1] The implication of this argument is that, when all the facts are known to both sides, the range of practicable bargains is necessarily a single point, representing a wage equal to the one which battle would have established. This, as we have seen, is not so. It is true that an arbitrator, if he is to be successful, must act as an interpreter, and not as a controller, of economic tendencies, in the sense that he must place his award within the range of practicable bargains—a range, be it remembered, which the appointment of the arbitrator has probably somewhat widened. It is also true that, if all the facts are known to both parties, the wage rate which battle would have established will necessarily be represented by a point within this range. But it is not true that this wage rate is the only award open to the arbitrator which the litigants would be prepared to obey. The range of practicable bargains is not limited to that point unless, not only are all facts known to both sides, *but also* the costs which a fight is expected to involve is, for both of them, nothing at all.[2]

---

[1] Schultze-Gaevernitz, *Social Peace*, p. 136.

[2] For a mathematical treatment of the problems discussed in this chapter, cf. Appendix A of my *Principles and Methods of Industrial Peace*.

CHAPTER VII

§ 1. OUR next problem has to do with the relation between economic welfare, as reflected through the size of the national dividend, and workpeople's hours of labour. The effect of improved shift systems, under which, with any given hours for workpeople, the hours for the employers' machinery are prolonged, and, therefore, the quantity of machinery required to maintain a given output correspondingly reduced, will not be discussed here. It is evident that, after a point, an addition to the hours of labour normally worked in any industry would, by wearing out the workpeople, ultimately lessen, rather than increase, the national dividend. Physiology teaches that, after a certain period of work of given intensity, the body requires a certain interval of rest in order to return to its initial state, and that this interval grows more rapidly than the period of work. Failing adequate intervals, our faculties become progressively blunted. The extra nourishment that enlarged earnings afford cannot be properly digested and yield little benefit. " Fatigue so closes the avenues of approach within that education does not educate, amusement does not amuse nor recreation recreate." [1] Furthermore, besides this direct injury to efficiency, indirect injury also comes about, in so far as recourse to stimulants or unhealthy forms of excitement is induced by the fact of exhaustion.[2] As a result, output suffers both from lost time, due to slacker attendance and unpunctuality, and from diminished vigour and application throughout the working spell. Of course the exact length of working day, beyond

[1] Goldmark, *Fatigue and Efficiency*, p. 284.
[2] Cf. Chapman, " Hours of Labour," *Economic Journal*, 1909, p. 360.

which an increase would contract the national dividend, varies with the climate. In very hot countries it may be more productive to work at low intensity for long hours, and in colder countries, where the food consumed is of a different kind, at high intensity for short hours.[1] It also varies with the class of workpeople affected. Children and women, particularly women who, besides industrial work, have also the burden of looking after their homes, can, in general, stand less than adult men. Further leisure for them yields a bigger return—for children in opportunities for healthy sleep and play, for women in opportunities for better care of their homes.[2] An important factor, too, is the kind of work that is done. Long hours of heavy muscular exertion and mental or nervous strain are much more injurious to efficiency than long hours of mere mild attention. Again, workers earning good money will be better nourished, and so likely to be able to stand more, than very poor workers. Yet again, the effects will vary according to the way in which the workpeople spend their leisure, whether in mere dissipation or in hard work on gardens of their own or in true recreation. It will also vary according as the shortened hours do or do not lead to greater intensity of effort and consequent strain during the hours that are worked—a matter which depends partly on whether wages are paid by piece or by time, partly on whether the work is of a sort that can be speeded up by improved ways of working or only by greater exertion, and partly upon whether or not the intervals of rest and the hour of starting work are based on careful tests of what best promotes efficient working.[3] In view of these considerations it is clear that no general statement as to the relation between hours of labour and the national dividend can be made. The relation will be different for different types of workpeople and different kinds of work. " Where output is controlled mainly by machinery the loss [due to long hours]

---

[1] Cf. Gini, *Report to the League of Nations on Raw Materials and Foodstuffs*, 1922, p. 41.

[2] Cf. Marshall, *Royal Commission on Labour*, Q. 4253.

[3] On the effects upon output of a pre-breakfast start, cf. [Cd. 8511], p. 58 *et seq.* This Report concluded that in certain types of munition work the start before breakfast might be abolished with advantage to the output (p. 66).

may be small. Where it depends more especially upon the worker it will be great. Purely mechanical work can sometimes be performed sufficiently well by tired men. Skilled work calling for judgement and discretion demands freshness and vigour." [1] It must be remembered, indeed, that even the feeding of a purely automatic machine can be done with greater or less regularity and completeness, and that the *number* of machines which can be entrusted to the control of an unfatigued worker is larger than can be entrusted to a fatigued one.[2] The essential point, however, is that, in each several industry, for each class of workers there is *some* length of working day the overstepping of which will be disadvantageous to the national dividend. A detailed official investigation into the condition of munition workers in 1916 led the investigators to conclude that the hours of work yielding maximum output were, for men on " very heavy work " about 56 hours a week, for men on " heavy work " about 60 hours, for men on " light work " about 70 hours, for women on " moderately heavy " work 56 hours, and for women on " light work " 60 hours.[3] It must be remembered, however, that, as the investigators point out, their *data* relate to those fittest persons among would-be munition workers, who did not drop out from the strain. Moreover, since in peace time workers naturally expect to have some surplus energy left for hobbies and amusements after their work is over, whereas in war time they may be ready to exhaust themselves completely, long hours in peace time are likely to cause more serious slackening of effort in each hour than they do in war time.[4] " Hence the *best* hours for work, suited for peace-time, are in every case considerably shorter than those mentioned." [5]

§ 2. *Prima facie* it might be thought that this conclusion is of academic rather than of practical importance, because the self-interest of employers and workpeople must prevent unduly long hours from being worked. There is, however, a large

---

[1] *Second Interim Report on Industrial Fatigue* [Cd. 8335], p. 50.
[2] Cf. Leverhulme, *The Six Hours Day*, p. 21.
[3] *Health of Munition Workers*, Memorandum, No. 12 [Cd. 8344], p. 9.
[4] " Report on Hours of Work and their Relation to Output," 1927 (International Association for Social Progress, British Section), p. 6.
[5] *Health of Munition Workers*, Memorandum, No. 12 [Cd. 8344], p. 10.

volume of experience, which contradicts this optimistic view and suggests that private self-interest has often seriously failed in this matter. It is not necessary to invoke the terrible history of the early days of the factory system. In quite recent times Dr. Abbe of the Zeiss works maintained, on the strength of experiments conducted by himself, that, among at least three-quarters of all industrial workers, a greater absolute product—not merely a greater product per hour—may be expected from regular work of between 8 and 9 hours a day than from regular work of any longer period.[1] In his own works, "in 253 different kinds of work, he found that a 4 per cent larger output was obtained in nine hours [than in ten], using exactly the same machinery";[2] and a number of similar instances are on record from elsewhere both before and during the period of the war.[3] It is, indeed, very difficult to draw confident conclusions from even the most careful experiments in this field. For the results will be misleading; (1) if the extra output per hour that is obtained is due to a mere spurt by men temporarily on their mettle, and not to a real increase of efficiency; (2) if the reduction of hours has been accompanied by improvements in the general organisation of the business, e.g. by the substitution of a three-shift for a two-shift system, involving an increase of from, say, a 15-hour to a 24-hour day for the machinery employed; or (3) if the reduction of hours has attracted to the experimenting works a grade of workmen superior to those formerly employed there. In spite, however, of these and other difficulties,[4] the evidence is fairly conclusive that hours of labour in excess of what the best interests of the national dividend require have often in fact been worked. This inference is strengthened when we reflect that any distant effect, which shorter hours may have in prolonging the working life of the persons concerned, cannot be displayed in these experiments.

§ 3. At first sight it is difficult to understand by what

---

[1] Conrad, *Handwörterbuch der Staatswissenschaften*, vol. i. p. 1214.

[2] Report of the Labour Association, *Special Committee on Hours of Labour in Continuous Industries*, p. 10.   [3] *Ibid.* pp. 10, 11.

[4] For a good discussion of the pitfalls to be avoided in a concrete study of the relation between hours of labour and efficiency, cf. Sargent Florence, *Use of Factory Statistics in the Investigation of Industrial Fatigue.*

process this state of affairs can be brought about: for it would seem to be contrary to the interest both of the workpeople and also of the employers to allow hours to be worked in excess of those that promote the largest production. The apparent paradox is, however, easily explained. First, workpeople, in considering for what hours per day they will consent to work, often fail to take account of the damage that unduly long hours may do to their efficiency. Their lack of forethought in this matter is on a par with the general inability of all classes adequately to foresee future happenings *in* themselves, as distinguished from future happenings *to* themselves. Secondly, employers also often fail to realise that shorter hours would promote efficiency among their workpeople, and so would redound to their own interest. Thirdly—and this, on their side, is the principal thing—except in firms which possess a practical monopoly in some department of industry, and so expect to retain the same hands permanently, the lack of durable connection between individual employers and their workpeople makes it to the employers' interest to work longer hours than are in the long run to the interest of production as a whole. This point was well brought out in some remarks of an employer who has successfully undertaken many schemes for the welfare of those whom he employs. " The employer as such," he said, " is not primarily interested in keeping labour in excellent condition. What he wants is a sufficient supply of efficient labour to meet his immediate demands ; and, though ultimately this supply will be curtailed unless the whole nation allows a margin for wear-and-tear and for the stimulation of progressive efficiency, he cannot afford, under our present competitive system, to take a very long view. He can act with others, but not much in advance of them. In so far then as he represents immediate and limited, rather than ultimate and general, interests, his economic outlook must stand in marked contrast to that of the nation as a whole." [1] This identification of the employers' interest with immediate, rather than with ultimate, output is especially important for the following reason. Where mobility and trade union

[1] Cf. Proud, *Welfare Work*, pp. 50-51.

organisation are imperfect, and where, therefore, as will be shown when we come to discuss "unfair wages," there is some range of indeterminateness in the bargain between an employer and his workpeople, the employer's bargaining power, as against his workpeople, is greater in the matter of hours of labour than it is in the matter of wages. For, whereas a workman striving to get better wages has only, as it were, to lift his own weight, it is, as a rule, impossible, for technical reasons, that any concession about the hours of labour should be made to him that is not general in character, and, therefore, less willingly granted. Moreover, if an employer succeeds in exploiting his workpeople in the matter of wages, the poverty, which he thus induces in them, will often make them *willing* to work for longer hours. It follows that, when exploitation is present at all, it is extremely likely to make itself felt in hours of labour too long for the best interests of the national dividend. The effect will be bad everywhere, but especially bad where the persons affected are women and young persons, whose aggregate efficiency throughout life is liable to suffer greatly from overstrain in youth.

§ 4. Moreover, in this matter it is misleading to confine attention to the effect produced on the national dividend. For, in general, the working day, whose length is adapted to maximise production over a long period, is not, given the existing distribution of wealth between workpeople and others, the *right* working day from the standpoint of economic welfare. What economic welfare requires is that workpeople should work for such hours per day that the wages due to the last hour—when account is taken of the fact that every extra hour worked lessens the opportunity for enjoying whatever purchases their wages may enable them to make—shall just compensate them for the unpleasantness of longer hours. There is a presumption that the working day which would satisfy this condition will be considerably shorter than the working day which would maximise production even in the long run. If then, as we have shown, the play of normal economic forces is liable to make the working day too long for the best interests of the national dividend, *a fortiori* it is liable to make it too long for the best interests of economic welfare.

§ 5. What has been said is sufficient to constitute a *prima facie* case for State intervention. This case, however, cannot be regarded as established, even in respect of badly organised industries where the danger of exploitation by employers is not countered by strong Trade Union action, until the possibility of evasions of the law has been considered. In laws about wages, as will appear presently, this point is of great practical importance. For example, when it is proposed to force up wage rates on the ground that an increase of pay would soon produce a corresponding increase of capacity, it can be objected that, since the reaction on capacity will not be immediate, employers will be tempted by an enforced increase in the wage rate to dismiss those workpeople who are not already worth what they are called upon to pay. But against proposals to reduce hours of labour this class of objection does not hold good. Provided that the hourly rate of wages is not raised, a shortening of the hours of labour does not, at all events until there has been time for it to bring about a reduction in the mechanical equipment of factories, make it to the interest of employers to employ fewer workpeople than before. It follows that a sufficient interval will be allowed, as it will not always be allowed when wage rates are increased, for the improvements in capacity, which they tend to produce, to work themselves out. This means that, by the time the danger of dismissals has become real, capacity will often be so far improved as to neutralise and abolish it. This consideration is important, but it is not, of course, decisive. It is still necessary to consider how far governmental authorities are competent to frame the delicately adjusted regulations which analysis shows to be desirable. Hitherto, the basis of systematic knowledge, upon which policy should be built up, has been small, and there is wide scope for further study. Meanwhile, it may be agreed that the general principle underlying legislation to limit the hours of work in industry is sound. The movement, which advanced with remarkable rapidity in many countries during the earlier post-war years, to fix a general maximum of eight hours a day in all industries, subject to certain special exceptions, may well be justified on broad social grounds. But it is very important that the different needs of different classes of workers should be recognised, and that the general maximum should not tend to become a general minimum also.

§ 6. One further aspect of this matter has to be considered. It is plain that, whatever limitation is imposed, it cannot be made absolutely rigid; because, if this were done, work would be prevented on some occasions when the immediate need for it was so urgent as to outweigh any indirect consequences. Certain materials, for example, become fit for use for a brief space only, and, if they are not worked upon then, are absolutely wasted. A good example is the fruit used in the fruit-canning industry. To refuse permission for occasional excessive hours of work in this industry might mean, from time to time, the total loss of very valuable crops.[1] Certain forms of repair work are in a similar position. They are urgent, in the sense that they must be executed *at once* on pain of very serious loss. It is evident that, when conditions of this kind prevail, some relaxation from rigid rules should be made, whether the authority behind these rules be legislation or a collective agreement between a Trade Union and an Employers' Federation. In other words, some amount of overtime beyond the hours normally permitted should *sometimes* be permitted. But it is very important that this concession should not be abused. It must be clearly understood that overtime is often injurious, even though it be followed by an equivalent period of slack time. "During overtime leisure and rest are cut down at the very same time that heavier and longer demands are made upon the human organism. It is practically inevitable that the metabolic balance should be thrown out of gear. . . . There is no rebound, or an infinitely slow one, when our elastic capacities have been too tensely stretched. It takes much more time, rest, repair than the working-girl can possibly afford to make good such metabolic losses. Compensation—off-time— comes too late. . . . After a doubled task muscle requires,

---

[1] As Miss Goldmark points out, however, this consideration affords no excuse for the overtime that in fact often prevails in the United States Canneries among the workpeople who label and stamp the cans after they have been sealed (*Fatigue and Efficiency*, p. 187).

not double, but four times, as long a rest for recuperation, and a similar need for more than proportionally increased rest after excessive work is true also of our other tissues and of our organism in its totality." [1]   " When once an individual has, through labour during ordinary hours, reached a certain degree of fatigue, and proceeds to further labour (overtime) without taking the repose necessary to dissipate the fatigue already produced, this further labour has a greater physiological effect and exhausts the organism more than would a similar amount of labour performed when fatigue was absent." [2]   These injurious effects follow from overtime work, in all industries where the normal hours already approach the maximum compatible with full efficiency, however cogent the excuses for it may be.   The excuses offered should always, therefore, be scrutinised with very great care.   In the conduct of this scrutiny it is essential to bear in mind that the immediate damage, which the prohibition of overtime would bring about, is often in fact much smaller than it appears to be at first sight.   For, first, in so far as pressure upon one set of firms in an industry occurs when other firms are slack, the prohibition need not kill the work they would have done, but may lead to its being given out, either on commission or by direct order, to other firms.   Secondly, in industries that manufacture goods capable of being made for stock, prohibition of overtime in periods of general boom will, indeed, directly lessen the hours of work done in these periods, but it will also indirectly increase the hours of work done in antecedent periods of depression.   Furthermore, in this connection, the notion " making for stock " should be given a significance more extended than usual.   Articles which have to be manufactured to individual order are not capable of being made for stock in the ordinary sense.   But, in so far as they are capable of being stored prior to need by their purchasers, they ought to be so regarded from the present point of view.   It is this class of commodity that the Minority of the Poor Law Commissioners had

---

[1] Goldmark, *Fatigue and Efficiency*, p. 88.
[2] Second Interim Report on Industrial Fatigue [Cd. 8335], 1916, p. 16.

in view when they wrote: " The variations in the consumers' pressure can be made much less extreme by means of a legal limitation of the hours of labour. When the hours of cotton operatives were settled by the individual mill-owner, cotton-spinning and weaving were extreme instances of seasonal trades; and the manufacturer was unable to resist the customers' insistence on instant delivery. Now that the maximum hours are legally fixed, the buyer has learnt to be more regular in his demands. The extreme seasonal irregularity of the London dressmaking trade would undoubtedly be mitigated, if dressmakers were absolutely prevented from working more than a fixed maximum day. Customers would simply not be able to insist on delivery in an unreasonably short time." [1] As a result, the output produced in *antecedent* times would be increased, thus partly offsetting the diminution of output directly consequent upon the diminution of overtime in periods of boom. Thirdly, there are certain things, whether or not they are capable of being made for stock in any sense, the demand for which can be *postponed* for a substantial period. Commodities and services that are consumed in a single use do not as a rule fall into this class. If a desire for bread or beer or doctor's services or railway travel existing now is not satisfied, that fact does not cause any greater desire for these things to exist in the future than would have existed if it had been satisfied. *Some* goods and services, indeed, even of an immediately consumable kind, are subject to demands which can be postponed. For example, a man may wish to do the Grand Tour once in his lifetime; if he cannot do it this year, he will desire to do it next year. But much the most important things for which the demand can be postponed are durable goods, such as boots, clothes, pianos, machinery and houses. The desire for these things is based upon an expectation of services to be rendered by them through a considerable period. Suppose, for example, that a bicycle has a normal life of seven years and that I desire to purchase one now. If I succeed in doing this, I shall have no desire to repeat my purchase next year; but, if I fail, the effect of failure will be to carry over

---

[1] *Report of the Royal Commission on the Poor Laws*, p. 1185, footnote.

to next year a demand at least six-sevenths as intense as my present demand. In all industries which make commodities of this class, the check, which the prohibition of overtime puts upon work in boom periods, is partially cancelled by a stimulus to work in *subsequent* periods of depression. Against these considerations it is, indeed, necessary to set one upon the other side. If overtime is prohibited, employers may find it to their interest to attach to themselves, through the offer of higher wages, a larger reserve of workpeople than they would otherwise have thought necessary. For, the more extensive this reserve is, the less likely it is that inability to work overtime will prevent them from fulfilling orders that they would like to fulfil.[1] When, however, the reserve is large, the workmen comprising the fringe of it are only actually employed during boom periods; in moderate and bad times they are attached in idleness to the industry which commands their services, instead of being employed, as they might otherwise have been, in some different industry. In so far as this happens, restriction of overtime leaves the amount of work done in the industry directly affected substantially unaltered both in boom periods and in depression periods, but makes the amount of work done throughout the whole body of industries smaller than it would otherwise have been in both sorts of period. This form of reaction is specially liable to be set up in industries where casual methods of engaging workpeople prevail. When it is threatened and cannot be, or is not, successfully resisted, the case in favour of close restrictions upon overtime is so far weakened.

[1] This point is illustrated indirectly by the small amount of overtime found among women workers, as compared with men workers, in the bespoke tailoring trade. The men are skilled hands whose number cannot easily be supplemented. But the women are unskilled hands, and "the readily available reserve of semi-skilled wives and daughters, who may at any time be pressed into work, tends to relieve the seasonal pressure upon the less skilled, or women's section of the trade" (Webb, *Seasonal Trades*, p. 87).

CHAPTER VIII

§ 1. An influence, less important, indeed, than the hours of labour, but still very important, is exercised upon the national dividend and, through it, upon economic welfare, by the methods of industrial remuneration. Whatever methods are adopted in any industry, the general tendency of economic forces will be to cause the wages offered for each class of workpeople to approximate, subject to qualifications which are not here relevant, to the value of the marginal social net product of that class. At first sight it might seem that, if this be so, things must work out in the same way whatever method of remuneration is in vogue. But the truth is otherwise. For, though under all systems a man will be paid over a year the worth of his work during the year, under some systems it will be to his interest to do more work, and so to have a larger worth, than under others. Thus payment may be made independently of the results achieved by the worker at any moment, being adjusted only to what experience shows he may be expected, under that method of remuneration, to achieve on the average; or it may be adjusted to results, not merely on the average, but continuously and in detail; or some compromise between these plans may be adopted. Broadly speaking, the worker's output will be larger, the more nearly the method of remuneration in vogue adjusts payments to individual results. This, no doubt, is not true invariably. There are certain sorts of work where interest in the work itself, or interest in the use to which it will be put, induces people to work as hard as they can without reference to the mode in which payment for their services is made. This is probably true of most work of original artistic creation, of the higher administrative work of the civil service and even of some kinds of private business. In these occupations the national dividend will be none the worse if a fixed salary by the year, or a fixed wage by the hour, is paid without any reference to what the worker actually accomplishes in any particular period. There is even an opening, if the jobs are sufficiently stable to make a high degree of mobility unnecessary, for payment by a life salary with yearly increments, adjusted not so much to presumed changes in the value of the employee's work as to presumed changes in his domestic status, and, therefore, in his needs. Most of the tasks, however, that ordinary manual workers have to perform, are routine tasks, and—owing to the division of labour—are so remotely connected with any finished product that interest in them sufficient to evoke continuous, spontaneous and disinterested effort can hardly be expected. Even here, no doubt, some men will be found, whom an ardour for excellence for its own sake or a stern sense of public duty will cause to exert themselves to the utmost without reference to expectations of reward; and the prospect that this will happen is specially favourable where systems of Labour Copartnership have succeeded in evoking in the workpeople a feeling of proprietorship in, and patriotism towards, the concern in which they are employed. From the main body of ordinary workpeople engaged in manual occupations this, however, is not at present to be looked for. The amount of work they will do in any hour, week or year will be greater if the payment made to them does, than it will be if it does not, vary as this amount varies. The national dividend will be larger the more nearly each increment of effort on the part of any individual worker is rewarded by a payment equal to the value of the difference which that increment of effort makes to the total product; and any enlargement of the dividend brought about by improved adjustment in this matter will, *prima facie*, carry with it an increase in economic welfare.[1] This does not, of course, imply that the pay should

---

[1] But cf. *post*, § 13.

be equal to the value of a man's output as ordinarily understood; for this output is in part due to machinery and equipment, which, if not engaged in assisting him, would have helped to increase the output of other workpeople. Nor does it even mean that the pay should be *exactly* proportioned to the value of a man's output so understood. In a factory —though not, of course, among home-workers—when a man works slowly he "occupies" the employer's machine or work-space for a longer period in producing a given quantity of output than he does when working fast; and so estops the machinery or work-space from being used by others. Hence, for a complete adjustment between wages and the value of marginal net product, we should need a payment that varied, not proportionately, but progressively, with the quantity of a man's output; and this point becomes more important the greater is the value of the plant in a factory relatively to the wages bill.[1] This, however, is a secondary matter. Subject to it, it is plain, from the present point of view, that pay should be *proportioned* (in a ratio calculable, and different in different occupations) to output as ordinarily understood. In other words, it should *correspond* for any worker, with the results, conditions remaining constant, actually achieved by him.

§ 2. In order to construct a wage system of this kind, under which a man's pay is based directly and immediately on his output, we must have some means of ascertaining, with greater or less accuracy, how large that output from time to time actually is. In the way of this there are a number of obstacles, the importance of which varies in different occupations. The first, though not the principal, of these is that a workman's output, when strictly interpreted, may include other elements in addition to the physical product that his labour, in conjunction with the machinery entrusted to him,

---

[1] This consideration is sometimes used as an argument against paying equal piece-rates to women engaged in the same operations as men. In certain engineering operations, for example, employers have claimed that women, being slower workers than men, involve much higher proportionate overhead charges (*Report of the War Cabinet Committee on Women in Industry*, p. 84). Plainly, however, reasoning of this type points to a lower piece-rate for all slow workers, whether male or female, than for fast workers, not to a lower piece-rate for women as such than to men as such.

brings to birth. For, as Jevons long ago observed : " In every works there are a thousand opportunities where the workman can either benefit or injure the establishment, and, could he really be made to feel his interests identical with those of his employers, there can be no doubt that the profits of the trade could be greatly increased in many cases." [1] Among these additional elements perhaps the most important are the suggestions which a workman may be able to offer for more effective or more economical methods of work, and the contribution which he may make by his influence towards a spirit of harmony and good-fellowship in the shop. These elements can, indeed, be taken account of in a rough general way, and money rewards designed to induce workpeople to provide them can be offered; but anything in the nature of approximate measurement of their value is obviously impossible. [2]

§ 3. The second difficulty is that the physical output for which an individual workman is responsible is liable to vary, not only in quantity, but also in quality. Ability to measure its quantity is, therefore, not sufficient, unless workmen can be prevented from making output larger at the expense of making it worse. In some circumstances this can be done by means of carefully thought-out schemes of inspection and supervision. Mechanical gauges can also be made use of in certain types of work. It has been said that " in the munition industry, where accuracy is of such vital importance, quite as many employees are engaged in gauging the output as will be actually producing it, and every single unit of output—not merely samples—will be subjected to the process." [3] These devices, however, cannot be effectively

---

[1] Jevons, *Methods of Social Reform*, p. 123.

[2] Arrangements are frequently made by progressive firms, both in America and in this country, for enabling workmen to submit suggestions that occur to them to the higher officials of the business, without the intervention of overseers and foremen, who might be actuated by motives of jealousy towards them ; and for rewarding with prizes and premiums such suggestions as it is decided to adopt. (Cf. Gilman, *A Dividend to Labour*, p. 230 ; Rowntree, *Industrial Betterment*, p. 31, and Meakin, *Model Factories and Villages*, p. 322.) In Van Marken's establishment a premium is given for "evidences of good-fellowship and co-operation, thus encouraging those whose behaviour conduces to the smooth working of the concern " (Meakin, *Model Factories and Villages*, p. 315).

[3] Sargant Florence, *Use of Factory Statistics in the Investigation of Industrial Fatigue*, p. 72.

applied either to work that has to be done by workmen acting in scattered places or to work the results of which— as in plumbing and sewer-making—are speedily covered up. In these types of work, since defects of quality threaten serious injury to health, it is generally thought better to refrain from any attempt at making the wage-payment depend on the quantity of output.

§ 4. Even where a proper standard of quality can be enforced and the danger of injurious reactions on quality eliminated, to measure the quantity of output by itself is often difficult. It is especially so when the work consists of general surveillance and attention, rather than of specific mechanical operations. The work done by seamen, telegraph and telephone operators, carmen and railway signalmen is of this kind. So also is much agricultural work. Thus M. Besse writes: "The essence of measurable things is their homogeneity, their identity with themselves. Harvesting and the weeding of roots, for example, allow of piece-wages, because the work remains the same for days and weeks, and, in order to measure its efficiency, all that is needed is to count the sheaves amassed or to calculate the surface weeded. The greater part of the work of cultivation is similar. But, on the other hand, the task of men who look after and manage animals varies from hour to hour of the day and begins again every morning in such wise that no summary or addition of it is possible. It consists of watching the pasture lands, grooming the animals, cleaning the stables, and so on, all operations complex in themselves, admitting of no common measure, needing to be done in a limited time and at a fixed hour, and often of such a kind that nothing would be gained by any extra stimulus to exertion. This is why piece-wages, very widespread in arable districts like the east and south-east of England, are so rare in the districts devoted to stock-raising."[1] In mechanical work the total product of *a body of men* is, in general, fairly definite and measurable. But even here it is sometimes very difficult to distinguish and measure separately the contribution that is made to it by separate individuals. This difficulty is

---

[1] *La Crise et l'évolution de l'agriculture en Angleterre*, pp. 99-100.

prominent in the work done by gangs of harvesters or navvies. It is also of some slight importance in that of shop-assistants, for it is the business of these people, not merely to serve customers, but also, when they are themselves engaged, to hand them over tactfully to some other assistant.

§ 5. Let us now suppose that we have to deal with occupations in which this difficulty has been, in some degree, overcome, so that a rough measure, or estimate, of the individual worker's contribution, as he works from day to day or week to week, can be made. It is required so to arrange things that pay is adjusted to this measure. To some extent—a more considerable extent than is often supposed —this can be, and is, done under ordinary systems of time-wages. Though it is not practicable to vary a man's time-wage from day to day or week to week with variations in his accomplishment, nevertheless, it is often possible so to arrange things that a man may reasonably expect higher rates on the whole as a reward for better work. Moreover, when there is no chance of this, he is almost certain to improve his prospects of being kept at work in bad times and of promotion to a better-paid post.[1]

§ 6. Plainly, however, a very much closer adjustment can be made by resort to the method of piece-wages. Under this plan workmen, working in given conditions and with given machinery, are paid exactly in proportion to their physical output. Of course it is recognised " that, if a manufacturer contributes anything directly toward reduction in the time by supplying an improved machine, or improved jigs or fixtures, or high-speed steel cutting tools, where previously carbon steel tools had been used at the original setting of the time, that then it would be perfectly proper and fair to lower the time set,"—which means, in effect, to lower the piece-rate. If this were not done, the benefit of improvements made in any industry would be seized by the particular workers engaged there—and they, in order to keep it, would have to form themselves into a close ring and exclude new-comers—instead of being spread, as normally it should be, over the general body of the purchasing public. In given conditions, however, under simple piece-wages

---

[1] Cf. *post*, Chapter XV. § 2.

a workman is paid, *from the standpoint of the moment,* in direct proportion to his output, the actual amount of the pay per unit of service being approximately equal to the (marginal) value of his services in assisting the machinery to make this output.[1] It is true, as was indicated at the end of § 1, that the adjustment is not exact. Even under piece-wages greater efforts are not rewarded directly in full proportion to their worth. Nevertheless, when account is taken of the fact that, on this system as well as on the time-wage system, the better a man works the more secure he is of regular employment, it may fairly be said that adjustment is *nearly* exact. Consequently, it would seem at first sight that this is the system under which, apart from possible overstrain to the workpeople, to be referred to presently, and provided that the level of the rate is properly adjusted, the largest practicable output is bound to be obtained.[2] The system has been for a long time established and has operated with great success in this country in coal-mining, the textile industries, the boot and shoe industry and a number of others.

§ 7. Experience has shown, however, that over a wide range of industries piece-wages have been a failure. When a piece-rate has been introduced, and, under its influence, the workers have increased their output, employers, thinking that some men were now earning too much money, have sometimes " cut " or " nibbled " the rate. The workers, perceiving this, realise that extra effort on their part is likely to involve, not only an immediate increase of earnings, but also a subsequent

---

[1] Of course, this statement does not hold good of "collective piece-wages," where each man's pay depends upon the output of the whole group of which he forms a part. When the group is very small, some inducement to exertion is offered by this form of piece-wage, but, when the group is large, practically none.

[2] It may be noted that, if piece-wages were substituted for time-wages throughout industry generally, with the result that a large increase of effort was put out by workpeople, the value per unit of workpeople's effort would by that fact be slightly depreciated, and, therefore, the payment for a given effort and output would have to be slightly less than before. Thus, if under time-wages at 1s. an hour two pieces had normally been produced, so that 6d. was paid for each, under a general system of piece-wages the basis of adjustment would have to be slightly less than 6d. per piece. When, however, a change from time to piece-wages is accomplished in one industry only, the effect in this direction (after the distribution of workpeople among different industries has been adjusted) will, in general, be very small.

reduction of the piece-rate, the effect of which will be to make it impossible for them to earn their original wage without working harder than before. To prevent this they tend, whether by formal agreement or otherwise, deliberately to limit their output, so that very little, if any, advantage is secured for the national dividend as against the output under time-wages.

§ 8. The apparently obvious solution of this difficulty, namely, that employers should rigidly abstain from rate-cutting in any circumstances, has occasionally been adopted. Thus, in the United States, "in the spring of 1902, the Moulders officially agreed with the Employers' Defence Association that no limit (of output) should be observed in the stone-moulding branch, in view of the agreement that the earnings of the individual moulders should not be considered in adjusting prices of work." [1]   Apart, however, from the fear of indirect cutting by slight alterations in the nature of a job and large accompanying alterations in the rate, which would enable unscrupulous employers to get round this kind of guarantee in a dishonourable way, the extreme difficulty of ensuring that rates are fixed reasonably in the first instance will make even the best employers hesitate to give such a guarantee. For, as a result of it, they might find themselves bound for a long time to pay four or five times as much for a piece of work as they could get the work done for in a free market. Some of them have, therefore, taken the line that, if there is to be an effective guarantee against "nibbling," they must be insured against the guarantee costing them too much. This is the origin of the various methods of remuneration embraced under the general title of *premium plans.* The essential characteristic of these is that the increases of wage, which correspond to increases of output above the standard, are proportionately smaller than these increases of output, but that, in compensation for this, the workpeople—in theory at least—are guaranteed against any cutting or nibbling of the rate, so long as the existing methods of production are maintained. The precise relation between the amount of the premium and the amount of increases of output above the standard varies

[1] McCabe, *The Standard Rate in American Trade Unions*, pp. 224-5.

with different systems. Under the plan known as the Halsey plan, for every 1 per cent increase of output above the standard output the wage rises above the standard wage by a *constant fraction* of 1 per cent: under the equally well-known Rowan plan, it rises by a *constantly diminishing fraction* of 1 per cent.[1] The advocates of these plans maintain that the low rate of the premium, as compared with that ruling under simple piece-wages, which is offered under them, and the consequent limitation of the employers' liability, make it possible for a really effective guarantee to be given against any nibbling of the rate, and that, therefore, on the whole, the adjustment of remuneration to output is closer than it would be under simple piece-wages. There is, indeed, considerable difficulty in the employment of premium plans except in workshops where all the workpeople are of more or less similar capacity. For, if their capacities are widely different, a strong man, who produces half as much again as a weak man, is paid much less than half as much again in wages ; and, in these circumstances, friction can hardly fail to result. But, when, for technical reasons, the differences of output between individuals cannot be great, this difficulty does not arise, and it is claimed that premium plans should prove an effective means of stimulating production.[2]

---

[1] These plans can conveniently be represented by the following formulae, which are convertible into those printed by Schloss in the *Journal of the Royal Economic Association* for December 1915.

Let W be the standard wage, P the standard output, w the actual wage earned by a workman, and p the actual output of that workman :

Then the general formula for the Halsey plan is

$$w = W\left\{1 + \frac{1}{n}\frac{p-P}{P}\right\}$$

when n is any integer. In the particular variety of this plan employed in Mr. Halsey's works, n has the numerical value 2. The general formula of the Rowan plan is

$$w = W\left\{1 + \frac{p-P}{P}f(p)\right\} \text{ when } f'(p) \text{ is negative.}$$

In the particular variety of this plan employed in the Rowan works $f(p)$ is given the value $\dfrac{P}{p}$: and the maximum value to which w can attain is, therefore, 2W. In England, but not in Germany, plans of this type are usually associated with the guarantee of a minimum time-wage irrespective of output ; that is to say, when p is $<$ P, the formula is not applied, but the standard wage W is paid.

[2] Cf. Chapman, *Work and Wages*, vol. ii. pp. 184-5.

R

§ 9. Now, it is quite possible that, if workpeople can be got to regard them as fair, and to trust the guarantee against cutting, these plans will be more effective than piece-wages under which cuts are feared. As a matter of fact, however, they are not fair. When a workman, other things being equal, doubles his output, he contributes, owing to his shorter occupation of machinery for a given product, rather more than twice as much as before to his employer's service. For the employer to give him, as under all premium plans he will do, considerably less than twice his former pay, is, and, when the position is realised, is felt to be, exploitation. Nor is it an adequate reply that the prospect of retaining a part of the resulting gain stimulates the employer to provide a number of conveniences and aids—"additional facilities, small tools, more power, improved lighting, better organisation, etc."[1]— which are themselves partly responsible for the worker's extra output. These things may or may not be provided. If they are provided, the rate should be adjusted to allow for them. But premium plans do not give any pledge that this will be done; they ensure that, even when conditions are absolutely unchanged and the whole additional output is due to the worker's effort, a doubled output shall mean much less than a doubled wage. This unfairness is bound sooner or later to be perceived, and, when it is perceived, the resentment which the worker will naturally feel at it is likely to drive down the output and nullify any good effect the plan may at first have had upon the national dividend. In any event, the only advantage that premium plans can claim over piece-wages is that they make possible effective guarantees against cuts. Clearly, therefore, they must be inferior to a piece-rate system so organised that the cut difficulty is overcome. The real problem is, not to evade the task of devising such a system, as premium plans substantially do, but to confront that task in those industries in which it is still formidable, and to overcome it there, as it has already been overcome in the textile industries and in coal-mining.

§ 10. The cutting or nibbling of rates may be attempted by an employer either quite honestly, when experience has shown that a particular rate was fixed too high relatively

---

[1] Rowan Thomson, *The Rowan Premium Bonus System*, p. 12.

to rates generally, or dishonestly in pure exploitation, *i.e.* in an attempt to pay the workpeople less than their marginal worth. It is plain that the first sort of cutting ought, in any satisfactory system, to be provided for, just as provision should also be made for raising rates which have accidentally been set too low. Elaborate precautions should be taken to ensure that both these sorts of error occur very rarely, but, when they do occur, machinery for correcting them should be available. If the machinery is regarded with confidence by the workpeople, the fear of this class of cut will do little harm. Exploitation cuts, on the other hand, must be absolutely prevented. With piece-wages settled by individual bargaining between separate wage-earners and their employers, neither of these things can be done. Furthermore, when a bad employer, under this arrangement, succeeds in "nibbling" the rate, his success makes it difficult for his competitors to refrain from following his example, and is apt, therefore, to start a cumulative movement. But it is not necessary that piece-rates should be fixed by individual bargaining. In this fact the solution of the problem may be found. For collective bargaining furnishes a guarantee against the kind of nibbling which is really exploitation, and also makes it easy to provide machinery — whether joint-committees or jointly appointed rate-fixers—to adjust particular rates, in the original fixing of which a mistake has been made. In this connection it is interesting to note that the rapid extension of piece-work in the engineering trade, which took place during the war —it was, no doubt, facilitated by the greater uniformity of products which was required—"led to a great variety of forms of collective bargaining. In some establishments a new piece-price is submitted to the Works Committee before it is discussed with the individual workman. In others an Appeals Committee has been instituted to consider and bring forward complaints against piece-prices or premium bonus times fixed by the management. In others again . . . prices have been discussed, not with the individual workman, but with the workman and two or three of his mates on similar work." [1]   These collective bargains within particular

---

[1] *Report on Works Committees*, 1918, p. 11.

works are, of course, not made in the air. They aim at such an adjustment of rates to the peculiar conditions of the works as will bring them into line with the standard conditions established for the industry as a whole by collective bargaining between representative associations of employers and employed.[1] In industries, such as textiles, coal-mining and the boot and shoe industry, where piece-wages have been successful and willingly accepted by the workpeople, they have always been associated with collective bargaining. Where there has been difficulty and opposition, as in engineering, woodworking and building, the real reason has been that subtle differences of quality and detail and great differences in the amount and kind of machinery in use in different shops have made anything like uniform piece-rates unsuitable, and so have stood in the way of successful collective bargaining. In these circumstances the supersession of time-wages by piece-wages would often have meant the surrender of collective bargaining in favour of rates really fixed by the arbitrary decision of employers or their representatives dealing with isolated workmen. In order that the piece-wage system, and the benefit to· production which it carries with it, may win further ground, what is required is to develop in these more difficult industries an adequate machinery for subordinating piece-wages, as they are subordinated in the textile industry, to the full control of collective bargaining.[2]

---

[1] Cf. *Report on Works Committees*, 1918, pp. 37-8.

[2] For an excellent discussion of this subject cf. Webb, *The Works Manager To-day*, chap. vi. ; also D. H. Cole, *The Payment of Wages, passim.* There is some evidence that "in Germany the strong antagonism to piece-work shown by organised labour in the early days of the German Republic is being displaced by a tendency to welcome its introduction, even in industries such as stone-cutting and the metal trades, in which it was formerly either quite excluded or bitterly opposed. According to the *Reichs-Arbeitsblatt*, this change of attitude is to be attributed, in the main, to the fact that the workers (under Article 165 of the German Federal Constitution) co-operate, on equal terms with the employers, in the regulation of wages conditions ; and that Section 78 of the Works Council Act of 1920 specifically grants to the Workers' Council (or the Works Council, as the case may be) the right to supervise the application of collective agreements, or, where these do not exist, to co-operate with the employer in the fixing of piece-rates or the bases thereof. Similar provisions have been inserted in a large number of collective agreements. Thus the workers have both a statutory and, in many cases, a contractual guarantee that a piece-work system accepted by them shall not be applied in a one-sided fashion in favour of the employer, but that the proceeds of any

§ 11. A word must here be said about a method of wage payment, different from both time-wages and piece-wages, which has been associated with some developments " of scientific management" under the name of task-wages. The essence of this method, of which there are several different forms, is as follows. Experiments are set on foot to ascertain how large an output a first-class workman, working under given conditions and exerting himself to his full capacity without overstrain, can produce in a given time. The output thus ascertained then becomes the standard task. The workpeople are so selected and trained that all those employed in establishments operating the system are first-class workmen—it would serve equally well if they were of any other class, provided all were similar—from the standpoint of the operations to be performed there ; and the wage system is adjusted in such a way that they earn very much better pay if they succeed in accomplishing the standard task than if they fail to do this.[1] The method has been described thus : " Under this system each man has his work assigned to him in the form of a task to be done by a prescribed method, with definite appliances, and to be completed within a certain time. The task is based on a detailed investigation by a trained expert of the best method of doing the work ; and the task setter, or his assistant, acts as an instructor to teach the workmen to do the work in the manner and time specified. If the work is done within the time allowed by the expert and is up to the standard for quality, the workman receives extra compensation (usually 20 to 50 per cent of the time allowed) in addition to his day's pay. If it is not done in the time set, or is not up to the standard for quality, the workman receives his day's pay only." [2] Under the Gannt

---

increased output shall be shared by them also " (*Labour Gazette*, November 1922, p. 440).

[1] It should be noted that, in effect, a very stringent form of this method is employed as regards the number of hours during which workpeople work per day ; for, if a man is not willing to work the regular factory day, he will not be employed at all and will get no wages. The reason for this is, of course, to be found in technical considerations of factory management. To have different men working in a factory different numbers of hours per day would be a much more serious inconvenience than to have them working with different intensities of effort.   [2] Going, *Principles of Industrial Engineering*, p. 135.

variety of the method ordinary time-wages are paid *plus* a large bonus to those who perform the standard task : under the Taylor variety ordinary piece-wages are paid, but the rate of piece-wages is abruptly raised by a large amount when the standard task is attained.

§ 12. Hitherto, when this plan has been employed in the United States, the standard has been fixed by the employers without resort to collective bargaining. When workpeople are prepared to allow this, and when employers are reasonable and liberal, there may, no doubt, be good results. But there is an obvious danger that unscrupulous employers may use their power to fix the standard as a means of exploitation ; [1] and it is certain that in Great Britain, where trade unions are strong, the workpeople would never consent to place this power in their hands. If the standard was fixed by collective bargaining, so that the workpeople were prepared to accept it, *and was fixed right,* the best result possible would be only equal to that given by a smoothly-working piece-wage system ; and, for a result as good as that to be achieved, it would be necessary that all the workpeople to whom any standard was applied should be *exactly* equal in capacity and temperament. Unless this impossible condition is fulfilled, adjustment under the task-wage system is bound to be less perfect than under a properly arranged piece-wage plan. On the whole, therefore,

---

[1] Certain investigations into the effect of the Taylor system upon some women employed under it do not suggest that this evil possibility has been realised in fact (*Quarterly Journal of Economics,* 1914, p. 549). But Mr. Hoxie (*Scientific Management and Labour,* pp. 44 *et seq.*) is less optimistic upon this point. He writes : " As a matter of fact, time study for task setting is found in scientific management shops in all its possible variations, both with reference to methods and results. In some the highest standards are maintained in regard to all the factors enumerated—all or a large proportion of the workers are timed, the largest practicable number of readings is made, cordial relations are established between the time study man and the workers, and the latter are cautioned against speeding up when being timed, and, if doubt remains, the allowances are purposely made large to cover all possible errors. Liberality of the task is the keynote. In other shops the maximum task is just as surely sought, and the method is warped to this end. The swiftest men are selected for timing, they work under special inducements or fear, two or three readings suffice, allowances are disregarded or cut to a minimum. The task of 100 per cent efficiency is to all intents and purposes arbitrarily fixed, sometimes practically before the time study, at what it is judged the workers can be forced to do. The main use of the time study is to prove to the workers that the task can be done in the time allowed " (*loc. cit.* p. 53).

since it is difficult to imagine circumstances in which it would be practicable to set tasks rightly but not practicable to arrange simple piece-wages, there is little to be said for introducing the task-wage system into this country.

§ 13. The practical conclusion, to which the reasoning of this chapter has tended, is that the interest of the national dividend, and, through that, of economic welfare, will be best promoted when immediate reward is adjusted as closely as possible to immediate results, and that this can, in general, be done most effectively by piece-wage scales controlled by collective bargaining. It is possible to urge against this conclusion that the large immediate output, which work-people produce under the piece-wage system, is obtained at the cost of exertions which wear them out prematurely and so damage their efficiency and output in the long run. If these charges were true, the advantage I have claimed for piece-wages would be proved to be, in part at least, illusory. It must be admitted that, when a piece-wage system is first introduced among workpeople not hitherto accustomed to it, it sometimes leads to a spurt of energy that could not be maintained for long without bad results. But experience does not show that it promotes overstrain, when once the men who have been brought under it have become, as it were, acclimatised to the new conditions. Moreover, it has to be remembered that greater intensity of work often means more thought, care and interest—which do not imply extra wear and tear—rather than greater muscular or nervous effort.[1] Little weight, therefore, need be assigned to this objection, and the conclusions set out above may be taken to hold good.

[1] Thus Mr. Cadbury writes of piece-wages : " If properly trained, the worker will try to find the quickest method of work, and the one involving the least strain ; and it has been found that, when a piece-rate has been fixed where previously there had been a time-basis, the output has doubled without any undue strain on the part of the worker, largely as the result of adopting better methods. This especially applies to hand processes " (*Experiments in Industrial Organisation*, p. 142).

CHAPTER IX

§ 1. THE subject-matter of this Chapter is the distribution of labour among different occupations and places. The supply of labour of various grades is taken as given; problems connected with the distribution of capital in the nurture and training of different persons, and so with the distribution of persons into different grades, being postponed to Chapter IX. of Part IV. The analysis of the preceding Part showed that, if the national dividend is to stand absolutely at its maximum, the values of the marginal social net products of every form of resource in all uses must be equal. It showed, further, that in many occupations marginal social net product differs from marginal private net product. Hence the maximisation of the national dividend does not require that the values of marginal private net products shall be equal in all uses. On the contrary, such a condition of universal equality is incompatible with maximisation. In spite of this, however, our argument showed that any departure from equality at any point, brought about otherwise than with the deliberate design of improving the dividend, *is likely* to indicate a lapse on the part of the dividend below the level at which it might have stood. This general result is applicable to labour. Any failure from equality in the values of the marginal private net products of labour of any grade—values that are always equivalent to the demand prices, and generally equivalent to the wages paid per efficiency unit, at different points—*probably* indicates a distribution of labour between different points other than the distribution most favourable to the national dividend. In general, therefore, causes of failure from equality in the demand prices and wage-rates of labour of given quality at different points are also causes of injury to the national dividend. These causes may be divided into three broad groups—ignorance or imperfect knowledge, costs of movement, and restrictions imposed upon movement from outside.

§ 2. One important qualification has, however, to be made to this generalisation. To some occupations and places disadvantages or advantages, not included in wage-rates, are attached, that are not common to all occupations and places. Thus in some occupations work has to be carried on in exceptionally unpleasant surroundings, in darkness and dirt or under a sense of social opprobrium—e.g. the work of the hangman. Some occupations again are exceptionally dangerous, unhealthy or subject to long bouts of unemployment. Some exhaust a man's strength and vitality after a few years, while others can be pursued easily to an advanced age. As between different places, in some house rent or other elements in the cost of living are higher than in others; in some climatic conditions are superior; in some there are more social amenities available than in others. In so far as these various incidental advantages and disadvantages of different occupations and places are fully realised and taken into account by those entering into employment, they will modify distribution in exactly the same way as occupational and local variations in wage-rates would do. Workpeople will be distributed to the occupations and places with smaller incidental advantages in less numbers and to the other occupations in greater numbers than they would be if these incidental advantages were everywhere equal : in such wise that the value of their several marginal net products—and so, in general, their wage-rates—tend not to be equal, but to differ by the value of the differences in the associated incidental advantages and disadvantages. Given the facts as to these discrepant incidental advantages and disadvantages, the national dividend is not injured, on the contrary it is augmented, by a distribution of workpeople involving departures of the types just described from equality in the values of marginal net products. When the incidental advantages and disadvantages can be brought easily into contact with a money measure this proposition is obvious. When they consist of such things as social amenities, the greater pleasantness of work in a clean than in a dirty place, and so on, it is necessary to stretch somewhat our formal definition of the national dividend in order to make the proposition true. Since, however, the national dividend is only of interest to us as a medium through which economic welfare is affected, we need not hesitate to carry out this stretching; for plainly failures from equality in the values of marginal net products of the kind here considered are, or rather the distribution of labour that implies them is, advantageous to the sum of economic welfare.

§ 3. From what has been said it follows at once that, when the incidental advantages and disadvantages attaching to different occupations and places are not fully realised and taken into account by workpeople entering employment, this fact causes labour to be distributed in a way that makes the values of marginal net products *more nearly equal* than in the interest of the national dividend they ought to be. Now there can be little doubt that wage-earners as a body under-estimate the disadvantages of dangerous, unhealthy and fluctuating trades, as against safe, wholesome and steady trades; on the other hand, they over-estimate the advantages of trades which yield a large immediate wage with little training of capacities, as against trades which yield a smaller immediate wage and more training. Both these forms of wrong estimate arise, in the main, out of a common cause, namely, the fact that people can grasp more easily the obvious, which forces itself into the field of vision, than the more remote, which has to be dragged there. The wage rate that is paid anywhere is obvious in this sense; but the chances of accident or unemployment, and the prospect of future gains through enhanced industrial capacity, cannot be fully realised without inquiry and a deliberate act of attention. Further-more, the exaggerated view which workmen hold of the advantages of dangerous, unhealthy and fluctuating industries—

the problem of training *versus* non-training occupations is deferred for separate treatment in Part IV.—is enhanced by the subconscious sentiment inherent in most men that they personally are somehow superior to the "average" man situated similarly to themselves. *They* do not need that machinery should be fenced; *their* constitution is not so feeble that deficiencies of light, air and sanitation in their place of work will injure them; *they* are not the sort of men who will lose their job in bad times. In short, workpeople are endowed, in Adam Smith's phrase, with "that natural confidence which every man has, more or less, not only in his own abilities, but in his own good fortune." This personal optimism towards the facts on the part of the persons directly concerned intensifies the maladjustment due to the difficulty, which they and their parents alike experience, of learning fully what the facts are. So far as false judgments in these matters prevail, labour is pressed into dangerous, unhealthy and fluctuating trades, till the value of its marginal net product there falls short of what it ought to be by the excess of the imagined advantage, which the false judgments attribute to these trades over their actual advantage; and, so far as the false judgments are corrected, the maladjustment in the values of marginal net products is correspondingly reduced. Against these definite false judgments specific measures of correction can be applied. Such specific measures are provided in Workmen's Compensation Acts and in State coercion towards insurance, to be financed separately by the several industries, against industrial accidents, industrial diseases (including the premature general wearing out of a man's strength by continued overstrain) and unemployment, in industries which are *more* dangerous, unwholesome and fluctuating than the industry least unfavourably situated in these respects. In one form or another, these devices exhibit the remote and unobvious chances of injury, illness or unemployment in the obvious shape of reductions in wages or immediate payments out of wages. They thus tend to lessen the proportion of people who enter dangerous, unwholesome and fluctuating trades, and so to make the value of the marginal net product of labour in these trades less nearly equal, indeed, to the value of the marginal net product of labour in general, but more nearly equal to what it ought to be. State bounties, so arranged as to *persuade* people to expend more money on insurance, serve, though less effectively, to promote the same object. On the other hand, State provision of insurance against accidents, industrial diseases and unemployment, whether the provision is financed out of taxes or out of general level-rate premiums, and whether it covers the *whole* cost or a *proportion* of it, differentiates in favour of dangerous, unhealthy and fluctuating trades, and causes an excess of people to enter them.

§ 4. A distribution of wage-earners that carries with it failures from equality in the values of the marginal net products, other than failures of the type we have been discussing in the two preceding sections, in general involves, as has already been made clear, injury to the national dividend and, through that, to economic welfare. The causes of " errors " of distribution that are present in actual life may be divided into three broad groups—ignorance, cost of movement and restrictions imposed upon movement from outside.

§ 5. The most fundamental way in which the first of these causes, ignorance, operates is by impairing the initial distribution of new generations of workpeople as they flow into industry. Those persons who direct the choice of avocations made by young men and women entering industry are ignorant both of the level at which the demand price for any given quantity of labour of any given grade will stand in different occupations at a later period of those young persons' lives, and also of what the quantity of labour offering itself in those different occupations at that period will be. A great part of this ignorance is, of course, inevitable in a world of change. Even though opinions were continually modified in the light of the most recent experience, yet newer experience would necessarily belie the best-based forecasts. But, besides the ignorance that is inevitable, there is also ignorance due to the frailty of individual minds and the paucity of organised information. About occupations for people this ignorance is likely to be more extensive than it is about occupations for capital; for the same reason that ignorance about the relative advantages of different forms of spending is more extensive than ignorance about the choice of investments. Those persons who have to direct their children's choice of a career are not rendered efficient by the selective influence of competition. Fathers who invest their sons' activities unremuneratively are not expelled by bankruptcy from the profession of fatherhood, but continue, however incapable they may be, to exercise in this matter the function of entrepreneurs. The grave errors that result are well known. " Many parents let their boys go into offices or as telegraph messengers, because they seem respectable jobs, but they have never considered, and, perhaps, have no means of knowing, whether there are any future prospects. This aspect is dwelt upon in the reports of many of the skilled employment committees. If the father is not himself in a position to get a boy into a good trade, he does not know in many cases how to manage it."[1] The point is well illustrated by Sir H. Llewellyn Smith's observation, some years back, that, among the Cradley Heath hand nailmakers, " although the trade has been decaying for more than half a century, children are still going into, and are further crowding, their parents' trade." Again : " A very large number of parents are ignorant of the relative advantages of different occupations. . . . The boys tend always to follow their older companions into the same factory or yard, or at any rate into the same kind of occupation ; and, where the prevailing trades are of a poor grade . . the boys will generally follow the line of least resistance."[2] This sort of ignorance may, of course, be overcome in part through the collection and spreading of information about the prospects of different trades, together with improved education enabling parents to make better use of the information that is open to them. It may be overcome still further

---

[1] Jackson, Report on Boy Labour, *Royal Commission on the Poor Laws*, Appendix, vol. xx. pp. 9-10.
[2] Jackson, Report on Boy Labour, *Royal Commission on the Poor Laws*, Appendix, vol. xx. p. 161. The general tendency of children to enter their parents' trades is illustrated by a very interesting special inquiry undertaken by Prof. Chapman and Mr. Abbot in the neighbourhood of Manchester (*Statistical Journal*, May 1913, pp. 599 *et seq.*).

if those parents, who are not themselves in a position to make any good study of the labour market, have access to the advice of persons who are in a position to do this. At the best, however, since the prospects that are relevant are the prospects that will prevail in future years when the children and youths now selecting an occupation are grown up, this type of ignorance must always be extensive.

§ 6. But this type of ignorance is not the only one that prevents labour of any particular grade from being initially distributed among different uses in such a way as to make the demand-prices — or values of marginal net products — equal. The same effect is produced by ignorance as *to what the grade is* to which any individual boy or girl, whose fate is being decided, belongs. For different children are born with different capacities and aptitudes. So far as some of those belonging to one grade drift into occupations more fitted to those of another grade, the value of their marginal net product there will be less than it might have been—less than that of children of the same grade who have been turned into occupations more suitable to that grade. Moreover, the loss, though lessened, is not done away with if people eventually find jobs that fit them, after drifting through one or more jobs that do not; for throughout the interval their efforts have been expended less usefully than they might have been. Hence it is important, from the standpoint of the national dividend, to provide for a rational sorting of children of different intellectual qualities, and for guiding them into lines of work for which their several qualities are fitted. " It is probable that labour exchanges for boys leaving school would be of very great value in securing that all the more intelligent and able boys had a chance of securing good openings. It is the ignorance of the boy which so often leads him into employment which is not suited to him."[1] There is—or was—an excellent example of the organisation required in Strasburg, where the Labour Exchange works in definite association with the teachers of the municipal schools. Our own Education

---

[1] Jackson, Report on Boy Labour, *Royal Commission on the Poor Laws*, Appendix, vol. xx. p. 31.

(Choice of Employment) Act, 1910, endeavours to foster an alliance of this kind. But, if this type of organisation is to be made thoroughly effective, the fitness of different boys for different occupations must not be judged by mere rough general impressions. There is required a scientific analysis, on the one hand, of the qualities for which various occupations call, and, on the other hand, of the qualities which different individual boys possess. The practical problems thus suggested have been discussed in a very interesting manner by Professor Munsterberg. He cites a bicycle factory in which the reaction times of different individuals were scientifically measured, and the results used as a test of fitness for the work of inspecting the balls of bicycle-bearings;[1] and he describes certain devices which he himself has invented for testing fitness for the work of motor-men. Tests with the same general purpose have recently been used by the military authorities to assist them in the selection of recruits for the Royal Air Force. Such methods can often guide the individual's choice of employment when he first steps into industry—or first moves from a boy's occupation to a man's occupation[2]—more effectively, and much less blindly, than the ordinary rough and tumble of trial and error. They would be made still more effective if a device could be invented for testing, not merely capacity at the moment, but also capacity to attain capacity through training. It

---

[1] *Psychology and Industrial Efficiency*, pp. 54-5.

[2] Cf. Sir Sydney Chapman's observation : "Certain occupations cannot be entered by any adequate number of people until they have nearly attained their full strength ; for instance, the occupations of manual workers on the railways, navvies, and dock labourers, and certain occupations in the building trades. This means that other callings must employ more young people than they can permanently find room for, unless some young people in search of work are to be left standing idle in the market-place. But to seek to obviate this tendency by making each industry more self-contained would not be a very wise proceeding, because it is poor economy to have a man doing a lad's work, or a lad doing a man's work, and from the operation of a certain amount of selection among the labour forces of the community productive efficiency results. . . . It may be that the partial *cul-de-sac* employment is a necessary part of a highly developed industrial system. If this is so, the establishment of labour-training institutes becomes doubly necessary, and an added importance attaches to Labour Exchanges with special reference to the claims of the rejected of certain trades, whom it is essential to deal with before they become demoralised or suffer in vigour or spirit " ("Industrial Recruiting and the Displacement of Labour," *Proceedings of the Manchester Statistical Society*, 1913–14, pp. 122-3).

is, therefore, of interest to learn that experiments " have been actually started to determine the plasticity of the psychological apparatus as an independent inborn trait of the individual." [1]

§ 7. When the initial distribution of new generations of workpeople among the various occupations open to them has been wrong for some little time, the aggregate distribution of the whole existing body of workpeople must also be wrong. The error may, of course, be corrected without any actual movement among established workpeople by a redirection of the flow of new recruits. This correction acts more rapidly in industries where the proportion of annual recruitment to total numbers is large than in those where it is small. It thus acts especially rapidly in women's industries, because the obligations of marriage make the average length of a woman's stay in industry especially short. Though, however, errors due to failures in the initial distribution of workpeople may be corrected without the need for movement, plainly they may also be corrected with the help of it. Moreover, even where there has been no error in initial distribution, maladjustment may come about because a man, who was fitted for a particular post when he first entered it, becomes either too good for it or too bad; either fitted for promotion to a higher

---

[1] Munsterberg, *Psychology of Industrial Efficiency*, p. 126. Initial testing of capacity is, perhaps, not very important among workpeople who begin their career in large and varied establishments, where employees found unsuitable for the job they first select can be rapidly transferred to other jobs. Of firms which follow Mr. Taylor's doctrine of scientific management it is said that, "by a careful study of each individual of a group of men in any department, it may be found that many are not physically or temperamentally adapted to performing the particular functions required in that department, and that they are adapted to the performing of functions in some other department. There follows a redistribution of men between departments, with the result that, without an increase in aggregate energy expended, there is an increase in aggregate productivity. It is the scientific method of adapting instrument to purpose" (Tuck School Conference, *Scientific Management*, p. 6). But in comparatively small and homogeneous establishments—and these employ a very large proportion of the world's workers —" the working man who is a failure in the work which he undertook would usually have no opportunity to show his strong sides in the same factory, or at least to be protected against the consequences of his weak points. If his achievement is deficient in quality or quantity, he generally loses his place and makes a new trial in another factory under the same accidental conditions, without any deeper insight into his particular psychical traits and their relation to special industrial activities" (Munsterberg, *Psychology of Industrial Efficiency*, p. 121).

grade or ripe for removal to less responsible work. Yet again, the distribution of labour, not only between occupations but also between places, may be made wrong from time to time by temporary fluctuations in the demand for and supply of different things, even though the initial direction given to new generations of workpeople was guided by perfect wisdom. Over a wide field, therefore, there is always opportunity for making the distribution of labour better by rightly directed movement between different places and different occupations.[1] The point we have now to consider is that ignorance, over and above the injury described already, inflicts a further injury on the national dividend by impeding and deflecting movement.

§ 8. Beyond doubt a great deal of ignorance prevails among workpeople in one place or occupation as to the comparative demand prices—by which the values of their marginal net products are represented—for their services prevailing there and elsewhere. The discussion of this matter is complicated by the fact that, since, from seasonal and other causes, work is less regular in some occupations than in others, wage rates per day or per week do not by themselves afford an adequate measure of comparative demand prices as a whole. Such a measure can only be obtained when both the wage rate for full employment and the prospect of unemployment have been taken into account. Clearly, workpeople can less easily gather information about the comparative liability of different occupations to unemployment than about comparative wage rates. This point, however, need not be enlarged upon here, and attention may be confined to wages. The extent of people's ignorance about the level of wage rates in any place or occupation depends, in great part, upon the form in which wage contracts are made. Some forms make the real prospect of earnings offered to workpeople much more difficult to calculate than other forms. In nearly all forms, indeed, there is a good deal of obscurity. For real wages, in the widest sense, embrace the conditions of a

---

[1] These considerations enable us to perceive that, though, when the distribution of labour between places or firms is right, a large labour turn-over is a social waste, when the distribution is wrong, it may be a means of overcoming social waste.

man's work in respect to sanitary arrangements, safety appliances, and so forth; and these cannot be fully known to any workman before he is actually working under them. But the obscurity is much enhanced when fines are charged for damaged work and information about these is suppressed, and when wages are paid partly in commodities on which some fictitious value may be set. It is, therefore, an important fact that wage contracts embracing these elements are restricted in most modern States. To meet direct suppression of relevant information, the law has intervened in this country through the Particulars Clause inserted in the Factory and Workshops Act, 1901. "That section provides that, in industries to which it is applied by Order of the Secretary of State, persons, to whom work is given out to be done, shall receive from the employer sufficient particulars of the rate of wages applicable to the work to be done, and of the work to which that rate is to be applied, to enable the worker to compute the total amount of wages payable in respect of the work. This provision, the enforcement of which is placed upon the Inspectors of Factories, is intended to secure to the outworker information beforehand as to the price he is to get for the work, and to protect him against arbitrary alterations or reductions when the work is brought in. The provision has been extended by Orders of the Secretary of State to the outworkers in a number of trades."[1] To meet indirect suppression of information through part-payment in objects of ambiguous value, the law in this country has adopted the broad policy of prohibiting such part-payment, despite the risk that in so doing it might incidentally suppress some useful institutions.[2] The fundamental provision of the Truck Act of 1831 was that "wages are to be made payable in current coin of the realm only," and that no condition should be made as to where or with whom any part of the wages should be expended.[3] This provision was made to

---

[1] *Select Committee on Home Work Report*, 1908, p. viii.

[2] Cf. C. D. Wright's account of some American systems of company stores in regions remote from ordinary shops (*The Industrial Evolution of the U.S.A.*, pp. 282 et seq.).

[3] *Report of the Select Committee on the Truck Acts*, p. 6. This provision can be evaded by a company establishing a provision store and informally

apply by the Act of 1887 to any one engaged in manual labour who has entered into, or works under, an expressed or implied contract with an employer; it did not include outworkers who contract in terms of product, not of work. It was decided by the Courts that to make deductions for rent of machines, standing-room, etc., was not incompatible with the Act, because wages meant what was left after such payments had been made. Fines were also held to be no contravention. By the Act of 1896, however, " deductions in respect of fines, in respect of loss to the employer by bad or spoiled work or materials, etc., and in respect of the supply of materials, tools and other conveniences to ·the worker were made subject to conditions intended to protect the worker against harsh or unfair charges on the part of the employer." [1] Some practical problems under this head still demand solution, and were discussed at length by the Committee of 1908.[2]

§ 9. Our study of ignorance as a cause of errors in the distribution of labour is now complete. We turn, therefore, to the second cause distinguished in § 4, namely, " costs of movement." The existence of these costs estops movements that

---

putting pressure on its workpeople to buy there. The French law of 1910 meets this danger by forbidding any employer to '' connect with his establishment any store at which he shall sell directly or indirectly to his employees or to their families provisions or goods of any description whatever " (*Labour Gazette*, May 1910, p. 156).

[1] *Report of the Select Committee on the Truck Acts*, p. 9.

[2] Thus, the Committee find that some deductions in respect of fines may be useful to secure discipline, and suggest that abuse be guarded against by a statutory provision that "the maximum fine or accumulation of fines in any one week permissible by law shall not exceed 5 per cent of the wages of the worker " (p. 29). Deductions for damage to materials and so on they hold may be usefully employed to prevent waste, under an arrangement, say, for charging for the material as given out and *adding* the value of it to the wage for the work in which it is afterwards incorporated (p. 41). Still, they conclude that, in view of the liability of such charges to become fraudulent, they should be prohibited, subject to a power of the Home Secretary to relax the prohibitions in special cases (*e.g.* of costly material). The Committee further hold that the general provisions of the Truck Acts should be extended to outworkers (p. 78). They discuss, but do not definitely recommend, rules prohibiting employers from making it compulsory for their hands to live in houses provided by them (p. 53). The real objection to such compulsion is, not so much that it may enable employers to veil the facts about real wages, as that it may enable them to put undue pressure on employees in times of strike.

would, in their absence, correct maladjustments in the distribution of labour. But there is, of course, no necessity for the maladjustments, when costs are present, to be such that, even apart from the factors considered in §§ 2-3, the values of the marginal net product of labour between two occupations and places must diverge by an amount equal to the costs of movement between them. The divergence cannot be greater than this, but there is no reason why it should not be less.[1] Most costs of movement, we have next to observe, are lump-sum costs of a single act of movement. Before these can be examined in detail, certain matters of a general character require elucidation. As was indicated ·in the footnote to p. 145, the cost of movement may most conveniently be regarded as equivalent to an annual (or daily) sum spread over the period during which the workman who has moved may expect to find profit in staying in his new place or occupation. The task of calculating this sum presents some difficulty. First, the costs of movement are not the same for all persons liable to move. Old workmen with families are, for example, rooted more firmly to their homes than young unmarried men. At first sight, indeed, it might seem that this fact does not greatly concern us, since the movement in which we are interested is the movement of those persons whose movement costs least—not fluidity in general, but fluidity at the edges. But the costs of movement of those persons whose movement costs least are themselves dependent upon the number of persons who are moving. Hence, for complete accuracy, we should need to treat these costs, not as a constant, but as a function of the volume of movement. For purposes of approximation, however, it is generally sufficient to take rough *discontinuous* groups, for which different fixed costs of movement can be set out. Thus, whether A and B represent different places or different occupations, and whether movement means movement in space or the acquisition of a new trade, we can in ordinary times—the position in the later period of the Great War was, of course, different—take for our costs those próper to the movement of young men without family encumbrances. It should, indeed, be noted that, as a trade or place decays and the young men

[1] Cf. *ante*, p. 138.

gradually leave, the relevant costs of movement will tend to rise, because the age distribution of the population will be modified. Statistical inquiry shows that in decaying trades the proportion of old men is above the normal, and becomes greater and greater as the decay proceeds.[1] But this complication is one of detail rather than of principle. Secondly, when the capital cost of movement is given, the annual (or daily) sum, to which we have to equate it, is not fixed, but is larger, the shorter is the period during which a workman who has moved expects to find profit in staying in his new place. For example, in the eyes of a man considering whether or not to move away from a point of slack demand, this sum will be larger if the depression is, say, a seasonal depression and likely to pass away rapidly than if it is likely to continue for a long time. Thirdly, from the present point of view, the costs of movement between any two places or occupations A and B are not necessarily the actual costs, but may be a lesser amount, which we may call the " virtual " costs, and which consist of the sum of the costs of movement along each of the separate stages that lie between A and B. When the costs in view are merely costs of physical transport, this point is not, indeed, likely to be important. For, in general, long-distance journeys are cheaper per mile than short-distance journeys, and, therefore, there will not exist any virtual cost smaller than the actual cost. If, however, the costs in view are those arising out of the need of learning particular accomplishments, it is very important. The costs of movement, in this sense, between the occupation of agricultural labourer and that of master manufacturer may be infinite; but those between agricultural labourer and petty shopkeeper, between petty shopkeeper and large shopkeeper, between large shopkeeper

---

[1] Cf. Booth, *Life and Labour, Industry*, vol. v. pp. 43 and 49. In like manner, Lord Dunraven observes that " Ireland has a larger population of aged than any other country in the king's dominions " (*The Outlook in Ireland*, p. 21). It must be noted, however, that we cannot *infer* decay or expansion unreservedly from such considerations, because, in some industries, the *normal* age distribution differs widely from the average. Messengers are young men who expect to become something else, and lightermen are generally retired sailors. Furthermore, some industries have an abnormal proportion of old workers, simply because they are abnormally healthy or attract abnormally healthy people.

and departmental manager, between departmental manager and general manager, between general manager and master manufacturer, may all be small. The same class of consideration is applicable to those costs which consist in the subjective burden of leaving one's home and settling elsewhere. Probably these costs, in respect of one movement of a thousand miles, greatly exceed those involved in two hundred movements of five miles each. A good illustration of this point is afforded by the following account of mediaeval France: "If Lyons had need of workmen, it called upon Chalon-sur-Saône, which supplied them. The void made at Chalon was filled by men drawn from Auxerre. Auxerre, finding that less work was offered than was required, called to its aid Sens, which, at need, fell back upon Paris. . . . Thus, all the different places were stirred at once by a demand for labour, however distant that might be, just as a regiment in column, marching in one piece and only advancing a few paces, would be."[1] This class of consideration is important.

§ 10. We may now look at the costs of movement somewhat more in detail. As between two given places, we perceive at once that they include, not only the sheer money cost of travel to a workman who contemplates moving, but also the sacrifice of the goodwill of shopkeepers to whom the workman is known, and the wrench involved in leaving his friends and the district with which he is familiar. The money cost, of course, becomes less in any country, as the means of communication are developed and transport, therefore, becomes cheaper. The other element of cost, in like manner, becomes less as the speed of travel is increased, because, as this happens, it becomes easier for workpeople to change the seat of their work without having at the same time to change their homes.[2]

---

[1] De Foville, *Transformation des moyens de transport*, p. 396. There is an exactly analogous phenomenon in the movement of capital between countries. People in the United States can move a given capital to Central or South America, and at the same time people in England move an equal capital to the United States at a less aggregate cost in uncertainty—because of differences of local knowledge—than that at which Englishmen could move that capital to Central or South America direct. Hence, this roundabout method of investment in fact occurs. (Cf. C. K. Hobson, *The Export of Capital*, pp. 29-32.)

[2] Cf. Mahaim, *Les Abonnements d'ouvriers*, p. 170.

As between two given occupations, the costs of movement become less, the more closely industrial progress causes the operations required in one occupation to resemble those required in another. Assimilation of this sort tends to come about more and more markedly the further the division of labour is carried. For division of labour means the splitting up of complex operations, formerly executed as wholes, into their elementary parts, and it so happens that a comparatively small number of elementary parts, when combined in different ways, make up nearly all the wholes. Consequently, the range of movements open to workmen helping to produce any given article, while " narrowed as regards the power of interchange among themselves, is, as a rule, widened as regards the power of interchange with those performing corresponding processes of other trades."[1] As M. de Rousiers well observes : " More and more the constantly developing applications of machinery are approximating the type of the mechanic to that of the shop assistant. The shop assistant passes readily from one kind of commerce to another, from drapery to provisions, from fancy goods to furniture, so much so that, at the present time, retail shopkeeping, in the hands of men of superior ability, is no longer confined to one or another single branch, but takes on the form of the large general store. Manufacture cannot yet pretend to so large a range, but, just as an assistant passes easily from one counter to another, so the workman passes easily from the supervision of one machine to the supervision of another machine, from the loom to bootmaking, from paper-making to spinning, and so forth."[2] In like manner, the same persons, at different times, may be found at match-box making, hopping, step-cleaning, and hawking; and the Poor Law Commissioners' investigators "found a tailoress working at bookbinding, a jam girl at screws, and a machinist giving pianoforte lessons at 1s. an hour."[3] In these developments there is evidence of great versatility. Specialised technical skill is coming to play a smaller part in industrial operations, relatively to general capacity, than it

[1] Llewellyn Smith, *The Mobility of Labour*, p. 19.
[2] *La Question ouvrière en Angleterre*, p. 334.   Cf. also Marshall, *Principles of Economics*, pp. 207 and 258.
[3] *Report of the Royal Commission on the Poor Laws*, p. 406.

used to do; and this means that the costs of the new training required to enable a workman to move from one occupation to another are becoming smaller. It should be added that, in so far as people's estimate of the cost of new training is greater than the actual cost, it is the estimated cost that is relevant to mobility; and, therefore, if they come to realise that the estimate has been excessive, mobility is increased. There is reason to suppose that the experience of the war has taught people that specialised skill can be gained more easily and quickly than used to be supposed.[1]

So far, we have spoken of movement between places and movement between occupations separately. But, of course, in the concrete, movement from one occupation to another may well necessitate, at the same time, movement from one place to another. Hence the aggregate costs of movement from one occupation to another are kept low when kindred occupations, in which the fluctuations of demand for labour more or less compensate one another, are carried on in the same neighbourhood. This is one of the advantages of the cottage industries of the country districts of India, where for three months of the year agriculture is almost at a standstill;[2] and also of recent extensions of small holdings and allotments, to which workpeople can resort during temporary unemployment in their main industry. The reduction of costs is still greater when the complementary occupations are conducted in the same establishment. It is, therefore, especially interesting to read in a Board of Trade Report issued shortly before the war: "The more competent and thoughtful employers endeavour to overcome the natural fluctuations of the seasons by superior organisation. With the manufacture of jam and marmalade they combine the making of sweets and the potting of meats. They thus occupy the time of the majority of their employees. An artificial florist, employing over two hundred girls and women in a trade which occupies six months of the year, has introduced a second trade, the preparing of quills for

---

[1] Cf. Cannan, *The Reorganisation of Industry* (Ruskin College), Series iii. p. 11.

[2] Cf. Muckerjee, *The Foundations of Indian Economics*, p. 323.

hat-trimming, and now the workers are employed all the year round. In Luton, where the staple trade is straw-hat making, and where work is always slack during six months of the year, felt-hat making has been introduced ; and it is now very usual to find the two trades carried on by the same firm, employing the same workpeople at different periods of the year." [1] Sometimes, no doubt, arrangements of this kind are introduced from philanthropic motives. But there is also a powerful motive of a purely self-regarding character at work in the same direction. It is clearly cheaper for one factory to work all the year round than for two to be built to work, one in one part, and the other in another part of the year ; and the gain in cheapness is particularly great when the plant and equipment are elaborate and costly. Hence, whenever it is practicable, it is to the interest of employers to adapt their factories—if they are engaged in seasonal production—to the manufacture of a series of different things so arranged that there is work to do at some of them in every part of the year. Anything that facilitates the adoption among employers of this policy necessarily reduces the effective costs of movement to labour.

§ 11. In the preceding sections we have permitted ourselves certain refinements of analysis. Turning back to coarser matters, we may conclude generally that workpeople's movements away from their present occupation to other occupations offering a higher wage, and, therefore, presumably yielding a larger value of marginal net product, are often impeded by considerable costs ; and that workpeople's movements from their present locality to other and distant countries, particularly if these are separated off by strong barriers of race, religion and language, may often be similarly impeded. But, so far as the forms of cost hitherto discussed are concerned, workpeople's movements to other parts of their native land, at all events in a small country such as England, will, in general, only be impeded by small costs. There remains, however, a peculiar form of cost obstructing movements from certain places to certain other places, which may be large even in a country like England. This cost arises out of the fact that husband, wife and young children generally live together. Because of this the movement

---

[1] *Cost of Living of the Working Classes* [Cd. 3864], p. 284.

of one member of the family implies the movement of the others, and the movement of the others may carry with it a large loss by cutting off the wages that they have hitherto been able to earn. This loss is really a part of the cost of movement of the member of the family who is tempted by higher wages to move elsewhere. For example, the men workers, in a district where there are opportunities for their women folk to earn wages, might know that they themselves could earn more in other districts where these opportunities do not exist. But, in reckoning up the advantages and disadvantages of movement, they would need to count as a true cost the prospective loss of their womenfolk's contribution. This cost may be very large and, consequently, may make possible wide differences in the values of the marginal net products, and, therefore, in the wages, of labour of a given grade in two districts of the same small country. As Marshall has well observed: " The family is, in the main, a single unit as regards geographical migration ; and, therefore, the wages of men are relatively high, and those of women and children low, where heavy iron or other industries preponderate, while in some other districts less than half the money income of the family is earned by the father, and men's wages are relatively low." [1] It is evident that all improvements in the speed and all cheapening in the cost of passenger transport, to which reference was made in an earlier section, because they enable different members of a family, while living together, to work in places more widely separated from one another, will mitigate the injury to the distribution of labour, and so to the national dividend, for which this kind of cause is responsible.

§ 12. In addition to ignorance and costs there remains the third cause of error in the distribution of labour, which was distinguished in § 4, namely, artificial restrictions upon movement imposed from without. These restrictions may assume any number of different forms. For example, until the end of the eighteenth century "place mobility" was seriously obstructed by the law of settlement, which, in order to prevent workpeople born in one part of the country from becoming chargeable on the rates of another part, greatly limited their right to move.

[1] *Principles of Economics*, footnote to p. 715.

" It was often more difficult," Adam Smith wrote, "for a poor
man to pass the artificial boundary of a parish than an arm of
the sea or a ridge of high mountains." Again, at the present
day, movement between occupations is, in some industries,
considerably impeded by the demarcation rules of Trade
Unions—rules which attempt to reserve particular jobs to
workers at a particular trade, and forbid, under threat of a
strike, their being undertaken by other tradesmen. A
bricklayer, for example, is not allowed by his union to do
stone-mason's work, or a pattern-maker to do joiner's work.
Nor can a man easily escape this kind of obstacle by
changing his union. For, apart from affiliation arrangements
among kindred unions, if he tries to do this, he is liable to
lose his old rights to trade union benefits without at once
acquiring new ones. This difficulty can be met by the
development of industrial unionism, as exemplified by the
National Union of Railway Workers, alongside of craft unionism, or by systems of affiliation among the craft unions
themselves and between the craft unions and unions of
unskilled workers. Probably, however, the most serious
artificial restrictions that are current in modern times are
certain traditions and customs, which obstruct and practically
prevent labour power, when embodied in a particular type of
person, from flowing to channels where similar labour power,
embodied in other types of persons, is yielding a more valuable
marginal net product than is obtainable in the channels to
which all labour has free access. In some countries traditions
and customs of this sort relate to industrial occupations open
to workpeople of different race and colour. But their most
important action—at all events, so far as Europe is concerned—
is in the sphere of women's work. There are a number of
occupations in which the value of the marginal net product,
and, therefore, the wage, of women's work would, if women were
admitted to them, be larger than it is in occupations where
they are in fact engaged; but they are excluded from these
occupations by tradition and custom. When new occupations,
such as the working of typewriters and telephones, are introduced, or when old occupations are transformed by the
introduction of new types of machinery, women are, indeed,

generally offered a free field. But in occupations which men have for a long time been accustomed to regard as their own, even though under present conditions women could adequately pursue them, tradition and custom frequently exercise a powerful excluding influence. The best known occupations in which such exclusion still prevails in fact, if not in form, are the two branches of the legal profession. Waiting in restaurants and railway clerical work were also, until a year or two ago, notable instances. The entrance of women into these occupations, prior to 1914, was hindered, as Prof. Cannan observes, "not so much by law as by the inertia of employers and their fear of inconvenience from the active resistance of the men employed at present."[1] This kind of resistance may be broken down by a world-shattering event like the Great War, but the difficulty with which it was overcome in 1915–16, even in munition-making trades, is witness to its strength. It is probable that employers do not battle with it so strongly as they otherwise might do, because women workers are liable to leave after a little while on getting married. As one employer put it: "There are many jobs one might teach women to do, but it does not seem worth while to risk a quarrel with the men, when you know that, the brighter a girl is, the more likely she is to go off and get married just as she is beginning to be of some use."[2] The men's opposition can, indeed, be modified by a stringent rule that women shall be paid equal wages with men of equal efficiency; for, when this rule exists, the men are less afraid of losing their jobs. But, on the other hand, the existence of such a rule sometimes makes employers less anxious to open the door to women workers than they otherwise might be.[3]

§ 13. We have now studied the principal causes that make the distribution of labour of various grades diverge from the most advantageous distribution. All these causes alike injure the national dividend—in the stretched sense of § 2—and it might, therefore, seem at first sight that, if the deflection of labour distribution, for which they are responsible, were overcome, the size of the national dividend would necessarily be

[1] Cannan, *Wealth*, p. 206.
[2] *The Round Table*, March 1916, p. 275.
[3] Cf. *post*, Chapter XIV. § 10.

increased. This conclusion, however, ignores the fact that there are three distinct and different methods by which the deflection can be overcome. The obstacles in the way of a nearer approach to what may be called the ideal distribution may *crumble from within*, or they may be *pulled down at public cost*, or they may be left as they are and *leapt over*. The effects of these three methods of overcoming them are not the same, but require separate investigation.

§ 14. When it is said that obstacles to ideal distribution *crumble from within*, it is meant that information and the means of movement are supplied more cheaply to workpeople, or that traditions hostile to movement are weakened, through the general progress of ideas, the introduction of large scale organisation into the machinery of mobility, or in other such ways. The essence of the matter is that the real costs to the community as a whole of providing information and transport, and not merely the expenses charged to particular workpeople purchasing these facilities, are lessened. When this happens, the actual distribution of labour will, *generally speaking*, be brought closer to the ideal distribution. It is true that, if the obstacle whose magnitude is diminished is costs of movement or tradition, this does not *necessarily* happen. For, as was pointed out in Part II. Chapter V., increased freedom to move may, when knowledge is imperfect, lead to movement in the wrong direction. Thus, it is sometimes an open question whether a *mere* cheapening of the costs of travel to workpeople, unaccompanied by any other change, will have a beneficial effect; though, of course, it is never an open question whether cheapening, coupled with intelligent direction to specific vacancies, will have such an effect. That this point is winning general recognition is suggested by the fact that, in England, travelling benefit, originally paid out by Trade Unions indiscriminately to all members in search of work, is now mainly used to enable selected members to reach places in which work has actually been found for them; by the fact that the British Labour Exchanges Act contains a clause permitting the Exchanges, subject to the approval of the Treasury, to authorise advances, by way of loan, towards the expenses of workpeople travelling to definite situations; and, finally, by the fact that, in Germany, the Exchanges provide cheap railway tickets, not to work-seekers in general, but to those only for whom they have found definite situations.[1] The difficulty thus exemplified is an important one. There would, however, be no dispute among economists that, with the organisation of knowledge concerning industrial conditions developed to the point at which it stands in modern civilised States, a reduction in the costs of movement, or a breach in traditions of exclusion, would, on the whole and in general, cause the distribution of labour to approach more closely towards the ideal. In so far as it has this effect, it must also increase the national dividend.

§ 15. When it is said that obstacles to ideal distribution are *pulled down at public expense*, it is meant that information or the means of movement are supplied more cheaply to workpeople, not because the real costs have been reduced, but because a part of these costs has been transferred to the shoulders of the tax-payers. This form of cheapening and that discussed in the preceding section do not react in the same way upon the national dividend. For this kind of cheapening implies that a greater quantity of resources is invested in the work of securing knowledge and effecting movement than would normally be devoted to that work. It implies, in fact, that a particular form of investment is being stimulated by means of a bounty; and there is a presumption that bounties hurt the dividend. As was shown, however, in Chapters IX. and XI. of Part II., this presumption, in respect of any particular industry, may be overthrown, if there are definite grounds for believing that, in the absence of a bounty, investment in that industry would not be carried far enough to bring the value of the marginal social net product of resources employed in it down to the general level. The industry of promoting the mobility of workpeople, partly because it yields a product difficult to sell satisfactorily for fees, is one about which there are definite grounds for believing this. Consequently, up to a point, it is probable that the expenditure of public money in promoting mobility would improve the national dividend. It is necessary, however,

[1] *Report of the Royal Commission on the Poor Laws*, p. 401.

for the State to watch this expenditure carefully; for, if it is carried too far, the cost at the margin will exceed the gain.

§ 16. When it is said that obstacles to ideal distribution are *leapt over*, it is meant that ignorance, costs of movement and tradition remain unaltered, but that, in spite of their existence, the distribution of labour is somehow forced towards what it would have been if they did not exist. This may be done by the compulsory removal of workpeople, or, more probably, as will be explained in Chapter XIV. § 5, by certain forms of authoritative interference with wage rates. The way in which it is done is not, however, important for our present problem. What we wish to ascertain is the effect on the national dividend of an "improvement" in the distribution of labour brought about *in spite of* the continued existence of obstacles. This effect is different with different obstacles. A redistribution of labour more conformable to ideal distribution, which is brought about in spite of opposing ignorance or tradition, necessarily benefits the national dividend. For the defiance of these obstacles involves no expense, and so leads to exactly the same consequences as would be produced by their crumbling from within. But the result is different with a redistribution brought about in spite of opposing costs of movement. For, when the obstacles to movement, which these costs present, are overborne, the costs themselves are by that very process incurred. Thus defiance does involve expense, and leads to the same consequences as would be produced if the obstacle were *pulled down at public cost.* That is to say, there is a presumption—which may, of course, in some circumstances be rebutted—that it will injure the national dividend.[1]

---

[1] This conclusion involves the verbally inconvenient result that the *ideal* distribution of labour, when brought about in certain ways, is not the *best possible* distribution. Confusion will be avoided, however, if we recollect that the distribution we have called ideal, namely, that which, subject to the qualifications of § 2, makes the values of the marginal net products of labour everywhere equal, is only ideal in an absolute sense. It is the best distribution accessible to a man who has unlimited power over all relevant circumstances, and can, therefore, at will abolish costs of movement. But it is not the best distribution accessible to one who must accept the costs of movement as brute fact, and has, therefore, to aim at maximising the national dividend subject to that limiting condition. Cf. *ante*, Part II. Chapter V. § 6.

CHAPTER X

§ 1. In the preceding chapter we have spoken as though the only movements of labour which take place, or which may be required in the interests of the national dividend, are movements from employment in one place or occupation to employment in another. In actual life, however, it often happens that workpeople find themselves, not merely employed at work of relatively low demand, but unemployed altogether. We are not now concerned to inquire into the causes of this, or to investigate the relation between the volume of unemployment and the wage policy of trade unions. From our present point of view the thing that matters is that, given this wage policy, workpeople are liable to find themselves unemployed at one place or in one occupation at a time when in other places or occupations work is on offer at the rate of wages which they demand, and they are held back from these places or occupations, not by costs of movement, but by ignorance of the facts. Plainly, this state of affairs involves an injury to the national dividend analogous to the injury involved when workpeople are held by ignorance in employments of low demand at a time when employments of high demand are calling for them. The form of ignorance that is responsible for this injury and the means by which it may be combated demand a brief study.

§ 2. If workpeople out of a job were completely ignorant about available vacancies, their only recourse would be to a perfectly haphazard and unguided search for work. They could do nothing but wander aimlessly round to the firms that have not, as well as to those that have, vacancies, engaging themselves in a weary " tramp from one firm to another, in the attempt to discover, by actual application to one after another, which of them wants another hand."[1] As a rule ignorance is somewhat less complete than this. Some sort of general information is available about the comparative state of the demand for labour in various places and occupations. This can be obtained through newspaper advertisements, the talk of friends and the reports about local conditions collected by trade unions. Mr. Dearle gives an interesting account of the development of these methods in the London building trades: " That system of mutual assistance in getting jobs, which a man and his mates render to one another, is extended and carried out in a more systematic manner by means of the vacant books of the trade unions. Each man, as he becomes unemployed, writes his name in the vacant book at the local branch office or meeting-place; and then every other member of the branch—and branches ordinarily number from 20 up to 400 or 500—is looking for a job for him, or, to be more exact, all members of the branch are on the look-out for vacancies to clear the vacant book. Obligations are imposed on all members to inform the branch secretary when men are wanted anywhere; and, whilst in some unions— for instance, the Amalgamated Carpenters and Joiners—a small sum, generally 6d. per member, is given to any one who will take unemployed men off the books, a heavy fine is imposed on any one known to be giving preference to non-union men. The usual thing is to inform the secretary where men are, or are likely to be, wanted, and the latter is bound to inform out-of-work members where best to look for jobs."[2] In England since 1893 still further information of this kind, in a more widely accessible form, has been furnished officially through the *Labour Gazette*. At the present time the Employment Exchanges also act as powerful informing agencies. They extend the inquiry work carried on by trade unions, and " enable the workman to ascertain, by calling at an office in his own neighbourhood, what enquiries have been made for his own kind of labour all over London."[3] When the Exchanges of different towns are inter-connected, the workman is

---

[1] *Royal Commission on the Poor Laws*, Minority Report, p. 1125.
[2] *Unemployment in the London Building Trades*, p. 133.
[3] *Royal Commission on the Poor Laws*, Minority Report, p. 1125.

brought into contact with a still wider range of information. Thus in Germany: " In order to ensure the mobility of labour, it is considered to be of importance that the agencies for obtaining employment in the different parts of the German Empire should be linked up by a system of inter-communication. This system is provided by the Federations of Labour Registries. . . . In the Grand Duchy of Baden all are telephonically in communication, and want or superfluity of labour in one place is immediately known in all the others."[1] In Bavaria the system is extended by the publication of lists of vacancies in villages in which no Exchange exists.[2] In England the development from the isolated to the connected form was consummated in the Labour Exchanges Act of 1910. It is evident that an organised system of this character may serve as a powerful instrument for facilitating the movement of workpeople out of jobs to vacancies having need of them.

§ 3. It might seem at first sight that, when once this system has been set up, nothing further can be required. That, however, is a mistake. Information that at the present moment there are two vacancies open in the works of a particular firm is not equivalent to information that the vacancies will be open when the men, to whom this fact has been narrated, arrive there in search of work. The ignorance that obstructs mobility may, therefore, be still further reduced if, in place of centres of information as to the vacancies there and then available in different establishments or departments of establishments, there are instituted centres at which hands can be definitely engaged for these different establishments or departments. When that is done, workmen are informed, not merely that there are so many vacancies now in certain places, but also that these vacancies will still be available when they arrive in quest of them. The probability that this kind of unification will be brought about is, naturally, different in different circumstances. The obstacles in the way of it are least when separate establishments belong to the same company —this is, *pro tanto*, an argument in favour of Trusts,—when they are fixed in position, and when they are physically close together. Thus in the London and India Docks unification

---

[1] [Cd. 2304], p. 65.   [2] *Ibid.* p. 93.

came about many years ago.[1] The obstacles are somewhat
more serious when the different establishments, though still
belonging to the same company or person, are scattered and
moving, as in the London building trade. No doubt, even
here unification is sometimes introduced. Before the Committee on Distress from Want of Employment, a witness,
referring to the building trade, observed: " In the case of one
employer, he said he did not hand over, as was the common
practice, the responsibility of taking on men to his foremen,
but did it himself, with this special object of having men
permanently, and being able, as the foreman is not able to do,
to move them on from job to job, the foreman being unable to
pass them on to another job of which another foreman would
be in charge. Although one understands why the other practice
is adopted, it seems a very desirable thing that the practice of
this individual employer should be more widely followed."[2] In
general, however, builders' workmen in London are engaged independently by the different foremen of the firm employing them.
The obstacles to unification are still more serious when the
separate establishments belong, not to one company or person,
but to several; for then, in order that unification may come
about, a definite organisation for engaging workpeople has to
be set up, either by the companies themselves or by some outside
body, and, having been set up, has to be used for this purpose.
This evidently involves the overcoming of considerable friction.

§ 4. If and when this friction has been overcome, it is
evident that the range over which ignorance is dissipated
and mobility improved will be greater, the larger is the
proportion of the vacancies occurring in any locality that are
filled by engagements negotiated through the local Employ-

[1] For an account of the introduction of the new policy at the Docks after
the strike of 1889, cf. *Report of the Royal Commission on the Poor Laws*, p. 356.
Sir William Beveridge summarises the changes introduced thus : " Formerly each
of the forty-seven departments of the Company's work was a separate unit for the
engagement of men ; each department had its insignificant nucleus of regular
hands and its attendant crowd of more or less loosely attached casuals ; 80 per
cent of the work was done by irregular labour. Now the whole Dock system is,
so far as the Company's work goes, the unit for the engagement of men ; 80 per
cent of the work is done by a unified staff of weekly servants directed from one
spot to another by a central office" (Beveridge, *Economic Journal*, 1907, p. 73).
[2] *Report of the Committee on Distress from Want of Employment*, Evidence
by Aves, Q. 10,917.

ment Exchange acting as an engagement agency. This proportion, under a voluntary arrangement, will be larger, the more attractive Exchanges are made to employers. Experience seems to show that, if they are to win an extensive clientèle, they should be public—not run as a private speculation by possibly fraudulent private persons—; that they should be managed jointly by representatives of employers and employed; that they should take no notice of strikes and lock-outs, but simply allow each side to post up in the Exchange a statement that a stoppage of work exists in such and such an establishment; that they should be wholly separated from charitable relief—association with such relief both keeps away the best men from fear of injuring their reputation as workers and makes employers unwilling to apply to the Exchanges—; that they should be given prestige by municipal or State authorisation, and should be advertised further, so far as practicable, by being made the exclusive agency for the engagement of workpeople employed by public authorities. The question whether fees should be charged to the workpeople making use of them is debatable. The French law of 1904 forbids even private Exchanges to charge fees to workpeople. But the Transvaal Indigency Commission points out that " the charging of fees is by far the most effective method of keeping away those who are not really in search of work ";[1] and, if such persons are driven off, the Exchanges will undoubtedly prove more attractive to employers. It is, further, open to the State, if it chooses, to increase the proportion of vacancies that are filled through Exchanges by some form of legal suasion. A step in this direction would be taken if the registration at an Exchange of all workpeople out of employment were made obligatory; for, if that were done, the inducement to employers to resort to these centres of engagement would be increased. Such a step is suggested by the Poor Law Commissioners in these terms: " We think that, if, as will be proposed subsequently, the State contributes to the unemployed benefit paid to each trade unionist, the State might well make it a condition of such payment that the trade unionist, when out of work, should register his

---

[1] *Report of the Transvaal Indigency Commission*, p. 135.

name and report himself to the local Labour Exchange, in addition (if it is so desired) to entering his name in the vacant book of his union. If the State supports and encourages the trade unions, it seems only reasonable that the trade unions should assist the State by supporting the national and nationally needed Labour Exchanges."[1] Under the practically universal system of unemployment insurance introduced by the Act of 1920 what was then suggested is, in effect, done. For insured persons are required to hand their insurance books to an Employment Exchange when they fall out of work. It has sometimes been argued that a further step should be taken by compelling employers to inform the Exchanges when they are in need of workpeople. In Germany, under an Act of 1922, the Federal Minister may require employers to give notice to the competent Exchange of vacancies for workers who are subject to compulsory sickness insurance.[2] Plainly, however, it must be very difficult to enforce a requirement of this kind should employers prove recalcitrant.[3] A still more drastic arrangement would be to provide by law that employers and workmen should never enter into a contract of work without reference to an Exchange. This plan already rules in England for sailors in the mercantile marine. Sir William Beveridge at one time suggested that, as regards short engagements, it should be enforced generally. " A new clause in the Factory Code, *e.g.* that no man should be engaged for less than a week or a month, unless he were taken from a recognised Labour Exchange, would be a legitimate and unobjectionable extension of the accepted principle that the State may and must proscribe conditions of employment which are disastrous to the souls and bodies of its citizens."[4] The British National Insurance Act, 1911, without going so far as this, offers the inducement of what is, in effect, a slightly reduced charge for the insurance of their workmen both against sickness and, where this form of insurance is provided, against unemployment, to those

---

[1] *Royal Commission on the Poor Laws*, Majority Report, p. 403.

[2] Report of the International Labour Office on *Remedies for Unemployment*, 1922, p. 70.

[3] Cf. *Report of the Committee on the Work of Employment Exchanges*, 1920, p. 13.

[4] Beveridge, *Contemporary Review*, April 1908, p. 392.

employers who engage their workpeople through Employment Exchanges.[1] In the Russian law of November 1923 all workers, with certain specified exceptions, must be engaged through the local branches of the Commissariat of Labour.[2]

§ 5. All these devices, in so far as they foster a more extended use of the Exchanges—if popular opinion oppose them they may, of course, not do this—tend, other things being equal, to break down ignorance of the conditions of the demand for labour, hence to lessen unemployment, and hence to increase the national dividend. The extent to which they do this is naturally greater, the smaller is the range of other agencies for bringing vacancies and unemployed workmen into contact. Thus, while in Germany, before the war, with her relatively undeveloped trade unions, the Employment Exchanges were as effective in finding places for skilled men as for unskilled men, in the United Kingdom their success was confined in the main, at all events as regards the finding of work in the immediate neighbourhood, to the latter class, among whom no strong union organisation existed.[3]

[1] Cf. National Insurance Act, § 99 (1).
[2] *Labour Gazette*, May 1923, p. 161.
[3] Cf. Schloss, *Economic Journal*, 1907, p. 78 ; *Bulletin de l'Association pour la lutte contre le chômage*, Sept. 1913, p. 839 ; and the *Report of the Committee on the Work of the Employment Exchanges*, 1920, p. 13.

CHAPTER XI

§ 1. THE general analysis of the two preceding chapters has an important bearing upon a problem from which it seems at first sight to be remote. This problem is to determine the comparative effects on the national dividend of the principal ways which are open to employers for meeting periods of depression. When, in consequence of lessened demand for his product, an employer finds that a continuance of output on his former scale will involve him in loss, he can accomplish the necessary reduction in any one of three ways: (1) by working full time and dismissing a part of his staff; (2) by working full time and retaining his whole staff, but rotating employment so that only a proportion (say 2/3rds) is actually at work at any one time; or (3) by working short time and putting the whole of his staff to work during the whole of the working period.

§ 2. As between the short-time plan and both the others the relevant influences are primarily technical. Resort to the short-time plan is easiest when the conditions are such that an appreciable advantage can be gained by cutting down the most expensive *hours* of work, those, for example, that involve extra charges for lighting and heating. But one or other of the rival plans is favoured when complete suspension of work for a little while would involve heavy costs of restarting—*e.g.* the relighting of blast furnaces that have been damped down.

§ 3. As between the dismissal plan and both the others the issue depends to a large extent upon how important it is to an employer to maintain a lien upon the services of the people who have so far been working for him. When the work to be done is skilled and specialised, it is often very important for him to do this.[1] Workpeople possessed of special aptitudes practically always acquire special value to the particular firms which have employed them for any length of time. This is partly because the detailed methods of different factories are different, and, therefore, workmen who have become accustomed to any given factory, particularly if the work they have to do in it is of an all-round kind, are more useful there than other similar workmen would be. It is partly also because skilled workmen often handle expensive materials or delicate machinery, and employers naturally prefer to entrust these things to men of whose qualities they have had continuing experience. Finally, among firms making certain proprietary articles, it is partly because workmen may be expected, after a time, to get an inkling of their firm's manufacturing secrets, and the firm is, therefore, unwilling to let them enter the service of its rivals.[2] Thus, "among goldsmiths and jewellers the masters share work among a permanent staff, since there are many secret and special patterns, and adjust production by overtime for short periods."[3] In like manner, employers are keenly anxious to retain a lien on the services of engine-drivers, domestic servants and specialised agricultural labourers.[4] Even when the work to be done is of such a sort that a man who has been employed before with a particular firm is not appreciably more valuable to that firm than one who has not, an employer in bad times, who knows, or hopes, that things will improve, will like to keep in touch with more men than he needs at the moment, so as to make sure that enough will be available later on. This consideration is especially likely to influence employers in industries where the fluctuations are known to be seasonal; for in these industries there is practical certainty that a full staff will be needed again shortly. It has been suggested

---

[1] It is to be expected, therefore, that the turn-over of labour will, in general, be lower for skilled than for unskilled workers. For evidence that this is so in the United States cf. Schlichter, *The Labour Turn-over*, pp. 57-64. But cf. also *ibid.* p. 73.

[2] Cf. Fay, *Co-partnership in Industry*, p. 90.

[3] Webb, *Seasonal Trades*, p. 43.   [4] *Ibid.* p. 23.

that seasonality of this kind is partly responsible for the prevalence of the short-time method in coal-mining and in agriculture. Moreover, even when employers, if left to themselves, would tend to the dismissal method, trade unions, which naturally dislike that method because it involves them in a larger burden of unemployment benefit, sometimes sway them in favour of one or other of the rival plans.

§ 4. In this choice between the dismissal plan and the other two another very important factor is the degree of accuracy with which wages are adjusted to efficiency. When the payment normally made to inferior workers is higher relatively to their efficiency than that made to better workers, there is a strong inducement to employers to meet bad times by dispensing with the least profitable part of their staff. It is, thus, natural to find that the dismissal method is relatively dominant in time-wage industries as compared with piece-wage industries. Discussing the principal ways in which a slackness of demand is met in this country, Sir H. Llewellyn Smith once wrote: "Looking at the question broadly, we may distinguish two main methods. The first general method is by short time, or short work, for all or the majority of those employed. A good example of that is mining, in which, for the most part, the contractions do not result so much in throwing out a certain number of colliers altogether, but in the colliery working a smaller number of days per week. Another example would be the boot and shoe trade (I mean apart, for the moment, from the great factories where machinery is used, but where it is carried on on the ordinary piece-work system), in which in slack times there are not many people entirely unemployed, but a very large number of people will have a short amount of work. The second method, which applies in other industries, is not by working short time, but by throwing out of work a certain proportion of the workers, who form a fluctuating margin of unemployed. Examples of such trades are the building, engineering and shipbuilding trades. I do not mean to say there is not short time known in any of those trades, or that overtime is not worked in times of inflation; but the main method by which they adjust themselves to a change in demand is by throwing out workers or taking on more workers."[1] An examination of the industries mentioned in this passage shows that those which Sir H. Llewellyn Smith classes among the short-time industries are just those in which piece-wages predominate, while those which he classes as dismissal industries employ time-wages. It may, indeed, be thought at first glance that the engineering trade belies this rule. Though, however, this trade contains a good deal of piece-work, it was until recently *mainly* a time-work trade, and so is no exception.[2] In like manner, it is natural to find that in Germany, where, before the war, trade unions were relatively weak, and where, partly as a consequence of this, a rigid standard rate in time-wage industries was much less effectively enforced than it was in this country, the practice of meeting slack periods by working short time, rather than by a reduction of staff, was considerably more general. "Some of the German authorities declare that the practice of short time in some industries reduces earnings by as much as one-fourth or one-third in the course of a year. It is certain that, though certain British industries, notably coal-mining and the cotton industry, resort to the system of short time, the extent to which this system operates to lower the figure of unemployed workmen in the United Kingdom is much less than in the German Empire."[3] I do not wish to stress these facts unduly. They seem, however, to illustrate the general tendency set out at the beginning of this section.

§ 5. As between rotation of hands and the two other plans the dominant fact is that the rotation method is troublesome to arrange and involves a good deal of organisation and collaboration with the workpeople. It appears to prevail among "the riverside corn porters working regularly at the Surrey docks";[4] it has been practised to some extent among the iron-workers of the north of England; and it was tried, alongside of the short-time plan, in the cotton industry during a part of

---

[1] *Third Report of the Committee on Distress from Want of Employment,* Evidence, Q. 4540.

[2] *Third Report of the Committee on Distress from Want of Employment,* Evidence, Q. 4541 *et seq.*

[3] *Report on the Cost of Living in German Towns* [Cd. 4032], p. 522. *Report of the Royal Commission on the Poor Law,* p. 1156, footnote.

1918. Yet again, as a result of negotiations with the Tailors' Trade Union, the Master Tailors' Association announced: "We fully recognise that the work ought to be fairly shared during the slack seasons (subject to certain explanations), and we urge upon our members throughout the country to carry these principles into effect."[1] But, broadly speaking, the inconvenience of this method has not permitted it to be adopted at all widely.

§ 6. The general result is that, in the main part of industry, depressions are met by either the short-time method or the dismissal method, or by a mixture of the two. Sir Sydney Chapman gives some interesting figures to illustrate the varying degrees in which different textile industries, all employing the same (namely, the piece wage) form of wage payment, have adopted the two methods respectively. Between November 1907 and November 1908 it appears that, in the cotton industry, among the firms investigated, a 13·3 contraction of output was met, to the extent of 5 per cent by reduction of staff, and to the extent of 8·3 per cent by short time; whereas, in the silk industry, an 8·1 per cent contraction of output led to a 6·2 per cent reduction of staff and 2·1 per cent short time.[2] As is well known, the method of short time is dominant in coal-mining, where it is carried out by a reduction, in times of depression, in the number of shifts worked per week; and the method of dismissal in the building, shipbuilding and engineering trades.[3] In a bill submitted to

---

[1] *Report on Collective Agreements*, 1910, p. xxviii.

[2] Cf. Chapman, *Unemployment in Lancashire*, p. 51. When a firm employs both factory workers and home workers, it is, of course, to its interest in bad times to withdraw work from home workers rather than to reduce factory work and home work equally, because it is thus enabled to keep its machinery going. It may be added that the power to treat home workers in this way indirectly checks employers from superseding home work altogether by factory work, because it enables them to face the prospect of periodic expansions without the need of erecting factories too large for the demand of ordinary times. (Cf. Vessilitsky, *The Home Worker*, p. 3.)

[3] Of course, it is not meant that in these trades no short time is known. On the contrary, even when the dismissal method is adopted for contractions of work from below the normal, what is, in effect, the short-time method is always adopted to some extent for contractions from above the normal. Thus, in the engineering trade, whereas the average amount of formal short time is very small, overtime adds on the average 3¾ per cent to the normal man's working time (Cd. 2337, p. 100), and, as against overtime working, normal hours are,

the Italian Parliament in 1921 it was proposed that, "in the event of a necessary reduction of the staff (in any concern), before dismissing hands, the hours of work must be reduced to a minimum of thirty-six hours a week with a proportionate reduction of wages." [1]

§ 7. *Prima facie* it would seem that, from the standpoint of the national dividend, the dismissal, or reduction of staff, method is certain to be more injurious than the short-time method, not only because the fear of unemployment may tend to make workpeople spin out their jobs unduly, but also because this method reacts injuriously on the quality of those men whom it condemns to longer or shorter periods of unemployment. The most obvious way in which it does this is through the larger and more concentrated loss of individual earnings, which unemployment, as compared with short time, involves. This threatens severe privation in food, clothing and firing, not only to the men directly affected, but also to their wives and children. If pushed far enough, this privation may easily lead to a lasting physical deterioration. Nor is this all. It may also cause those who suffer from it to supply their needs by means which threaten a permanent weakening of moral fibre. *Inter alia*, it may lead to resort to the Poor Law; for, as is well known, the curve of pauperism in this country follows about a year behind the curve of unemployment. [2] Resort to the Poor Law, however, or to vagrancy, marks, according to some, a definite stage of descent. There is a definite line between poverty, where struggle and independence prevail, and pauperism. "Paupers are not, as a rule, unhappy. They are not ashamed; they are not keen to become independent; they are not bitter or discontented. They have passed over the line which separates poverty from

---

of course, really short time. All that is meant is that "the main method by which these industries adjust themselves to a change in demand is by throwing out workers or taking on more workers" (Llewellyn Smith, *Third Report of the Committee on Distress from Unemployment*, Evidence, Q. 4540).

[1] *Economic Review of the Foreign Press*, July 22, 1921, p. 190.

[2] The interval is probably partly due to resistance made possible by savings, the pawning of household goods, children's earnings, etc. ; partly to the fact that a check to the *inflow of pauperism* will not involve a diminution of pauperism until the inflow falls below the outflow brought about by death and other causes. (Cf. Beveridge, *Unemployment*, p. 49.)

pauperism." [1] Again : " The men who enter the workhouse or go on tramp, leaving their families to the Poor Law, are, as a rule, those whom adversity, combined, no doubt, with their own weaknesses, has made no longer able-bodied or respectable. Having once entered, they seldom return to industry again." [2] Sir H. Llewellyn Smith sums the matter up thus: " It is, I think, a definite induction from history and observation that, when risk falls outside certain limits as regards magnitude and calculability, when, in short, it becomes what I may call a gamblers' risk, exposure thereto not only ceases to act as a bracing tonic, but produces evil effects of a very serious kind." [3] Leroy-Beaulieu in like manner declares, and is surely right in declaring : " It is not the insufficiency of pay which constitutes, in general and apart from exceptional cases, the social evil of to-day, but the precariousness of employment." [4] Nor is it only through the sense of insecurity that harm is done. The mere fact of idleness, apart altogether from the privation by which it is normally accompanied, is likely, unless, indeed, it is mitigated by opportunities for work on land belonging to or rented by themselves,[5] to exercise a seriously deteriorating influence—an influence, too, which grows rapidly as the amount of the idleness grows—upon the economic and general efficiency of those affected by it. The Royal Commissioners on the Poor Laws have in evidence : " The enforced idleness on completion of a job naturally throws the men upon their own resources, which is, in nine cases out of ten, the nearest public-house. The frequent change from strenuous hard work to absolute indolence to men of this character naturally tends to gradual moral and physical degeneration, and ultimately the individuals become unfit for work, even when opportunity offers." [6] A large employer of labour is

---

[1] Hunter, *Poverty*, p. 3. [2] Beveridge, *Unemployment*, p. 50.
[3] *Economic Journal*, 1910, p. 518.
[4] *Répartition des richesses*, p. 612.
[5] In Belgium the cheapness of workmen's tickets on the railways enables many workers to live in cottages with gardens attached to them, to the cultivation of which they turn when out of ordinary work. (Cf. Rowntree, *Unemployment*, p. 267.)
[6] Quoted in the *Minority Report*, p. 1138. It has been abundantly proved, however, that the aggregate consumption of drink in the United Kingdom is greatest in periods of good employment, for the reason, no doubt, that good employment is usually associated with high spending power among the people

reported to have said: "Between 5 and 6 per cent of my skilled men are out of work just now. During the long spell of idleness any one of these men invariably deteriorates. In some cases the deterioration is very marked. The man becomes less proficient and less capable, and the universal experience of us all who have to do with large numbers of working men is that nothing has a worse effect upon the calibre of such men than long spells of idleness."[1]   The Transvaal Indigency Commission report: "Unemployment is one of the most fruitful causes of indigency of a permanent and hopeless kind. However skilled a man may be, he is bound to deteriorate during a long period of unemployment. His hand loses some of its cunning and he acquires the habit of idleness. The tendency is for the unemployed to sink to the level of the unemployable."[2]   There is evidence that the men who have once become casuals are not readily reconciled again to regular work.[3]   Reference may also be made to the results of a recent American inquiry: "If a period of enforced idleness were a season of recuperation and rest, there would be a good side to lack of employment. But enforced idleness does not bring recuperation and rest. The search for labour is much more fatiguing than labour itself. An applicant, sitting in one of the charity offices waiting for the arrival of the agent, related his experiences while trying to get work. He would rise at 5 o'clock in the morning and walk three or four miles to some distant point, where he had heard work could be had. He went early so as to be ahead of others, and he walked because he could not afford to pay car fare. Disappointed in securing a job at the first place, he would tramp to another place miles away, only to meet with disappointment again. . . . As the man told his story, he drove home the truth that lack of employment means far more than simply a

---

generally.   Cf. A. D. Webb, "The Consumption of Alcoholic Liquors in the United Kingdom" (*Statistical Journal*, Jan. 1913), and Carter, *The Control of the Drink Trade*, pp. 90-94.   It does not follow, of course, that those *who are actually unemployed* must drink less than they did when employed.

[1] Alden, *The Unemployed, a National Question*, p. 6.

[2] *Report of the Transvaal Indigency Commission*, p. 120.

[3] Some evidence before the Unskilled Labour Committee of the C.O.S. relates how an attempt to convert casual dockers into permanent hands failed through the men refusing to turn up regularly (*Report*, p. 183).

loss in dollars and cents; it means a drain upon the vital forces that cannot be measured in terms of money."[1] Moreover, the evil consequences of lean months are not balanced by good consequences in fat months. Indeed, it may well be that, when, as often happens, the fat months imply long hours of overtime, they will not yield any good effects to set against the evil effects of the lean months, but will themselves add further evil effects.

§ 8. It is at this point that the analysis of the two preceding chapters becomes relevant. The inference that the short-time method of meeting depressions is always more advantageous to the national dividend than the dismissal method, to which the foregoing observations seem to lead, must not be accepted out of hand. There is an important consideration to be set on the other side. When, in the analysis just referred to, costs of movement were discussed, it was tacitly assumed that the gains from movement to be set against them were definitely determined by the economic situation, and needed no special investigation. In fact, however, this assumption is not wholly warranted. If, in a factory (or industry) employing 100 men, the demand so falls that, at the current rate of wages, —which we assume to be maintained—$\frac{1}{100}$th part less work than before is required, this state of things may be met either by short time all round to the extent of $\frac{1}{100}$th part of normal time or by the dismissal of one man. It is plainly in the interest of the national dividend that one man should move elsewhere if the cost of movement, translated into terms of daily payment in the way described on p. 500, is less than the whole of the daily wage. If the method of dismissal rules, one man—the one who has been dismissed—will, in fact, given that he has the necessary knowledge, move elsewhere when this condition is fulfilled. But, if the method of short time (or rotation of work) rules, nobody will move unless the cost of moving, translated as above, is less than $\frac{1}{100}$th part of the daily wage. On this side, therefore, the method of short time must be more injurious to the national dividend than the method of dismissal. When the costs of movement are so large (*e.g.* when it is a question of moving from one skilled

[1] *United States Bulletin of the Bureau of Labour*, No. 79, pp. 906-7.

industry to another), or when the depression of demand is only expected to last for so short a time, that movement would not take place on either plan, there is, indeed, nothing to set against the direct and immediate advantages of short time. But, when the conditions are such that movement would have taken place on the dismissal plan, but does not take place on the short-time plan, the national dividend so far suffers. This is more likely to happen if a single firm adopts short time to meet a depression peculiar to itself, while there is a good demand for work in other parts of the industry, than if it adopts it to meet a depression shared by other firms; for the costs obstructing movement between firms are less than those obstructing movement between industries. The above objection to the short-time plan deserves attention, but is not, of course, decisive. It is interesting to observe that an objection on exactly the same lines lies against the cotton industry's war policy of rotating such work as there was among all the workpeople and providing out-of-work pay for those "playing" from a special levy upon such employers as were working more than the normal proportion of their machinery.[1] It also holds, in some degree, against all plans of unemployment insurance; for these plans lessen the gain that a man will get if he moves to a new trade where work might be obtained.[2] This objection also, it need hardly be said, is not decisive. The difference made to movement will generally be small, while,

---

[1] For an account of the work of the Cotton Control Board during the war, cf. H. D. Henderson, *The Cotton Control Board*. In August 1918, the rota system, which had been established in September 1917, was abolished, and it was decided that the proceeds of the special levy should, henceforward, only be used for giving out-of-work pay to men played off definitely and continuously. The Jute Control in March 1918 introduced a scheme for compensating workers dismissed owing to a decision to stop certain machinery with a view to reducing jute consumption by 10 per cent. But the compensation was specifically confined to workpeople who were not able to find other employment, and any workman who refused suitable employment without reasonable cause was to receive no further benefit (cf. *Labour Gazette*, 1918, p. 135). A similar condition was made in a plan adopted in Germany at about the same time for compensating workpeople whose work was stopped through shortage of coal (*Labour Gazette*, 1918, p. 141).

[2] Under the British Insurance Act of 1927 an applicant for benefit may be asked to accept work, under suitable conditions, in an occupation other than his own : but naturally this is only likely to be done as a last resort.

on the other hand, many men will be saved from the grave injury which unemployment, if no provision has been made against it, may inflict. Still, the fact that the objection exists ought not to be ignored. In the very peculiar circumstances of 1921–23 in the United Kingdom, when, as it appears, the engineering and shipbuilding industries were overcrowded as a result of the movement into them during the war,[1] and the general interest required a substantial shifting of men out of them, it was of dominating importance.

§ 9. In the foregoing analysis attention has been confined to methods of dealing with manual workers that play an important part in current practice. It will not have escaped notice, however, that salaried employees in the highest posts of business and other undertakings are not dealt with in any of these ways. They are retained continuously and receive their salaries without reference to the amount of work they are called upon to do from time to time. Judges are neither dismissed nor do they receive diminished pay in periods when litigation is slack. The same thing is true of civil servants, University professors, soldiers and sailors, whether officers or men, and the principal officials in private and joint-stock businesses. Why, it is sometimes asked, should not this plan be applied also to manual workers in industry? Why should they not, when once engaged, be regarded as permanently on the strength, and, on condition of their presenting themselves for work, be paid full wages whether, in any particular period, there is much, little, or no work for them to do? It must be conceded at once that, in concerns in which the demand for labour is perfectly steady, the introduction of the permanent salary method would leave the national dividend unaffected. The men, if their wage level were rightly adjusted, would all be employed continuously at full wages anyhow. Where, however, the demand for labour is liable to vary, things would work out differently. In view of the fact that workpeople would now get wages when they were not working, the mean level of wage rates would fall, so as to keep the annual earnings of an average man at about the old level. Labour

---

[1] Cf. *The Third Winter of Unemployment*, by Dr. Bowley and others, pp. 24-5.

would have become a fixed charge, in the way that interest payment on capital equipment and the salaries of the higher staff are now a fixed charge; but the employer would pay in the aggregate, over good and bad times together, much the same aggregate wages as at present. On the surface, therefore, it might seem that this contemplated arrangement would differ from the present arrangement in book-keeping appearance rather than in essence. This, however, is not really so. Like resort to short time in periods of depression, but much more forcibly, it would stop workpeople from moving away from concerns that were temporarily or permanently depressed to others that were in need of labour. For the higher staff, who must be retained in these concerns in any case, this does not matter. No harm is done by tying to his place a man who will stay there anyhow. But for ordinary manual workers it does matter. Though, therefore, this plan might be applied, without injuring the national dividend, to a certain proportion of the ordinary workers that a firm employs, it could not be applied to all of them; and to apply it to some and not to others would be difficult in practice. There is more to be said for a modified arrangement which has recently been proposed. This is that manual workers should become, as it were, salaried employees, not of particular concerns, but of the whole of the industry to which they belong. When once registered to the industry, they should receive full wages on condition of presenting themselves for work at a bureau entitled to send them to any concern in the industry that has need of labour. This modified plan—which, in effect, amounts to a system of unemployment insurance by industry with a benefit equal to the full wage rate—would not interfere with movement from one firm to another within the same industry. It would, however, no less than the unmodified plan, obstruct movement from one industry to another. There would, moreover, be some technical difficulty in defining the conditions under which a man might become registered to a particular industry and those under which he should cease to be so registered. A full discussion of these matters cannot, however, be undertaken here.

CHAPTER XII

§ 1. THE purpose of the remainder of this Part is to inquire whether, and if so in what circumstances, the size of the national dividend can be increased by interference designed to raise the rate of wages in any industry or part of an industry above the "natural rate." The natural rate is here taken to mean the rate that would prevail apart from interference by some person or body of persons external to the workmen and employers directly concerned. Monopolistic action, whether by employers or by employed, is thus included in the "natural course of things"; and the only interference that we have to consider is interference by consumers and interference by public authorities, acting, not as consumers, but as governors.

§ 2. Interference by consumers consists in attempts by customers to compel employers to grant better conditions to their workpeople by agreeing to confine their custom to those whose treatment of their workpeople comes up to a standard that is considered fair. The scope of this method varies greatly in different industries. It can be applied more readily, for example, to the hours of labour of assistants in retail shops, whom the customers actually see, than to those imposed on factory or domestic workers, whom they do not see.[1] It is always much restricted by the imperfections of customers' knowledge, and by the fact that many articles pass through a number of stages of manufacture before they reach the man who ultimately sells them to the consumer. Associations of private persons have, nevertheless, sought to employ this method through the devices of the White List and the Trade Union

[1] Cf. Mény, *Le Travail à domicile*, p. 173.

Label.[1]   It has been employed with greater effect by public bodies which have extensive contracts to offer.   The Fair Wages Resolution of the British House of Commons in 1893 endeavoured to secure that Government Departments should use it by demanding that, on Government contracts, not less than " the rate of wages current (in the district) should be paid to employés."   The London County Council furnish a schedule of wages, which all firms tendering on their contracts must agree to pay to the workpeople they employ on them.   Some municipal authorities insist, further, that no contract shall be given to a firm that fails to pay " fair " rates, not merely on the town's contract, but regularly on all its work.   Thus " Belfast and Manchester have standing orders, under which contractors tendering for, or executing, work must be paying all their workpeople the rate of wages, and observing the hours of labour, agreed upon by the organisations of employers and workpeople, and must not prohibit their workpeople from joining trade unions ; while at Bradford the contractor gives an assurance that, for three months immediately preceding his tender, he has paid all his workmen the rate agreed upon between the employers' association and the trade union." [2] Interference by public authorities—acting in their capacity, not as consumers, but as governors—has been made familiar by Australasian experience, and now plays a considerable part in this country also.   To determine the way in which these different sorts of interference are likely to affect the national dividend is a complicated problem, which it is necessary to approach by stages.   In this chapter I shall ask the preliminary question whether it can in practice be made operative, and whether, therefore, it can really affect the size of the national dividend at all.

[1] The Australian Trade Marks Act of 1905, which directed that all goods sold should be marked with a label, showing whether or not their makers employed Union labour exclusively, was ruled by the High Court to be unconstitutional, on the ground that the Federal title to legislate about trade marks did not permit legislation in respect of marks not designed for the benefit of the manufacturer using them (*Economist*, Sept. 19, 1908, p. 532).

[2] *Report of the Fair Wages Committee*, p. 50.   Unless the requisition that contractors shall pay standard wages is made to apply to all their work, and not merely to their work on particular contracts, unscrupulous contractors can evade it by employing the same men for part of their time on contract work at full wages and for another part of their time on other work at exceptionally low wages.

§ 3. The answer to this question depends in part on the further question whether it is possible for employers and workpeople to evade the recommendations or decrees of the intervening body without being detected. Detection is made difficult by the fact that the contract, which an employer makes with his workpeople for their services, is complex, including, besides the money wage, explicit or implicit conditions as to speed of work, arrangements for the workers' comfort during the work, and also sometimes provision for certain payments in kind. By operating on one or other of these items it may be possible for an employer, if he wishes to do so, to neutralise apparent additions to the money wage.[1] It is not, however, only in this way that undetected evasion can come about. Since a poor man will often prefer to accept a low wage rather than lose his job, collusion may take place between employer and employed, and, as is well known to happen in the Chinese factories of Victoria, a lower wage may be paid actually than is paid nominally. When workpeople are unorganised—and they are specially likely to be unorganised if they are very poor or if they work apart from one another in their own homes [2]—even a strong Government, not to speak of a Consumers' Association, must have immense difficulty in enforcing its will. This fact may be illustrated from the experience of our own laws about sanitation, safety and hours of labour for women and children. It has always been found very difficult to bring the smaller and less obvious units of a trade under effective control—especially as to hours of labour—since, in "domestic workshops" and among solitary workers, household and workshop labour can so easily be intermingled.[3]   In England at present any place, where employers,

[1] In this connection it is interesting to observe that the State Wages Boards of California, Oregon, Washington and Wisconsin are given power to regulate, not merely wage rates, but also hours of work and "conditions of labour" for the women whom they cover (*The World's Labour Laws*, Feb. 1914, p. 78).

[2] Mr. Lloyd writes: "The chief reason why the grinders both in Sheffield and Solingen have been better organised than the cutlers is that they are more congregated at their work" (*Economic Journal*, 1908, p. 379).

[3] It is sometimes suggested that the law could be enforced more easily if the giver-out-of-work, or even the landlord, as well as the employer, in a domestic workshop, were made legally responsible for breaches of the law. (Cf. Webb, Evidence before the Royal Commission on Labour [C. 7063-1], Q. 3740.) In Massachusetts responsibility is sometimes thrown on the giver-out-of-work.

working in their own houses, employ persons from outside, is a "workshop," and is subject to the ordinary provisions of the factory law. Any place where employers, working in their own houses, employ only members of their own family, is a "domestic workshop," and its sanitary arrangements, and also, though in a less degree than ordinary workshops, the hours of young persons and children working in it, are regulated. But, when a home-worker works alone in her house for an outside firm, these things are not regulated. Even in workshops and domestic workshops, it is doubtful whether, with the existing staff of inspectors, the rules are satisfactorily enforced.[1] Throughout, the inspectors' task is exceedingly heavy; so much so that, in England, the demand for a larger staff is continually being made. If, however, the kind of regulation we have just been discussing is thus difficult, wage-regulation is more difficult still. As has been well observed, wage rates are not, like sanitary arrangements, hours and so forth, things easily detected by the watch or nose of an inspector.[2] Hence the violation of rules about them can scarcely be discovered except through overt action by the workers; and, when they are not organised, individual workers will often fail to act for fear a worse thing should befall them. The administration of the English Trades Boards Act has been much hampered by this difficulty, especially in its relation to home-workers.[3] Where, however, an effective workers' association exists, this difficulty can be overcome. For the workers, having a sense of solidarity among themselves, will not be terrorised into accepting less than the union rate by fear of losing their job, but will complain to the union officials; and, even when individual workmen do not do this, their officials will play the part of a body of lynx-eyed unpaid inspectors. It is, therefore, encouraging to learn that State action designed to raise wages in depressed industries (e.g. the chain-making industry) has several times led to an improve-

[1] Cf. the difficulties experienced in New Zealand and Victoria in enforcing the law limiting the hours of shop assistants. In New South Wales these difficulties are partly avoided by means of a general law regulating the hours for all shops, whether employing assistants or not. (Cf. Aves, *Report on Hours of Employment in Shops*, p. 12.)

[2] Mrs. Macdonald, *Economic Journal*, 1908, p. 142.

[3] Cf. Vessilitsky, *The Home Worker*, chap. vii.

ment in the workpeople's organisation. " One especially
hopeful feature in the situation (connected with the establishment of Trade Boards) is that women in the industries
affected are taking heart to join their trade unions, some
of which have received large accessions of members. A
frequent objection to wages regulation has been that it would
be useless for unorganised trades, which are the very ones
that need it most. The actual fact seems to be that the
prospect of wages regulation is encouraging organisation by
giving these poor workers the sense of some public support at
their back." [1]   At the same time, of course, by giving them
more money, it makes it easier for them to pay trade union
subscriptions. These considerations seem to show that interference, though it may *sometimes* be baffled by undetected
evasion, cannot be thus baffled generally.

§ 4. This broad statement, however, does not do full
justice to the difficulty involved in setting up a really water-
tight system of regulation. When it is practicable for the
regulating authority itself to construct and impose a complete scale of piece-rates, there is, indeed, nothing further
to be said. But this procedure can only be resorted to over
a limited field, because in many industries differences of
machinery, factory arrangements, quality of work required
(*e.g.* in making button-holes) and so on, make a different piece-
rate " appropriate " to different firms ; and it is seldom practicable for a Trade Board or other official authority to have the
knowledge needed to deal with these differences.[2] Consequently, as the Boards appointed under the British Trades
Board Act have often found, the best they can do is to lay
down a so-called minimum day-wage as a standard, at the same
time authorising employers to draw up a piece-list, subject to
the condition that the piece-rate shall allow an " ordinary "
worker in their industry to earn the equivalent of this day-
wage. In view of the fact that payment by the piece is expected

---

[1] Hutchings and Harrison, *History of Factory Legislation*, p. 269. For
evidence as to the favourable reaction of Trade Boards upon organisation in
the tailoring trade, cf. Tawney, *Minimum Rates in the Tailoring Industry*,
pp. 90-94.
[2] For illustrations of this difficulty cf. Tillyard, *The Worker and the State*,
p. 58.

to evoke greater effort by the workers than payment by time, the Trade Board Act of 1918 empowered the Trade Boards to fix a higher minimum day-wage as the standard for piece-workers than the minimum day-wage decreed for workers actually employed on day-wages, and most Trade Board industries in which factory work is done on the piece-wage system have availed themselves of this power.[1] There is, however, yet another difficulty. Unless some further provision is made, there is a subtle opportunity for evasion on account of the ambiguity attaching to the term "ordinary." To shut this loophole some definition of that term must be furnished. In the wage-determination given by the Trade Board controlling the paper-box-making trade this is done by providing that any piece-work operation must yield not less than the minimum day-wage to 85 per cent of the group of piece-workers employed upon it by any firm. Thus the 85th worker (out of a hundred) from the top of the scale of capacity is taken to represent the worst "ordinary" worker. But even a numerical definition of this kind will not make evasion impossible. It is still in the power of employers in effect to force down the general standard of pay by dismissing their worst workmen, engaging better men instead of them, and then fixing a piece-rate below what would have been necessary to enable 85 per cent of their original workpeople to earn the standard day-wages. To escape this danger the Trade Board in the tailoring trade fixes a minimum time-wage for " ordinary " workers, and lays it down that, if 85 per cent of a firm's employees are earning this minimum, there is *prima facie* evidence that the piece-rates established there are adequate. But it permits this *prima facie* evidence to be rebutted by information that the number of slow workers employed by a firm at a particular rate has been substantially reduced. The 85th man in a hundred is only to be regarded as the lowest "ordinary" worker when the firm has not specially selected its workpeople.[2] The rule established by the Trade Board in the box-making industry is similar.[3] Such a rule obviously

---

[1] Cf. Tillyard, *The Worker and the State*, p. 60.
[2] Cf. Tawney, *Minimum Rates in the Tailoring Industry*, pp. 50-51.
[3] Cf. Bulkley, *Minimum Rates in the Box-making Industry*, pp. 21-2.

leads to delicate questions of detail, which must be referred, in the last resort, to some form of joint Board. Thus, under the Minimum Wage (Coal Mines) Act, the question whether any workman, whom an employer wishes to treat as below the ordinary, can rightly be so regarded, is adjudicated upon by a joint Committee of employers and employed. Under an arrangement of this kind evasion, if not stopped altogether, can, at all events, be effectively checked.

§ 5. Granted, however, that evasion cannot take place without an overt breach of law that is capable of being detected, this does not by itself make interference with the natural course of wages really operative. For it might happen that no sanction was available to restrain evasion even when it was detected. In fact, however, sanctions are available. Even a Consumers' Association commands the weapon of the boycott, and, when it is backed by a trade union, can also call upon that body to exercise in its behalf the weapon of the strike. A public authority controls a large armoury of sanctions. Of these the least stringent is a simple appeal to informed public opinion, like that relied upon in the Canadian Industrial Disputes Investigation Act. On this model, a law passed shortly before the war in the State of Massachusetts sets up a Commission with authority to investigate—through a Wages Board—any trade in which there is good reason to believe that the wages paid to women workers are " inadequate to supply the necessary cost of living and to maintain the worker in health." After a public hearing, the Commission recommends rates of wages, and " issues a decree of its award, together with a list of the employers who fail or refuse to accept it. This list is there-upon published in at least four newspapers, but no further penalty is imposed." [1] It would be an error to belittle the power of this form of sanction. There can be little doubt that the rates of pay of our low-grade workers " would be lower than they actually are but for the effective force of conventional or customary standards." [2] It is probable, too, that the

---

[1] *The World's Labour Laws*, Feb. 1913, p. 49. A summary of this law and of the similar laws of other American States is given in Marconcini's *Industria domestica salariata*, pp. 546 *et seq.*

[2] *Report of the Royal Commission on the Poor Laws*, Appendix, vol. xvii. p. 377.

frequency with which the wage of women workers used, before the war, to approximate to 10s. a week was, in some measure, due to the sanction of public opinion. A somewhat more stringent sanction is made use of, for a special and limited purpose, in the English Trades Boards Act of 1909. This Act provides that, in the preliminary period before the determinations of Boards are made obligatory, Government contracts shall only be given to firms which pay the wage rates they have recommended. A more stringent sanction still was proposed by the Australian Excise Tariff Act of 1906, which was afterwards declared by the Supreme Court to be unconstitutional.[1] A differential excise duty was to be imposed upon native manufacturers who paid less than " fair and reasonable " rates to their workpeople. A policy substantially equivalent to this has actually been carried through in a kindred sphere of Australian legislation. " The Bounties Act 1907, the Manufacturers' Encouragement Act 1908, and the Shale Oil Bounties Act 1910, in providing for the encouragement of native industries, provide also for the refusal or reduction of a bounty if the production of a commodity is not accompanied by the payment to the workers employed in the production of a fair and reasonable rate of wages." [2] If these lesser sanctions fail, resort may be had to fines, a sanction which is embodied, not only in the well-known laws of Victoria and other Australian colonies and in the British Trades Boards Act, but also in more recent laws—applicable only to women and minors—which were passed by the States of Oregon and Washington in 1913.[3] In some of these laws there is added also the sanction of imprisonment. Nor has the last word even yet been said. There is a sanction more powerful than fines and imprisonment. For there is always a margin between rates of wages, which

---

[1] Mr. St. Leger, in his book, *Australian Socialism*, pp. 394 *et seq.*, prints the judgment of the Supreme Court.

[2] *Federal Handbook*, p. 476. Cf. Bryce, *Modern Democracies*, vol. ii. p. 245.

[3] Cf. *Labour Gazette*, Jan. 1913, p. 204. By the end of 1923 seventeen States of the U.S.A. had passed some kind of minimum wage legislation, but decisions of the courts have since that time ruled most of the laws to be unconstitutional. New laws relying on the sanction of public opinion only, have been passed in Massachusetts and Wisconsin (cf. *Minimum Wage-fixing Machinery* (Intermediate Labour Office, 1927), pp. 113 *et seq.* ; and *Report of the Delegation to study Industrial Conditions in Canada and the U.S.A.* [Cmd. 2833], 1927, p. 92).

employers resent and would elect to resist by a temporary stoppage of work, and rates which would drive them to abandon their industry altogether. Of this margin the State or other public authority can make use in two distinct ways. First, in certain specially situated industries, it can threaten to expel employers from their occupation unless they consent to pay the wage rate which it decrees. When, for instance, as in ordinary or street railways, a business depends upon franchises granted by authority, the terms of the concession may provide that any refusal to accept the authority's decision about wage rates shall cause it to lapse.[1] Secondly, in industries in general, if obdurate employers try to pay less than the decreed wage, the State can subsidise workpeople who strike against them, or can even close their works by force. By these devices it can deprive them of any third way between surrender and a permanent change of occupation. Nor is resort to such measures rendered impracticable by the chaotic character of the procedure which they would involve. They cannot be laughed out of court as meaning a ceaseless conflict between the Executive and rebellious associations of employers. For their success is so certain that, if once the Government was understood to be determined upon them, resistance would hardly ever take place. At the worst, a single exhibition of force would be sufficient:

> That great two-handed engine at the door
> Stands ready to strike once and strike no more.

This form of sanction is the most powerful of all that are available.[2] Of course neither it nor any of the other sanctions is absolute and compelling in all circumstances. Critics can easily show that, when employers are extraordinarily obstinate, interference to raise wages cannot be successfully carried out. But this fact is not relevant to the practical issue. When it is asked how people can be compelled to continue in a particular industry at a loss, the answer is that they cannot be so compelled. But, as was indicated in the chapter dealing with compulsory arbitration, to prove that a law will *sometimes* fail in its purpose is a very different thing from proving that

---

[1] Cf. Mitchell, *Organised Labour*, p. 345.
[2] Cf. my *Principles and Methods of Industrial Peace*, pp. 191-2.

it is futile. It is not *impossible* for murderers and incendiaries both to break the law and to escape the penalty. Judges may order a mother to deliver up her child to the custody of such and such a person; but, if she chooses to disappear, or, in the last resort, to destroy either the child or herself, they cannot compel her to obey. Nobody, however, cites these facts as evidence that the general body of our laws is without powerful sanctions. In like manner, nobody ought to cite the fact that the sanctions to authoritative decisions about wages are imperfect as evidence that they are non-existent. They are real and potent. With their help interference to raise wages *can* be made operative in practice.

CHAPTER XIII

METHODS OF ENGAGING LABOUR

§ 1. BEFORE the effect of interference to raise wages is examined, it is necessary to make a preliminary inquiry into the methods of engaging workpeople; for the effect produced by interference depends in part upon what these methods are. The reason for this dependence is that, when wages in any place or occupation are raised, an influence is set at work, which, according to circumstances, may draw new workpeople from outside into the place or occupation, or, *per contra*, may push out workpeople who are already there. This influence acts through the change which the wage movement brings about in the attractiveness of the place or occupation, on the one hand, to people outside it, and, on the other, to those already belonging to it. The change in attractiveness to these two sets of people is not determined solely by the amount of the change in wage and the nature of the relevant demand for labour, but also by certain other conditions associated with the methods of engagement in vogue. This can be proved as follows. The mathematical expectation of earnings in any place or occupation is measured by the aggregate annual earnings of all the workpeople of given quality attached to it at any time, divided by the number of those workpeople. If the methods of engagement are such that everybody of given quality, whether already engaged there or at present outside, has an equal chance of obtaining a share of employment in it, the attractiveness of the place or occupation to outsiders and insiders alike corresponds to this mathematical expectation, and, from the standpoint of both these classes, changes in the mathematical expectation correspond roughly to changes in attractiveness. This correspondence is not, indeed, complete, because to many men a given " expectation of earnings " made up of a higher nominal wage coupled with a worse prospect of employment is more attractive than an equal expectation made up of a lower nominal wage coupled with a better prospect of employment. Thus the Poor Law Commissioners report: " In Liverpool it is freely said that the nominally high wages attract men from the country and from Ireland, under the impression that they can get regular work at these rates." [1] Mr. Dearle speaks to like effect of the London building trades.[2] Sir William Beveridge again, before the war, wrote: " Men can be got to follow up work which gives them five shillings a day about four times in a fortnight, when they would repudiate with scorn a regular situation at fifteen or eighteen shillings a week." [3] But this consideration need not be pressed here. It is enough that, in the conditions contemplated, there is a rough general correspondence between changes in the mathematical expectation of earnings and changes in the attractiveness of the industry both to outsiders and to insiders. If, however, the methods of engagement are of such a sort that anybody of given quality, who has already been employed in the industry, will be taken on rather than a new man from outside, the attractiveness to outsiders of the industry, when the rate of wages there is forced up—and the quantity of employment available thereby reduced—is necessarily zero, whatever the effect of the change may be upon the mathematical expectation of earnings. Yet again, if the methods of engagement are such that, among the workpeople of given quality who have already been employed, men are always selected for employment in accordance with a formal or informal preference list, an enforced rise in the wage rate must press the attractiveness of the place or occupation to those insiders who are near the bottom of the list down to zero. Of course, divergencies in the methods of engagement are more or less blotted out from the point of view of people considering a long time beforehand for what industries their

[1] *Report of the Royal Commission on the Poor Laws*, p. 353.
[2] *Unemployment in the London Building Trade*, p. 127.
[3] *Unemployment*, p. 197.

children shall be trained. This, however, does not lessen their relevance to the effect produced by interference designed to raise wages. In the face of an enforced rise there are three possibilities : (1) the attractiveness of the place or occupation affected may correspond after the change, both for outsiders and for insiders, to the mathematical expectation of earnings there; (2) for all insiders it may correspond to this mathematical expectation, but for all outsiders to zero; and (3) for displaced insiders, as well as for all outsiders, it may be zero. The first of these possibilities will be realised if the method of engagement of labour is entirely haphazard and engagements are for short periods; the second if the method is such that all insiders are preferred to any outsiders, but among themselves are on an equal footing; the third if all workpeople interested in the place or occupation are implicitly or explicitly arranged, for purposes of engagement, upon a preference scale. Of the three methods thus distinguished the obvious label for the first is the *casual* method and for the third the *preference* method. For the second no satisfactory label is available, and it is necessary to invent a name : I shall call it the *privileged class* method.

§ 2. The distinction between these three methods can be made clear by examples. The casual method reigns when all comers of given quality (not necessarily all comers of different qualities) are accepted indifferently. The general nature of the method is obvious. It is sometimes supposed that, when workpeople for a number of firms are engaged through a central institution, it is necessarily ruled out by that fact. But this is a confusion. It is open to Employment Exchanges, just as much as to single firms, to engage men by the casual method ; and, in fact, the rules of many of them provide that they *must* do so. Thus, in a number of Employment Bureaux organised by trade unions in France, the officials " allot situations to their members strictly in order of *priority of application*." [1] " The Antwerp Bureau adopts the rule of sending workmen to situations in the order in which they apply at the office—a method which has been the subject of much criticism." [2] In the Labour Bureau of the Berlin brewers

[1] *U.S.A. Bulletin of Labour*, No. 72, p. 761.   [2] *Ibid.* p. 766.

" a workman must wait his turn before he is placed, *i.e.* on registration he gets a number and must then wait till all the numbers on the list prior to his own have been satisfied." [1] Under all these arrangements the method of engagement that rules is the casual method. The privileged class method was formally established under the Liverpool docks scheme of 1912. All workmen who were dockers at a given date were furnished with a tally, possession of which gave them preference over workmen not holding tallies, while leaving certain classes of them still equal among themselves. [2] The preference method, whether formally or informally applied, is of wide scope. It implies that different workpeople of given quality are not hired indifferently but in some sort of more or less definite order, so that whatever work there is tends to be concentrated upon certain individuals, while the others get nothing. When an actual preference list is used it does not matter, from the present point of view, upon what basis this list is drawn up. One made by placing the names of applicants in order of their length of service in the industry—a specially good arrangement in a decaying trade—or even in alphabetical order, would answer the purpose. In practice, when preference lists among similar men exist, they are always a mere bye-product of lists designed to set in order of capacity a number of workpeople presumed to be dissimilar. Thus the Central (Unemployed) Body for London suggested, among its model rules, that " the superintendent will recommend applicants for employment according to suitability, but employers may select from the registered applicants any one whom they consider suitable." [3] Broadly speaking, this policy is pursued by the Berlin Central Labour Registry. [4] In so far as it involves the placing in order of precedence of a number of men of *equal* capacity, it implies preference of the kind relevant to this discussion.

[1] Schloss, *Report on Agencies and Methods for dealing with the Unemployed*, p. 84.

[2] Cf. Williams, *The First Year's Working of the Liverpool Docks Scheme*, chapter i.

[3] *U.S.A. Bulletin of Labour*, No. 72, p. 803.

[4] Cf. Schloss, *Report on Agencies and Methods for dealing with the Unemployed*, p. 87.

§ 3. It need hardly be said that the methods of engagement ruling in different places and occupations are not sharply separated into the three types that have just been described. Rather, actual existing arrangements are, in general, compromises tending towards, but not identical with, one or another of them. The influences which determine the choice made between them are very similar to those which were discussed in Chapter XI. in connection with the choice between different ways of meeting periods of depression. Many of the considerations which make employers unwilling to resort to a reduction of staff in these periods—fear of losing men who for any reason have a special value to them, and so on—also make them hostile to the casual method. Therefore this method is likely to be adopted only when the men are so unskilled, and the detailed conditions of particular plants or works so similar, that a man's value to an employer is not appreciably increased by his having been employed by him before. The preference method is favoured when the conditions are such that continuity of work by the same man is important, while to retain in bad times a larger number of men than is necessary by resort to short time would be costly or otherwise injurious. Where the technical objections to short time are less serious the way is open for the privileged class method. It will be readily perceived that in a "stationary state" the last two methods would lead to identical results.

§ 4. It is interesting to observe that there is a connection between the casual method and the custom of short engagements. Long engagements are not, indeed, incompatible with some degree of casualness, because, even with annual engagements, provided the hirings of different people terminate irregularly, there will always be a certain number of jobs on offer; whereas, if the hirings of different individuals all terminate at the same times, at those times all the jobs that there are will be on offer. With very short engagements, however, practically all the jobs that there are will be continuously on offer. Since it is only in respect of jobs on offer that casualness is possible, it follows that the casual method cannot be developed so completely when long engagements

T

prevail as when short engagements do; or, more generally, that every increase in the length of the normal period of engagement, in an industry in which the casual method prevails, will, to some extent, undermine that method. In great measure, long engagements are a bye-product of the same causes that make employers prefer the preference or privileged class method to the casual method, and have not themselves any causal influence. Sometimes, however, long engagements are fostered by causes other than these, and then the long engagements, or, more strictly, the causes which bring them about, operating through them, are properly regarded as additional factors making against the casual method. Among skilled manual workers, in industries where continuous service to the public is extremely important, long engagements have sometimes been introduced as a device for obviating strikes. An example is afforded by the agreement of the South Metropolitan Gas Company with its " co-partners." " The agreement is a definite engagement on our part to give a man work for a period varying from three months to twelve months, and the great bulk of our men work under such agreements. The origin of it was, as perhaps you may have heard, in order to prevent a large number of men giving notice to us at the same time. At the time of our strike in 1889 all the stokers gave notice at one time. In order to obviate that, we instituted a series of agreements, to fall in so many every week. It is not compulsory. The men can sign them or not as they please, but those who do sign partake in the prosperity of the Company. At present, the men who have signed are getting 10 per cent on their wages as a result of being under agreement, so you may realise that there is no difficulty in getting the bulk to sign."[1] Among unskilled workpeople, not only is this positive motive for long engagements generally weak, because, in the event of a strike, their work can be more easily replaced, but there is sometimes a negative motive working definitely in the opposite sense. For, whereas, among skilled men, their own greater intelligence and the existence of strong union organisation make

---

[1] *Report of the Charity Organisation Society's Committee on Unskilled Labour*, 1908, p. 170.

disciplinary machinery unnecessary, among the rougher class of the unskilled, foremen may find it impossible to enforce a fair day's work unless the weapon of instant dismissal is ready to hand.[1] Moreover, it must be remembered that, among all classes of workers, short engagements *may*, as was indicated in § 1, be preferred by the men themselves, just because they make casualness possible. The majority of the Poor Law Commissioners write : " The ' docker's romance,' as it is called, is that he, alone of all tradesmen, can take days off when he likes, without suffering for it. . . . At Southampton docks several cases have come under notice, where permanent hands have asked to be given casual employment." [2]   Mr. Walsh, in like manner, writes that a large percentage of men have taken to the docks, " because the work there is intermittent and, therefore, more congenial to them than other occupations, where regularity in attendance is required." [3]

§ 5. It is possible for the Government, by direct action designed to encourage the re-engagement of the man whose engagement has just terminated rather than of a new man, to combat the casual method in the same way that the establishment of a system of long engagements would do. Thus the Poor Law Commissioners write : " One method of discouraging casual labour would be the imposition of what we might call an ' employment termination due.' That is to say that, to the termination of an engagement, either by the master or by the man, should be attached a small payment, both by the master and the man, in the nature of a fine or stamp duty to the State. The tax, or ' employment termination due,' could be very easily levied by means of stamps placed upon a ' termination of employment' form, which it might be made incumbent upon every workman to produce to the labour exchange upon registration. It is urged that the advantages of this system, if it could be adopted, would be threefold. In the first place, it would discourage the, so to speak, wanton termination of employment either by the employer or the employee. In the

---

[1] Cf. Messrs. Pringle and Jackson's *Report to the Poor Law Commission*, Appendix, vol. xix. p. 15.

[2] *Report of the Royal Commission on the Poor Laws*, pp. 335 and 354.

[3] *Report on Dock Labour*, p. 19.

second place, it would discourage also the employment of casual labour, inasmuch as, the more casual the labour employed in a concern, the greater would be the amount of 'employment termination due' which would have to be paid. And, thirdly, to the extent to which it did not deter either of these practices, it would afford a source of revenue, which might be devoted to defraying the cost of one or other of the proposals which we shall make."[1] Devices of this sort, if introduced, would undoubtedly strengthen the desire of employers to keep posts occupied as far as possible by the same men, and so would enhance the stimulus, which this desire affords, towards the adoption of methods of engagement other than the casual method. The provision of the National Insurance Act of 1911 (not continued in the Act of 1920), to the effect that, "when an employer has employed a man continuously throughout a period of twelve months, he may recover one-third of the contributions paid for that man,"[2] was a device of the kind contemplated. We must not forget, however, that all such devices not only encourage employers to fill posts, which they have decided in any event to fill somehow, with the same man continuously, but also encourage them, in some slight measure, to keep men on in posts which otherwise they would have been inclined temporarily to close down. *Pro tanto*, the effect of this is to check the free movement of labour from centres of falling demand to centres of rising demand, thus impeding its most advantageous employment. The direct injury which these devices would in this way inflict on the national dividend needs to be set against whatever indirect benefit they may confer upon it.

---

[1] *Report of the Royal Commission on the Poor Laws*, pp. 410-11.
[2] Explanatory Memorandum [Cd. 8911], p. 5.

CHAPTER XIV

INTERFERENCE TO RAISE WAGES IN PLACES AND OCCUPATIONS WHERE THEY ARE UNFAIR

§ 1. IT is convenient to use the term money wages in a wide sense, so as to include a money estimate of any payments in kind that there may be. Thus something should be added to the literal money wages recorded for food and drink provided for agricultural labourers, for coal provided for coal-miners, for housing and food provided for domestic servants, and so on. For the purpose of this chapter wages are taken to mean money wages corrected in this way. Provided that the wages paid to workpeople in all places and occupations were equal to the values of the marginal net product of their work—possible divergences between private and social net product are, for the present purpose, ignored—and provided that the distribution of all grades of workpeople among different places and occupations were such as to maximise the national dividend in the wide sense of Chapter IX. § 2, there would be established between different people's wages a certain relation. *This relation I define as fair.*[1] As between similar persons it is equivalent to the relation of *equality*, subject to adjustment for differences in incidental advantages and disadvantages as described in Chapter IX. § 2. My

---

[1] If we were considering the relative earnings of all classes in the population, it would be convenient to define as fair the relation which would prevail if not only the conditions postulated in the text were satisfied, but also the inequalities of opportunity for education and training referred to in Chapter IX. § 1 were removed. The discussion as to when interference with what is unfair in this wider sense is socially advantageous would follow the same lines as the discussion in the text. Here, however, we are concerned with fairness inside the wage-earning class where inequalities of opportunity play a comparatively unimportant part.

definition thus conforms to that given by Marshall when he writes that, in any given industry, wages are fair relatively to wages in industries in general, if, allowance being made for differences in the steadiness of the demand for labour, " they are about on a level with the payment made for tasks in other trades which are of equal difficulty and disagreeableness, which require equal natural abilities and an equally expensive training."[1] As between persons who are not exactly similar, fairness implies wages which, after adjustment for incidental advantages and disadvantages, are proportioned to " efficiency "; the efficiency of a worker being measured by his net product conceived as marginal,[2] multiplied by the price of that product. While, however, it implies this, it, of course, does not imply only this.[3] On the above basis, and utilising the results of Chapter IX., I shall ask, first, whether, and, if so, in what circumstances, the national dividend will be benefited by interference—in the form, for example, of the legal enforcement throughout a district or occupation of piece-rates equal to those paid by reputable firms there—designed to raise wages in a particular centre that are unfairly low relatively to those ruling in industries in general; and secondly, whether, and, if so, in what circumstances, it will be benefited by interference designed to raise wages that are already fair. In the present and following chapters I shall endeavour to answer these questions upon the assumption that the reactions produced by the earnings of workpeople upon their capacity can

---

[1] Marshall, Introduction to L. L. Price's *Industrial Peace*, p. xiii. I have ventured to substitute *equal* for Marshall's *equally rare* natural abilities, which does not seem to be quite correct. (Cf. *post*, Chapter XVI.)

[2] Cf. *ante*, Part II. Chapter II. § 4. As will appear more in detail presently, efficiency thus conceived is not merely a function of a worker's personal quality, but also of surrounding circumstances. But, none the less, *other things being equal*, an enhancement of physical, mental, and moral strength in general carries with it an enhancement of efficiency. It is necessary to distinguish this use of the term from two other uses. Efficiency does not mean for us, as it means for engineers, the ratio of the output of energy to the intake of fuel, or, in other words, the ratio of the value of a workman's product to his wage. Nor yet does it mean for us, as it means for Mr. Emerson, the ratio of a man's actual output to the output which the tasksetter holds that he ought to be able to produce without undue strain, a man of 100 per cent efficiency being one who produces exactly the allotted task.

[3] Cf. *post*, Chapter XVI.

be ignored, and I shall reserve for Chapter XVIII. the inquiry how far our results must be modified when that assumption is removed. Let us turn then to the theme of the present chapter, namely, the effect, apart from the reactions on workpeople's capacity, of interference with *unfair* rates of wages.

§ 2. In real life, when the wage rate ruling at any point is unfairly low, the unfairness may be the resultant of two or more separate elements of unfairness, produced by different causes, which operate perhaps in the same, perhaps in contrary, directions. In the practical treatment of a case of this kind the consequences of interference against each of the different elements of unfairness would need to be examined separately, since it might happen that interference was desirable against one element and undesirable against another. But, though this consideration creates a difficulty for practice, it makes no difference to the form of our analysis. For purposes of exposition, therefore, we are justified in ignoring it and in confining attention to those forms of unfair wages in which the unfairness consists of a single element. This is the method that I propose to adopt in the following discussion.

§ 3. It is of the utmost importance to distinguish between two principal sorts of unfair wage. On the one hand, wages may be unfair in some place or occupation, because, though they are equal to the value of the marginal net product of the labour assembled there, this is not equal to the value of the marginal net product, and, therefore, to the wage rate, of similar labour assembled elsewhere. On the other hand, wages may be unfair in some place or occupation, because workpeople are exploited, in the sense that they are paid less than the value which their marginal net product has to the firms employing them. The effects of interference with these two kinds of unfairness are by no means the same, and the discussion of them must be kept sharply separate. In the next three sections I shall be considering exclusively interference with wages, which, though unfair, are equal to the value of the marginal net product of the workers directly affected, and thus involve no exploitation.

§ 4. One preliminary observation of a general character should be made. Given that the number of workpeople (of

given quality) assembled in a particular place or occupation
is such that, in the existing conditions of demand there, the
value of the marginal net product of labour is not sufficient
to carry with it a fair wage rate, the effect which interference
would have on the national dividend is entirely independent of
the reason why the conditions of demand there are what they
are. On reflection this is obvious. But in popular argument
it is frequently ignored. Thus manufacturers in out-of-the-
way districts often urge that the inferiority of their machinery
or the magnitude of their freight - charges—factors which
depress the level of their demand for labour—" justify " the
payment of a wage lower than that paid by their competitors.
In an agreement made in the coal industry of Illinois, Indiana,
Ohio, and Pennsylvania, the validity of this plea was formally
recognised, and " the scale nicely adjusted so that the districts
with the better quality of coal and the lower railway charges
are required to pay enough higher wages than other districts
to counterbalance their superior natural advantages." [1]
Much argument has been expended upon the question
whether pleas of this type are sound or unsound. The truth
of the matter is that they are neither the one nor the other,
because they are irrelevant. The effect which interference
with unfairly low wage rates at any point produces on the
national dividend will be good or bad according to the way
in which it reacts on the distribution of labour power between
different places and occupations (including the occupation of
idleness). The character of this reaction is not made different
by any difference in the causes through which the existing
conditions of the demand for labour at the point affected have
come about. It depends exclusively on the causes which
have prevented the number of workpeople attached to that
point from so adjusting itself to the existing conditions of
demand there as to make the value of the marginal net
product of labour equal to what it is elsewhere, or, in districts
where the cost of living for workpeople diverges from the
normal, different from what it is elsewhere by the appropriate
amount.[2] We have, therefore, to distinguish the principal

---

[1] Clause 8 of agreement, *U.S. Bulletin of Labour*, January 1897, p. 173.
[2] Cf. *ante*, Chapter IX. § 2.

causes to which failure of adjustment may be due, and to examine in turn the effects of interference with each of the different types of unfair wages for which these several causes are responsible.

§ 5. First, the wage rate in some place or occupation may be unfairly low because the costs of movement prevent workpeople there from moving to other places or occupations where the wage rate is higher. Among unfairly low wages of this kind are included the abnormally low wages that may rule (1) in some country distant from others and differing from them in race, language, or religion; (2) in some occupation, movement from which to other occupations would involve much loss of skill; (3) in some occupation mainly filled by low-grade unskilled workpeople, the failures of higher classes, who have spent their energies in attempting a skilled trade or in confidential service to a particular firm, and are, consequently, incapable of becoming either high-grade unskilled labourers or skilled workers of another kind; (4) in some district, movement away from which would involve, for the workmen who move, the loss of special opportunities for earnings which that district offers to their women folk, or, for women workers, to their men folk; and (5) in some form of work, to wit, home work, to which more people are tied by the non-economic compulsion of family cares—a very large proportion of home workers are married women or widows [1]—than, in the existing highly developed state of factory manufacture, economic considerations alone would warrant. It can be shown in a summary manner that interference designed to raise any of these forms of unfairly low wages will, apart from reactions on capacity, be injurious to the national dividend. The only part of the effect which even *appears* to be advantageous is the movement—if any such is set up—of certain workpeople away from low-waged places or occupations to others; for the diminution of work available to those workpeople who do not move away obviously involves nothing but loss. But the argument of Chapter IX. has already shown that that movement of workpeople, though it appears to be advantageous, is not

---

[1] Cf. Vessilitsky, *The Home Worker*, p. 13.

really so. For no doctoring of the wage rate can alter the costs of movement; it can only cause the obstacles set up by them to be leapt over or forced. So long, however, as the costs of movement are what they are, that distribution of labour which differs from the absolute ideal only on account of the costs of movement was shown in Chapter IX. to be the ideal distribution *relatively to the fact of those costs*.[1] Any change of distribution, therefore, so long as those costs remain, must actually make the dividend smaller than it would otherwise have been. Plainly, therefore, no loop-hole is left for any gain.[2]

§ 6. Secondly, the wage rate in some place or occupation may be unfairly low because ignorance retains there workpeople, who, if costs of movement alone were in question, would find it advantageous to move. To determine the effect of interference in these conditions is more difficult than it was in the conditions discussed in the preceding section. For, as was shown in Chapter IX., while the forcing of obstacles set up by costs of movement involves a loss to the dividend, the forcing of those set up by ignorance involves a gain. Hence, so far as the effect of pushing up wages in a low-wage place or occupation is to transfer workpeople from employment in that place or occupation to employment elsewhere, the national dividend will be increased. The apparent advantage involved in movement, where movement occurs, is also a real advantage. Before, however, any conclusion can be drawn as to the *net effects* of interference, we need to inquire how far, and in what circumstances, the pushing up of wages will transfer superfluous workpeople elsewhere.

When the method of engagement that prevails is the preference method, it is plain that, whether the demand for labour is elastic or inelastic, no superfluous new employees will be tempted to attach themselves to the place or occupa-

---

[1] It should be noted, however, that, as old employees die off, these costs will disappear ; for to young men contemplating a choice between the occupation we are considering and others there will be no costs. Hence, if wages there are still unfairly low after a number of years, this will presumably not be because of costs, and the above argument against interference does not apply.

[2] Thus, in so far as home workers earn a wage equal to their marginal worth — which is often low because they are in direct competition with machinery of great efficiency — and are prevented from moving into factory work by family necessities, the national dividend, apart from possible reactions on capacity, would be injured by any forcing up of their wage rate

tion where the wage rate has been raised, and that all persons dislodged from employment there will know themselves to be definitely and finally dislodged. For, under this method, certain men are formally preferred to others, and it is known that whatever work is available will be wholly concentrated upon them. In these circumstances, since, if the others do not move, they must expect to earn nothing at all, they will be under a very strong inducement to move. Hence the whole effect of the enhancement of wages will consist in the transference of some workpeople from points of less effective employment to points of more effective employment. Except as a temporary incident in the process of transition, no unemployment or partial employment will be created anywhere as a set-off against this gain. Consequently, interference designed to force up wages to the fair level *must* benefit the national dividend.

When the method of engagement of labour is either the privileged class or the casual method, the effect on the national dividend is different according as the demand for labour, in the place or occupation where the wage rate is raised, has an elasticity less than, or greater than, unity. If the elasticity is less than unity, the attractiveness of that place or occupation to workpeople already assembled there will be increased, because the mathematical expectation of earnings will be increased. Consequently, under either of these two methods of engagement, there is no reason to anticipate any movement of workpeople away from that place or occupation to others; and under the casual method there will probably be some movement in the opposite direction. It is certain, however, that the amount of work available in that place or occupation will be diminished. Hence the national dividend will necessarily suffer. If the elasticity of the demand for labour is greater than unity, the attractiveness of the place or occupation to the workpeople assembled there, as well as to outsiders, will, under both these methods of engagement, be diminished when wages are raised. Therefore, it is *prima facie* probable that some workpeople will move away; though it should be remembered that, in so far as workpeople are better acquainted with, and so attach more importance to, the nominal wage than to the prospect of continuous employment, the tendency to move may meet with considerable obstruction. This obstruction is the greater in that those workpeople who could move most easily, namely, the young men, are not likely to be hit by unemployment so much as the "average" worker. To the extent that movement does occur, the national dividend will be made larger. But, on the other hand, some workpeople, who formerly were fully employed, are likely, at all events for some time, to remain in the place or occupation in partial employment. The injury which the national dividend suffers from this cause may either exceed or fall short of the benefit which it receives from the movement of the other workpeople. It is impossible to say generally whether the net result will be advantageous or disadvantageous. It will be different in different circumstances. There is, however, one case in which a definite solution is obtainable. Where the elasticity of demand is so great that the raising of the wage rate to the "fair" level reduces the demand for labour to zero, the attractiveness of the place or occupation to all workpeople is also reduced to zero, and those assembled at it *must*, therefore, move away. This condition is satisfied when individual employers are so incompetent, or individual factories or mines are so badly situated, that the enforcement of fair wages causes them to collapse altogether before the competition of others. When it is fulfilled—it will be remembered that we are here discussing cases in which movement on the part of workpeople is obstructed, not at all by costs (*e.g.* the cost of learning a new trade) but only by ignorance—the national dividend is bound to be increased by interference designed to enforce fair wages.

§ 7. We now turn to the second main class of unfair wage rates that was distinguished in § 3, namely, wage rates that are unfair, not because the value of the marginal net product of labour at the points where they occur is insufficient to yield a real wage equal to wages elsewhere, but because exploitation on the part of employers forces workpeople to accept in payment for their services less than the value which the marginal net product of their services has to these employers.

There is, indeed, something artificial in this statement of the problem, because, if any employer, or body of employers, exploits the workpeople in his service, he will, in general, not be able to hire as much labour as would have been available for him otherwise, and, consequently, the value of the marginal net product of such labour as he does hire will be indirectly raised. Hence, in general, if an employer exploits his men by paying them 5s. a week less than the value of their marginal net product to him, this will not mean that they are getting 5s. a week less than the fair wage obtainable for similar work elsewhere, but perhaps only 4s. or 3s. less than this.[1] This being understood, we may proceed to investigate the way in which unfairly low wages due to exploitation may be brought about.

It was explained in Chapter VI. that, if perfectly free competition prevailed everywhere, the wage rate paid by any employer in any occupation would be determinate at a definite point. The value of the marginal net product of labour of given quality would be the same to all employers —to simplify the exposition we ignore for the moment local differences in the cost of living—and, if one employer offered a man less than others, that man would know that he could at once get as much as this value of his marginal net product from others. In so far, however, as movements of workpeople are hampered by ignorance and costs, a monopolistic element is introduced into the wage bargain. Consequently, there is created *a range of indeterminateness*, within which the wages actually paid to any workman can be affected by individual "higgling and bargaining." The upper limit of this range is a wage equal to the value of the marginal net product of the workman to the employer engaging him, it being understood that this value is not fixed from outside, but depends in part upon how many men the employer concerned chooses to engage. The lower limit is a wage equal to what the workman believes he could obtain by moving elsewhere, *minus* an allowance to balance the costs of the movement. The width of the gap

[1] Cf. Appendix III. § 30.

between the workers' minimum and the employers' maximum varies in different circumstances. It is made larger when the employers in a district tacitly or openly enter into an agreement not to bid against one another for labour, since, in that event, the alternative to accepting terms from them is to seek work, not near by, but perhaps in an unknown district. For example, in some districts the rate of pay to agricultural labourers had, before the war, become a matter of tradition and custom. Though conditions had become quite different from what they were when this tradition crystallised, nobody ventured to take the initiative in breaking away from it. "The farmer," says the *Report of the Land Inquiry Committee*, "has been accustomed to pay a certain wage and to feel that the conditions of farming would not allow him to go beyond that limit, and we have found instances of his going without labour for a time rather than grant a rise in wages. . . . His line of defence is greatly strengthened by the solidarity of interests among farmers. If an employer in the town wishes to make a substantial advance in wages, he can afford to be indifferent to the resentment, if any, among other employers. But the personal bonds between farmers are extremely close, and the best employer of labour is sensitive to social ostracism. From many parts of the country we have heard of cases where farmers would willingly raise wages but for fear of local opinion. Thus, a farmer told us that, to avoid the appearance of paying higher wages than the farmers round him, he had actually resorted to subterfuge and adopted a bonus method of payment." [1] The width of the gap is also greater the more free employers are to make use of devices likely to aggravate the ignorance of their workpeople as to the real amount of the earnings they are receiving—such devices as are combated by the "particulars clause," the Truck Acts and the other forms of protective legislation that were discussed in Chapter IX.

§ 8. Whenever any gap exists, exploitation of the workpeople up to the measure of this gap is *possible*.[2]

---

[1] *Report of the Land Inquiry Committee*, 1914, vol. i. p. 40.

[2] It is sometimes thought that an employer's power of exploitation is always greater under a piece-wage than under a time-wage system. But this is not so. Workpeople engaged in operations, the pace of which is dependent upon

Whether and how far, when the extent of the gap is given, exploitation will actually take place, depends partly on the relative bargaining power of the employers and workpeople concerned and partly on the willingness of the stronger party to exercise its power. Even when the gap is large, the occurrence of exploitation is not certain, and, in occupations where the workpeople have been able to organise themselves into strong Trade Unions, supported by a reserve fund and bargaining for their wage rates as single collective wholes, it is not even probable. But, in occupations in which the workpeople—whether because they are widely scattered in space, or because they are poor and ignorant, or because they are women who do not expect to continue in industry after marriage, or for any other reason—are unorganised, there are grounds for fearing that exploitation will often occur. The chief of these is that, when workpeople are unable to combine, an employer generally possesses considerably greater strategic strength than his opponents. First, the actual process of bargaining is one to which he is accustomed and to which he is, in a sense, trained, while these things are not true of the generality of workpeople. Women workers and children are especially weak from this point of view. Secondly, partly because he is richer and partly because he employs a considerable number of workmen, an employer usually stands to suffer a smaller loss of well-being when a bargain with an individual workman fails to be consummated than that individual workman stands to suffer. He is, therefore, in a better position to push things to extremes. The significance of the number of people employed is brought out by the comparative weakness of employers in bargains about domestic service: "The alternative to the well-to-do woman of doing without a servant for a single day is perhaps as disagreeable to her as the alternative to the servant of being out of a place; and the worry and inconvenience to

machinery controlled by employers, often prefer piece-wages on the ground that, under that system, they will be subjected to *less* overstrain through speeding-up than they would have to put up with under time-wages. The cotton operatives and the operatives in those sections of the boot-trade where machinery is largely employed appear to take this view. (Cf. Lloyd, *Trade Unionism*, pp. 92-4.)

the mistress of finding another servant is at least as great as the discomfort to the servant of getting another situation."[1] Thirdly, in some circumstances for a workman to refuse an employer's terms involves for him further evil in addition to loss of wages. This will happen if, besides being a workman, he is also a tenant to his employer, and so liable to eviction from his house. In view of these considerations, if an employer of unorganised workpeople chooses to exercise his bargaining power, he *can* pay wages much nearer to the workman's minimum than to his own maximum. Where employers reckon to keep the same workpeople for a long time, fear of injuring these workpeople's future efficiency may induce them in their own interest to concede terms more liberal than they need have done. Furthermore, it is to be expected that feelings of generosity and kindliness will often prevent employers from fully exercising their power. But, when they are themselves very poor, there is little scope for generosity; and, even when they are not very poor, if they work through foremen or sub-contractors employed upon piece-profits, there is little prospect of it.[2] It follows that, among unorganised workpeople unable to bargain collectively, a number of men and women are likely to be paid wages approaching much more nearly to the lower than to the upper end of the range of possible rates. Such wages are, in general, lower than the wages for similar work that are paid elsewhere ; that is to say, they are " unfair."[3]

[1] Webb, *Industrial Democracy*, p. 675.

[2] There is reason to believe that the excessive pressure to which children were subjected under the old factory system was partly due to the fact that overseers were paid piece-wages. (Cf. Gilman, *A Dividend to Labour*, p. 32.) In like manner, the " sweating " that is sometimes found among the employees of sub-contractors is probably traceable, not to the system of sub-contract, but to the fact that sub-contractors are generally small masters on piece profits.

[3] It may possibly be argued against the above analysis that, though an employer may succeed, by bargaining, in forcing upon workmen, *other than the man most expensive to him*, a wage below the value of their marginal net product, it cannot pay him to treat *this* man so. For it will be to his interest to go on engaging fresh hands till the wage and the value of the marginal net product of the workman most expensive to him are equal. Hence, it is impossible for any employer who pays to all his workpeople the same efficiency-wage to pay to any of them less than the value of the marginal net product of their work. This argument, however, tacitly assumes that an employer, whom it *would pay* to engage fresh hands at an exploited wage rate, *will be able* to do this to an indefinite extent. No such assumption is warranted.

§ 8. The establishment anywhere of unfair wages of this type does not involve, at all events directly, any divergence in the actual distribution of labour from the most advantageous distribution. All that it involves directly is that in some places certain workpeople, who would in any event have been employed there, are mulcted of part of their possible earnings by the greater strategic strength of opposing bargainers. Thus it appears *prima facie* that, though the abolition of this type of unfairness would presumably benefit economic welfare as a whole by preventing the relatively rich from taking money from the relatively poor, it would make no difference to the magnitude of the national dividend. This *prima facie* conclusion omits, however, to take account of certain important indirect effects. These are three in number, and have now to be noticed in turn.

First, the forcing down of wages in particular places or occupations, though it does not reduce the labour supply sufficiently to compel employers to refrain from it, may easily reduce it to some extent by driving some workpeople away.[1] When this happens, the quantity of labour employed there will be so far contracted that the value of the marginal net product of labour there becomes greater than it is elsewhere. This involves injury to the national dividend. Consequently, a forcing-up of the wage rate, by bringing in men from other occupations which yield a smaller marginal return, would benefit it. In so far, for example, as the wages of agricultural labourers before the war were kept down by tacit understandings among farmers, the legal enforcement of a higher wage would have increased the number of these labourers in a way unambiguously advantageous to the national dividend.[2]

[1] It is *possible* that exploitation may lead the exploited workpeople to do *more* work than they would have done with better wages, and *may* thus, despite the considerations that follow, involve an increase in the national dividend. In view, however, of the reactions that are likely to be set up in their capacity, it is very unlikely that an effect of this kind will be permanent. In any event, this sort of increase in the dividend, if it were to come about, nobody would regard as a sufficient atonement for the exploitation. I propose, therefore, while noting here this possible economic disharmony, to ignore it in the body of my argument.

[2] It is thus perfectly correct to attribute a portion of the transference from arable to grass farming that has taken place in England since the 'seventies to the low rates of wages driving the labourers off the land. (Cf. Hall, *Agriculture after the War*, p. 121.) Another and a larger portion of it is, however, due to

Secondly, it was pointed out in Part II. Chap. IX. § 16, that, "when their clients, be they customers or workpeople, can be squeezed, employers tend to expend their energy in accomplishing this, rather than in improving the organisation of their factories." To prevent them from seeking profit along the line of bargaining power indirectly impels them to seek it along that of technical improvement. Thus Mr. Mallon writes: "An employer, compelled by the Trade Board [through the institution of a minimum wage] to scrutinise his factory, found that, through lax organisation, its workers were often kept waiting for work to their, and his own, considerable loss. Applying himself to the removal of this cause of waste, he was soon able to provide for the steady and continuous employment of the workers, the outcome being substantial gain to them and, in at least an equal degree, to himself. Such cases could be multiplied indefinitely. In many factories and workshops for the first time methods and equipment are being overhauled, with results at which many of the employers, not at the outset in favour of the Act, are pleased and astonished." [1] With this passage may be compared a kindred observation of Miss Black's: "It has been shown over and over again that, when employers are prevented from developing their business along the lines of cheap labour or bad conditions, they proceed to develop it along the lines of improved methods, and that the improved methods tend both to increased output and to greater cheapness." [2] This view, the correctness of which nobody seriously doubts, is not, it should be understood, equivalent to the view that, if in any country labour in general is abundant and, therefore, cheap, employers are discouraged from making use of machinery. Since machinery is itself the product of labour,

the cheapening of imported food, which has rendered the employment of British resources in direct food production less profitable relatively to other employments than it used to be. To substitute grass farming for arable farming is merely one way of reducing the resources devoted to food production in this country, as against the production of other things by the sale of which food can be purchased from abroad; for, as Sir A. D. Hall observes, "land [apart, of course, from special sorts of land] under arable cultivation produces nearly three times as much food as when under grass and employs ten times as many men" (*ibid.* p. 127).

[1] *Industrial Unrest and the Living Wage*, p. 155.
[2] Black, *Makers of our Clothes*, pp. 185 and 192.

that view is not correct.[1] If, however, in a particular district or occupation employers are able to exploit a particular class of labour, they are discouraged from making use of machinery, because machinery embodies the services of other classes of labour, which, not being exploited, are more expensive relatively to their efficiency.

Thirdly, if particular employers outbargain their workmen, in such wise as to compel some or all of them to accept a wage below the value of their marginal net product, it necessarily happens that these employers are receiving more than the normal earnings of persons of their degree of competence;— a state of affairs which, in view of the imperfect mobility of employing power between occupations, may continue for some time. If the exploiting employers were persons of the ordinary competence of their grade, interference, which forced up the wages paid by them to the fair level, would simply compel them to hand over to workpeople profits formerly exacted from them by *force majeure*, and would have no other effect. As a matter of fact, however, exploitation of this kind is much more often practised by incompetent or badly situated employers, who, without it, could not maintain themselves in business, than by competent and well-situated men. The small masters have, throughout history, been always the worst exploiters. Hence exploitation provides, in the main, a bounty at the workers' expense for relatively incompetent and badly situated employers; and the prevention of exploitation would tend to hasten their defeat at the hands of more efficient rivals. This consideration, in conjunction with the others that have preceded it, makes it plain that external interference to prevent that type of unfair wages which I have described as exploitation is desirable in the interest of the national dividend as well as upon other grounds.

§ 9. All that has been said hitherto, both of unfair wages that are equal to the value of marginal net product, and of unfair wages that are exploited below the value of marginal net product, is of quite general application. It holds good equally of men's wages and of women's wages;

[1] Cf. Hayes, "The Rate of Wages and the Use of Machinery," *American Economic Review*, September 1923, pp. 461 *et seq.*

and, of course, in view of their inferior organisation, the danger of exploitation is especially great with women. Any specific plea that the wage of either sex in any place or occupation is unfair would need to be reviewed in the light of it. There still remains, however, a somewhat special problem arising out of *the relation between men's wages and women's wages*, which our analysis does not cover. It may happen that women's wages in some place or occupation are fair relatively to women's wages in other places or occupations, but unfair relatively to men's wages in that place or occupation. This statement has not, of course, anything to do with the well-known fact that women's day wages on the average are considerably lower than men's day wages. Women, looking forward, as they do, to matrimony and a life in the home, are not trained to industry as men are, and do not devote to it that period of their lives when they are strongest and most capable. Thus between the age-periods of 18−20 and 25−35 there is a great decrease in the percentage of women who are engaged in wage-earning occupations, and this is due, no doubt, to the withdrawal of many of them at marriage. Prof. Sargant Florence writes : " The common age at marriage being between 21 and 25 for spinsters, the typical length of industrial life for a woman would be eight years.[1] " In these circumstances, even though women's natural endowments of mind and muscle were equal to those of men, which, on the average, they are not, it would be surprising if their day wages were not lower. Certainly, the fact that they are lower involves no unfairness in the sense in which that term is here used. In some places or occupations, however, it may happen that not only the day wages, but also the piece wages, or, more accurately, the efficiency wages, of women are lower than those of men. This state of things may come about because women's wages in those places or occupations are

---

[1] *Economic Journal*, Mar. 1931, p. 20. In the later age-groups, it may be noticed, alongside of a continuing efflux, there is also a certain reinflux into industry of women whose husbands have died. Sir Sydney Chapman refers to this point in connection with home work, pointing out that much of this work requires only such skill as can be acquired by anybody at any time of life, and is taken up by untrained persons, who "suddenly find it necessary to do something, or have to make money " (*Home Work*, Manchester Statistical Society, Jan. 1910, p. 93).

unfair relatively to women's wages elsewhere. In that event there is nothing special about it, and the analysis relevant to it has already been given in preceding sections. But it may also come about because women's wages in those places or occupations are unfair relatively to men's wages there, although they are fair relatively to women's wages elsewhere. It is this state of things that constitutes our present problem.

In order to understand the matter rightly, analysis is necessary. The common idea is that women are normally paid less than men because men's wages have, in general, to support a family, while women's wages have only to support the women themselves. This is very superficial. The correct line of approach would seem to be as follows. The productive efficiency of a representative woman relatively to that of a representative man is different in different occupations: in some, such as nursing and the tending of infants, it is much greater; in others, such as coal-mining and navvy work, it is much less. If we knew enough of the facts, we could draw up a list of all occupations, giving for each of them the amount of normal man's labour to which a day or week of normal woman's labour is equivalent. The relation between the demand schedules for women's work and for men's work is determined by the facts embodied in this list, in conjunction with the general conditions of demand for the products of the several occupations. The relation between the supplies of women's work and of men's work is determined partly by the physiological fact that male and female children survive in nearly equal numbers, whatever the comparative wages ruling for men's work and women's work may be; and partly by the economic fact that the proportions, respectively, of the men and women in existence who offer their work in industry depend, not only on the wages offered to members of either sex separately, but also, since women are the less likely to work at industry the more money their husbands are earning, on the aggregate amount of the joint family income. These two sets of influences together govern and determine the relation between the general level of the wages per day paid to representative members of the two sexes.[1]   In equilibrium there is one general rate of representative men's day wages and one general rate of representative women's day wages, the one or the other being higher according to the circumstances of supply, and according as the commodities demanded by the public are chiefly commodities for the manufacture of which the one or the other sex is specially well fitted.[2]

[1] This analysis may be formulated mathematically as follows :

Let w_1 be the rate of women's wages per day,

w_2 the rate of men's wages per day.

Then, since the amount of women's labour offered in industry at any given wage depends in part upon the rate of men's wages—being, in general, smaller the larger these are—the supply of women's labour may be written $f_1(w_1, w_2)$. In like manner, the supply of men's labour may be written $f_2(w_1, w_2)$.

And we know that $\dfrac{\delta f_1(w_1, w_2)}{w_1}$ and $\dfrac{\delta f_2(w_1, w_2)}{\delta w_2}$ are positive, and $\dfrac{\delta f_1(w_1, w_2)}{\delta w_2}$

and $\dfrac{\delta f_2(w_1, w_2)}{\delta w_1}$ are negative.

Again, since the amount of women's labour demanded in industry at any given wage depends upon the rate of men's wages—being, in general, smaller the smaller these are — the demand for women's labour may be written $_1\phi(w_1, w_2)$, and the demand for men's labour $\phi_2(w_1, w_2)$. And we know that $\dfrac{\delta \phi_1(w_1, w_2)}{\delta w_1}$ and $\dfrac{\delta \phi_2(w_1, w_2)}{\delta w_2}$ are negative, and $\dfrac{\delta \phi_1(w_1, w_2)}{\delta w_2}$ and $\dfrac{\delta \phi_2(w_1, w_2)}{\delta w_1}$ are positive.

The two equations, which suffice to determine our two unknowns, are :

$$(1) \quad f_1(w_1, w_2) = \phi_1(w_1, w_2)$$
$$(2) \quad f_2(w_1, w_2) = \phi_2(w_1, w_2).$$

It may be added that, if the proportion of women and men offering work in industry were determined solely by the proportion of women and men in existence, we should have to do with a straightforward problem of joint-supply; for, obviously, the comparative numbers of the two sexes are determined by physiological causes outside the range of economic influences.   In these conditions, therefore, both the supply of women workers and the supply of men workers would be functions of one variable, this variable being some symbol of a normal family income, such as $(w_1 + w_2)$.   For $f_1(w_1, w_2)$ and $f_2(w_1, w_2)$ we should have to write $f(w_1 + w_2)$ and $kf(w_1 + w_2)$: and in countries where males and females survive in equal numbers, k would be equal to unity.

[2] It is interesting to note that in the European War, while the withdrawal of men from industry for the army naturally tended to raise men's wages relatively to women's wages, the character of the commodities demanded by the public was changed in a way tending in the opposite direction.   Ordinary tailoring and munition making, the demand for both of which enormously expanded, appear to be better adapted for women's work than the general run of industries.   In the Report of the Conference of the British Association on *Outlets for Labour after the War* it is suggested that, on the whole, the special war demand of the Government was "a demand for a class of goods in the production of which a greater proportion of women rather than men can be more usefully and economically employed than under normal peace conditions" (*Report*, 1915, p. 8).

Men alone are employed in all occupations where the ratio of their efficiency to women's efficiency exceeds the ratio of their day wages to women's day wages; women alone in all occupations in opposite case; and men and women indifferently in the marginal occupations in which their respective efficiencies bear to one another the same ratio as their respective day wages. In these marginal occupations, that is to say, the efficiency wages of the two sexes are equal. This equality of efficiency wages means, with certain allowances, equality of piece wages. The principal allowances are, first, a small extra for men, because, since, at need, they can be put on night-work and can be sworn at more comfortably, it is rather more convenient to employ them; secondly, a small extra to the more skilful workers, whether men or women, because they occupy machinery for a shorter time than less skilful workers in accomplishing a given job. In equilibrium the piece wages paid to the members of the two sexes in the marginal occupations are, with these limitations, equal.[1] This is the state of things which the play of economic

---

[1] It so happens in fact—as indeed is probable *a priori*—that the range of these marginal occupations is in this country small. The Poor Law Commissioners report: "About four-fifths of the occupied male population are engaged in employments which they monopolise, or in which women are a negligible factor as regards possible competition, such as agriculture, mining, fishing, building, transport, wood, gas and water, and the staple metal and machine-making trades, all of which are virtually male preserves. Only one-fifth of the males are engaged in trades where women enter to the extent of 1 per cent of the whole number of occupied females" (*Report*, p. 324). Mr. and Mrs. Webb witness to the same effect: "There are a very small number of cases in which men and women compete directly with each other for employment on precisely the same operation in one and the same process" (Webb, *Industrial Democracy*, p. 506. Cf. also Smart, *Economic Studies*, p. 118.) When one sex appears to be invading the province of the other, the fact generally is that the process, as well as the workers, is being changed. Thus, machinery and males have come into lace and laundry work: machinery and females into boot-making and tailoring. The Poor Law Commissioners report: "In the boot and shoe trade—which has been distinctively a male industry—women are certainly obtaining a relatively stronger hold, owing to the division of labour which now furnishes certain lighter processes, suitable for women, that were formerly done as part of the general work of male shoemakers. Slipper-making, for instance, is now passing entirely into female hands" (*Report of the Royal Commission on the Poor Law*, p. 324). Also, on the authority of the Board of Trade inquiry into the *Cost of Living of the Working Classes*: "The same phenomenon occurs in other fields; for instance, in Sheffield, file-cutting, an occupation which used to be largely done by female out-workers—the work requiring rather dexterity than strength—is now being done by heavy machinery requiring male attendants" (*ibid.* p. 324). The Commissioners

forces tends to bring about; and, so far as it in fact brings it about, it is not possible for women's wages in any place or occupation to be fair relatively to women's wages elsewhere and yet unfair relatively to men's wages there.[1]

In real life, however, it happens from time to time that economic equilibrium in this matter is not attained. In particular occupations employers may pay to women workers an efficiency wage, which, though fair relatively to women's wages elsewhere, is less than the efficiency wage they are paying to men workers, and yet may still employ some men. They may

summarise their views thus: "The conclusion is that, while women and juveniles are now engaged in many industries in which the specialisation of machinery enables them to take part, they are not, in any considerable trade or process, displacing adult males in the sense that they are being more largely employed to do work identical with that formerly done by men. The great expansion of women's labour seems to have been in new fields of employment, or in fields which men never occupied. It should also be borne in mind that, even when women are employed where men used to be employed, this is largely due to the men going into more highly paid industries. Mining, machine-making, and building have of late years attracted an abnormal number of men and boys" (*ibid.* p. 325). This view is fully borne out by what occurred during the European War. The British Association Conference of 1915 on *Outlets for Labour after the War* reported: " Even during the present time of stress, when women are to a certain extent doing work which would normally be done by men, the work, as shown in the detailed portion of this Report dealing with separate trades, is very rarely similar either as regards process or conditions. With the introduction of women the work has often to be subdivided, and the men generally have at least the arduousness of their work increased, with oft-times the addition of over-time and night-work and a larger amount of work entailing a greater strain. Where workshops have been recently built for women workers, they have been equipped with machines of a different type from what would have been installed had the management been able to procure trained men" (*loc. cit.* p. 15). Cf. also *Report of the War Cabinet Committee on Women in Industry*, 1919, pp. 21-2.

[1] The scheme of analysis worked out in the text can also be applied to the case in which one class of worker is not more efficient in any job than another class, but is *as efficient* in some jobs. If the number of persons in this class is more than enough to fill the jobs in which they are as efficient as the others, their wage-rate will, in equilibrium, be less than that of the others, but, if their number is not more than enough for this, their wage-rate will, in equilibrium, be equal to that of the others. In this connection the following passage from Mr. Henry Ford's book *My Life and Work* is of interest: " The subdivision of industry opens places that can be filled by practically any one. There are more places in subdivision industry that can be filled by blind men than there are blind men. There are more places that can be filled by cripples than there are cripples. And in most of these places the man who short-sightedly might be considered as an object of charity can earn just as adequate a living as the keenest and most able-bodied. It is waste to put an able-bodied man in a job that might just as well be cared for by a cripple " (*loc. cit.* p. 209).

do this either for a short time, while they are in process of substituting the one sex for the other; or for a long time, because trade union pressure or custom either compels the retention of some men, or vetoes the entry of more than a limited number of women. In these conditions is the claim "equal pay for workers of equal efficiency" justified? In what way would interference to raise the women's efficiency wage to the level of the men's affect the national dividend?

If the power of tradition, custom or trade union pressure is such that neither the number of women attached to the occupation under review nor the number of women employed there will be different if employers are allowed to pay them the lower rate from what it will be if they are forced to pay the higher rate, the national dividend will not be affected at all. This, however, is a very improbable state of affairs. For even though the number of women who may be *employed* in the occupation is rigidly limited, it is likely that the number trained for and attached to it will be made greater by the higher wage rate; and, if this happens, the dividend obviously suffers from the enforced idleness of those who are attached but not employed. Furthermore, in real life permission to pay the lower wage rate will seldom be without effect on the number of women who are employed there and take the place of men. For example, "in Stoke-upon-Trent it appears that women and girls are very largely employed in the pottery industry. In some branches of this trade they are being employed to an increasing extent upon work which, a few years ago, was performed almost exclusively by men; they are now acting in competition with male labour; and, as they are able to do similar work for lower wages, they are gradually driving men from certain sections of the trade." [1] This consideration confirms Professor Cannan's contention, that "the most powerful lever for increasing the opportunities of women is taken away if they are not allowed to do the work cheaper." [2] It follows that, generally speaking, to compel the payment to them of an efficiency wage equal to that paid to men in occupations which they are seeking to enter, and in which

---

[1] *Report of the Royal Commission on the Poor Laws*, p. 323.
[2] *Wealth*, p. 206.

such a rate would give them higher earnings than similar women can obtain elsewhere, must obstruct their entry either directly, or indirectly by relaxing employers' efforts to break down the customs and rules that hinder it. But, since, *ex hypothesi*, they are more efficient, relatively to men, in these occupations than they are in marginal occupations common to both sexes, their entry would necessarily be beneficial to the national dividend. Hence, generally speaking, interference designed to enforce the payment to them of a "fair" wage, as compared with the wages paid to men, in circumstances when this means an unfairly high wage as compared with women's wages elsewhere, would injure the national dividend.[1] Interference may still conceivably be advocated by those who wish to exclude women from industry, as far as that can be done, on general social grounds. Such a defence for it is, however, insecure, because interference of the type here discussed not only lessens the aggregate number of women in industry, but distributes them among different occupations in a wasteful manner. The social argument for excluding women from industry generally cannot sustain a policy which has this effect.

§ 10. In view of the distinctions that have been found, in the course of this chapter, to exist between different forms of unfair wages, it is plain that interference directed indiscriminately against all forms must do harm as well as good. The procedure, which, if practicable, would most advantage the national dividend, would be to examine and deal separately with every place or occupation where there was *prima facie* reason to believe that wages were unfair in any of the senses studied in the text. It may, however, be argued that this plan is an impracticable one, and that it is necessary either to interfere against unfair wages by

---

[1] It is possible to employ the term "unfair" wages in reference to women's wages in a somewhat different sense, and to hold that women's wages in general are unfairly low, because they fall short of what they would have been, were it not that custom and tradition permanently exclude women from certain occupations suited to their powers, and so force some of them to take up work for which they are relatively ill-fitted. As was shown in Chapter IX., the removal of all artificial barriers of this kind would benefit the national dividend. But, so long as the barriers are left standing, reasoning analogous to that employed in § 6 of the present chapter proves that any attempt to force up women's wages towards what they would be if the barriers were removed, will injure the national dividend.

broad general rules or else not to interfere at all. Thus, it may be said, it is practicable to pass and administer a law like the French law of 1915, which provides that female outworkers shall be paid a piece-wage that will yield to the average outworker earnings equal to those of an average factory worker;[1] but it is not practicable to enact that a wage lower than this shall be permitted when it is due to family ties which restrain home workers from going into factories, and forbidden when it is due to exploitation. When the issue raised is of this type, policy must be based on a balancing of conflicting considerations.

[1] *Labour Gazette*, Sept. 1915, p. 357.

CHAPTER XV

§ 1. IN Chapter VIII. methods of industrial remuneration were discussed from the point of view of their effect in stimulating the productive activity of the individual worker. We have now to consider them from the standpoint of fairness between different workers. To be fair, the wages of different men in any industry engaged in the same class of job must, as we have seen, be proportioned to their efficiency in the sense defined in Chapter XIV. § 1. I propose to inquire how far under the two principal methods of industrial remuneration, time-wages and piece-wages, we may expect this requirement to be satisfied.

§ 2. Under time-wages a good deal more can be accomplished in this sense than is sometimes supposed. By means of careful records and corresponding adjustments wage-rates can be arranged at differing levels adapted to the different efficiencies of individual workpeople.[1] It is frequently urged, indeed, that, where standard rates for average workpeople are established, either by bargaining between associations of employers and employed or by authoritative intervention on the part of the State, adjustment is bound to be very imperfect, alike for workpeople below the average of capacity and for workpeople above it. Experience, however, does not altogether bear out this view.

---

[1] Cf. for an elaborate attempt on these lines, Gannt, *Work, Wages, and Profits*, ch. iv. In the Birmingham brass trades "the executive of the National Union of Brass Workers grades each worker according to his ability, and places him in one of seven different classes, for each of which a minimum wage is set by collective bargaining. If an employer challenges the qualifications of any man, a practical examination in the processes of the trade is given him by the manager of the Municipal Brass Trades School" (Goodrich, *The Frontier of Control*, p. 165). This, however, is a very unusual arrangement.

As regards workpeople below the average, when their relative inferiority arises out of some definite physical cause, such as old age, adjustments are made very freely. Trade unions often have special arrangements permitting men over sixty to accept less than the standard (time) rate. Such arrangements, Sir William Beveridge states, "occur in the rules of several furnishing trade unions, and of others in the printing, leather, and building trades. In one union, indeed, members over fifty-six years of age may not only be allowed, but may be compelled, by their branches to accept less than the standard rate (so as to clear the unemployed fund)."[1] "It is," he adds, "of course, possible that, in some of these cases, the formal rule of exception is seldom put in force, or that the branch refuses its consent to a lower rate. On the other hand, it is quite certain that many unions in fact make exceptions for their aged members without possessing any formal rules on the subject. This is done by the Amalgamated Society of Carpenters and Joiners, and, to a less extent, by the Amalgamated Society of Engineers. The question is, indeed, very largely one of the strength and feeling of the particular branch concerned. If the standard rate is firmly established, it may appear safe to make exceptions for the older men."[2] There are, however, many relatively inefficient men in industry, even among the members of trade unions with fairly stringent capacity tests at the time of admission, whose inefficiency is not associated with a definite objective thing, such as old age or infirmity. For these men adjustment is more difficult. The

[1] *Unemployment*, p. 124, footnote.

[2] *Ibid.* p. 124. The peculiarity and uncertainty of these arrangements is brought out in Mr. Barnes' evidence to the Poor Law Commissioners: "In the Amalgamated Society of Engineers we do not require a man to shift from one town to another after he is fifty years of age, and, putting it generally, we do not require him to get the standard rate of wages—according to the discretion of the committees who may deal with the matter—after about fifty-five years of age." But the percentage of men who take advantage of this is very small. "In fact, although we allow men to work under the rate at fifty-five years of age, it is rather the case that the men at fifty-five, or even sixty, do not avail themselves of the opportunity. So strong is the sense of discipline in the trade unions, and their sense of loyalty to their fellows, that in most cases a man would rather give up work altogether than accept work at the lower rate. So that, instead of trade unions standing in the way of the men accepting lower rates, the opposite is the fact, and the trade unions rather encourage it" (Evidence of Mr. G. N. Barnes, M.P., quoted in the Report of the Commission, p. 313, footnote).

nature of the difficulties involved may be illustrated from the much discussed case of the "slow workers" under the New Zealand Arbitration Law. In connection with its award of "minimum" wages, it is usual for the Arbitration Court to provide for a tribunal to fix an "under-rate" for slow workers.[1] In the earlier years of the Act permits to claim the under-rate used to be obtainable from the president or secretary of the trade union concerned. But it was found that, for slow workers, as distinct from those who are more obviously afflicted by age, accident, or infirmity, these officials hesitated to issue permits. Under the revised Act, therefore, the power of issue is entrusted to the chairmen of local Conciliation Boards, after hearing the representatives of the unions. In Victoria the issue is in the hands of the Chief Inspector of Factories, subject to the condition that the persons working with licences in any factory must not exceed one-fifth of the adult workers who are employed there at the full minimum rate.[2] The unwillingness of the unions to sanction permits is due to the fear that, through them, the standard required of the ordinary grade of workmen in the industry may be raised, and the minimum thus insidiously lowered.[3] This unwillingness tends, of course, to be checked when the unions are under obligation to pay large out-of-work benefit to unemployed members. In all circumstances, however, it is likely to operate to some extent. Under the British Trades Boards Act permits may not be issued at all to slow workers as such—only to those suffering from physical or mental incapacity. Thus it would

---

[1] Cf. Broadhead, *State Regulation of Labour in New Zealand*, p. 66.

[2] Cf. Aves, *Report on Wages Boards*, p. 61, and Raynaud, *Vers le salaire minimum*, p. 96.

[3] The danger of allowing under-rating to become a means of evasion of awards is clearly seen by those in charge of the Acts. "In granting permits, the Chief Inspector is guided by claims based on personal disability of some kind, and not by the exigencies either of an industry or of a particular business. If conditions have changed, making the applications for permits more urgent on that account, the view is held, very consistently, that the occasion would then have arisen for the reconsideration of its determination by the Board concerned. While the determinations are in force, wages conditions, it is held, should conform to them, and in their power to arrest or postpone a fall some consider that they will in the future prove their greatest value. Such is the hope, but to that form of testing they have not yet been subjected. The point, which it is necessary to emphasise here, is that at such a period the permit is not regarded as the appropriate instrument on which to fall back" (Aves, *Report on Wages Boards*, p. 63).

be idle to pretend that, for under-rate workers, adjustment is a perfectly smooth and simple matter. Even for them, however, a good deal is done.

As regards workpeople above the average of capacity, there is, of course, never any formal rule precluding payment to them of more than the standard rate. But, it is often asserted, employers as a matter of fact refuse to pay more than the standard rate for capacity in excess of the standard, for fear that trade unions should make this action an excuse for demanding a rise in the standard itself;[1] and it is, no doubt, true that, especially among large employers, the convenience of a uniform rate acts strongly to prevent adjustment to individual differences. "The secretary of the Composition Roofers estimates that not more than two per cent of the members in New York City receive more than the minimum. An official of the Steam Filterers estimates that for his union in New York City the proportion is not less than five nor more than ten per cent."[2] On the whole, however, the tendency for the minimum rate to become the maximum does not appear to be nearly as strong as is generally supposed. Thus the Inspector of Factories in Victoria in 1902 stated that, in the clothing trade, while the minima for men and women workers respectively were 45s. and 20s., the average wages were 53s. 6d. and 22s. 3d.[3] Furthermore, in the Report of the Bureau of Labour for 1909, it is stated that "out of 2451 employees in factories in Auckland City, excluding under-rate workers and young persons, 949 received the minimum rate, and 1504, or 61 per cent of the whole, received more than the minimum. In Wellington the percentage receiving more than the minimum was 57, in Christchurch 47, and in Dunedin 46."[4] The same point is illustrated in a rough way by the

---

[1] It should be noted that, when it is a question of an excess of wage sought by particular men above the standard time-wage, the unions under a time-wage system are not in a position to resort to collective bargaining, and that, therefore, the employers' bargaining power is more likely to be superior to the workpeople's than it is as regards the standard itself. (Cf. McCabe, *The Standard Rate in American Trade Unions*, p. 114.)

[2] McCabe, *The Standard Rate in American Trade Unions*, p. 118 *n.*

[3] Cf. Webb, *Socialism and the National Minimum*, p. 73.

[4] *Quarterly Journal of Economics*, 1910, p. 678. The tendency of the minimum to become the maximum is, of course, stronger in some circumstances than in others. Thus, Mr. Broadhead writes of New Zealand : "In those

policy of certain American unions, which enter into agreements with employers concerning both a standard and a minimum wage. In the Norfolk and Western Railway shops in Roanoke the minimum wage was at one time 20 cents, while the standard rate was that received by the largest number of men in the shop, namely, 24 cents per hour. Again, in an agreement made in 1903 between the "Soo" Railway and the International Association of Machinists, "it is stipulated that in the machine shops of the railway company the minimum rate shall be 30 cents per hour, and the standard rate $34\frac{1}{2}$ cents per hour."[1] The whole matter is well summed up by the Reporter to the United States Bureau of Labour in 1915: "Employers have frequently said to me that they believed there was a tendency in that direction—i.e. for the minimum to become the maximum—but they have seldom been able to furnish evidence to that effect from their own establishments. At times I have found on enquiry that not a single man in their own plants was receiving the minimum wage. The employers' opinion seems to be more the result of a priori reasoning than the result of experience. Nor on reflection is it easy to see why the minimum should become the maximum. . . . There seems to be no reason why under this system there should not be the same competition among employers as under the old system to secure the most efficient and highly skilled workmen, and there is no reason why such men should not get wages based on their superior efficiency. Victorian statistics on this point are lacking, but in New Zealand, where minimum wages are fixed by the arbitration court, statistics as to wages tabulated in 1909 by the Labour Department showed that, in the four leading industrial centres of the Dominion, the percentages of workers in trades where a legal minimum wage was fixed, who received more than the

---

trades, in which there is no competition with the outside world, many of the workers, according to their degree of skill, are paid more than the minimum wage fixed by the court, but in others, in which there is competition with the imported article, the practice of making the minimum the maximum wage is, I believe, pretty general. In the latter case the employers contend that they cannot afford to pay to any worker any more than is fixed by law" (State Regulation of Labour in New Zealand, p. 72).

[1] Holland and Barnett, Studies in American Trade Unionism, p. 118.

minimum, varied from 51 per cent in Dunedin to 61 per cent in Auckland. There is no reason to think that a dissimilar situation would be revealed by a statistical investigation in Victoria."[1] Even where the open payment of higher time-wages as a reward of higher efficiency is prevented by friction and jealousy, the result aimed at may sometimes be attained by secret payments.[2] It should be remembered, too, that, when time-wages are fixed rigorously and there is no machinery for making payments above the standard rate, the standard rate is usually fixed at different levels in different centres, and men of more or less similar quality tend to be concentrated at each several centre. Thus, even when a specially capable workman cannot obtain exceptional earnings while remaining at the place where he is, he can do so by migrating to one where higher wages and larger output are the rule.

Yet again, even when extra efficiency is not rewarded by any addition to the wage-rate, it may be rewarded by selection for continued employment in bad times and, in businesses where, as in railway service, there are a number of grades of employees receiving different rates of pay, for promotion when opportunity offers. The former of these processes is particularly important. Its working is well illustrated from the records of the Amalgamated Society of Engineers made in the days when the trade worked predominantly upon time-wages. The "vacant books" of the Society, after the results of a number of years, some good and some bad, had been averaged, yielded the following table of days lost through want of work:

---

[1] "Minimum Wage Legislation," *U.S. Bulletin of Labour Statistics*, 1915, p. 136, No. 167.

[2] For example, a New Zealand employer told Mr. Aves that "he was alive to the danger of a rigid scale of remuneration, and that to some of his men he was paying 'something extra' a day. But this was done ' on the quiet.' The men are paid in paper and metal currency, the loose coinage being folded in the notes. The array of little packages was shown me. All are paid with great rapidity, and 'no one can tell what any one else receives'" (*Report on Wages Boards* [Cd. 4167], p. 109). In like manner, an English employer told the Charity Organisation Society's Committee on Unskilled Labour: "If one man is better than another, we give him 1s. or 2s. extra at the end of the week. We have to be careful that other men do not know that, or they want to know why. They cannot understand that it is because the man has served us better. You cannot say openly, 'I will give you 2s. more.' The man would be considered a favourite, and he would have a warm time in the stable at night" (*Report*, p. 109).

Loss less than 3 days per annum   . 70·4 % of the Union.
  „   between 3 days and 4 weeks   . 13   %   „
  „   from 4 to 8 weeks   .   .   . 4·6 %   „
  „   from 8 to 12 weeks .   .   2·8 %   „
  „   over 12 weeks   9   %   „

Thus the greater part of the unemployment that occurred
was concentrated upon a comparatively small number of men.[1]
That its distribution was associated with inefficiency is suggested by the annexed table showing the age-distribution
of the men who drew unemployment benefit in 1895 (a
medium year).[2]

		Average number of days lost in a year.
Members between 15-25 years old		8·8
„	25-35 „ ·	13·1
„	35-45 „	12·3
„	45-55 „	20·1
„	55-65 „	33·1
„	65 and over (excluding superannuated)	26·9

These tables take no account of time lost through "short
time," sickness, unpunctuality or trade disputes, or of time
gained through overtime. They indicate that the older, and
presumably less efficient, men suffer most.[3] Moreover, "a
comparison of 1890 with 1893 yields the rather striking
result that almost as large a proportion of members (21·4
per cent) were unemployed during one of the best years
as during the worst (26·4 per cent)."[4] In 1926 the Ministry
of Labour investigated the circumstances of a large sample of

[1] Cf., for confirmatory evidence from America, Schlichter, *The Turnover of
Factory Labour*, pp. 44-5.

[2] Cf. *British and Foreign Trade and Industry*, Second Series, p. 99.

[3] There is evidence that in the industrial depression of 1922 in Great
Britain the incidence of unemployment among men, which was, as might have
been expected, least between the ages 25-40, was higher in the early twenties
than among elderly men. (Cf. Mozley, "The Incidence of Unemployment
by Age and Sex," *Economic Journal*, December 1922, p. 484.) A possible
explanation is that men in the early twenties would be those who had been
prevented by the war from learning a skilled trade, that the wages of unskilled
workers were unduly high relatively to those of skilled workers, and that,
therefore, unskilled workers, among whom these young men were abnormally
numerous, found it harder to obtain employment than skilled workers. This
"explanation" is, however, little better than a guess. It is interesting to note
that in 1921 a law was passed in Italy to the effect that, "in the case of dismissals being necessary, preference in the retaining of hands be given to the
oldest workmen and to those having the largest families" (*Review of the Foreign
Press*, July 1921, p. 191).

[4] Beveridge, *Unemployment*, p. 72.

persons insured under the Unemployment Insurance Act. It
appeared that, over a period of two and a half years (from
October 1923 to April 1926), 63 per cent of the males and
66·2 per cent of the females in the sample did not draw
benefit at all, while, of those who drew benefit, nearly half
drew it for less than 10 per cent of the period.[1] The report
adds that, despite some complicating considerations, "it is
clear that age has been a factor in the problem of unemployment from age forty-five onwards in the case of males and age
thirty-five onwards in the case of females."[2] The implication of
these facts is emphasised in the blunt statement of the (pre-war)
Transvaal Indigency Commission. "The really efficient man
is rarely unemployed except for short periods between jobs,
because, being competent, he is the last to be thrown out of
employment, and has generally sufficient money to enable him
to migrate to some place where his services are wanted."[3]

The general result of this discussion, therefore, is that
under time-wage systems it is not impossible so to arrange
rates that wages, as between the various workpeople employed
in an industry, are not seriously unfair.

§ 3. Under piece-wage systems the difficulty of attaining
fairness is *prima facie* much less. For these systems are
deliberately designed to make payment proportional to output,
which is precisely what, subject to the qualification set out
in Chapter IX. § 1, fairness appears to require. A moment's
reflection shows, however, that payment proportional to output
is only fair when the various workers concerned are operating
under similar conditions. Except when this is so, payment
proportional to output and payment proportional to efficiency
are not the same thing.[4] In order, therefore, that a piece-
wage system may yield fair wages, various allowances must
be made under it to provide for divergent conditions of work.

§ 4. First, allowance must be made for differences in the
assistance which different men receive in their work from

---

[1] *Report on an investigation into the employment and insurance history of
a sample of persons insured against unemployment in Great Britain*, 1927,
pp. 46-7.
[2] *Ibid.* p. 38.
[3] *Report of the Transvaal Indigency Commission*, p. 121.
[4] Cf. *ante*, Part II. Chap. II. § 4.

machinery or from Nature. Thus the piece-rate must be higher for men working with obsolete machinery, or in mines where the easiest seams have been used up, than it is for men assisted by the most modern appliances, or hewing coal from a face that is easy of access. Allowances of this kind have frequently been provided for in the wage-agreements of important industries. For example, "in mining the tonnage rates paid to hewers vary almost indefinitely, not only from colliery to colliery, but from seam to seam within the same pit, according to the nature of the coal and the conditions under which the coal has to be won in each place; yet in some districts (as, for example, in Northumberland and Durham) the agreement which governs wages requires that the tonnage rates throughout the county shall be so fixed that each collier shall be able to make certain agreed earnings, *i.e.* the ' county average.' " [1] There is abundant evidence that men of local and trade experience can calculate with very close accuracy what this kind of allowance ought in different circumstances to be.

§ 5. Secondly, allowance must be made for differences in the exact character of the article which different workpeople in the same industry are engaged in making. These allowances also have often been provided for in important industries by means of piece-wage lists. The general method by which they are arranged is well described in a report of the Labour Department as follows: "A close inspection will show that, notwithstanding the variety of detail which these lists exhibit, there are certain salient features of construction and arrangement common at least to the more important among them. The most noteworthy of these common features will be seen to be the definition of a 'Standard' article or process, with a corresponding piece-price fixed in relation to this unit. From this point of departure the whole wage-scale starts, all other articles or processes having their price fixed by means of extras, deductions and allowances, specified in the list, and corresponding to clearly defined variations from the standard. In this manner it is possible to provide for a very large number of processes with very fine shades of difference under

[1] *Report on Standard Price Rates*, 1900, p. xiv.

a single price-list. As an example of a standard unit we may take the basis of the book-work scale for compositors in the London printing trade:

All works in the English language, common matter, including english and brevier, are to be cast up at 7½d. per 1000 [ens]; minion 7¾d., nonpareil 8½d., ruby 9d., pearl 9½d., diamond 11½d., head and white lines included.

Here we have the piece-rates for the simplest form of the work; if the language be foreign, if the matter involve special difficulty, if any other variation or extra be required, the scale will be found to provide for the case, and to specify the amount of extra remuneration due in respect of the particular departures from the standard work which the compositor may be required to make."[1] In industries whose "output consists of a limited range of staple articles, more or less uniform in character, and produced in considerable quantities, year after year, by identical or very similar processes of manufacture,"[2] experience shows that technical experts can calculate with close accuracy how large the various allowances ought to be.

§ 6. For operations which have not been standardised by frequent use, such as the great bulk of repairing work, and, during the period of their novelty, all new operations of which experience is lacking, the task of calculating these allowances correctly is naturally much more difficult. But of late years it has been made easier by the device of "elementary rate-fixing." This device is based on the fact that the great bulk of industrial operations consist of some out of a comparatively small number of elementary movements combined together in various ways. As a consequence of this fact, it is possible, by determining from experience the time appropriate for each elementary operation, to calculate beforehand the time appropriate for new complex jobs which have never been done before. Of course the process of combining any set of elements can be performed more rapidly by men who undertake it frequently than by those to whom the task falls on compara-

[1] *Report on Standard Price Rates*, 1900, p. xvi.

[2] Schloss, *Report on Gain-sharing*, p. 113. For a detailed account of the arrangements by which piece-scales in the United States are adjusted to variations in the sizes and patterns of products, the materials used and the physical conditions of the work, cf. McCabe, *The Standard Rate in American Trade Unions*, chapter i.

tively rare occasions, and, therefore, our reckoning of the
piece-rate appropriate to any job will be somewhat different
according as it is, or is not, carried out often enough to make it
worth while for a group of workmen to become specialised upon
it. But this difficulty is *comparatively* unimportant. The
general character of the device of elementary rate-fixing is
illustrated in the following description : " Suppose the work to
be planing a surface on a piece of cast iron. In the ordinary
system of piece-work the rate-fixer would look through his
records of work done by the planing machine until he found
a piece of work as nearly as possible similar to the proposed
job, and then guess at the time required to do the new piece
of work. Under the elementary system, however, some such
analysis as the following would be made :

WORK DONE BY MAN.

Minutes.

Time to lift piece from floor to planer table

Time to level and set work true on table .

Time to put on stops and bolts

Time to remove stops and bolts

Time to remove piece to floor .

Time to clean machine

WORK DONE BY MACHINE.

Time to rough off cut $\frac{1}{4}$ in. thick, 4 ft. long, $2\frac{1}{2}$ in. wide

Time to rough off cut $\frac{1}{8}$ in. thick, 3 ft. long, 12 in. wide, etc.

Time to finish cut 4 ft. long, $2\frac{1}{2}$ in. wide .

Time to finish cut 3 ft. long, 12 in. wide, etc. .

Total

Add — per cent for unavoidable delays .

It is evident that this job consists of a combination of
elementary operations, the time to do each of which can be
readily determined by observation, and, while this exact combination of operations may never occur again, elementary operations similar to some of those given will be performed in
differing combinations almost every day in the same shop.
The rate-fixer soon becomes so familiar with the time for each
of the elements that he can write them down from memory.
For the part of the work which is done by the machine he
refers to tables, which are made out for each machine, giving
the time required for any combination of breadth, depth, and

length of cut."[1]   This method is not, of course, perfect; for to determine what interval shall be allowed for passing from one elementary process to another is still a matter of more or less arbitrary judgment.[2]   Nevertheless, the method undoubtedly makes it feasible to ascertain what rate of wage is a fair one in a number of jobs, for which, apart from it, this could not possibly be done.

§ 7. Thirdly, allowance must be made for differences in the assistance which different workpeople receive in their work from the co-operation of managing power.   When the organisation of a factory is bad, so that men are kept waiting for their material, and so on, a man of given efficiency will be able to produce a smaller output, and, therefore, ought to be paid a larger piece-wage, than when the organisation is good. That this point is very important is suggested by the following comment of an experienced observer : " The methods and distribution of work vary surprisingly in different places, and the real wage received is greatly affected by the degree of organising and administrative ability that may happen to be possessed by the person in command.   It is a common thing for groups of workers employed in different rooms of the same factory, doing precisely the same work under identical outward conditions, and at the same piece-work rates, to show weekly general averages, one of which will be always steadily larger than the other." [3]   It is obvious that very great difficulties—not the least of them being that the quality of the management in all firms is liable to vary from time to time—must be met with in any attempt to calculate with accuracy the allowances that ought to be made under this head.   These difficulties cannot be completely overcome.   When, however, they seem likely to be serious, they may, to some extent, be met by the establishment, as an adjunct to the piece-wage system, of a minimum time-wage, below which the earnings of workmen of average quality shall in no circumstances be allowed to fall.   Strong trade unions generally aim at securing this,[4] and the Minimum Wage (Coal Miners) Act enforces it by law.   This arrangement,

---

[1] *Engineering Magazine*, 1901, p. 624.
[2] Cf. Hoxie, *Scientific Management and Labour*, p. 51.
[3] Black, *Makers of our Clothes*, p. 145.
[4] Cf. Cole, *The Payment of Wages*, p. 4.

in effect, makes an allowance for *extremes* of incapable management. It also makes an allowance for accidental fluctuations of management. Within any factory or mine, in
which managing ability stands on the whole at the average
level, there will necessarily occur from time to time accidental
variations in the facilities afforded to individual workmen in
the conduct of their operations. " Suppose a gang is unloading
coal cars at so much per ton, and the switching crew is tardy
in moving away empties and setting in loaded cars, and so
keeps them idle for considerable periods, or suppose that, in
setting in the new cars, it places them badly, so that the men
have an extra long throw and work at a disadvantage. Again,
the workmen may be unable to make fair wages through no
fault of their own. Suppose, once more, a working gang is
made up by the foreman so that green men are mixed with
skilled, and these green men by their awkwardness cut down
the output of the whole gang. Here, again, if they are
working at piece-rates, their earnings are reduced without
their fault." [1] On the average of a long period, no doubt,
accidents of this kind would be spread fairly evenly among
all the workpeople employed, so that everybody would get
approximately fair wages on the whole. Wide occasional
variations from a man's ordinary weekly wages are, however,
injurious, and ought, if possible, to be prevented. The addition of a properly constructed minimum time-wage does prevent
them. In order that it may provide against extremes of bad
management and against these accidental fluctuations, without
also bringing about other and unintended consequences, it
must possess the following characteristics. First, when the
minimum time-wage is introduced, the general level of the
prevailing system of piece-rates should be slightly lowered;
for, if this is not done, the average efficiency-wage paid in the
industry is, in effect, raised ; and that is an unintended consequence. A corollary is that the minimum time-wage should
change when the general average piece-rate of a district
changes. Secondly, the minimum time-wage should be
such as to yield somewhat lower day earnings to the man of
normal efficiency than such a man might expect to earn, with

[1] Going, *Principles of Industrial Engineering*, p. 123.

average good fortune, upon piece-wages. For, otherwise, the stimulus to effort, which piece-wages are designed to afford, will be, in great measure, destroyed, and, as a result, output may be much reduced; and this is a second unintended consequence. Thirdly, provision should somehow be made to secure that the full minimum time-wage is only payable to workmen of normal capacity. If it is a perfectly general minimum, it will imply—yet a third unintended consequence —an enforced enhancement, above the general level, of the efficiency wages of incompetent men. There is, therefore, required a rule, such as is provided under the British Minimum Wage (Coal Miners) Act, that those workmen who frequently fail to turn out a stipulated amount of output in a normal week, when they are not hindered by accident, sickness, or abnormality in their work-place, shall be placed outside the scope of the minimum time-wage.

CHAPTER XVI

§ 1. As between persons exactly similar in quality fair wages mean, in accordance with what is said in § 1 of the last chapter but one, equal wages, subject only to adjustment for differences in the incidental advantages enjoyed ; and they mean this in all circumstances whatever. As between dissimilar persons fair wages mean, in like manner, in any given set of circumstances, wages which are proportioned to efficiency and which, therefore, bear to one another a certain definite numerical relation. At first sight it may be supposed that this numerical relation, like the relation of equality required for fairness between similar persons, will be the same in all circumstances. This, however, is not so ; for the reason that the comparative efficiencies of different persons possessing given qualities and capacities are not the same in all circumstances. It is the task of the present chapter, to make this matter clear. For that purpose it is convenient to distinguish differences between workpeople under two heads : (1) differences in the degrees of a given kind of ability ; (2) differences in the kinds of ability that they severally possess. I shall begin by ignoring differences of kind, and assume that there is only one kind of ability distributed to different people in different degrees.

§ 2. The key here is given by Marshall in his discussion of the fertility of land. He shows, it will be remembered, that, even when we are considering only fertility in respect of one kind of crop—which corresponds to my one " kind " of ability—the fertilities of two dissimilar pieces of land do not bear to one another a single numerical relation which is the same in all circumstances. On the contrary, this relation

will be different in different states of demand, different
conditions of capital supply, and so on; and it may even
happen that a piece of land, which is more fertile than another
in one set of circumstances, will be the less fertile of the two
in another set. In like manner we now find that the net
product (conceived as marginal) and, therefore, the efficiency
of workman A, is liable to bear a numerical relation to the
net product (similarly conceived) of workman B, which varies
as the supply of tools and so on, with which their labour is
assisted, varies. Thus, though in any given set of conditions
there is some definite numerical relation between the wages
of the two men which is fair, this relation does not depend
simply upon their personal qualities, but is liable to change as
external circumstances change.

§ 3. Marshall's analysis of fertility suggests the further
inference that progress tends in a general way to level up
the efficiency of workers possessing less ability relatively to
that of workers possessing more ability, and so to make the
fair ratio between their wages approach more closely towards
unity. He writes: "Independently of any change in the
suitability of the prevailing crops and method of cultivation
of special soils, there is a constant tendency towards equality
in the value of different soils. In the absence of any special
cause to the contrary, the growth of population and wealth
will make the poorer soils gain on the richer."[1] If this is
so, it would seem that an analogous proposition ought to hold
good of workpeople possessing different degrees of ability
engaged in producing the same thing. Marshall's proposition
can be rigidly proved for pieces of land which differ from
one another in such wise that the yield to an rth unit of
investment in one exceeds the yield to an rth unit in the
other by the same constant amount for all values of r.
Marshall illustrates this case by means of a diagram.[2] But,
of course, pieces of land need not be related to one another
in this way. It may be that acre A yields a lower return
than acre B for each dose of investment up to the Rth dose,
and thereafter yields a progressively greater return. In this

---

[1] *Principles of Economics*, p. 162.
[2] *Ibid.* p. 162, footnote.

case acre B is the worse when (R+k) doses are being invested, but its rentability—which is a measure of its fertility—so far from approaching towards that of acre A, is likely to fall further behind it, when a rising demand for the products of land causes the number of doses to increase beyond (R+k). Hence the question whether or not the rentabilities of acres of different capacities for producing a given crop tend towards equality as demand grows depends upon what sort of relation usually holds between what Marshall calls the produce-curves (*i.e.* the lists of yields to various doses of investment) of different acres picked at random. In my judgment the usual (probable) relation is such as to warrant Marshall's conclusion.[1] If this is so, we may add, by parity of reasoning, that the wage rates, that tend to be paid and are "fair" between workpeople possessing different degrees of the same ability, will tend towards equality as population and wealth increase.

§ 4. Account has next to be taken of the fact that men are born with different *kinds* of ability as well as with different degrees of it. No doubt, it is *possible* for two men or two acres of land to differ from one another in such a way that the ratio between their capacities, when the price of capital stands at any given level, is the same for all purposes. This, however, is not likely to happen often. With capital at a given price, one man will generally stand in one relation to another in respect, say, of physical strength and in a different relation in respect, say, of mathematical ability; just as one acre will be 10 per cent better than another for growing barley but 20 per cent better for growing wheat. Indeed, it may easily happen that the order of merit between two men is different for different purposes. Mr. Tunney has the

---

[1] If the produce-curves for two acres are parallel to one another, then, as Marshall shows, whatever the shape of these curves, an increase of demand for the product (say wheat) makes the rentability of the inferior acre a larger proportion than before of the rentability of the other. If the curves are straight lines and one lies above the other throughout its length, the same thing is true, even though the curves are not parallel. If the curves are straight lines and cut one another, it is not true. If they are straight lines and if they coincide initially (*i.e.* in respect of the first dose of investment) the ratio between the rentabilities of the two acres is the same in all states of demand. If they are not parallel and are not straight lines, no general statement can be made. These results are easily demonstrated by means of simple diagrams.

advantage of Herr Einstein in a boxing ring but not in a laboratory. It follows that, when either the public demands for the services which different sorts of ability can render change relatively to one another (whether as a result of changes in taste or of changes in the distribution of income among people with different tastes), or when developments of technique alter the relative importance of different sorts of ability in producing services and things, (1) it will be profitable to alter the relative amounts of capital invested in training different types of men, and (2) the relative efficiencies of different types, both net and gross (*i.e.* reckoned as including interest on capital), and so the relative earnings that are "fair" between these types, will change. Thus, when the war raised greatly the demand for the services of common soldiers, the efficiency and earnings of unskilled workers rose while those of musicians fell; and, had the war gone on for ever, children born with a special faculty for soldiering would have had a relatively high, and those born with a special faculty for music, a relatively low, expectation of earnings. On the other hand, technical developments enabling a great many industrial operations to be performed by elaborate machines associated with highly skilled attendants cause the efficiencies and the earnings expectation of intelligent children to rise relatively to those of children born with the temperament and physique of an ox. Again, if an invention causes blindness to be less of a handicap in some occupation than it has been hitherto, blind men will tend to flow into that occupation and other men out of it, until finally, their relative efficiency having risen, the earnings of blind men are everywhere slightly higher than before relatively to those of other men. With a wider sweep but a like aim Bateson wrote: "The fact that families or individuals rose into prominence or dropped into obscurity when the great industrial development of this country began, does not prove that the strains from which they came ought previously and in differing circumstances to have been in different relative positions. In various circumstances various qualities are required for success."[1] The efficiencies of different types of people

[1] *Biological Fact and the Structure of Society*, p. 32.

are thus determined, not merely by their natures alone, nor yet by their natures in conjunction with the supply price of capital, but by these things together with the state of demand for different sorts of service and the state of industrial technique in various occupations. It is not possible, I think, to say what kind of change in relative efficiencies, and so in relative earnings—a scattering or a tendency towards greater equality — future developments in tastes and technique are likely to bring about.

§ 5. The significance of the preceding analysis becomes apparent when the question is asked whether or not the wage ruling in some one industry is or is not fair relatively to that ruling in others. The main issue here is, of course, concerned with the relation between the wages of *average* workpeople in different industries. For, when the wage that is fair for an average worker in one industry relatively to that of an average worker in another is known, to discover the allowance that should be made for those above or below the average is a comparatively simple matter. If we knew, by direct judgment or otherwise, that these average workers were in all respects exactly alike, we should know also, in accordance with what was said in Chapter XIV. § 1, that fair wages would be equal wages. But, if we do not know that the workers in the industries we are comparing are exactly alike, the problem is much more complicated. It is true, as was shown in the section cited above, that, if wages are not proportioned to efficiency—as measured by marginal net product multiplied by price—they cannot stand in a fair relation to one another. But it is not true that, if they are proportioned to efficiency in this sense, they *must* stand in a fair relation. They only do this if a second condition is also fulfilled; namely, if labour as between the industries is distributed ideally, *i.e.* so as to maximise the national dividend in the wide sense of Chapter IX. § 2.[1] How in these circumstances is it possible in practice to decide whether or not the wage ruling in one industry relatively to others is or is not fair? In certain conditions a workable method is available. It may be possible to find some model, or standard, year, in which there was a general agreement

[1] Cf. *ante*, Chap. XIV. § 1.

among employers and employed in an industry that the wage rate there was fair relatively to that ruling in other industries. This wage rate will be our starting-point. Having ascertained it, we try to discover by statistical inquiry in what proportion wage rates in other industries have changed since our standard year. Suppose that they have risen by 20 per cent. Then, if no obvious change has occurred in the comparative average qualities of the workpeople in our industry and in other industries, we conclude that the fair wage for our industry now is the wage that ruled there in the standard year *plus* a rise of 20 per cent. This method, which during the pre-war period was, in effect, pursued for a long time by Conciliation Boards in the coal industry, often enables a reasonably close determination of fair wages to be made. The analysis of the present chapter shows, however, that it only does this, and is, therefore, only applicable, provided that nothing has happened meanwhile to modify appreciably the relative aggregate demands for the kinds and degrees of ability that are chiefly utilised in our industry and in other industries respectively. If the popular taste for horse-racing had greatly expanded and that for litigation greatly diminished since the date of our model year, the abilities which go to make a good jockey would have become much more valuable relatively to those that go to make a good lawyer, and the fair wage for jockeys as against lawyers would now be much higher than it was in that year. So far, of course, as the relative supplies of the two sorts of abilities depend, not on natural endowment, but on differences in the amount of money invested in the training and nurture of persons initially similar, we should expect that the number of persons entering the occupation where the demand had risen would increase relatively to the number entering the other, and, therefore, that after a time the difference between the new and the old fair relation would be *pro tanto* lessened. Thus a falling off in the relative demand for skilled as compared with unskilled workers would alter the fair relation between the wages of the two classes to a less extent in the long run than it did immediately. If we may suppose that a relative rise in the demand for the services of people possessing the natural endowments of a jockey, as compared with those possessing the natural endowments of a lawyer, would cause the former class to have relatively more children—sharing, we may presume, their natural endowments—the difference between the new fair relation, as ultimately attained, and the old one, would be lessened still further.

CHAPTER XVII

INTERFERENCE TO RAISE WAGES IN PLACES AND OCCUPATIONS WHERE THEY ARE ALREADY FAIR

§ 1. In the analysis of Chapter XIV. attention was confined to the effects of interference designed to force up wages in places and occupations where they are unfairly low to a rate equivalent to that paid for similar labour enjoying similar incidental advantages elsewhere. It is sometimes claimed, however, that wages which are low and fair, as well as those which are low and unfair, may often be forced up with advantage to the national dividend. We have now to inquire how far and in what circumstances this claim is valid.

§ 2. In his very interesting book, *Wages in Practice and Theory*, Mr. Rowe urges strongly that the forcing up of wage rates may stimulate employers to improve their methods of organisation and technique, not only where, as in the case described above on p. 562, exploitation is taking place, but throughout the general body of industry.[1] The extent to which this kind of reaction occurs must depend on how far, in different industries, the best known practice is already adopted by the main body of the employers there and on the openings that there are for bettering that practice. But *some* favourable reaction may be looked for not infrequently. As a result of it, the marginal net product of any given quantity of labour of given capacity will be indirectly raised, and the national dividend *pro tanto* enhanced; just as it will be if increased wage rates lead to an improvement in the workpeople's capacity in the manner described in the chapter that follows. This consideration creates some presumption in

[1] *Loc. cit.* pp. 204-214.

favour of a policy that would push wages upwards gradually and by small degrees, even where they are already fair and where there is no question of reactions on workpeople's capacity. In this chapter, however, reactions of this kind are left out of account, and our problem is studied on the assumption that employers' technique and methods of organisation are not appreciably affected by wage policy.

§ 3. First, as was implied in the course of Chapter XIV. § 2, fair wages at particular points may sometimes emerge as the result of a conflict and cancelling among two or more unfair elements. Thus in some place or occupation the value of the marginal net product of labour may be abnormally high because the number of workpeople there is kept down by custom or by heavy costs of entry. If this circumstance operated alone, the wage rate would be unfairly high. But it may also happen that these workpeople are out-bargained by their employers, and compelled to accept a wage less than the value of the marginal net product of their work. If this circumstance operated alone, the wage rate would be unfairly low. Conditions are *possible* in which these opposing tendencies exactly balance one another, so that the resultant wage stands precisely at the level of fairness. But this fairness embodies two elements of unfairness, interference with one of which would not benefit, while interference with the other would benefit, the national dividend. The interest of the dividend requires that the wage rate should not be fair, but should be put at a level that embodies the former of the two cancelling elements of unfairness. Interference, therefore, is desirable in spite of the fact that the wage is fair. It is obvious, however, that an exact cancelling of elements of unfairness that act in opposite senses is, in a high degree, improbable. Consequently, wage rates that, as wholes, are fair cannot reasonably be suspected, except on very special grounds, of embodying any element of unfairness. Hence the considerations set out in this paragraph, though they point to complications in certain sorts of unfair wages, are only of academic interest as regards fair wages.

§ 4. Secondly, in order that, in any particular place or occupation, a wage that is *fair* as compared with other places or occupations may also be *right* from the point of view of the national dividend, a certain definite condition must be fulfilled. This condition is that in places or occupations in general workpeople are receiving as wages the value of the marginal net product of their work. If they are receiving less than this, they are without the normal inducement to give as much work as the general interest demands. The pushing up of their wages to a level that equates demand price and supply price would lead to an increase in the size of the dividend more than sufficient to compensate them for their extra sacrifice of leisure. Now, when things have settled down in more or less stable conditions, the play of economic forces tends to secure that in industries in general wages do correspond to the value of the marginal net product of labour. But conditions are liable to change, on account, for example, of new mechanical discoveries, the accumulation of capital, the opening up of foreign trade, or an expansion in the supply of the substance used as money. Any one of these changes necessarily tends to raise the value (in money) of the marginal net product of labour throughout occupations generally. The old wage, therefore, though still fair, will, nevertheless, be too low. It is to the interest of the national dividend that all wages should be raised. If, however, fairness in every individual wage rate was regarded as a conclusive reason against altering it, this change could never come about. Suppose, for example, that wage rates over the whole of industry were settled by Boards of Conciliation and Arbitration, whether wholly voluntary or partly controlled by State authority; and that the principle which each of these Boards followed was that of making its own wage rate equal to that paid for similar work in other occupations. The result, in the face of changing general conditions, would be a complete *impasse*. In like manner, it is conceivable that workpeople might, even in stable conditions, have their wages "exploited" everywhere to exactly the same extent, and for this reason might be everywhere receiving less than the value of their marginal net product. Here again a rigid rule against interfering with fair rates would make any correction of the abuse impossible. Hence it follows that fairness in a wage rate must not be taken as a conclusive reason against interference to raise it.

§ 5. If it were the fact, either that workpeople were exploited over the general body of industry, or that, over the general body of industry, wages were settled by Joint Boards whose sole principle of action was to establish fairness, the results of the preceding section would be of great practical importance. There would be a wide field over which interference to raise wages that are already fair would benefit the national dividend. As a matter of fact, however, the general body of industry is not controlled by Joint Boards actuated by the single principle of fairness, and there is good reason to believe that the places and occupations in which workpeople are exploited form but a small part of the whole. Hence these special reasons for interfering with wage rates on some occasions, in spite of their being " fair," are not of wide application. It must, however, be conceded that, when a large and sudden change, such as might be brought about by the issue of a large quantity of paper money, takes place in the money costs of living, money wages in general will not respond immediately, and, therefore, for a time real wages all round will tend to be too low. Hence a policy which only interferes to raise unfair wages will lose opportunities for speeding up the required adjustment. If an external authority could force wages in any industry or group of industries from that old level, which is at the moment still " fair," to the new level which will be " fair " in a short time, it would benefit the national dividend. It will, of course, be understood that, when the money cost of living undergoes a large and sudden change, the response on the side of money wages, which it is the function of the authority to expedite, is not the same in all circumstances. If a given rise in the money cost of living is a part of an equivalent rise in prices generally, caused by a banking or currency change, the proper response is a rise in money wages sufficient to make real wages equal to what they were before. If the given rise in the cost of living is a part of an equivalent rise in prices generally, caused by diminished facilities for production, such as might result from the destruction of real capital in war, the proper response is either no rise in money wages, or, at all events, a rise less than sufficient to establish the old real wage; for the real demand for labour will have fallen off. Again, if the given rise in the cost of living is the result of a real rise in the cost of producing the things on which wages are predominantly spent, unaccompanied by any similar rise in the real cost of producing other things, the proper response is, for the same reason, either no rise in money wages, or, at all events, a rise less than sufficient to establish the old real wage. These distinctions are not always perceived clearly. There is also another complication of a different kind. The "cost of living" is not a single definite thing, which necessarily changes in equal proportion for all classes of the population. It may reasonably be argued that, since better-to-do persons, accustomed to more varied purchases, have a greater power of substituting things that have risen less for things that have risen more in price than poorer persons have, the sort of price movement that took place during the war really raised the cost of living proportionately more the lower we descend in the scale of earnings. This consideration affords a defence for the practice adopted in the cost-of-living sliding scales, introduced during and immediately after the war, of making wages vary less than in proportion to the Board of Trade cost-of-living figure, except for persons in the lower wage-groups. Had wages been raised equally for all wage-earners, the relative position of better-paid workers, as against worse-paid workers, would, it might be argued, have been improved and not kept constant.

§ 6. We have now to consider a much broader claim. This is that, in any occupation where wages are low, whether or not they are fair (relatively to the degree of efficiency among the workers engaged in them), they ought to be raised far enough to yield a decent subsistence to the average worker; a "decent subsistence" for the average man and the average woman respectively being interpreted in the light of the fact that the former has, and the latter has not, to support a family. Some approach to a recognition of this claim was made in a modification introduced into the British Trades Boards Act of 1918, as against the original

Act of 1909. Whereas under the original Act a condition precedent to the establishment of a Trade Board in an industry is that wages there are *exceptionally* low, under the later Act it is sufficient that the trade be unorganised and, therefore, likely to be in receipt of wages *unduly* low. Elsewhere the claim has been accepted explicitly. Thus the South Australian Industrial Arbitration Act 1912 provides that "the Court shall not have power to order or prescribe wages which do not secure to the employees affected a living wage. 'Living wage' means a sum sufficient for the normal and reasonable needs of the average employee living in the locality where the work under consideration is done or is being done." [1] In the Western Australian Act it is laid down that "no minimum rate of wages or other remuneration shall be prescribed, which is not sufficient to enable the average worker to whom it applies to live in reasonable comfort, having regard to any domestic obligations to which such average worker would be ordinarily subject." [2] In the New South Wales Act of 1918 these general rules are given a statistical interpretation. The Board of Trade is ordered, after public inquiry into the cost of living, to declare from year to year what shall be the living wages respectively of male and female adult employees (other than those who are abnormally inefficient) in the State or any defined area thereof, and no industrial agreement shall be entered into, and no award made, for wages lower than such living wages. In the Arbitration Court of the Australian Commonwealth Mr. Justice Higgins proceeded (as regards unskilled workers) on the same principles, seeking to establish basic wages dependent on the cost of living for a normal man presumed to be the head of a family of five persons and for a normal woman presumed to support herself alone. [3] In most of the American States, which have minimum wage laws for women, the minimum

---

[1] *Bulletin of the U.S. Bureau of Labour Statistics*, No. 167, pp. 165-6.
[2] *Ibid.* p. 167.
[3] Cf. his interesting book, *A New Province for Law and Order.* For skilled workers he aimed at adding to the basic wage "a secondary wage," in the determination of which a dominant part should be played by considerations as to what the trade would bear. It will be noticed that, on Mr. Justice Higgins' principles, the *real* rate of wages for unskilled workers would never change at all.

wage is defined as one sufficient to supply the necessary cost of living and to maintain the employee in health.[1]

§ 7. In popular discussion the issue which these proposals raise is sometimes blurred by a confused idea that a living wage implies, for workmen of normal capacity in any industry which enjoys it, a "living income." This, of course, is not so. A living wage, as ordinarily conceived, for a man, is a wage that will enable the person who receives it, if he has an average family to maintain and if he has average good fortune in the matter of sickness, to earn an income sufficient for a good life. But a rate of wages that will achieve this end in these conditions will not achieve it for a man with a family in excess of the average or subjected to an unusual amount of sickness.[2] Nor can the "living wage" take account of the fact that some workpeople need to support parents who are past work as well as their own children, or of the further fact that the wives of some workpeople contribute nothing towards the family income, while those of others contribute largely. Moreover, a wage for the breadwinner, which would provide a "living" for his family at one stage of its growth, would be quite inadequate at another stage. This consideration is very important. Dr. Bowley, for example, on the basis of his investigations into the condition of the poor at Reading in 1912, estimated that the minimum expenditure necessary for the attainment of a reasonable standard of living "at marriage would be 16s. weekly and would rise gradually to about 25s. in five years and 28s. in ten years, provided that there were four children all surviving. It would remain at 28s. for another five years, and then fall back to 16s. as the children became self-supporting."[3] For women workers the connection between living wage and living income is even more remote, in view of the great differences between the positions of women mainly supported

---

[1] Cf. *Bulletin of the U.S.A. Bureau of Labour*, No. 285. These laws, so far as they affect minors, do not stipulate for a wage that shall cover subsistence, but merely for one that is "suitable" and "not unreasonably low."

[2] Mr. Rowntree has shown that in York, if a minimum wage based on a family of as many as five dependent children were established, no less than 20 per cent of the children born would be inadequately provided for for five years or more (*The Human Needs of Labour*, p. 41).

[3] *The Measurement of Social Phenomena*, pp. 179-80.

by their husbands, self-supporting single women, and women who are themselves the principal bread-winners of a family. These various considerations taken together make it plain that the enforcement in any industry of a living wage, in any plausible sense of that term, would go a very little way towards ensuring a " living income " even to those workpeople who regularly received it. Our natural desire to ensure in every industry a living income is thus not really relevant to the " living wage." The policy of forcing up wage rates in industries employing workpeople of such a low grade that fair rates, as defined in Chapter XIV., are less than living rates—however we may choose to define these—has, therefore, to be considered separately on its own merits.

§ 8. An argument by which it is widely supported is as follows: " An industry, which uses up the human capital without replacing it, is not self-supporting and does positive harm to the community. When, therefore, a woman is partially maintained by some other source, such as by a father, husband, etc., the industry which employs her is being subsidised from these other sources to the extent by which her wages fall short of proper maintenance." [1] In other words, to allow the low wages, which make this subsidisation necessary, to continue, is to allow a process to go on, by which productive power and, consequently, the national dividend of the future, are steadily eaten away. This argument is invalid. It depends upon an ambiguity in the phrase " uses up." If the setting to work of people at some industry wears out and destroys productive powers, which, had they not been set to work in that industry, would be available to augment the national dividend, then the destruction of this productive power ought strictly to be debited against that industry. Its social net product falls short of its private net product to that extent. But there is no general presumption that an industry employing low-grade workers and paying them a wage equivalent to what they could obtain elsewhere is using up human capital in this sense. For, if it did not employ them, they would either be employed in another industry at the same wage or they would not be

[1] Women's Supplement to *New Statesman*, Feb. 21, 1914.

employed at all; and in either event there is no reason to suppose that their productive powers would be worn out any less soon. The industry, therefore, only uses up their productive powers in the sense of using or employing them, not in the sense of wearing them out. Hence there is no difference between the (marginal) social and the (marginal) private net product of the work done in it, and no damage is caused to the national dividend by its continuance. Nor is this conclusion affected by the fact—when it is a fact—that the workers engaged in the industry are "subsidised" from other sources; because, if they were not engaged in this industry, they would still have to be "subsidised" to at least as great an extent. It is true, as was argued at length in Chapter XIV., that, if an occupation or section of an occupation is maintaining itself in being by its power to pay to workpeople of a given grade of capacity less wages than such workpeople *could*, and, apart from the existence of that occupation or section of occupation, *would* earn elsewhere, then the continuance in existence of that occupation or section involves a waste of the resources of the community. Here there is true parasitism. The essence of it, however, lies in the fact that workers are paid less than they could and would earn elsewhere. When this is not happening there is no parasitism, even though workers are being paid much less than is required to maintain them in independent self-support. The thesis that industries which pay less than "fair wages" ought to be forbidden by law to do this, even though such prohibition involves their destruction, is quite different from, and lends no support to, the thesis that industries which pay less than a "living wage" to workpeople who are in fact worth, for all purposes, less than a living wage, ought to be subjected to a similar prohibition. This common argument, therefore, breaks down, and our problem must be studied without reference to it.

§ 9. We suppose that a particular industry is employing low-grade workers, and that these workers are being paid a wage, which, in view of their comparative inefficiency, is fair relatively to that paid in other industries; and we suppose further that equality of efficiency wages in this industry and elsewhere is accompanied both by equality in the values of marginal net products there and elsewhere and also by a general equality between wages and these values. In these conditions, if the wage rate in our industry is forced up, a strong inducement is offered to employers to distribute inferior workpeople away from the occupations in which they are specially privileged, leaving these occupations to be occupied exclusively by more capable men. For example, the establishment of different (real) trade union rates of wages in different towns is met, in the main, by the abler workpeople gravitating to the towns with higher real wages, just as the establishment of the "dockers' tanner" in 1889 was met by the substitution, in part, of strong immigrants from the country for the weaker men among the old dockers. If this class of reaction occurs, it will not really happen to any substantial extent that the workers aimed at are paid higher wages than before. All that will be accomplished will be a redistribution of workers of different grades between different occupations. Consequently, no significant effect, either favourable or adverse, will be produced upon the size of the national dividend. The attempt at interference in favour of particular workpeople will, in fact, be parried by evasion. Let us suppose, however, that for some reason this reshuffling of workpeople is impracticable. Then, unless, of course, the demand for labour is perfectly inelastic, it must happen that some labour is ejected from employment in the industry where wages have been raised, with the result that, according to circumstances, it is either not employed at all or is employed elsewhere in conditions such that the value of the net product of most of it is less than it was. That this must be so follows directly from the analysis sketched out in Chapter XIV. The inference is that, employers' technique being given, apart from reactions on workpeople's capacity, to force up wages to a "living" standard in an industry where the fair wage is less than a living wage must injure the national dividend.

§ 10. At first sight it is natural to suppose that the damage done will be roughly proportionate to the number of occupations to which the interference extends; so that the dividend will be reduced three times as much if a living wage is enforced in all of three similar industries, where the fair wage is less than a living wage, as it would be if only one of them was touched. This, however, is an underestimate. When labour—and, consequently, capital also—is driven out of one occupation, it moves, in the ordinary course, into others; and, though it produces there less than it was producing before, it still produces a good deal. If only a little labour and capital are thus sent seeking a new home, and there is a large field open to them, the new contribution of each unit will be worth very nearly as much as the old contribution. But, if, with a given field open to them, more labour and capital are sent to seek work, they will have to be pushed into less highly valued uses, and the new contribution made by each unit will be less. Hence a doubling or trebling of the amount of interference, and, consequently, of the quantity of labour and capital turned loose, will involve more than a doubling or trebling of the damage done to the dividend. This consideration must be borne in mind when any inference is attempted from Australian experience as to the probable effect of forcing up the wages of low-paid industries in this country. For " industrialism is relatively simple in form and limited in extent in the Australian colonies. Agriculture is the chief occupation, and this, being untouched by the arbitration laws, is a vent for any labour or capital driven out of the industries." [1] In this country the proportionate part played by agriculture is enormously smaller, and, therefore, the vent available, if a wide-reaching policy of forcing up industrial wages were attempted, would be far less extensive. Moreover, it is practically certain that in the United Kingdom this policy could not be applied to industry without being applied to agriculture also. The danger to the national dividend would, therefore, be very much greater than Australian experience suggests.

§ 11. Up to this point we have tacitly assumed that the old-established practice of disregarding conjugal and family estate in fixing wages will be maintained. Of recent years,

[1] Chapman, *Work and Wages*, vol. ii. p. 263. Since the passing of the Industrial Arbitration (Further Amendment) Act of 1918, it is no longer wholly true, for New South Wales, that agriculture is untouched by the arbitration laws.

however, considerable attention has been paid to proposals for regulating wages on a family basis. These proposals involve a departure from the ideal of fair wages even larger than is involved in the policy of " a living wage " as described above. For they require that different men of equal quality shall be paid wages that differ in accordance with the number of children that they have. During the Great War the wages paid to soldiers (pay and maintenance allowances being counted together) were, in effect, regulated on this principle; and the war bonuses on account of the increase in the cost of living, that were paid to members of the police force, were also on a family basis. It has long been understood that a public authority, if it chooses, is free to adopt a plan of this kind for the payment of its own servants, but it has been felt that no such arrangement could be introduced into the general body of industry without causing whatever unemployment there is at any time to be concentrated upon men with large families. In the last few years, however, there has been a very marked movement in several countries towards what has come to be called the " family wage system." In Germany, owing to the serious fall in real wages, a man with a family cannot live on the ordinary rate. In consequence of this, " the system of paying extra allowances in respect of family is now very widespread. An analysis, from this point of view, of the terms of current collective agreements was recently undertaken by the German Ministry of Labour. It shows that, while there are scarcely any trades in which the family-wage principle is not applied to some extent, there are a number of important industries in which it is universally recognised, amongst the latter being coal-mining, mechanical engineering, textile and paper and cardboard manufacture." [1] In France the system first began to assume importance in 1916, and has since developed so far that, by 1923, some $2\frac{1}{2}$ million workers were affected by it. In separate industries " compensation funds " are established, to which the separate employers contribute in proportion to their wages bill, and from which the whole of the family allowances are paid.[2] By this device, an employer makes the same total payment in respect of each worker employed by

---

[1] *Labour Gazette*, March 1923, pp. 86-7.   [2] *Ibid.* p. 86.

him whatever the size of his family, and there is, therefore, no inducement to anybody to engage single men in preference to married men. In Belgium, Holland and Austria this system has also had some vogue.[1] It is easy to see that, on plans of this type, a given aggregate wage payment would yield a bigger direct return in social benefit than it would have done under a living-wage rule of the ordinary type. But the family wage, in any form, is open to a serious objection from another side. It necessarily implies the taxing of bachelors in order to provide a bounty for men with large families—a sort of bounty on parenthood. I do not now raise the question whether this is, in principle, a good or a bad thing; a question in connection with which it is relevant to observe that those bachelors who afterwards marry get compensation in later life for the damage they have suffered in youth. Plainly, however, different bachelors of equal earning power ought to be taxed equally. But, if the family-wage plan is adopted, those of them who happen to work in industries where the proportion of bachelors, as compared with family men, is small will be hit very much more severely than their *confrères* in industries where the proportion of bachelors is large. If taxation is to be raised for the purpose of giving bounties to the heads of large families, it would seem better to raise it through the ordinary machinery of taxation, rather than in this hidden and uneven way. This consideration is applicable to a family-wage system applied universally by State decree to all industries. As against such a system confined to particular industries there is the further objection that it must tend to fill those industries with married men with large families, and to leave there no bachelors to be taxed in their interest.[2] In 1927 New South Wales passed a Family Endowment Act, which provides for a payment of 5s. per week to the mother for each child in families with incomes of less than the official

[1] Cf. Rathbone, *Economic Journal*, 1920, p. 551.
[2] Cf. Heimann, "The Family-Wage Controversy in Germany," *Economic Journal*, December 1923, p. 513. For an account of "family-wage" arrangement in France, cf. Douglas, "Family Allowances and Clearing Funds in France," in the *Quarterly Journal of Economics*, February 1924. An interesting discussion of family wages and alternative forms of family endowment is contained in Miss Rathbone's book, *The Disinherited Family*. Cf. also Cohen, *Family Income Increase*.

living wage for a man and wife without children, plus £13 a year in respect of each child, and raises the necessary revenue by contributions from employers in all industries proportionate to their wages bill.[1]

[1] For an account of this Act cf. *The Quarterly Journal of Economics*, May 1928, pp. 500 *et seq.*

CHAPTER XVIII

§ 1. THE whole of the analysis of the three preceding chapters has been conducted without reference to the effects which interference to raise wages may produce upon the physique, mentality and morale, and so upon the efficiency of the workpeople. But, as we have just seen, certain industries exist whose operations require little or no skill, and in which even the normal so-called able-bodied workers are of an exceedingly low grade. In these industries—simple sewing at home is one of them—even a fair rate of wages, and, still more, an unfair rate, is necessarily an exceedingly low rate. In such industries it seems probable *prima facie* that interference designed to force up wage rates would react upon the capacity of the workpeople and so might indirectly increase the national dividend, even though the direct effects, taken by themselves, would have been adverse. The reaction to be expected is partly physical, resulting from increased strength due to better food and better conditions of life. It is also partly psychological, resulting from a sense of fair treatment, an increased feeling of hopefulness, and the knowledge that, with the increased wage, slack work is more likely to lead to a loss of employment. Hence, in occupations employing exceptionally low-grade workpeople—and an argument of the same kind, though of less force, can be advanced about those employing better workpeople—there would seem to be a stronger case for interference to raise wages than the considerations advanced in the preceding chapters by themselves indicate. This suggestion has now to be examined.

§ 2. It is sometimes thought that light can be thrown

upon it by comparing the capacities of workpeople employed in occupations or firms where the earnings are high and low respectively. It is found that people who earn good money are very much more capable than those who earn bad money, and it is inferred that, if the latter were paid as much as the former, they would thereby be raised to their standard. This reasoning is inadequate. The fact that workpeople in high-wage districts are, in general, more capable than workpeople in low-wage districts does not prove that high wages cause high capacity; for there is available the alternative explanation that high capacity causes high wages. Nor does the fact that workpeople, who have moved from low-wage to high-wage districts, are soon found to be earning the wages proper to these latter districts prove this; for the people most likely to undertake such journeys are just those who feel themselves already more capable and worth a larger wage than their neighbours. All statistical arguments of the above type must be regarded with the greatest suspicion. In order to discover experimentally how increased earnings react upon capacity, we should need to investigate the output of *the same individual workman in the same environment* under both low-wage and high-wage conditions. It is only thus that we could ascertain the extent of the reaction which improved pay would produce in workpeople of different income grades. Unfortunately investigations of this kind are not available. The rapid improvement which took place in the appearance of the men recruited and trained for the new armies in the Great War does, indeed, suggest that human quality is more quickly and completely plastic, at all events in youth, than we had been accustomed formerly to suppose. The good effects, as reported by those who have studied them, of the increased wages that have been awarded by the Trade Boards in the tailoring and box-making industries point in the same direction.[1] These things give ground for hope, but they do not enable us to formulate

---

[1] Cf. Tawney, *Minimum Wages in the Tailoring Trade*, pp. 121-34; and Bulkley, *Minimum Wages in the Box-making Trade*, p. 51. In the box-making industry the workpeople's capacity has also been benefited in an indirect way, because the enforcement of higher rates has induced employers to pay more attention to their training; "every worker has to be trained to earn the minimum, whereas formerly it did not matter how little they earned" (*loc. cit.* p. 51).

any precise conclusions. We are thus in the end thrown back on the vague guess-work called common sense. This suggests that the reaction will be most marked among work-people who are exceedingly poor, and in whom, therefore, there is large scope for physical improvement through better food, clothing and house accommodation; that it will vary with the age of the people affected and with their previous condition; that it is more likely to occur where employment is fairly regular, so that a definite standard of life can be built up, than it is among people whose employment is "casual" and intermittent; and that, the longer the improved payment lasts, the greater is the chance that capacity will benefit to an appreciable extent.

§ 3. In places and occupations, where wages are low because low-grade workpeople are being "exploited" by employers and paid less than they are worth, there is no reason to expect that the forcing of the wage rate up to a fair level will cause any of the people affected to lose their jobs for any length of time; for it will not pay employers to dispense with their services. Consequently, all that has to be considered is the direct effect upon the capacity of the people who actually receive the better wage. It is, therefore, practically certain that there will be some net benefit to the national dividend. Moreover, there is reason to expect that this benefit will be cumulative. If exploitation is allowed, and a bad bargain by workmen leads to a reduction of their capacity and so to a diminution in the value of their marginal net product, they will start for the next round of bargaining from a lower level; if they again get slightly the worse of the deal,— and, being weaker, they are now more likely to do so,—they will again, in the same manner, be driven yet lower. Thus their capacity, as well as the wage they receive, is cumulatively and progressively reduced, and the national dividend suffers thereby a serious injury. If, however, exploitation is prevented and wages are forced up to a fair level, the benefit to capacity will start an upward movement exactly analogous to this downward movement. High earnings will lead to greater capacity; greater capacity will lead to the power of obtaining higher earnings, both because the workers' services are worth more and because, being better off, they are in a stronger position for bargaining; the higher earnings so obtained will react again to increase capacity; and so on cumulatively. This consideration is of special importance among those extremely poor workpeople, whose very poverty, so long as it continues, makes them easy victims to the superior bargaining power of employers. In these circumstances, therefore, the conclusion reached in Chapter XIV. that the national dividend will be increased by the forcing up of wage rates, which are rendered unfairly low by exploitation, is confirmed and enforced when account is taken of reactions upon capacity.

§ 4. In Chapters XIV. and XVII. it was shown that, in certain somewhat special conditions, the forcing up of wage rates, which are either already fair or are unfair from other causes than exploitation, would benefit the national dividend apart from reactions on capacity. A study of these conditions, as there described, makes it evident that, when any of them are present, the forcing up of wage rates may easily produce beneficial reactions on the capacity of the workpeople as a whole, and is extremely unlikely to produce injurious reactions. Here too, therefore, the indirect effects on the dividend operated through capacity are in line with the direct effects. When, however, conditions are such that, apart from reactions on capacity, the forcing up of a wage rate would damage the national dividend, the way in which these reactions will work is much more difficult to determine. The reason is that, in these conditions, some workpeople will be ejected from employment in the place or occupation where the wage is raised, and either reduced to unemployment or, at best, set to work where the value of their output is less than it was before. For, unless one of these things happens, the dividend will not be damaged, and we are now assuming that, apart from reactions on capacity, it is damaged. But, if some workers are made worse off than before, the net effect on capacity will not consist merely of benefit done to those who actually receive the better wage rate, but also of injury done to these others. *Prima facie* it seems reasonable to suppose that, if, after the increase of wage rate in one particular industry, the aggregate sum paid in wages throughout the grand total of industries is less than before, the aggregate capacity of the workpeople as a whole will not be enhanced. The conditions in which an increase of wages in a particular industry may increase the real earnings of wage-earners as a body, in spite of damaging the national dividend, will be examined at length in the course of Part IV. It is evident that the prospects are best when the demand for labour in the occupation whose wage rate is forced up is highly inelastic. From the standpoint of a short period, which alone is relevant to reactions on capacity, the causes making for inelastic demand are, in general, much more powerful than they are from that of a long period. For example, if the wage of any group were forced up, employers would not generally dismiss many of their workpeople so long as existing orders were still in hand. If, then, the "reaction time" of wages upon capacity is fairly rapid, the chances of a favourable reaction may be taken, at all events when the commodity affected by the increased wage rate is not one largely purchased by working men, to be reasonably good. They are particularly so if the rate fixed for any group of workpeople is not raised suddenly much above the existing rate—in which event a large number of dismissals might take place—but is pushed up gradually by small stages. Hence, it may not infrequently happen that, in circumstances where, apart from reactions on capacity, the forcing up of a wage rate would inflict damage on the national dividend, the damage will be at least partially cancelled by these reactions. When a State authority is available to help people who may have been incidentally thrown out of work, the extra State contribution, which is an indirect effect of the forcing up of the wage rate, will make this cancelling benefit somewhat larger than it would have been otherwise. Whether the cancelling benefit will be large enough to outweigh the direct damage to the dividend, against which it has to be balanced, cannot be determined generally, but will depend on the detailed conditions of each separate problem.

§ 5. It should be added that, in any event, such interference to raise wages as is warranted by the considerations set out in the preceding section is essentially a temporary interference. Where wages are paid by the piece it is temporary in form as well as in substance. For, though an enhanced piece-wage, by providing larger earnings, may so improve a workman's capacity that he can produce more pieces in the day, and is thus enabled permanently to make larger earnings at the old piece-rate, it cannot cause him to become worth the new piece-rate. Hence, there is no case for retaining that rate for a longer time than is necessary for its reaction upon capacity to be completed—no case, at least, from the standpoint of the national dividend. If it is maintained for longer than this, it will add nothing further to capacity, but will injure the national dividend by preventing labour from distributing itself among different uses in the most advantageous manner. When wages are paid by time, the interference warranted is no longer temporary in form, and there is no reason why the enhanced time-wage should ever be reduced. But it is temporary in substance, because, after a while, the workpeople, in consequence of their improved capacity, will become worth the new time-wage, and, therefore, this wage will become the "natural" wage, for the maintenance of which no interference is necessary.

CHAPTER XIX

§ 1. In Chapter XVII. we considered the effects of interference designed to raise the wages of a low-paid industry, or part of an industry, above the "fair" level. The centre of the problem was the wage of the "average" worker, and it was tacitly supposed that the rates paid to workers above and below the average would be adjusted according to their comparative efficiencies. We have now to consider a different type of interference, directed not so much towards trades as towards individuals. Granted that the average worker in all — or in most — industries is suitably remunerated, the very inefficient worker in some of them will, on account of his inefficiency, if paid on a like scale, often earn so small a sum of money that the public conscience is shocked. It is widely held that this state of things ought to be prevented by the legal establishment of a national minimum day-wage, below which no workman whatever can be legally engaged. This policy, it must be clearly understood, differs in essence from, and goes much beyond, the mere establishment of a national minimum day-wage from which under-rate workers are exempt, as described in Chapter XV. § 7. It is illustrated —though very imperfectly, since the minimum fixed was very much below the worth of anybody except an extraordinarily inefficient apprentice—by certain of the labour laws of Australasia. The Parliaments of Victoria and South Australia "have decided that no person whatsoever can be employed there in a registered factory, without receiving some minimum remuneration—in Victoria, 2s. 6d. a week, and in South Australia, 4s." [1]

---

[1] Aves, *Report on Wages Boards*, p. 88.

In like manner, the New South Wales Minimum Wage Act of 1908 provided that no workman or shop assistant shall be employed, unless in receipt of a weekly wage of at least 4s., irrespective of any amount earned as overtime.[1] Again, in the Factory Act of New Zealand, it is enacted that every person who is employed in any capacity in a factory shall be entitled to receive from the occupier payment for the work at such rate as is agreed on, in no case less than 5s. per week during the first year of employment in the industry and, thereafter, an annual increase of not less than 3s. weekly till a wage of 20s. per week is attained.[2] This clause in its original form—the form given above is the slightly modified form of the 1907 amendment—was passed in order to prevent persons being employed in factories without "reasonable remuneration in money." Payment is always to be made irrespective of overtime, and premiums are forbidden.[3] The same idea is embodied in the statute by which the State of Utah in 1913 fixed a minimum wage for all "experienced" adult women of 1·25 dollars per day, no exceptions to this minimum being allowed even for defective workers,[4] and in a flat-rate law of the same general character enacted in the State of Arizona in 1917.[5]

§ 2. Now, as was shown in Chapter XVII. § 8, any attempt to force the wage rate of low-grade workpeople above their "fair" level, so long as the area over which it is extended is narrow, may be rendered inoperate by a perfectly legal form of evasion, namely, a reshuffling of workpeople of different grades between this area and occupations not included in it. When, however, the State interferes to establish a national minimum time-wage, the area affected by its action will not be a narrow one. On the contrary, it will be more or less nation-wide, leaving no field free into which low-grade workers can be pushed to be paid a derisory wage. Evasion by way of a redistribution of work among workers of various qualities is, therefore, altogether excluded. Hence the effect pro-

---

[1] *Labour Gazette*, March 1909, p. 103.

[2] Cf. Aves, *Report on Wages Board*, p. 88 ; and Raynaud, *Vers le salaire minimum*, p. 335.

[3] *Ibid.* p. 88.

[4] *The World's Labour Laws*, Feb. 1914, p. 77.

[5] Cf. Douglas, *American Economic Review*, December 1919, p. 709. Cf. also *Bulletin of the U.S. Bureau of Labour*, No. 285, pp. 22 *et seq.*

duced upon the national dividend may prove serious and substantial.

§ 3. It is probable that the enactment of a national minimum time-wage will incidentally prevent the payment of certain low wages that are unfair, in the sense that they are the result of exploitation, i.e. the payment by employers of less than their workpeople's services are worth to them. The forcing up of *this* sort of low wage will, as was explained in Chapter XIV., react favourably upon the size of the national dividend, by strengthening competent employers in their competition with incompetent rivals. Nor is it only in this field that advantage will be won. Even when low wages are fair wages, in the sense of being proportioned to efficiency, it does not necessarily follow that a higher wage will not be fair also. For, as was shown in the preceding chapter, if only an incapable worker can be secured good payment for a little while, he or she may be so far improved in capacity as to become worth the higher wage. In so far as these things happen, the national dividend will be *pro tanto* benefited. Obviously, however, these are mere incidents, by-products as it were, of the establishment of a national minimum wage, and not the main consequence of it.

§ 4. This main consequence is the expulsion from private industry of a number of low-grade workers—the number being greater the higher the level at which the national minimum wage is fixed. When it is enacted that low-grade workpeople shall not in future be paid rates as low as many of them are now receiving, it necessarily follows that some of them will no longer be worth employing. Of course, not all those who are now worth less than the new wage will be affected in this way, because the withdrawal of some workers from private industry increases the worth of those that remain. Some, however, of those not now worth the new wage will still not be worth it when it is established. The proportion that these make of the whole will be greater or less according as the demand for labour is elastic or inelastic. It is sometimes argued that this demand is highly inelastic, upon the ground that in certain special industries, such as the chain trade, there is statistical evidence that the demand is of this

character.   But, when it is a question of a general minimum
wage, it is the demand for labour as a whole, and not merely
in particular industries, that is relevant; and, whether from a
short-period or from a long-period point of view, there can be
little doubt that the elasticity of this aggregate demand is
much greater than the elasticity of the special demand of the
chain trade.[1]   Hence the number of low-grade workers, that
the establishment of a national minimum wage substantially
higher than the wage they are now worth will render not worth
employing in private industry, is likely to be considerable.
Some of these, no doubt, employers will still keep on from
kindliness or old association.   But many will lose their jobs,
and, consequently, will have no opportunity to reap improved
capacity from improved earnings.   As far as they are concerned,
therefore, there will be no indirect gain to the national dividend;
and there will be the obvious direct loss that their labour
is withdrawn from production in private industry.   No doubt,
some of them might be set to work in State-controlled
institutions.   But the enforced labour of assisted persons in
institutions invariably yields but little product; and, therefore, the main part, at all events, of their capacities would be
wasted.

§ 5. Under a régime of complete aloofness and passivity on
the part of the State this effect would be dominant, and there
can be no doubt that the national dividend would be injured.
In the actual world, however, it must be remembered that a
well-organised system of care for the poor may rebuild the
strength of persons who, through unemployment, fall in need
of public relief, and may accord to them, in farm colonies or
elsewhere, an economic training of which they can afterwards
make use.   It follows that the establishment of a national
minimum time-wage, though it will, for a time, cause the
withdrawal of some persons from effective production, need
not, even in respect of these persons, harm the national dividend in the long run, provided that it is associated with a
well-organised State policy towards the poor on the pattern
that will be exhibited in Part IV. of this volume.

A little reflection shows, however, that the benefit to

---

[1] Cf. *post*, Part IV. Chapter III. § 8.

be looked for in this connection is more apparent than real. The establishment of a national minimum time-wage would accomplish very little more than could be accomplished without it. If there is not a well-organised system of care for the poor, there is no reason to suppose that any of the persons expelled from private industry by the operation of the minimum will be trained and rehabilitated ; and, even if there is such a system, only those persons will come in contact with it, and so secure its benefit, who do not belong to families able and willing to support them without State help. But, if there were no national minimum, most of the people, whom the minimum expels from private industry, would, since the minimum itself will presumably be a low one based on a consideration of what is essential for subsistence, be earning so little that they would be nearly sure, in one way or another, to come into contact with the State organisation for looking after poor persons. This organisation, therefore, will have much the same opportunity for withdrawing from private industry those suitable for training, or those needing treatment for sickness, as it would have if there were no national minimum wage.

Nor is this all. It has to be remembered, further, that by no means all those persons, who are prevented from working at ordinary industry by the establishment of a national minimum time-wage, will be in a position to derive benefit from State training. There will be no hope of this kind for old men who have hitherto done a little work and have derived the remainder of their support from their families and friends. These men will simply be precluded from rendering those partial and occasional services to industry which they are both able and willing to render. Elderly women home workers and younger women workers in factories, who are of low capacity and are partly supported by husbands and fathers, will be in like case. So also will State pensioners and others who would gladly work up to their capacity and thus help to support themselves if they were permitted to do so. The driving of these persons into idleness will inflict definite and uncompensated damage upon the national dividend. Consequently, if damage is not to be done, it is essential that, in any law establishing a national minimum time-wage, provision shall be made for excepting from its operation would-be workers of the above type, whom there is no serious prospect of rendering more efficient by training. But a satisfactory arrangement effecting this, which should not at the same time effect a number of other things that are not desired, is extremely difficult to devise. Until it is devised we may fairly conclude that the establishment of an effective national minimum time-wage (effective in the sense of being substantially above what a considerable number of people are earning now) is likely, on the whole, to damage, rather than to benefit, the national dividend. No doubt, in the absence of such a minimum a number of low-grade workers, particularly low-grade women workers with families, will be left in private industry with earnings insufficient to maintain a decent life. This evil, as will be urged with emphasis in Part IV., it is imperative to remedy. But the cure for it consists, not in establishing a national minimum time-wage at a level that will drive low-grade women workers out of private industry altogether, but by the direct action of the State, in securing for all families of its citizens, with the help, if necessary, of State funds, an adequate minimum standard in every department of life.

CHAPTER XX

§ 1. WHEN in practice it is decided to interfere with wages anywhere, either because they are " unfair " or for any other reason, there is at once presented a new problem. Effective interference involves either the authoritative award of a new wage rate or encouragement to employers and employed to agree upon a new wage rate. Equally whether an award or an agreement is made, it would be ridiculous that the terms laid down should be fixed for ever. The industrial situation generally, no less than the circumstances of particular trades, is in a continuous state of flux. Every award and agreement, therefore, must be restricted, either explicitly or implicitly, to a short period of time. How short the period shall be before revision can be called for depends entirely upon the practical difficulties that revision would have to face. Apart from this, it would seem, on the face of things, that, since conditions may change fundamentally at any moment, revision should be permitted whenever either side desires it. In practice, however, considerations of convenience alone would make it imperative that some minimum interval should be provided for. But there are also other considerations. Except where the relations between employers and employed are exceptionally good, it is dangerous to reopen fundamental wage controversies more frequently than can be avoided. In view of this it often happens that the governing decisions are given a currency of not less than, say, two years from the date when they are launched. For the purpose of this discussion we will suppose that that practice is adopted

619

generally. It does not, however, follow from this that, whenever a governing award or agreement about wages is made, the rate must, thereafter, be fixed rigidly for at least two years. For it may be possible to devise methods by which the governing award or agreement shall provide for variations in wages in response to temporary changes in demand—we may provisionally regard the conditions of supply, from the standpoint of this sort of period, as given—during the period that it covers. A choice, therefore, has to be made between a rigid arrangement and a plastic arrangement, and our investigation is not complete until the comparative effects of these have been ascertained.

§ 2. Let us postulate a single industry in general equilibrium, which is neither expanding nor decaying on the whole, but in which the demand for labour now falls below and now rises above its mean level. We also assume for the present that the conditions of demand in other industries are stationary. The argument of Chapters XIV. to XVII. has shown that, allowance being made for certain obstacles and for possible reactions on capacity, the wage rate that will most advantage the national dividend will be a rate that, subject to what was said in Chapter XIV. § 1, is equal, over the period of the agreement or award, to the rate paid for work of a similar grade elsewhere. Is it in the interest of the national dividend that this rate should be single and constant, or that it should vary about a mean ?

In the first place, let us consider a rise in the demand for labour. If a fixed wage system is adopted, this implies that the nominal rate remains unaltered. Hence we might expect that the amount of labour provided will also be unaltered, and, consequently, that the aggregate amount of work done will be less than if the wage fluctuated. It must be remembered, however, that, though the wage per man remains the same, the wage per efficiency unit of labour is, in effect, raised for new employees. An adjustment is brought about, either by employers taking on inferior men at the wage formerly paid to good men only,[1] or by resort to overtime at special rates.

---

[1] It may be suggested that under a piecework system this device is impracticable, since a given wage bears the same relation to a given output, whoever the worker may be. But (1) equal pieces are not always of the same

In either event more is paid for the new labour units than for the old.   It is conceivable, if the rise in demand is small, that the same addition will be made to the aggregate amount of labour employed as would have been made had the general wage rate been raised in an equal proportion.   The difference is that the employer, by fixing what practically amounts to two prices as between his new labour and his old, preserves for himself a sum of money, which, under a one-price system, would have been added to the remuneration of the latter. This result is best illustrated under the method of overtime. Suppose that the normal working day is six hours at a shilling per hour—a shilling being the equivalent payment for the disenjoyment caused to the workman by the sixth hour's work.   Suppose, further, that the disenjoyment of an extra hour's equally efficient work, to a man who has already worked six hours and received six shillings pay, is measured by fifteen pence.   Then the employer can obtain seven hours' work from that man, either by raising the general rate per hour to fifteen pence, or by paying the same as before for a six hours' day and offering fifteen pence for one hour of " overtime."   The amount of work done is approximately the same on either plan ;[1] the only difference is that, if the former is adopted, the employer pays over to the workman an extra eighteen pence, which, under the latter, he retains for himself.   This point is of some importance.   As a general rule, however, particularly if the rise in demand is large, not all the extra labour that employers would like to have can be got by working overtime and taking on inferior men.   Though, therefore, there will be some expansion in the dividend under the fixed wage plan, the expansion is not likely to be so big as it would be under the fluctuating plan.

---

quality, and are not always obtained with the same amount of injury to the employer's property (*e.g.* in coal-mining, a ton of coal badly cut may damage the general conditions of the mine in the neighbourhood) ; and (2) even when two pieces are similar in all respects, one man, in finishing his, may occupy the fixed plant of his employer for a longer time than his neighbour.

[1] Since on the overtime plan workpeople get less money and, therefore, the marginal utility of money to them is slightly higher, the amount of work forthcoming under the overtime plan should in strictness be slightly larger than under the other.

In the second place, let us consider a fall in the demand for labour. If the wage rate remains at the old level, the quantity of labour which it will pay the employer to keep at work will be diminished. If the rate is lowered, it may still be diminished, but not in so high a degree. The point is well illustrated by a comparison, made shortly before the war in a Report of the British Board of Trade, between conditions here and in Germany. " Trade Union standard rates of wages do not prevail in Germany to the same extent as in Great Britain. In consequence workpeople have greater liberty in accepting work at wages lower than those at which they have previously been employed, especially in bad times. A more speedy return to employment of some kind and a consequent reduction in the percentage of trade union members unemployed results from this."[1] That is to say, in bad times more work is done under the plastic than under the rigid form of wage system.

From a combination of these results it follows that, over good and bad times together, a wage system fluctuating on both sides of the mean level, in accordance with temporary movements of the demand for labour, means more work and, therefore, a larger national dividend than one permanently fixed at that level. This gain arises directly out of superior adjustment between demand and supply. It is the fruit of improved organisation, and is similar to the gain produced by improved machinery. It is not retained for long as an exclusive possession of the industry which first secures it, but is distributed over the community as a whole, with the result that a new general equilibrium is established somewhat more advantageous than the old. The interest of the national dividend thus requires that the wage should not stand at the mean level for periods as long as two years, but should undergo short-period oscillations about this level, in such wise as always to make the demand for labour and the supply of it equal.

§ 3. To this conclusion there is an objection, the limits of whose validity require careful investigation. It has been urged that fluctuations in the wages of individual workpeople

[1] *Report on the Cost of Living in German Towns* [Cd. 4032], p. 521.

tend indirectly to impair both their moral character and their economic efficiency. Thus Professor (now Sir Sydney) Chapman writes : " It may be argued that there is far more chance of a somewhat steady wage, which varies infrequently and by small amounts only, contributing to build up a suitable and well-devised standard of life, than a wage given to sudden and considerable alterations." [1] If this is true, it follows that the direct advantages of a wage rate fluctuating with fluctuations of demand may be more than counteracted by indirect disadvantages. For, though the national dividend will, indeed, be enhanced for the moment, it may ultimately be diminished, in a more than corresponding degree, through the injury done to the quality of some of the nation's workers.

In examining this argument we at once observe that the term " wages " ought to be deleted in favour of the term " earnings." It is stability of earnings that enables a well-devised standard of life to be built up, and not stability of wages. Hence, if, for the moment, questions connected with distribution between different individuals are left out of account, we may put aside, as unaffected by Sir Sydney Chapman's argument, all occupations in which the earnings are not liable to be pushed to so low a point under a fluctuating wage as they are under a fixed wage. The occupations thus excluded comprise all those in which the elasticity of the demand for labour is greater than unity. It may, indeed, be objected that, though, in these occupations, the workpeople collectively earn more in bad times under the fluctuating system, yet the particular workpeople who are so skilful as always to command employment earn less, and that it is stability in *their* earnings rather than in those of others that is of especial importance. Since, however, these superior workpeople are presumably better off than their less skilful fellows, this latter statement is highly disputable. For there can be little doubt that fluctuations in the income of a poorer man cause more suffering, and, hence, more loss of productive capacity, than fluctuations of the same size in that of a richer man of similar temperament. Hence the rejoinder fails, and

[1] *Economic Journal*, 1903, p. 194.

it follows that, where the elasticity of the relevant part of the demand for labour is greater than unity, Sir Sydney Chapman's argument is of no force against a fluctuating wage.

In occupations where the demand, from a short-period point of view, is highly inelastic, the result may be different. In these conditions the total earnings of the workpeople will touch a lower level in bad times under the fluctuating system. If it were the fact that in good times adequate provision were regularly made for bad times, the consequent evil effects on capacity, and, therefore, on the national dividend, would not be great. But, as everybody knows, the ordinary workman does not "conform his expenditure and his savings to the standard wage, and regard what he sometimes gets above that standard as an insurance fund against what he will at other times get below it."[1] Hence it is probable that there is a considerable net evil effect on capacity. Against this, however, there has to be set the fact that, under a fixed wage, unless the demand is perfectly inelastic, the available employment in bad times will be smaller, and more workpeople are likely to be thrown out of work altogether. It is not, of course, certain that this will happen. In some industries—most notably the cotton industry—a constriction of employment is met by short time all round instead of by a reduction in the numbers of the staff, and, in others, by a sharing of work more or less in rotation. But, in general, the actual number of unemployed persons in bad months will be greater under a fixed than under a fluctuating wage system; and the capacity of totally unemployed persons is likely to suffer in a very special measure. Hence, even in occupations where the demand for labour is highly inelastic, so long as it is not absolutely inelastic, the evil effect on capacity due to a fluctuating wage is matched by another due to a fixed one. This does not, of course, show that circumstances can never arise in which fluctuating wages are, on the whole, more injurious to capacity, and so indirectly to the national dividend, than fixed wages. It does, however, throw the burden of

---

[1] This is the advice given him by Smart, *Sliding Scales*, p. 13. It may be noted that the pawn-shop and the power to get credit afford, for short periods of unemployment, a partial, though sometimes an injurious, substitute for saving.

proof upon those who maintain, in any particular instance, that such circumstances have arisen. For the two evils noted above are so vague and indefinite that it will often be practically impossible to weigh them against one another. In the absence of special detailed information our decision must then be based upon the one fact which is known, namely, that a wage fluctuating with fluctuations in the demand for labour has the better *direct* effect upon the national dividend. In general, therefore, the defence of a system of rigid wage rates examined in this section must be adjudged to have failed.

§ 4. If then it is agreed that a wage fluctuating with fluctuations in the demand for labour is desirable, it becomes necessary to determine how frequently adjustments should be made. In pure theory it would seem that adjustments should be made continually from day to day or even from moment to moment. To this sort of adjustment, however, there are insuperable practical obstacles. Time is required for the collection and arrangement of the statistics upon which the changes must be based. Considerations of book-keeping and ordinary business convenience come upon the stage, and fix a lower limit, beyond which the interval between successive adjustments must not be reduced. Of course, this limit is not always the same. In a small local industry, for example, it will probably be lower than in a great national one. But in every industry it must lie considerably above the infinitesimal level which pure theory recommends. So far as it is possible to judge from the practice of those industries in which the interval is determined, as under a sliding scale, by considerations of convenience alone, it seems as though this interval should not be less than two or three months.[1]

§ 5. Having thus satisfied ourselves that the interest of the national dividend requires a wage-system fluctuating within the normal period of agreement or award, and having determined the intervals that should elapse between successive fluctuations, we have next to determine on what plan the fluctuations themselves should be organised. It is evident that, other things being equal, the larger any fluctuation of demand is, the larger the corresponding change of wage should

---

[1] Cf. for illustrations, L. L. Price, *Industrial Peace*, p. 80.

be. This principle has now to be worked out in the concrete; and to that end the chief factors upon which the magnitude of demand fluctuations depends must be described. These fall into two divisions: (1) movements in the employers' demand schedule for the commodity which the labour we are interested in is helping to produce; and (2) movements in the supply schedule of the other factors that co-operate in production with that labour. These two sets of influences will now be reviewed.

§ 6. Movements in the employers' demand for the commodity the labour is helping to make are derived directly from movements in the public demand for the commodity. The liability to oscillation of that demand is, of course, different for different classes of commodities. The most obvious distinction is between articles which are desired for immediate personal use "for their own sake" and articles which are desired largely as means to distinction through display. The demand for articles of the former sort is likely to be the more stable, because, as Jevons suggests, people's desire for them is generally steady for a longer period. For example, we may notice the stability of the pinafore industry: "No clothing trade (in Birmingham) suffers so little from short time."[1] On the other hand, commodities that are largely display articles are liable to fluctuations of desire, as opinion transfers the distinction-bearing quality from one thing to another. Thus the demand would seem to be less variable for common objects of wide consumption than for luxuries. To these special considerations should be added the more general one, that an industry which supplies a wide market made up of many independent parts is likely to enjoy a steadier demand than one which supplies a narrow market. This is merely a particular application of the broad proposition, familiar to statisticians, that "the precision of an average is proportionate to the square root of the number of terms it contains."[2] It is well illustrated by the interesting study of M. Lazard on *Le Chômage et la profession*. Using figures from the French census of 1901, he takes the percentages of unemployment

---

[1] Cadbury, *Women's Work and Wages*, p. 93.
[2] Bowley, *Elements of Statistics*, p. 305.

there recorded in a number of industries, and sets them alongside of the average number of men (*moyen effectif*) per establishment in the several industries, and finds, on a method of his
own, an inverse correlation. Connecting large unemployment
with variable demand, he explains this correlation by the
relation, which he believes to subsist, between a large *moyen
effectif* and *l'extension des débouchés commerciaux.* " The connection between this latter phenomenon and the size of the
personnel is evident. Large establishments exist only when
the markets to be served are considerable. Now, a large
market must also be a relatively stable market, because in it
considerable decreases in the consumption of some customers
have a chance of being balanced by increases in the consumption of others ; and this stability, implying, as it does, stability
of production, implies at the same time the absence or, at all
events, a diminution of unemployment." [1] In like manner, he
argues : " If unemployment seems to grow as we pass upward
from primary towards finishing industries, this circumstance is
explained by the fact that the industries at the top of the
scale, being more specialised, have narrower markets. On
the other hand, the industries that deal with raw products
provide the material needed by numerous other industries,
and, therefore, enjoy the advantages which a multitude of
outlets confer." [2] The same principle may, of course, be invoked
to explain the stability of the demand for railway transportation, as compared with the demand even for such things as

[1] *Le Chômage et la profession*, pp. 336-7. M. Lazard adds : "A ce premier
avantage, propre aux grandes entreprises, du fait de leur organisation com-
merciale, il s'en ajoute d'autres, résultant du mécanisme de la production.
Lorsque la direction de l'industrie est concentrée dans un petit nombre de
mains, les chefs d'entreprises connaissent le marché qu'ils fournissent mieux
que ne font, dans leurs sphères respectives, les petits ou moyens entrepreneurs
des autres branches industrielles. Sachant sur quelle consommation ils peuvent
compter, ils règlent leur production en conséquence. . . . Notre hypothèse
demanderait d'ailleurs à être vérifiée, car plus d'une industrie fait apparemment
exception à la règle indiquée ; on remarque, par exemple, que l'agriculture,
l'industrie humaine par excellence, est assez épargnée par le chômage, bien
que l'effectif moyen des établissements y soit très réduit. Il semble que l'on
puisse attribuer cet état de choses au fait que les débouchés sont plus stables
dans l'agriculture que dans l'industrie proprement dite ; en outre, le nombre
des entreprises agricoles est naturellement limité par l'inextensibilité de la
surface cultivée " (*ibid.* pp. 337-8).

[2] *Ibid.* p. 337.

coal, sugar, or iron. In like manner, an industry, which sells largely in foreign markets as well as in the home market, is likely, other things equal, to have a more stable demand than one which sells in the home market only—except, indeed, when it is disturbed by changes in the rate of duty imposed on its products by an important foreign customer.

§ 7 When the oscillations of the public demand for any commodity are given, it is natural to suppose that the oscillations of the employers' demand for it will be exactly equivalent to them. As a fact, however, the employers' demand usually oscillates through the smaller distance of the two. The reason for this is the common practice of making for stock. In bad months the employer is glad to acquire and warehouse more goods than he wishes, for the moment, to sell, while in good months, because he has these goods to fall back upon, his demand for new ones rises less for them than the demand of the public whom he supplies. His demand this month is, in short, derived from the anticipated public demand of a considerably longer period, thus divesting itself to some extent of temporary oscillations. Naturally the extent to which making for stock takes place is different in different industries. The practice is less attractive to employers, the greater is the cost of carrying a unit of the commodity affected from one point of time to another. This cost depends, of course, in part, upon a circumstance affecting all commodities equally, namely, the rate of interest. For all carriage across time implies a loss of interest through holding commodities unsold. It also depends upon a number of circumstances which differ for different commodities. Of these the most obvious is the expense of storage. One important determinant of this expense is the resistance that the commodity makes to *physical* wear and tear in transit across time, or, more broadly, its durability, in respect both of decay and of accidental breakage. In this quality the precious metals and hard materials, like timber, are specially favoured. As we should expect, things that are extracted from the earth are, in general, more durable than things that are grown on it. It is interesting to note that, in recent times, the development of refrigerating and other preserving processes has rendered a number of commodities, chiefly articles of food, much more durable than they used to be. The Committee on Hops, for instance, wrote in 1908 : " At the time of the previous inquiry in the year 1856, attention was called to the fact that ' the deterioration which hops suffer when kept prevents the superabundance of one year from adequately supplying the deficiencies of another.' The advent of cold storage has effected an adjustment between years of plethora and years of scarcity, with the resultant effect upon prices." [1] It may be added that such things as the direct services rendered by missionaries, doctors, teachers, train-drivers, and cab-drivers are wholly incapable, and such things as gas and electricity are in great measure incapable, of being stored. A second important determinant of the expense of storage is the resistance that the commodity makes to *psychical* wear and tear in transit across time, or, more broadly, its steadiness of value. The contrast I have in view is between staple goods of steady demand—Charles Booth once cited philosophic and optical instruments as instances of this class of goods [2]— and fashion goods of unsteady demand. Clearly, there is a higher cost of carriage and less inducement towards storage for a commodity, which, next week, nobody may want, than there is for one for which a constant· market is assured. Thus the turned and pressed parts of bicycles, which are much the same whatever type of frame is in vogue, are largely made for stock, whereas this is not done with completed bicycles, the form of which is liable to fashion changes. An extreme instance of unfitness for stock-making is afforded by commodities, such as ball-dresses, which every purchaser will wish to have constructed to her own special order, and which, when " readymade," have practically no appeal for her. It is possible that things at one time customarily made to individual order may, subsequently, become more generalised ; and *vice versa*. Houses are sometimes built to the order of would-be private owners, and sometimes as a speculation. The boot industry has developed from an earlier stage, in which the individual order method predominated, to its present condition, in which most boots are ready-made. In certain textiles, on the other

[1] *Report*, p. x.   [2] *Industry*, v. p. 253.

hand, there is evidence of a movement in the opposite direction. A recent Report on unemployment in Philadelphia observes: "Twenty years ago a manufacturer made carpet or hosiery or cloth and then went out and sold *that* carpet or hosiery or cloth. To-day the order comes in for a particular design, with a certain kind of yarn or silk and a certain number of threads to the inch, and the manufacturer makes that particular order. Formerly a manufacturer produced standard makes of his particular line, and simply piled up stock in his warehouse in the off-season. . . . To-day manufacturers make, as a rule, very little to stock and run chiefly on orders."[1] It is evident that every development towards the standardisation of products renders making for stock more practicable, while every development away from standardisation renders it more difficult.

§ 8. There is another point to be made in this connection. Granted that the practice of making for stock causes the oscillations of employers' demand for any commodity to be less than the associated oscillations in the public demand, it might be thought by the hasty reader that the relation between these two oscillations can be expressed by a constant fraction, different in different industries, but the same in any one industry whatever the size of the oscillation. This is a mistake. If, in response to a given percentage elevation or depression of the public demand, the employers' demand is elevated or depressed through a percentage five-sixths as great, it is not to be expected that the same proportion will hold good for larger changes of public demand. As a rule, making for stock is carried up to a certain point for a small inducement, and, after that, is extended only with great reluctance. Hence the public demand is apt to undergo slight oscillations without producing on the employers' demand any appreciable effect. But, after a point is passed, further oscillations in it tend to be accompanied by further oscillations in the employers' demand, the magnitude of which rapidly approaches towards equality with theirs. These considerations justify the provision, which is found in most sliding scales, that

[1] "Steadying Employment," *Annals of the American Academy of Political Science*, May 1916, pp. 6-7.

alterations in the price of the commodity must exceed some definite amount before any alteration takes place in wages.[1] They also serve as a ground for the rule, which in practice is universal, that, when wages are conjoined to prices under a sliding scale, the percentage change in wages shall be smaller than the percentage price change to which it corresponds.[2]

§ 9. Let us now turn to the second determinant of fluctuations in the demand for labour in any occupation, which was distinguished in § 5. Among the co-operant agents whose supply schedule is liable to move the most obvious are the raw materials used in the occupation. In extractive industries, such as coal-mining, these do not play any significant part; but in the majority of industries they are very important. In accordance with what was said in § 6, it is evident that, when they are obtained from a large number of independent sources, the oscillations of supply are likely to be less than when reliance has to be placed on a single source. For this reason the imposition of high protective duties upon any material, with a view to ousting foreign sellers, may be expected to bring about increased fluctuations. In addition to raw materials, the co-operant agents include the services of auxiliary labour and the services of machines. Mechanical improvements, for example, involve, in effect, a lowering of the supply schedule of the services rendered by capital invested in the occupation that is affected by them. Moreover, in some industries, Nature herself, as represented by the light and heat received from the sun, is a very important co-operant factor in production. Thus there is a high degree of seasonal variability in the demand for labour in the building trades, because the advent of frost in winter seriously interferes with brick-laying, masonry and plastering, while the shortening of the hours of daylight, by necessitating resort to artificial illumination, adds to the costs and further handicaps such work. No doubt, recent developments, such as the substitution of cement for mortar, are doing something to lessen the influence of climatic changes upon this industry,[3] but their

---

[1] Cf. Price, *Industrial Peace*, p. 97.
[2] Cf. Marshall, *Economics of Industry*, p. 381 *n.*
[3] Cf. Dearle, *Economic Journal*, 1908, p. 103.

influence is still very important. The same remark applies
to the industry of discharging cargoes at the London Docks,
which is liable to serious interruptions by frost and fog. On
the other hand, indoor trades and trades little dependent on
weather conditions, such as engineering and shipbuilding—
dress-making is obviously not relevant here — display a
relatively small amount of seasonal variability. Thus, according to a study by Sir H. Llewellyn Smith extended over some
years, the mean difference in the percentage of unemployment
between the best month and the worst month was $3\frac{1}{4}$ per
cent in the building trades and only $1\frac{1}{3}$ per cent in the
engineering and shipbuilding trades.[1]

§ 10. When the demand for labour in any industry
fluctuates in a given measure, the appropriate consequent
fluctuation in the rate of wages is not, of course, determined
by the size of the demand fluctuation alone. It depends
also on how elastic the demand for labour in the industry is
and how elastic the supply. The more elastic the demand is,
the larger the appropriate wage change will be : the more
elastic the supply (from the short-period standpoint here
relevant), the smaller it will be. The former of these propositions does not call for special comment. But of the
application of the latter to practice something should be said.
The supply of labour is elastic in occupations so situated that
a small change in the wage rate offered in them suffices to
divert a considerable quantity of labour between them and
other occupations. In general, therefore, the following results
hold good. First, when, as with the Scottish shale and coal-
miners,[2] a small industry is neighbour to a kindred and very
large one, the wage change corresponding to a given oscillation of demand should be less than in an isolated industry.
Secondly, a set of circumstances, which would justify a given
change in the wages of workmen specialised to a particular
industry or locality, would justify a smaller change in those of
labourers, whose lack of skill, or of managers, the generalised
character of whose skill, renders them more mobile.[3] Thirdly,

[1] Cf. *Committee on Distress from Want of Employment*, Q. 4580.
[2] Cf. Sheriff Jameson's award in a shale-miners' arbitration (*Economic
Journal*, 1904, p. 309).
[3] When specialisation, either to trade or place, is very high, the labour

among workmen trained to a particular job, the wage fluctuations corresponding to given changes in the demand of one industry employing them should be smaller when there are other industries in which their services are required. Thus, in a boom or depression in the coal trade, the wages of mechanics employed in the mines should fluctuate less than those of hewers. Fourthly, when wages are paid by the piece, the percentage fluctuation corresponding to a given fluctuation in demand should be smaller than when they are paid by the time. For, since, under the latter system, a rise of pay has not the same effect in inducing workmen to pack more labour into an hour, the elasticity of the supply of efficiency units is lower. Fifthly, broad changes, such as the spread of information, improvements in communication, or an increased willingness on the part of workpeople to work at a distance from their homes, will tend to increase the elasticity of the labour supply and so to diminish the wage change appropriate to any given fluctuation of demand. Lastly, in industries subject to regular seasonal fluctuations, many of the workpeople will have prepared themselves for the slack periods by acquiring some form of skill for which the demand at these times is apt to increase. Hence, within the normal limits of seasonal fluctuations, the supply of labour will be fairly elastic, and, therefore, seasonal demand changes should not seriously alter wages. Thus, despite the great fluctuations in the demand for gas stokers between summer and winter, wages should not, as indeed they do not, fluctuate much, because these workers are often also employed in making bricks, the demand for which expands in the summer.

§ 11. So far our discussion has been confined to the

supply will, for considerable variations of wage, remain practically constant. The workman may know that his skill is useless in other districts or occupations, and may, therefore, be driven to accept a great drop in wages before leaving. Nor (except for navvies and other labourers, the muscular character of whose work makes it specially dependent upon their nourishment) need his capacity suffer appreciably. Thus the supply may be perfectly inelastic. It may also be inelastic on account of conservative feeling among the workers affected. For example, Dr. Clapham writes of the decline of the hand-loom industry : "The independence and professional pride of the old race of weavers made them hate the thought of the factory, and stick to their home work with a tenacity that, in the long run, did them no good " (*Bradford Textile Society*, June 1905, p. 43).

general nature of the relation between demand changes and the wage changes that should be associated with them. We have still to inquire whether the wage fluctuation that corresponds to a given change in the demand for labour in any industry should be related to it in the same way, whatever the amount and direction of this latter change may be. The answer must be in the negative, since the supply of labour will not have the same elasticity for all amounts and both directions. We may, indeed, presume that the elasticity will not vary greatly for changes in demand fairly near to the mean. The entrance and the exit to most trades are about equally open. In the North of England mining districts, for example, " the migratory miners include a large number of skilled mechanics, who divide their time between mining and their other handicraft according as either industry offers a better chance of profit." [1] A moderate upward movement in demand should, therefore, in general be met by about the same percentage of wage change as an equal downward movement. But for large upward and downward movements this symmetry no longer obtains. When the demand for labour falls considerably, there is a limit beyond which the wage cannot be reduced without reducing the available amount of the labour in question to zero. This limit will be determined, for unskilled men, by the conditions of life when they are unemployed altogether and subsisting on unemployment insurance and so on, and, for skilled men, in the last resort, by what they can earn in unskilled occupations. Thus, if the demand for labour has fallen in more than a moderate degree, a further fall should be accompanied by a less than proportionate fall, and eventually by no fall, in wage.[2] On the other hand, when the demand for labour rises considerably, the effect upon unskilled wages should be proportionate to that produced when it rises a little. For skilled labour the percentage of wage increase should be even greater. For, while the power of those already in a trade to work extra hours, and the probable presence of a floating body of

---

[1] *Statistical Journal*, Dec. 1904, p. 635.

[2] These considerations justify the establishment, in connection with sliding scales, alike for skilled and unskilled work, of a minimum wage uncompensated by any corresponding maximum.

unemployed, will enable a moderate addition to the supply of labour to be made fairly easily, these resources will be ineffective when a large addition is required.[1]

§ 12. In the light of this general analysis, we have now to inquire how far it is possible to provide, in the terms of a governing award or agreement, automatic machinery for adjusting the wage rate to changes in demand occurring within the period covered by it. The best-known instrument intended for this purpose—an instrument at one time widely used in the coal industry, and still popular in the iron and steel trades [2]—is a sliding scale connecting the wage rate of an industry with the price of its finished product. Changes in the price of the product are regarded as indices of changes in the demand for the labour that produces it; and a definite scheme relating different amounts of price change to different amounts of wage change is set up. This scheme varies, of course, with the particular conditions of different industries, and is, or should be, based on the considerations adduced in the seven preceding sections of this chapter. The hope is that a skilfully devised scheme will cause the rate of wages to vary in the way in which those considerations show that it ought to vary.

§ 13. To any one looking critically at this machinery it will naturally occur that, since it makes wage changes depend, not upon contemporaneous, but upon antecedent, price changes—*e.g.* price changes as recorded in the preceding quarter—the adjustment made under it must necessarily be incorrect. This, however, is not so. For the connection between the employers' and the public's demand for any commodity always bridges an appreciable interval. Oscillations in the employers' demand lag behind the primary oscillations to which they correspond. It is generally only after prices have remained up for some little while that employers think seriously of expanding their business, and they hesitate in a similar manner about reducing production

---

[1] This consideration affords an argument in favour of the device of the "double-jump" after a certain point has been reached, which found a place in a former scale in the South Wales coal industry and also in certain English sliding scales.

[2] Cf. *Industrial Negotiations and Agreements*, published for the Trade Union Congress, 1922, pp. 46 *et seq.*

when a depression sets in. Their demand for labour at any time is thus derived from the public demand for the commodity which existed at an earlier time. It follows that the supposed defect in sliding scales, that they fix future wages by past prices,[1] is really an advantage. It is, indeed, sometimes objected that an intelligent anticipation of events before they occur is coming to influence more and more the conduct of industrial concerns; and that, so far as this tendency prevails, the adequacy of past prices as an index of future demand necessarily diminishes. "Why, then, should wages automatically fall when the leaders of industry have cast their eyes over the future, and proclaimed the need of an enlarged output and more hands? Or why should wages rise when employers see that good trade is behind, and are preparing for a period of marking time?"[2] The answer to this argument is found in a closer analysis of the phrase "public demand." In the present connection it signifies the demand, not of the ultimate consumers, but of those intermediate dealers who buy from the manufacturers, and whose operations are the proximate cause of changes in wholesale prices. Where such persons are present, it is extremely improbable that prices will fall when the anticipation of the leaders of industry are roseate, or rise when they are gloomy. For these anticipations will generally be shared by the dealers, and, if so, will be reflected in their present demand and, hence, in present prices. The foregoing objection is, therefore, only relevant on occasions when the forecasts of manufacturers and of dealers are at variance. Since, however, the former forecasts are, in the main, based upon the latter, these occasions will be exceedingly rare.

§ 14. There is, however, a much more serious objection to be urged against sliding scales. Changes in the price of the finished product only constitute a good index of changes in the demand for the labour that makes it, on condition that other things are equal. But in real life other things are often not equal. For these other things include the supply conditions of raw material, of the services of auxiliary work-

---

[1] Cf. Ashley, *Adjustment of Wages*, pp. 56-7.
[2] Chapman, "Some Theoretical Objections to Sliding Scales," *Economic Journal*, 1903, p. 188.

people, and of the services of machinery : all of which supply
conditions are liable to vary.   It is evident that a given
oscillation in one direction of the supply schedule of any one
of these things causes the employers' demand for the labour,
whose wages we are considering, to oscillate in exactly the
same manner as an equal oscillation in the opposite direction
in his demand schedule for the finished commodity.   Hence, in
order to infer the oscillations in labour demand from those in
the employers' commodity demand, we need to subtract from
the latter whatever oscillations occur in the supply schedules
of the other factors of production.   It is true that no provision
has to be made for corrections under this head (1) when the
supply schedules of the other factors are certain not to
oscillate, or (2) when the part they play in the cost of the
commodity is so small that their oscillations can be neglected
without serious inaccuracy.   It is not easy to imagine an
industry in which the former of these conditions could be
postulated ; but the latter holds good in extractive industries,
such as coal-mining, where nearly the whole cost of production
is labour cost.   Except in these industries the index afforded by
price changes is seriously defective.   A fall in price will occur
in consequence of a fall in the demand for the commodity, and
also in consequence of a cheapening in the supply of the raw
material.   Thus there are two routes connecting changes in
price with changes in labour demand.   A price movement
caused in one way indicates a fall ; caused in another way, a
rise.   If, for example, the price of iron goes up on account
of an increase in the public need for iron, there is a rise in
the demand for iron-workers' services ; if, however, it goes up
because a strike in the coal trade has rendered one of the constituents used in making it more expensive, there is a fall in this
demand.   It is obvious that, in the latter event, wages ought
not to follow prices, but should move in the opposite direction.

§ 15.   As a way of escape from this difficulty, it is sometimes proposed that the index should be, not the price of the
finished commodity, but the margin between its price and that
of the raw materials used in making it.   " Margins " are
utilised with apparent success by the officials of the Cotton
Workers' Union, who obtain them by " subtracting the price

of raw cotton (calculated from the five leading sorts) from the price of yarn (of eleven kinds) or of calico (of twenty-three kinds),"[1] and order their wage negotiations accordingly. This index has the advantage of moving in the same way in response to a fall in the demand for the commodity and to an increase in the expense of obtaining raw material. The solution it affords is not, however, perfect. Among the contributory factors to the production of the finished article raw material is only one. The conditions of supply of auxiliary labour and of the services of machines are also liable to vary, but their variations are not reflected in any change in the " margin." Mechanical improvements, for example, mean, in effect, a cheapening of the help rendered by machines. When such improvements are occurring, margins are liable to mislead in the same manner as, though in a less degree than, crude price statistics. Furthermore, margins, equally with prices, and because prices enter into their construction, are subject to a serious practical inconvenience. They are not likely to afford a good index in industries where the general level of elaborateness and so forth in the goods produced is liable to vary. In these industries an apparent change in price may really indicate nothing more than a change in the kind of article manufactured. This difficulty is specially likely to occur when prices are deduced from the quantities and values of exports, since there is reason to expect that the cheaper varieties of goods will gradually yield place in foreign trade to the finer and more valuable varieties.

§ 16. Yet another plan, and one which avoids some of the above difficulties, is to base a sliding scale, neither on prices nor on margins, but on " profits." The report of the wage negotiations in the cotton trade in 1900 makes it clear that, in that trade at all events, it is exceedingly hard to arrive at a satisfactory estimate of what " representative " or aggregate profits are.[2] What reckoning, for example, is to

---

[1] Schultze-Gaevernitz, *Social Peace*, p. 160.

[2] Mr. L. L. Price, in discussing these negotiations, speaks of a "profits" scale in the cotton trade as a "closer approach to the conception of profit-sharing than that made by the usual type of sliding scale" (*Economic Journal*, 1901, p. 244). The view appears to be erroneous, so long as the "profits" of the *representative firm* are taken as the index. Of course, a system which should make the wage paid by individual firms fluctuate with their own particular "profits" would be an entirely different thing.

be made for firms which have failed altogether and disappeared ? It is interesting to observe, however, that the agreement, which settled the great coal strike of 1921, provided what is in effect a sliding scale based on profits. *For each district* standard wages and standard profits (aggregating 17 per cent of the cost of the standard wages) were set up ; and, every month, the balance, after the costs other than wages had been met, was to be divided between profits and wages in the proportion of 17 to 83. The coal industry is, perhaps, better adapted for this kind of arrangement than the majority of other industries would be.

§ 17. The preceding discussion, while it has revealed explicitly or implicitly many difficulties in the way of constructing an effective sliding scale, has, nevertheless, made it plain that scales adequate to take account of all changes in the demand schedule for labour are theoretically possible. In favourable circumstances, when, for example, as in coal-mines, labour is by far the most important element in the cost of production, there is no reason why a fairly close approach to the theoretical ideal should not be made. Obviously, when this can be done, an award embodying a scale is much superior to one embodying a single fixed wage for the whole period covered by it. But, while this is so, we have to recognise the very serious disability from which even a perfectly constructed scale must suffer. A given rise or fall in the price of a commodity or in the profits of an industry covered by a scale may be brought about either by a change in the real demand for the commodity or by an expansion or contraction of money or credit, which affects the general level of money prices but leaves real conditions substantially unaltered. It is plain that, if the price of coal or the profits of coal-owners go up, say 50 per cent, as a part of a general 50 per cent rise due to a purely monetary cause, the proper response in the wages of coal-miners is a 50 per cent rise. But, if the price of coal or the profits of coal-owners go up 50 per cent in consequence of an increase in the real demand for coal, the proper response, as indicated in § 8, will be a rise of considerably less than 50 per cent. It follows that any scale, which provides for the right adjustment of wages when the price of coal or the profits of coal-owners change from a cause special to coal, must provide a wrong adjustment when these change from a general monetary cause. Something might be done to remedy this defect by making wage changes depend *both* on changes in the price of coal, or the profits of coal-owners, *and* on changes in general prices, or, if we prefer it, in the "cost of living."[1] Thus there might be a scale of the type described in previous sections, referred not to absolute changes in coal prices, but to differences between the changes in coal prices and in general prices; and, superimposed upon this, there might be a second scale making wages vary in the same proportion as general prices, or, alternatively, as the cost of living. Thus, if coal rose 50 per cent while general prices rose 20 per cent, wages should rise 20 per cent *plus* whatever fraction of 30 per cent (the rise peculiar to coal) the special coal scale might decree. This arrangement, however, though it would work satisfactorily when changes in general prices were due to monetary or credit causes, would not, as was shown in Chapter XVII. § 4, give a right result when these changes were due wholly or in part to such causes as the destruction of capital in war, bad harvests, general improvements in transport methods, and so on.

§ 18. There is yet another disability, even less open to remedy, from which any form of sliding scale necessarily suffers. These scales, being designed to relate changes in wage rates to changes in the demand for labour in the particular industries they cover, cannot from their nature recognise or in any way allow for changes in the supply of labour to these industries, such as might be brought about, for example, by the development or decay of some other industry employing the same type of labour. Plainly, however, wage rates ought to be adjusted to meet changes of this type equally with changes in the demand for labour. The failure of scales to do this has sometimes led to results so plainly unreasonable that it has been necessary for one party

---

[1] Scales based, like several post-war scales, *solely* on the "cost of living" index are inadequate because they ignore changes in demand. Scales of this sort were adopted in 1922 in the wool, hosiery, cable-making, paper, and several other industries (*Industrial Negotiations and Agreements*, Trade Union Congress, 1922, p. 22).

to a scale agreement voluntarily to concede to the other terms more favourable than those which the scale decreed.

§ 19. From these considerations it appears that, though we may expect from scale agreements better adjustments than could be got from fixed wage agreements covering periods of equal length, better adjustments still will be obtained if the relations between employers and employed are good enough to allow the two-monthly or quarterly variations of the wage rate, which take place during the currency of the governing agreement or award, to be based, not exclusively upon the variations of a mechanical price or profits index, but also upon any other relevant considerations that may present themselves. There are several examples of this type of settlement. In the Scottish coal agreement of 1902, the relevant portion of which remained unchanged till 1907, it was provided " that the net average realised value of coal at the pit bank for the time being, *taken in conjunction with the state of the trade and the prospects thereof*, is to be considered in fixing miners' wages between the minimum and the maximum for the time being, and that, in current ordinary circumstances, a rise or fall of $6\frac{1}{4}$ per cent in wages on 1888 basis for each $4\frac{1}{2}d.$ per ton of rise or fall in the value of coal is reasonable." [1] In like manner, in the agreement entered into in the Federated Districts in 1906, it was provided that " alterations in the selling price of coal shall not be the sole factor for the decision of the Board, but one factor only, and either side shall be entitled to bring forward any reasons why, notwithstanding an alteration in the selling price, there should be no alteration made in the rate of wages." [2]   Under schemes of this type reasoned and agreed action, instead of automatic action, is required every two or three months. The successful introduction of them is, therefore, only practicable in industries where cordial relations prevail between employers and employed.

[1] *Report on Collective Agreements* [Cd. 5366], 1910, p. 32.
[2] *Report on Collective Agreements* [Cd. 5366], p. 27.

PART IV

THE DISTRIBUTION OF THE NATIONAL DIVIDEND

CHAPTER I

IN the two preceding Parts we have examined the way in which the size of the national dividend is affected by certain important groups of influences. It is not, of course, pretended that *all* the influences that are relevant have been brought under review. On the contrary, many of the more remote *causae causarum,* such as those that determine the general attitude of people toward work and saving, as well as many less remote causes that affect the development of mechanical inventions and improved methods of workshop management, have been deliberately left on one side. This deficiency I do not propose to remedy. There is, however, another deficiency, which cannot be thus lightly left unfilled. From the propositions laid down in Chapters VII. and VIII. of Part I. it follows that, while, in general and apart from special exceptions, anything that either increases the dividend without injuring the absolute share of the poor, or increases the absolute share of the poor without injuring the dividend,[1] must increase economic welfare, the effect upon economic welfare of anything that increases one of these quantities but diminishes the other is ambiguous. Plainly, when this kind of disharmony exists, the aggregate effect upon economic welfare, brought about by any cause responsible for it, can only be determined by balancing in detail the injury (or benefit) to the dividend as a whole against the benefit (or injury) to the real earnings of the poorer classes. No general solution of problems of that class is possible. It is important, therefore, to determine how

[1] That is to say, without injuring it either from the point of view of the period before the change or from the point of view of the period after the change. Cf. *ante,* p. 54.

far they are likely to arise in real life; to discover, in other words, whether causes acting discordantly upon the dividend as a whole and upon the absolute share of the poor are frequent or rare. When disharmonies are found, certain practical problems arising out of them will have to be examined.

CHAPTER II

§ 1. THE mere statement of this problem brings us into contact with an interesting thesis, which, if valid, would immediately dispose of it. This thesis is that no cause operating in opposite senses upon the aggregate amount of the dividend and upon the absolute share of the poor can possibly exist. It is backed by an inductive proof. The data for the induction are derived from some remarkable investigations conducted by Pareto and published by him in his *Cours d'économie politique.* Statistics of income in a number of countries, principally during the nineteenth century, are brought together. It is shown that, if x signify a given income and N the number of persons with incomes exceeding x, and if a curve be drawn, of which the ordinates are logarithms of x and the abscissae logarithms of N, this curve, for all the countries examined, is approximately a straight line, and is, furthermore, inclined to the vertical axis at an angle, which, in no country, differs by more than three or four degrees from $56°$. This means (since $\tan 56° = 1·5$) that, if the number of incomes greater than x is equal to N, the number greater than mx is equal to $\frac{1}{m^{1·5}}$·N, whatever the value of m may be. Thus the scheme of income distribution is everywhere the same. "We are confronted, as it were, with a great number of crystals of the same chemical composition. There are large crystals, middle-sized crystals and small crystals, but they are all of the same form."[1] These are the facts as found by Pareto.

[1] *Cours d'économie politique,* ii. pp. 306-7.

The inference which he appears to draw from them in the *Cours d'économie politique* contains two parts. He defines diminished inequality among incomes thus: "Incomes can tend towards equality in two quite different ways; that is, either because the larger incomes diminish, or because the smaller incomes increase. Let us give this latter significance to the diminution of inequality among incomes, so that this will take place when the number of the individuals having an income less than an income x diminishes compared with the number of persons having an income greater than x."[1] On this basis he finds: First, "we may say generally that the increase of wealth relatively to population will produce either an increase in the minimum income, or a diminution in the inequality of incomes, or both these effects in combination."[2] Secondly, "to raise the level of the minimum income or to diminish the inequality of income, it is necessary that wealth should grow more rapidly than population. Hence we see that the problem of improving the condition of the poor is, before everything else, a problem of the production of wealth."[3] Now, on Pareto's definition, "to increase the minimum income, or to diminish the inequality of income, or both," is substantially equivalent to "to increase the absolute share of the national dividend accruing to the poor." Hence, what this thesis amounts to in effect is that, on the one hand, anything that increases the national dividend must, in general, increase also the absolute share of the poor, and, on the other hand—and this is the side of it that is relevant here—that it is impossible for the absolute share of the poor to be increased by any cause which does not at the same time increase the national dividend as a whole. Hence disharmony of the type referred to in the preceding chapter is impossible: we cannot be confronted with any proposal the adoption of which would both make the dividend larger and the absolute share of the poor smaller, or *vice versa*.

§ 2. Now it is quite evident that a sweeping proposition

[1] *Manuale di economia politica*, p. 371.
[2] *Cours d'économie politique*, ii. p. 324.
[3] *Ibid.* p. 408.

of this kind, based upon an inductive argument, requires very careful consideration. It is, therefore, necessary at the outset to call attention to certain defects in its statistical basis. The sum of what has to be said is that, though the various distributions that are brought under review are similar in form, the likeness among them is by no means complete. In all of them, it is true, the logarithmic income curve—at least for incomes of moderate size—is approximately a straight line; but the inclination of this line, though it does not differ widely, still does differ distinctly, for the different groups of statistics that have been observed. Pareto's lowest figure from adequate data for the tangent of the angle made with the vertical axis is, for instance, 1·24 (Bâle, 1887), and his highest 1·89 (Prussia, 1852). Nor is this all. As Dr. Bowley has pointed out, in the most important set of figures observed over a long period (those for Prussia) the slope of the curve has been decreasing with the lapse of time. The figures which Dr. Bowley gives differ slightly from those of Pareto, but the general effect is the same in both sets. According to Pareto, however, a smaller slope of the curve means a greater equality in his sense—a sense the appropriateness of which, it will be remembered, is matter for debate—in the distribution of income.[1] Dr. Bowley, therefore, naturally offers as an explanation of the Prussian figures: "The incomes are becoming more uniformly distributed in Prussia, and the result is, from these figures, that the Prussian income is getting to the more uniform distribution of the English."[2] Hence, interesting as Pareto's comparisons are, to build upon them any precise quantitative law of distribution is plainly unjustifiable.

§ 3. But, if the position is to be fully understood, it is well that this point should be waived. Let us suppose that the statistical basis of Pareto's reasoning is not defective in the way that has been indicated. Even so, much material for criticism remains. For let us consider what exactly this scheme, or form, of distribution is, for the

---

[1] Cf. *ante*, p. 96.
[2] Select Committee on the Income Tax, 1906, *Evidence*, p. 81.

existence of which a mysterious necessity seems to have been discovered. If we were to plot it out, not as Pareto does, but in the simpler form of a curve so drawn that the abscissae represent amounts of income, and the ordinates the number of people in receipt of these amounts, the curve would rise very quickly to its highest point and, thereafter, fall much less quickly. This would express in a picture the well-known fact that there are a very large number of people with incomes much below the average income, and, comparatively, a very small number with incomes above the average income. In short, the essential characteristic of current income distributions is that the great bulk of incomes are massed together near the lower end of the income scale. This fact is significant for the following reason. There is clear evidence that the physical characters of human beings—and considerable evidence that their mental characters—are distributed on an altogether different plan. When, for instance, a curve is plotted out for the heights of any large group of men, the resulting picture will not, as with incomes, have a humped and lop-sided appearance, but it will be a symmetrical curve shaped like a cocked-hat. It will, in short—to use a technical term —be the characteristic Gaussian curve, or curve of error, symmetrical about the mean in such wise that there is no massing near either end, but an equal number of heights above the mean and below it and a lessening number of people at every height as the distance from the mean in either direction is increased. Now, on the face of things, we should expect that, if, as there is reason to think, people's capacities are distributed on a plan of this kind, their incomes will be distributed in the same way. Why is not this expectation realised? A partial answer to this question may, perhaps, be found in a closer analysis of the word "capacities." For our purpose this must mean income-earning capacities. But people earn incomes by means of several different sorts of capacity, among which the principal division is between manual capacity and mental capacity. From the point of view of income-getting, therefore, it cannot properly be assumed that we are dealing with a single homogeneous group. If we examined together the members of a University and the members of a junior school, the table of heights obtained for these two groups jointly would not accord with the normal curve. If the number of persons in the University was much smaller than the number in the junior school group, heights very much above the average of the two groups combined would be unduly numerous. It may be that brain-workers constitute a homogeneous group and hand-workers a homogeneous group, but that, for the purpose of income-earning, they do not jointly constitute a homogeneous group ; that the normal law rules in each separately, but, as with the University and the school, not in both together. On these lines the peculiar form of the income-distribution curve might be partly explained. There is, however, a more important and more certain explanation. Income depends, not on capacity alone, whether manual or mental, but on a combination of capacity and inherited property. Inherited property is not distributed in proportion to capacity, but is concentrated upon a small number of persons. Even apart from the fact, to be referred to in a moment, that the possession of a large property enables the property-owner to improve his capacity by train-ing, this circumstance necessarily deflects the curve of income distribution from the " normal " form. The significance of this, from the standpoint of our present problem, is obvious. If the form of the income-distribution curve is partly determined by the facts of bequest and inheritance, the particular form which is found to be dominant in current conditions cannot possibly be *necessary*, except upon the assumption that the broad scheme of inheritance now generally in vogue is main-tained. An alleged law, then, that should speak of any form as necessary in an absolute sense, runs counter to this appar-ently irrefutable reasoning.[1]

§ 4. The statistics adduced by Pareto do not provide a basis for any counter-argument. For, as a matter of logic, it is plain that, if all the different groups to which his statistics refer possess any common characteristic in addition to the fact that they are all in receipt of income, no general inference about income distribution that is based upon them can be extended to groups not possessing these characteristics. But, in fact, all these groups are communities enjoying the

[1] Cf. Benini, *Principii di statistica metodologica*, p. 310.

general type of inheritance laws common to modern Europe.[1] It follows at once that no inference can be drawn as to how the form of the income distribution would be affected if these laws were abolished or fundamentally changed. In his *Manuale di economia politica,* published some years after the *Cours,* Pareto himself explicitly recognised this. He wrote: "We cannot assert that the form of the curve would not change if the social constitution were to change radically; if, for example, collectivism were to take the place of the system of private property." [2]

§ 5. Nor is it necessary to imagine so large a change as the destruction of inheritance laws, in order that the form of the income-curve may be largely affected. There is ground for believing that a like result would come about in consequence of anything that affected, in a marked way, the proportion between "earned" income and income derived from investments. The reason for this opinion is twofold. First, it is found by experience that incomes from property are distributed much more unevenly than incomes from either head-work or hand-work. Mr. Watkins, in his *Growth of Large Fortunes,* after printing an interesting table, comments on it as follows: "In making the comparisons made possible by this table, the criterion must be relative, not absolute. Convenient relative numbers are the ratio of the upper decile, or the upper centile, to the median. It will be observed that, in the statistics of wages, the upper decile is always somewhat less than twice the median, and, in one occupation of the nine, it is little more than one-fourth greater. In the distribution of salaries the upper decile is approximately twice the median, the inequality thus being not greatly different from that prevailing among wage-incomes. But there is a great gap between this and the prevailing distribution of income from property. In the Massachusetts

---

[1] Of course it is not suggested that the inheritance laws of all modern European countries are exactly identical. They differ considerably in detail. The French laws, for example, force a more even division of estates among children than the English laws and deny special privileges to the eldest son. It is interesting to connect this fact with the observation of Benini (*Principii di statistica metodologica,* p. 191), that the distribution of wealth is more even in France than it is here. (Cf. also Ely, *Property and Contract,* vol. i. p. 89.)

[2] *Loc. cit.* pp. 370-71.

probate statistics the upper decile is eight or nine times
the median, and the error is doubtless in the direction of
under-statement, since the figures are not net, so that large
deductions for debts should be made from the smaller estates,
and also since many very small properties do not pass through
the courts. Among French estates the upper decile is
thirteen times the median." [1]   For this country also the
available statistics show a much more marked concentration
of wealth than of income.   This is well illustrated by
Professor Clay's comparison between his own estimate for the
distribution of capital in the United Kingdom in 1912 and
Dr. Bowley's estimate for the distribution of income in 1910.
He wrote: "94·5 per cent of persons have 56 per cent of
the national income, while 96·2 per cent of persons have only
17·22 per cent of the national capital; 98·9 per cent of
persons have 71 per cent of income, while the same percentage of persons have only 33 per cent of the capital." [2]
Secondly, the distribution of earned income itself is likely
to be more uneven, the greater is the importance of
the unevenly distributed income from investments.   This
result comes about because differences in income from
investments make possible different degrees of educational
training and afford different opportunities for entering
lucrative professions.   The correlation between the two sorts
of income is illustrated by Benini in a table, in which he
divides the figures for certain Italian incomes into two parts:
"The one represents the income that people derive from
property, supposed to be invested for all the different
categories at a uniform rate of, say, 5 per cent; the other
represents the strictly personal income, due to work, enjoyed
by the same people.   For example, a total income of
2000 lire, accompanied by a property of 9016 lire, may be
regarded as composed of 451 lire, the fruit of investment, and
of 1549 lire, the fruit of professional activity.   Calculating in
this manner, we obtain the following table:

---

[1] *The Growth of Large Fortunes*, p. 18.
[2] *Proceedings of the Manchester Statistical Society*, 1924-26, pp. 64-5.   For
a useful summary of the available statistics concerning income and capital
distribution, cf. Carr-Saunders and Jones, *Social Structure in England and
Wales* (1927), chapters ix. and x.

Total Income (lire).	Income derived from Property.		Income derived from Personal Activity.
1,000	=	143 +	857
2,000	=	451 +	1549
4,000	=	1,458 +	2542
8,000	=	4,285 +	3715
16,000	=	11,665 +	4335
20,000	=	15,885 +	4115
32,000	=	28,640 +	3360
40,000	=	37,500 +	2500

It will be noticed, of course, that, so soon as total incomes begin to exceed 16,000 lire, the part derived from personal activity diminishes; but this does not mean that the remuneration of the profession followed diminishes; it only means that many will now live wholly on the income derived from their property without following any gainful profession, and that this conduct of theirs reduces the average of the income due to work for the class to which they belong."[1] Moreover, there is yet another way in which the form of the income-curve might be modified. A change in the distribution of training and so forth, that is, of investment of capital in people, may take place apart from variations in income from investments. When this happens, the change must tend directly to alter the distribution of earned income, even though original capacities are distributed in accordance with some (the same) law of error. It is perhaps some change of this kind that accounts for the conclusion, which Professor Moore derives from his study of American wage statistics, that the variability of wages (as between different people at the same time) was less in 1900 than it had been in 1890.

§ 6. When these points are conceded, the general defence of " Pareto's Law " as a law of even limited necessity rapidly crumbles. His statistics warrant no inference as to the effect on distribution of the introduction of any cause that is not already present in approximately equivalent form in at least one of the communities—and they are very limited in range—from which these statistics are drawn. This consideration is really fatal; and Pareto is driven,

---

[1] *Principii di statistica metodologica*, pp. 336-7.

in effect, to abandon the whole claim which, in the earlier exposition of his formula, he seemed to make. In the *Manuale di economia politica* he insists that that formula is purely empirical. " Some persons would deduce from it a general law as to the only way in which the inequality of incomes can be diminished. But such a conclusion far transcends anything that can be derived from the premises. Empirical laws, like those with which we are here concerned, have little or no value outside the limits for which they were found experimentally to be true." [1] This means that, even if the statistical basis of the " law " were much securer than it is, the law would but rarely enable us to assert that any contemplated change *must* leave the form of income distribution unaltered. As things are, in view of the weakness of its statistical basis, it can *never* enable us to do this. Disharmony between movements of the national dividend as a whole and of the absolute share accruing to the poor cannot be proved by statistical evidence to be impossible, and a detailed study of the matter must, therefore, be made.

[1] *Manuale di economia politica*, pp. 371-2.

CHAPTER III

§ 1. In undertaking that study we are forced to avail ourselves of a somewhat rough method of approximation. Our
inquiry is concerned with the comparative effects of certain
causes upon the size of the national dividend and upon its
distribution among rich and poor persons. No machinery
exists by which effects upon distribution in this sense can be
directly investigated. But economists have carried through,
and have made common property, a very full analysis of the
influences that affect distribution in another sense, namely,
distribution among the various "factors of production."
These two sorts of distribution are not the same. They
would be the same if each factor were provided exclusively
by a set of persons who provided nothing of any other
factor. But, of course, in real life the same man often
provides portions of several factors, obtaining part of his
income from one and part from another. A landlord is
not merely the owner of "the original and indestructible
properties of the soil." On the contrary, he frequently
invests a great deal of capital in his land, and sometimes
also considerable mental labour in choosing his tenants,
exercising a certain control over their methods, and deciding,
it may be, upon the necessity of evictions. A shopkeeper
provides capital, or waiting, to some extent, but he also
provides, especially if his sales are on credit, much mental
labour in judging the "standing of his customers" and not
a little uncertainty-bearing in respect of bad debts. A
large capitalist employer is still more obviously capitalist,
brain-worker, and uncertainty-bearer combined. Finally, an

ordinary manual worker is frequently, in some measure, also a capitalist. In view of these considerations, it is plain that doctrines about distribution among factors of production cannot be applied directly and unreservedly to problems concerning distribution among people. The difficulty is not, however, as it so happens, of decisive practical importance. By far the largest part of the poorer classes in this country consists of wage-earning workpeople. It is true, of course, that " there is no definite line between wage-earners and ·persons working directly for customers and small employers and small farmers, . . . nor is there any clear and uniform division between wages and salaries."[1] But the dominant position of wage-earners among the poor is illustrated by the fact that, whereas, before the war, they numbered some fifteen and a half millions, persons other than wage-earners with incomes below £160 a year numbered, say, three and a half millions.[2] Moreover, it is reasonable to suppose that a large number of persons earning small salaries or small incomes from working on their own account are affected by the main body of relevant economic causes in much the same way as wage-earners proper. For the purpose of the present discussion, therefore, though not, of course, for all purposes, we shall not commit any serious error if we treat manual workers and the poor as roughly equivalent classes. Furthermore, statistics show that by far the most important income-yielding instrument actually possessed by the poor of the United Kingdom, as thus defined, is manual labour. Persons in receipt of wages number, as I have said, some fifteen and a half millions, and it is probable that persons dependent upon wages amount to 30,000,000, or nearly two-thirds of the population. The accumulated property of these persons before the war—it is, of course, a good deal larger now—was estimated at £450,000,000, and the interest on it might, therefore, be put at some £20,000,000 a year. This was probably little more than $\frac{1}{35}$th part of the total income of the wage-earners, all the rest being received as wages of labour.[3] Hence, just as we have agreed roughly to identify

[1] Bowley, *The Division of the Product of Industry*, p. 12.
[2] *Ibid.* p. 11.   [3] Cf. Chiozza-Money, *Riches and Poverty*, p. 49.

the poor with the wage-earners, we may agree also to identify
the earnings of wage-earners with the earnings of the factor
labour. No appreciable error is introduced by this simplification. When we have made it, the familiar analysis of
economists can be directly applied.

§ 2. We may divide the factors of production, from whose
joint operation the national dividend results, into two broad
groups, labour and the factors other than labour. Of course,
neither labour nor the factors other than labour constitute
a homogeneous group made up of similar units. Labour
embraces the work both of wholly unskilled workpeople and
of numerous sorts of skilled artisans. The factors other than
labour embrace, along with the work of Nature, the work of
many kinds of mental ability and of various sorts of capital
instruments. This circumstance is not, however, relevant to
our present problem. That problem is to determine whether
and how far economic causes, which affect the national dividend as a whole in one sense, can affect the receipts of the
factor labour in the opposite sense. In the present chapter
attention will be concentrated upon two sets of causes of the
broadest kind, namely, those that act respectively on the
supply of capital in general and on the supply of labour
in general. It will be convenient to begin with capital.

§ 3. Capital, or to put the same thing in concrete terms,
capital instruments, are the embodiment of labour itself, waiting for the fruits of labour and uncertainty-bearing. Consequently, apart from inventions and improvements, which will
be considered presently, an increase in the supply of capital
instruments can only mean that people have been willing to
undertake more waiting for the fruits of labour and more
exposure of those fruits to uncertainty. In other words, the
supply of waiting, or of uncertainty-bearing, or of both, has
been increased. It is obvious that a cause of this kind will
make for an increase in the national dividend as a whole.
Can it at the same time make for a decrease in the real income of labour ? The analysis relevant to this question has
been developed by Marshall. Subject to certain important
qualifications, which do not affect the present argument, this
analysis shows, first, that every factor of production, including

entrepreneurs' work,[1] tends to be remunerated at a rate equivalent to its marginal net product of commodities in general. It shows, secondly, that, other things being equal, the marginal net product, in this sense, of every factor diminishes as the supply of the factor increases beyond a fairly low minimum.[2] For, as the supply of any factor increases, the supplies of all the other factors being given, it pushes forward an irregular boundary along a great number of routes;[3] and, the more of it there is, the smaller is the quantity of other factors, with which to co-operate and from which to derive assistance, that each new unit finds available. This proposition expresses what may be called the *law of diminishing returns to individual factors of production.* This law must not be confused with the law of *diminishing returns to resources in general invested in a given occupation,* referred to in Part II. Chapter XI.

§ 4. From this analysis an important proposition directly relevant to our present problem can be derived. This proposition has two sides, and is to this effect : If the quantity of any factor of production is increased, the reward per efficiency unit reaped by all factors completely rival to that factor (in the sense of being perfect substitutes) will be diminished, and the reward per efficiency unit reaped by all factors completely co-operant with it, and in no degree substitutes, will be increased. The former

---

[1] The special case of the entrepreneur's earnings is discussed in detail by Professor Edgeworth in the *Quarterly Journal of Economics* for February 1904 ; it is also touched upon in his paper on " Mathematical Theories " in the *Economic Journal* of December 1907.

[2] This idea is well expressed by Turgot in an elaborate figure (cf. Cassel, *Nature and Necessity of Interest,* p. 22). In illustration, it may be noticed that, as the rate of interest falls, instrumental goods come to be built more solidly and to be repaired and renewed more readily when need arises.

[3] The significance of this qualification is that, in a given state of the other factors, an increase in the supply of one factor *up to the amount required to provide a single group-unit on the optimum scale—e.g.* a sufficient number of men to lift a heavy tree or a sufficient number to run one factory of *optimum* size in *each* occupation—need not yield diminishing returns. It is not relevant to the present argument that an increase in the scale of population, by generating closer contacts and mutual stimulation of thought, may indirectly lead to an increase in the supply of capital and to improved organisation, and that, *therefore,* output may increase in a larger proportion than population. The law of diminishing returns is concerned with the effects of an increase in the supply of one factor of production when the supply of other factors is *not* increased.

half of this proposition is obvious. The advent of Chinese immigrants in the retailing business *must* injure the British retail shopkeepers of New Zealand, and the steady flow of low-grade European immigrants *must* keep down the wages of unskilled workmen in the United States.[1] The latter half of the proposition is easily proved as follows. Since each unit of the increased factor must be paid at the same rate, and the rate for the new units is less than the old rate, a part of the product of the old as well as of the new units is handed over to the co-operant factors.[2] As an illustration, we may note that a high level of wages generally prevails in new countries, because, first, there is a large quantity of land available, and, secondly, by mortgaging the land to foreigners, the inhabitants can obtain a large quantity of capital also.[3]

§ 5. If, as is, of course, generally true in the concrete, different factors are partly co-operant and partly rival, the effect of an increase in the quantity of one of them upon the reward obtained by the others can be analysed in this wise. Suppose that the quantity of factor A increases from A to $(A + a)$, and that x of the new units are substituted in uses formerly occupied by mx units of the other factor B. Then the effect produced on the reward per unit of B is equal to that which would have been produced had the two factors been entirely co-operant, and had the quantity of A increased

---

[1] Professor Taussig wrote in 1906 that, whereas most money incomes in the United States have increased, "the wages of ordinary day labour and of such factory labour as is virtually unskilled seem to have remained stationary and sometimes seem even to have fallen" (*Quarterly Journal of Economics*, 1906, p. 521). Whether the unskilled immigrants are mainly rival or mainly co-operant with the skilled workers of America is another and more difficult question. Dr. Hourwich writes on this point : "It is only because the new immigrants have furnished the class of unskilled labour that the native workmen and older immigrants have been raised to the plane of an aristocracy of labour" (*Immigration and Labour*, p. 12). In the same sense Prof. Prato (*Le Protectionisme ouvrier*, p. 72) maintains that, in general, the low-grade immigrant takes on occupations which native-born workpeople wish to leave, and that this is true, not only of the Chinese and European immigrant into the United States, but also of the Italian and Belgian immigrant to France, Switzerland, and Germany.

[2] It is not relevant to the present argument to note, though the point may be added for completeness, that, in response to the improved demand, the co-operant factors tend to increase in quantity, but, since their supply curve is inclined positively, not to a sufficient extent to reduce their receipts to the old level.

[3] Cf. Marshall, *Royal Commission on Labour*, Q. 4237-8.

from A to $(A + a - x)$ and the quantity of B from B to $(B + mx)$. It is obvious that this effect *may* represent either an increase or a decrease in the reward per unit of B, and that it is more likely to represent an increase, the larger is $\dfrac{A + a - x}{A}$ relatively to $\dfrac{B + mx}{B}$. It is not possible, in the absence of knowledge as to the form of the function representing the relations between the factors and their product, to make any statement more precise than this. Interpreted roughly, the condition, under which, on the hypothesis taken, an increase in the quantity of A would lead to an increase in the reward per unit of B, is that the predominant part of the extra units of A can be profitably turned to uses other than those formerly occupied by units of B. Hence, in general, where two factors are partly co-operant and partly rival, an increase in the quantity of the one will augment the reward per unit, and, therefore, the absolute share of the dividend, enjoyed by the other, if the relation of co-operation between the two factors is more important than the relation of rivalry.

§ 6. The question whether the relation between waiting and uncertainty-bearing in general and labour in general is, in the concrete, mainly co-operant or mainly rival is not one to which an *a priori* answer can be given. If the only sort of capital instruments which mankind had learned how to make were a kind of Frankenstein monster capable of exactly duplicating the labour of manual workers, and not capable of doing anything else, this relation would be wholly one of rivalry. What it is in actual fact, therefore, chiefly depends on the nature of the things which people are able, by combining labour with waiting and uncertainty - bearing, to create. If we consider realistically what these things in the main are—and, of course, when what is contemplated is a general increase in the supply of waiting and uncertainty-bearing, we must imagine the new supplies to be used in an all-round addition to existing capital instruments—it is apparent that their work is mainly co-operant. Railways, ships, factory buildings, machines, motor cars and houses, whether in the hands of private people or of business men who let them out on hire, taken broadly, are tools for, and not rivals to, men. By giving help, they enable any nth worker to produce more stuff or service than he could have produced without them ; they do not, by supplanting him, compel him to produce less. This is the general teaching of experience. In particular instances, indeed, the relation is predominantly one of rivalry. But, *comparatively*, these are unimportant. As Marshall well writes : " There is a real and effective competition between labour in general and [waiting to which should be added uncertainty-bearing] in general. But it covers a small part of the whole field, and is of small importance relatively to the benefit which labour derives from obtaining cheaply the aid of capital, and, therefore, of efficient methods in the production of things that it needs." [1] In other words, the relation between capital as a whole and labour as a whole is predominantly one of co-operation. It follows that the question set out for discussion in § 2 must be answered in the negative. It is not, in present conditions, practically possible that a cause (other than inventions and improvements, which will be considered in the next chapter) operating to expand the national dividend by increasing the supply of capital generally should at the same time lessen the real income of labour. Similarly, of course, it can be shown that a cause operating to contract the dividend by diminishing the supply of capital generally cannot at the same time increase the real income of labour. In this field, in short, disharmony cannot occur.

§ 7. This conclusion leads up to the difficult problem of capital investments abroad. Apart from the special qualifications indicated on page 188, it may be presumed that, since nobody will invest abroad rather than at home unless he expects a better return, freedom to invest abroad will augment the national dividend. As against this, it seems at first sight that it will diminish the real income of labour. The funds for investment must be obtained either by exporting goods or by refraining from the import of goods to which we have a claim. It makes very little difference whether or not the granting of a loan is made conditional

[1] *Principles of Economics*, p. 540.

upon the proceeds of it being expended in purchasing the railway material, or other things, which it is destined to pay for, in the lending country.   If this is done, the *kind* of goods that we export may be altered, but the volume of them will not be substantially affected.   In any event the volume of things immediately available in this country will be diminished.   This is practically certain to involve a direct injury to labour, either by making the things workpeople buy more expensive, or by reducing the supply of tools and machines that help them in production.   It is true that, since some capital will have been withdrawn from home uses, the rate of interest here will go up, and this will encourage saving to create more capital.   But this tendency can only mitigate, and not wipe out, the initial injury to labour.   It follows that labour must be less well-off *in terms of things in general* than it would have been if the opening for investing capital abroad had been closed.

This result, however, is not decisive.   In certain circumstances, even though this happens, labour may, nevertheless, be better off in terms of the particular things which workpeople are interested to buy.   For, as an indirect effect of our foreign investments, these things may have been substantially cheapened.   In actual fact this has happened.   Sir George Paish, writing in 1914, stated : " In the aggregate, Great Britain has supplied the world outside these islands with nearly £600,000,000 for the construction of railways in the last seven years (out of a total so supplied by her of upwards of eleven hundred millions), and all of the money has been placed in countries upon which we depend for our supplies of food and raw material." [1]   When our foreign investments are of this character, the real income of labour, in the only sense that signifies, is fairly certain to be increased, so that no disharmony arises.   No doubt, if there were special reason to believe that, had the export of capital been forbidden, the funds set free would have been devoted to domestic uses specially beneficial to workpeople, such as the erection of a large number of healthy workmen's cottages, this conclusion

[1] " The Export of Capital and the Cost of Living," *Manchester Statistical Society*, Feb. 1914, p. 78.

would not hold good. But there is not, in general, special reason to believe this.

Moreover, it is necessary to take account of certain more remote consequences of foreign investment. When the export of capital is free, the opportunity to obtain higher interest abroad both causes more British capital to be created—in lieu of consumption—than would have been created otherwise, and also enables a part of it to be invested in enterprises yielding a larger return than would otherwise have been open to it. Thus freedom to export capital at one time exercises a twofold influence in enlarging the aggregate real income of the country at a later time. It follows that, other things being equal, the amount of new capital that can be created there at a later time will be enlarged. This effect will repeat itself cumulatively year after year. In the end, therefore, if we suppose the amount of capital annually exported to remain constant —though not, of course, if we suppose the interest earned on capital invested abroad always to be itself invested there— the extra capital created at home as an indirect result of past exportation must exceed the amount withdrawn by contemporary exportation. On this supposition, in the end, labour as a whole will be benefited and not injured. Though, therefore, disharmony may prevail from the point of view of a short period, in the higher unity of the long view it may well be resolved. The practical inference is that all proposals to restrict the export of capital in the interests of labour—apart from the special reasons discussed on page 188 cited above— should be subjected to a very cautious and critical scrutiny.

§ 8. We turn to the second main group of causes distinguished in § 2, those, namely, which operate through the supply of labour. It is evident that, if this supply is increased, whether the increase comes about through an addition to the number of workpeople or through an addition to their average capacity, the national dividend must be increased. Our problem, therefore, is to ascertain the effect that will be produced upon the aggregate real income of labour. The analysis set out in the preceding section shows that the marginal net product of labour, in terms of things in general, and, therefore, its real earnings *per unit*, must be diminished. Whether its *aggregate* earnings will be increased depends, therefore, on whether the elasticity of the demand for labour in general is greater or less than unity. If this elasticity is greater than unity, labour in the aggregate will receive a larger absolute quantity of dividend than before ; whereas, if the elasticity is less than unity, it will receive a smaller absolute quantity.[1] It is, therefore, necessary to determine whether in fact the elasticity of demand is greater or less than unity.[2]

Let us begin by ignoring the fact that an addition to the supply of labour available in industry is likely to react upon the supply of other factors co-operating with it. It may then be observed that there is a certain field of personal service where labour works practically unaided

---

[1] The general proposition, of which the statement in the text is a special instance, is that, other things being equal, an increase in the quantity of any one factor of production will be accompanied by an increase in the *absolute share* of product accruing to that factor, provided that the demand for the said factor has an elasticity greater than unity. The condition on which it will be accompanied by an increase in the *proportionate share* of product accruing to the factor is different from this, and can be determined as follows. The supply of the other factors being given, the aggregate output P depends on the quantity of the variable factor, in such wise that, if x represents this quantity, $P = f(x)$. The *absolute share* accruing to the variable factor is, therefore, represented by xf', and the *proportionate share* by $\dfrac{xf'}{f}$. The condition that this latter magnitude shall increase when x increases is that

$$\frac{1}{f}\left\{f' + xf''\right\} + xf'\left\{\frac{-f'}{[f']^2}\right\} \text{ is positive.}$$

Let e represent the elasticity of demand for the factor in question. Then

$$e = -\frac{f'}{xf''} ;$$

and the above condition can be expressed, by easy substitution, in the form

$$e > \frac{1}{1 - \dfrac{xf'}{f}} \text{ or } e > 1 + \frac{\dfrac{xf'}{f}}{1 - \dfrac{xf'}{f}}.$$

Thus e exceeds unity by a larger amount, the larger is the proportionate share of the product accruing, before the variation, to our variable factor. The condition set out above in symbols can be expressed in words, as Dr. Dalton has pointed out, by the statement that " the elasticity of demand is greater than the reciprocal of the relative share of all other factors taken together " (*The Inequality of Incomes*, p. 187).

[2] The term elasticity of demand, as employed by Marshall and in the text above, signifies proportionate change in quantity divided by proportionate change in price when the changes are very small (strictly infinitesimal). It is what Dr. Dalton calls " point elasticity " (cf. *The Inequality of Incomes*, pp. 192-7). Hence, in order that the argument of the text may hold good of substantial

by other factors, where, therefore, its productivity per unit
would not appreciably fall with an increase in its quantity,
and where a good deal could be absorbed without greatly
reducing the value of its product in terms of other things.
This circumstance points, *pro tanto*, to a fairly low rate of
diminution in the (real) demand for labour in general as the
quantity of it increases; though exactly *how rapid* the rate of
diminution would be, or, in other words, how elastic is the
demand for labour, it is quite impossible to say. In real life,
however, it is illegitimate to ignore reactions, indirectly
brought about by an increase in the supply of labour, on
the supply of other factors. In particular, the supply of
capital is known to be very far from rigidly fixed. When
the quantity of labour increases, and, hence, indirectly, the
return per unit of capital is enhanced—though, no doubt,
those people who have decided to leave some definite sum to
their descendants will not be willing to save so much as before—
people in general will be willing to save more than before,
and so to create a greater quantity of capital.[1] Moreover,
owing to the greater size of the national dividend, their
ability to save will be increased. The resultant increase in
the supply of capital will react to increase the marginal productivity of any given quantity of labour. On the whole,
therefore, it is probable that the demand for labour, even
viewed from the general standpoint of the whole world, is
fairly elastic.[2] The probability is far stronger as regards
the demand for labour in any single country. For capital
is so mobile that a small increase in the return per unit
obtainable by it in any one country must inevitably—
apart from complications due to double income-tax, about
which it may be hoped that international arrangements will
soon be made—bring about a large influx from foreign
countries, or, what comes to the same thing, a large contraction

---

increases of supply, we must suppose that the elasticity of demand is greater or
less than unity, as the case may be, not merely in respect either of the old or of
the new quantity of supply, but also in respect of all the quantities intermediate
between these two.

[1] Cf. Marshall, *Principles of Economics*, p. 235.

[2] Cf. Edgeworth, "On the Use of the Differential Calculus in Economics,"
Rivista di Scientia, vol. vii. pp. 90-91.

of the outflow that formerly went to foreign countries. Hence the elasticity of the aggregate demand for British labour is greater than the elasticity of that part of the demand which depends on British capital alone. It is, indeed, so much greater that, with any reasonable assumption as to this latter elasticity, the elasticity of the aggregate demand is practically certain, from the standpoint of a long period, which is alone in question here, to be immensely larger than unity.

Hence it follows that an increase in the supply of labour, whether through an increase in the number of units of labour of given efficiency that the average workman provides, or through an increase in the number of workmen providing, on the average, a given number of units of labour, must increase the absolute quantum of dividend that labour in the aggregate receives. It is, no doubt, true that, within the broad group labour, an increase in capacity, which only affected some of the sub-groups, might involve injury to other sub-groups, whose capacity has not been improved. Even this danger, however, is likely to be avoided where the different sub-groups are not strictly homogeneous, but are partly co-operant, and where, as occurs when some unskilled labourers are trained to trades, the group, which is not made more capable, is diminished in numbers by the indirect operation of the change that has occurred. Furthermore, these incidents within the broad group labour are, in any event, of subordinate interest. So soon as it is shown that the absolute share of labour as a whole possesses, along with the aggregate dividend, the property of increasing with increases in the supply of labour, the only proposition that is of direct relevance to the present argument is established.

§ 9. When the increase in the supply of labour comes about through an increase in the capacity of labouring people, it is obvious that the consequent increase in the absolute share of dividend accruing to them carries with it, in accordance with the argument of previous chapters, an increase in their economic welfare. When, however, the increase of supply comes about through an increase in numbers, the absolute share *per man* is lessened, despite the fact that the absolute share of the group as a whole is increased. If there were reason to believe that the loss per man were large, we should hesitate to conclude that an increase of this sort in the supply of labour involves an increase in the economic welfare of labour. In fact, however, it can be shown that, under the conditions now existing in this country, the loss per man would be very small. That it would be very small in terms of commodities in general follows from the fact already established, that the elasticity of the demand for labour in England is large. If the conditions were such that an increase in numbers would lead to a material increase in the price of food or other articles predominantly consumed by the working-classes, it might, indeed, be large in terms of the things that are of significance to them. At present, however, the fact that we are able to import food freely from abroad, makes it impossible that an increase in the population of a small country such as ours should, to any important extent, evoke the law of increasing supply price in respect of it. Hence, in all senses, the diminution of real wages per head of the working-classes would be very small.[1] Consequently, it seems reasonable to conclude that an increase in the absolute share of labour, even when it results from an increase in the numbers of the population, will carry with it an increase in the economic welfare of working people. It is not necessary, therefore, to qualify our conclusion, that causes impinging upon the supply of labour affect the aggregate amount of the dividend and the aggregate real earnings of labour in the same sense, by emphasising the caution that the welfare of labour is sometimes diminished by causes that increase its wealth.

§ 10. The results that have been reached in this chapter serve to rebut two popular opinions. The first of these has to do with hours of labour, and is to the effect that a general shortening of the working day, because it will cut down the supply of labour, will enable workpeople as a whole to secure terms so much better than before that their aggregate real income must be increased. The truth is that, in so far as a diminution in the hours of work leads to a more than corresponding increase in capacity, both the national dividend and the absolute share of labour will benefit.

[1] Cf. Marshall, *Principles of Economics*, p. 672.

But, if the reduction of hours is pushed beyond this point, so that it injures the national dividend, the real income of labour must, in view of the elasticity of the demand for labour, necessarily be injured also. The second popular opinion is that the compulsory withdrawal from work of persons in receipt of State assistance would increase the aggregate real earnings of the poor, and, therefore, from the point of view of labour, ought to be encouraged. Two schemes were submitted to the Royal Commission on the Aged Poor, one of which contained, as a condition for the receipt of a pension, "the abstention from all work of pensioners, male and female," while the other would have awarded pensions to "every one over sixty, and prohibited work beyond that age." [1] The defence proffered for those schemes was that, if pensioners did not abstain from work, independent workpeople would find their earnings diminished. From a long-period point of view, however, the interests of the poor should be identified, not with those of independent workpeople only, but with those of all workpeople ; for all workpeople are liable to become dependent at some period of their lives. But it follows directly from what was said in the preceding section that, if the supply of labour is contracted, the aggregate earnings of independent and dependent workpeople together will be diminished. Hence, so far as the present argument goes, it is inadvisable to adopt the policy embodied in these two pension schemes. It should be noted, however, that the cessation of work by pensioners can be defended from a more special point of view. It may be held desirable that the qualification for a pension should be, not age, but declining strength. This cannot be tested directly, but, if abstention from work were made a condition for receiving, say, a 10s. pension, conformity to the condition would ensure that recipients were really incapable of earning much more than 10s. regularly. Hence such an arrangement, though it would abolish work on the part of many persons below the 10s. line, might, nevertheless, be desirable as a means of preventing many other persons from obtaining pensions, and, in consequence of obtaining or expecting them, from

[1] *Report of the Royal Commission on the Aged Poor*, p. 72.

relaxing their efforts in industry.   The pension policy pursued
by certain friendly societies seems to be based on considerations of this order.[1]   Clearly, however, this argument is not
relevant where the condition for the receipt of a pension is,
not declining strength, but the attainment of some definite age.

---

[1] *Royal Commission on the Aged Poor, Minutes of Evidence* (Q. 10,880).

CHAPTER IV

§ 1. WE have thus seen that in existing conditions causes acting through the supply of capital in general and also causes acting through the supply of labour in general operate harmoniously. They either increase both the national dividend and the real earnings of labour, or they decrease both of them. A more complicated problem has to be faced when the initiating cause is an invention or improvement in processes or methods. All developments of this kind, since they enable something to be produced which was not being produced at all before, or enable something which was being produced before to be produced more easily, must increase the national dividend. Unless at the same time they indirectly alter distribution adversely to labour, they must also increase the real income which falls to labour. Hence, of any invention considered in the abstract, there is an initial presumption that its effects will be harmonious, in the sense that it will benefit labour as well as increase the national dividend. But it is *possible* that a given invention may change the parts played by capital and labour in production in such a way as to make labour less valuable relatively to capital than it was before ; and, if this happens, the absolute share received by labour *may be* diminished. Our problem is to determine in what, if any, conditions this result will come about. It is interesting to observe that exactly the same analysis is appropriate when the initiating cause is, not an invention in the ordinary sense, but a development which enables a country to obtain some commodity more cheaply than before by making something else with which to purchase it from elsewhere, instead

671

of making the commodity itself. Here too more of what people want is made available ; and here too the proportionate parts played by labour and capital in production may be changed.

§ 2. The popular solution of our problem is very simple. It is thought that workpeople will be injured if an invention causes less labour to be employed in the industry to which it refers, and benefited if it causes more labour to be employed there. Such a view leads at once to optimism. Mr. Hobson has, indeed, shown that inventions do not always cause more labour to be employed in the industry where they are introduced : " The introduction of spinning and weaving machinery into Lancashire and Yorkshire afforded a considerable increase of employment, and a number of successive inventions and improvements during the second and third quarters of the last century had a similar result, but later increments of machinery have not been attended by similar results ; on the contrary, there has been a decline in the number of persons employed in some of the staple textile processes. The introduction of typesetting machines into printing works has been followed by a large increase of employment ; the introduction of clicking machinery into the shoe trade has been followed by a net reduction of employment." [1] A broader illustration of a diminution of employment in a particular sphere, in consequence of an invention in that sphere, may be found in agriculture : for it is well known that agricultural machines have displaced a substantial number of agricultural labourers. An occasional failure of this kind is fully admitted by all. Still, in the main, inventions are believed by those who have studied the matter to increase, and not to diminish, employment at the point at which they act. Thus M. Levasseur writes : " The common opinion is that ' the machine drives out the workman ' and robs a part of the working-classes of work. It is certainly true that a shop furnished with powerful machinery yields in a given time a greater product, with the help of a much smaller number of employees, than a shop where the same goods are made by hand. It is this

[1] Hobson, *The Industrial System*, p. 281.

that one perceives in the first instance. What one only perceives later, by dint of study, is that the goods made economically by machinery, being sold, in general, at a lower price, often find such a number of new purchasers that the increased production, thus made necessary, provides employment for a greater number of workpeople than were employed before the machinery was introduced."[1] Again, the Poor Law Commissioners are gratified to find among manufacturers a remarkable consensus of opinion concerning the effects of improvements in machinery. They believe that such improvements " do temporarily reduce the demand for labour within the department where such changes occur; that the displacement does not, as a rule, reduce the labour employed in each producing unit, the workers dispensed with being readily absorbed within the same business—particularly in shipbuilding, where changes are slowly introduced and affect only a few men at a time—and that the final result is that more labour is required instead of less."[2] Now, I am not concerned to deny the empirical part of these conclusions. I do not dispute the Poor Law Commissioners' assertion that the conditions necessary to secure that increased employment in any sphere will ultimately result from an invention in that sphere are, as a matter of practice, usually fulfilled. I do dispute, however, the very widespread opinion that these facts are directly relevant to the question whether inventions and improvements are beneficial allies or injurious foes to the fortunes of labour, and so of the poor as a whole. To elucidate that issue a different and more far-reaching analysis is necessary.

§ 3. Every invention or improvement either facilitates the manufacture of some commodity or service that is already being produced, or makes possible the manufacture of some new commodity or service. It is certain, therefore, to lead to a cheapening and an increased consumption of the commodity affected by it. With the differently made and enlarged output, a different amount of labour, and also a different amount of capital (or waiting), will be employed in the industry and in the subsidiary industries engaged

---

[1] *Salariat et salaires*, p. 421.   [2] *Report*, p. 344.

Z

in making machinery for it. Let us suppose that work
people purchase absolutely none of the product which the
invention has cheapened. Then the effect of the invention
upon their real income depends upon its effect on the
marginal net product of things for which labour is responsible
in other industries; for, when equilibrium is established,
it will get, in the industry where the invention has taken
place, the same real wage as it gets in these industries. For
the present purpose we may reasonably leave out of account
factors of production other than labour and capital. It
will then follow that, if, as a result of the invention,
the quantity of labour in industries other than the improved industry and its subsidiaries is diminished in a larger
ratio, or increased in a smaller ratio, than the quantity
of capital, the marginal net product of labour in terms of
the things workpeople buy—and, therefore, the aggregate real
income of workpeople—must be increased. In the converse
event this aggregate real income must be diminished. If
the two ratios of change are equal, it must be left unaltered.
Inventions which have these several effects I shall call, respectively, capital-saving inventions, labour-saving inventions
and neutral inventions. It will, of course, be observed that
this use of terms is different from the common use, according
to which every invention that enables a given amount of
product to be got with the help of less labour is labour-saving.

§ 4. It is easy to apply this analysis to practice, provided
we have to do with an industry in which (and also in its
subsidiaries) the proportion of the country's total labour
employed is equal to the proportion of its total capital. In
this class of industry anything which changes in one direction
the ratio between the labour and capital employed there must
change in the opposite direction the ratio outside. Hence, on
my definition, an invention or improvement which reduces the
ratio of capital to labour in the industry where it applies will
be capital-saving, one which increases it, labour-saving, and one
which leaves it unchanged, neutral. In these conditions, therefore, we are able with fair confidence to distinguish in the concrete the several classes of inventions. Thus, assuming the
above conditions to prevail, the introduction of two-shift or three-

shift systems, making possible the more continuous working of machinery, *must* be a capital-saving invention. For, if, instead of only 12 hours being worked in each 24-hour period, the whole 24 hours are worked, a staff of 100 men, 50 working by day and 50 by night, will only require half as much machinery to produce a given output as they would need if the whole 100 worked by day only. Of course, the machinery will wear out more quickly when it is worked for a longer time per day. But for many kinds of machinery the working life is—on account of obsolescence—much shorter than the physical life. Consequently, though the substitution of two twelve-hour shifts for one twelve-hour shift would not reduce the capital required for a given scale of production by as much as a half, it would, in general, reduce it a good deal. In whatever way, therefore, the absolute quantity of output is changed, the ratio of capital to labour employed must be diminished. The same result holds good of developments that enable the manufacturers, wholesalers or retailers, who deal in any commodity, to conduct their business equally efficiently with a smaller amount of capital locked up in the form of stocks. For, here again, whatever happens to absolute amounts, the ratio of capital to labour employed must be diminished. This point is of some importance in view of the economy in the matter of stock-holding, which, as will be shown in Appendix I., modern improvements in communication have made practicable. Among developments more ordinarily named inventions, we might, still assuming the industries to which they apply to have previously employed capital and labour in normal proportions, count as capital-saving such things as Marconi's invention of wireless telegraphy, by which the need for cables is removed. Probably, however, the majority of inventions in the narrower sense would have to be reckoned as "labour-saving," because, as Dr. Cassell has observed, "almost all the efforts of inventors are directed towards finding durable instruments to do work which has hitherto been done by hand."[1] These results, it must be remembered, are not necessarily valid, unless, before the invention, the industry (and its subsidiaries), in which the invention is

---

[1] *Nature and Necessity of Interest*, p. 112.

made, was employing labour and capital in the same proportion as the general average of all industries.   If it was employing an abnormally large proportion of labour or of capital, an invention, which changed the ratio in it in any direction, might change the ratio in other industries in the same, and not in the opposite, direction.   Suppose, for example, that in a particular industry 3000 units of labour and 1000 units of capital are being employed, and in the rest of industry one million units of each.   In consequence of an invention in this particular industry only 2000 units of labour and 500 units of capital come to be needed there.   The ratio of labour to capital there is, therefore, increased from 3 to 1 to 4 to 1. At the same time in the rest of industry it is increased from 1 to 1 to 1,001,000 to 1,000,500.   It is thus evident that a knowledge of the effect on the ratio in the improved industry would not by itself enable us to determine whether the invention is labour-saving or capital-saving or neutral.   But, plainly, we have no ground for supposing that labour-saving inventions in my sense are impossible.   If they take place in the conditions contemplated up to this point of our analysis, disharmony must result.   The national dividend will be increased, but the real earnings of labour will be lessened.

§ 5.   The conditions so far contemplated are not, however, in conformity with the facts.   It has been assumed that workpeople purchase absolutely none of the commodity or service which the invention or improvement has cheapened. Obviously this assumption is highly unfavourable to the prospect of their obtaining an increased real income.   When conditions are such that, even on this assumption, they would gain, in so far as in fact they do purchase the commodity they will gain still more;   and, when conditions are such that, on this assumption, they would lose, nevertheless in real life they may gain.   In short, the more important is the part played by the commodity to which the invention refers in the consumption of poor people, the more likely it is that the net effect of the invention will be advantageous to them.

In the light of this result it is a very significant fact that the things principally purchased by the working-classes are relatively crude things, which can be readily made on a

large scale by machinery, while the things principally purchased by the well-to-do are of higher quality, and, therefore,
involve a larger use of human labour. Marshall writes:
"Probably about twice as much horse-power is used in
providing for each pound's worth of expenditure on commodities by the poor as by the rich." But it is just in
things of this kind that the readiest opportunities are found
for mechanical inventions and improvements, and in which,
as a matter of fact, these are most extensively made. No
doubt, the consumption of the poor embraces a much larger
proportion of house-room and food than the consumption of
the rich, and both building labour and agricultural labour are
relatively little aided by those mechanical instruments, in
respect of which technical improvements and devices of
organisation have the widest scope. This qualification is
especially applicable to the very poor. "The fall of prices
does not benefit the various grades of wage-earners in direct
ratio to their wages. Rent and certain other necessary
elements of expenditure, such as fuel, which have risen in
amount for the large majority of workers, play a relatively
larger part in the budget of the lower grades of workers,
reducing to that extent their gain from the general fall of
prices. The poorest classes, whose retail purchases are made
in very small quantities, also gain least from the lower prices
of other commodities than housing and fuel."[1] But these
qualifications leave the main result untouched. On the whole,
the poor spend a larger proportion of their income than other
classes on things the manufacture of which specially lends
itself to inventions. Thus Leroy-Beaulieu notes : "The man of
fashion, who is fitted for his clothes by a tailor, gains nothing
from the great reduction of prices which shops selling clothes
ready-made offer to the less comfortable section of the population."[2] He contrasts with these things "all those objects,
which the mass of the people have hitherto done without, but
which have now come into general use, and which contribute
either to better hygiene or to increased decency and dignity
in the homes of the workpeople. Stockings, handkerchiefs,

[1] *Report of the Royal Commission on the Poor Laws*, p. 309.
[2] *La Répartition des richesses*, p. 37.

more varied and more suitable garments, curtains for the
windows, carpets on the floors, a less exiguous array of
furniture, these things constitute democratic luxury, the fruit
of the development of mankind's powers of production." [1]
Nor is this all. It has to be added, as Marshall has strongly
urged, that the staple articles of food mainly consumed
by the poor are, so far as this country is concerned, largely
brought from abroad, and that one of the most marked features
of recent times has been the development of improvements
in the machinery of transport, and the consequent heavy fall
in transport charges. To this may be added the important
improvement in the machinery for retailing goods to poor
persons, which has been realised by co-operative stores, and the
consequent heavy fall in the cost of the service of retailing.

Of course the historical fact that recent inventions have
largely affected commodities, which enter directly or indirectly
into the consumption of the working-classes, is not a proof
that further inventions will be predominantly of a like kind.
It is, however, open to us to urge that this historical fact is
conformable to a priori expectation, because, not only are the
openings for profit, and, therefore, the stimulus to invention,
exceptionally great among " mass-goods " of wide consumption,
but also, as Marshall has pointed out, and as the history
of the motor car, culminating in the petrol-driven lorry and
motor omnibus, illustrates, even those improvements, which were
originally designed exclusively for the luxuries of the rich,
are apt soon to spread themselves to the comforts of other
classes.[2] These considerations lead to the conclusion that it
is less likely than the argument of the preceding section
alone would suggest that any given invention will injure the
real income of labour.

§ 6. Yet another qualification must be added to the
analysis of §§ 3-4. That analysis tacitly assumed that the
invention, whose consequences were examined, had no effect
on the quantity of new waiting, or capital, which people are
prepared annually to create. This assumption, however, is
not warranted. Certain sorts of invention, by giving a new

[1] *La Répartition des richesses*, p. 440.
[2] Of. *Principles of Economics*, p. 541.

field for "spending," may cause rich people to save less and so to provide less new capital to help labour in production. The invention of luxurious motor cars for private travel, by inducing people to spend more of their income on petrol, chauffeurs' wages and so on,[1] has probably had this effect, and the impending invention of comfortable private air cars probably will have it. Nor is the effect necessarily confined to inventions which create opportunities for new forms of consumption. It may also follow from those that cheapen consumption goods which are already known, provided that they are of highly elastic demand. People who could have saved and created capital may be tempted to spend instead. On the other hand, inventions that cheapen things for which the demand is highly inelastic, by enabling people to get what they want at less cost, will leave them a greater margin out of which to make savings, and so will indirectly increase the annual creation of new capital. Whether the tendency thus set up by inventions is towards a decrease or towards an increase in the annual addition that is made to capital, it is cumulative, in the sense that in each successive year that year's check to the flow of new capital is added to the total check imposed on the *stock* of all capital. For this reason it is more important than it might be thought to be at first sight. When the indirect effect of an invention is to diminish savings, it may injure labour even though it is capital-saving; and, when the indirect effect is to increase savings, it may benefit labour even though it is both labour-saving and also concerned with some product which does not enter at all into workpeople's consumption. There is reason to believe that hitherto the general body of inventions has had the effect of increasing, and not of diminishing, the opportunity and the will to accumulate new capital.

§ 7. From these various considerations it is plain that no rigid and exact conclusions can be drawn. The general impression created by our study is that, though inventions

---

[1] This statement is not incompatible with the facts (1) that the resources devoted to making the motor car itself are turned into "capital" uses, and (2) that the existence of a private motor car of given value may tend to push up wages (by drawing people into service with it away from other employment) as much as the existence of a machine employed in industry.

and improvements injurious to the real income of the working-classes *may* occur, they will not occur often. The great majority of inventions and improvements will increase the real income of labour as well as the aggregate national dividend. Disharmony, as a result of inventions, is a possible, but a decidedly improbable, contingency. Nobody would seriously propose to interfere with, or to obstruct, inventions in order to provide a safeguard against it.

CHAPTER V

THE MANIPULATION OF WAGES

§ 1. In the latter portion of Part III. I examined at length the conditions under which an enforced increase in the wages rate paid in a particular occupation or place would injure the national dividend. We have now to consider the effect that will be produced on the real income of workpeople, and so of the poor, as a whole. For simplicity we may take for examination—no difference is made in the substance of the argument—the state of things contemplated in Part III. Chapter XVII. §§ 8-9. The wage rate was there supposed to be forced up in an occupation where it had formerly been both "fair" relatively to other industries and equal to the value of the marginal net product of the work for which it was paid. It was assumed that no difference was made either to employers' technique or to the capacity of the workpeople to whom the increased wage was given : and, on this assumption, it was proved that the national dividend *must* be diminished. In what, if any, conditions will the real income of labour as a whole, nevertheless, be increased ?

§ 2. The first step towards answering this question is to determine in what circumstances the enforcement of an uneconomically high wage—that is a convenient term for a wage that damages the dividend—will increase the real earnings of the particular group of workpeople in whose behalf it is won. It should be noticed in passing that an uneconomic enhancement of the wage rate in any occupation may take the form either of a special enhancement of the rate per unit of labour paid to inferior workpeople—*e.g.* such workpeople may be given the same time-wages as competent workers—

or of a general enhancement of the rate per unit of capacity paid to all workpeople. It is evident that an uneconomic enhancement of the former kind must either throw all the inferior workpeople out of work altogether, or must diminish the aggregate quantity of labour employed to exactly the same extent as an equal enhancement in the rate per unit of capacity paid to *all* the workpeople in the occupation. Hence it is bound to have a less favourable effect on the aggregate earnings of the whole group of workpeople concerned than the latter kind of enhancement. In what follows, therefore, it will be sufficient to consider that type of uneconomically high rate which affects equally the wages per unit of capacity paid to all workpeople in an occupation. To determine in the abstract the conditions in which the establishment of this type of uneconomically high wage will increase the real earnings of this group of workpeople is perfectly simple. It will increase them if the demand for the labour of the group has an elasticity less than unity, and it will diminish them if the elasticity is greater than unity. This result—on the assumption, of course, that the workpeople concerned are not themselves purchasers to any appreciable extent of the commodity they produce—is an obvious arithmetical truism, following at once from the definition of elasticity. To fill it out in the concrete, to investigate, that is to say, the conditions that determine whether the demand for the services of any assigned group of workpeople is likely to have a high elasticity or a low one, is the task we have now to essay.

§ 3. In the fifth section of Part II. Chapter XIV., an analysis was given of the determinants of elasticity with reference to the demands for different classes of commodities. This analysis is applicable to the demands for different classes of labour also. In that application it may be set out as follows.

First, we have the general fact that the demand for anything is likely to be more elastic, the more readily substitutes for that thing can be obtained. This fact has an important bearing on the relation between labour and machinery; for, in some industries, a very small addition to the cost of working a process by hand would induce employers to adopt mechanical appliances. Aves, for example, quotes the statement of an ex-inspectress that, in the Victorian clothing trade, where minimum wage determinations have unintentionally discriminated against home work, employment was transferred to factories using machinery, and "practically all outside work was stopped."[1] In like manner, the tanners of Victoria, commenting on the effects of the Wages Board in their industry, state : " Labour-saving machinery is forced into use, so much so that the tannery trade has been practically revolutionised since the Wages Board system was applied to the trade."[2] In circumstances of this kind the high elasticity of demand for labour is, in effect, due to the fact that there is a readily available and closely competing substitute for its services in the rival factor capital, or, more strictly, other labour accompanied by a greater amount of waiting. Since it is easier to introduce this substitute after an interval than immediately, elasticity in demand due to this cause is greater from the standpoint of a long period than of a short period.

Secondly, we have the general fact that the demand for anything is likely to be less elastic, the less important is the part played by the cost of that thing in the total cost of some other thing, in the production of which it is employed. This general fact enables us to point out certain occupations in which the demand for a particular class of labour is likely to be especially inelastic. One of these is the occupation of women in sewing on the covers of racquet and fives balls.[3] Another is that of making trouser-buttons. Lord Askwith writes : " The rich man's trousers may be cut by an expensive

---

[1] *Report on Wages Boards*, p. 197. This "determination" fixed both an hour rate and a piece-work rate, compelling the latter to be paid to outworkers. The intention was that the two should be equivalent, but employers in practice found the hour, or wages, rate much the cheaper. The ex-inspectress added : " When the wages rate and the piece-work rate were nearly the same, as in the shirt and underclothing trade, the trouble did not occur, and, after ten years' working of the determination, these trades count many outworkers to-day." The choice between an out- and an in-worker is affected by the fact that, when employing outworkers, the employer escapes charges for working space, light, firing, and so forth. " The savings upon factory rent, upkeep, and superintendence appear to be larger factors in the cheapness of home work than the lowness of wages" (Black, *Makers of our Clothes*, p. 44). Cf. also Marconcini, *L' industria domestica salariata* (pp. 432-3). On the other hand, of course, economies of superintendence and, sometimes, of power are to be obtained in factory work.

[2] *Report on Wages Boards*, p. 179. Cf. *ante*, Part III. Chapter XIV. § 8.

[3] Cf. Lyttleton, *Contemporary Review*, February 1909.

tailor. The buttons on those trousers may be made by sweated industry. High payment for those buttons would be but a minute part of the cost of the whole article."[1] The engineering work done by engineers engaged by building firms, since these persons are employed only incidentally and as a trivial part of the total producing force, is in a similar position. In like manner, the part played by the original labour is small in commodities for which the addition to wholesale price made by the work of the retailer is large. "For example, when we find that the maker of a lady's costume is paid 10d. or 1s., while the article is sold for 25s. to 30s., it is obvious that the wage paid is so small in relation to the retail price that, even were the wage doubled, it need necessarily affect the price but little, if at all."[2] This condition, that the part played by labour in a particular act of production shall be small, is probably fulfilled fairly often, and it is likely to be fulfilled still more often as the relative importance of installations of plant and machinery in production increases. One writer has even suggested that "the labour cost of production in most industries is usually not sufficient materially to affect the price of the finished article." It should be noticed, however, that, in the important work of coal production, hewers' labour constitutes a very large part of the total cost, and the condition stipulated for is, therefore, not fulfilled.

Thirdly, we have the general fact that the demand for anything is likely to be more elastic, the more elastic is the supply of co-operant agents of production. This fact makes it evident that the demand for labour will be specially inelastic in industries which make use of raw materials of highly inelastic supply. Apart from raw materials, the principal co-operant agents working with labour in any industry are capital instruments, managing ability and other labour. From the standpoint of a long period the supply of these to any single industry is, beyond doubt, exceedingly elastic. But, from the standpoint of a short period or a period of moderate length, it is likely to be inelastic; for

---

[1] *Fortnightly Review*, August 1908, p. 225.
[2] Cadbury and Shann, *Sweating*, p. 124.

specialised machinery and managing skill, and even other labour, can neither be created or brought from elsewhere, nor yet destroyed or carried off elsewhere, in the twinkling of an eye. Here again, therefore, the forces making for elasticity of demand are stronger from the standpoint of a long period than of a short period. It should be added that in some industries, notably coal-mining, Nature herself acts as a very important co-operant factor of production. In times of expanded demand new men have to be set to work on seams much more difficult and less productive than those ordinarily worked.[1] This means, from a short-period point of view, a highly inelastic demand for labour.

Fourthly, we have the general fact that the demand for anything is likely to be more elastic, the more elastic is the demand for any further thing which it contributes to produce. This fact implies that the demand will be specially inelastic for the services of workpeople engaged in the manufacture of commodities of highly inelastic demand. When the elasticity of the public demand for any commodity is given, it is obvious that, from a short-period point of view, the elasticity of the demand for new production of it will be greater or less, according as the thing can or cannot be readily made for stock. Apart from this, the circumstances upon which the elasticity of demand for various classes of commodities depends were discussed in the fourteenth chapter of Part II. The most significant of them for our present purpose is the presence or absence of foreign competition. Thus a critic comments on some of the effects of New Zealand wage regulation: " In some trades employers have not been able to cope with the extra cost of production owing to competition with the imported article. They have, therefore, had to give up the producing part of their business and increase their importations. In the tanning and fellmongering business some serious results have followed the fixing of a minimum wage. I will mention two instances. Some years ago a firm in the district of Dunedin closed down its works and removed its plant to Australia, largely owing to the conditions imposed by the Arbitration Court. A member of a Christchurch firm has

---

[1] Cf. Hooker, *Statistical Journal*, 1894, p. 635 n.

informed me that, since the Court's award in the Canterbury
district was made about six years ago, a much larger proportion of sheepskins have been shipped to London, without being
handled by the local fellmonger, than was formerly the case.
Hides, which should have been tanned here, have been shipped
raw. Prior to the award, my informant's firm paid from
£10,000 to £15,000 in wages; now the wages sheet amounts
to only about £5000. The number of bales of wool scoured
annually by the same firm since the award came into force
has not been more than 2000; formerly the number was
from 6000 to 8000."[1] In connection, however, with this
matter of foreign competition a word of caution is necessary.
Let us imagine that there are a dozen industries in this
country, all of about the same size and all subject in about
equal measure to foreign competition in the home market.
Looking at any one of these industries singly, we conclude,
perhaps, that the elasticity of demand for its product is such
that an increase of 10 per cent in the cost of making it in this
country would stimulate importation and reduce the demand
for the home-product by 50 per cent. It is natural to infer
that a 10 per cent increase in costs in all twelve industries
together would reduce the demand for the home-product in
all of them by 50 per cent. This, however, is not so.
Foreign imports collectively constitute the foreign demand for
British exports. When, therefore, for any reason it becomes
advantageous to increase the sendings of one kind of import,
other kinds of import will tend to fall off, the adjustment
being brought about *through*—but not *by*—a change in price
levels. Thus, when an extra flow of imports, stimulated by
increased home-costs, helps to bring about a contraction in
the demand for the home-product in one industry, the
contraction will be, in part, cancelled by an expansion, made
possible by lessened imports, in other industries. In other
words, the demand for the whole body of British products
subject to foreign competition is less elastic than the demand
for a single representative item among these products. It
follows that, other things being equal, the workpeople
immediately affected are more likely to be benefited by inter-

---

[1] Broadhead, *State Regulation of Labour in New Zealand*, p. 215.

ference to raise their wages if the interference is extended to several industries subject to foreign competition than they would be if it were confined to one.

§ 4. With these results in mind we may proceed to the next stage in our inquiry, and ask in what conditions the establishment at one point of an uneconomically high wage, which raises the real earnings of the workpeople there, will also raise the real earnings of workpeople as a whole. Let us still suppose that the commodity, to the makers of which an uneconomically high wage has been assigned, is exclusively consumed by persons other than workpeople. It may be noted, in passing, that, when a factor making for inelasticity in the demand for the services of the particular group of workpeople in whom we are interested is inelasticity of supply and, therefore, "squeezability" in some co-operant group, a part of the gain to the first group will be offset by loss to the second. For the purpose of a general analysis, however, we may neglect this rather special point.

If the elasticity of demand for labour in the occupation where the wage rate has been raised is less than unity, the aggregate earnings of labour as a whole, and not merely the earnings in that occupation, will be increased, provided that either the casual method or the privileged class method of engaging labour, as described in Chapter XIII. of Part III., prevails in that occupation. Under the casual method workpeople will be attracted into the occupation from outside until the prospect of earnings per man inside and outside are brought to equality ; and, since the number of workpeople left outside is diminished by this drain, the wage rate there will be raised. This proves that aggregate earnings inside and outside together must be raised. Under the privileged class method of engagement no one will be attracted from outside and no one will be driven out. Hence earnings outside will be unchanged. Since, therefore, earnings inside are, ex hypothesi, increased, it again follows that earnings as a whole are increased. If the preference method of engagement prevails, conditions are conceivable in which earnings as a whole would not be increased. For some persons must be driven out of the industry where the wage is raised, and, though those left there will be getting more than they were getting before, the influx of labour into other industries might, if the demand in these industries had an elasticity less than unity, so lower earnings outside as to outweigh the gain inside. Since, however, as was shown in Chapter III., the demand for labour in industry in general is highly elastic, the conditions necessary to this result are not fulfilled. In real life, therefore, the earnings of labour as a whole must be increased whenever an uneconomically high wage is enforced in a selected occupation, provided that the elasticity of the demand for labour there is less than unity.

If the elasticity of demand in the occupation where the wage rate is raised is greater than unity, analogous reasoning shows that earnings as a whole cannot be increased, provided that either the casual or the privileged class method of engagement prevails in the occupation. For some workpeople will be driven out of the occupation, and a new equilibrium will be established, with an expectation of earnings for every one equal to the earnings in other occupations; and these will have been made lower than before by an influx of new workers. If, however, the preference method prevails, earnings as a whole may be increased even though the elasticity of demand is greater than unity. Those who are left in the industry where the wage is raised will be getting more than they were getting before; and, though everybody else will be getting less than before, yet, if the demand for labour in other industries is sufficiently elastic, their loss need not be so great as the others' gain.

§ 5. It is now time to remove the assumption set out in § 2, that the commodity produced by the group of workpeople, whose wage is being interfered with, is exclusively consumed by persons other than workpeople. On the strength of that assumption we have been able, up to this point, to ignore the distinction between effects on money earnings and effects on real earnings. Where the assumption is unwarranted we are not justified in doing this. An increase of money earnings may be associated with a decrease of real earnings, and may, therefore, be delusive. If the commodities produced by the favoured workers are consumed by nobody except members of the working-classes, it *must* be delusive, for it is bound to involve a more than equivalent loss to workpeople (those inside the privileged industry and those outside it together) in their capacity as consumers. If the consumers consist partly of workpeople and partly of others, it is not possible to say absolutely whether the workpeople's gain as producers or loss as consumers will be greater. All we can lay down is that, the more important the part of the consumption for which non-wage-earners are responsible, the more likely it is that the establishment of an uneconomically high wage rate will succeed in bringing about an increase in the real income of workpeople as a whole. When, therefore, the main part of the product of any group of workers is consumed by other workers, though the establishment of an uneconomically high wage rate may enhance the aggregate real income of the favoured workers, it is not probable that it will enhance that of all workers collectively. This point is important, because, in real life, it is rich people who make, or otherwise provide, a great part of the luxuries of the rich, while poor wage-earners make things for other wage-earners. Thus, Mrs. Bosanquet writes: "Nothing strikes one more forcibly in studying the position of the lowest-paid workers than that they are almost always engaged in producing goods for the consumption of their own class. . . . Badly paid tailors are making cheap clothing that no rich man would look at ; badly paid servants are rendering services that would not be tolerated by any one of refinement and culture ; while the real requisites of refinement and culture, if by these we mean such things as art, music, and literature, are produced by professional people."[1]   Again : "*The great majority of wage-earners are engaged in producing for the benefit of other wage-earners*, and have no direct connection with the non-wage-earning classes. The majority of builders are building houses for wage-earners ; the very large majority in the clothing trades are making clothing for the wage-earners ; the majority of food-preparers are preparing food for the wage-earners. More especially of the sweated trades is it literally true, almost without exception, that they are working for the wage-earners alone, and that a rise in the

[1] Bosanquet, *The Strength of the People*, p. 71.

price of their products would be paid by the wage-earners alone. How would it be possible that the propertied classes should pay any share in the increased price of ready-made suits, or cheap blouses, or shoddy boots and shoes, or Pink's jams ? The burden must fall on the consumers of these articles, and they are the wage-earners." [1]   Mrs. Bosanquet would not, of course, pretend that there are no rich men's luxuries, towards which poor men's labour contributes an important part. It would seem, however, that not much of the labour of poor persons in the United Kingdom is devoted to the supply of luxuries of this sort.[2]   It follows that the establishment of an uneconomically high wage rate for a particular group of workpeople is much less likely to involve a real increase in the earnings of workpeople as a whole than it appears to be when the distinction between money earnings and real earnings is ignored.[3]   So far, however, the possibility that it may involve this remains.

§ 6. But against the realisation of this possibility there is at work a corrective tendency. If the real earnings of labour in the aggregate are increased by the manipulation of wages in any industry, a smaller portion of the productive power of the community is left available to provide payment for the services of capital. Had there been no alteration in the constitution of the national dividend, this would have meant a fall in the real rate of interest offered to new capital. The change in the constitution of the dividend, consisting, as it does, in a shifting of production away from its natural channels, cannot prevent this fall from coming about. It would seem, therefore, that manipulation of wage rates cannot benefit labour in the aggregate without causing the reward offered to savings to be diminished. Now, it is no doubt true

[1] *The Strength of the People*, pp. 294-5.

[2] For examples of things made by "sweated" workers and consumed by others than wage-earners, cf. Cadbury and Shann, *Sweating*, p. 123.

[3] The reason why this conflict between the interests of a particular class of wage-earners and those of wage-earners as a whole, when the particular class endeavours to force up its rate of wages above the normal, is not generally recognised may well be, as Mr. H. D. Henderson suggests, that most wage movements are associated with trade cycles. In consequence of this, the wage rates of different groups generally move up and down together, and, therefore, to the casual observer, there appears to be a greater harmony of interest than there really is (*Supply and Demand*, p. 157).

that a fall in the real rate of interest will not cause every-body's savings to be diminished. The savings of those people, whose object it is to leave a definite sum to their children at death, will actually be increased ; and the savings of the very rich, who merely put by what is left over after their accustomed standard of life has been satisfied, will not be affected at all. There can be little doubt, however, that, on the whole, a fall in the rate of interest will diminish savings to *some* extent, and, of course, a diminution of savings carries with it a diminution in the rate at which new capital equipment is provided. In this way an indirect influence is set in play tending to make the remuneration of labour in future years decrease. Here, plainly, is a tendency adverse to disharmony. Furthermore, this tendency is quantitatively important. For suppose a policy to be adopted, which, while increasing the real income of labour at the moment, causes the supply of new capital each year to be one per cent less, not necessarily than it was before, but than it would have been apart from the policy. In any one year the loss to the aggregate stock of capital equipment in the country will be small. But the annual losses are *cumulative*. After, say, ten years, the capital stock that is available to assist labour in its activities may be considerably smaller than it would otherwise have been.[1] Moreover, the reduction of this stock is aggravated by the fact that it must itself cause a reduction in the national dividend ; that, therefore, the transference to labour of any given annual sum must throw a continually increasing burden on profits ; that, therefore, the diminution (or check to the growth) of the national dividend must be greater in the second year than in the first, greater in the third year than in the second, and so on ; and that, therefore, the rate of fall in the capital stock must be progressively accelerated. As this stock falls in amount below what it would otherwise have been, the annual earnings of labour also fall continuously. In the end it would seem that, as against any policy, which, in the first instance, benefits labour at the expense of injuring the national dividend, this cumulative tendency is bound to prevail, and that, there-fore, from the standpoint of a sufficiently long period, any

---

[1] Cf. Marshall, *Economics of Industry*, pp. 372-3.

disharmony that may have been set up must disappear. Since, however, relatively to the stock of capital, the annual creation of new capital is small, and, consequently, any probable change in the annual creation very small, the harmonising tendency will work slowly. This implies that, for some time after the establishment of an uneconomically high wage in particular occupations, disharmony may prevail.

§ 7. Up to this point we have been concerned with the consequences of fixing an uneconomically high wage, as if this were a single self-subsistent act. In actual life, however, it is inevitably mixed up with State policy as regards the protection of persons in distress. If the enforcement of an uneconomically high wage in some occupation throws a certain number of people out of work for a long time, the State will have to help these people. Consequently, if we count as a part of the real income of the poor what the State provides for assisted persons, their real income in this wider sense may well be raised by a policy which lowers the earned part of their real income. Thus, by a forcing up of the wage rate in some occupations, we may suppose that the national dividend is injured, and that those workers who are left in industry gain a little less than those who are thrown out of it lose. There is then harmony between the effects on the national dividend and on the real income of the poor in the narrower sense. But, if, in consequence of increased unemployment, the expenditure of State aid to poor persons becomes £1,000,000 bigger than it would otherwise have been, there may be disharmony between the effect on the dividend and the effect on the real income of the poor in the wider sense. The way is thus opened for a somewhat special argument in favour of forcing up wage rates in low-grade occupations. It may be granted that both the national dividend and the real earnings of labour as a whole will be diminished. But, it may be claimed, at all events if the preference method of engagement prevails, that a number of people, who otherwise would have earned too little to maintain independently a decent life, will now get adequate earnings. A number of others will, indeed, earn less than before—possibly nothing at all—but, owing to the action of the State, they

need not *receive* less than before.   Thus we shall have, instead
of a large body of people, all of them occasionally or partially
supported by the State, one moderate-sized body fully self-
supporting and another moderate-sized body scarcely self-
supporting at all.   From the point of view of economic
welfare as a whole, particularly if the conditions are such as
to make the fully self-supporting body much larger than the
other, the latter state of things may be deemed the better, in
spite of the fact that it involves a smaller national dividend.
It may be objected, no doubt, that the persons now rendered
fully self-supporting will really be sustained by the help of
what is, in effect, a special tax upon the people who purchase
the things they happen to make ; and that the care of
relatively incapable citizens is an obligation upon the whole
community, and not merely upon those members of it who
buy racquet balls, or whatever the article may be.   It may
be replied, however, that, in so far as relatively incapable
citizens are responsible for products of general consumption,
or in so far as they do work for municipalities or the State
in connection with commodities or services not designed for
sale, this objection loses the greater part of its force ; and
that, in any event, since every indirect tax must hit some
people " unfairly," it is not of *very* great weight.   Moreover,
since the workers who benefit will not think of themselves as
being in any sense " relieved by their customers," there is no
danger that any injurious moral effect analogous to the " taint
of pauperism " will be produced upon them.   Plainly, an issue
turning upon considerations of this kind is not susceptible of
any general solution.   Whenever it is proposed to enforce
an uneconomically high wage in any occupation upon the
grounds suggested in this section, a decision can only be
reached by a careful balancing of conflicting tendencies, after
all the relevant circumstances have been studied in detail.

CHAPTER VI

§ 1. In Chapter XIII. of Part II. some discussion was undertaken of the policy of rationing, as an adjunct to State control over the prices of commodities produced under competitive conditions. A brief study of this policy is now required from another point of view. The rationing of essential commodities to the better-to-do classes, whether coupled or not with price control, may be advocated as a means of ensuring that sufficient supplies at reasonable prices shall be available for the poor. *Prima facie* it would seem that this policy may affect the size of national dividend in one way and the absolute share of it accruing to the poor in another, thus involving disharmony. The question whether or not this is in fact so will be examined in the present chapter.

§ 2. In the special emergency of the Great War, supplies of certain things were short as a result of causes which could not have been got over, whatever prices sellers had been allowed to charge. Price regulation and rationing did not, therefore, as was argued in Part II. Chapters XII. and XIII., substantially reduce the size of the national dividend. At the same time they jointly saved the poor from a disaster that could not otherwise have been avoided. The grant of large bonuses on wages would not have enabled poor people to obtain essential articles of which the supply was short and the demand of the rich inelastic. The prices of these things would, indeed, have been forced up, but the rich, at the cost of paying more money, would still have obtained as much as before out of the shortened supply, and would have correspondingly cut

694

down the share available for the poor. Thus the poor would have suffered enormously in respect of real income, even though their money income had risen proportionately to the rise in general prices, because particular things of vital importance to them would have been practically unobtainable. Moreover, the fixing of maximum prices without rationing would not have been sufficient; for the presumption is that the rich, by various pulls, would still have skimmed the market. From the joint facts that in the war price control coupled with rationing did not injure production and did benefit distribution it has sometimes been inferred that the same policy continued in normal conditions would produce the same harmoniously beneficial result. That is the issue we have to judge.

§ 3. In attempting to elucidate it we have to make clear, from the present point of view, the relation between rationing and price-fixing. Clearly in a brief period of shortage it is possible, with a given system of rations, to have any one of a large number of regulated price maxima, because, for the time being, the output and (within limits) the amount offered for sale are independent of the price. But, when we are contemplating a policy for normal times, the position is different. Suppose, first, that a given scale of rations is established unaccompanied by any price restriction, and that everybody is purchasing the whole of the ration to which he is entitled. This implies a definite quantity demanded; and there is, in general, only one price that will call out this quantity. If the State fixes a maximum price higher than this, the sellers will not be able to realise it, and the maximum price will become otiose. If, on the other hand, the State fixes a price less than this, not enough will be produced to enable everybody to get his ration: and, consequently, if the rations are to be effective, in the sense that whoever wants his allotted ration can obtain it, the whole ration scale will have to be altered to fit the new price. Suppose, secondly, that a given ration scale is established, but that, while the scale limits the purchases of some people, others are buying less than their ration allowance. As before, to whatever aggregate quantity is being

purchased there corresponds one single price that will call out
that quantity; and, as before, if the State fixes a maximum
price higher than this, the maximum will become otiose.
If the State fixes a maximum lower than this, it seems
at first sight that a new equilibrium may be established, in
which some of those now buying less than their ration will
buy the full amount. But, in fact, the lower price must
mean a lower output, so that nobody can buy more, or even
as much as before, unless others buy less. It must happen,
therefore, that some of those who before were purchasing
their full ration are now unable, although they still wish,
to do so. Here again, therefore, the ration scale becomes
ineffective, and a new and lower ration must be established
to fit the new price. Hence, generally, to any *effective* ration
scale only one price level can correspond; and it is
impossible for the State to establish any other price level
without at the same time establishing another *effective* ration
scale. This conclusion is a very important one for my
present purpose: because it makes it unnecessary to study
both rationing by itself and also rationing accompanied by
price regulation. The two things work out, when the
numerical constants are adjusted, in exactly the same way;
and the whole problem is exhausted when the consequences
of rationing alone have been examined.

§ 4. It is evident that any rationing system, which aims
at benefiting the poor, must be so designed as to cut down
the consumption of the rich. Such facts as that, for example,
a *uniform* bread ration on a scale tolerable to the poor would
not accomplish this, because, normally, poor people eat more
bread per head than rich people, are not really relevant. We
are not concerned here with technique, but with principle;
and any rationing scheme, that pretends to increase the
supplies available for the poor as a body, *must* be so devised—
the scale need not, of course, be uniform—that it cuts down
those available for the rich. So much being understood, our
analysis of rationing in normal times may proceed. It works
out differently for commodities produced under conditions of
decreasing supply price and of increasing supply price.

§ 5. With decreasing supply price from the standpoint

of the industry, the ultimate consequence of extruding from the market a part of the demand of the relatively well-to-do is necessarily to contract the production of the commodity and, therefore, since, as was shown in Part II. Chapter XI., too little of it is being produced anyhow,—for decreasing supply price from the standpoint of the industry usually implies also decreasing supply price from the standpoint of the community —to lessen the national dividend. At the same time the rise in price, which a diminution in the supply of an article produced under conditions of decreasing supply price must involve, forces poor people both to buy less of the commodity than they would have done and also to pay more for what they do buy. Thus they are unequivocally damaged. The aggregate dividend and their share of it alike suffer, and disharmony is impossible.

§ 6. With increasing supply price from the standpoint of the industry the extrusion of part of the demand again, of course, contracts the production of the commodity. If the conditions are such that increasing supply price from the standpoint of the industry implies constant supply price from the standpoint of the community, the amount of production that would take place in the absence of interference will be the right amount to maximise the national dividend, and an enforced contraction in it will lessen the national dividend. If, on the other hand, the conditions are such that increasing supply price from the standpoint of the industry implies also increasing supply price from the standpoint of the community, the amount of production that would take place in the absence of interference will — as was shown in Part II. Chapter XI.—be too large to maximise the national dividend, and an enforced contraction in it will, if it does not go beyond a certain definite limit, benefit, and not injure, the national dividend. In either event the price of the commodity will be reduced, so that the poor probably get more of it, and certainly get it at a lower price. Hence the poor must gain. In the second case distinguished above, therefore, if the slice cut off the demand of the rich is not too large, there is harmony of an opposite sort to that which comes about under decreasing supply price ; the national dividend and the slice accruing to the poor are both increased. But, if the check to the purchases of the rich is pressed beyond a certain point, there is disharmony, the poor still getting a benefit but the national dividend as a whole suffering loss. In the first case distinguished above there is disharmony of this sort whatever the size of the check to the purchases of the rich.

§ 7. This analysis makes it plain that conditions *may* exist in which a system of rationing in normal times, if conducted with perfect skill and without any friction, would yield a net social benefit. It does not prove, however, that in practice the rationing of any commodity is in normal times desirable. Not only is the skill of government officials limited, but also a large adverse balance of inconvenience and irritation would have to be neutralised before any positive advantage could begin. Moreover, it must be remembered that, since the rich are relatively few in number, and their consumption of common articles—with the exception of coal, the consumption of which is regulated by the size of a man's house and not by his bodily capacity—a small proportion of the whole, a very large percentage cut in their *per capita* purchases would involve only a very small percentage cut in the consumption of the country as a whole, and an almost negligible cut, for most things, in the consumption of the world. In general, therefore, its effect in cheapening the supplies to poor persons of articles of increasing supply price would be scarcely perceptible. The practical conclusion seems to be that, while it may redound slightly to the general interest for well-to-do persons voluntarily to restrict their purchases of these articles, yet, in the present state of economic knowledge and administrative efficiency, it would, in ordinary times, do more harm than good for the State to force them to do this by any system of compulsory rationing.[1]

---

[1] It must be remembered, however, that, if only 500 rich men cut down their consumption of this type of article in a given proportion, the benefit to the poor will be less than half what it would have been had 1000 done so ; because what one rich man voluntarily refrains from consuming another rich man, tempted by the resultant lowering of price, may be tempted to bid for. This is, *pro tanto*, an argument for compulsory (and, therefore, universal), as against voluntary, rationing.

CHAPTER VII

§ 1. In a community in which wage-rates are everywhere adjusted to the conditions of demand and supply, so that no wage-rates are uneconomically high and there is no unemployment beyond what is necessary to allow adjustments to be made to industrial fluctuations, for the State to subsidise wages in particular industries must, in general,[1] worsen the distribution of productive resources and damage the national dividend. A policy of wage subsidies applied to all industries would not necessarily damage the distribution of productive resources, but it could not improve this distribution; and, though in some circumstances it might increase the dividend, it would probably only do so at the cost of causing too much work to be done, and, therefore, in a manner injurious, and not beneficial, to economic welfare. Hence, subject to qualifications which the reader can readily provide, we may conclude that in a community, in which, apart from subsidies, rates of wages would be everywhere adjusted to the conditions of demand and supply, any policy of wage subsidies is likely to prove anti-social.

§ 2. In real life, however, it may happen that either in particular industries or, it may be, throughout industry as a whole, wage-rates are established at an uneconomically high level; that is to say, at a level too high to allow the demand for labour to absorb the supply, in such wise that more people are unemployed than are accounted for by the movements they have to make in consequence of industrial fluctuations. Thus there is some reason to believe that in England during

[1] Cf. Part I. Chaps. IX.-XI.

the post-war depression, partly through direct State action and partly through the extra bargaining strength given to workpeople's organisations by the development of unemployment insurance, wage-rates over a wide area were set at a level uneconomically high in the above sense. Where conditions of this kind prevail and where public opinion insists that unemployed persons shall be somehow provided for, a policy of wage subsidies is no longer *prima facie* anti-social, but needs more particular consideration.

§ 3. The possibility of social gain is made clear most easily by means of a highly simplified imaginary case. Consider an agricultural community in which farmers own the land and employ labourers, all of whom are of equal skill. Let nothing else be produced except wheat, and let wages be paid in kind. Let the conditions be such that, with wages at one bushel of wheat per day, all the labourers would find employment, but that, when the rate is put at one and a quarter bushels per day, 10 per cent of them are out of work and the aggregate output of wheat, instead of being A bushels, is cut down to $(A - a)$ bushels. Let the State insist, for humanity's sake, that a man out of work shall, nevertheless, receive, say, one-third of a bushel of wheat for maintenance, and let it take from farmers whatever amount of wheat is needed to permit of this. In such a case it is easy to see in a general way that, if a tax is imposed on the income of farmers or on the rental value of their land, and the proceeds used to give a subsidy of so much per cent on wages, the labourers are bound to gain, and the farmers—when their loss through the tax is balanced against the extra output of wheat and their savings in respect of unemployed labour— *may* gain. For a full understanding of the situation it is, however, helpful to make use of a few symbols.[1]

§ 4. Let $(x + h)$ workpeople be attached to a given industry, *whose products are not exported*. Let w_2 be the wage at which all of them would find employment; w_1 the wage which is actually established, and x the number of men that are actually employed. If then things are allowed to take their " natural "

---

[1] The analysis which follows was suggested to me by Mr. Ramsey of King's College, Cambridge.

course, h workpeople will be unemployed in the industry. For humanity's sake these must be somehow provided for; so we suppose that a payment r is made to each of them, and—to make the case as strong as possible—that the whole sum hr is taken from non-wage-earners. This is the position in the absence of any subsidy. Now let a subsidy at a rate $s = (w_1 - w_2)$ be paid in respect of each workman employed; and let the funds for it be raised by taxation imposed on non-wage-earners (e.g. income tax). The wage (including the subsidy) paid to each workman will hereafter still be w_1—the workmen already in work will receive no more than before—but it will now pay employers in the industry to take on $(x + h)$ workpeople instead of x workpeople. The output of the new h workpeople taken on will have a value equal to some amount (dependent on the slope of the demand curve for labour) intermediate between hw_1 and hw_2. Let it be $\{hw_2 + hc\}$; which, in the special case where the demand curve for labour is a straight line, $= \{hw_2 + \frac{1}{2}h(w_1 - w_2)\} = \{hw_2 + \frac{1}{2}hs\}$. From these data it is easy to calculate loss and gain. Workpeople as a body obviously gain; for h more of them are employed at the full wage w_1 for which they stipulated. Non-wage-earners neither gain nor lose in respect of the x workpeople who would be employed anyhow. In respect of the others they make a payment in wages plus subsidy equal to hw_1: they obtain an extra product of a value equal to $(hw_2 + hc)$, which is less than hw_1; and they save a payment to unemployed workpeople equal to hr. Their net gain is, therefore, equal to $\{hw_2 + hc + hr - hw_1\} = h(r + c - s)$. This is necessarily positive, provided that the rate of subsidy required is less than the rate of contribution which would have been paid to unemployed workmen. When this condition is satisfied it is obvious that both the absolute receipts of labour and also the national dividend as a whole must be larger than they would have been had other things been equal but no subsidy paid.[1]

§ 5. The foregoing analysis was explicitly confined to

[1] In the special case where the demand curve for labour is a straight line the net gain is equal to $h(r - \frac{1}{2}s)$; which is necessarily positive, provided that the rate of subsidy is less than twice the rate of contribution to unemployed workmen.

industries whose products are not exported. If the policy of subsidies were applied to export industries, the balance of gain and loss would work out less satisfactorily, because foreigners, instead of domestic users, would get the benefit of the price reduction due to the subsidy; in effect British non-wage-earners would be paying a part of the costs of work done for foreigners, which, had there been no subsidy, foreigners themselves would have paid. Here, therefore, there would only be a net gain to British non-wage-earners if the foreign demand were so extremely elastic that employment would be increased from x to $(x + h)$ by a subsidy s, such that $(x + h)s$ is less than hr. The case for subsidies as a means of mitigating the ill-effects of uneconomically high wage-rates is, therefore, substantially weaker for export industries than for others. Even so, however, it is clear that the subsidy device is applicable over a considerable range. It will lessen the volume of unemployment in any industry (with uneconomically high wages) to which it is applied; and, so long as it is on an appropriate scale and is confined to industries whose products are not exported, it will correspondingly increase the real income of the country.

§ 6. The foregoing analysis is in principle favourable to a policy of wage subsidies, at all events in industries other than export industries, provided that the maintenance of uneconomically high wage-rates is taken for granted. When, however, we pass from generalities to more detailed considerations, pitfalls are revealed. The most obvious difficulty has to do with the comparative treatment of workpeople in different occupations. If all occupations were rigidly separated from one another, so that, not only could no one pass directly from one to another, but also the choice among them to be made by each new generation coming to industrial age was rigidly fixed, everything would be quite simple. Each occupation could be treated as a single problem. In real life, however, different occupations are not rigidly separated, and account must, therefore, be taken of possible effects of a policy of subsidies in modifying the proportions of workpeople attached to different occupations. If exactly equal fiscal encouragement were given to all occupations, no effects of this kind would tend to come about. In practice, however, it can hardly be doubted that larger subsidies would be paid in industries with low wage-rates and large unemployment than in others. For example, at the present time the relatively distressed engineering and ship-building industries would certainly demand more favourable treatment than, say, the railway industry. As the demand for the products of any industry fell off and distress became more pronounced, higher subsidies, both absolutely and relatively to those ruling in other industries, would always be called for. Such pleas would often be acceded to. As a consequence, too many people would be set to and kept at work in some industries and too few in others. Extraordinary strength and competence on the part of the Government would be needed to prevent a policy of wage subsidies from acting in this way. If these were not forthcoming the resulting social loss might well be large. There is also a second serious danger. If the Government were in a position to control the wage demands of the workpeople as well as the amount of the subsidies, and if it were absolutely impervious to political pressure, the adoption of the above policy would not lead to any change in the rate of wages demanded. In practice, however, once the policy was adopted and, as a result of it, unemployment reduced to a low level, there would be a strong temptation to workpeople to demand higher wage-rates, while employers, hoping to recoup themselves from an increased subsidy, might not resist these demands very strenuously. In this way both wage-rates and the rates of subsidy would be subjected to a continuous upward pressure. This tendency, which would exist even in a static community, would be accentuated in the actual world ; for in times of boom wages would tend, as now, to go up ; and, when, subsequently, depression came, there would be a powerful demand, very likely on the part of employers and workpeople acting together, for an addition to the subsidy to prevent them from falling again. The annual revenue required to provide the subsidy would thus tend to grow larger and larger continually. The burden imposed on non-wage-earners would be raised above the benefit accorded them, and the gap would grow always wider. The supply of the services rendered by them in work and saving would be discouraged; and in the end both the national dividend and the real absolute share of it enjoyed by workpeople would be diminished.

§ 7. The broad result then is this. If wage-earners insist on maintaining a real rate of wages above the economic level in the sense defined above, and if no mitigating action is undertaken by the State, an abnormal volume of unemployment, with all the material and moral waste that this implies, is the inevitable concomitant. In principle it appears that this evil is susceptible of large alleviation, of a kind not involving injury to society at large, by a system of wage subsidies. But in practice it is probable that the application of such a system would be bungled, and that a community which relied upon it would lose more than it gained.

CHAPTER VIII

DIRECT TRANSFERENCES FROM THE RELATIVELY RICH
TO THE RELATIVELY POOR

§ 1. WE now turn to what is in practice by far the most important field of possible disharmony. In a great number of ways, and for a great variety of reasons, poor people in civilised countries are given help, in the main through some State agency, at the expense of their better-to-do fellow-citizens. In Great Britain in 1925 the contribution from central government funds towards social services, chiefly for old-age pensions, education, unemployment insurance, health insurance and housing, amounted to 113 millions, and the contributions from the funds of local authorities, chiefly for education and Poor Law relief, to 79 millions.[1] Evidently a large part of these 192 millions represent what is, in effect, a transfer of income from relatively rich for the benefit of relatively poor persons. *Prima facie* the transference, which this help implies, *must* increase, and it can certainly be so arranged that it *shall* increase, the real income available for the poor. Hence the question whether any particular form of help to the poor involves disharmony is often equivalent to the question whether its indirect consequence is to increase or to diminish the national dividend. This question, in one or another of its various aspects, will be the theme of the next four chapters. But, before we embark upon it, a brief comment is needed upon two popular arguments, one of which asserts that no transference of resources to the poor is possible, because, in effect, all money taken from the rich is really taken from the poor, while the other asserts that it

---

[1] Cf. Carr-Saunders and Jones, *Social Structure in England and Wales*, p. 158.

is not possible, because the beneficiaries will give back what they have received by agreeing to accept lower wages.

§ 2. The position taken up in the former of these arguments is that any levy of money, whether voluntary or compulsory, from the well-to-do for the benefit of some poor persons necessarily implies the infliction of a substantially equivalent burden upon other poor persons, through the reduction which the rich are compelled to make in their purchases of the services rendered by them. The foundation of this view may be set out as follows. It is obvious that a great part of the expenditure of the rich involves, directly or indirectly, the employment of labour ; and it is equally obvious that, if the incomes of the rich are diminished by, say, £20,000,000 of taxation, their expenditure for consumption and for capital investment together must be contracted to a corresponding extent. Some persons, concentrating attention upon these facts, immediately conclude that the workpeople, whose services this expenditure would have called into being if the tax had not been there—and an exactly analogous argument applies to a voluntary contribution—must suffer a loss of income approximating to the twenty million pounds levied in taxation. To argue thus, however, is to ignore the fact that the twenty million pounds collected from the rich is, *ex hypothesi*, transferred to the poor, and that the expenditure of it by them is likely to be no less productive of employment than the expenditure of it by the rich would have been. No doubt, if we are contemplating the immediate effect of the addition of twenty millions to the taxation of the rich for the benefit of the poor, it is relevant to observe that the men who lose jobs on the one side will not be the same persons as those who find them on the other ; and that, therefore, a certain number of men, who have been trained to special aptitudes, may find their immaterial capital of acquired skill rendered permanently worthless. This loss, however, is the result, not of taxation, but of *change* in taxation, and would emerge equally in consequence of a *reduction* by twenty millions in imposts levied on the rich for the benefit of the poor. Our problem is not concerned with incidents of this character. The comparison we have to make is between one permanent system, under which nothing is collected from the rich and handed over to the poor, and another permanent system, under which twenty millions is so collected and handed over. To this comparison the incident we have just been discussing is irrelevant. Speaking broadly and apart from special circumstances, we may say that it makes very little difference to the employment of, and wages paid for, labour, whether twenty millions is annually transferred or not transferred from any one class to any other class. The idea that reactions in this field will render attempts at transference of no effect is, therefore, illusory.

§ 3. The latter of the two arguments distinguished above asserts that, if any group of poor persons are accorded any form of subsidy, they will, in consequence, be willing to work for less than the worth of their services to their employer, and so will, in effect, transfer back the subsidy they have received to members of the richer classes. This view rests partly upon *a priori* reasoning and partly upon what is called experience. It needs, therefore, a twofold discussion. The *a priori* reasoning starts from the fact that a Poor Law subsidy *enables* a person to accept lower wages than it would be possible for him to accept otherwise without starvation, or, at all events, serious discomfort; and it proceeds to assert that, if a person is *enabled* to work for less, he will be *willing* to work for less. Now, no doubt, in certain special circumstances, when a workman, in receipt of a subsidy insufficient to enable him to live up to his accustomed standard of life, is confronted by an employer occupying towards him the position of a monopolist, this inference may be valid. In general, however, where competition exists among employers, it is quite invalid. A person who, by saving in the past, has become possessed of a competence, is *enabled* to work for less than one who has not. A millionaire is *enabled* to work for less even than a relieved pauper. So far from this ability making it probable that he will strike a worse bargain in the higgling of the market, it is likely, in general, to have the opposite effect. It is not the fact that the wife of a man in good work is likely to accept abnormally low wages. On the contrary, the woman who, for this or any other reason, can afford to "stand out," is, in general, among those who resist such wages most strenuously.[1] Let us turn, then, to the reasoning from what is called experience. This starts from two admitted facts. The first fact is that old and infirm persons in receipt of a Poor Law subsidy very frequently earn from private employers considerably less than the ordinary wage per hour current for the class of work on which they are engaged. The second fact—given in evidence before the Poor Law Commission of 1832—is that the refusal of guardians to grant relief in aid of wages "soon had the effect of making the farmer pay his labourers fairly." From these facts the inference is drawn that, where a Poor Law subsidy exists, workpeople accept a wage lower than the worth of their work to their employers. This inference, however, is illegitimate. There is an alternative and more probable explanation. As regards old and infirm persons, may it not be that the low wage per hour is due to the circumstance that the work they can do in an hour is poor in quality or little in quantity? As regards the old Poor Law, may it not be that the unreformed system of relief, so long as it prevailed, caused people to work slackly and badly, that, when it was abolished, they worked harder, and that this was the cause of the alteration in their wages? The view that the true analysis of experience is to be found along these lines, and not in the suggestion that relieved persons work for less than they are worth to their employers, is made likely by general considerations. It has been further confirmed by recent investigations, which tend to show that, where two people differ solely in the fact that one does, and the other does not, receive a Poor Law subsidy, their wages are in fact the same. Thus investigators appointed by the Poor Law Commission of 1909, as a result of their inquiry into the effects of out-relief on wages, write: "We found no evidence that women wage-earners, to whose families out-relief is given, cut rates. Such wage-earners are invariably found working at the same rates of pay as the much larger number of women not in receipt of relief, who entirely swamp them. . . . We could find no evidence that

---

[1] For an illustration of this among home-working tailoresses cf. Vesselitsky, *The Home Worker*, p. 17.

the daughters of paupers accepted lower rates than others, or earned less than others, because of their indirect relation to pauperism."[1] This argument, therefore, like that set out in § 2, breaks down. The direct transference of resources from the relatively rich to the relatively poor, by way of philanthropic or State action, whatever its ultimate consequences may prove to be, is at least not impossible. Of course, this conclusion does not deny that *additional work* by assisted, or any other, workers slightly lowers the general *rate* of wages.[2] But that proposition is quite different from the proposition that assistance to persons who are working anyhow has this effect.

§ 4. In view of this result we may proceed undisturbed to our main problem — that of determining the effect of various sorts of transference upon the size of the national dividend. Some sorts, it would seem, are likely to increase that dividend and others to diminish it. We have, therefore, to investigate the conditions upon which the occurrence of the one or the other of these opposing consequences depends. These conditions can be examined most effectively by means of an analysis in which the distinction between the effect of the fact, and the effect of the expectation, of transference is made fundamental. Of course, when we have to do with a levy, which is made once and for all to meet some exceptional need, and the regular continuance of which is not anticipated, effects operating through expectation do not have to be considered. In ordinary times, however, the fact of a tax levy imposed one year carries with it the expectation that it will be continued in future years, so that both fact and expectation are relevant. I shall consider first the expectation of transferences *from* the rich; secondly, the expectation of transferences *to* the poor; and thirdly, the fact of transferences.

---

[1] *Report of the Royal Commission on the Poor Laws*, Appendix, vol. xxxvi. pp. vi-vii.

[2] Cf. *ante*, Chapter III. § 10. Dr. Hourwick, in his book *Immigration and Labour*, seems to miss this point ; for, having shown that immigrants into the United States do not earn less wages for equally efficient work than native Americans, he treats this conclusion as implying that they do not *affect* the wages of native Americans.

CHAPTER IX

§ 1. THE expectation of levies from the relatively rich, as
from any other class, acts upon the national dividend differently according as the levy is voluntary or coercive. The
contribution of a voluntary levy implies that a new use has
been found, into which people wish to put some resources
more keenly than they wish to put them into other available
uses. This means that their desire to possess resources is
enhanced, and, therefore, that the provision they are willing to
make of waiting and effort, in order to obtain resources, is also
enhanced. Hence the expectation by the rich of voluntary
transferences from the rich is likely to make for an increase
in the size of the national dividend. " Though it would
have disastrous effects if the State should attempt to enforce
universal benevolence, yet only beneficial results would follow
if all men were to become wisely benevolent." [1] It is, therefore, important to consider briefly what scope there is in the
modern world for this type of transference.

§ 2. The most obvious form which it can and does take
is that of generous conduct towards their workpeople on the
part of wealthy employers of labour. Since these workpeople
spend a great part of their lives in buildings provided by
their employers and in conditions largely under their control,
the employers have the power to spend money in their
interest with exceptional effect. Acting in careful collaboration with chosen representatives of the workpeople, they can
contribute conveniences, opportunities for recreation and

---

[1] Carver, *Social Justice*, p. 142.

opportunities for education, and can make it a condition of employment for their younger workers that these things shall be used. Thus Messrs. Cadbury at Bournville require all their employees under eighteen to take part in regular gymnastic classes and in regular and elaborate courses of education, in part provided by, and in part paid for by, the firm.[1] The special opportunities which they enjoy for effective action may well create in wealthy employers a special sense of obligation. This sense was admirably expressed by the well-known Dutch employer Van Marken, when he declared : " It seems to me the duty of an employer to aid his subordinates by every means at his command—his heart, his intellect, his money— to attain that highest stage which alone makes life worth living. My own conviction is that in doing so the employer will make no sacrifices. But, if he needs must make them, be it from the material or the moral point of view, let him make them up to the limit of his capacity. It is his sacred duty."[2] With the education of opinion among well-to-do employers of labour we may look increasingly for a growth of this sense of patronal obligation. Furthermore, this sense may be fortified and extended by the egoistic consideration that generous treatment of workpeople is often a splendid advertisement, leading indirectly to large profits. On this point I cannot do better than adopt Ashley's excellent words : " Instead of cynically pooh-poohing it [employers' welfare work] for that reason, I think this is a particularly encouraging fact, and highly creditable to human nature. It shows that there is such a thing as a consumers' conscience. The whole essence of the Consumers' League work in America and of the White Lists of the Christian Social Union in this country is to make it 'good business' to be known to manufacture under satisfactory working conditions; and, with increasing publicity and an increasing fellow-feeling among all classes, I expect that this is going to be the case more and more."[3]

§ 3. Voluntary transference of resources may also take

---

[1] Cf. Cadbury, *Experiments in Industrial Organisation*, p. 17.
[2] Meakin, *Model Factories and Villages*, p. 27.
[3] Preface to Cadbury's *Experiments in Industrial Organisation*, p. xiii.

the form of generous conduct on the part of the wealthy to those poor persons who are united to them through common citizenship of the same town. Here, too, there is a special relation and, consequently, a special spur towards generous action : for the wealthy donor of such things as public parks and playgrounds has the satisfaction of choosing the form of his gift, of directing the use of it in some measure, and of seeing the fruits of it develop before his eyes. This localised generosity may easily expand into a wider patriotism, which interests itself, not merely in fellow-citizens of a common city, but in fellow-citizens of a common country. Pure public spirit often leads wealthy persons voluntarily to provide, partly in their lifetime and partly by legacies at death, large sums for the service of the poor. Often, too, public spirit is reinforced by the craving, strong in some men, for that sense of power which the fact of giving conveys.

§ 4. The normal motives prompting men to these and other forms of voluntary transference of resources to public ends are already of considerable force, and it is open to us to stimulate them still further. "No doubt," Marshall writes, " men are capable of much more unselfish service than they generally render ; and the supreme aim of the economist is to discover how this latent social asset can be developed more quickly and turned to account more wisely."[1] Not much has yet been accomplished in this direction. It is well understood, however, that Government, if it so chooses, has power to harness to the nobler motives for generosity others of a lower order. Much will be done for the sake of fame and praise, and fame of a sort may be offered as a reward for private munificence. Thus the transference of resources from the rich can be purchased, in a delicately veiled manner, by honours and decorations that cost nobody anything. These things are at once symbols and conveyers of reputation ; for, when a worthless man is decorated, those who feel, or pretend to feel, respect for the decorator, offer a vicarious respect to the decorated also. No doubt, in some degree, the issue of fresh decorations may diminish the value to their possessors of those already issued. To confer the Order of Merit broadcast

---

[1] *Principles of Economics*, p. 9.

among excellent bricklayers would annihilate its attractive power for the class in whose behoof it was originally designed. This difficulty can, however, be overcome to a great extent by the creation of new orders, instead of the extension of old ones. It is not impossible, therefore, that, along these lines, inducements might be provided adequate to secure the transference of a good deal of income from rich people, without the expectation of the transference involving any diminution, but, rather, some appreciable increase, in the waiting and effort furnished by them towards the upbuilding of the national dividend.

§ 5. Unfortunately it is quite certain that, in present conditions, voluntary transferences will fall very much below the aggregate of transferences from relatively well-to-do people which the general sense of the community demands. A considerable amount of coercive transference is, therefore, also necessary. This means, in one form or another, taxes, and probably, in the main, direct taxes graduated against the owners of large incomes and properties. The taxes, to which resort is in practice most likely to be had, are taxes on incomes and taxes on property passing at death. In what follows attention will be confined to these taxes. It is proposed to examine the kind of reactions on the national dividend to which the imposition of the one or the other kind is likely to lead.

§ 6. Let us consider first an income tax in which there is no differentiation against saving. As I have shown elsewhere, this means, broadly speaking, an income tax under which either savings themselves or the incomes subsequently yielded by these savings are exempted.[1] When such an income tax is graduated so as to yield a substantial contribution from the relatively well-to-do, in what way will the expectation of the levies to be made under it react on the size of the national dividend ? Three possible lines of reaction may be distinguished. First, the knowledge that this tax is there might drive men capable of earning large incomes by their work to live and work abroad rather than in the taxing country. Secondly, it might drive men with large powers of saving to make their

---

[1] Cf. *A Study in Public Finance*, Part II. chapter x.

investments abroad rather than in the taxing country. Thirdly, it might cause men capable of earning large incomes by their work, while continuing to reside in England, to work less (or conceivably, as will be argued in a moment, to work more) than they would have done had there been no tax. These three lines of reaction will now be considered in turn.

§ 7. If one country has a much higher income tax on large incomes than others, this fact will certainly constitute some inducement to men capable of earning large incomes to go and live abroad. There is reason to believe, however, that residence in their native land means so much to many rich men— particularly since the advantage of wealth is largely social advantage—that it would need a very large excess of tax to affect many of them in this way. Moreover, the movement towards high income tax on large incomes has a wide sweep, and the man who contemplates leaving his home to escape taxes there must reflect that similar taxes may before long be imposed in the country to which he goes. Along these lines, therefore, the reaction on the national dividend is not likely to be very important.

§ 8. At first sight it might seem that the second line of reaction is, on the other hand, almost certain to be very important. For, whereas a rich man will dislike moving himself abroad, he will not, it would seem, as a rule object to sending his capital abroad. The fear, however, that high income taxes will, in this way, drive capital abroad in large quantities, arises, at all events so far as the United Kingdom is concerned, from an imperfect knowledge of the exact scope of the British income-tax law. It is, no doubt, true that a tax striking the fruits of capital, in so far as it impinges on the investments of foreigners in England, lessens the advantage to foreigners of investment here, and, *pro tanto*, stimulates foreign individuals to withdraw their capital, and foreign corporations with plant abroad to withdraw their head offices. This, however, is a minor matter, for foreign investment here is admittedly small in amount. The substantial fear is that high income tax will drive British-owned capital to foreign fields. This fear is not well grounded. Since the English income tax, unlike the income taxes of the colonies, is levied on incomes *received* in England, and not merely upon those *earned or built up* there, high income tax here, in general, constitutes no inducement to an Englishman resident in England to send his capital abroad for investment. He will have to pay income tax when he brings the income derived from it home from abroad; and, under an amendment of the income-tax law passed in 1914, he must even pay if he leaves it abroad for investment there. Nor is this all. As things are at present, the income from English capital invested abroad will often have to pay a foreign income or other tax as well as the British income tax; so that a man, by sending his capital abroad, so far from escaping taxation, would actually encounter more of it. Hence, apart from deliberate and purposed fraud, if English capital is to be driven abroad, English capitalists must be driven there also. Nor is it even true that the supposed indirect effect of high income tax, namely, the fear of " Socialism," could rationally drive capital abroad without driving its owners abroad also; for, presumably, " Socialism " would not fasten on British factory-owners and leave British owners of foreign securities unscathed. Hence the same fact that limits the tendency of high income tax to drive able men to do their work abroad—namely, the desire to live in their native land—also limits the tendency to drive their capital abroad.

§ 9. There remains the third line of reaction—that, namely, on the amount of work which those persons who are subjected to a high income tax will do. This is a more complicated matter. At first sight it might seem that the expectation of having to pay any tax upon the fruit of work *must* in some degree discourage the performance of work. This, however, is not so, because, if a man's income is reduced by taxation, the addition of a £ to his income will satisfy a more urgent want than it would have done had his income not been reduced, and, consequently, though extra work will yield a less net return of money, it may, under certain types of tax, yield a greater net return of satisfaction. Proceeding on this line of thought, we observe that if an income-tax scale is so drawn as to impose equal sacrifice on all tax-payers (of similar temperament) whatever their incomes, the amount of work which they elect to do will not be altered at all by the expectation of it. As Professor Carver writes : " The minimum of repression (on industry and enterprise) is secured by so distributing taxes that an equal sacrifice is required of all. No one is discouraged from the acquisition of wealth or a large income, or from entering this or that occupation, if there is equal sacrifice involved in either case." [1] Now, we do not know enough about the relation between differences in the sizes of incomes and differences in the amounts of satisfaction yielded by them to be able to say what scale of income-tax graduation would conform to the canon of equal sacrifice. It would, however, be generally agreed that a proportionate income tax would involve a heavier sacrifice to poor people than to rich people, and that *some* degree of progression in the tax rate could be introduced without making the sacrifice imposed on the rich exceed that imposed on the poor. It is not an untenable view, therefore, that taxes on the better-to-do classes adequate to yield the revenue we require for trans- ference to the poor could be contrived on equal sacrifice principles, and, therefore, in a way innocuous to the national dividend. In view of the fact that, when an able man is actually engaged in work, a large part of his aim is simply " success," and that that is not interfered with by any tax that hits his rivals equally with himself, it may well be that, in the upper part of the tax scale, a fairly steep rate of progression might be adopted without the limits set by the principle of equal sacrifice being overstepped. It will be easily understood, however, that the scale of progression which conforms to the principle of *equal sacrifice* is very much less steep than that required to bring about minimum aggregate sacrifice. Most people will agree, therefore, that a scale somewhat steeper than that yielding equal sacrifice is desirable. If such a scale is adopted, *some* repressive influence on the amount of work done and, therefore, on the size of the national dividend must be exercised. It is important to realise, however, that, contrary to common opinion, the extent of this repressive influence upon any particular tax-payer depends, not on the absolute amount, or the absolute

Annals of the American Academy, 1895, p. 95.

percentage, of his income that he is required to pay in taxes, but on the relation between this amount or percentage and the amount or percentage which he would be required to pay if his income were a little more or a little less.

§ 10. When an income tax of a type that does not differentiate against savings cuts down the national dividend of the moment by checking work, it will also indirectly cut down the dividend of future years, because, with the smaller dividend of the moment, there will be less to invest as well as less to consume. An income tax, which is constructed on the same general plan and yields an equal revenue, but which *does* differentiate against saving, may be expected to have a larger effect. We need not suppose that it will affect the amount of work done and, therefore, the size of the dividend of the moment otherwise than the non-differential tax would have done. The non-differential tax lessens in a given degree the advantage that work yields, whatever is done with the fruit of work ; the differential tax lessens in a smaller degree the advantage which the part of it devoted to spending yields, and in a larger degree the advantage which the part devoted to saving yields. The net effect on the quantity of work done is likely to be much the same in either case.[1] It may be expected, however, that the differential tax will discourage savings more seriously—in spite of the fact that it may cause the savings of certain persons to increase [2]—than the non-differential tax, and, therefore, to contract more seriously the dividend of future years. How far it will do this it is impossible, with our present knowledge, to determine. All that can be said is that, if we take the point of view of a fairly long period, the succession of national dividends spread

[1] If the desire for income to save is decidedly more elastic than the desire for income to spend, the differential tax can be shown to be more restrictive of work than the other ; in the converse case it can be shown to be less restrictive. But we have no reason to suppose that the desire for one of these uses is, from a long-period standpoint, much more or much less elastic than that for the other.

[2] Cf. *ante*, p. 666. The possibility that, for some people, a tax on savings might cause more savings to be made is parallel to the possibility that, for some people, a tax on work might cause more work to be done. The maximum amount that could in any circumstances be added to savings or to work is an amount sufficient to discharge the whole tax, in such wise that the taxed persons would be left with the same amount of available income as they would have had if there had been no tax.

over a series of years is likely to be damaged somewhat more by the expectation of an income tax which differentiates against saving than it would be by that of a non-differential income tax yielding the same revenue.

§ 11. The second fiscal instrument, distinguished in § 5, through which substantial levies on the relatively well-to-do can be made, is the system of graduated taxes upon property passing at death. These duties, which are actuarially equivalent to deferred income tax on income derived from property, plainly differentiate against savings. The expectation of them will, therefore, check savings and so contract the national dividend of future years. Since, however, they do not as a rule hit savings till some years after they are made, this repressive effect need not be very great. For let us suppose that twenty million £'s a year are to be raised. This can be done either by collecting, say, £100 every year from each of a group of 200,000 people (income tax), or by collecting £2000 from each of them at death, say, on the average, once in twenty years (death duties). The choice between the two methods is indifferent to the State. But it is not indifferent to the persons concerned. Since these persons discount future taxes precisely as they discount all future events, and since their concern in any event is largely diminished if the event is known to fall due when they themselves are no longer alive, the expectation of taxes levied after the second method will have the smaller restrictive influence upon the quantity of capital created by them. Moreover, there are additional reasons why death duties should impose a relatively small check upon the creation of capital. A part of the stimulus to accumulation consists in the power and prestige that riches confer. In persons of only moderate fortune, who have, or hope to have, children, this motive is not, indeed, likely to play a dominant part. A desire to provide for their children will be the main motive, and, if it were removed, many of them would elect to "retire" from work much earlier than they do now. But, as Professor Carver observes : " After one's accumulation has increased beyond that which is necessary to safeguard one's offspring and to provide for the genuine prosperity of one's family, the motive to further accumulation changes. One then engages in business enterprises because of a love of action and a love of power. Accumulated capital becomes then one of the instruments of the game. So long as the player is left in possession of this instrument while he is one of the players, he is not likely to be discouraged from accumulation merely by the fact that the State, rather than his heirs, gets it after he is through with it." [1] In a like spirit the late Mr. Carnegie wrote : " To the class whose ambition it is to leave great fortunes and to be talked about after death, it will be even more attractive, and, indeed, a somewhat nobler ambition, to have enormous sums paid over to the State from their fortunes." We may add the similar saying of Walter Rathenau : " The object of the business man's work, of his worries, his pride and his aspirations, is just his undertaking, be it a commercial company, factory, bank, shipping concern, theatre, or railway. The undertaking seems to take on form and substance, and to be ever with him, having as it were, by virtue of his book-keeping, his organisation, and his branches, an independent economic existence. The business man is wholly devoted to making his business a flourishing, healthy, living organism." [2] Hence very heavy death duties could probably be levied on large fortunes—particularly on such parts of them as are left out of the direct line—without the knowledge that these taxes exist and will have ultimately to be paid exercising any large influence in discouraging rich men from saving.

§ 12. The general result of this analysis is, unfortunately, very nebulous. It is probable on the whole that, unlike the expectation of voluntary transferences from the rich, the expectation of coercive transferences from them by taxation will do harm to the dividend, particularly if the taxation imposed is heavy or steeply graduated. But we cannot determine the size of the adverse influence, even when the quantity of revenue to be raised and the scheme of taxation to be enforced are exactly set out.[3]

---

[1] *Essays in Social Justice*, p. 323. Professor Fisher even writes : "The ordinary normal self-made American millionaire is rather disposed, I believe, to look on the inheritance of his millions by his children with some misgiving " (*Journal of Political Economy*, vol. xxiv. p. 711).

[2] A. G. Sombart, *The Quintessence of Capitalism*, p. 173.

[3] For a fuller discussion of the comparative effects of various forms of taxation, cf. *A Study in Public Finance*, Part II.

CHAPTER X

THE EFFECT ON THE NATIONAL DIVIDEND OF THE EXPECTATION
OF TRANSFERENCES TO THE POOR

§ 1. IN turning to examine the effect on the national dividend of the expectation of transferences to the poor, we come at once into contact with a widely held opinion. The experience of the old Poor Law has made people very much afraid that any expectation of assistance from public funds will tempt the poor into idleness and thriftlessness. It is common—or at all events was common before the war—to hear proposals for State aid towards housing accommodation, insurance premiums, or even education, denounced on the ground that they constitute relief in aid of wages, and are, therefore, a reversion to the discredited policy of Speenhamland. This reasoning is based on defective analysis. Underlying it is the tacit assumption that the expectation of any one sort of transference to the poor acts in the same way as the expectation of any other sort. In reality different types of transference act in different ways, and nothing of importance can be said that does not take account of this fact. The main lines of division are between transferences which differentiate against idleness and thriftlessness, transferences which are neutral, and transferences which differentiate in favour of idleness and thriftlessness.

§ 2. The first of these groups is made up of those transferences which are conditional upon the recipients making provision for themselves on a scale that is fairly representative of their individual capacity. These transferences can be arranged as follows. First, the poorer members of the community are classified according to the amount of provision that they " could

720

reasonably have been expected to make " for themselves, apart from any transference of resources in their favour. The standard of capacity set up is, of course, different for different sorts of people with different opportunities. For example, the income from savings, which a man can reasonably be expected to have secured at a given age, varies with his situation in life. If, before the war, a man on 12s. a week had secured for himself an annuity of 1s. a week, his thrift was much more real than if a man on 50s. had got an annuity of 3s. a week. The classification of different people into different groups with different standards may be carried out with any degree of roughness or exactness, according to the scope and skill of the various classifying authorities. In ideal conditions a separate standard capacity would be estimated for every individual. Secondly, the standard having been set up, resources are transferred to poor persons on condition that their productive activity comes up to the standard assigned to them, an extra amount, perhaps, being transferred in recognition of any excess above standard to which they may attain. It is not, of course, necessary that the same grant should be made to all persons who live up to their capacity ; and, in general, we may presume that a poorer man satisfying this condition will receive more than a less poor man who also satisfies it. The kind of arrangement which this policy embodies has been advocated for certain purposes by Marshall. "Should not indoor and outdoor relief," he asks, " be so administered as to *encourage providence,* and to afford hope to those whose means are small, but who yet desire to do right as far as they can ? "[1] Practically the adoption of this ideal would mean that persons coming up to, or exceeding, the standard adjudged reasonable for them would be treated more favourably than similar persons failing to do this. A rough application of it is made in the rules governing the grant of old-age pensions in Denmark. In order to qualify for a pension, a man must have worked and saved enough to keep off the rates between the ages of fifty and sixty. Under this system, though, possibly, thrift, labour and private charity are discouraged, so far as they touch the provision for maintenance after sixty, "on the other hand,

[1] *Economic Journal,* 1891, p. 189.

both thrift and private charity have been stimulated, so far as they are concerned with provision for maintenance between the ages of fifty and sixty. The motive for maintaining independence during these years is strengthened, and its effectiveness is greatly increased, by the consideration that a limited task, the completion of which is not so distant and uncertain as to deter men from attempting it, is all that is now imposed on the honest and industrious, though indigent, person, or on friends, former employers or others, who may be interested in helping him. Many shrink from trying what seems impossible of achievement, and much effort, which would otherwise have remained latent, has been evoked by bringing the task within the reach of a wider circle of persons."[1] There can be little doubt that openings exist for a further application of methods of this kind. It is plain that the expectation of transferences to poor persons, engineered by means of them, will stimulate, and will not diminish, the contribution which potential recipients make towards the upbuilding of the national dividend.

§ 3. The second group, neutral transferences, is made up of those transferences which are dependent on the attainment of some condition, not capable of being varied by voluntary action in the economic sphere, on the part of possible beneficiaries. It thus includes schemes for universal old-age pensions (dependent only on the attainment of a certain age), the universal endowment of motherhood (dependent only on the fact of motherhood), or the universal gift to everybody of a sum deemed sufficient to furnish by itself the essential means of subsistence. These wide-reaching arrangements are, hitherto, nowhere more than projects. But less ambitious examples of neutral transferences have been embodied in actual law. Under them grants of help are made to depend, not on the performance of the recipient, nor on the relation between performance and estimated

---

[1] "Denmark and its Aged Poor," *Yale Review*, 1899, p. 15. The following sentence from the first report on the working of the British Unemployment Insurance Scheme is of interest in this connection : "Twenty of our Trade Unions, with an estimated membership of over 86,000 in the (compulsorily) Insured Trades, have begun to make provision for unemployment since the passing of the Act ; while other Associations making such provision have much increased their membership" ([Cd. 6965], p. iv.). The help given towards insurance would thus seem to have stimulated private effort.

capacity, but upon estimated capacity itself. The root idea
of this system was approached in a Report made to the Poor
Law Authority in 1872 by Mr. Wodehouse, in which he
endeavoured to distinguish between relief in aid of wages
and relief in aid of earnings. " Relief in aid of earnings,"
he wrote, " is clearly inseparable from any system of out-relief.
Thus, in all unions, relief is afforded to able-bodied widows
with children, and it is clear that all such relief is in aid of
an income obtained by the widow by washing, charing, or
other similar employments. So, again, in almost every union
that I visited, relief is given to old and infirm men, who,
though past regular work, are from time to time employed
on occasional odd jobs of various sorts. Relief to these two
classes of paupers may, I think, be distinguished from that
system of relief in aid of wages, which was so generally prevalent prior to the introduction of the present Poor Law." [1]
A closer approach to the above idea is made in the treatment
which many Boards of Guardians before the war accorded to
old and infirm women and to widows with several children.
They appeared to hold that, whereas most of the regular trades
followed by men provide persons of average capacity, in full
employment and without encumbrances, with fairly adequate
earnings, most women's trades do not do this. It is not at
all obvious that a widow of ordinary ability, even without
children, *can*, with reasonable hours and so forth, earn enough
to " maintain herself and provide for the ordinary vicissitudes
of life." [2]   Hence we read : " Once a woman is put on the
roll (for out-relief), provided she is not guilty of immorality or
frequent intemperance, she is not disturbed. Her earnings
may rise and fall, but the relief will not vary. The inquiry
as to her earnings is made at her first application and rarely

---

[1] Quoted in Appendix, vol. xvii., to the *Report of the Royal Commission on the
Poor Laws* [Cd. 4690], p. 355.

[2] Cf. *Report to the Poor Law Commission* by Mr. Steel Maitland and Miss
Squire, Appendix, vol. xvi. p. 5. The position of widows is, of course, especially
likely to be difficult in districts where there is no established women's trade.
In such districts " widows left destitute come at once for poor relief and remain
throughout their widowhood on the rates." Where opportunities for home work
exist, pauperism may be postponed—often at the expense of hours far longer
than a proper interpretation of the minimum standard, to be stipulated for in
chapter xii., would allow. (Cf. *ibid.* p. 182.)

afterwards. . . . One officer put the common practice into a
few words: 'We never bother about what the women earn.
We know they never earn ten shillings. They can always
find room for half-a-crown.' It follows that, in unions where
minute inquiry is the exception—that is to say, in most
unions—the pauper worker is not discouraged from working up to her full capacity."[1] The French law of 1893
concerning sick relief is of kindred character. It provides
that in every commune there shall be drawn up periodically a list of persons who, if they become sick, will be
entitled to assistance, the persons on the list being placed
there on the ground that they have not the capacity
to make provision against sickness for themselves. Yet
again, the same principle is embodied in the English
system of exacting payment (whether through recoverable
loans or otherwise) from persons adjudged capable of making
some contribution, to whom medical aid has been given, or
whose children have been fed by public authority. A charge
is made, based, not on what the actual service rendered to the
poor man has cost, but on an estimate of the provision which,
apart from the hope of outside help, he might have been
expected to make. Thus Circular 552 of the Board of
Education urges that, when the parents cannot pay the full
cost of meals provided for their children, "it is better that
they should pay what their means permit, rather than that
meals should be given free of cost."[2] In other words, an

[1] *Report to the Poor Law Commission* by Miss Williams and Mr. Jones,
Appendix, vol. xvii. p. 334.
[2] *Loc. cit.* Par. 4. The Board's Report on the Working of the Act in 1910
showed that the amount of money actually recovered from parents was insignificant.
([Cd. 5131], p. 9.) This, however, was largely due to the facts (1) that many
local Education Boards deliberately limit their provision of meals to necessitous
children, and (2) that, when they do not do this, parents who can afford to
pay dislike sending their children to meals where no distinction is made between
payers and non-payers. (Cf. Bulkley, *The Feeding of School Children*, pp. 107-9.)
In these circumstances not many children whose parents are capable of paying
anything are likely to be affected. In respect of lunatics the conditions are
different, and considerable contributions from relatives are collected. (Cf.
Freeman, *Economic Journal*, 1911, pp. 294 *et seq.*) It must be admitted, however,
that there are considerable practical difficulties in the way of exacting payment
for a service which it is understood will be rendered whether payment is
made or not. Further objection is often taken to the device of "recoverable
loans," on the ground that they divert energy from industrial effort to attempts
at evading payment. As Mrs. Bosanquet observes: "Many a shilling is

attempt is made so to arrange the State's contribution to different families that it shall depend upon, and vary inversely with, their estimated capacity to make provision for themselves.

§ 4. The way in which the expectation of a neutral transference will react on the size of the national dividend depends on the kind of things in which the transference is made. As a general rule, of course, it is made in money. In these circumstances it might be thought at first sight that the contribution of effort and waiting which potential recipients make, and, therefore, the size of the dividend, will be wholly unaffected. This, however, is not so. For, if a man of any given presumed capacity knows that he will receive, say, a pound a week as a gift, independently of anything that he may earn for himself, his desire for any nth unit of money earned by himself is lowered. But his aversion to any rth unit of work that he may do remains unaltered; or, since the extra money creates new opportunities for a pleasurable use of leisure, may even be increased. Consequently, if he continued to do the same amount of work as before, his aversion to the last unit of work done would exceed his desire for the money received in exchange for it. It follows that the expectation of a weekly grant will cause the recipient to contract the amount of work that he does, and, therewith, his contribution to the national dividend. The extent of this effect varies with the magnitude of the grant and the forms of (1) the schedule representing his desire for various amounts of money and (2) the schedule representing his aversion from various amounts of work; but, in any event, *some* contraction in his contribution to the dividend is likely, *ceteris paribus*, to occur.

§ 5. The transference may, however, be made in the form, not of money, but of things. If these things are things which, apart from the transference, a recipient would have purchased out of his own earnings, or if, not being such things, they are capable of being sold or pawned and thus converted into money, the effect is the same as if money had been transferred. But transference of objects not capable of

recklessly wasted, because, if not spent, it will only go to the debt collector" (*Economic Journal*, 1896, p. 223).

being sold or pawned, and designed to satisfy needs, which, apart from the transference, a recipient would have left unsatisfied, have a different effect. The last unit of money which a man earns for himself in industry will be required to satisfy the same needs, and will, therefore, be desired with the same intensity as it would have been if no transference had been made. Hence no contraction will occur in the contribution which, by work and waiting, he makes to the national dividend. Thus public parks for the collective use of the poor, or flowers for their private use, can be transferred to them, without the expectation of the transference reacting injuriously upon the dividend. The same remark holds good of general sanitary measures. The grant from State funds of the expenses involved in such things is on a different footing from the grant of funds for ordinary medical treatment. As the Poor Law Commissioners write: " Sanitary measures, for the most part, lie beyond the reach of the individual, and are a common need, which must be provided for in common; while medical treatment is essentially an individual need, and is, for the most part, easily attainable by the individual." [1] Similar considerations hold good, in some degree, of the gift of free school education, or of a portion of the costs of it— when the amount of education to be covered is authoritatively fixed—to the children of the poor. For some persons are so poor that, if left to themselves, they could not devote any of their earnings to the purchase of school education, and, therefore, the free provision of it by the State does not lower their desire for any unit of these earnings. Since, when children are taken to be educated, their parents are deprived of the wages they might otherwise have obtained, it may be that, even when to free education free meals are added, there is no net lightening of the costs of living to parents, and, therefore, no diminution in the contribution of work and waiting which they find it profitable to make. In these circumstances the expectation of this variety of neutral transference will leave the size of the national dividend unaltered.

§ 6. There remains the third possibility. There are some commodities and services, the demand for which is so correlated

[1] *Report of the Royal Commission on the Poor Law*, p. 231.

with that for certain other commodities and services that the gift of them increases the recipient's desire for these others, thus increasing his desire for any rth unit of purchasing power that he may be able to earn, and thus, finally, increasing the work and waiting that he is willing to provide in exchange for purchasing power. It is claimed, for example, that the gift of medical treatment to children in some elementary schools reacts beneficially on the energy of their parents by enlisting co-operation and thought from them. The possibility thus opened up is illustrated in the following passage from Mr. Paterson's *Across the Bridges* :

> At present the difficulty of school dinners centres round the position of the mother. Her apathy towards the education of her child, her severance from any sense of partnership with the school, makes her sometimes ready to snatch advantages, but slow to bear her proper share. Her lack of responsibility arises, not from the fact that so much is done for her, but that so much is done without her. As long as the education of the boy is taken completely out of her hands, so long will she be apt to stand aloof, regard every committee as a natural enemy, and grasp at all that she can by any manœuvre hope to be given. The absence of home work, visiting, reports, and all natural ties between school and home are the real enemies of parental responsibility. No mother is harmed by kindness done to her child, so long as every such kindness exacts from her a higher standard and ensures her active co-operation with the school.[1]

A like suggestion is contained in the following extract from the *Letters of Octavia Hill* :

> I sometimes dream about the time that shall come, " when we shall try to keep up the spirit of our poor," not by shutting up their hearts in cold independence, but by giving them others to help, and thus rousing the deepest of all motives for self-help, that which is the only foundation on which to build our service to others.[2]

An illustration of what is meant is furnished by the late Canon Barnett thus :

> The Children's Country Holiday Fund, for instance, by giving country holidays to town children, and by making the parents contribute to the expense, develops at once a desire for the peace

---

[1] *Loc. cit.* p. 110.   [2] *Loc. cit.* p. 207.

and beauty of the country and a new capacity for satisfying this
desire. When parents realise the necessity for such holiday, and
know how it can be secured, this fund will cease to have a reason
for existence.[1]

In undertakings of this kind there is a field for neutral
transferences of resources, the expectation of which not
merely leaves the national dividend undiminished, but, by
creating a new inducement for work and saving, actually
increases it.

§ 7. We now pass to the third main group of transferences—namely, those which differentiate in favour of
idleness and thriftlessness by making the help that is given
larger, the smaller is the provision the recipients have made
for themselves. Some resort to this type of transference is
involved in all Poor Law systems that fix a state of minimum
fortune below which they will not allow any citizen to fall.
For, in so far as they raise to this level the real income of all
citizens whose provision for themselves falls below it, they
implicitly promise that any reduction in private provision shall
be made good by an equivalent addition to State provision. It is plain that the expectation of these differential
transferences will greatly weaken the motive of many poor
persons to make provision for themselves. For, whatever the
standard is below which the State has determined that nobody
shall fall, any person, who could not provide as much as this
for himself but could provide something, will be equally well
off if he provides nothing. In so far, therefore, as what a
person provides for himself corresponds to what he contributes
to the national dividend, transferences that differentiate in
favour of small provision threaten grave injury to the national
dividend.

§ 8. A recognition of this fact has led many persons to consider plans for limiting the scope of this class of differential
transference. Since everybody agrees that in a civilised State
no citizen shall be allowed to starve, this can only be done
by so enlarging the scope of neutral transferences that the
elementary needs of practically all persons, whatever their
income, are met through them. The movement in this

---

[1] *Practicable Socialism*, p. 237.

direction is well illustrated by the debate between advocates and opponents of a universalised system of old-age pensions.[1] If, say the advocates of this plan, all persons over a given age, irrespective of their income, are awarded a given pension, there will be no differentiation tempting people in old age to earn smaller incomes than they are able to earn; whereas, if only those persons above the given age who are in receipt of an income below some specified maximum are awarded a pension, there will be an inducement to all persons, who could have earned an income between this maximum and this maximum *plus* the pension, to earn less than this maximum: and an effect similar in kind, though less in extent, will be produced by sliding-scale pension schemes. On the other side, however, it is pointed out, in accordance with the reasoning of the last chapter, that money cannot generally be collected through taxation without some injurious reaction on the national dividend being produced. This reaction is likely to be more extensive, the greater is the amount of the money that is raised. Since, therefore, universal old-age pensions necessarily cost more than limited old-age pensions, the argument in favour of the universal form is confronted with an argument of the same order that tells against it. Exactly the same issue, somewhat complicated in this instance by eugenic considerations,[2] is raised between persons who wish to confine State aid for mothers to those families with young children in which the parents are unable, out of their own resources, to provide for their children adequately, and advocates of the " endowment of motherhood " generally; and again between the advocates of free meals for all school children in elementary schools and advocates of free meals only to those whose parents cannot afford to pay for them. In this last case there has also to be considered the social awkwardness in the schools themselves of distinguishing between two classes of children, and also the practical difficulty of determining which parents can, and which cannot,

---

[1] This controversy is presented in a clear-cut form in the Report of the Departmental Committee on Old-Age Pensions [Cmd. 410], 1919. The majority of the Committee recommended that the means limit for pensions should be abolished, but the minority dissented from this recommendation.

[2] Cf. Darwin, *The Racial Effects of Public Assistance*, pp. 13-15.

afford to pay.[1] To strike a balance between the conflicting considerations in controversies of this kind is a very delicate task, and one that need not be attempted here. If, however, the method of obviating differential transferences contemplated by the advocates of universal pensions and universal endowment of motherhood were itself universalised, in such wise that the minimum required for subsistence were paid out by the State to everybody, whatever his income might be, the task of balancing gain against loss would no longer be delicate. In these circumstances there can be little doubt that the type of reaction described in § 7 would operate so strongly that the dividend would be seriously injured. In any event, among practical politicians the device of universalising grants to large categories of persons, irrespective of their individual needs, is greatly disliked. There is no real question of pressing it far enough to do away with the need for differential transferences based directly on the poverty of recipients.

§ 9. The expectation of these transferences must, as we have seen, damage the national dividend. If, however, to the receipt of the help they give deterrent conditions are attached, the damage can be mitigated. Consequently the question arises, in what circumstances it is desirable, in the interest of the national dividend, to attach deterrent conditions to State aid, and what form the deterrent conditions, if decided upon, can best assume. To answer this question correctly we need to revert to the concluding sentence of § 7, in which it was indicated that differentiation in favour of people who make small provision for themselves injures the national dividend, *only in so far as what a person provides for himself corresponds to what he contributes to the national dividend.* It is common to assume that the provision which a person makes for himself must correspond exactly to his contribution to the national dividend, and that, therefore, the contraction of the aggregate provision thus made——which results from the establishment of a system of differential transferences to poor people——implies an equal contraction of the national dividend. This is substantially true of provision made through work and through savings invested in industry and not sub-

---

[1] Cf. Brooks's *Labour's Challenge to the Social Order*, p. 228 *et seq.*

sequently withdrawn. But it is not true of provision made in the form of a claim to benefit from a mutual insurance society, secured by the payment of previous contributions to that society. For what a sick or unemployed member draws from this source is only in small part the fruit of savings that have been built up into productive capital investments. In the main it consists of payments made out of the contemporary earnings of other members—payments which they are willing to make in return for a promise that they themselves shall, at need, receive similar assistance; but payments, none the less, which represent a transference of real income, just as the gift of a friend would do, and not a creation of real income. In practice the chief part of the provision which poor people make for themselves, otherwise than by contemporary work, is made by way of some form of insurance, though it is loosely and popularly credited to saving. Consequently, we may conclude broadly that, while any check, caused by differential transferences, to the provision that poor people make for themselves through contemporary work involves a corresponding diminution of the national dividend, any check to the provision they make otherwise than through work involves a very much less than corresponding diminution in the dividend. It follows that there is little to be gained by imposing deterrent conditions upon those recipients of State help who have failed to make this sort of provision.

§ 10. But differentiation in favour of small provision made through contemporary work is a serious matter. If, for example, it is understood that everybody's income will, at need, be brought up by State aid to, say, £3 a week, it will, generally and roughly, be to the interest of everybody capable of earning by work any sum less than £3 a week to be idle and earn nothing. This *must* damage the national dividend. How much it damages it will, of course, depend on how large the sum fixed on as a minimum is, and how many people in the country would normally earn by work less than that sum. If the sum exceeds the normal earning power of a large part of the community, the damage done must necessarily be very great. It is probable that this consideration lay behind the recommendation of the 1832 Commission, that " the situation on the whole of able-bodied paupers should not be made really, or apparently, so eligible as the situation of the independent labourer of the lowest class "—that is to say, of the ordinary unskilled labourer of full age and in good health. At that time unskilled labourers formed a very large proportion of the population. To have guaranteed to everybody a situation better than these labourers could ordinarily earn would, therefore, have threatened the nation with the withdrawal from work of a mass of people whose aggregate efforts were responsible for an important slice of the dividend. It may be observed, however, that to guarantee now a situation better than that represented by the earnings of an unskilled labourer of 1832 would inflict a much smaller proportionate injury upon the dividend, because the proportion of the population, who are not capable of attaining a situation better than this, has become much smaller. Even to guarantee now a situation represented by the situation of the unskilled labourer of to-day would have a smaller proportionate effect, because the proportion of the dividend contributed by unskilled labour now is smaller than it was in 1832. Plainly, however, for the State, tacitly or openly, to guarantee any standard high enough to affect a substantial number of people must threaten considerable injury to the dividend. Here, therefore, there is real scope for the association with State help of deterrent conditions. Of course, there is no object in attaching such conditions to help given to a man who is idle because he is genuinely unable to find work. The knowledge that he cannot get help without these conditions will not remove this inability. But there is an object in attaching them to help given to those who are idle because they are unwilling to find (or to keep) work. The deterrent conditions will make them less unwilling. Until recently the practical difficulty of distinguishing between these two classes of persons, coupled with a general and justified unwillingness to deal hardly with the former of them, made it impossible to arrange these conditions satisfactorily. A compromise was accepted, under which, instead of no deterrence on the one class and strict deterrence on the other, mild deterrence was imposed on both. This plan did, indeed, save the innocent from gross tyranny, but at the expense of leaving the guilty relatively immune and, therefore, inadequately deterred. Of late years, however, the establishment of employment exchanges has provided machinery by which the truth of a man's plea that he is out of work through no fault of his own can be, in some measure, tested. In trades where the jobs, once obtained, are of " presumed permanence," if the employment exchanges are unable to find employment for a man who applies to them, more particularly if that man has a definite settled home, the plea that he is a victim of misfortune, and not of laziness, may be provisionally accepted. This test is, indeed, not easily applicable to casual trades, where workpeople continually alternate between work and idleness; for in these trades a man might be prepared to accept work for a day or so, whenever it was offered through an employment exchange, and yet might deliberately spend a much longer period out of work than there was any need for him to do. This difficulty must be recognised ; and it must be admitted, further, that in the exceptional period of free insurance granted by the British Government after the armistice of November 1918, a number of persons obtained unemployment donation who might, had they wished, have been employed. But, in spite of this, there can be no doubt that the development of employment exchanges has made it possible, over a wide field, to distinguish directly those who cannot from those who will not find work. Consequently, since the former class can be withdrawn altogether from the range of deterrent conditions, it is now feasible so to stiffen up the conditions against the latter class —people who are in need because they *will* not work with reasonable continuity in private industry—as to make them really effective.

§ 11. Some guidance as to the form that deterrence should take can be obtained from English Poor Law experience. It is clearly suggested, for example, that some degree of enforced labour is an essential ingredient. The importance of this element is well illustrated in some of the evidence given before the Royal Commission of 1832. Thus one witness, in a

Memorandum on Liverpool, stated: "The introduction of
labour thinned the house very much; it was sometimes
difficult to procure a sufficient supply of junk, which was
generally obtained from Plymouth; when the supply was
known to be scanty, paupers flocked in; but the sight of
a load of junk before the door would deter them for any length
of time."[1] In the same spirit, the Comptroller of the Accounts
for the township of Salford stated: "Finding work for those
who applied for relief in consequence of being short or out of
work has had a very good effect, especially when the work
has been of a different kind from that which they have been
accustomed to. In Salford employment to break stones on
the highways has saved the township several hundred pounds
within the last two years; for very few indeed will remain
at work more than a few days, while the bare mention of
it is quite sufficient for others. They all manage to find
employment for themselves, and cease for a time to be
troublesome; although it is a singular fact that, when the
stock of stones on hand has been completely worked up before
the arrival of others, they have, almost to a man, applied
again for relief, and the overseers have been obliged to give
them relief; but, so soon as an arrival of stones is announced,
they find work for themselves again."[2] The information
given in a later Report on the Poplar Union points in the
same direction. But, though enforced labour seems to be
an essential ingredient in deterrent conditions, it is not by
itself sufficient. The chief reason for this is the extraordinary
difficulty of making a man work for the Poor Law Authorities
with anything approaching the energy that he would need to
put forth for a private employer. It is practically impossible
to set relieved persons to work, each at his own trade. Consequently some general form of labour has to be required:
and it is impossible to fix, for a miscellaneous assortment of
different people, any single standard of performance. Hence
the standard exacted has to be measured to each man "with
due regard to his ordinary calling or occupation, and his age
and physical ability." Since this cannot be tested objectively,

---

[1] *Report of the Poor Law Commission of 1832*, p. 161.
[2] *Ibid.* p. 162.

"no specified task can be enforced. The capability of the persons employed varies, and it can only be required that each person shall perform the amount of work that he appears to be able to accomplish. . . . The standard of accomplishment is practically fixed by the unwilling worker."[1] The fact that resort cannot be had to the ordinary practice of dismissal leaves the Poor Law Authority without any real defence against this tendency. Consequently potential beneficiaries are aware that the labour which will be imposed upon them if, through unwillingness to work in private industry, they become candidates for public assistance, will not be severe labour. Furthermore, even if this difficulty could be overcome, work for the Poor Law, because its certainty and continuity absolve those engaged in it from the risk, trouble and cost involved in occasional loss of employment and the need of finding a new job, might still prove more attractive than independent labour. Thus, for effective deterrence, something more than enforced labour is required. Disfranchisement (abolished in England in 1918) and the stigma of pauperism are, in the opinion of practical administrators, quite inadequate. Consequently, for those who need support, but will not work to get it, resort must be had to disciplinary measures. This implies detention under control without excessive leave of absence. On the Continent of Europe able-bodied men who fail to support themselves because they will not work are subjected to long periods of detention in labour colonies. In Belgium such persons may be committed to the penal colony of Merxplas for not less than two years nor more than seven years.[2] The cantonal law in Berne provides for their internment in a labour institution for any time between six months and two years.[3] The German Imperial Penal Code has a similar provision.[4] The practice of the Continent is coming to be proposed seriously for adoption in this country also. Thus the Committee on Vagrancy recommended "that a class of habitual vagrants should be defined by Statute, and that this class should include any

---

[1] *Report of the Committee on Distress from Want of Employment*, quoted by Beveridge, *Unemployment*, p. 153.
[2] Cf. Dawson, *The Vagrancy Problem*, p. 136.
[3] *Ibid.* p. 179.   [4] *Ibid.* p. 193.

person who has been three or more times convicted, during
a period of, say, twelve months, of certain offences now
coming under the Vagrancy Act, namely, sleeping out,
begging, refusing to perform his task of work in casual
wards, or refusing or neglecting to maintain himself so that
he become chargeable to the poor rate."[1]   There is no
reason—much the contrary—why the conditions of deterrence should not be arranged with a view to "improving" the
deterred persons, if that be possible; for to a man wishing to
be idle the prospect of improvement, whether by training or
by education or in any other way, will be as deterrent as anything else.   Detention, however, is essential.   Its adoption—
which the development of employment exchanges as a means
of separating the sheep from the goats has made practicable—
would enable a far more effective system of deterrence to be
associated with State aid to the deliberately idle than is at
present known in this country.   We cannot, however, seriously
expect that the system will ever become perfect enough to
prevent the expectation of differential transferences from contracting, in some degree, the size of the national dividend.

[1] *Report of the Departmental Committee on Vagrancy*, vol. i. p. 59.

CHAPTER XI

BOUNTIES ON THINGS PURCHASED BY THE POOR

§ 1. So far we have been considering transferences of a direct kind. There remain transferences through bounties or devices substantially equivalent to bounties. These take three principal forms: first, bounties, provided out of taxes, on the whole consumption of particular commodities which are predominantly purchased by poor persons; secondly, bounties, similarly provided, but confined to that part of the whole consumption which is actually enjoyed by defined categories of poor persons; thirdly, authoritative interference with prices, so contrived that the richer purchasers of particular commodities have to bear part of the cost of what is sold to poorer purchasers. The first of these methods is illustrated by the special subsidies which were paid on bread and potatoes during the Great War to enable prices to be kept down to what was considered a reasonable level. The second and third methods are only practicable in connection with commodities and services which are non-transferable in the sense explained in Part II. Chapter XVII. The second is illustrated by the Irish Labourers Acts, under which, not all house-building in the districts affected, but only house-building for labourers was subsidised, and by the more general provisions which were adopted to meet the post-war house shortage. The third method is illustrated by special arrangements often made in connection with the services supplied by monopolistic "public utilities." Whether these services are actually produced by private concerns or by the public authorities themselves, public authorities can, if they choose, compel sales to selected poor persons to be made at a

2 B

loss, and can arrange for this loss to be made good through charges to other persons higher than would otherwise have been permitted. This plan is adopted under a number of Tramway Acts, where provision is made for a convenient service of workmen's cars at specially low fares. Thus " a recent report of the Highway Committee of the London County Council estimates that the loss involved by running the workmen's car service is £65,932 per annum."[1] The same policy is illustrated in another connection by the (pre-war) practice of the municipality of Wiesbaden, where gas supplied by means of prepayment meters—a more expensive method of supply—was charged for at the same rate as gas supplied by ordinary meters to all persons the annual rent of whose house was less than 400 marks.[2] It should be noted that this method is not necessarily confined to commodities and services produced under conditions of monopoly. Provided that the goods are, or can be made, non-transferable, it is open to public authorities to fix a charge at which anybody undertaking a named business or profession must sell whatever quantity of service is demanded by persons in a given category. The result will be to limit the number of persons entering that business or profession, till the expectation of earnings therefrom—derived jointly from sales to the poor and to other persons, for whose purchases the charges are fixed by the normal play of demand and supply—becomes about equal to that ruling in other businesses or professions of a similar difficulty and disagreeableness and involving an equally expensive training. This, of course, implies that the low charges made to the favoured category of persons are associated with charges to other categories higher than would have prevailed if the low charges had not been enforced.

§ 2. To all these methods it has been objected that they necessarily benefit unequally different poor persons whose circumstances are substantially similar. Professor Knoop writes, for example: " It is difficult to see why artisans, mechanics, and day labourers, who travel in the early morning,

---

[1] Knoop, *Principles of Municipal Trading*, p. 266.
[2] *Ibid.* p. 213.

should receive privileges which men and women serving in shops, clerks, and others, who are no better off financially, do not enjoy."[1] It may be replied that, if a thing is good in itself, the partial realisation of it cannot rightly be condemned on the ground that complete realisation is impracticable. We are not, however, concerned with the validity either of this objection or of the different and more forcible objection, from the side of fairness, which can be urged specially against the third method, namely, that it throws the cost of helping the poor upon particular persons, instead of upon the taxpayers generally.[2] For the present purpose it is enough to know that all three of the methods distinguished above have, as a matter of fact, been adopted over a fairly wide field.

§ 3. The first of the three necessarily, and, if the categories are so chosen that people cannot practically be drawn by the bounty into a benefited category, the other two also involve "neutral transferences" in the sense explained in § 3 of the last chapter, and not differential transferences. Hence the expectation of them operates on the productive activity of the poor only through their effect on the marginal desiredness which money has to them. But they differ from the kind of neutral transferences so far examined in one respect. They will check to a small extent the contribution of work made by the poor, if they are granted upon things for which the demand of the poor has an elasticity less than unity ; but they will increase this contribution to a small extent, if they are granted on things for which this demand has an elasticity greater than unity. For in the former event the marginal desiredness of money to the poor will be lowered, since more is left over for other things; and in the latter event it will be raised. As a matter of fact, bounties are most likely to be given on things of urgent need and, therefore, of inelastic demand. The check to output resulting from the consequent relaxation of effort on the part of potential recipients means *some*, though probably a very small, diminution of the national dividend.

---

[1] Knoop, *Principles of Municipal Trading*, p. 266.
[2] Cf. *ante*, Part IV. Chapter V. § 7.

§ 4. So far it would seem that there is little to choose between help to the poor by bounties and by direct neutral transferences. If the amount of the bounty-fed commodity which each recipient is to consume is fixed authoritatively, as under the British system of free and compulsory elementary education, this is in fact so. It is so, too, if the amount is not fixed authoritatively, but is, for other reasons, not liable to change in consequence of the bounty. Thus poor people are accustomed to buy some things through a common purchase fund, so organised that the payment a member has to make does not vary with the amount of his individual purchases. Sick clubs are arranged on this plan. There will be no inducement to a member of a sick club to increase the amount of the doctor's services that he calls for in a year merely because the fixed amount, that he has been accustomed to pay for membership of the club, is taken over and paid by the State. These conditions, however, are exceptional. In general, when a bounty, or the equivalent of a bounty, is given on any commodity, the purchasers, having regard to the bounty, will buy more of the commodity than they would have done had they received an equivalent subsidy in the form of a direct money grant. In this way resources are diverted out of the natural channels of production, and there is a presumption—which may, of course, as was explained in Part II. Chapter XI., be rebutted by special knowledge—that this diversion will inflict an extra injury on the national dividend, over and above that set out in the preceding paragraph. If the bounty is large enough, it may happen that the output of the bounty-fed commodity will be expanded so far that to the poor themselves the supply price, not merely in terms of money, but in terms of satisfaction, exceeds the demand price, or, in other words, that the economic satisfaction they get from the last increment consumed is less than the economic dissatisfaction involved in producing it. In general the expectation of a transference to the poor through bounties on particular commodities is likely to damage the national dividend rather more than the expectation of a direct neutral transference of equal magnitude. In spite of this, however, the bounty method may still sometimes be better than the other, not only because there may be special economic or non-economic reasons for encouraging the consumption of the particular thing on which the bounty is given, as compared with other things, but also because the element of " charity " is less obvious and, therefore, less damaging to the *morale* of the beneficiaries, when it is concealed in a bounty than when it is displayed in a direct dole.

CHAPTER XII

§ 1. In the three preceding chapters we have been concerned with the effect on the national dividend of the expectation of transferences from the rich and of the expectation of transferences to the poor. These things, we have seen, are liable to modify the dividend of any year by reacting both on the contribution of work provided during that year and on the quantity of capital equipment made ready in former years against the needs of that year. The whole story, however, has not yet been told. In the year—any year—that we are considering, the dividend, as determined by these expectations, will be of such and such a size. Thereupon occurs *the fact of transferences* from the rich to the poor. This, for the years yet to come, superimposes upon the effects we have been considering so far a new set of effects. For it involves a shifting, additional to any shiftings that are brought about by expectations, in the uses to which the dividend of the year we are considering is put. For the present purpose the accessible uses may be taken to be the provision of goods consumable by the rich, the provision of machines to assist future production, and the provision of goods consumable by the poor. When a transference of resources from the rich to the poor takes place, the third of these three divisions of the dividend is increased at the expense of the other two. Our problem is to determine the effect of this alteration in the distribution among different uses of the dividend of one year upon the magnitude of the dividend of later years.

742

§ 2. If no transference had occurred, the portion of the dividend due to assume the form of machines would have contributed to enlarge the dividend in later years. The portion devoted to the consumption of the rich, in so far as it served to make them more efficient producing agents, would also have done this to some extent. Among rich persons, however, it is improbable that any practicable reduction of consumption—the effect might, of course, be different if a levy were imposed so large as to bring down incomes from £5000 to £100—would diminish efficiency in an appreciable degree. Hence we may say roughly that that part of the sum transferred to the poor in any year, which, if it had not been transferred, would have been converted into capital, is the only part that would have made a substantial contribution to the dividend of the future. How large that part of the transferred sum is will depend to some extent on the method of taxation that is employed. Under the income-tax method we may suppose that in one year twenty million £ is collected from 200,000 people by a levy of £100 on each; under the death-duty method that an equal sum is collected from 10,000 people by a levy of £2000 on each. Things *could*, no doubt, be so arranged that these two plans would come to substantially the same thing. For under the death-duty method each person might furnish about £100 annually to insurance companies, to be handed over by them in payment of the death duties falling due during the year, instead of furnishing it, as under the income-tax method, to the Treasury. In actual life, however, it is not likely that a tax falling due from any estate every twentieth year will be fully provided against in the untaxed years that precede or follow. Consequently it is probable that under the death-duty method a good deal more than £100 will have to be furnished towards the tax from the resources accruing in the actual year of the tax, and a good deal less from those accruing in other years. It is fairly clear, however, that, as the amount withdrawn from the resources of any year grows, people will be less and less willing, owing to the wrench threatened to their habits, to take it out of consumption. Consequently there will be a tendency for a large part of it to come out of such part of the taxpayers' resources

as would normally have been saved; and, if these resources
are not sufficient, for it to be raised by the sale of capital.
This last arrangement does not, of course, imply the handing
over to the State in taxation of actual capital goods, but it
does imply that somebody else, who would otherwise have
devoted resources to building plant and machinery, will devote
them instead to buying the existing plant and machinery
that the taxpayer is forced to sell; with the result that the new
savings of the community as a whole are contracted by an
amount approximately equivalent to the amount of existing
capital that the taxpayer throws on the market.   In general,
then, the fact that death duties consist of large levies at long
intervals in place of small levies at short intervals suggests
that the resources transferred through them are likely to be
drawn from potential capital more largely than would be the
case if equal resources were collected through income tax.   This
suggestion is confirmed and emphasised by the further fact
that, under death duties, the moment chosen for the tax levy
is one at which the heir is entering into an entirely new
fortune.   At this moment he will not have accustomed himself
to think of his new property as " belonging to him " in the
ordinary sense: he will look upon what comes after death
duties have been paid as his " inheritance," and will not be
spurred on to replenish with new special savings the gap that
these duties have made in its original amount.   This incident
also makes *pro tanto* for the payment of the duties out of
potential capital.   The distinction between death duties and
income tax in this respect is, however, a secondary matter.
Even under death duties, when any given quantity of resources
is collected from the rich, it is practically certain that some of
it will be taken (perhaps *via* insurance premiums) from that
part of their income which would, in the ordinary course, have
been consumed.   This implies that the part which would have
become capital will not be reduced by the whole amount of
the levy.   It follows that any given transference of resources
from the rich to the poor is bound, in itself and apart from
the reactions discussed in the preceding chapters, to increase
the national dividend of the future, provided that the return
yielded by investment in the poor, through additions to

their industrial capacity, is not less than the return yielded by investment in material capital—that is to say, roughly, than the normal rate of interest.

§ 3. Now it must be admitted at once that there are certain classes of poor persons whom no transference of resources could render appreciably more efficient. These classes include the great mass of those who are morally, mentally or physically degenerate. The history of Labour Colonies both at home and abroad and the experience of our own special schools for the feeble-minded make it clear that, for this class of person, real cure is practically impossible. " The officials of the colonies, on being asked their opinion as to whether it could be said with truth that any large proportion of the men sent to Merxplas were rehabilitated, morally or socially, by their stay at Merxplas, replied that in very few cases is such reclamation effected ":[1] and this is the experience of more than one colony elsewhere devoted to the care of the worst class of the non-criminal population. The fact is that, in the economic, as in the physical, sphere, society is faced with a certain number of incurables. For such persons, when they are found, the utmost that can be done is to seclude them permanently from opportunities of parasitism upon others, of spreading their moral contagion, and of breeding offspring of like character to themselves. The residue of hopelessly vicious, mentally defective, and other unfortunates may, indeed, still be cared for humanely by society, when they come into being, and it would be wrong to neglect any method of treatment that might raise the lives of even a few of them to a higher plane. But our main effort must be, by education and, still more, by restricting propagation among the mentally and physically unfit, to cut off at the source this stream of tainted lives. To cure them in any real sense is beyond human power. The same thing is true of those persons who suffer from no inherent defect and have lived in their day the life of good citizens, but whose powers have been worn out by age or ruined by grave accident. Here again, from the standpoint of investment, the soil is

[1] *Report of the Royal Commission on the Poor Laws*, Appendix, vol. xxxii. p. 17.

barren. The transference of resources to these persons, in whatever form it is made, may be extremely desirable for other reasons, but it cannot yield any significant return in industrial capacity.

§ 4. Fortunately, however, these classes constitute only a small part of the whole body of poor persons. With the poor regarded generally there is no frozen fixity of quality, but investment is capable of real effect. At a first glance we might, perhaps, expect the marginal return obtainable in this field to be equal to what it is in industry proper. This, however, is not so. In a perfectly adjusted community capital would be invested in the nurture, education and training of different persons, no matter in what class they were born, in such wise that, given the existing state of capital supply, the existing relative demand for services requiring different sorts of ability, and the existing state of industrial technique, the values of the marginal net product yielded by it would be equal everywhere. Thus, as between men with different degrees of the same kind of capacity—duke's sons and cook's sons alike—more would be invested in the abler than in the less able ; and, as between men of different kinds of capacity, more would (in general) be invested in those whose kind was in keener demand. There is, however, reason to believe that the ordinary play of economic forces tends unduly to contract investment in the persons of the normal poor, with the result that the marginal return to resources invested, not, indeed, in all, but in a great number of the poor and their children is higher than the marginal return to resources invested in machines. The ground for this belief is that poor persons are without sufficient funds to be able themselves to invest adequately in their own and their children's capacities, while they are also so situated that other persons, who have sufficient funds, are, in great measure, debarred from doing this for them. Under a slave economy, or under a social system so organised that those, in whom alien money was invested, could somehow pledge their capacities as security for loans, the case would be different. But in the actual world there is no easy way in which capitalists can ensure that any considerable part of the return, on money invested by them in the capacities of the poor shall accrue to themselves. If they make a loan, they cannot exact security for repayment; if they invest directly, by providing instruction for their own employés, they have no guarantee—unless, indeed, they are manufacturers of proprietary goods requiring a more or less specialised kind of labour, which is of less value to others than to them—that these employés will not shortly quit their service; and, even when there is such security, the employers must expect that the workers, having become more competent, will endeavour to exact a wage increased proportionately to their efficiency, and so to annex for themselves the interest on the employer's investment. In fact, investment in the persons of the poor is checked in a way analogous to that in which investment in land tenanted by rich occupiers and owned by poor men may be checked. The owners cannot afford to invest, and the occupiers, living without proper security as regards tenants' improvements, and receiving, therefore, as private net product, only a portion of the social net product of their investment, are unwilling to invest as much as the interest of the national dividend requires. In view of these considerations there is strong reason to believe that, if a moderate amount of resources were transferred from the relatively rich to the relatively poor, and were invested in poor persons with a single-eyed regard to rendering the poor in general as efficient as possible, the rate of return yielded by these resources in extra product, due to increased capacity, would much exceed the normal rate of interest on capital invested in machinery and plant.[1] Of course, however, in real life transferences from the rich to the poor are not all made subject to the condition that they shall be employed in the way most productive of efficiency. It is, therefore, necessary to examine separately the effects of certain principal sorts of transference.

§ 5. First, consider transferences in the form of industrial training to selected persons among able-bodied adult workers. In this class of persons there are always a number who are

---

[1] It should be noted that, if the transference is very large, the resultant shortage of material capital may cause the rate of interest to increase appreciably; and that then the advantage of investment in the capacities of the poor will have to be balanced against the advantage of investment in machines yielding this increased rate.

making exceptionally low earnings, because they are ill-adjusted to the job in which they are engaged, but who are, nevertheless, of good natural ability. Resources transferred to these persons in the form of training are likely to yield a large return. This fact was recognised, not merely in the special arrangements made for demobilised officers and men after the war, but also in the National Insurance Act of 1911. The hundredth clause of that Act provided that, if, after test and inquiry, "the insurance officer considers that the skill or knowledge of a workman (who repeatedly falls out of employment) is defective, but that there is a reasonable prospect of the defect being remedied by technical instruction, the insurance officer may, subject to any directions given by the Board of Trade, pay out of the unemployment fund all or any of the expenses incidental to the provision of the instruction, if he is of opinion that the charge on the unemployment fund in respect of the workman is likely to be diminished by the provision of the instruction." The class of persons to whom this policy is especially applicable are workpeople not too far advanced in years, whose special skill has been rendered useless by some invention enabling the work they have learnt to do to be performed more economically by unskilled labour in attendance upon an automatic tool. They include, too, those persons whom accident or illness has deprived of some specialised capacity, as well as the victims of permanent changes of fashion. Money spent in teaching these persons a new trade in place of the one they have lost is likely to yield a substantial return. The same thing is true of instruction given to those persons, if in practice they can be distinguished, who, with an aptitude for one sort of occupation, have accidentally, or through perversity, drifted into another. In this category should be included men bred in the country and well fitted for rural life, who have been enticed by the glamour of some city to abandon their proper vocation. It is, however, essential that the men selected for agricultural training should be carefully chosen from among persons with a real turn for agricultural life. Frequently this has not been done.[1]

[1] On the continent of Europe, "the Farm Colonies, as distinguished from penal workhouses, do not, in general, receive the genuine unemployed, i.e. those

The comparative failure which attended early British experiments in farm colonies may have been due to that fact. The agricultural training centres established by the Ministry of Labour at Brandon and at Clayton in Suffolk in 1925 appear to have had considerable success.[1] The usefulness of such centres might perhaps be enhanced if they were not confined to the service of persons who have fallen out of employment, but were general training schools of agriculture, open to members of the public, and so endowed with an industrial rather than a remedial atmosphere.[2]

§ 6. Secondly, we may distinguish transferences in the form of medical attendance and treatment to persons suffering from temporary sickness. If these persons are not assisted in time—delayed help may be comparatively useless—they may well suffer a permanent break-down in health. Resources transferred to them in the form of medical care and appropriate food are likely to prevent a large loss of capacity Of course, in order that good results may be attained, the transferences must be adequate and the medical attendance or supervision must not be abandoned at too early a stage. On this point the Minority Report of Poor Law Commissioners made a serious complaint against the administration of English Poor Law Infirmaries : " No attempt is made to follow into their homes the hundreds of phthisical and other patients discharged every week from the sick wards of the Workhouses and Poor Law Infirmaries, in order to ensure at any rate some sort of observance of the hygienic precautions, without which they, or their near neighbours, must soon be again numbered among the sick."[3] Given, however, that the transferences to sick persons are reasonably made, there is good hope that they will lead to a large increase of capacity.

---

who are out of work against their will. The great majority of the frequenters are the shiftless loafers, who, in the severer seasons of the year or in times of special distress, seek the shelter they offer rather than expose themselves to continued want or run the risk of entering the penal workhouse " (*Bulletin of the United States Bureau of Labour*, 1908, No. 76, p. 788).

[1] Cf. Webb, *English Local Government*, vol. iv. p. 692.

[2] Cf. *Report on The Transference of Functions of Poor Law Authorities* [Cd. 8917], p. 26.

[3] *Royal Commission on the Poor Laws, Minority Report*, p. 867.

§ 7. Thirdly, attention may be directed to transferences in the form of training and nurture to the normal children of the poor. Here there is immense scope for profitable investment. It is just when their children are young, and, therefore, in many ways afford the most fruitful soil for investment, that poor families find themselves in the greatest straits, and, therefore, least able to provide adequately for them. The proportion of *children* who pass their earlier years in great poverty is much larger than the proportion of *families* who are in this condition at any one time. Thus, taking a standard of life analogous to Mr. Rowntree's poverty line, Dr. Bowley found, just before the war, that "more than half the working-class children of Reading, during some part of their first fourteen years, live in households where the standard of life in question is not attained." [1] The same point is brought out by Miss Davies's observation about the village of Cowley, that "from the insignificant one-eighth of the households in primary poverty two-fifths, or nearly half, of all children in the parish are drawn, and that only one-third of all the children are in households above the line of secondary poverty." [2] As was observed in Part I. Chapter VIII. § 6, the position in this matter has greatly improved since the war, partly through the rise in the real wages of unskilled labour and partly through the falling-off which has taken place in the average number of children per family. Thus in 1923–24 in Reading the proportion of children under 14 living in houses where the standard specified above could not be reached had fallen (assuming no unemployment) from 1 in 2 to 1 in 7. [3] Even yet, however, the position is sufficiently deplorable. Reviewing the statistics collected from the five towns (Northampton, Warrington, Reading, Bolton and Stanley), Dr. Bowley concluded in 1924 : "More than 1 in 6 (of the children) are in present circumstances below the line (his calculated poverty line) at some period of their young lives ; a smaller proportion are below it for many years consecutively." [3] Properly arranged help for these children may do much towards

[1] *Journal of the Royal Statistical Society* June 1913, p. 692.
[2] *Life in an English Village*, p. 287.
[3] *Has Poverty diminished ?* pp. 24-5.

building up, in the most plastic period of life, strong bodies and minds trained, at least in general intelligence, and, perhaps, also in some form of technical skill.

Of course, if these transferences are to be fruitful, they must be reasonably conducted. It is useless, for example, to spend money on educating children while leaving them the prey to demoralising home conditions. If they are not properly looked after at home, a part of the transference to them must be utilised in boarding them out with carefully chosen families, or in sending them compulsorily to an institution or industrial school. Thus both the Majority and the Minority of the Poor Law Commissioners agree that children, who are neglected in the homes of parents in receipt of relief, should be forcibly "sent to an institution or industrial school," [1] and that, for the children of " ins and outs," " power should be taken to keep these children in institutions while the parents are detained in a detention colony." [2]

Again, it is useless, and may be even harmful, to spend money on educating children so ill-nourished that they cannot learn and merely exhaust their nervous system in trying to do so.[3] Underfed children must be provided with meals as well as with education, and, it need hardly be added, these meals must be regular and not spasmodically offered to different children twice or three times in a week. Probably the meals should be continued during the school holidays, for otherwise much of the benefit will be lost. In like manner, it is useless to spend money on educating children, if, at the same time or immediately afterwards, they are permitted to engage in occupations which inquiry shows to be destructive of whatever benefit education might be expected to yield. There is reason to suppose that many of the forms of unskilled labour at present open to boys not merely fail to train, but positively untrain, their victims. In a report presented to the Royal Commission on the Poor Laws Mr. Jackson well writes: " Mere skill of hand or eye is not everything. It is character and sense of responsibility which requires to be

---

[1] *Royal Commission on the Poor Laws, Report*, p. 620.
[2] *Ibid.* p. 187.
[3] Cf. Bulkley, *The Feeding of School Children*, p. 179.

fostered, and not only morals, but grit, stamina, mental energy, steadiness, toughness of fibre, endurance, must be trained and developed." But these general qualities can ill withstand the conditions, if these are unalleviated, of many forms of unskilled boy-labour. Mr. Jackson reports the view that " the occupation of van-boys is very calculated to destroy industry," and adds that " opinion is practically unanimous that street-selling is most demoralising to children. It is not so much a question of a skilled trade not being taught as of work which is deteriorating absorbing the years of the boy's life when he most needs educative experience in the wider sense." [1] It is plain that, if investment in the children of the poor is to be truly fruitful, it must be accompanied by prohibition, or at all events by restriction, of the right of entry into these occupations.

Yet again, as with the sick, so too with the children, the care expended on them must be adequately prolonged. " It is not sufficient to send a child of fourteen to a situation which may prove unsuitable, and leave it there to look after itself." [2] In short, stupidly organised investments in children's capacities—like other stupidly organised investments—will yield little return ; but well organised investments, and, more especially, investments adjusted in amount to the natural abilities of the various children affected, hold out large promise. Nor is this promise exhausted when account has been taken of the effect produced on *average* children. Among the great number of working-class families there are sure to be born from time to time children of exceptional power. Investment in the education of children generally should be credited with the effect it produces in *these* children. This point and the implications of it are put with great force by Marshall in the following passage : " There is no extravagance more prejudicial to the growth of national wealth than the wasteful negligence which allows genius that happens to be born of lowly parentage to expend itself in lowly work. No change would conduce so much to a rapid increase of national wealth as an improvement in our schools, and especially those of the

---

[1] *Royal Commission on the Poor Laws*, Appendix, vol. xx. pp. 23-7.
[2] *Royal Commission on the Poor Laws, Report*, p. 188,

middle grade, provided it be combined with an extensive system of scholarships, which will enable the clever son of a working man to rise gradually from school to school till he has the best theoretical and practical education which the age can give." [1]

§ 8. Up to this point we have been considering transferences made in selected forms and to selected groups among the poor; and we have seen that for such transferences there are "openings," in which the return probably obtainable is very much superior to that offered by investment in machines. It follows that the fact of these transferences, when they are managed by competent persons, is practically certain to benefit the national dividend. The effect of transferences made in a general way, in the form of command over purchasing power, cannot be determined so easily. The main difficulty is that many poor persons are unable, through lack of knowledge, to invest resources in themselves or their children in the best way. Thus, in a recent report of the Board of Education, we read: "A large proportion of the badly nourished children suffer from unsuitable food rather than from lack of food. It is probably no exaggeration to say that the improvement, which could be effected in the physique of elementary school children in the poorer parts of our large towns, if their parents could be taught or persuaded to spend the same amount of money as they now spend on their children's food in a more enlightened and suitable manner, is greater than any improvement which could be effected by feeding them intermittently at the cost of the rates." [2] In like manner, Mrs. Bosanquet notes that some two-ninths, out of Rowntree's three-ninths, of poverty is "secondary" poverty. She writes: "The weight of the problem rests with the ignorance and carelessness of parents who do not lack the means to do better; and this view is further enforced by the

---

[1] Marshall, *Principles of Economics*, p. 213. Furthermore, it should be noticed that such a policy will react to the advantage even of those members of the manual working class who are not directly touched by the improved educational opportunities; for it will both increase the demand for their services, by increasing the number of persons capable of acting as business managers, and also diminish the supply of their services by withdrawing these men from among them.

[2] [Cd. 5131], p. 5.

large amount of evidence that most of the malnutrition is due to misdirected feeding rather than underfeeding."[1] To charge the whole body of the poorer classes with ignorance and lack of capacity for management would, indeed, be to utter a gross libel. A sharp distinction must be drawn between poor families whose income, though small, is fairly regular, and poor families where the fathers are in casual and intermittent employment. Families of the latter class, disorganised in their mental habit no less than in their homes, never knowing from day to day or week to week what their income will be, *cannot* arrange their expenditure well. But families of the former class are in a position, if they choose, to build up a fairly definite standard of life. Among them there are many whose spending is even now arranged with extraordinary competence and wisdom; and, if they were better off, so that the wife was less burdened with work and worry, it may be supposed that their present high standard would be still further raised. Still, though, as against some members of the poorer classes, the charge of incapable management is ridiculous, as against many members it is undoubtedly true. Nor from the nature of things could it be otherwise. The art of spending money, not merely among the poor, but among all classes, is very much less developed than the art of making it. The investments which people make in industry are usually made with the help of specialists, who are in competition with one another and among whom bad judgment ultimately means elimination; but the investments which people make in their own capacities are conducted by themselves—that is to say, by persons who are not specialists, acting in circumstances where the selective influence of competition is excluded. This distinction can be brought out by an illustration drawn from within the business sphere itself. Those entrepreneurs who produce goods for the market are subject, in general, to keen competition among themselves. The result is that the stupid and ignorant tend to be extruded, and those only continue to act as entrepreneurs, who approach fairly closely to the average level of intelligence among their class. In occupations where

---

[1] "Physical Degeneration and the Poverty Line," *Contemporary Review*, Jan. 1904, p. 72.

commodities are produced, not for sale in the market, but for domestic consumption, and where, therefore, the competitive struggle is relaxed, the standard of competence tends, other things being equal, to be lowered. This point is well illustrated by the history of the English textile industries. Wool and linen, at the time of the industrial revolution, were associated with the ordinary routine of peasant life, but the treatment of cotton was not so associated. " Everywhere a professional employment, not a by-product, those who followed it did so for gain."[1] The result was that improvements developed and spread much more rapidly in cotton manufacture than in the other textiles. It is plain that the conditions under which the art of spending money is conducted are on a par with those prevailing in domestic, and not with those prevailing in professional, employments. It follows that the main stimulus making for competence and the power of wise choice between different ways of using resources is lacking. Thus, Professor Mitchell writes : " The limitations of the family life effectually debar us from making full use of our domestic brains. The trained intelligence and the conquering capacity of the highly efficient housewife cannot be applied to the congenial task of setting to rights the disordered households of her inefficient neighbours. These neighbours, and even the husbands of these neighbours, are prone to regard critical commentaries upon their slack methods, however pertinent and constructive in character, as meddlesome interferences. And the woman with a consuming passion for good management cannot compel her less progressive sisters to adopt her system against their wills, as an enterprising advertiser may whip his reluctant rivals into line. For the masterful housewife cannot win away the husbands of slack managers, as the masterful merchant can win away the customers of the less able. What ability in spending money is developed among scattered individuals we dam up within the walls of the single household."[2] The inevitable consequence is that among all classes, and among the poor along with the others,

---

[1] Cf. Clapham, *Cambridge Modern History*, vol. x. p. 753.
[2] "The Backward Art of Spending Money," *American Economic Review*, No. 2, p. 274.

there is a very great amount of ignorance concerning the comparative (marginal) advantages of different ways of spending money. Consequently it is idle to expect that resources transferred to poor persons in the form of general purchasing power will be employed by them exclusively in the openings that are likely to yield the largest return of capacity. When the mistakes made are very grave, the national dividend may gain less from the improvements wrought in the capacity of the poor than it loses by the withdrawal from ordinary investment of that part of the transferred resources, which, if they had not been transferred, would have been devoted to that use.[1] There is a danger that resources transferred to poor persons, in the form of command over purchasing power, will, from the point of view of the national dividend, be wasted. The Royal Commissioners on the Poor Laws complain, for example, that out-relief, as administered in many parts of Great Britain, serves merely " to perpetuate social and moral conditions of the worst type." [2] Many Boards of Guardians take no measures to ascertain what recipients do with the relief granted to them.[3] " With significant exceptions, Boards of Guardians give these doles and allowances without requiring in return for them even the most elementary conditions. . . . We have seen homes thus maintained out of the public funds in a state of indescribable filth and neglect, the abodes of habitual intemperance and disorderly living." [4]

§ 9. The practical inference from this discussion is that transferences to the poor, made in the form of command over purchasing power, have a much better chance of benefiting the national dividend of the future if they are associated with some degree of oversight over the persons to whom the transferences are made. This oversight, and whatever control it may be necessary to couple with it, must, of course, be very carefully guarded. It

---

[1] It may possibly be objected that of £100 invested in industry, £50 or more goes as wages, and, therefore, is also invested in the poor. This is a misconception. When £100 is invested in industry, £100 worth of labour and tools is devoted to making machinery : when it is invested in the persons of poor people, £100 worth of labour and tools is devoted to making consumable goods for their use.

[2] *Royal Commission on the Poor Laws, Majority Report,* p. 102.

[3] *Ibid.* p. 267.

[4] *Royal Commission on the Poor Laws, Minority Report,* p. 750.

should be based on a full recognition of the fact that people are not machines, and that their industrial—not to speak of their human—capacity is a function of their moral, as well as of their material, surroundings. If the arrangements are such that persons hitherto respectable are compelled, for any considerable time, to associate with vagabonds and ne'er-do-weels, their industrial character is endangered. If, on the other hand, the gift of material aid is accompanied by the interest, sympathy and counsel of friends, willingness to work and save may be largely and permanently encouraged. Out of a full experience Canon Barnett wrote: "Many have been the schemes of reform I have known, but, out of eleven years' experience, I would say that none touches the root of the evil *which does not bring helper and helped into friendly relations.*" [1]   A system of administration, in which, as in the Elberfeld and Bergen plans—copied in essentials by the voluntary Guilds of Help now growing up in many English towns [2]—the elements of personal care are largely utilised, is thus likely to prove, even from a purely monetary point of view, a better investment than one dependent on mechanical rules. This consideration emphasises the great importance of associating voluntary effort with the official machinery of State aid to the poor.

[1] *Practicable Socialism,* p. 104.

[2] Cf. Mr. Snowden's *Report of the Local Government Board on Guilds of Help* [Cd. 5664].

CHAPTER XIII

A NATIONAL MINIMUM STANDARD OF REAL INCOME

§ 1. WHEN we desire to determine whether the fact and the expectation of the fact, taken together, of any given annual transference of resources from the relatively rich to the relatively poor are likely to increase the national dividend, all the various considerations set out in the preceding chapters must be taken into account. There is little doubt but that plans could be devised, which would enable transferences, involving a very large amount of resources, to be made with results advantageous to production. Since the generality of these transferences will also increase the real incomes of the relatively poor, they must redound to the advantage of economic welfare in a wholly unambiguous way. Transferences which diminish the national dividend, on the other hand, are liable, through various reactions which have been indicated in the course of this discussion, to diminish the real earnings of the relatively poor; and, if their amount is kept constant, they may do this to so great an extent that the earnings per year of the relatively poor *plus* the transference made to them will *ultimately* be less than their earnings alone would have been, had no transference been made. When this happens, these transferences also affect economic welfare in an unambiguous way : this time by injuring it. There remains, however, one further sort of transference, the results of which cannot be unambiguous. I refer to a system of transferences varied from year to year in such a way as to compensate for any reduction that may come about in that part of the income of the poor which accrues to them through earnings. An arrangement of this sort is implicitly introduced whenever a government

758

establishes a minimum standard of real income, below which it refuses to allow any citizen in any circumstances to fall. For the establishment of such a minimum standard, implying, as it does, transferences to the poor of a kind that differentiate in favour of poverty, is likely to diminish the national dividend, while it will, at the same time, for an indefinitely long period, increase the aggregate real income of the poor. To determine the effect, which the establishment of this kind of minimum standard is likely to exercise upon economic welfare, involves, therefore, a balancing of conflicting considerations.

§ 2. Before this balancing is attempted, it is desirable to obtain a clear notion of what precisely the minimum standard should be taken to signify. It must be conceived, not as a subjective minimum of satisfaction, but as an objective minimum of conditions. The conditions, too, must be conditions, not in respect of one aspect of life only, but in general. Thus the minimum includes some defined quantity and quality of house accommodation, of medical care, of education, of food, of leisure, of the apparatus of sanitary convenience and safety where work is carried on, and so on. Furthermore, the minimum is absolute. If a citizen can afford to attain to it in all departments, the State cares nothing that he would prefer to fail in one. It will not allow him, for example, to save money for a carouse at the cost of living in a room unfit for human habitation. There is, indeed, some danger in this policy. It is a very delicate matter for the State to determine authoritatively in what way poor people shall distribute scanty resources among various competing needs. The temperaments and circumstances of different individuals differ so greatly that rigid rules are bound to be unsatisfactory. Thus Dr. Bowley writes: " The opinion is quite tenable that the poor are forced (by the effect of the law to enforce a minimum quality and quantity of housing accommodation) to pay for a standard of housing higher than they obtain in food, and that they would make more of their income if they were worse housed and better fed." [1] This danger must be recognised ; but the public spirit of the time demands also that it shall be faced. A man must not be permitted to fall below the minimum in one department

[1] *The Measurement of Social Phenomena*, p. 173.

in order that he may rise above it in others. Again, if a citizen cannot afford to attain the minimum in all departments, but, by failing in one, can remain independent, that does not justify the State in standing aside. The State must not permit anywhere hours of child labour or of women's labour or conditions of housing accommodation incompatible with the minimum standard, on the ground that, by resort to them, some given family could, and, without resort to them, it could not, support itself; for, if that is the fact, the family ought not to be required to support itself. There is no defence for the policy of "giving poor widows and incapable fathers permission to keep their children out of school and take their earnings."[1] Rather, the Committee on the Employment of Children Act are wholly right when they declare: "We feel, moreover, that the cases of widows and others, who are now too often economically dependent on child labour, should be met, no longer by the sacrifice of the future to the present, but, rather, by more scientific, and possibly by more generous, methods of public assistance."[2] The same type of reasoning applies, with even greater force, to the common plea that women should be allowed to work in factories shortly before and shortly after confinement, because, if they are not allowed to do this, they and their children alike will suffer shocking poverty. In these circumstances it is the duty of the State, not to remit the law, but to defend those affected by it from this evil consequence.

§ 3. There is general agreement among practical philanthropists that *some* minimum standard of conditions ought to be set up at a level high enough to make impossible the occurrence to anybody of extreme want; and that whatever transference of resources from relatively rich to relatively poor persons is necessary to secure this must be made, without reference to possible injurious consequences upon the magnitude of the dividend.[3] This policy of practical philanthropists

---

[1] Cf. Henderson, *Industrial Insurance in the United States*, p. 301.

[2] *Report*, p. 15.

[3] It is sometimes suggested that those very improvements in the capacity of labour, which have been discussed in previous parts of this book, are calculated to push some men below the minimum standard. It is true, as a point of analysis, that increased capacity of labour is, in effect, equivalent

is justified by analysis, in the sense that it can be shown to be conducive to economic welfare on the whole, if we believe the misery that results to individuals from extreme want to be indefinitely large; for, then, the good of abolishing extreme want is not commensurable with any evils that may follow should a diminution of the dividend take place. Up to this point, therefore, there is no difficulty. But our discussion cannot stop at this point. It is necessary to ask, not merely whether economic welfare will be promoted by the establishment of *any* minimum standard, but also by *what* minimum standard it will be promoted most effectively. Now, above the level of extreme want, it is generally admitted that increments of income involve finite increments of satisfaction. Hence the direct good of transference and the indirect evil resulting from a diminished dividend are both finite quantities; and the correct formal answer to our question is that economic welfare is best promoted by a minimum standard raised to such a level that the direct good resulting from the transference of the marginal pound transferred to the poor just balances the indirect evil brought about by the consequent reduction of the dividend.

§ 4. To derive from this formal answer a quantitative estimate of what the minimum standard of real income established in any particular country at any particular time ought to be, it would be necessary to obtain and to analyse a mass of detailed information, much of which is not, in present circumstances, accessible to students. One practical conclusion can, however, be safely drawn. This is that, other things being equal, the minimum can be advantageously set higher, the larger is the real income per head of the community. The reason, of course, is that every increase in average income implies a diminution in the number of people unable by their own efforts to attain to any given minimum standard; and, therefore, a diminution, both absolute and proportionate, in the damage to the dividend which an external

---

to an addition to its supply, and, therefore, involves a slight reduction in the real wage of a labour unit of given quality. In view, however, of the elastic character of the demand for labour in general, the number of the unimproved men whom this change would push over the line of self-support would almost certainly be very small.

guarantee of that standard threatens to bring about. It follows that, when we have to do with a group of pioneer workers in rough and adverse natural circumstances, the minimum standard may rightly be set at a low level. But, as inventions and discoveries progress, as capital is accumulated and Nature subdued, it should be correspondingly raised. Thus it is reasonable that, while a relatively poor country makes only a low provision for its "destitute" citizens, a relatively rich country should make a somewhat better provision for all who are "necessitous."[1]

§ 5. In this connection it is important that there should be no confusion as to what is meant by a rich country. For the present purpose country means, not Government, but people. There is a widespread impression that a nation's duty to make provision for its poorer citizens depends upon the amount of money that the Government has to provide for other purposes; and from this it is inferred that the great increase in the British Budget required to meet the annual charges on the war debt justifies, and, indeed, commands, large retrenchments in social expenditure. This idea is, in great measure, illusory. It is true, of course, that the indirect effect in checking production of the expectation of continuous taxation sufficient to yield 800 million post-war £s annually is a good deal greater than that of the expectation of taxes yielding 200 million pre-war £s. But this, though important, is a secondary matter. The essential fact is that, when interest is paid to domestic holders—the case is, of course, different with foreign holders—of Government securities, no part of the real income of the country is directly *used up*. Resources are merely transferred from one group of citizens to another. No doubt, when a nation has to provide funds for a large internal debt in consequence of a war, this is a *sign* that resources have been expended on war that might have been expended on building up capital equipment and so making the real income larger. It must not be forgotten, however, that a large part of the resources that were lent, for example, to the British Government by its citizens in the Great War, was not withdrawn

[1] This is the term employed by the Majority Commissioners of the 1909 Report on the Poor Laws.

from what would have been real capital, but was the result of economies in consumption and special activities in production, which, but for the war, would not have taken place. Even, therefore, as a sign of a country's capacity to give help to its poor, the magnitude of an internal war debt is of little use. The true test of this capacity is the direct one—aggregate real income compared with population. It is, indeed, proper to subtract from this the resources which are necessarily used up in unproductive ways. Thus, when a country is so situated that it has to devote an exceptionally large proportion of its real income to the upkeep of powerful armaments, or to the payment of interest to foreigners, who, in the past, have lent money to its Government, or to machinery for preserving internal order, account must be taken of these things. As a rule, however, they are *relatively* unimportant. The amount of the aggregate real income in relation to the number of the population is the dominant relevant fact.

§ 6. For the United Kingdom the best available estimate gives an aggregate national income, for 1913–14, represented at then prices by some 2250 million pounds. Deducting some 250 millions for rates and taxes and some 230 millions for new investments, we have left a sum sufficient, if it could have been divided up equally without being diminished in the process, to yield an income of £162 to each representative family of $4\frac{1}{2}$ persons.[1] Of course, as a matter of fact, it would have been quite impossible to pool the national income in this way without a large part of the flow of goods and services, which this money figure represents, disappearing altogether. Apart from great improvements in productive organisation, which may, perhaps, be hoped for, but certainly cannot be predicted with confidence, there is no reason to expect that the real income per head of the country—we need not trouble about its swollen reflex in the glass of money—will be substantially greater in the near future than it was in 1913–14. In view of these facts it is plain that, wealthy as this country is, as compared both with itself in the past and with most of its neighbours in the present, it is not wealthy in an absolute sense. As

[1] Cf. Bowley, *The Division of the Product of Industry*, pp. 20 *et seq.*

things are it is literally impossible for it, by any manipulation of distribution, to provide for all its citizens a really high standard of living. In so far, therefore, as social reformers rely upon improvements in the distribution of wealth, as distinguished from improvements in production, they are bound to chasten their hopes. The national minimum may rightly be set now much higher than it could have been set a hundred or fifty years ago. But, with the *national average* no larger than it is, it is inevitable that the *national minimum* must still be set at a deplorably low level.

§ 7. So far nothing has been said of the common view that, in determining the minimum standard which it will establish for itself, one country must have regard to the policy of other countries. It is widely held that the prohibition in England of socially undesirable practices, such as the employment of women at night, the use of unfenced machinery, the building of factories without proper sanitary arrangements, or the working of unduly long hours, involve a larger real cost to us if undertaken here alone than if undertaken by all industrial countries together. The reason commonly given for this view, that isolated action here would cause a flood of imports from abroad destructive of our industries, fails to take account of the fact that, subject to certain well-known qualifications, imports cannot expand in the long period without exports expanding correspondingly ; so that our industries *as a whole* could not suffer injury in the manner contemplated. It is true, however, that, if a handicap is imposed on productive methods in one country only, there will be a tendency for employing power, capital and labour to leave that country. If all leave in equal proportions, the general scale of the country's industry will be correspondingly reduced, the rate of pay per unit of every factor remaining much as before. The national dividend need not fall as much as production falls, because capitalists may still live and receive income here while employing their capital elsewhere. Since, in fact, capital—at all events if we suppose the obstacle of double income-tax to be done away with by international and intra-imperial agreement—is more mobile than labour, the presumption is that capital will leave in a somewhat larger proportion, and that, therefore, the earnings per head of work-people will fall. In whatever way the detail of the movement is worked out, it is plain that economic welfare in the country affected is likely to be lessened. The injury thus inflicted on it cannot, it should be observed, be prevented by setting up a tariff against imports from countries where labour legislation is less advanced. On the contrary, such a tariff, by interfering with the normal distribution of the country's resources among different occupations, would, in general, make the national dividend smaller, and the injury, therefore, worse. If, however, the handicap of these high minima is extended to all important countries by international labour legislation, the danger that our capital will be driven abroad is removed—at the cost of some slight damage to us in the terms on which our goods exchange against foreign goods.

§ 8. From these considerations it appears that the extension by international labour legislation of regulations, which are both desirable in themselves and also a real handicap to industry, is likely, though in a way different from that commonly supposed, to lessen the burden which these regulations would inflict on any country adopting them in isolation. To this extent it will, therefore, really be easier for a country to rule out injurious methods and processes, if it can persuade other nations to move forward in company with it. Moreover, when the injurious methods specially affect particular industries, an international agreement will really make it easier for the persons engaged in those industries to accept a veto upon injurious methods; and it will almost always be *thought to* make this easier both for those persons and for the community regarded as a whole. Hence the development of machinery for international labour legislation may be expected to accomplish something solid in speeding up improvements in industrial conditions. The advantage to be looked for is the greater in that many improvements in method, which are not really handicaps at all, but, through their effect on efficiency, net benefits, are, nevertheless, popularly believed to be handicaps, and are, therefore, unlikely to be adopted by cautious statesmen without some outside stimulus. International negotiation may often furnish such a stimulus and give strength to reformers in a country where the social movement is slack or the power of vested interests strong. There can be little doubt, for example, that the Franco-Italian treaty of 1906 led indirectly to a general improvement in Italian practice in the supervision and enforcement of labour laws. At the same time it would be a mistake to expect from the lever of internationalism more than it has power to give. Inevitably international minima, if they are to secure general or wide assent, must lag behind the practice of the most advanced nations. It would be disastrous if a custom should grow up of regarding these international minima as national maxima ; for that would check the forward movement of pioneer nations, and so indirectly of the whole world. Just as a "good" employer, while welcoming the Factory Acts, will keep his own practice well in advance of the legal standards, so also a "good" nation will always maintain national laws more ambitious than those which at the time have international sanction.[1]

§ 9. One word should be added in conclusion. In spite of what was said in Part I. Chapter IX. about the probable reaction of improved fortunes upon the standard of living, it must be conceded that the establishment by the State of an effective national minimum, since it must in effect, if not in name, differentiate to some extent in favour of large families, may somewhat increase the birth-rate among the poor. It is reasonable to hope that this tendency would not be very pronounced, since the people affected would be mainly those the size of whose families is not determined to any large extent by economic considerations. As much cannot be said, however, of an associated tendency. The establishment of an effective minimum standard, if adopted in one country alone, might well lead to a considerable increase in the numbers of the population through the immigration of relatively inefficient poor persons attracted by the prospect of State aid. If it did lead to this, the new immigrants would consume more than they con-

---

[1] The International Labour Conference of 1919, in framing its convention on Women's Employment, aimed at a high standard. On each separate provision of the Convention it fell behind the practice of some countries, but the existing law of no country covered the whole requirement of the Convention (G. Hetherington, *International Labour Legislation*, p. 90).

tributed to the dividend; and, as their numbers grew, the native-born citizens of the country concerned would be more and more heavily mulcted to maintain them. It is, therefore, to the advantage of a State, which has established a minimum standard above that enjoyed by its neighbours, to forbid the immigration of persons who seem unlikely to attain this minimum without help from the public funds. To this end idiots, feeble-minded persons, cripples, beggars and vagrants, and persons over or under a certain age may be excluded, unless they are either accompanied by relatives able to support them, or themselves possess an adequate income derived from investments.[1] Unfortunately, however, it is exceedingly difficult to devise machinery which shall be effective in excluding all " undesirable " immigrants without at the same time excluding some that are " desirable."

[1] For a summary of a number of laws on this matter, cf. Grünzel, *Economic Protectionism*, pp. 281 *et seq.*

APPENDICES

APPENDIX I

UNCERTAINTY-BEARING AS A FACTOR OF PRODUCTION

§ 1. It is customary in economic discussion to class together as factors of production, along with the services of Nature, waiting and various sorts of mental and manual labour. In a world in which all future events were perfectly foreseen this catalogue would be substantially adequate. But in the actual world some future events are not perfectly foreseen. On the contrary, in the vast majority of enterprises, in the conduct of which resources are waited for, they are also exposed to uncertainty; they are turned, that is to say, into a use, the result of which cannot be certainly predicted. In these circumstances it is proper that there should be added to the list of factors of production enumerated above a further group comprising various sorts of uncertainty-bearing.

§ 2. The principal reason why this arrangement is not usually adopted seems to be that, in practice, uncertainty-bearing is bound up in such intimate association with waiting that the possibility of separating the two in analysis is not immediately apparent. Reflection, however, makes it plain that the connection between them is not a necessary or inherent connection,—that they are, in fact, two things generally found together, and not a single thing. Thus let us imagine a man in possession of a vase, which, as a vase, is worth £100, but, if broken, would be worth nothing; and let us suppose the owner to know that this vase contains something, whose value is equally likely to be anything between nothing and £250. If the owner breaks the vase, he is, then, equally likely to lose any sum up to £100 or to gain any sum up to £150. The actuarial value of his chance is, therefore, £25, and, if there were a million people in his position, and they all elected to break their vases, the aggregate wealth of them all would probably be increased by about £25,000,000. In other words, the services of these million people, in bearing the uncertainty of placing £100 each in a position where it is equally likely to become anything between nothing and £250, are responsible for an addition of £25,000,000 to national wealth. This example shows that uncertainty-bearing,

771

though generally associated with waiting, is analytically quite distinct from it. Nor was it really necessary to seek an illustration so far removed from actual life. If a man contracts to deliver 100 bushels of wheat six months hence, with the intention of buying them for that purpose on the day of delivery at a price which he hopes will be lower than his contract price, that man, no less than the breaker of the vase, provides uncertainty-bearing without providing any waiting. Uncertainty-bearing is thus seen to be an independent and elementary factor of production standing on the same level as any of the better-known factors.

§ 3. In the way of this general conception there are two serious difficulties. The first of them can be set out as follows. It is well known that the ordinary factors of production are two-dimensional, in the sense that a unit of any of them can only be expressed as a quantity of stuff multiplied by a quantity of time. Waiting consists in the provision of a given quantity of resources, and labour in the provision of a given quantity of labour, during a given period. Thus the unit of waiting is said to be a year-pound, and the unit of labour a year-labourer.[1] It would seem, therefore, that, if uncertainty-bearing, as a factor of production, is to stand on a level with waiting and labour, it must somehow bear a relation to time analogous to that which they bear. But uncertainty-bearing, unlike waiting and labour, is in its essence independent of time, and, so far as pure theory goes, capable of instantaneous consummation. Consequently, the provision of a given quantity of uncertainty-bearing of any sort for a given period seems at first sight a mere phrase without substantial meaning. The difficulty thus suggested is, however, obviated by the fact that, as a matter of practice, the consummation of any act of uncertainty-bearing is not instantaneous, but involves a process in time. The uncertainty-bearing, for example, which a company promoter undertakes, is not completed until the public has come in and allowed him to unload, and this, of course, will not happen till a considerable interval has elapsed. This circumstance enables us to fashion a unit of uncertainty-bearing on the same plan as the units of waiting and of labour. This unit is the exposure of a £ to a given scheme of uncertainty, in an act the consummation of which occupies a year. The exposure of a £ to a succession of like schemes of uncertainty during a year, in acts the consummation of which occupies on the average, say, ten days, will thus embrace $\frac{365}{10}$ of these units. We have in this way obtained a two-dimensional unit of uncertainty-bearing analogous to the units of waiting and of labour, and the difficulty, which this section was designed to discuss, has been overcome.

---

[1] Cf. *ante*, pp. 161-2, footnote.

§ 4. The second difficulty is in this wise. Labour and waiting are objective services, the aversion to providing which may vary with different people, but which, in themselves, are the same for everybody. Uncertainty-bearing, however, it may be said, is in its essence a subjective state, invoked, indeed, by external conditions but bearing a quite different relation to these conditions for people of different temperaments and with different information. It would seem, therefore, at first sight that the amount of uncertainty-bearing involved in carrying through any operation must depend, not only on the nature of the operation, but also on the temperament and knowledge of the people who bear the uncertainty. Such a conception, however, is fatal to the symmetry of our analysis. If there is to be any real parallel with labour and waiting, we *must* define uncertainty-bearing objectively. Thus the uncertainty-bearing involved in the investment of any given amount of resources means for us the uncertainty-bearing which that investment would involve if it were made by a man of representative temperament and with representative knowledge. If the investment is actually made by a man who never feels subjective uncertainty, whatever the evidence, or by a man who possesses information adequate to destroy subjective uncertainty, we shall say, not that less uncertainty-bearing has been taken up, but that a given amount has been taken up by a person, who, from temperament or information, is an exceptionally ready bearer of uncertainty. There is, it must be admitted, an arbitrary and artificial appearance about this method of defining our key term ; but there appears to be no way in which this can be avoided.

§ 5. Up to this point we have taken no account of the fact that uncertainty-bearing, like labour, is a term embracing a large group of factors of production, rather than a single factor. It must now be observed, however, that, just as there are many different sorts of labour, so there are many different sorts of uncertainty, embodied in many different schemes of prospective returns, to which, in the course of industry, resources may be exposed. A scheme of prospective returns can be represented diagrammatically in the following manner. Along a base-line OX mark off all possible yields that may result from the exposure of a £ to the scheme in question ; and, through each point on OX, draw an ordinate proportionate to the probability, on the evidence, of the corresponding return. Join the tops of all these ordinates, as in the figure on the next page. Evidently any scheme of prospective returns can be represented by a curve formed upon this plan. Furthermore, the principal species of schemes that are liable to occur can be distinguished into certain broad groups. Find on OX a point B, such that OB represents the actuarial value of the chances of the returns indicated on the curve, or, in other words, such that OB is equal to the sum of the products of each several ordinate multiplied by the corresponding abscissa, divided by the sum of the ordinates ; and let the ordinate through B cut the curve in H.   In like manner, find on OX a point M, such that OM represents the most probable, or most "frequent," return relevant to the scheme of prospective returns under review ; and let the ordinate through M cut the curve in K.   On this basis we may distinguish, in the first place, between curves which are symmetrical, in such wise that BH and MK coincide, and curves which are asymmetrical.   The symmetrical group includes schemes of such a sort that, if r is the actuarial value of a pound exposed to any scheme, the chance of obtaining a return $(r - h)$ is equal to the chance of obtaining a return $(r + h)$, for all values of h.   The asymmetrical group includes all other schemes.   The symmetrical

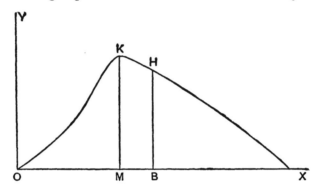

type is only possible when the conditions are such that the exposure of a pound to uncertainty cannot yield a gain greater than a pound, since, from the nature of things, it cannot yield a loss greater than this.   Secondly, within the symmetrical group we may distinguish curves which are spread out, like open umbrellas, and curves which are narrow, like closed umbrellas.   The former sort represent schemes in which a wide divergence, the latter schemes in which only a small divergence, of the actual from the most probable return is probable.   Thirdly, within the asymmetrical group we may distinguish curves in which MK lies respectively to the right and to the left of BH.   The former sort represent schemes in which the most probable outcome is a moderate return on the money invested, but a small return is more probable than a large one.   A scheme of this kind would be embodied in a lottery offering a great number of small prizes and one or two blanks. Again, a £ might be lent to somebody : and there might be 96 chances of its return in full, 1 chance that 10s. would be returned, 1 chance that 5s. would be returned, and 2 chances that none would be returned. The actuarial value of this scheme of prospect is $£\frac{999}{1000}$: the most probable return is £1. The latter sort of curves represent schemes in which the most probable outcome is a small return, but large returns are possible. A lottery of the ordinary kind, containing a few large prizes and many blanks, affords an example of this sort of scheme. Within each of the groups thus distinguished an indefinite number of further subdivisions could be made. Of course a great many schemes of prospective returns are not represented by continuous curves, but by a few isolated points with gaps between them, these gaps corresponding to returns which are not possible.

§ 6. The existence of the great variety of schemes of prospective returns, each representing different sorts of uncertainty, might seem at first sight to vitiate the attempt, which was made in an earlier section, to treat "the factor uncertainty-bearing" and "the factor waiting" on the same footing. For waiting is a single thing, while uncertainty-bearing is a group of different things. The meaning of a change in the supply of waiting is, therefore, clear; but how are we to conceive of a change in the supply of uncertainty-bearing? This difficulty, though it is a natural one to raise, is easily overcome. For, after all, uncertainty-bearing in this regard stands in exactly the same position as labour. Labour in general includes an immense variety of different sorts and qualities of labour. This circumstance does not prevent us from making use of the general concept labour alongside of the concept waiting. In order to render this procedure legitimate, all that we need do is to select in an arbitrary manner some particular sort of labour as our fundamental unit, and to express quantities of other sorts of labour in terms of this unit on the basis of their comparative values in the market. In this way all the various sorts of labour supplied or demanded at any time can be expressed in a single figure, as the equivalent of so much labour of a particular arbitrarily chosen grade. Exactly the same device is available for uncertainty-bearing. The uncertainty involved in exposing a pound to a particular arbitrarily chosen scheme of prospective returns can be selected as a fundamental unit, and the uncertainty involved in other exposures can be reduced, on the basis of comparative market values, to its equivalent in terms of this unit. So soon as this is understood, an apparently formidable obstacle in the way of assimilating uncertainty-bearing to the other factors of production can be successfully overcome.

§ 7. When the assimilation is accomplished, and all the various sorts of uncertainty, to which, in different industries, people submit resources, are translated into terms of the uncertainty-bearing involved in some representative scheme of prospective returns, there will be a supply schedule and a demand schedule for pounds to be exposed to this scheme, just as there are a supply and a demand schedule for pounds to be exposed to "waiting." The demand price or the supply price for the exposure of any given quantity of pounds is the excess of money offered or asked above the actuarial value of a £ so exposed. For different quantities of uncertainty-bearing the demand price and the supply price will, of course, both be different. For some quantities the supply price will be negative. Up to a point, people will gamble because they like the excitement, even though they know that, on the whole, they are likely to lose money. But, though some amount of uncertainty-bearing, like some amount of labour, would be forthcoming for industry, even if there were no expectation of reward, in present conditions more is wanted than can be obtained on those terms. The main reason is that an uncertain prospect actuarially worth £100 of money is much less satisfactory than a *certain* prospect also worth £100 of money. This follows from the law of diminishing utility. One income of £90 plus one of £110 carry less satisfaction, other things being equal, than two incomes each of £100. Thus, in respect of such quantities of uncertainty-bearing as are actually made use of in modern industry, the supply price, like the supply price of the other factors of production, is positive; and the general conditions determining the value, or price, of uncertainty-bearing are similar to those determining the price of those factors.

§ 8. It must be clearly understood that the payment thus asked and offered for uncertainty-bearing is by no means the same thing as the exceptional profits obtained by persons who have succeeded in risky businesses. An uncertain undertaking is a risky undertaking. But the term risk is generally used to mean the chance of obtaining a smaller return than the actuarially probable return. This must be compensated by a corresponding chance of obtaining a larger return than this. Even though no payment whatever is made for uncertainty-bearing, the *successful* undertakings in a risky business would still need to make exceptional profits as an offset to the exceptional losses of those which fail. Otherwise the whole body of investors in the business, taken collectively, would be obtaining less than normal returns from investment in it. The payment for uncertainty-bearing, therefore, consists, not in the whole of the excess above normal profits earned by these successful undertakers, but only in that (generally small) part of this excess which is not cancelled by the corresponding losses of other undertakers who have fallen out of the race.

§ 9. It has next to be observed—and here we follow the line

of thought indicated in § 4—that the supply of uncertainty-bearing, as defined in the objective manner there set out, will be increased by anything that enables people with more knowledge to undertake risky enterprises in lieu of people with less knowledge. Every form of organisation that enables risks to be shifted on to the shoulders of specialists—the resort of farmers to speculators in grain prices through hedging on the produce exchange, the resort of bankers to specialist bill-brokers in negotiating the discount of bills, the resort of manufacturers for the foreign market to specialist export houses, and so on, has this effect. It may be added that a similar effect is produced when risky undertakings are taken over by rich persons instead of by poor persons. For, if a man possesses $(x + 100)£$, to expose £100 to a 5 per cent range of uncertainty is to accept an even chance of having $(x + 105)£$ or $£(x + 95)$. But there is reason to believe that, not merely the desire for an extra unit of resources in general, but also the rate of diminution of this desire, diminishes as the number of units in our possession grows. It follows that the probable loss of satisfaction involved in accepting the above even chance instead of a certain $(x + 100)£$ is smaller the larger is the value of x.

§ 10. Like any other factor of production, uncertainty-bearing may improve in technical efficiency. The central fact, upon which the improvements in it that have actually taken place depend, is that forecasts based upon existing knowledge are, in general, more certain when they are made about collections than when they are made about individual members of collections. If all the individual members were so linked together that they necessarily always acted in the same way, this, of course, would not be so. But in many collections there are some individual members that are complementary to one another. Thus, on a holiday, it is uncertain whether indoor entertainers will make a great deal of money or very little money, because it is uncertain whether the weather will be wet or fine. In like manner and for the same reason it is uncertain whether outdoor entertainers will make very little money or a great deal of money. But the amount that the two sorts of entertainers together will make may be susceptible of nearly accurate forecast.[1] The case is similar with exporters and importers between countries the mutual exchange rate of whose moneys is varying; the exporters and importers will be affected in opposite senses if the exchange moves up or down between the making and the completion of foreign trade contracts. In circumstances such as these, so soon as an organisation is set up that combines the two complementary uncertainties under

[1] Cf. Marshall, *Industry and Trade*, p. 255.

a single head, they neutralise or destroy one another. Nor is it only when uncertainties are complementary that combination reduces them. The same result follows, though in a less marked degree, when they are simply independent. The measure of reduction to be expected from combination in these circumstances is indicated in the familiar corollary to the normal law of error, which asserts that the "precision of an average is proportional to the square root of the number of terms it contains."[1] This implies that, if there is an even chance that the investment of £100 in one assigned venture will yield a return greater than £95 and less than £115, there is an even chance that £100 scattered among a hundred similar investments will, if all the causes affecting the different investments are independent, yield a return lying between £104 and £106. If only some of the causes are independent and some common, the range within which it is more probable than not that the return will lie will be greater than that enclosed between £104 and £106, but it will still be smaller than that enclosed between £95 and £115. It follows, that, if out of a hundred people, each of whom has £100 to invest, every one divides his investment among a hundred enterprises, the aggregate amount of uncertainty-bearing undertaken by the group is smaller than it would have been had every investor concentrated on a single enterprise. The physical results of the investments taken together must, however, be the same. Therefore, whenever more or less independent uncertainties are combined together, a given result can be attained by a smaller amount of uncertainty-bearing, or, to put the matter otherwise, the factor uncertainty-bearing has been made technically more efficient.[2] The principle thus explained is fully recognised by business men, and has long lain at the root both of insurance and of much speculative dealing on 'Change. Thus the segregation of the speculative element in certain forms of business and its concentration upon a relatively small number of speculators have not only changed the distribution, but have reduced the aggregate amount, of uncertainty-bearing required in industry. In modern times the range over which this principle can be applied has been greatly extended by three important developments. Of these the first is a legal change, namely, the concession to joint-stock companies of the privilege of limited liability ; the second an economic change, namely, the develop-

---

[1] Bowley, *Elements of Statistics*, p. 305.

[2] This circumstance, of course, permits the release, partly for immediate consumption and partly for investment, of resources which must otherwise have been stored. For example, the combination of the community's gold reserves in a central bank lowers the amount of aggregate gold reserve necessary, increases the capital available for investment, and *pro tanto* lowers the rate of interest. (Cf. H. Y. Brown, *Quarterly Journal of Economics*, 1910, pp. 743 *et seq.*)

ment of organised speculative markets ; the third also an economic change, namely, the development of the means of transport and communication. The ways in which these three changes have facilitated the application of the above principle will now be examined.

§ 11. So long as liability was unlimited, it was often against a man's interest to spread his investments ; for, if he did so, he multiplied the points from which an unlimited call on his resources might be made. The English Limited Liability Act of 1862 and its foreign counterparts enabled investments to be spread without evoking this danger. Furthermore, intermediary organisations, themselves fortified by limited liability, have been developed, capable of spreading investments on behalf of persons whose resources are too small to allow of their spreading them for themselves. Since the minimum share in industrial enterprises is seldom less than £1, the small investor's capacity for direct spreading is narrowly restricted. Savings banks, friendly societies, trade unions, building societies, co-operative societies, trust companies and so forth—all of them limited liability associations—are able, however, to put him in a position as favourable in this respect as is occupied by the large capitalist. Nor is it only the spreading of investments that the system of limited liability has facilitated. It has also made possible the spreading, or combination, of risks in a wider sense. For, in general, each business deals directly or indirectly with many businesses. If one of them fails for a million pounds, under *unlimited liability* the whole of the loss falls on the shareholders or partners—provided, of course, that their total resources are adequate to meet it—but under *limited liability* a part of it is scattered among the shareholders or partners of a great number of businesses. Hence any shareholder in one business combines with the uncertainty proper to his own business some of that proper to other businesses also. It follows that the range of uncertainty, to which a normal £100 invested in industry is subjected by reason of failures, is still further diminished in amount. This advantage is additional to, and quite distinct from, any direct national gain which limited liability may give to a country by throwing a part of the real cost of its unsuccessful enterprises upon foreigners.

§ 12. The development of organised speculative markets enables the producing classes to shift uncertainty-bearing on to speculators, in whose hands they in great part cancel out. Thus the miller, who is contracting to deliver flour at a fixed price some months hence, can protect himself by buying "a future" in wheat at the same time that he makes his contract, and afterwards selling the "future" *pari passu* with purchases of "spot" wheat of various grades as he needs them for his milling. In like manner, the farmer can protect himself by selling a future at an early stage, and afterwards buying to cover it in the speculative market at the same time that he sells his actual wheat in the spot market. Plainly these processes involve a large reduction in the amount of uncertainty-bearing that has to be undergone to accomplish a given result. The chief conditions needed to render any class of products suitable to be handled in the type of organised market that permits of their use have been succinctly stated by Marshall as follows: "(1) That the product is not quickly perishable; (2) that the quantity of each thing can be expressed by number, weight, or measure; (3) that the quality can be determined by tests that yield almost identical results when applied by different officials, assumed to be expert and honest; and (4) that the class is important enough to occupy large bodies of buyers and sellers." [1]

§ 13. There remains the development of the means of communication. This facilitates the combination of uncertainties in one very simple way. It puts investors into contact with a greater number of different openings than were formerly available. This effect, though of great importance, is so obvious and direct that no comment upon it is required. There is, however, a more subtle way in which the development in the means of communication works. Dr. Cassel has observed that industrial firms have, in recent times, been lessening the quantity of stock that they carry in store waiting to be worked up, relatively to their total business. The improvement in this respect applies all round. As regards production, "there is, in the best-organised industries, very little in the way of material lying·idle between two different acts of production, even if these acts have to be carried out in different factories, perhaps at great distances from each other. A modern iron-works has no large stock either of raw materials or of their product, yet there is a continuous stream of ore and coal entering, and of iron being turned out of it." [2] In like manner, factories are coming to keep a smaller amount of capital locked up in the form of reserve machines not ordinarily in use. The same tendency is apparent in retail trading. The ratio of the average amount of stock kept to the aggregate annual turn-over is smaller than it used to be. "Under modern conditions the trade of the country is conducted on a retail system which is growing year by year. The practice of keeping large stocks has almost ceased, and goods are ordered

[1] *Industry and Trade*, p. 256.
[2] *The Nature and Necessity of Interest*, p. 126.

in quantities only sufficient to meet the current demands."[1] One reason for this is the improvement in the means of communication. " The trunk lines of America, with their wide-spreading branches, enable merchants in the cities and the larger towns to replenish their counters and shelves every day. Stocks, therefore, need not be so large as of old, when, let us say, a whole winter's goods were laid in by October. . . . The inter-urban roads are extending these advantages to the village storekeeper, who, in the morning, telephones his wants to Toledo, Cleveland, or Detroit, and, in the afternoon, disposes the ordered wares on his shelves."[2] Now, *prima facie*, this change of custom would seem to be of little significance. After all, a reduction in the amount of finished goods held by retailers, of reserve machinery held by manufacturers, and so on, does not necessarily imply a reduction in the aggregate amount of these things held by the whole body of industrialists. On the contrary, we are naturally inclined to suggest that the wholesaler and the machine-maker must increase their stocks *pari passu* with the decrease in the stocks of their clients. As a matter of fact, however, this suggestion is incorrect. The reason is that the wholesaler and the machine-maker represent points at which uncertainties can be combined. The development of the means of communication, therefore, in so far as it directly transfers to them the task of bearing uncertainty, indirectly lessens the amount of uncertainty that needs to be borne. Uncertainty-bearing, in short, is rendered more efficient. The same result as before can be achieved with a smaller quantity of it, or, what comes to be the same thing, with a smaller quantity of waiting designed to obviate the need for employing it.

[1] Inglis, *Report of the Board of Trade Railway Conference*, 1909, p. 33.
[2] Iles, *Inventors at Work*, p. 488.

APPENDIX II

THE MEASUREMENT OF ELASTICITIES OF DEMAND

§ 1. WITH the information at present available it is not possible to lay down any propositions about the elasticity of demand for different commodities beyond those general propositions that are set out in Part II. Chapter XIV. As has been pointed out by Marshall,[1] attempts to determine the elasticity of demand for any commodity in any market by a direct comparison of the prices and the quantities consumed at different times are exposed to very great difficulties. If it could be presumed that the reactions exercised by price-changes upon quantity demanded came about immediately, if the association of actual price - changes with people's expectation of connected future price-changes in the same or the opposite direction could be eliminated, and if allowance could be made for those upward and downward shiftings of demand schedules, for which movements of confidence and alterations in the supply of monetary purchasing power are responsible, a comparison of the percentage changes of price between successive years with the percentage changes in consumption between the same years might, for commodities about which adequate statistics exist, yield a rough numerical measure of elasticity for amounts of consumption in the neighbourhood of the average actual consumption.[2] It seems that for certain commodities the above presumption can reasonably be made. On the basis of it Professor Lehfeldt calculated, immediately before

[1] *Principles of Economics*, pp. 109 *et seq.*

[2] Professor Moore, in his *Economic Cycles* (chapters iv. and v.), makes calculations of the "elasticity" of demand for certain commodities without resort to the allowances stipulated for in the text. But, as he himself fully recognises, the elasticity, which his method enables him to measure, is not the same thing as, and is not, in general, equal to, the elasticity of demand as defined by Marshall and employed here. Marshall's elasticity, if known, would make it possible to predict how far the introduction of a new cause modifying supply in a given manner would *affect* prices ; Professor Moore's to predict with what price-changes changes in supply coming about naturally, in company with such various other changes as have hitherto been found to accompany them, are likely to be *associated*. That this distinction is of great practical importance is shown by the fact that, whereas the elasticity of the demand for pig-iron, in Marshall's sense, is, of course, negative—that is to say, an increase in

782

the war, that the elasticity of the aggregate demand for wheat in the United Kingdom was about -0.6.[1] But there is little hope that many elasticities will lend themselves to calculation in this direct way. It is, therefore, important to inquire whether any indirect method of calculation is available for overcoming difficulties due to the slowness with which reactions work themselves out.[2]

§ 2. Some years ago I devised a method, the basis of which is a comparison of the amounts of a commodity consumed by persons of different incomes at a given price, instead of a comparison of the amounts consumed by persons of given incomes at different prices.

---

supply involves a fall in price—the elasticity in Professor Moore's sense, as calculated from his statistics, is positive. The reason for this is that the principal changes in the price of pig-iron that have in fact occurred are mainly caused by expansions of demand (general uplifts in the demand schedule), and not by changes in supply taking place while the demand schedule is unaltered. In certain conditions it might be possible to *derive* Marshall's elasticity from Professor Moore's elasticity, provided that the reactions exercised by supply changes upon prices could be presumed to take place very rapidly. Apart from this presumption derivation would be impossible, however ample the statistical material.

[1] *Economic Journal*, 1914, pp. 212 *et seq.*

[2] The direct method and any possible indirect method are seriously hampered by the fact that the elasticity of demand for a thing may be different in respect of different amounts. Thus suppose we start with a consumption A at a price P : that the price rises by p per cent, and that this rise is the direct and sole cause of a fall in consumption of a per cent. We cannot infer that the

elasticity of demand either for consumption A or for consumption $A\left(1-\dfrac{a}{100}\right)$

is equal to $-\dfrac{a}{p}$ unless p is small—strictly unless it is infinitesimal. If p is not small, some assumption as to the relation of neighbouring elasticities must be made before any inference can be drawn. One possible assumption is that the demand curve is a straight line. On this assumption the elasticity of demand in

respect of consumption A will be $-\dfrac{a}{p}$: and in respect of consumption

$A\left(1-\dfrac{a}{100}\right)$ it will be $-\dfrac{a}{p}\cdot\dfrac{100+p}{100-a}$. Another possible assumption is that the elasticity of demand is constant for all amounts of consumption from A to

$A\left(1-\dfrac{a}{100}\right)$. On this assumption it can be proved, as Dr. H. Dalton has

pointed out to me, that the said elasticity is not $-\dfrac{a}{p}$, but

$$\frac{\log\left(1-\dfrac{a}{100}\right)}{\log\left(1+\dfrac{p}{100}\right)}.$$

This must lie between $-\dfrac{a}{p}$ and $-\dfrac{a}{p}\cdot\dfrac{100+p}{100-a}$: and is probably not far from

$$-\frac{a}{p}\sqrt{\frac{100+p}{100-a}}.$$

Statistical data needed for this method are found in family budgets. Considerable attention has been paid both by State Departments and by private persons to the study of these budgets; and a number of tables have been printed to show the proportion of their income which families in different income groups expend upon the various principal sorts of commodities. It is possible so to manipulate these data as to derive from them information about certain elasticities of demand.

§ 3. Let us suppose that the data are better than they are, and that our tables give the expenditure of the group of workpeople whose wages lie between 30s. and 31s., of the group whose wages lie between 31s. and 32s., and so on continually for all wage levels. With this close grouping we may fairly assume that the tastes and temperament of the people in any two adjacent groups are approximately the same. That is to say, the desire for the xth unit of any commodity (or group of commodities), the demand for which is not markedly correlated with the demand for other commodities, is equal for typical men in the 30s. to 31s. group and in the 31s. to 32s. group. Let the quantity of desire for the xth unit of the commodity be $\phi(x)$: or, in other words, y being the desire for the xth unit, let the desire curve for the commodity be represented by $y = \phi(x)$. We are entitled to assume further, in the absence of special knowledge as to the existence of correlation, that the desire curve of both groups for the commodity is independent of the quantity of other commodities consumed and, therefore, of the marginal desiredness of money. Let this marginal desiredness to the lower and higher income groups respectively be μ_1 and μ_2, and the quantities of the commodity consumed by these groups x_1 and x_2. Then, since the price paid for the commodity must be the same for both groups, we know that this price p is equal both to $\dfrac{1}{\mu_1}\phi(x_1)$ and to $\dfrac{1}{\mu_2}\phi(x_2)$. These two expressions are, therefore, equal to one another. But, if, as it is reasonable to suppose when the incomes of the two groups are close together, x_2 differs only slightly from x_1, $\phi(x_2)$ may in general be written $\phi(x_1) + (x_2 - x_1)\phi'(x_1)$;

$$\therefore \phi'(x_1) = \frac{1}{x_2 - x_1} \cdot \frac{\mu_2 - \mu_1}{\mu_1}\phi(x_1).$$

But the elasticity of the desire curve in respect of any consumption x_1 is known to be equal to $\dfrac{\phi(x_1)}{x\phi'(x_1)}$. Let this elasticity be written η_{x_1}. It follows that

$$\eta_{x_1} = \frac{x_2 - x_1}{x_1} \cdot \frac{\mu_1}{\mu_2 - \mu_1}.$$

But, since a small change in the consumption of any ordinary commodity, on which a small proportion of a man's total income is spent, cannot involve any appreciable change in the marginal desiredness of money to him,[1] the elasticity of the desire curve in respect of any consumption x_1 is equal to the elasticity of the demand curve in respect of that consumption. Therefore the elasticity of demand, as well as the elasticity of desire, of the lower income group, in respect of its consumption of x_1 units, may be represented by η_{x_1}, when :

$$\eta_{x_1} = \frac{x_2 - x_1}{x_1} \cdot \frac{\mu_1}{\mu_2 - \mu_1}.$$

§ 4. If we knew the relative values of μ_1 and μ_2, this equation would enable us to determine the elasticity of demand of the lowest income group for any commodity, the demand for which is not markedly correlated with the demand for other commodities, in respect of such quantity of the commodity as that group is consuming. Similar equations would enable us to determine the corresponding elasticities of each of the other income groups. If it is objected that our result would in practice be impaired by the fact that the higher income groups are apt to consume a better quality of commodity, and not merely a greater quantity, than the lower income groups, the difficulty is easily overcome by substituting in our formula for the quantities of the commodity that are consumed by the different groups figures representing their *aggregate expenditures upon it*. This device escapes the suggested objection by treating improved quality as another form of increased quantity. In order to obtain the elasticity of demand for the commodity as a whole, it would be necessary to calculate the separate elasticities for all income groups and to combine them on the basis of the quantity of purchases to which they respectively refer.

§ 5. Unfortunately we do not know, and cannot ascertain, the relative values of μ_1 and μ_2. Consequently we are estopped from using the above analysis to determine the elasticity of the demand for any commodity in absolute terms.[2] But this does not block

---

[1] Strictly, of course, such a change must involve *some* alteration in the marginal desiredness of money, unless the demand for the commodity in question has an elasticity equal to unity. If the elasticity is anything other than this, a change in the consumption of the commodity will be accompanied by a transference of money from expenditure upon it to expenditure upon other things, or *vice versa*. This must affect the marginal desiredness of money spent on these things, and its marginal desiredness, if affected in one field, is, since it must be the same in all, affected in all.

[2] Professor Vinci, in his very interesting monograph *L' elasticità dei consumi*, suggests that the method described above can be extended to yield an absolute measure of elasticity by reference to the distinction between nominal and real prices. The money price paid by the higher income group is the same as that

our investigation. For, by the process indicated above, the elasticities of demand in any income group can be determined, for all the things consumed in that income group, in expressions into which μ_1 and μ_2 enter in exactly the same way, namely, as the term $\dfrac{\mu_2 - \mu_1}{\mu_1}$. If, then, the several elasticities be η_x, η_y, η_z, and so on, any one of them can be expressed in terms of any other without reference to μ_1 and μ_2. These unknowns are eliminated, and we obtain the formula

$$\eta_y = \eta_x \cdot \frac{x_1}{x_2 - x_1} \cdot \frac{y_2 - y_1}{y_1}.$$

This result, it should be observed, only follows directly from the preceding argument, provided that the commodities concerned are both such that only a small part of a typical man's income is normally spent upon them. In general, however, though the absolute formula for elasticities, from which the result is derived, is only valid on this assumption, the above comparative formula is approximately valid also for two commodities on which a large part of a typical man's income is spent, so long as the part spent on the one does not differ greatly from that spent on the other. The reason for this is that the errors in the two formulae for absolute elasticities, which have to be combined, will tend to balance one another. Our comparative formula is seriously suspect only when it is used to obtain the relative elasticities of the demands of a group for two things, on one of which that group spends a large proportion, and on the other a small proportion, of its income. Apart from this, the formula, when applied to the statistics of quantities of, or expenditures upon, different commodities by neighbouring income groups, enables us to determine numerically the ratio of the elasticity of demand of any income group for any

---

paid by the lower income group. But the real price is, he holds, less than this, in the proportion in which the income of the higher income group exceeds that of the lower. Thus, if the higher income group has 10 per cent more income, an equal money price paid by it implies a real price $\frac{10}{11}$ths as great ; and the elasticity of demand is obtained by dividing a virtual price difference of $\frac{1}{11}$th into whatever fraction represents the associated consumption difference (*loc. cit.* p. 22). This procedure is, however, illegitimate, because, on the assumptions taken, the virtual price of *all* commodities to the higher income group is $\frac{10}{11}$ths of what it is to the lower income group. Consequently, the difference in the consumption of *any particular* commodity is not due solely to the difference in price of that commodity, and cannot, therefore, in general, be inserted in the formula for elasticity of demand. Professor Vinci has, in fact, tacitly assumed that the marginal desiredness of money is equal for the two groups—an assumption which would only be warranted if the demand of both for the sum of commodities other than the particular one under investigation had an elasticity equal to unity.

one commodity (in respect of the quantity of the commodity actually consumed by it) to the elasticity of demand of the group for any other commodity. This information will often be valuable in itself. It is important to know whether the demand of workers with 35s. a week for clothes is about twice, or about ten times, as elastic as their demand for food. But the information is also valuable indirectly. For, if we can in some other way—through the examination of shopkeepers' books or otherwise—determine the elasticity of demand of any income group, or collection of income groups, for one thing, we have here a bridge along which we may proceed to determine the elasticity of their demand for all other things.

§ 6. In explaining the above method I have, as indicated at the outset, assumed that our data are better than they are. This, I think, is legitimate, because there is no reason in the nature of things why these data should not be improved; and, indeed, there is little doubt that they will be improved. Even then, of course, any one attempting a detailed application of the method is certain to encounter serious difficulties, among which, perhaps, not the least will be that of deciding how far to treat different commodities separately and how far to group them together according to the purpose which they jointly serve. When put to the test, these difficulties may, no doubt, in some applications, prove insurmountable. From the results of an experiment made upon figures given in the second Fiscal Blue-book (pp. 215 and 217), I am, however, tempted to hope for better things. The figures refer to the expenditure upon "food" and "clothing" of groups of workpeople whose wages were respectively under 20s., between 20s. and 25s., between 25s. and 30s., between 30s. and 35s., and between 35s. and 40s. My method gave the ratio of the elasticity of demand for clothes to that for food for the several groups as follows:

Workmen under 20s.	.	.	.	.	.	1·16
From 20s. to 25s.	.	.	.	.	.	1·31
From 25s. to 30s.	.	.	.	.	.	1·62
From 30s. to 35s.	.	.	.	.	.	1·25
From 35s. to 40s.	.	.	.	.	.	2·46

Apart from the drop in the ratio for workpeople earning from 30s. to 35s.—and it may be remarked in passing that the instances from which the average in this group is made up are only half as numerous as those in the two adjacent groups—these figures are continuous and in no wise incompatible with what we should expect from general observation. It is natural that among the very poor the demand for clothes should be nearly as inelastic as the demand for food, and that, as we proceed to groups of greater wealth, its relative elasticity should grow.. This small experiment, therefore, is not discouraging, and it is much to be desired that some economist should undertake a more extended study along similar lines.[1]

[1] Cf. my article "A Method of Determining the Numerical Value of Elasticities of Demand," *Economic Journal* of December 1910.

APPENDIX III

A DIAGRAMMATIC AND MATHEMATICAL TREATMENT OF CERTAIN
PROBLEMS OF COMPETITION AND MONOPOLY

THE purpose of this Appendix is to investigate certain matters
of pure theory which cannot be handled easily without the help
of some sort of technical apparatus.

I

NORMAL SUPPLY PRICE

§ 1. I define the normal supply price of any quantity of
output as the price which will just suffice to call out a regular
flow of that quantity when the industry under review is fully
adapted to producing that quantity and no monopolistic action is
undertaken. *Prima facie* the supply price of an industry may fall,
remain stationary or rise, as the output of the industry increases.
According as it does one or other of these things, the industry
will be said respectively to obey the law of decreasing, constant
or increasing supply price.[1] The same industry may, of course,
obey one of these laws in respect of some quantities of output and
another in respect of other quantities. It is proposed to study
generally the way in which the relation between variations in
normal supply price and the variations in quantity of output is
determined.

§ 2. Most industries are made up of a number of firms, of
which at any moment some are expanding, while others are
declining. Marshall, it will be remembered, likens them to trees
in a forest. Thus, even when the conditions of demand are
constant and the output of an industry as a whole is correspondingly constant, the output of many individual firms will not be
constant. The industry as a whole will be in a state of equilibrium ;
the tendencies to expand and contract on the part of the individual
firms will cancel out ; but it is certain that many individual firms

---

[1] Cf. *ante*, Part II. Ch. XI.

will not themselves be in equilibrium and possible that none will be. When conditions of demand have changed and the necessary adjustments have been made, the industry as a whole will, we may suppose, once more be in equilibrium, with a different output and, perhaps, a different normal supply price ; but, again, many, perhaps all, the firms contained in it, though their tendencies to expand and contract must cancel one another, will, as individuals, be out of equilibrium. This is evidently a state of things the direct study of which would be highly complicated. Fortunately, however, there is a way round. Since, when the output of an industry as a whole is adjusted to any given state of demand, the tendencies to expansion and contraction on the part of individual firms cancel out, they may properly be regarded as *irrelevant* so far as the supply schedule of the industry as a whole is concerned. When the conditions of demand change, the output and the supply price of the industry as a whole must change in exactly the same way as they would do if, both in the original and in the new state of demand, all the firms contained in it were individually in equilibrium. This fact gives warrant for the conception of what I shall call the *equilibrium firm*. It implies that there *can* exist some one firm, which, whenever the industry as a whole is in equilibrium, in the sense that it is producing a regular output y in response to a normal supply price p, will itself also individually be in equilibrium with a regular output x_r.[1] The conditions of the

[1] Marshall's statements about his "representative firm" show that this is conceived as an "equilibrium firm." But it is also something more. It is a firm of, in some sense, average size. Marshall pictures it as a "typical" firm, built on a scale to which actual firms tend to approximate ; for some purposes he suggests that it might be well to picture to ourselves several different typical firms, one, for example, in the company form, another, probably smaller, in the private business form. That this conception is appropriate to actual conditions is well shown by the studies of the sizes of a number of actual businesses carried out in 1914 by Sir Sydney Chapman and Mr. Ashton. They conclude : "Generally speaking, there would seem to exist in industries, or branches of industries, of adequate size, under given sets of conditions, a typical or representative magnitude to which businesses tend to grow, typical proportions between their parts and typical constitutions. . . . As there is a normal size and form for a man, so, but less markedly, are there normal sizes and forms of businesses." (The sizes of businesses mainly in the textile industry. *Statistical Journal*, 1914, p. 512.) This is not surprising. For, if we so far abstract from reality as to suppose that there are large numbers of people of each grade of managing ability, each industry will tend to call to its firms men of that grade whose "comparative efficiency" is greatest there. If y be the output of the industry, x the output of the typical firm, and $F(x,y)$ the total cost to that firm of its output, F will be a definite function determined by technical conditions, and for any assigned value of y, x will be given by the equation

$$\frac{\partial}{\partial x}\left\{\frac{F(x,y,)}{x}\right\} = 0.$$

For my more limited purpose, however, it is not necessary to postulate that

industry are compatible with the existence of such a firm; and the implications about these conditions, which, whether it in fact exists or not, would hold good if it did exist, must be valid. For the purpose of studying these conditions, therefore, it is legitimate to speak of it as actually existing. For any given output, then, of the industry as a whole, the supply price of the industry as a whole must be equal to the price which, with the then output of the industry as a whole, leaves the equilibrium firm in equilibrium. The industry, therefore, conforms to the law of increasing, constant or decreasing supply price according as the price which leaves the equilibrium firm in equilibrium increases, remains constant or decreases with increases in the regular rate of output—we are not here concerned with short-period fluctuations—of the industry as a whole. In industries which consist, not of many firms but of one firm only, the industry as a whole and the equilibrium firm are, of course, identical, and there are no firms other than the equilibrium firm. In what follows we are concerned (1) with industries in which the outputs of the individual firms are small relatively to the output of the whole industry, which implies that x_r, the output of our equilibrium firm, is small relatively to y; (2) with industries consisting of one firm only. The difficult intermediate case of an industry in which x_r is neither small relatively to y nor yet equal to y—a case involving some measure of indeterminateness —will be left out of account. It is assumed throughout that outsiders are not excluded from the industry under review by legal rules or clubbing devices.

II

MANY-FIRM INDUSTRIES

§ 3. Marshall's discussion of internal and external economies has made familiar in a general way the idea that the long-period production costs of an individual firm in a many-firm industry some-times depend, not on the size of its own output only, but also on that of the industry as a whole. This idea needs, however, to be set out in precise form. Three stages may be distinguished. In the simplest stage the individual firm's costs depend solely upon its own output. There are no external economies or diseconomies, and such internal economies or diseconomies as there are are wholly unaffected by variations in the scale of the industry as a whole. If we write y for the output of the industry as a whole

---

there is any representative or typical size of firms. Firms might be of all varieties of size, not concentrated about any norm. All that is required is that one firm is—or, rather, that the conditions are such as to make it possible for one firm to be—an " equilibrium firm " in the sense defined above.

and x_r for the output of the equilibrium firm, the money costs of the equilibrium firm are measured by $F_r(x_r)$. In the next stage the individual firm's money costs consist of two parts, one depending on the size of its own output, the other on that of the output of the whole industry. We may call the former, if we will, internal costs, the latter external costs. The latter will consist of the firm's expenditure on the materials, machinery and so on which it buys, and the price of which will vary with variations in the demand for them on the part of the industry as a whole. Here the money costs of the equilibrium firm are measured by $F_r(x_r) + \dfrac{x_r}{y}\psi(y)$. In the third stage the relation between costs and the individual and collective outputs are more complex. It is no longer proper to regard the individual firm's money costs as consisting of two separate and independent parts. These costs will undergo different variations in consequence of a given change in its output according to the level at which the output of the industry as a whole stands ; and they will undergo different variations in consequence of a given change in the output of the industry as a whole according to the level at which the individual firm's own output stands. The costs of the equilibrium firm are measured by $F_r(x_r, y)$. This last formula, which is a general one, of course includes the two simpler formulae as special cases. It will, therefore, be convenient in the first instance to conduct our analysis by means of it.

§ 4. Let y be the output of an industry as a whole ; x_r the output of the equilibrium firm ; $F_r(x_r, y)$ the total costs of the equilibrium firm ; and p the supply price of the industry's product. The following quantities have then to be distinguished.

First, the *marginal additive cost* to the equilibrium firm, *i.e.* the difference made to the total cost of that firm by increasing its output from x_r to $(x_r + \Delta x_r)$, the output of the other firms remaining unchanged,

$$= \frac{\partial F_r(x_r, y)}{\partial x_r} + \frac{\partial F_r(x_r, y)}{\partial y}.$$

Secondly, the *marginal substitute cost* to the equilibrium firm, *i.e.* the difference made to the total cost of that firm by increasing its output from x_r to $(x_r + \Delta x_r)$, the output of the industry as a whole remaining unchanged (*i.e.* that firm's increase being balanced by an equal decrease elsewhere),

$$= \frac{\partial F_r(x_r, y)}{\partial x_r}.$$

Thirdly, the average cost to the equilibrium firm

$$= \frac{F_r(x_r, y)}{x_r}.$$

§ 5. When a firm is considering what difference will be made to its total costs by adding to or subtracting from its output a small increment, it will measure the difference by marginal additive cost if it reckons that the output of other firms will not be altered in consequence of its action, and by marginal substitute cost if it reckons that other firms will be driven by its expansion to contract their output correspondingly, so that the output of the whole industry, including itself, will be unaltered. It may reckon that something intermediate between these two things will happen, in which case it will look to something intermediate between marginal additive cost and marginal substitute cost. If the total cost to any one firm producing a given output is the same, whatever quantity other firms are producing, these two sorts of marginal cost coincide. In any event, so long as the output of the industry as a whole is large relatively to the output of any one firm, they are not likely to differ very much. The technique of the discussion will be slightly different according as we suppose that the equilibrium firm reckons that a small increase in its output would involve an equal, nil or intermediate addition to the output of the industry as a whole, but no difference will be made to the broad result. Since, therefore, the analysis is simplest if the equilibrium firm thinks of small changes in its output as involving equal and opposite changes in the output of its competitors, I shall proceed on the assumption that it in fact does this. Hence, so long as we are considering many-firm industries, no further reference will be made to marginal additive cost; and the term marginal cost will be used without adjective to signify marginal substitute cost, namely,

$$\frac{\partial_r F(x_r, y)}{\partial x_r}.$$

§ 6. It is then easy to see that, if the supply price of the industry were less than the marginal cost of the equilibrium firm, sales at the supply price would involve a loss to it and it would tend to contract. If the supply price were greater than the marginal cost to the equilibrium firm, that firm would gain by expanding at the expense of other firms, because, while the cost of its old output would still be covered by the selling price—which would be unchanged, since aggregate output is unchanged—the cost of its new output would be more than covered.[1] Hence in neither case would the equilibrium firm be in equilibrium. Since then, *ex hypothesi*, it must be in equilibrium, the supply price of the

---

[1] The argument here would have a slightly different form if marginal additive cost were the relevant form of marginal cost, but the result would be the same. Cf. *post*, footnote (2) to § 14.

industry must be equal to the marginal cost of the equilibrium firm. That is,

$$p = \frac{\partial F_r(x_r, y)}{\partial x_r}.$$

§ 7. If the supply price were less than the average cost of the equilibrium firm, it is obvious that that firm would be making a loss and, therefore, would tend to contract, thus belying its nature as an equilibrium firm. Therefore, the supply price cannot be less than the average cost of the equilibrium firm. Again, if the supply price is greater than the average cost of the equilibrium firm, outsiders will be tempted to come into the industry, forming themselves into similar firms and thus increasing the producing capacity of the industry, until the supply price of an output y is no longer in excess of the average costs of the equilibrium firm. Therefore the supply price cannot be greater than the average costs of the equilibrium firm. Hence the supply price is equal to the average costs of the equilibrium firm,[1] i.e.

$$p = \frac{F_r(x_r, y)}{x_r}.$$

§ 8. Expressed in words, this condition and the preceding condition together state that the normal supply price of the product of a many-firm industry is, in respect of all quantities of output, equal both to the marginal cost and to the average cost of the equilibrium firm; cost being understood, of course, in the sense of money cost. These two conditions are fundamental and of general application. The resultant equality

$$\frac{\partial F_r(x_r, y)}{\partial x_r} = \frac{F_r(x_r, y)}{x_r}$$

can also be derived directly from the proposition that, when y is given, x_r must be such as to make $\dfrac{F_r(x_r, y)}{x_r}$ a minimum. To obviate a possible misunderstanding, it may be added that, since x_r is an implicit function of y, the supply function of the industry as a whole can, if desired, be expressed as a function of one variable, and is, therefore, capable of being represented by a plane diagram.

§ 9. There are three sorts of equilibrium—unstable equilibrium, neutral equilibrium, and stable equilibrium. A system is in stable equilibrium if, when any small disturbance takes place, forces come into play to re-establish the initial position; it is in neutral equilibrium if, when such a disturbance takes place, no re-establishing forces, but also no further disturbing forces, are

---

[1] It will be noticed that neither the preceding argument nor the condition set out in § 3, that the tendency of the various non-equilibrium firms to expand and to contract must balance one another, necessarily implies that the supply price is equal to the average cost *of the industry as a whole.*

evoked, so that the system remains at rest in the position to which it has been moved; it is in unstable equilibrium if the small disturbance calls out further disturbing forces which act in a cumulative manner to drive the system away from its initial position. A ship with a heavy keel is in stable equilibrium; an egg lying on its side in neutral equilibrium; an egg poised on one of its ends in unstable equilibrium. Obviously for practical purposes unstable equilibrium is no equilibrium at all: its presence would involve the system running down to one in which the industry consists of a single firm. In order that the equilibrium may be neutral, we require the further condition that $\dfrac{\partial F_r(x_r, y)}{\partial x_r}$ is constant over a certain range: in order that it may be stable, the further condition that

$$\frac{\partial^2 F_r(x_r, y)}{\partial x_r^2} > 0.$$

§ 10. Let us now consider in turn the three cases distinguished in § 3. In the simplest of these, where the costs of the equilibrium firm are dependent only on its own output and not at all on the output of the industry as a whole, the expression $F_r(x_r, y)$ degrades to $F_r(x_r)$. The two conditions of equilibrium become

$$p = F_r{}'(x_r), \qquad \bullet \quad \bullet \quad \bullet \quad \bullet \quad (1)$$

$$p = \frac{F_r(x_r)}{x_r}, \qquad \bullet \quad \bullet \quad \bullet \quad \bullet \quad (2)$$

and the condition that the equilibrium shall be neutral or stable becomes $\qquad F_r{}''(x_r) = > 0. \qquad \bullet \quad \bullet \quad \bullet \quad \bullet \quad (3)$
In a many-firm industry condition (3) in conjunction with condition (1) rules out the law of decreasing supply price in respect of outputs equal to or greater than what is being actually sold. For, if that law holds for the industry as a whole, it must hold for some individual firm belonging to it, and such a firm, once getting an accidental start, would cumulatively undersell and oust all the others. Condition (3) is not, however, really necessary to exclude the law of decreasing supply price. For conditions (1) and (2) in conjunction exclude both this law and also the law of increasing supply price. This is easily proved. The two conditions together yield $\qquad \dfrac{F_r(x_r)}{x_r} = F_r{}'(x_r).$

This implies that x_r, and consequently $F_r{}'(x_r)$, are determined independently of the output of the industry as a whole; and this implies in turn that the supply price of the industry is the same whatever the magnitude of its output. In other words, the industry is necessarily conducted in accordance with the law of constant supply price.

§ 11. In this simple case, since the cost function of the equilibrium firm can be — as of course it cannot in the more complex cases—represented by a plane diagram which is valid and

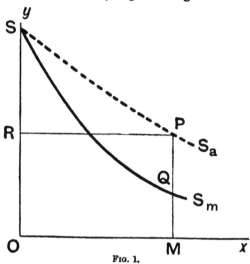

FIG. 1.

the same whatever the output of the industry as a whole, it may be of service to persons who prefer diagrams to algebra to set out the implications of the foregoing analysis by these means.

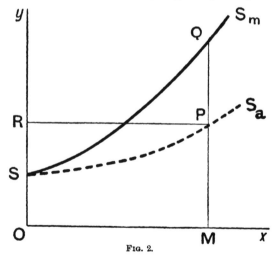

FIG. 2.

In the annexed figures the curve SS_m represents the marginal costs that various amounts of output involve to the equilibrium firm, and the curve SS_a the average costs. These two curves are, of course, bound together by a rigid relation ; such that, if M be any point on Ox and a perpendicular be drawn through M cutting SS_m in Q and SS_a in P, the area SQMO is equal to the rectangle RPMO, whatever be the shapes of the two curves.   It is easy to

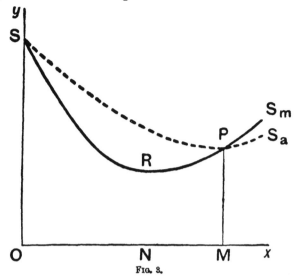

Fig. 3.

see that, if either curve slopes downward throughout (as in Fig. 1), the other must also do this; and, if either slopes upward throughout (as in Fig. 2), so also must the other.   If SS_m slopes down-

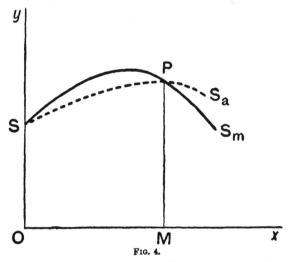

Fig. 4.

ward at first, then turns upward and thereafter continues to rise, the curve SS_a will continue to slope downward until the point at which the now upward moving SS_m intersects it, and will then itself turn upward. This case is represented by Fig. 3. If SS_m slopes upward at first, then turns downward and thereafter continues to fall, SS_a will, in like manner, slope upward until SS_m

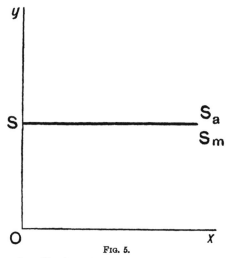

FIG. 5.

intersects it, and will then itself turn downward. This case is represented in Fig 4. Finally, if, either initially or after a point of intersection between the two curves, either of them hencefor-

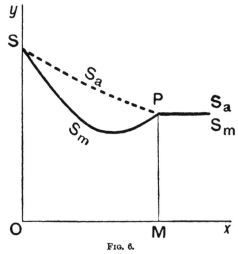

FIG. 6.

ward moves horizontally, the other must coincide with it and do the same. This case is represented in Figs. 5, 6 and 7.[1] The

[1] We could, of course, if we wished, draw more complicated figures, in which the curves should reverse their direction of movement more than once, but no new principle would be brought to light by this proceeding.

conditions of equilibrium for the equilibrium firm, set out in the preceding section, imply that it is producing such a quantity of output OM that an ordinate drawn perpendicular to OM cuts the curves SS_m and SS_a at the same point. Hence in the conditions represented in Figs. 1 and 2 no equilibrium of any sort is possible. In those represented by Fig. 4 there is a single point of unstable equilibrium: in those represented by Figs. 5 to 7 there are ranges of neutral equilibria: and in those represented by Fig. 3 there is a single point of stable equilibrium; the point, namely, at which internal economies have reached their limit, in such wise that the average cost of production is at a minimum. Unstable equilibrium is, as we have seen, for practical purposes impossible. If neutral

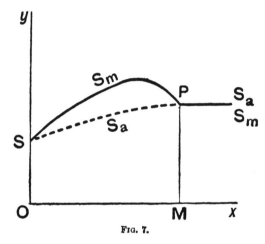

FIG. 7.

equilibrium prevails, changes in the output of the equilibrium firm may take place, but cannot be caused by associated changes in the output of the industry as a whole. If stable equilibrium prevails, the output of the equilibrium firm cannot change. It is fixed rigidly, and changes in the output of the industry as a whole can only come about through an alteration either in the number of firms employed or in the magnitude of the non-equilibrium firms. In any event, whether neutral or stable equilibrium prevails, the average (and marginal) cost of the equilibrium firm, and so the supply price of the industry, is the same for all outputs of the industry: *i.e.* the industry conforms to conditions of constant supply price.

§ 12. In the second class of case distinguished in § 3 the formula for the costs incurred by the equilibrium firm degrades to

$$F_r(x_r) + \frac{x_r}{y}\psi(y).$$

The two conditions of equilibrium become

$$p = F_r'(x_r) + \frac{\psi(y)}{y}, \qquad . \qquad . \qquad . \qquad . \qquad (1)$$

$$p = \frac{F_r(x_r)}{x_r} + \frac{\psi(y)}{y}, \qquad . \qquad . \qquad . \qquad . \qquad (2)$$

and the condition that the equilibrium shall be neutral or stable becomes, as before,

$$F_r''(x_r) = >0. \qquad . \qquad . \qquad . \qquad . \qquad (3)$$

As in the previous case, conditions (1) and (2) yield $\dfrac{F_r(x_r)}{x_r} = F_r'(x_r)$.

So far, therefore, as the internal position and what we may term the internal costs of the equilibrium firm are concerned, everything is exactly the same as it was in that case. Internal costs per unit of product are determined at a fixed level independent of the output of the industry as a whole, and the size of the equilibrium firm is also independent of that output. In this case, however, these results do not imply that the industry as a whole must conform to the law of constant supply price. For, though $\dfrac{F_r(x_r)}{x_r}$ is fixed independently of y, the element $\dfrac{\psi(y)}{y}$, and, therefore,

$$\frac{F_r(x_r)}{x_r} + \frac{\psi(y)}{y}$$

are, so far as the present argument goes, free to vary up or down as y varies. Thus, if a growth in the output of the cotton industry led to a rise in the price of its material, raw cotton, the cotton industry as a whole would conform to the law of increasing supply price; if its expansion led to a fall in the price of raw cotton, to the law of decreasing supply price. To determine whether in fact the price of materials, machinery and so on supplied to an industry by others will rise, fall or remain constant when the output of that industry increases, we should need to step outside the industry primarily under review and investigate the conditions of production in the others.

§ 13. In the third and most general case distinguished in § 3 it is obvious that the three governing conditions impose no restrictions on the relations that may subsist between variations in the supply price and in output. It is still true that, for any given output of the industry as a whole, the output of the equilibrium firm must be such as to make its marginal costs and its average costs equal. But, as the output of the industry as a whole varies, both the output of the equilibrium firm which will make these two things equal and also their magnitude when they are equal may vary indefinitely in either direction. Even, therefore, if the prices of the materials and machinery bought from outside do not vary with variations in the scale of our industry, its own supply price may vary. Many-firm industries of the generalised type are thus perfectly free to conform to the law of increasing supply price, constant supply price, or decreasing supply price, or to any combination of these laws in respect of different quantities of output. Fig. 3 on p. 797 still correctly represents the conditions of supply in the equilibrium firm *when the aggregate demand is such that* OM *units are being purchased from that firm at a price* PM *per unit*. But now, when the aggregate demand alters, the curves SS_m and SS_a alter also. They move upwards or downwards, or they change their shape, or they do both these things. After the change, as before, equilibrium is only attained when the selling price is equal to both the average cost and the marginal cost of the equilibrium firm. The output of that firm is still measured by OM, where M is the base of a perpendicular drawn from the point of intersection of SS_m and SS_a; but, nevertheless, both the selling price and the output of the equilibrium firm may be different from what they were before the change.

III

ONE-FIRM INDUSTRIES

§ 14. Let us now revert to the laws of supply price in relation to an industry of one firm only. Here the equilibrium firm and the industry as a whole become identical, so that there is no need to employ a function of two variables. Moreover, marginal cost is no longer ambiguous : it must signify marginal additive cost, since there is no such thing as marginal substitute cost. If we were to follow blindly the lead of the preceding discussion, we should conclude that equilibrium requires that

$$p = \frac{F(y)}{y} = F'(y).$$

This would mean that there can only be a supply price in respect of one, or, if the curves of marginal cost and of average cost cross one another several times, in respect of a few isolated quantities of output, unless the industry conforms to conditions of constant supply price. Only then, it would seem, is the existence of a continuous supply schedule of the ordinary type possible. It is not difficult to see, however, that the foundation of this argument is unsound. For the equilibrium firm of a many-firm industry it is true that equilibrium is only attainable if both its average cost and its marginal cost are equal to the supply price of the industry. But for the equilibrium firm of a one-firm industry that is not true.

2 D

There can, indeed, be no equilibrium if the average cost is greater than the supply price and the industry is selling at the supply price; for, in such conditions, there will be a tendency to contraction. Likewise there can be no equilibrium if the marginal cost is greater than the supply price and the industry is selling at the supply price; for here, again, there will be a tendency to contraction. But, since we have to do with one firm only, equilibrium does not necessarily forbid average cost to be *less* than the supply price.[1] Again, if, where average cost is equal to the supply price, marginal cost is less than this, and the industry is selling at the supply price, there is no tendency for output to expand, since any expansion would necessarily involve a loss, and, therefore, equilibrium is not incompatible with this arrangement.[2] Hence we conclude that in a one-firm industry the supply price of any given quantity of output is equal to average cost or to marginal cost, according as the one or the other of these is the greater. So far as formal considerations go, the industry is free to conform to decreasing, constant or increasing (money) supply price. If it conforms to decreasing supply price throughout, the supply curve is coincident with the curve of average cost: if it conforms to increasing supply price throughout, with the curve of marginal cost: if it conforms to constant supply price throughout, with both these curves. If it conforms to conditions of increasing supply price in respect of some outputs, and of decreasing supply price in respect of other outputs, the supply curve lies along the curve of average cost where this is higher than the curve of marginal cost, and along the curve of marginal cost where that is the higher of the two.

IV

THE IDEAL OUTPUT IN A MANY-FIRM INDUSTRY

§ 15. I call the output in any industry which maximises the national dividend, and, apart from the differences in the marginal utility of money to different people, also maximises satisfaction, the ideal output. As was shown in Chapter XI. of Part II. this output is attained—the possibility of multiple maximum positions

---

[1] It does not forbid it if the firm's supply schedule is of the type depicted in Fig. 3 *and* if OM in the figure constitutes a large proportion of the total output which the market is capable of absorbing at a price PM ; for in those conditions the one firm may make an abnormal profit without calling new competitors into the field.

[2] This matter is best elucidated by means of a diagram. Let DD' be the demand curve, SS_m the curve of marginal costs, and SS_a the curve of average costs of a one-firm industry. Let OM units be produced and sold at a price PM, where P is the point of intersection between DD' and SS_a. If the

being ignored—when the value of the marginal social net product of each sort of resource invested in the industry under review is equal to the value of the marginal social net product of resources in industries in general, or, more strictly, in the central archetypal industry of Part II. Chapter XI. § 1. In this central archetypal industry each sort of productive resource will have a value in money per unit equal to the value of the net product of a marginal unit of it. Hence the ideal output in our particular industry will be that output which makes the demand price of the output equal to the money value of the resources engaged in producing a marginal unit of output; in other words, it will be

industry were to increase its output beyond OM, say to ON, the extra units would cost less than PM per unit to produce. But, nevertheless, on the assumption that all units are sold at the same price, ON units could not be sold at a less price than QN without involving the industry in a loss. Since, however, the portion of DD' that is to the right of P necessarily lies below SS$_a$, it

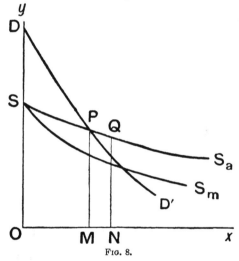

Fig. 8.

is impossible for an output ON to be sold at a price as high as QN. Hence, if the industry expands its output beyond OM, it will make a loss ; and, therefore, it has no tendency to expand. When the curves SS$_m$ and SS$_a$ represent the circumstances of one equilibrium firm among many firms, the position is quite different. It is not now proper to draw a demand curve of the form of DD'. The price in the market would be absolutely unaltered by an expansion on the part of the equilibrium firm if its expansion were balanced by the corresponding contraction in other firms, and approximately unaltered—the equilibrium firm being supposed small relatively to the industry as a whole—if the output of other firms remained unchanged. Therefore the equilibrium firm could expand to ON and still sell at approximately the old price PM. Thus it could sell an enlarged output at more than the average cost of that output, and so make a gain. Hence, for one firm among many others, a state of things in which the supply price of the industry is equal to the average cost of the equilibrium firm, but greater than its marginal cost, is not a state of equilibrium.

the output that makes demand price and marginal supply price *to the community* equal.

§ 16. Let the quantities of the several domestically owned ingredients (including, of course, factors of production), which are required, directly or through things made by them, to produce an output x_r in the equilibrium firm of an industry, whose total output is y, be respectively a, b, c, and the prices p_1, p_2, p_3. Let the quantity of foreign owned ingredient (*e.g.* imported machinery or raw material) be q and its price p_q. We may then, in a many-firm industry, distinguish the following quantities:

First, *the supply price equals*

$$\frac{ap_1 + bp_2 + \cdots + qp_q}{x_r}. \qquad \cdot \qquad \cdot \qquad \cdot \quad (1)$$

Secondly, *the marginal supply price to the industry, i.e.* the difference made to the total money expenses of the industry by adding a small increment of output,

$$= \frac{d}{dy}\left[\frac{y}{x_r}\left\{ap_1 + bp_2 + \cdots + qp_q\right\}\right]$$

$$= y\left[\left\{p_1\frac{d}{dy}\left(\frac{a}{x_r}\right) + p_2\frac{d}{dy}\left(\frac{b}{x_r}\right) + \cdots + p_q\frac{d}{dy}\left(\frac{q}{x_r}\right)\right\}\right.$$

$$\left. + \left\{\frac{a}{x_r}\cdot\frac{dp_1}{dy} + \frac{b}{x_r}\cdot\frac{dp_2}{dy} + \cdots + \frac{q}{x_r}\cdot\frac{dp_q}{dy}\right\}\right] + \frac{ap_1 + bp_2 + \cdots qp_q}{x_r}. \quad (2)$$

Thirdly, the *marginal supply price to the community, i.e.* the difference made to the total money expenses of the community by adding a small increment of output,

$$= y\left[\left\{p_1\frac{d}{dy}\cdot\left(\frac{a}{x_r}\right) + p_2\frac{d}{dy}\left(\frac{b}{x_r}\right) + \cdots + p_q\frac{d}{dy}\left(\frac{q}{x_r}\right)\right\} + \frac{q}{x_r}\cdot\frac{dp_q}{dy}\right]$$

$$+ \frac{ap_1 + bp_2 + \cdots + qp_q}{x_r}. \quad (3)$$

Fourthly, *the rate of change from the standpoint of the industry in the supply price* as output increases

$$= \frac{d}{dy}\left\{\frac{ap_1 + bp_2 + \cdots + qp_q}{x_r}\right\}$$

$$= \left\{p_1\frac{d}{dy}\left(\frac{a}{x_r}\right) + p_2\frac{d}{dy}\left(\frac{b}{x_r}\right) + \cdots + p_q\frac{d}{dy}\left(\frac{q}{x_r}\right)\right\}$$

$$+ \left\{\frac{a}{x_r}\cdot\frac{dp_1}{dy} + \frac{b}{x_r}\cdot\frac{dp_2}{dy} + \cdots + \frac{q}{x_r}\cdot\frac{dp_q}{dy}\right\}. \quad (4)$$

Fifthly, *the rate of change from the standpoint of the community in the supply price as output increases*

$$= \left\{ p_1 \frac{d}{dy}\left(\frac{a}{x_r}\right) + p_2 \frac{d}{dy}\left(\frac{b}{x_r}\right) + \cdots + p_q\left(\frac{q}{x_r}\right) \right\} + \frac{q}{x_r} \cdot \frac{dp_q}{dy}. \qquad (5)$$

This last expression is derived from the preceding one by eliminating the elements that represent increments of transfer between the equilibrium firm in our industry and domestic owners of the ingredients it employs.

§ 17. The foregoing expression (4) multiplied by y measures the excess of expression (2) over expression (1); and the expression (5) multiplied by y measures the excess of expression (3) over expression (1). Hence:

(1) In all industries where the rate of change from the standpoint of the industry in the supply price, as output increases, is positive (*i.e.* where conditions of increasing supply price *simpliciter* prevail), the supply price is less than the marginal supply price to the industry: in the converse case it is greater.

(2) In all industries where the rate of change from the standpoint of the community of the supply price is positive (*i.e.* where conditions of increasing supply price from the standpoint of the community prevail) the supply price is less than the marginal supply price to the community: in the converse case it is greater.

§ 18. It was shown in § 10 of Part II. Chapter XI. that the expression

$$\left\{ \frac{a}{x_r} \cdot \frac{dp_1}{dy} + \frac{b}{x_r} \cdot \frac{dp_2}{dy} + \cdots + \frac{q}{x_r} \cdot \frac{dp_q}{dy} \right\}$$

is unlikely to be negative: and in § 7 of the same chapter that the expression

$$\left\{ p_1 \frac{d}{dy}\left(\frac{a}{x_r}\right) + p_2 \frac{d}{dy}\left(\frac{b}{x_r}\right) + \cdots + \frac{d}{dy}\left(\frac{q}{x_r}\right) \right\}$$

is extremely unlikely to be positive. We may take it that, though exceptions are possible, both these inequalities hold good *in general*. On the other hand, the expression

$$\left\{ p_1 \cdot \frac{d}{dy}\left(\frac{a}{x_r}\right) + p_2 \frac{d}{dy}\left(\frac{b}{x_r}\right) + \cdots + p_q\frac{d}{dy}\left(\frac{q}{x_r}\right) \right\} + \frac{q}{x_r}\frac{dp_q}{dy}$$

may be positive if $\frac{dp_q}{dy}$ is positive: and, of course, the expression for the rate of change from the standpoint of the industry in the supply price may be either positive or negative.

Hence:

(1) In general the rate of change from the standpoint of the industry in the supply price, as output increases, is greater than or equal to the rate of change from the standpoint of the community in the supply price. Hence decreasing supply price (*simpliciter*)

implies decreasing supply price from the standpoint of the community : but increasing supply price (*simpliciter*) does not imply increasing supply price from the standpoint of the community.

(2) In general, except in industries that make use of imported materials of increasing supply price, the rate of change in supply price from the standpoint of the community, as output increases, is nil or negative, and the supply price is equal to or greater than the marginal supply price to the community.

(3) In the generality of industries the marginal supply price to the industry is equal to or greater than the marginal supply price to the community.

§ 19. The ideal output is attained, as was stated above, when the marginal supply price to the community is equal to the demand price.

The output proper to simple competition is attained when the supply price is equal to the demand price.

The output proper to discriminating monopoly of the first degree is attained when the marginal supply price to the industry is equal to the demand price.

The following inferences hold good in general (*i.e.* when the inequalities set out in § 18 are valid) :

(1) Except in industries that make use of imported materials of increasing supply price, the output proper to simple competition is equal to or less than the ideal output.

(2) In any industry the output proper to discriminating monopoly of the first degree is less than the ideal output if the marginal supply price to the community and the marginal supply price to the industry differ, *i.e.* if the rate of change from the standpoint of the industry in the supply price and the rate of change from the standpoint of the community in the supply price differ : it is equal to the ideal output if they coincide.

(3) The output proper to simple competition is less or greater than the output proper to discriminating monopoly of the first degree according as the industry conforms to conditions of decreasing or increasing supply price *simpliciter*.

(4) When decreasing supply price *simpliciter* prevails, the output proper to simple competition falls short of the ideal output by more than the output proper to discriminating monopoly of the first degree falls short of it. But, when increasing supply price (*simpliciter*) prevails, the output proper to simple competition, while greater than the output proper to discriminating monopoly of the first degree, may be either greater or less than the ideal output. In the former case the national dividend fares better than it would do under discriminating monopoly : in the latter it may fare better or may fare worse.

§ 20. The analysis of head (4) in the preceding paragraph may be illustrated thus. Suppose that wheat-growing conforms to the law of constant supply price from the standpoint of the community, but to that of increasing supply price from that of the industry (*i.e. simpliciter*), because, and only because, the price of land is raised when more of it is wanted for wheat-growing. In this case the supply price is equal to the marginal supply price to the community, and the output proper to simple competition is identical with the ideal output. But, if wheat farmers, *who are supposed to hire their land from landlords*, combine and exercise discriminating monopoly of the first degree, they will cut down their wheat-growing, because, by so doing, they will cause the rent per acre that they have to pay to fall. Their output will then be less than the ideal output, instead of being, as it was before, equal to it. If wheat farmers own their land, and do not hire it, the distinction between the interests of the industry and of the community disappears; and the output of wheat will be the same under discriminating monopoly of the first degree as under simple competition, *i.e.* equal to the ideal output.

V

THE IDEAL OUTPUT IN A ONE-FIRM INDUSTRY

§ 21. In a one-firm industry when $\dfrac{F(y)}{y} > F'(y)$, and the supply price of an output y is, therefore, $\dfrac{F(y)}{y}$, the analysis of the preceding discussion is applicable, the formal expression of it needing to be modified only so far as to provide for the identity of x_r and y. In a one-firm industry, in which marginal cost exceeds average cost, something different is needed. The marginal supply price to the industry and the supply price are both equal to $F'(y)$. Therefore, if no transfer elements are involved, so that the marginal supply price to the industry is equal to the marginal supply price to the community, an output equating supply price and demand price—which, in this case, is the output proper alike to simple competition and to discriminating monopoly of the first degree—will be equal to the ideal output, in spite of the fact that the industry conforms to the law of increasing supply price. This case in general can only occur when imported ingredients of increasing supply price are being used. If transfer elements are involved, an output which equates supply price and demand price will be less than the ideal output.[1]

[1] It should be noted that, when, in one-firm industries, actual investment differs from ideal investment, the grounds for this divergence cannot be

VI

DEMAND PRICE AND MARGINAL DEMAND PRICE

§ 22. In the preceding discussion it has been tacitly assumed that the demand curve is also what may be called, by analogy with supply, a curve of marginal demand prices. This is not necessarily so. The marginal demand price of a quantity y of any commodity is the difference between the desiredness (as measured in money) to consumers in the aggregate of annual (or weekly) purchases of a quantity y and of a quantity $(y + \Delta y)$ respectively. The demand price of y units is the price that maintains an annual (or weekly) purchase of a quantity y. Hence it is equal to the desiredness (as measured in money) of the least desired increment (Δy) in a quantity y to the purchaser of that increment. If then the purchase of the marginal unit indirectly increases or diminishes the desiredness of their holdings to the purchasers of other units, the marginal demand price and the demand price will be different. For commodities the desire for which is partly a desire for the uncommon the curve of marginal demand prices, which, for a nil purchase, coincides with the demand curve, will fall further and further below it as purchases increase : for commodities the desire for which is partly a desire for the common the opposite of this is true ; while for commodities which are desired solely on account of the direct satisfaction they confer, the two curves are identical.[1] When the curves diverge, maximum satisfaction—the parties concerned being assumed to be similar in wealth and temperament—is attained with an output that equates marginal supply price, not with demand price, but with marginal demand price.

VII

SIMPLE MONOPOLY AND MAXIMUM PRICES

§ 23. If the State, seeking to protect consumers against a monopoly, fixes a maximum price at the level proper to free competition, it is obvious that, under decreasing or constant supply price, the monopolist will gain by increasing his output up to the

---

translated into terms of a difference between marginal social and marginal private net products. Since there is only one firm these two net products necessarily coincide. The ground of divergence, when such exists, is that, owing to the absence of competition, marginal private (which is here equal to marginal social) net product is not equal to average net product. If the one-firm industry is making normal profits, the value of the average net product is equal to the value of the marginal social net product in the imaginary central industry of Part II. Ch. XI. § 1 : and, therefore, the value of the marginal social net product in the one-firm industry is not equal to that value.

[1] Cf. Part II. Ch. XI. § 13.

amount that would have been produced under free competition. If, however, conditions of increasing supply price prevail, the amount which it will pay the monopolist to produce, namely, the amount which will maximise output multiplied by the excess of the regulated price of sale over the supply price, is necessarily less than the competitive output. It *may* be either greater or less than the output that would result under unregulated monopoly. If the curves of demand and supply are both straight lines, it will be exactly equal to this amount. This is readily seen by inspection of a suitably drawn diagram.

§ 24. If, under conditions of increasing supply price, the State fixes a maximum price, less than the monopoly price but greater than the competitive price, it is *probable* in general that the output will be intermediate between the competitive output and the output proper to unregulated monopoly. If the curves of demand and supply are both straight lines, this result is *certain*. Construct a diagram (Fig. 9), such that PM represents the competitive price, and OM the competitive output; while QN represents the

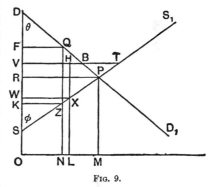

FIG. 9.

monopoly price, and ON the monopoly output. Let the State-controlled price, measured by OV, be greater than the competitive price, but less than the monopoly price. Through V draw a horizontal line VBT cutting DD_1 in B and SS_1 in T. It is easily shown that the monopoly output ON is one-half of the competitive output OM, and that the output, which it will pay the monopolist to produce when the price is fixed at OV, will be measured by one-half of the line VT, drawn horizontally through V to cut SS_1 in T, or by the line VB, according as the one or the other of these lengths is smaller. But, since OV is greater than PM, it is obvious that VT is greater than OM. Consequently one-half of VT is greater than one-half of OM. This proves that the output at the controlled price is greater than the monopoly output; and, since VB must be less than RP, it is necessarily less than the competitive output. That is, it lies somewhere between the two.

§ 25. An extension of the foregoing argument shows that, in the conditions contemplated, when the demand and supply curves are straight lines, the level of controlled price, which will make the output larger than any other level would do, will be that which causes the intersection point of VT and DD_1, namely, the point B.

to be identical with the middle point of VT, namely, the point H. If the ∠ SDP be θ and the ∠ DSP be ϕ, this output can be shown to be equal to the output proper to simple competition multiplied by the fraction

$$\frac{\tan \theta + \tan \phi}{2 \tan \theta + \tan \phi}.$$

VIII

SOME PROBLEMS OF DISCRIMINATING MONOPOLY

§ 26. Consider an industry in which conditions of decreasing supply price prevail, but in which the supply curve lies wholly above the demand curve, so that neither under simple competition nor under simple monopoly can any output take place. Draw the demand curve DD_1 and the supply curve SS_1 as in Fig. 10. Through S draw a curve SS_2 such that, if a perpendicular be drawn from any point P on SS_1, to cut SS_2 in Q, and the figure be completed as drawn, the area SQMO is equal, for all positions of P and Q, to the rectangle KPMO. If DD_1 lies throughout below both SS_1 and SS_2, it is obvious that no output can occur under monopoly *plus* discrimination of the first degree, just as none can occur under simple competition. It may happen, however, in some industries of decreasing supply price, that DD_1, while lying below SS_1, cuts SS_2. If it cuts it once it must obviously cut it a second time. Let it cut it in R and Q. Then, under conditions of simple competition, no output can occur. But under conditions of monopoly *plus* discrimination of the first degree, provided that the area RQ is greater than the area DRS, an output OM will yield aggregate receipts in excess of aggregate costs, and will, therefore, be forthcoming. This result is more likely to be achieved, the more steeply the curve SS_1 slopes downward (that is to say, the more strongly the law of decreasing supply price works); because, the steeper is SS_1, the larger, when the distance OM is given, is the area PQS, and, therefore, the greater is the range of demand curves that will make the area

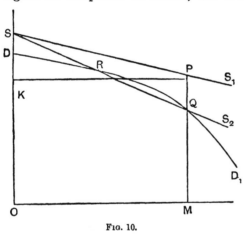

FIG. 10.

RQ greater than the area DRS. Given the inclination of SS_1, it is also more likely to be achieved, if the demand curve does *not* slope downward steeply in its earlier stages (that is to say, if the demand is elastic till fairly low price levels have been reached).

§ 27. Monopoly *plus* discrimination of the second degree, as defined on p. 279, approximates in its effects towards monopoly *plus* discrimination of the first degree, as the number of different prices which it is possible for the monopolist to charge increases. This result, which is obvious in general, can be worked out exactly in a particular case. Let the output proper to discrimination of the first degree be a, and let n be the number of different price-groups. On the hypothesis that the demand and supply curves are straight lines, it can be shown that, when the commodity obeys the law of constant supply price, the output will be equal to $\dfrac{n}{n+1}a$ for all values of n. That is to say, if one price only can be selected, the output will be $\dfrac{1}{2}a$: if two prices can be selected, $\dfrac{2}{3}a$, and so on. When the commodity obeys the law of decreasing supply price, the output, if n is equal to 1, will still be equal to $\dfrac{n}{n+1}a$, but, if n is greater than 1, it will be somewhat less than this.

§ 28. Our next problem has to do with the relative outputs under discriminating monopoly of the third degree—as defined on p. 279—and of simple monopoly re-spectively. Let con-ditions of constant supply price prevail, and let there be two markets only. Then if the curves of de-mand in both markets are straight lines,

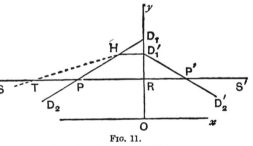

FIG. 11.

precise results can be obtained. Let D_1D_2 and $D'_1D'_2$ represent the demand curves of the two markets, and let SS' be drawn at a vertical distance OR above the base line, where OR measures the constant cost of production. Through D'_1 draw D'_1H parallel to SS', and, through H, draw a straight line HT, such that PT is equal to RP'. Then under discriminating monopoly the output for the two markets will be respectively $\frac{1}{2}RP'$ and $\frac{1}{2}RP$. Under simple monopoly, *if PH is greater than HD_1*, the output will be $\frac{1}{2}RT$. But, since

PT is equal to RP', $\frac{1}{2}$RT = $\frac{1}{2}$RP' + $\frac{1}{2}$RP. Therefore, subject to the condition italicised above, the outputs under simple monopoly and under discriminating monopoly will be the same. If PH is less than HD_1, the output under simple monopoly will, *in some conditions*, be $\frac{1}{2}$RP, and there will be no consumption in the less favourable market. When these conditions prevail, so that under simple monopoly nothing would be consumed in one of the two markets, the substitution of discriminating for simple monopoly increases the output; but except in these conditions the output is not changed. When the assumption of constant supply price is removed and it is allowed that increasing or decreasing supply price prevails, the results reached above are not modified, since it is only through a change in the quantity of output that increasing or decreasing supply price can be called into play.[1] Decreasing supply price, however, opens up a possibility referred to in Part II. Chapter XVII. § 13, and analogous to that examined in § 26 above, to which the preceding discussion has no relevance. This is that, in some conditions under which neither simple monopoly nor simple competition would have led to *any* output, discriminating monopoly may lead to *some* output.

IX

METHODS OF INDUSTRIAL REMUNERATION

§ 29. The central argument of Part III. Chapter VIII. can be brought into clear light by means of a diagram. Let us suppose the number of workpeople employed in any industry and the length of the working day to be given. It is then possible to construct a demand curve representing the employers' demand prices (in terms of product) for different amounts of exertion per unit time from a typical workman, and a supply curve representing the workman's supply prices (in terms of product) for different amounts of exertion. Units of exertion are marked off along Ox, and the demand and supply prices (in terms of product) of different amounts of it along Oy.

Since every increase of exertion on the part of workpeople enables employers to finish any given job more quickly, and so to start their machinery upon some other job, the demand curve DD' will slope upwards towards the right. Since, if a man is at work at all, neither public opinion nor his own comfort will allow him to do absolutely nothing, the supply curve SS' will start at a

---

[1] In conditions such that a simple monopoly would sell in market A only, while a discriminating monopoly would sell in B also, it can easily be shown that the introduction of discrimination will affect consumption and price in A as

point some distance along O*x*, and, thereafter, will slope upward somewhat steeply. Let it cut DD' in P. Through P draw PM perpendicular to O*x*, and PR perpendicular to O*y*. Then, apart from possible injurious reactions on capacity that are not here considered, the amount of exertion by a typical workman, which is most advantageous to the national dividend and economic welfare, is measured by OM, and the corresponding amount of his output by the rectangle OMPR. If the wage paid to him is wholly independent of his exertions and consequent output, the amount of his exertions will approximate to OS, and his output to OSQK. An amount of exertion OM, and consequent output OMPR, can be obtained *either* by the offer of a rate (in product) PM for each unit of exertion (which means each PM units of output); *or* by the offer of an aggregate wage (in product)— per day or whatever the time-unit may be—equal to OMPR, conditional upon the man producing OMPR units of output, any failure to reach this standard involving the payment of a considerably lower wage.

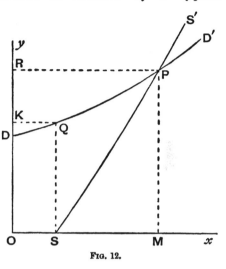

Fig. 12.

X

THE MEANING OF EXPLOITATION

§ 30. Let DD' be the employers' demand curve for labour and SS' the workers' supply curve in any district or occupation. Let PM be the wage that would result from free competition, *i.e.* that is equal to the general rate of wages for workpeople of the grade concerned; QM'' the wage most profitable to the

follows. Under constant supply price both will remain unchanged ; under increasing supply price consumption will be diminished and price increased ; under decreasing supply price consumption will be increased and price diminished. These considerations are of practical importance to a government considering whether native cartels should be allowed to sell abroad at less than the home price.

workpeople if they were combined; and RM' the wage most profitable to the employers. Then the range of indeterminateness described in Part III. Chapter VI. is constituted by all rates between QM" and RM'. There

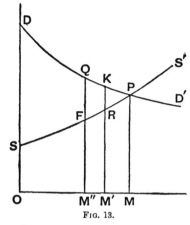

Fig. 13.

is necessarily exploitation if the employers succeed in paying any wage less than PM. Let us suppose that they succeed in paying a wage RM'. It follows that, if they obtain an amount of labour represented by OM', then the measure of *unfairness* in the wage is the excess of PM over RM', but the measure of *exploitation* is the excess of KM' over RM'. If the workpeople succeeded in establishing a wage larger than PM, the exchange index would necessarily fall on the demand curve to the left of P, say at the point Q, and we might speak of an exploitation of employers by workpeople, measured by the excess of QM" over FM".

APPENDIX IV

(To Part I, Chapter III) [1]

THE MEASUREMENT OF REAL INCOME IN RELATION TO TAXES

§ 1. LET us define (i) real income as the aggregate of all items produced by factors of production, and (ii) money income as the sum of the payments made to these factors for their services in providing the said items. Any tolerable method of measuring real income through prices must satisfy the following condition—namely, that, provided only one sort of commodity is being produced, money income divided by the price index shall be equal to the number of (in this case) homogeneous units of real income. We have to ask what way or ways of treating indirect taxes in the construction of price index numbers are compatible with this condition. To answer that question will not, of course, enable us to decide any of the larger problems of index number construction. But none the less it should be useful.

§ 2. First, suppose that a tax is imposed on those units of our commodity that are sold to private persons, and the proceeds used to pay factors of production for producing other units for the service of the Government.

Write Q_1 for output not for Government; Q_2 for output for Government:

c for cost of production per unit of output in either section.
p for the price of the taxed goods as sold cum-tax.
t for the rate of tax.
P for the price index number.
I for money income as defined above.

Evidently $Q_1 t = Q_2 c$.

[1] From the *Economic Journal*, December 1940.

To satisfy our condition the price index P must be such that $\dfrac{I}{P} = Q_1 + Q_2$. Since obviously $Q_1 p = I$, this is so if P is taken *either* as

$$\frac{Q_1 p + Q_2(o)}{Q_1 + Q_2} \quad or \text{ as} \quad \frac{Q_1(p - t) + Q_2 c}{Q_1 + Q_2} :$$

that is to say, either if (1) the prices of non-Government goods are reckoned cum-tax and Government goods are assigned a nil price, or (2) the prices of non-Government goods are reckoned ex-tax and Government goods are assigned a price equal to cost ; money income in both cases being reckoned as defined above. Plainly, however, the condition is also and equally satisfied if (3) P is taken as

$$\frac{Q_1 p + Q_2 c}{Q_1 + Q_2}$$

and money income is inflated, for the purpose of measuring real income, by the yield of the tax, so that it reads $(I + Q_1 t)$. Any of these methods of reckoning satisfies our condition. But it is *not* satisfied if the price of non-Government goods is taken cum-tax, Government goods are priced at cost and money income is not inflated, but reckoned as I. Dr. Bowley's method, as set out in his paper to the Manchester Statistical Society (November 1939), agrees with method (1) above.

§ 3. Secondly, suppose that money collected by the Government through indirect taxation is expended in making gratuitous transfers to pensioners and so on—forms of incomings which are not included in money income as here defined. In this case, to satisfy our condition it is obvious that *either* the price of taxed goods must be taken ex-tax *or* money income must be inflated, for the purpose of measuring real income, by the yield of the tax.

§ 4. Thus, provided we decide to assign to Government goods prices equal to cost—which seems the natural thing to do—we can satisfy the requirements of both of the above two cases either by reckoning the price of taxed goods ex-tax or by inflating money income by the yield of the tax. But we must not do both these things.

APPENDIX V

(To Part I, Chapter IV) [1]

OBSOLESCENCE AND KINDRED MATTERS

FOUR matters treated in Part I, Chapter IV, need, I now think (1951), further comment.

§ 1. The first is obsolescence. According to the text, changes in the value of capital objects, consequent upon changes in taste for the things they help to produce or upon the introduction of new types of capital goods that compete with them in satisfying given tastes, are irrelevant to the size of the capital stock. Business practice, on the other hand, holds that, in order to maintain that stock intact, allowances against obsolescence must be made. I suggest that a partial reconciliation between these two views may be obtained by distinguishing between elements that are actually standing in the capital stock and elements that have been discarded from it. So long as an element stands in the stock, its quantity is a matter for physical measurement, with which valuation has nothing to do. But elements may be discarded from the stock on account of something that has happened to valuation. When they are discarded, the stock is *pro tanto* reduced. Thus valuation, though irrelevant to the quantity of such elements as are at any time standing in the stock, is, or may be, relevant to what elements do stand there, and so in this indirect way does, or may, affect the quantity of the stock. Thus a machine will stand in the stock so long as there is *some* quantity of labour in conjunction with which it can, or is expected soon to be able to, produce more value than it could earn elsewhere. Otherwise it will be discarded.

§ 2. The second matter concerns the treatment of an element of capital which has deteriorated physically in some measure but still stands in the stock of capital. A distinction should be drawn between physical changes which, while leaving the element still as

[1] Based on "Net Income and Capital Depreciation," *Economic Journal*, June 1935.

productive as ever, bring nearer the day of sudden and final break-down, and physical changes which reduce its current productivity and so rentable value. With the former sort of change, until the breakdown occurs, the capital stock is, I suggest, best regarded as intact. With the latter sort of change we may conveniently conceive of physical discards being made, whose quantity is measured by the original quantity of the decaying instrument multiplied by the proportionate fall in its rentability. This is, of course, a subordinate matter; and a different view might be taken without the main argument suffering damage. In any event, even though we hold that certain sorts of capital affected by physical change (or by obsolescence) are discarded, not gradually in parts but suddenly as wholes, this does not imply that the aggregate of all sorts of capital together must experience a discontinuous discarding. Nor is anything that has been said inconsistent with the view that particular business concerns subject to discarding of a discontinuous type are well advised to make provision against it in a continuous manner by means of regular annual payments into a depreciation fund.

§ 3. The third matter concerns the line to be drawn between the depletions of capital that are and depletions that are not compatible with maintaining the capital intact. The attempt to justify the distinction between other depletions and depletions due to acts of God and the King's enemies and ordinary depletions on the ground that the latter are incidental to the use of the capital instrument affected, which is made in Part I, Chapter IV, § 4, is not satisfactory as regards weathering through lapse of time and losses through fire and accident. It is not enough to argue, as was done in the text, that a necessary condition of use is subjection to the passage of time and so to the risk of these kinds of loss. For exactly the same argument could be used in regard to earthquakes and wars. A better approach is to say that capital is maintained intact if allowance has been made for such part of capital depletion as may fairly be called " normal " ; the practical test of normality being that the depletion is sufficiently regular to be foreseen, if not in detail, at least in the large. This test brings under the head of depreciation all ordinary forms of wear and tear, whether due to the actual working of machines or to mere passage of time—rust, rodents and so on— and all ordinary discarding through obsolescence, whether due to technical advance or to changes of taste. It brings in too the con-sequences of all *ordinary* accidents, such as shipwreck and fire, in short, of all accidents against which it is customary to insure. But it leaves out capital depletion that springs from the act of God or the King's enemies, or from such a miracle as a decision to-morrow on the part of this country to forbid the manufacture of whisky or beer. These sorts of capital depletion constitute, not depreciation to be made good before current net income is reckoned, but capital losses that are irrelevant to current net income. The line between the two sorts of capital depletion cannot be drawn precisely. It may vary between different times and different places, between a country such as England, for example, and one in which earthquakes are familiar events, against which provision by insurance is usual.

§ 4. The last observation I should like to add is this. Clearly when any discarding has occurred, in order to make good the depletion of capital implied in it, that quantity of resources must be engaged which would suffice in actual current conditions of technique to compensate for the discarded element. But what of the *direction* in which this quantity of resources should be engaged ? Ideally this should be so chosen that the maximum possible addition is made to the present value of the stock of capital. If a machine has suffered damage and, in order to continue working, needs repair, in general much the most productive use for the resources engaged to offset the depletion of capital implied in this will be that of repairing the machine. But, if the demand for one sort of product has fallen off and some instruments so far engaged in making that product have in consequence been discarded, the most productive use for the offsetting resources will be in making machines for some industry the demand for whose product has meanwhile been enhanced. Here we have a clear principle. A basis for it may be found in the concept of capital as an entity capable of maintaining its quantity while altering its form and by its nature always drawn to those forms on which, so to speak, the sun of profit is at the time shining. But in view of the fact that different firms, whether in the same or in different industries, are often controlled by different people, to apply this principle in its ideal form is seldom practicable.

APPENDIX VI

(To Part I, Chapters V and VI) [1]

REAL INCOME AND ECONOMIC WELFARE

In the appendix to an article entitled " The Evaluation of Real National Income," published in *Oxford Economic Papers* for January 1950, Professor Samuelson made, very courteously, some effective criticisms of parts of Part I, Chapters V and VI, of this book. The Editor invited me to comment. Not wanting to challenge Professor Samuelson's argument on any substantial matter, I thought that the most useful way of doing this would be by saying directly in my own language how these things seem to me to stand now. The following paragraphs are reproduced from what I wrote in reply.[1]

I

For any investigation in this field the starting-point is plain. If real income consisted of a single sort of measurable homogeneous commodity, it would vary from time to time in proportion to the quantity of this commodity contained in it. But in actual life real income is made up of a large number of heterogeneous commodities. If these were bound together in such a way that their several quantities always altered in the same proportion, real income would vary in accordance with this proportion. We should still have an unambiguous physical measure of change. If conditions were such that, when the quantity of one commodity embraced in real income increased (or decreased), the quantity of none decreased (or increased), we would be able to say of the real income in one situation that it was greater or less than the real income in another ; though we should not be able to specify a proportion in which it was greater or less. In actual life it will only happen rarely that even the second less stringent of these conditions is satisfied. In general, therefore, it is impossible, by means of any physical test, to say

[1] " Real Income and Economic Welfare," *Oxford Economic Papers*, February 1951.

whether one real income is larger or smaller than another in a specified proportion, or even to say whether it is larger or smaller at all. When we read that real income, or the part of it represented by industrial production, is 5 or 10 per cent larger in one year than in another, this cannot be a true statement of *physical* fact. The real incomes of the two years are physically incommensurable, and no algebraic manipulations, useful as these may be for some purposes, can get over that. Where do we go from here ?

II

THE PROBLEM

Let there be two situations, I and II, in which there are equal numbers of persons, and let their aggregate money incomes (all of which are expended in buying real incomes) be equal. In both situations real income is made up of the same various kinds of heterogeneous measurable items. In the first situation the quantities of these items respectively are x_1, x_2 ... and their prices a_1, a_2 ... In the second situation the quantities are y_1, y_2 ... and the prices b_1, b_2 ...

It follows, of course, that $a_1x_1 + a_2x_2 + \ldots = b_1y_1 + b_2y_2 + \ldots$

Suppose that the values of the x's, a's, y's, and b's are such that (1) $a_1x_1 + a_2x_2 + \ldots$ is $>$ or, alternatively, is $< b_1x_1 + b_2x_2 + \ldots$ in a given ratio and (2) that $b_1y_1 + b_2y_2 + \ldots$ is $>$ or, alternatively, is $< a_1y_1 + a_2y_2 + \ldots$ in a given ratio.

What inferences about (1) real income and (2) economic welfare respectively can be derived from these statistical data ? This is our problem.

III

INFERENCES ABOUT INCOME

Under this head consider first the relation between the actual real income of the first situation and the potential real income of the first situation's pattern in the second. That is to say, given that the real income of the first situation comprises x_1, x_2 ... amounts of the several items, is, so to speak, of x pattern, what can be said about the relation of this actual income to the potential income *of this pattern* in the second situation ?

If we know that in the second situation constant supply price rules everywhere, we can infer that the price of any nth item will be the same in that situation if x_n units of it are being produced as if y_n units are being produced. The prices actually found in this situation will, then, also be those that would rule for the quantities proper to the first situation. Hence $b_1x_1 + b_2x_2 + \ldots$ is the aggregate price for which the real income of the first situation could be purchased in the second. Hence, given that $a_1x_1 + a_2x_2 \ldots >$ or $< b_1x_1 + b_2x_2 + \ldots$ in a given ratio, the potential x pattern real income in the second situation is greater or less than the actual real income of the first situation in this ratio.

If we do not know that in the second situation constant supply price rules everywhere, we cannot claim that b_1, $b_2 \ldots$ (or some multiple of them) were being produced instead of the actual y_1, $y_2 \ldots$ Hence to know that $a_1x_1 + a_2x_2 + \ldots$ is $>$ or is $< b_1x_1 + b_2x_2 \ldots$ in a given ratio does not enable us to say that the potential x pattern real income in situation II is greater (or less) in a given ratio than the actual real income of situation I, or even that it is greater (or less) at all. We may, indeed, hold in a general way, as I did in the text,[1] that the " errors " may be expected so far to cancel out that the potential x pattern real income of situation II is *probably* greater (or less) in some degree—though not in a given degree—than the actual real income of situation I. But this sort of *a priori* hunch is perhaps not worth much.

Consider, secondly, the relation between the actual y pattern real income of the second situation and the potential real income of the second situation's pattern in the first. The arguments developed above obviously hold good here also with appropriate verbal adjustments.

There is clearly nothing to prevent *both* the potential x pattern real income in situation II being greater (or less) than the actual x pattern real income of situation I ; *and also* the potential y pattern real income in situation I being greater (or less) than the actual y pattern real income of situation II. There is nothing, that is to say, to prevent this *in a general way*. As we shall see immediately, however, in a certain special case this state of things entails a contradiction and is, therefore, impossible.

IV

INFERENCES ABOUT ECONOMIC WELFARE

Case 1. First suppose that in situation I all purchasers' tastes and purchasing power are alike ; that no change in any of them takes place in situation II ; but that in that situation there is a change either as regards aggregate resources at work or as regards technique in some or all industries.

Here *prima facie* we may argue as follows. If in situation II potential x pattern income is *smaller* than actual x pattern income

---

[1] Cf. *ante,* p. 62.

in situation I, we know that purchasers prefer the actual y pattern income of situation II to *something less than* the actual x pattern income of situation I. But this does not imply that they prefer it to that actual x pattern income itself, and so allows no inference about economic welfare. If, however, in situation II potential x pattern income is *larger* than actual x pattern income in situation I, then, since each purchaser must prefer what he actually buys to what he could have bought, and since each could have bought more x pattern income in situation II than he does buy in situation I, his economic welfare must be larger.

This, however, as Professor Samuelson has shown, is not exact. Each individual consumer, when y pattern income is actually being produced, knows that whatever he individually does will not make prices differ from b_1, b_2 . . . Therefore the prices *which he thinks* of when deciding how much of anything to buy are b_1, b_2 . . . What matters to him is his share of the potential x pattern income, *as he thinks it would be*, in situation II. Given then that this *imagined* potential x pattern income in situation II is larger than the actual x pattern income in situation I, it follows that economic welfare in situation II is larger than in situation I irrespective of what the potential x pattern income of situation II actually is. That is to say, in the conditions I have here supposed, if $a_1x_1 + a_2x_2 + \ldots >$ $b_1x_1 + b_2x_2 + \ldots$, economic welfare is larger in situation II.

In these circumstances it follows that imagined potential y pattern income in situation I cannot be larger than actual y pattern income in situation II. That is to say, $b_1y_1 + b_2y_2 + \ldots$ cannot be $> a_1y_1 + a_2y_2 + \ldots$ For that would entail economic welfare being larger in situation I than in situation II : which contradicts what was established above. When constant supply price rules in both situations, so that imagined and true potential incomes coincide, what has been said of imagined potential incomes also holds of true potential incomes. A restrictive condition is, in fact, imposed in this special case excluding a relationship which, as we saw above, is *in general* admissible.

Case 2. Secondly, suppose that, as before, everybody's tastes and purchasing power are the same in situation II as in situation I, but that the tastes and (or) purchasing power of different purchasers differ from one another ; while, as before, there is a change on the supply side.

In this case it is never possible to infer from price and quantity statistics how economic welfare will differ in situation II from situation I. Given that $(a_1x_1 + a_2x_2 \ldots) > (b_1x_1 + b_2x_2 \ldots)$, it is necessary, as before, that the actual y pattern income bought in situation II must be preferred to the imagined x pattern income which might have been bought. But it is not necessary that this imagined x pattern income of situation II, though it is larger than the actual x pattern income of situation I, yields more economic satisfaction than that does. For people who get more may have less keen desires for the additional things they get than people who get less had for the things of which they are deprived. Thus suppose that there are only two sorts of commodities, bread and beer, bread only being desired by one set of consumers and beer only by another set ; and that bread becomes cheaper, but beer dearer. Economic welfare may obviously be rendered greater if the forms of the utility functions of the two groups for bread and beer are of one sort and less if they are of another sort.

Case 3. As in Case 1 ; but here tastes are supposed to be changed uniformly ; while the quantity of resources at work and technique are not changed at all. If $(a_1x_1 + a_2x_2 \ldots) > (b_1x_1 + b_2x_2 \ldots)$, we know, indeed, that in situation II the y pattern real income that prevails is preferred to the imagined x pattern real income which might prevail. But we do not know whether the imagined x pattern real income would yield more satisfaction in situation II than the smaller actual x pattern income of situation I, because tastes in the two situations are different. No inference can, therefore, be drawn about comparative economic welfare. Thus, suppose that real income consists only of a single sort of commodity, the aggregate supply of which is fixed. It is obvious that, if people come to care much more than before for this commodity, their economic welfare (satisfaction) will be increased ; if they come to care much less, it will be diminished. But price quantity statistics cannot distinguish these cases.

More Complicated Cases. It is unnecessary to discuss more complicated cases, where tastes and purchasing power, being alike for all, both these and also technical conditions of production have changed, or, where, tastes and purchasing powers not being uniform, they and technical conditions have both changed. It is evident from what has already been said that no inference about changes in economic welfare can be drawn from price quantity statistics.

Thus it is only in our Case 1 above, where quantity of resources and technical conditions have changed and tastes and the purchasing power are alike for all purchasers and have not changed, that inferences about economic welfare are possible.

APPENDIX VII

DUOPOLY [1]

THE discussion of Duopoly in § 2 of Part II, Chapter XV, is not, I now think, satisfactory. The following paragraphs are intended to emend and supplant it.

§ 1. Let us suppose that there are two sellers only, with given productivity functions, engaged in producing the same commodity for a perfect competitive market, throughout the whole of which the commodity is sold at a uniform price; and that each seller always endeavours to maximise his current net receipts. Let us suppose further that production and sale proceed in a succession of rounds, each occupying, say, a year. This is unrealistic, but not, I think, in such a way as to upset the argument. Then in respect of any given round there are four relevant quantities: A's actual output, which we may call x_a, B's actual output, y_b, the output from A which B expects, x_b, and the output from B which A expects, y_a. Given the state of the market's demand, A will then produce that output which, granted B's expected output, will maximise his own net receipts; and B will proceed in a similar manner. These conditions provide us with two equations. But, since there are four unknowns, they are not sufficient to determine anything. For that two further equations independent of these two are needed. Now A must expect, or, what for our purposes comes to the same thing, act as though he expected, something definite about B's output; and the same thing is true of B. The word definite is important. It is not enough that A shall merely expect B to try to maximise his net receipts in the light of his expectations about A and that B shall do the same thing. For that would merely mean writing the two first already given equations over again. A and B both expect something definite from the other. These expectations provide two further independent equations. They do not, indeed,

[1] This Appendix is not, except for a short paragraph, a reproduction of, but it is partly in line with, " A Comment on Duopoly," *Economica*, December 1948.

imply that the price-quantity situation in respect of any given round is *uniquely* determined. For it may be that our equations are equally well satisfied by a number of alternative sets of values. But it does mean that that situation in each round is mathematically determinate.

§ 2. This being so, we have to inquire into the forms that our second pair of independent equations may assume. Broadly, each of A and B may expect either of two things ; first, that the other's output will be a definite constant independent of what he himself may do ; secondly, that the other's output will be some function of his own output. Practically speaking, we may take it that, if A expects B's output to be a constant, this means that he expects it to be the same as B's actual output during the preceding round, or possibly some derivative of the output of several preceding rounds ; he will not frame his expectation by thinking of a number in the abstract and writing it down. The same thing, of course, holds of B's expectation. If A expects B's output to be a function of his own output, the function may be either a simple multiple or something more complicated. These expectations may, and, as we shall see in a moment, will often, in fact, be constrained to be different in different rounds. But in respect of any given round they are what they are and the system is determinate.

§ 3. But to be determinate, while it implies being in short-run — one-round — equilibrium, does not imply being in long-run equilibrium. A system is in long-run equilibrium if, apart from shifts in the governing factors, there is no tendency for it to alter from one round to another *and if there is nothing inherent in the system to make any governing factor shift.* These factors are, of course, always liable to shift, so to speak, on their own merits. For example, tastes may change, or techniques of production, or A's forecasts about B may become more optimistic because A has taken a dose of benzedrine, or more pessimistic because he has contracted influenza or, indeed, for any cause not inherent in the system. Such things do not prevent the system from being in long-run equilibrium in the sense just explained, though they entail that different long-run equilibrium situations exist at different times. But the system is prevented from being in long-run equilibrium at all if A's expectation entertained in round I about what B is going to do in round II is presently contradicted by the facts ; and similarly for B. For in that case expectations in round II must be altered from what they were in round I. We shall have a long-run equilibrium situation if and only if the expectations entertained by each about the other's conduct turn out to be correct, that is to say, if $x_a = x_b$ and $y_b = y_a$.

§ 4. We are thus led on to investigate the character of the long-run equilibrium that emerges provided that the foregoing condition is satisfied. Let x without subscript be the output that A does *and* (since there is to be long-run equilibrium) is expected by B to produce, and y similarly for B. Then $\phi(x+y)$ is the price and $(x+y)\,\phi(x+y)$ the gross receipts of A and B together. If there are no costs of production, as with Cournot's imaginary mineral springs, $(x+y)\,\phi(x+y)$ is also the net receipts—the monopoly revenue—of A and B together. Let us begin with this case.

§ 5. In order that there may be long-run equilibrium two equations must be simultaneously satisfied, namely,

$$\frac{d}{dx}\left\{x\phi(x+y)\right\}=0 \quad \text{and} \quad \frac{d}{dy}\left\{y\phi(x+y)\right\}=0.$$

Hence
$$\phi(x+y)+x\frac{d\phi(x+y)}{d(x+y)}\left\{1+\frac{dy}{dx}\right\}=0. \qquad \text{. . (3)}$$

$$\phi(x+y)+y\frac{d\phi(x+y)}{d(x+y)}\left\{1+\frac{dx}{dy}\right\}=0. \qquad \text{. . (4)}$$

This entails that
$$x\left(1+\frac{dy}{dx}\right)=y\left(1+\frac{dx}{dy}\right):$$

from which it follows that
$$\frac{dx}{dy}=\frac{x}{y}.$$

Hence from (1)
$$\phi(x+y)+(x+y)\frac{d\phi(x+y)}{d(x+y)}=0.$$

This implies that $(x+y)$ must have the value which maximises $(x+y)\phi(x+y)$; that is to say, the value which would have been obtained if A and B were acting together as a single monopolist. *Prima facie* it might seem that $\frac{dy}{dx}$ and $\frac{dx}{dy}$ may be equal to -1; in which case our equations would be satisfied if $\phi(x+y)=0$: that is to say, in a nil cost situation, with aggregate output the same as it would be in competitive conditions. But since, as we have seen, $\frac{dx}{dy}=\frac{x}{y}$, that would imply that either x or y is negative, which is obviously impossible. Hence the only possible long-run equilibrium situation is that in which the joint output of A and B is the output they would produce if joined together in a single monopoly.[1]

[1] This result is in conflict with that reached by Cournot, who, as is well known, found that there is a long-run equilibrium position with aggregate output intermediate between that proper to a single monopolist and that

§ 6. Consider next the case in which there are costs of production, but the average cost per unit of each monopolist depends not at all on his individual output, only on the aggregate output of the two together—whether this rises as output rises or falls or remains constant. Let us write $f(x+y)$ for the average cost of production. We have then merely to write throughout each of our equations $\{\phi(x+y)-f(x+y)\}$ instead of $\phi(x+y)$, and the same results as were reached in the preceding paragraph immediately follow.

§ 7. Turn then to the case in which each seller's average cost of production depends on his own output only, not on the aggregate output. If they both produce under conditions of constant supply price and *their supply prices are equal*, it is evident that the situation is again the same as before. Otherwise, however, it is more complicated and the equations that need to be satisfied in order that long-run equilibrium may exist are different. Putting $f_a(x)$ for A's average cost of production and $f_b(y)$ for B's, they are

$$\phi(x+y) + x\,\frac{d\,\phi(x+y)}{d(x+y)}\left\{1+\frac{dy}{dx}\right\} -f_a(x)-xf'_a(x)=0 \qquad . \quad (3)$$

$$\phi(x+y) + y\,\frac{d\,\phi(x+y)}{d(x+y)}\left\{1+\frac{dx}{dy}\right\} -f_b(y)-yf'_b(y)=0. \qquad . \quad (4)$$

It is thus no longer necessary to long-run equilibrium that

$$x\left(1+\frac{dy}{dx}\right)=y\left(1+\frac{dy}{dx}\right),$$

---

proper to competition. What Cournot did in effect was to consider a single round in isolation. For this round he postulated that A has a certain expectation with regard to B's output, and he then inquired how much A would have to produce in order to maximise his net receipts if that expectation was fulfilled. A's expectation about B being regarded as a constant, this method gives a determinate output in that round for A, and a similar procedure gives a determinate output for B. For long-run equilibrium, however, as we have seen, these expectations have to turn out correct. This is incompatible with regarding both A's and B's expectations as constants ; in order to be correct each of them must depend on the actual output of the other. In respect of a single round Cournot's assumptions are self-consistent and, if satisfied, yield a determinate result. But they are not legitimate in an inquiry about long-run equilibrium. This is easily seen from my equations. For Cournot's assumption implies that $\frac{dx}{dy}$ and $\frac{dy}{dx}$ are both equal to 0, which, with x and y both measuring actual outputs, is obviously impossible. Hence Cournot's (long-run) equilibrium position cannot exist.

implying $\dfrac{dx}{dy} = \dfrac{x}{y}$.[1]   There must, however, be at least one pair of

values of x and y that satisfies these two equations and so leads to a long-run equilibrium situation. Except in the special conditions described in the footnote, this is not the pair that maximises aggregate net receipts—a pair that would result from a unified monopoly. But, none the less, the situation is one of long-run equilibrium.

§ 8. We have thus found in all our three cases that, *if* the expectations entertained by A and B about the other's output are so related that the actual outputs emerging as a result of them are equal to the expected outputs, a long-run equilibrium situation will establish itself, and we have seen how in the several cases the equilibrium will be constituted. But this does not tell us whether under Duopoly a long-run equilibrium situation is likely to emerge in fact. If it is very unlikely that the expectations entertained by A and B will be co-ordinated in the way we have described, it is very unlikely that there will be long-run equilibrium. Now, of course, it is *possible* that expectations so correlated may emerge spontaneously when a given set of conditions as to productivity and demand are first set up. The range covered by pairs of expectations that are not is, indeed, much larger than that covered by pairs that are thus co-ordinated. This, however, is not decisive. Thus it is very unlikely that a single monopolist confronted with a competitive market will at the outset correctly gauge what the demand schedule of that market is, and so be able to adjust his output in such a way as to maximise his net receipts. By a process of trial and error he will, however, presently do this ; for he will be continually impelled nearer and nearer to a correct judgment. Is there any similar tendency for two firms acting as duopolists, by a similar process of trial and error, to hit presently upon a pair of expectations compatible with a long-run equilibrium situation ? Obviously, if there is, it is immaterial whether the expectations initially and spontaneously entertained are or are not so compatible. Suppose then that A finds his first spontaneous expectation about B wrong—*e.g.* that B is in fact producing more than he expected him to do. A may thereupon react by raising his expectation attitude about B and, consequently, producing less himself. If B's conduct was independent of what

---

[1] Except where each producer expects the other's output to be an assigned multiple of its own output, the same whatever that output may be (compare " A Comment on Duopoly," *Economica*, November 1948, pp. 255 *et seq.*). In that special case $\dfrac{x}{y} = n$ (a constant). Therefore $\dfrac{dx}{dy} = n$, or $\dfrac{dy}{dx} = \dfrac{1}{n}$: whence $x\left(1 + \dfrac{dy}{dx}\right) = y\left(1 + \dfrac{dx}{dy}\right)$ in all circumstances.

A does in the way that the general demand schedule of the market is, he would have to do this. But B's conduct is not thus independent. A may, therefore, react by producing *more* himself, expecting that, as a consequence of this, B will be induced to produce less. There is, of course, a like uncertainty about B's reactions. Thus there is no tendency for trial and error to promote the formation of a pair of expectation attitudes so adjusted to one another as to allow a long-run equilibrium situation to emerge. There is no influence at work tending to convert expectation attitudes arising spontaneously that are not compatible with a long-run equilibrium situation into expectation attitudes that are so compatible. We should rather look for an indefinitely prolonged series of successive situations, none of which are long-run equilibrium situations. Such a situation *may* emerge, so to speak, by accident. But, in general, duopoly will be associated with long-run disequilibrium, and so with fluctuations.

§ 9. The limits within which the fluctuations must lie are easy to see. It will plainly pay neither A nor B in any round, no matter what he expects the other to do, to produce less than nothing. We cannot, I think, say more than this unless we regard the range of A's and/or B's expectations about the other as somehow restricted. At the other extreme it would pay neither to produce so much that, whatever the other produces, the price must fall below his own average cost of production—unless, regardless of loss to himself, he is out deliberately to destroy a rival. In that case, so long as this intention held, the upper limit of the disequilibrium range might be extended indefinitely.

§ 10. In this discussion I have supposed, apart from a special case of cut-throat competition just referred to, that each of our sellers is seeking independently, without formal or informal agreement with the other, to maximise his net receipts. On this assumption no long-run equilibrium position can be established except by a fluke, even when one of our duopolists is enormously larger and is producing enormously more than the other. It may perhaps be urged that in that case the range of disequilibrium will be very small, and *de minimis non curat lex*. This, however, is not very satisfactory. What actually happens, I imagine, is that the larger producer does not in fact set himself, as we have so far supposed, to maximise his current net receipts, but decides on an output or price that comes, in his view, near enough to doing that to be satisfactory, and then sticks to it without bothering about what his small rival does. This small rival will then do the best he can for himself, taking account of what the big one is doing. This gives a long-run equilibrium situation. The conditions for it, however, are not likely to be satisfied where the two duopolists are at all comparable in size and power.

APPENDIX VIII

(To Part II, Chapter XVI) [1]

ALL-ROUND MONOPOLY

§ 1. In the text some study was made of the consequences of substituting simple monopoly for competition in a single industry. It is of interest to ask further how a system in which all industries are monopolised would compare with one in which they are all operated under conditions of competition. We suppose that under both systems the same volume of resources is employed and every individual firm is of optimum size. We also suppose, to make the analysis more tractable at the expense of making it unrealistic, that all the several commodities are independent of one another, neither substitutes nor complements in the Marshallian sense.

§ 2. A preliminary issue to decide is whether a system of this kind will be determinate without further data. Doubt might be raised about this by reflecting on the case of a monopolist buyer and a monopolist seller bargaining with one another. But in our case each monopolist sells to individual members of the public, whether his own employees or not, not to other monopolist organisations. Each of them, in other words, is dealing with a competitive market and that situation is clearly determinate.

§ 3. Since the controllers of every monopoly are supposed to aim at maximising their net receipts, the condition that the same aggregate volume of resources shall be engaged under the monopolistic as under the competitive system implies that under the former factors of production are " exploited " and forced to work for a lower return (except in so far as they themselves are controllers and enjoy the fruits of monopolisation) than they would do under competition. The rate of return obtainable by the factors must be supposed in our highly abstract world to be the same in all industries. Thus in effect a uniform cut in costs is made in all industries at the

---

[1] This matter is discussed on a different method with similar results in *The Economics of Stationary States*, chapter 41.

expense of the factors of production (other than the controllers). This should enable us to determine how a shift to monopolisation would modify the distribution of resources among different industries.

§ 4. Consider first the simplest case in which the demand and supply curves may be represented by straight lines. Then in any industry, if monopoly were substituted for competition and no cut in costs were introduced, output would be contracted as against competition by one-half. The cut in costs will, therefore, affect output everywhere in the same proportions when monopoly rules as it would do if competition ruled. With constant supply prices it is evident that the cut in costs will expand output, and so the quantity of resources employed, in a larger proportion in industries the demand curve of whose products is less than in those in which it is more steeply inclined. Thus we may conclude that, when all-round monopoly is substituted for all-round competition and the total volume of resources employed is held constant, output and the volume of resources employed will be increased in industries with flattish demand curves and decreased in those with steepish demand curves ; while industries with some intermediate degree of demand steepness will produce the same output, and engage the same volume of resources, as they would do under all-round competition. When constant supply price does not rule, this conclusion still holds. For we may exclude the possibility of increasing returns acting so sharply that less resources are required to produce a larger than a smaller output. Further, as between industries with similar demand conditions, when all-round monopoly is substituted for all-round competition, the volume of resources employed in any industry is more likely to be increased the steeper is the supply curve if downward-sloping and the less steep if upward-sloping, *provided that the demand curve does not slope so steeply as to make expenditure on a larger less than expenditure on a smaller output.* If the demand curve does slope more steeply than this, the opposite conclusion holds. It is not difficult to show this by means of a diagram.

§ 5. If we abandon the assumption of straight line demand and supply curves and substitute for steeper and less steep the vaguer notion of less and more elastic in a general way, the same results hold good broadly. A more exact analysis would need the help of mathematics.

APPENDIX IX

IMPERFECT COMPETITION

§ 1. No reference is made in the body of this book to the now familiar topic of imperfect competition. The first sustained attempts to investigate this subject were made by Mrs. Robinson and Professor Chamberlin in the early thirties. Had their work appeared a few years earlier, I should, no doubt, have given a proper place to this subject in my book. For it is evident that the presence anywhere of imperfect competition is liable, like the presence of simple monopoly, to modify the allocation of resources among different uses, and so to affect the national dividend ; and, moreover, to affect this yet again by interfering with the influences pushing individual firms towards optimum size. But Mrs. Robinson and Professor Chamberlin came on the scene too late to help me and I had not the vision to help myself.

§ 2. From the standpoint of this book the most important consequence of the new analysis may be set out as follows. In the second division of Appendix III it was shown that in conditions of competition—by which is there meant perfect competition—in any industry marginal cost and average cost in the equilibrium firm must be equal. This obviously implies that the size of that firm must be such that average cost is the smallest possible.

§ 3. Now the characteristic of perfect competition is that the demand for the output of any one firm is infinitely elastic, in such wise that, if it varies its price in any degree above that of the others, it will lose the whole of its custom. In imperfect competition, however, the elasticity of demand for the output of any one firm is not infinite. If it raised its price a little relatively to the others, it would lose a part of its custom, but, owing to some people preferring it to others, not the whole of it. In view of this firms will be stimulated, in the hope of monopoly gain, to charge higher prices and operate on a smaller scale than they would do under perfect competition. They cannot, in fact, secure a monopoly gain because, as is further supposed in the theory of imperfect competition, factors of production can move freely between industries, so that their attempt to do so will be frustrated by new rival firms entering the industry. But they will try to do that.

§ 4. It follows that in an industry in which imperfect competition prevails there will be a larger number of firms and the equilibrium firm will be smaller in size than would have happened had perfect competition ruled. But under perfect competition the size of the equilibrium firm would have been such as to make marginal cost and average cost equal. A smaller size will entail marginal cost being different from (greater than) average cost. Average cost will not, therefore, be the smallest possible.

§ 5. Thus imperfect competition in any industry, as compared with perfect competition, entails a wasteful use of resources by bringing them together in firms of less than the technically most efficient size.

APPENDIX X

(To Part IV, Chapter III)

THE ELASTICITY OF SUBSTITUTION [1]

§ 1. THE concept of Elasticity of Substitution was developed and discussed in the early thirties by a number of writers, notably Dr. Hicks, Mrs. Robinson and Mr. Kahn. It does not, like that of Imperfect Competition, open up a new field of inquiry. It provides a new phrase and a new technique. Thus, in the footnote to p. 665 above it is shown (in effect) that the condition required, in order that a small increase in the quantity at work of one of two factors of production—there being no other factors—shall leave the proportionate shares of the two factors unchanged, is that the elasticity of demand for the expanded factor is numerically equal to the aggregate output divided by the share of the other factor. In the new terminology this condition can be expressed by saying that the elasticity of substitution between the two factors is numerically equal to unity. (A proof that these two statements are equivalent is given in *The Economics of Stationary States*, p. 310.) What we want to know, therefore, about this concept, after the meaning of it has been explained, is how far it is likely to be *useful* as a tool of thought in comparison with other tools.

§ 2. The elasticity of substitution in its most fundamental form may be defined as " the proportional change in the ratio of the amounts of the factors (engaged in producing any commodity) divided by the proportional change in the ratio of their marginal physical productivities." [2] This definition—applied to industries, not, as Mrs. Robinson, from whom this wording is taken, applies it, to individual firms—may be expressed symbolically thus : let a and b be the quantities of any two factors of production A and B— it is immaterial how many factors there are—engaged in producing some commodity, and p_a and p_b their marginal products. When a

---

[1] Reprinted with modifications and with a substituted first paragraph from the *Economic Journal*, March 1933.

[2] Robinson, *The Economics of Imperfect Competition*, p. 330, n., and Kahn, *Review of Economic Studies*, October 1933, p. 72.

increases to $(a + \Delta a)$, b becomes $(b + \Delta b)$, p_a becomes $(p_a + \Delta p_a)$ and p_b becomes $(p_b + \Delta p_b)$. The elasticity of substitution, which we may call η, is then equal to

$$\frac{\Delta \dfrac{a}{b}}{\dfrac{a}{b}} \div \frac{\Delta \dfrac{p_a}{p_b}}{\dfrac{p_a}{p_b}}.$$

Let us write α, β, π_a and π_b for $\dfrac{\Delta a}{a}$, $\dfrac{\Delta b}{b}$, $\dfrac{\Delta p_a}{p_a}$ and $\dfrac{\Delta p_b}{p_b}$. Then by an easy reduction we have, in the limit, $\eta = \dfrac{\alpha - \beta}{\pi_a - \pi_b}$.[1]

§ 3. This way of defining the concept implies that there is, between any two factors that it relates, a single unambiguous elasticity of substitution, irrespective of the manner in which the initial equilibrium situation is supposed to be disturbed. As will be shown presently, this implication is, in fact, correct in the special case where the relevant productivity function is homogeneous in the first degree—*i.e.* where conditions are such that equi-proportionate changes in the quantities of all the associated factors entail a change in the same proportion in the quantity of output [2]—and where only two factors of production are operating. In the general case, however, it is clear that no implication of this sort holds. When the proportional quantities of any two factors alter in a given measure their proportional marginal productivities will, in general, alter differently according to the nature of the disturbance that has taken place—according as it is brought about by a shift in A's supply function, or in B's or C's or D's. Thus there is not, between any two factors, a single elasticity of substitution, but a large number of such elasticities. As between factors A and B there are elasticities, which we may write $_a\eta_{ab}$, $_b\eta_{ab}$, $_c\eta_{ab}$, and so on, according as the initial equilibrium has been disturbed by a move in A's, B's or C's supply function. Similarly, as between any two factors Q and R, there are a series of elasticities of substitution, which, with a like significance, may be written $_a\eta_{qr}$, $_b\eta_{qr}$, $_a\eta_{qr}$, and so on. Thus, if there are n factors of production, there are, in general,

$$\frac{n^2(n-1)}{2}$$

---

[1] The writers who have so far made use of this concept have usually preferred, when treating the matter formally, to define the elasticity of substitution as $-\dfrac{a - \beta}{\pi_a - \pi_b}$. This is a matter of taste. I prefer not to insert the *minus* sign, and shall proceed on that plan in the discussion that follows.

[2] In a many-firm industry this implies that the marginal physical productivity of any factor to the firm by which it is employed is equal to its marginal

elasticities of substitution. The fact that in the special case of two factors and a homogeneous function of the first degree the two elasticities $_a\eta_{ab}$ and $_b\eta_{ab}$, which this formula allows, happen to be identical does not, of course, invalidate the rule.

§ 4. Let us now investigate the particular elasticity of substitution $_a\eta_{ab}$ in the general case where there is no proviso either that the productivity function is a homogeneous function of the first degree or that there are only two associated factors. It will be enough for our purpose to consider a system containing three factors. The presence of a larger number would extend the algebraic analysis, which is, in any event, cumbrous, without introducing any new point of interest. Write for the productivity function F and for the quantities of the several factors a, b, c : so that the quantity of product is $F(a, b, c)$. For simplicity of working let us choose units such that $a = b = c$. This, of course, makes no difference to the result reached. For the marginal product of A, namely, $\dfrac{\partial F(a, b, c)}{\partial a}$, write p_a ; analogously for the marginal products of B and C. Next distinguish a series of elasticities, to be called *elasticities of partial productivity*. For each factor there is an elasticity of partial productivity in respect of shifts in the supply functions of itself and of each of the others. The elasticity of partial productivity of factor A in respect of B is the proportional change in the marginal productivity of A due to a given proportional change in the quantity of B, when the quantities of all the other factors are unaltered, divided into that proportional change. Thus write $_a\epsilon_a$ for A's elasticity of partial productivity in respect of changes in A ; $_b\epsilon_a$ for A's elasticity of partial productivity in respect of changes in B ; and so on. Then—

$$\frac{1}{_a\epsilon_a} = \frac{a}{p_a} \cdot \frac{\partial p_a}{\partial a}$$

$$\frac{1}{_b\epsilon_a} = \frac{b}{p_a} \cdot \frac{\partial p_a}{\partial b}$$

$$\frac{1}{_c\epsilon_a} = \frac{c}{p_a} \cdot \frac{\partial p_a}{\partial c}$$

$$\frac{1}{_a\epsilon_b} = \frac{a}{p_b} \cdot \frac{\partial p_b}{\partial a}$$

$$\frac{1}{_b\epsilon_b} = \frac{b}{p_b} \cdot \frac{\partial p_b}{\partial b}$$

$$\frac{1}{_c\epsilon_b} = \frac{c}{p_b} \cdot \frac{\partial p_b}{\partial c}$$

productivity to the whole industry, *i.e.* that marginal private and marginal social product coincide.

while $\dfrac{1}{a^{\epsilon}c}$, $\dfrac{1}{b^{\epsilon}c}$ and $\dfrac{1}{c^{\epsilon}c}$ have corresponding meanings.

Write db and dc for the changes in the quantities of B and C that are brought about when the quantity of A is changed, through a shift in A's supply function, from a to $(a+da)$. Finally, write e_a, e_b, e_c for the elasticities of the supply functions of A, B and C. Then the elasticity of substitution between A and B in respect of shifts in A's supply function, namely—

$$a\eta_{ab} = \left\{ \dfrac{\dfrac{d}{da}\left\{\dfrac{a}{b}\right\}}{\dfrac{a}{b}} \div \dfrac{\dfrac{d}{da}\left\{\dfrac{p_a}{p_b}\right\}}{\dfrac{p_a}{p_b}} \right\} = \dfrac{p_a b}{p_b a} \cdot \left\{ \dfrac{d}{da}\left\{\dfrac{a}{b}\right\} \div \dfrac{d}{da}\left\{\dfrac{p_a}{p_b}\right\} \right\}$$

Hence, by algebraic manipulation, we obtain

$$\dfrac{1}{a\eta_{ab}} = \left\{ \left\{\dfrac{1}{a^{\epsilon}a} - \dfrac{1}{a^{\epsilon}b}\right\} + \dfrac{db}{da}\left\{\dfrac{1}{b^{\epsilon}a} - \dfrac{1}{b^{\epsilon}b}\right\} + \dfrac{dc}{da}\left\{\dfrac{1}{c^{\epsilon}a} - \dfrac{1}{c^{\epsilon}b}\right\} \right\} \div \left\{1 - \dfrac{db}{da}\right\} \tag{1}$$

§ 5. This formula contains two unknowns, $\dfrac{db}{da}$ and $\dfrac{dc}{da}$, and is, therefore, without significance until the values of these have been determined. For that to be possible some assumption must be made about the relation between the rates of payment of the factors B and C and their marginal products. The natural assumption is that the relation is one of equality. If the productivity function is homogeneous in the first degree, and if conditions of perfect competition prevail, this assumption must conform to the facts. The rate of payment of every factor must then be equal to its marginal product. If the condition of homogeneity is not satisfied, it is *impossible* for this to be true of *all* the factors ; for payment on that plan would involve aggregate receipts for all the factors together either greater than or less than aggregate output. But that the two factors B and C should be paid in accordance with their marginal productivity is still possible. Let us suppose that they are, in fact, so paid. It follows that, for equilibrium, the marginal product of B must be equal to the supply price of the extant quantity of it ; and similarly for C. Hence the change in the marginal productivity of B consequent on the shift in A must be equal to the change in its supply price ; and similarly for C.

Hence $\dfrac{d}{da}p_b = \dfrac{db}{da} \cdot \dfrac{p_b}{b} \cdot \dfrac{1}{e_b}.$

But $\dfrac{d}{da}p_b = \dfrac{\partial}{\partial a}p_b + \dfrac{db}{da} \cdot \dfrac{\partial}{\partial b}p_b + \dfrac{dc}{da} \cdot \dfrac{\partial}{\partial c}p_b.$

Hence

$$\frac{db}{da} \cdot \frac{1}{e_b} = \frac{1}{_a\epsilon_b} + \frac{db}{da} \cdot \frac{1}{_b\epsilon_b} + \frac{dc}{da} \cdot \frac{1}{_c\epsilon_b}.$$

In like manner,

$$\frac{dc}{da} \cdot \frac{1}{e_c} = \frac{1}{_a\epsilon_c} + \frac{dc}{da} \cdot \frac{1}{_c\epsilon_c} + \frac{db}{da} \cdot \frac{1}{_b\epsilon_c}.$$

Writing $\left(\dfrac{1}{_b\epsilon_b} - \dfrac{1}{e_b} \right) = m$ and $\left(\dfrac{1}{_c\epsilon_c} - \dfrac{1}{e_c} \right) = n$, we derive from these equations

$$\frac{db}{da} = \frac{-\dfrac{1}{_a\epsilon_b} + \dfrac{1}{n} \cdot \dfrac{1}{_a\epsilon_b} \cdot \dfrac{1}{_a\epsilon_c}}{m - \dfrac{1}{n} \cdot \dfrac{1}{_c\epsilon_b} \cdot \dfrac{1}{_b\epsilon_c}} \qquad \bullet \quad \bullet \quad \bullet \quad (2)$$

and

$$\frac{dc}{da} = \frac{-\dfrac{1}{_a\epsilon_c} + \dfrac{1}{m} \cdot \dfrac{1}{_b\epsilon_c} \cdot \dfrac{1}{_a\epsilon_b}}{n - \dfrac{1}{m} \cdot \dfrac{1}{_b\epsilon_c} \cdot \dfrac{1}{_c\epsilon_b}}. \qquad \bullet \quad \bullet \quad \bullet \quad (3)$$

By substituting the values of $\dfrac{da}{db}$ and $\dfrac{dc}{da}$ thus obtained in equation (1) we are able to express $\dfrac{1}{_a\eta_{ab}}$ in terms of e_b, e_c and the various ϵ's. It is not necessary to write out the highly complex expression that results. The essential point is that e_b and e_c, representing the elasticities of supply of B and C, are contained in it.

§ 6. Let us now suppose, not only that the factors B and C are paid in accordance with their marginal products, but also that they are associated in a homogeneous function of the first degree. This condition entails the equality

$$\frac{\partial}{\partial a}p_a + \frac{b}{a} \cdot \frac{\partial}{\partial b}p_a + \frac{c}{a} \cdot \frac{\partial}{\partial c}p_a = 0,$$

and the two analogous equalities. For the marginal product of each factor is, with a homogeneous function of the first degree, unaltered by an equal proportional change in the quantities of all of them.

Hence we have

$$\frac{1}{_a\epsilon_a} + \frac{1}{_b\epsilon_a} + \frac{1}{_c\epsilon_a} = 0 \qquad \bullet \quad \bullet \quad \bullet \quad (4)$$

$$\frac{1}{_a\epsilon_b} + \frac{1}{_b\epsilon_b} + \frac{1}{_c\epsilon_b} = 0 \qquad \bullet \quad \bullet \quad \bullet \quad (5)$$

$$\frac{1}{_a\epsilon_c} + \frac{1}{_b\epsilon_c} + \frac{1}{_c\epsilon_c} = 0. \qquad \bullet \quad \bullet \quad \bullet \quad (6)$$

No essential simplification is made in the complex final expression for $\dfrac{1}{a\eta ab}$. In particular, the elements e_b and e_c are not eliminated from it. Thus, equally whether or not we assume that the productivity function is homogeneous, the elasticity of substitution between A and B in respect of shifts in A does not measure any characteristic either of the general productivity function or of any supply function, but is a complex consequence of interactions between productivity and supply.

§ 7. The next step takes us to the special case in which there are only two factors of production. If we require the factor B to be paid according to its marginal productivity, but do not require the productivity function to be homogeneous in the first degree, the formula for the elasticity of substitution between A and B in respect of shifts in A's supply function is greatly simplified. The element $\dfrac{dc}{da}$, of course, disappears. The element $\dfrac{db}{da}$ is then derived from the single equation

$$\frac{db}{da}\frac{1}{e_b} = \frac{1}{a\epsilon_b} + \frac{db}{da}\frac{1}{b\epsilon_b}.$$

Hence
$$\frac{db}{da} = \left\{ -\frac{1}{a\epsilon_b} \div \left(\frac{1}{b\epsilon_b} - \frac{1}{e_b} \right) \right\}$$

Inserting this value in the general equation (1), we obtain

$$\frac{1}{a\eta ab} = \left[\frac{1}{a\epsilon_a} - \frac{1}{a\epsilon_b} - \left\{ \frac{1}{a\epsilon_b}\left(\frac{1}{b\epsilon_a} - \frac{1}{b\epsilon_b} \right) \div \left(\frac{1}{b\epsilon_b} - \frac{1}{e_b} \right) \right\} \right] \div \left\{ 1 + \frac{\dfrac{1}{a\epsilon_b}}{\dfrac{1}{b\epsilon_b} - \dfrac{1}{e_b}} \right\}$$

$$= \frac{\dfrac{1}{a\epsilon_a} \cdot \dfrac{1}{b\epsilon_b} - \dfrac{1}{a\epsilon_b} \cdot \dfrac{1}{b\epsilon_a} - \dfrac{1}{e_b}\left(\dfrac{1}{a\epsilon_a} - \dfrac{1}{a\epsilon_b} \right)}{\dfrac{1}{a\epsilon_b} + \dfrac{1}{b\epsilon_b} - \dfrac{1}{e_b}} \qquad \cdot \quad \cdot \quad \cdot \quad \cdot \quad (7)$$

This expression is, of course, very much less cumbrous than that proper to the case of three (or more) factors of production. But, it will be observed, the elasticity of supply of B, namely e_b, is still contained in it.

§ 8. Finally, let us add the condition that the productivity function is a homogeneous function of the first degree. In accordance with what is said in § 6, this entails, when there are only two factors,

$$\frac{1}{a^\epsilon_a} + \frac{1}{b^\epsilon_a} = 0 \qquad . \qquad . \qquad . \qquad . \qquad (8)$$

$$\frac{1}{a^\epsilon_b} + \frac{1}{b^\epsilon_b} = 0. \qquad . \qquad . \qquad . \qquad . \qquad (9)$$

Hereupon the complex formula of the preceding section reduces to the very simple expression :

$$\frac{1}{a\eta_{ab}} = \frac{1}{a^\epsilon_a} + \frac{1}{b^\epsilon_b}, \qquad . \qquad . \qquad . \qquad . \qquad (10)$$

an expression which is also obtainable direct from equation (1). The companion expression $\frac{1}{b\eta_{ab}}$ obviously has an identical value. This value, *if the rule of diminishing returns for factors of production is obeyed*, and if my usage of not inserting a *minus* sign is followed, must be negative, since each of a^ϵ_a and b^ϵ_b is negative. In any event, whether this is so or not, the element e_b has been eliminated, while the element e_c does not, of course, exist. The elasticity of substitution describes certain characteristics of the productivity function, and is not connected with supply conditions in any way. It is an elementary fact, and not a consequence of a series of complex interactions.

§ 9. Having thus completed our analysis, we have to consider how far this concept is a serviceable one. Let us first consider the special case of two factors only, associated in a productivity function homogeneous in the first degree. If the characteristics of the productivity function, which the elasticity of substitution in this case defines, can be shown to be relevant to the solution of any important problem, there is so far reason for disentangling them and giving them a name. This can and has been shown. Thus, as was indicated in § 1, when, subject to the above conditions, the quantity of one of two factors is increased, the effect on that factor's proportional share of the product can be expressed by reference to the way in which the magnitude of the elasticity of substitution is related to unity. Again, Dr. Hicks has used the concept—once more, of course, subject to the above conditions—to extend and generalise an important theorem of Marshall's. Marshall, it will be remembered, worked out, in respect of a commodity made up of two elements whose proportions are fixed, *e.g.* knives containing one blade and one handle each, rules relating the elasticity of demand for one element to the elasticity of demand for the whole commodity, the elasticity of supply of the other element and the comparative parts played by the two elements in the total cost. He had also observed, without furnishing formal proof, that these rules are not substantially modified if the commodity is of such a sort that the proportions between the elements are different when different amounts are being produced.[1] It is easy to see that, when some commodity is being produced by the joint action of two factors of production, the factors play a part analogous to that of the elements, handles and blades, in Marshall's case. If, therefore, the proportions between their respective quantities are rigidly fixed, or if, not being fixed, they are functions of the quantity of commodity that is being produced, Marshall's elasticity rules apply. But of course, in fact, when we are dealing with factors of production, and not with elements such as the handles and blades of knives, these conditions are not satisfied. For the proportions in which the factors are employed will depend in part upon their prices, and, at all events with a commodity that engages large amounts of the factors, these prices will be modified when the output of the commodity is modified. Hence it is important to find, in respect of this more general case, rules corresponding to those which Marshall found in the particular case where the proportions of the constituent elements are independent of their prices. For two factors associated in a productivity function homogeneous in the first degree Dr. Hicks has done this. Write E for the elasticity of demand for the commodity ; e for the elasticity of supply of factor B ; m for the proportional part of the total cost that consists in payments to A ; and λ for the elasticity of demand for factor A. Then, when Marshall's conditions are satisfied, his rules can be expressed in the formula

$$\lambda = \frac{mEe}{E(1-m)+e}.$$

Dr. Hicks has shown in effect [2] that, if we write η for the elasticity of substitution between A and B,

$$\lambda = \frac{\eta(E+e)+me(E-\eta)}{E+e-m(E-\eta)}.$$

In Marshall's simple case η is nil : so that, in that case, the generalised formula reduces, as of course it is bound to do, to his formula. Dr. Hicks' result is an important one, and the use of the symbol η

---

[1] *Principles*, Mathematical Note XV.

[2] *The Theory of Wages*, p. 244. In this formula, which is translated directly from Dr. Hicks' version, η is defined on his plan as $-\dfrac{a-\beta}{\pi_a-\pi_b}$, not on my plan, which omits the minus sign.

enables it to be expressed in a very compact form. A third interesting application of the new concept has been made by Mrs. Robinson. She has shown—again, of course, only for the case of two factors and a productivity function homogeneous in the first degree—that, when the quantity of one factor is increased, the demand price per unit for the existing quantity of the other is increased or diminished according as the elasticity of demand for the commodity is (numerically) larger or smaller than the elasticity of substitution.[1] Thus in the somewhat rarefied atmosphere in which alone it has so far been employed the new concept has proved its worth.

§ 10. If, however, we pass beyond the case of two factors only this is no longer so. For here the elasticity of substitution is a complex describing characteristics of one or more functions of factor supply interwoven with characteristics of the productivity function. If and when we have expressed the conditions of some event in a formula embodying the elasticity of substitution, we have merely entangled together different elements which have presently to be disentangled. No elasticity formula, of course, can itself constitute realistic knowledge ; at best it is only a bridge towards such knowledge. But a formula containing the elasticity of substitution, except where there are only two factors of production and conditions are such that elements connected with the supply of these can be eliminated, is an *unnecessary* bridge. It does not dispense us with crossing the *necessary* bridges ; it provides a roundabout way of coming to them. It is no easier to go by the roundabout way than by the direct way ; and it takes a longer time.

§ 11. In these circumstances it is open to us either to retain the definition for elasticity of substitution that I have been studying and recognise frankly that the concept is serviceable only in the narrow class of cases discussed in § 9, or to modify the definition in such wise as to exclude the *e*'s *ab initio*. One definition that would accomplish this has been suggested to me privately by Dr. Hicks. Under it $_a\eta_{ab}$ is equal to

$$\frac{\Delta\frac{a}{b}}{\frac{a}{b}} \cdot \frac{\Delta\frac{p_a}{p_b}}{\frac{p_a}{p_b}}$$

---

[1] *The Economics of Imperfect Competition*, p. 259. For these two last applications the elasticity of substitution must be defined as the proportional change in the ratio of the quantities of the two factors divided by the proportional change in the ratio, not of their marginal products, but of their money prices. Provided, however, as is here assumed, that the factors are paid according to their marginal productivities, the elasticity of substitution is obviously the same whether it is defined in the one way or in the other.

when a small amount of A *is substituted for* B *in such a way as to leave the total product unchanged, and the amounts employed of other factors,* C, D, *etc., remain constant.* This implies that $\dfrac{dc}{da}=0$ and that $\dfrac{db}{da}$ is such as to make $\dfrac{d}{da}\{ap_a+bp_b+cp_c\}=0$. Hence from equation (1)

$$\frac{1}{{}^a\eta_{ab}}=\frac{\left\{\dfrac{1}{{}_a\epsilon_a}-\dfrac{1}{{}_a\epsilon_b}\right\}\left\{p_a\cdot\dfrac{1}{{}_b\epsilon_a}+p_b\left(1+\dfrac{1}{{}_b\epsilon_b}\right)+p_c\cdot\dfrac{1}{{}_b\epsilon_c}\right\}+\left\{\dfrac{1}{{}_b\epsilon_b}-\dfrac{1}{{}_b\epsilon_a}\right\}\left\{p_a\left(1+\dfrac{1}{{}_a\epsilon_a}\right)+p_b\cdot\dfrac{1}{{}_a\epsilon_b}+p_c\cdot\dfrac{1}{{}_a\epsilon_c}\right\}}{p_a\left(1+\dfrac{1}{{}_a\epsilon_a}+\dfrac{1}{{}_b\epsilon_a}\right)+p_b\left(1+\dfrac{1}{{}_a\epsilon_b}+\dfrac{1}{{}_b\epsilon_b}\right)+p_c\left(\dfrac{1}{{}_a\epsilon_c}+\dfrac{1}{{}_b\epsilon_c}\right)}.$$

The companion expression for $\dfrac{1}{{}^b\eta_{ab}}$ is obviously identical with this. A much simpler method of extruding the e's is to define ${}^a\eta_{ab}$ as above, substituting for the words there italicised the words *when a small amount of* A *is added and the amounts employed of all the other factors, including* B, *are constant.* This implies that $\dfrac{dc}{da}=0$ and also $\dfrac{db}{da}=0$. Hence from equation (1)

$$\frac{1}{{}^a\eta_{ab}}=\left\{\frac{1}{{}_a\epsilon_a}-\frac{1}{{}_a\epsilon_b}\right\}.$$

The companion expression for $\dfrac{1}{{}^b\eta_{ab}}$ is $\left\{\dfrac{1}{{}_b\epsilon_b}-\dfrac{1}{{}_b\epsilon_a}\right\}$. When there are only two factors of production associated in a homogeneous function of the first degree, both the above ways of defining the elasticity of substitution come to the same thing as the way followed in earlier sections. All the ways make $\dfrac{1}{{}^a\eta_{ab}}$ and $\dfrac{1}{{}^b\eta_{ab}}$, both equal to $\left\{\dfrac{1}{{}_a\epsilon_a}+\dfrac{1}{{}_b\epsilon_b}\right\}$. For this case, therefore, any of the definitions may be used indifferently. But for the general case this is not so. Both new definitions have the advantage that they describe characteristics of the productivity function without any intrusions from the side of factor supply. The second is obviously much the simpler of the two. Whether either of them can be turned to a useful purpose in treating the problem of distribution among more than two factors of production remains to be seen. In my own work I have found it more convenient to deal with the elasticities of partial productivity individually rather than with combinations of them.[1]

[1] Cf. *The Economics of Stationary States*, Appendix XI.

APPENDIX XI

MEASURABILITY AND COMPARABILITY OF UTILITIES

THIS Appendix comprises the first half of an article entitled " Some Aspects of Economic Welfare," which appeared in the *American Economic Review* of June 1951.

I

THE PURPOSE OF WELFARE ECONOMICS

Welfare Economics is concerned to investigate the dominant influences through which the economic welfare of the world, or of a particular country, is likely to be increased. The hope of those who pursue it is to suggest lines of action—or non-action—on the part of the State or of private persons that might foster such influences. Nobody supposes that economic welfare is coincident with the whole of welfare or that the State ought to pursue it relentlessly without regard for other goods—liberty, for instance, the amenities of the family, spiritual needs and so on. But here we are not concerned with these things; only with economic welfare, that is to say, the part of welfare that is associated with the economic aspects of life. First and foremost we have to satisfy ourselves as to what that is and, more particularly, to decide whether or not it is the sort of thing to which the notions of greater or less and increase or decrease can properly be applied. For, if they cannot, Welfare Economics, every part and aspect of it, vanishes and leaves not a wrack behind.

II

THE MEANING OF ECONOMIC WELFARE

Let us consider first a single individual. What do we mean by the economic welfare of such an individual ? It will be generally agreed that this must be somehow resident in his state of mind or

845

consciousness. When we speak loosely of " material welfare," in the sense of a man's income or possessions, that is not welfare as we are thinking of it here. Material welfare may be a *means* to welfare, but it certainly is not identical with or a part of it. As it seems to me, welfare must be taken to refer either to the goodness of a man's state of mind or to the satisfactions embodied in it. If we were prepared to say that the goodness of satisfactions depended simply on their intensity it might not be necessary to make this distinction. But it is generally felt, in a vague way, that some sorts of satisfaction are in their nature better than others, and that quite irrespective of whether or not they entail dissatisfactions later on. If this is right, a situation containing more satisfaction is not necessarily " better " than one containing less. For the present purpose, I propose to make welfare refer to satisfactions, not goodness, thus leaving it possible that in certain circumstances, a government " ought "— granted that it " ought " to promote goodness—to foster a situation embodying less welfare (but more goodness) in preference to one embodying more welfare.

A man's welfare then consists in his satisfactions. But what does satisfaction mean ? Not simply happiness or pleasure ; for a man's desires may be directed to other things than these and may be satisfied. It might seem that, when his desire attitude is given, his satisfaction depends straightforwardly on the extent to which his desires are fulfilled. But the satisfaction yielded when a desire is satisfied does not always bear the same proportion to the intensity of the desire. Not only may people make mistakes, desiring certain objects in the hope of satisfactions which they do not in fact yield, but also, as Sidgwick observed, " I do not judge pleasures to be greater or less exactly in proportion as they exercise more or less influence in stimulating the will to actions likely to sustain or produce them." [1] Some economists, neglecting this point, have employed the term " utility " indifferently for satisfactions and for desiredness. I shall employ it here to mean satisfactions, so that we may say that a man's economic welfare is made up of his utilities. For a full treatment we should need to bring into account also such dissatisfactions or disutilities as men may suffer from work, or, what is not quite the same thing, such further satisfactions or utilities as leisure yields to them. It would not be difficult to do this, but doing it would complicate and lengthen the discussion. I shall not, therefore, trespass into that field.

[1] *Methods of Ethics*, p. 126 ; quoted in the text, *ante*, p. 24.

III

MEASURABILITY AND COMPARABILITY IN PRINCIPLE OF
SATISFACTIONS ENJOYED BY THE SAME INDIVIDUAL

I said in Section I that, if economic welfare were not something to which the notion of greater or less were applicable, Welfare Economics would vanish away. It is sometimes thought that this notion *cannot* be applicable unless satisfactions are measurable. Now for magnitudes of any kind to be measurable means that a unique and reciprocal correspondence, a one-one relation, can be established between the magnitudes in question and cardinal numbers. Extensive magnitudes, such as length, are, in general, measurable in this sense. Pleasures, satisfactions, utilities, are intensive magnitudes and are not measurable. They are not the sort of thing that we can correlate with a series of cardinal numbers.

It is true, no doubt, that an intensive magnitude may sometimes be correlated with an extensive magnitude and so may be capable of being measured indirectly. This would be true of satisfactions if, by a miracle, they were correlated rigidly with levels of temperature or speed of pulse. Moreover, there is, in fact, available in our field an " extensive " magnitude of the kind required, namely, the amount of money that a man would be willing to pay in order to avoid losing a given satisfaction or pleasure. Marshall, it will be remembered, laid stress on the advantage which economics has over other social sciences in possessing this measuring rod. Apart, however, from complications about the relation between the intensity of desires and the intensity of the satisfactions that result when a desired object is secured, to which I have already referred, neither Marshall nor anybody else claims that money enables us to measure anything more than small parts of a man's satisfaction. If I have an income of £1000, it is reasonable to say that the satisfaction I get (or, more strictly, expect) when I spend £2 on a small increment of one commodity is likely to be twice as great as what I get when I spend £1 on a small increment of another. But nobody supposes that the satisfaction I get from the whole of my £1000 income will be only 1000 times as large as what I get from the expenditure of a single marginal pound. Money does not, therefore, enable us to correlate satisfactions with a series of cardinal numbers, that is, to measure it in the sense understood here. We must concede that they are not measurable in that sense.

This, however, is far from entailing that satisfactions are not in principle *comparable*. The following passage from Bertrand Russell makes this clear. " Those mathematicians who are accustomed to an exclusive emphasis on numbers will think that not much can be said with definiteness concerning magnitudes incapable of measurement. This, however, is by no means the case. The immediate judgments of equality, upon which (as we saw) all measurements depend, are still possible where measurement fails, as are also the immediate judgments of greater and less. Doubt only arises where the difference is small ; and all that measurement does in this respect is to make the margin of doubt smaller—an achievement which is purely psychological and of no philosophical importance. Quantities not susceptible of numerical measurement can thus be arranged in a scale of greater and smaller magnitudes, and this is the only strictly quantitative achievement of even numerical measurement. We can know that one magnitude is greater than another and that a third is intermediate between them ; also, since the differences of magnitudes are always magnitudes, there is always (theoretically at least) an answer to the question whether the difference of one pair of magnitudes is greater than, less than, or the same as the difference of another pair of the same kind. . . . Without numerical measurement, therefore, the quantitative relations of magnitudes have all the definiteness of which they are capable—nothing is added, from the theoretical standpoint, by the assignment of correlated numbers." [1]

A corollary follows—or seems to follow. Given that we are able in principle to say that the difference between one pair of magnitudes is greater or less than the difference between another pair, we must presumably also be able to say that about differences between differences. This entails that, in spite of the fact that utilities are not measurable, it is still legitimate in principle to imagine a marginal utilities curve and to say, not merely that it slopes down or up, but also that it slopes more or less steeply as we move along it from right to left.

It is, indeed, impossible even in principle to draw a base line for the curve. Non-measurability entails that. It is thus meaningless to say that the utility derived by one individual in a given period from x units of a commodity is twice, or any other multiple, of the utility derived from y units, or to say, for example, that the curve is a rectangular hyperbola or bears some specifiable relation to a rectangular hyperbola. This entails that we cannot compare the damage done to welfare by a given proportionate change in a man's income when he is enjoying incomes of different sizes. Such questions as whether a tax proportioned to income will inflict equal sacrifice upon him whatever the size of his income or whether a tax progressive in some given form and degree is required to do this, are unanswerable, not merely from lack of data, but in principle. Thus the non-measurability of utility rules out one type of question,

[1] Russell, *Principles of Mathematics*, pp. 182-3.

which, were utility measurable, it would be legitimate to ask—and which, assuming that it *is* measurable, I did ask in Chapter 7, Part II, of my *Study in Public Finance*. This does not, however, reduce the domain of Welfare Economics very seriously, nor does it seriously matter that such questions as whether aggregate welfare would be increased if the population were larger but individual satisfactions smaller, are in principle, not merely in practice, unanswerable.

IV

COMPARABILITY IN FACT

So far I have been discussing comparability in principle ; are satisfactions or utilities the sort of things which can be held in the relation of greater or less, or is it nonsense to maintain this of them in the way that it is nonsense to maintain that one is more red or more liquid than another ? I have answered that question. But, granted that these things are comparable in principle, it is a quite different question whether they can be actually compared. If we found that they could not be actually compared, it would not follow that they are incomparable in principle. If all thermometers and kindred gadgets were destroyed, this would not upset at all the comparability in principle of temperatures. *Per contra*, to find, as we have done, that utilities, differences among utilities and differences among these differences are comparable in principle does not imply that all or any of them can be compared in fact. Subject, however, to a qualification to be mentioned presently, it is generally agreed that, when an individual chooses satisfaction A in preference to satisfaction B, this *indicates* that satisfaction A is, or, more strictly, is expected to be, greater than satisfaction B. Choice thus provides an objective test of the comparative magnitudes of different utilities or satisfactions to a given individual. It does the same for marginal utilities or satisfactions, that is, the utilities derived from marginal increments of different sorts of goods. But nobody chooses or can choose between the *excess* of marginal utility A over marginal utility B and the *excess* of marginal utility C over marginal utility A. Hence these second differences, though, as I have maintained, comparable in principle, are not comparable in fact—at all events, by means of this kind of test. The point, however, is not important for our main argument.

V

INTER-PERSONAL COMPARISONS

So far we have been considering only the comparability of satisfactions as affecting the same person. Once we reject solipsism and admit the existence of other people, what has already been said should suffice to show that the utilities enjoyed by different people are not in their nature incomparable—it is not nonsense to say that A is happier than B. But the question whether they are comparable in fact is a more difficult one. The test of choice is not available here as it is for intra-personal comparisons. No doubt, a parent can choose satisfaction A for one of his sons as against satisfaction B for another; and, if he is impartial between them, this should mean that he judges satisfaction A to be the greater. But I do not think we can appeal to this, because the parent's choice is not a direct one and, in framing his decision, he is really faced with the very problem that confronts us here. We cannot, therefore, shift our burden upon him. The issue for Welfare Economics is important. For, if the satisfactions of different individuals cannot be compared, a large part of that subject is undermined. We are not, indeed, precluded from saying that, if one person has more of something and nobody else has less of anything, the welfare of the whole group, so long as their desires are unchanged, is increased. But we are precluded from saying anything about the implication of transfers between richer and poorer persons. To ask whether inter-personal comparisons of satisfactions or utilities are, in fact, possible is thus not an idle question.

Now, if we take random groups of people of the same race and brought up in the same country, we find that in many features that *are* comparable by objective tests they are on the average pretty much alike ; and, indeed, for fundamental characters we need not limit ourselves to people of the same race and country. On this basis we are entitled, I submit, to infer by analogy that they are probably pretty much alike in other respects also. In all practical affairs we act on that supposition. We cannot prove that it is true. But we do not need to do so. Nobody can prove that anybody besides himself exists, but, nevertheless, everybody is quite sure of it. We do not, in short, and there is no reason why we should, start from a *tabula rasa*, binding ourselves to hold every opinion which the natural man entertains to be guilty until it is proved innocent. The burden is the other way. To deny this is to wreck, not merely Welfare Economics, but the whole apparatus of practical thought. On the basis of analogy, observation and intercourse, inter-personal comparisons *can*, as I think, properly be made ; and, moreover, unless we have a special reason to believe the contrary, a given amount of stuff may be presumed to yield a similar amount of satisfaction, not indeed as between *any* one man and any other, but as between representative members of groups of individuals, such as the citizens of Birmingham and the citizens of Leeds. This is all that we need to allow this branch of Welfare Economics to function. Of course, in working it out, positive conclusions can only be reached subject to very important qualifications.

INDEX

INDEX FOR APPENDICES IV–XI

876 ECONOMICS OF WELFARE

ERRATUM

p. 822, lines 8 and 9 should read :

"we cannot claim that b_1, b_2 ... are the prices that would prevail in that situation if x_1, x_2 ... (or some multiple of them) were being produced instead of the actual y_1, y_2 ..."

Pigou : Economics of Welfare

For Product Safety Concerns and Information please contact our EU
representative GPSR@taylorandfrancis.com Taylor & Francis Verlag GmbH,
Kaufingerstraße 24, 80331 München, Germany

Printed and bound by CPI Group (UK) Ltd, Croydon, CR0 4YY
08/05/2025
01864548-0001